Ted Turner
It Ain't As Easy As It Looks

Ted Turner
It Ain't As Easy
As It Looks

The Amazing Story of CNN

Porter Bibb

This edition first published in Great Britain in 1996 by
Virgin Books
an imprint of Virgin Publishing Ltd
332 Ladbroke Grove
London W10 5AH

First published in Great Britain in 1994

Originally published in the USA in 1993 by Crown Publishers, Inc.,
201 East 50th Street, New York, New York 10022. Member of the
Crown Publishing Group.

A catalogue record for this book is available from the British Library.

ISBN 0 86369 892 1

Printed and bound in Great Britain by
Cox & Wyman Ltd, Reading, Berks

Introduction

The student audience was eating out of his hand as Ted Turner, sporting a CNN tie emblazoned with tiny logos of his new all news network, barreled along in the midst of one of his trademark dissertations on the evils of network television. Vintage stuff, but the kids had heard it all before—this wasn't Turner's first visit to Washington's Georgetown University and certainly not his last. The local reporter who had stopped by hoping to get a quote or two was beginning to wonder what he was doing there. So was the bleached trophy blonde in the front row Turner brought along for the ride.

It was late 1981 and Ted Turner had just slapped all three major broadcast networks with a landmark antitrust suit, claiming they were conspiring to keep Cable News Network out of the White House television press pool. For good measure, Turner was also suing Ronald Reagan, the president of the United States; James Brady, his press secretary; and General Alexander Haig, the secretary of state. And as if that were not enough, he was about to petition Congress to investigate CBS, NBC, and ABC for "polluting the minds of the American people."

Turner's quixotic takeover attempt of CBS was still to come, as was his bold acquisition of MGM and many of his other astounding triumphs, but at forty-two Ted Turner was already widely recognized as a world-class yachtsman, sports impresario, and maverick media personality. Three years earlier he had been included in *Forbes* magazine's first listing of the "400 Richest People in America." His personal net worth was estimated to be close to $100 million.

Waving a well-thumbed copy of the latest issue of *Success* magazine, Turner was just beginning to hit his stride when he stopped suddenly, flattening out the publication so no one could possibly miss the fact that his own handsome profile graced the front cover. Turner's loud, unmistakable, rasping voice—a cross some wag once said between Huey Long and a dying duck—which had ricocheted off the walls of Georgetown's Gaston Hall all afternoon, suddenly trailed off to a whisper.

"Is this enough?" he beseeched plaintively, his eyes rolling back into his head as he stared up at the rafters, holding the magazine high over his head. "Is this enough for you, Dad?"

Robert Edward Turner III has spent the better part of his life waiting for an answer to that question, an answer he knows will never come. He has set ocean racing records that will never be equaled. He has revolutionized the broadcast industry and made Marshall McLuhan's "global village" real by tying the world together into one live television network. He has even rewritten the very definition of news as something that *is* happening rather than something that *has* happened. On the brink of bankruptcy in 1963, Turner has now amassed a personal fortune of more than $3 billion. He has also become a one-man diplomatic corps with access, thanks to CNN's enormous influence, almost anywhere.

Ted Turner grew up lonely and unloved. He was tormented by an abusive, alcoholic father who hoped to provoke his son to greatness by beatings, which as often as not were administered with a wire coat hanger. If he cried, the punishment was doubled. His mother, who graced Ted with her own good looks and ebullient, outgoing personality, eventually left his father—in great part, she said, because of her husband's severe treatment of their only son.

Despite the beatings, Turner's father loved him dearly and bequeathed to his son a modest fortune and an unquenchable competitive spirit. He also gave his son a mind that could soar into the ethereal while his feet were planted firmly on the ground. Ted Turner's most telling inheritance, however, was the insidious manic depression passed down to him from a father so overcome by imagined jeopardies that he took his own life at the age of fifty-three.

I first met Ted Turner in early 1974 and recognized him immediately as my way out of an awkward situation. I had sold CBS a prime-time television special documenting that summer's America's Cup in Newport, Rhode Island, the first time in history the Cup would be featured on network television. Trying to capture the intense drama and excitement of ocean racing, however, without today's lightweight electronic equipment was proving almost impossible. Then I discovered Ted Turner. His instant love affair with our cameras lasted all summer. The New York Yacht Club had somewhat reluctantly allowed him into their charmed circle, although he had the predictably impossible task of sailing a radical, aluminum-hulled twelve-meter in his first America's Cup. His valiant but losing effort aboard *Mariner*—one of the few major setbacks in sixteen glorious years of ocean racing—helped make our film a sailing classic. And began Turner's new life as a media celebrity.

I continued to follow his progress as the Ted Turner story began to assume almost legendary proportion. I saw him come back in 1977 to succeed in defending the America's Cup, and I heard him make the first announcement of his daring new Cable News Network before a less-than-impressed convention of cable television executives in 1979. As an investment banker and media specialist, I have had the opportunity to witness firsthand Ted Turner's incredible impact on the broadcast industry. His programming innovations helped jump-start the cable industry and accelerated the decline of the three major television networks. Last year Turner's CNN alone was more profitable than either CBS, NBC, or ABC. No one today doubts his ability to acquire any one of the three. They are all for sale. Both the odds and the economic logic are compelling that Turner Broadcasting will combine with one of them before the 1996 Summer Olympics, which just happen to be in Turner's own Atlanta.

Ted Turner is a journalist's dream. His disarming candor and unflinching sincerity are unusual, if not unique. He may be the only honest billionaire in history. Stories of his enormous successes and egregious excesses have long served as common currency in the media. Ted Turner is also one enormous bundle of contradictions. Acutely aware of his own image, Turner continues to perpetuate his myth with frequent, passionate diatribes against everything from pollution to overpopulation to organized religion. On occasion he's even been known to take on the Almighty. Now nearly fifty-five, he is still trying to figure out what he wants to be when he grows up.

By his own admission, however, Ted Turner does not have much time for introspection. It took a ghost writer to draft the autobiography he agreed to write for Simon & Schuster almost seven years ago. The publisher was eventually forced to send a representative to Atlanta to collect the $1.2 million advance when an acceptable manuscript did not appear to be forthcoming. Turner's unique insight, which has often allowed him to see well into the future, fails whenever he is forced to look back inside himself. He operates on pure adrenaline and feeds on unmitigated competition. Turner's uncanny ability to obliterate anything and everything peripheral to his immediate objective makes any kind of self-examination all but impossible.

In attempting to discern the real Ted Turner, define his character, and plumb his motives, I have looked at the man himself and beyond, to the people who surround him, who have stood at his side, followed behind him, and sometimes been bowled over by his inexorable ego. Written without his permission or approval, this biography is based on personal interviews with more than two hundred of Turner's close associates, friends, and family —people who have known Ted Turner well and have been witness, usually with no small amount of awe and amusement, to his transformation over the years into the true American folk hero he once sought so hard to become.

Although he finds any comparison "inappropriate," Ted Turner is rightful heir to the legacy of broadcast pioneer William S. Paley. Both men were enormous risk takers, both defied the odds and conventional wisdom and succeeded in changing the face of television. Both also recognized and responded to the public trust inherent in any media franchise. And both were consummate showmen, personifications of the broadcast empires each had built. Turner has taken Paley one better, however, and turned his business into a bully pulpit of social conscience.

Where this will lead and what the consequences of such open advocacy will be remain to be seen. But there are no hidden motives in Ted Turner's larger agenda—he is as serious about population control and environmental pollution as Rupert Murdoch may be about tabloid television or Barry Diller about cable shopping.

A new revolution is under way within the broadcasting industry, a revolution that promises to turn the television set into an interactive information highway of five hundred channels or more. Can there be a place for Ted Turner in the new world of high-density television, fiber optics, and digital compression?

Turner already controls the largest news-gathering organization in the world. And it's growing larger every day. He also controls the largest library of motion pictures anywhere, one of the largest collections of animated film, and more individual programming networks than any other broadcaster. His CNN already airs in Spanish and Portuguese to all of Latin America. Turner is rapidly ramping up cooperative ventures, like his recent forays into Germany and Finland, to provide twenty-four hours of all news in local language throughout continental Europe. On January 1, 1993, Turner switched on the first advertiser-sponsored, Russian-language television station in the Soviet Union, a joint venture between TBS and Moscow Independent Broadcasting Company. Next comes the first Soviet superstation.

Turner scorns the idea of spending hundreds of millions of dollars to develop HDTV or billions to wire the country with fiber optics, when two-thirds of the world still goes to bed hungry every night. Instead he invests in what he believes—Native American film projects, Cousteau documentaries, *National Geographic* specials, and mass educational ventures like the animated series "Capt. Planet," which all have a legitimate business rationale but which also carry important messages Turner wants the world to hear. Will he be left at the post as the new information age unfolds? Not bloody likely.

We are living through a watershed in history as cataclysmic as the invention of movable type or the Industrial Revolution. The basic economic currency is no longer capital or natural resources or labor. The only currency that matters now is knowledge. Economic performance, theorist Peter Drucker contends, is no longer the sole purpose of a business. "Organizations have a responsibility," he suggests, "to find an approach to basic social problems that can match their competence." If Drucker is right, Turner may once again have got himself out on the cutting edge, as Turner Broadcasting System becomes a prototype of the new age corporation.

No one who has ever met Ted Turner can remain indifferent to the man. He is complicated and contradictory, but utterly compelling. He says he carries the burden of saving the world on his shoulders, but his own children have called him an abusive and irresponsible parent. His better qualities are often overshadowed by the monumental banality of his public persona. In spite of it all, Ted Turner remains a charismatic, kinetic life force. As his new bride and third wife, Jane Fonda, has observed, "There is nobody who can so quickly recognize a truth and internalize it." In addition to a lightning-quick mind, Turner also has a sixth sense that allows him to cut through cant and conventional wisdom like the old Confederate saber he has often used to rally his troops.

Ted Turner at fifty-four has already outlived his father, no mean triumph itself for this man who predicted his own demise for decades. Despite the daily doses of lithium he began taking in 1986 and several game attempts at analysis, he still runs on a high octane mixture of insecurity, charm, intelligence, cunning, and ambition. *Vicarious* is not a word he is ever likely to experience. There is nothing phony about Ted Turner. That, in the end, and not the measure of his extraordinary material successes— may finally be enough to lay his father's ghost to rest.

New York City
June 1993

*What e'er soon creetur Brer Rabbit is, dat
nobody can't fool him. Nobody can't outdo
him. He is one of deze yere graveyard rabbits.
Dat's what he is.*

JOEL CHANDLER HARRIS
Tales of Uncle Remus

Chapter One

The wedding was supposed to be a secret. "You'll know when it happens. We don't want helicopters buzzing around over our house," Ted Turner told the media. And since he *was* the media, he added thoughtfully, "It's not likely I'll let anybody scoop me on the story." Not even Turner, however, could stop the two news copters that hovered incessantly over his 8,100-acre Avalon Plantation that bright winter morning. Their ear-shattering clatter finally drove the bridal party from the plantation's small private chapel into the relative sanctuary of the main house nearby.

Once everyone had reassembled inside, Reverend A. I. Dixie, a local Baptist minister who had been sworn to secrecy, was able to complete the simple fifteen-minute nondenominational ceremony. The bride herself had stayed up late the night before to compose the couple's vows, a proper new age promise that pointedly omitted any reference to the word *obey*. Shortly after noon on December 21, 1991, in the sun-splashed sitting room of this classic old square-columned Florida plantation house, Robert Edward Turner III and Jane Seymour Fonda Plemiannikov Hayden were formally and, according to most observers, fittingly joined together in holy matrimony.

It turned out that Ted Turner was scooped, however, when the Associated Press flashed news of the nuptials across its wire minutes before he was able to pick up a telephone himself to call

Michael Oglesby, Turner Broadcasting's vice-president of corporate communications in Atlanta, who cleared the story for CNN. "It's a fact," Turner's all-news network was finally able to announce breathlessly. "That long awaited wedding has just happened."

Culminating a very public two-year courtship, Ted Turner's wedding day was a remarkable contrast to the celebration of the marriage a little more than seven months before, of his firstborn, Laura Lee Turner, to Rutherford Seydel II. On that notable occasion, a red-letter day on Atlanta's social calendar, the bride and groom pronounced their vows before the sixty-two-member Atlanta Boys Choir, twenty groomsmen, ten bridesmaids, over eight hundred invited guests, and several dozen working press. Laura Lee had worn a hand-stitched, champagne silk-and-organza wedding dress, with a long-sleeved bodice hand-embroidered in France with rhinestones and pearls. In spite of all the pomp, the show had been stolen that day by Ted and Jane who held hands in their seat near the front of the church and went on to charm half of Atlanta at his daughter's reception.

For his own wedding day, Ted Turner was decked out in a wilted white linen suit, white open-collar shirt, and brown leather shit-kicker boots. With a white rose pinned to his lapel, he looked every inch the contemporary southern country squire. Jane Fonda, celebrating her fifty-fourth birthday as well as her betrothal, wore a formal high-waisted, high-necked Empire gown resurrected from her 1980 film, *Rollover*. Completing the ephemeral but utterly incongruous effect, Fonda had pinned up her own frosted auburn hair into a halo of fresh yellow and white freesias.

The small coterie in attendance included the couple's seven children from their four previous marriages and a dozen loyal members of the Avalon household staff. Also present were Jane's brother, Peter; her stepmother, Shirlee Fonda; Dee Woods, Ted's personal assistant and right hand for the past twenty-two years; Barbara Pyle, an attractive Turner intimate who serves as his conscience on environmental affairs; and Peter A. Dames, Sr., a longtime business associate who worked for both Ted and Ted's father.

Wandering among the guests was the only outsider present, a pretty young woman in dark glasses and a bizarre red-and-black satin smoking jacket, who had been hired to videotape the entire proceedings for posterity.

Jane Fonda had chosen her eighteen-year-old son, Troy Hayden, to give the bride away. The only other formal wedding attendant was a tall, heavyset black gentleman named Jimmy Brown, who served as Ted's best man.

How appropriate that this graying, round-faced man with the million-dollar smile and congenitally withered left arm should once again be at Ted Turner's side. After all, Jimmy Brown had served three generations of the Turner family as houseman, chauffeur, and general factotum. He had raised Ted Turner almost singlehandedly—taught him to fish, to hunt, and, not incidentally, to sail in the treacherous tidewaters of the Skidaway and Savannah rivers. "My father worked a lot," Ted has said, generously understating reality, "and didn't spend much time with me. I was really raised by this black man."

A Gullah from Isle of Hope, Georgia, Jimmy Brown was just seventeen when he first came to work for Ed Turner. He still speaks the lilting Geechee dialect his Gola forebears brought with them from west Africa. His first job had been to take care of *Thistle*, the forty-foot Great Lakes schooner Ed sometimes kept down in the Bahamas. He later came into the Turner household as cook, chauffeur, and what in Geechee is called a "da," or nanny, to Ed's only son. Jimmy Brown had been there for Ted through the many years when Ted's father never was. And he was still there today, through nearly half a century of service and his own difficult times overcoming a personal battle with the bottle.

"It's an Uncle Remus–type relationship," Ted Turner once tried explaining. "That's the way it is. I love him like my own father. You can say he's a servant if you want to, but I don't think of him like a servant."

Now approaching seventy, Jimmy had been more than surrogate father and big brother to Ted Turner; he had also been the one constant in his employer's tumultuous life—the closest, perhaps the only, true friend Ted Turner had ever really known.

Ted's eighty-two-year-old mother, Florence Rooney Turner Carter, was conspicuously absent from this intimate family affair. Suffering from complications brought on by a persistent heart condition, she had planned to be there, had even picked out her dress, but was too weak to make the trip from Cincinnati. Florence would pass away just three weeks later, leaving Jimmy Brown as Ted Turner's only real link with his past.

As usual, Jimmy had done his best to ensure that this day would be as perfect as possible. He knew exactly how his Mr. Ted liked everything and piled the wedding table high with Avalon's native bounty—wild rice, candied yams, collard greens, corn bread, and fresh quail, shot by none other than the bride herself. The wedding cake was a glorious three-tiered affair, redolent with the fragrance of fresh gardenias.

Once the short service was over, everyone moved outside under the natural awning of Spanish moss that graced the beautifully tailored grounds of the turn-of-the-century plantation, softening the harsh December sun of that warm winter day. Barbara Pyle, who was a *Time* magazine photographer when Turner met her during the 1980 America's Cup in Newport, Rhode Island, cranked off several rolls of film as everybody took turns dancing with the bride. Then the assembled guests did their best with two or three politically correct rounds of "Amazing Grace." Even Ted's two black Labrador retrievers, both sporting gaily colored bandanas in honor of their master's nuptials, joined in and tried crooning a few bars. After a long, leisurely lunch in Avalon's ample dining room, glasses were raised, principally by the younger generation, since the bride and groom both claimed to be abstemious. An endless series of overblown champagne toasts then followed, threatening to last well into the evening.

"It was a wonderful and joyous moment," Peter Fonda remembered. "We were all crying and laughing." Ted and Jane took a few turns around Avalon's ballroom, doing their best to keep in step with the music of a pickup band led by the son of Ted's plantation manager, George Purvis. That effort took its toll on Ted, however, who had never been comfortable on the dance floor. And so, promptly at nine o'clock, just as everyone else was getting a wind, the blissful newlyweds said good night and retired upstairs, where Jane would try on, a little sheepishly, the negligee she had picked out a few weeks earlier at Frederick's of Hollywood for their wedding night. The couple surfaced three weeks later, after a New Year's stopover at Ted's huge Montana ranch, for a postnuptial celebration three thousand miles away in Los Angeles, where Hollywood finally got to meet Hotlanta.

This time the crowd was considerably larger and significantly more self-conscious: 125 strictly A-list guests, each with some legitimate tie to either the bride or the groom. Braving the evening's unseasonable heat to crowd into Los Angeles' elite L'Orangerie restaurant, they sanctioned by their presence the union of their town's newest power couple. The eclectic gathering, which included a smattering of old Turner cronies like Bill Barthalomay, who sold Ted the Atlanta Braves in 1976 and still sits on his

board of directors, took turns downing Dom Pérignon and gawking at the likes of Barbara Walters, Lily Tomlin, Meg Ryan, Charl-
ton Heston, Mike Ovitz, Barry Diller, Jeff Bridges, Quincy Jones,
Jon Voight, and Gregory Peck, all of whom had worked with
either Jane or Ted and were counted by the couple among their
closest friends.

By arriving characteristically late, the newlyweds made a
smashing entrance and lost no time working the room with their
usual professional aplomb. Drifting onto the dance floor, they
gamely attempted a tango but soon lapsed into an evening-long
dance floor embrace, leaving everyone with the distinct impression they were watching a couple of teenagers in love. It was well
past midnight when things finally quieted down enough for a
delirious Dolly Parton to begin tapping her glass as she asked the
crowd for silence. Then she cleared her throat and raised a champagne flute in tribute to "the Man of the Year. The Woman of the
Hour. The Couple of the Century!"

Thirty years ago Ted Turner could hardly have imagined he
might one day find himself in such surroundings. Or running a
global media conglomerate worth more than $6 billion. Or fea-
tured on the cover as *Time* magazine's Man of the Year. Let alone
married to Jane Fonda.

Back then he liked to catalog, for virtually anyone who would
listen, the triumphs he was certain he could achieve. These included becoming a millionaire, winning the America's Cup, and
being elected president. But Turner in 1961 could not have been
particularly sanguine about his future. Expelled from Brown University after an earlier suspension, he had watched his sister,
Mary Jane, succumb to the ravages of lupus cerebritis, a horribly
debilitating disease that led to a five-year siege of violent fits and
agonizing pain before she finally died. He had also seen his parents' twenty-two-year marriage unravel. And now even his own
tempestuous two-year attempt at matrimony was coming apart
at the seams.

Ted Turner was descended on his father's side from English, Scot-
tish, and French forbears and on his mother's from rather more
substantial German, Irish, and Dutch stock, a genealogical legacy
responsible for many of the contradictions that would influence
the way he came to view the world and the way he would live his
life. "I got my thrift," Turner has said, trying valiantly to explain

his uniquely inexplicable individualism, "from the Scots, my work ethic from the Germans, and my colorfulness from the French and the British. My judgment and conservatism come from the Dutch, and the Irish—well, the Irish, they're all off their rockers, unbalanced."

Ted's father was a garrulous, gregarious southerner born and raised in Sumner, Mississippi, a once prosperous planters' town and the seat of Tallahatchie County. The town made headlines in the 1960s as the site of Emmett Till's murder, although Ted Turner had been oblivious of the growing civil rights movement then sweeping the South and would hardly have thought twice about the coincidence. The Turners of Sumner were the last in a long line of well-to-do but hardworking cotton farmers who began a migration into northwestern Mississippi early in the nineteenth century.

Simon Theophilus Turner, Ted's great-great-grandfather, was born in North Carolina in 1809. A cousin of Captain Robert Turner, who served with General Francis Marion, the famed "Carolina Swamp Fox," Simon Turner believed his future lay farther west. He brought his Bible and his faith in a Methodist God with him as he crossed over the Great Smoky Mountains into Tennessee. Then he followed the Natchez Trace all the way to Memphis, where he met Mary Ann Eddings, an Alabama girl five years his junior. The couple married and remained in Memphis long enough to have two sons before deciding to join the Mississippi land rush that occurred in the early 1830s when a large tract of Choctaw tribal land in the northwestern quarter of the state was opened up to settlers. Drawn to this rich, bayou-country farmland, Turner and his young family sank their roots near the new county seat of Carrollton. By the time Mississippi's first census was taken in 1850, the Turner household had expanded to include six more children, plus "one male and two female Negro slaves."

Through a prudent marshaling of his resources, Simon Theophilus accumulated a respectable amount of Carroll County cotton land, often trading properties with one James Wellons, another North Carolinian who had arrived in Mississippi shortly ahead of the Turners. In due course Simon's oldest daughter would marry into the Wellons family, thus creating a modest Turner-Wellons dynasty that was to survive well into the mid-twentieth century.

Decades of cotton crops, however, began to wear out the once fertile fields. By the end of the nineteenth century Robert Edward Turner and his younger brother, Frank Wellons Turner, were ready to move on. They traveled farther west to Sumner, Mississippi, where they settled down to seek their fortunes. Both young men were still in their teens.

Without benefit of a formal education and with only the barest hint of an inheritance, Robert Edward Turner soon proved he was no less adept than his grandfather at piecing together opportunistic land purchases. Before he was twenty-one, R.E., as he now called himself, had accumulated enough acreage to become a full-fledged cotton planter. A few years later he was feeling substantial enough to venture downriver in search of a wife. In Indianola, Mississippi, he found Maggie Dill Gaston. A handsome young farmer's daughter with traces of Cajun blood, "Dillsey" Gaston was as enterprising as she was independent. The couple married in 1908, and before long Dillsey had helped her husband parlay their Sumner holdings into a very considerable amount of agricultural real estate.

In 1911 Robert Edward Turner, Jr., Ted's father, was born. Two younger sisters, Frances and Gaston, followed in quick succession. The land in Sumner, however, proved to be no kinder to the growing Turner family than the Carroll County fields had been to their forebears. As the Great War raged in Europe, R. E. Turner found it necessary to open a grocery and general store in Sumner to augment his declining income. Shortly thereafter he moved his family into town, taking a large house on Cassidy Street.

A staunch and active citizen, R. E. Turner was also a devout Christian and elder of the Sumner Methodist Church. He was determined that his only son should not be deprived, as he himself had been, of the advantages of a formal education, and in 1929, just three weeks before Black Tuesday and the start of the Great Depression, he sent Ed Turner off to Ole Miss, the state university in Oxford. R.E.'s financial situation, however, continued to deteriorate, and shortly thereafter he was forced to give up the house, close the grocery store, and move his wife and daughters back onto the farm. Like many other Delta planters in those early Depression years, R.E. could not afford the necessary help to work his fields and was forced to depend on the meager income generated by his sharecropping tenant farmers.

Ed Turner knew from the moment he left home he would have to rely on his ingenuity to cover his expenses. When he got to Oxford, he tried stringing tennis rackets and working as a cabinet maker's assistant. He even apprenticed himself out as a butcher. None of these jobs lasted long enough for him to pay his way through school, however, and Ed Turner was finally forced to leave Ole Miss without the degree he knew was so important to his father.

Disheartened, yet sustained by the fierce ambition that had fired generations of Turners before him, Ed made his way to Memphis, where he unexpectedly found work as a traffic counter for General Outdoor Advertising, the largest billboard company in the country. Ed was intrigued by the potential of this new business, but before he could learn much about it, an acquaintance from Oxford offered to introduce him to the owner of a large automobile dealership in Cincinnati, Ohio. Ed Turner knew he was a natural-born salesman and was certain somebody up in heaven was merely confirming the fact. Without a moment's hesitation he packed up his belongings and headed north. Ed not only landed the job when he got to Cincinnati; he also proved to be Queen City Chevrolet's new star salesman.

One of Ed Turner's first customers was a gentleman by the name of George F. Rooney, Jr., grandson of Henry Sicking, one of Cincinnati's most prominent citizens. Founder of the first chain grocery in the Midwest and proprietor of a popular Cincinnati livery stable, Henry Sicking was just forty years old when he stepped off one moving trolley car directly into the path of another. Sicking was killed instantly. His portrait shows him to have been a tall, handsome man with sharply chiseled features, a prominent, dimpled chin, a close-cropped mustache, and deep-set, piercing blue eyes. "He looked enough like Ted Turner," says Lucy Rooney, Ted's mother's cousin by marriage, "to have been his brother." Despondent over reversals in the stock market, the unfortunate Henry Sicking nevertheless left his wife and seven-year-old daughter, Florence, a sizable fortune.

In 1905 Florence Sicking, Ted Turner's grandmother, married George F. Rooney, Sr., and bore him two children, George Jr. and Florence, Ted's mother. When the Rooneys divorced in 1915, Florence and the two children went to live with her mother in Mrs. Sicking's elegant residential apartment hotel.

Raised in a strict Irish Catholic household, Florence Rooney was sent off to a succession of exclusive convent schools. She always relished returning home to her grandmother's hotel, however, where she would sit for hours in the building's grand lobby, mesmerized by the beautiful young flappers who breezed in and out on the arms of some of Cincinnati's most eligible young men.

When she was twenty, Florence became engaged to a prominent young Irishman named Paul McCoy, whose singular misfortune it was to suffer an attack of acute appendicitis the night before they were to be married. Florence was heartbroken when he died two days later and spent most of her twenty-first year in mourning. Her mother, however, was so taken with the McCoy family that she married Paul's father a little less than a year after his poor son passed away. It would be nearly a decade before Florence could become serious about another man. By then, says Lucy Rooney, "she was in total command of herself and her attributes. And she thought she knew exactly what she wanted."

Despite a well-developed eye for the ladies, or perhaps because of it, Ed Turner also had a pretty good idea of what it was he wanted. When his new friend, George Rooney, introduced him to his beautiful sister, Ed decided on the spot that he was going to marry Florence.

There were, however, several other eligible young men ahead of him. So Ed mustered all his southern charm and laid down an eight-month siege for Florence's hand. Occupying as much of her time as he could, Ed managed, sometimes with great difficulty, to hold on to his job and still not leave Florence alone for even one evening. Another suitor, a fine young man from an old northern Virginia family, was equally determined that she should be his. When Ed bundled Florence and her mother into the new Chevrolet he had won in a sales contest and headed down to Mississippi to introduce them to his parents, this other fellow followed right behind, on the off chance that the Turners might not approve of Florence. It was love in vain, however, when a few weeks later Ed Turner and Florence Rooney stood at the main altar of Cincinnati's magnificent old St. Francis deSales Cathedral to plight their troth to each other.

As may have been the custom of some well-bred convent girls in those days Florence Rooney simply assumed that her religion would be their religion. She never even bothered to discuss the subject with her new husband. When she finally did, Ed was adamant. Anything but Catholic! he declared, ensuring that the honeymoon would indeed be short-lived. Hoping to keep the peace, Florence became an Episcopalian on the spot. Though he had been brought up Methodist by his parents, Ed Turner had never professed to any religion and let Florence go off alone each Sunday to acquaint herself with her new high church Episcopal God. (Florence would have the last word, however, when she quietly arranged years later for Ed to be buried as an Episcopalian.)

Another detail that Florence discreetly overlooked during their whirlwind courtship was Ed's increasingly obvious drinking problem. The Rooneys were hardly Irish teetotalers. Florence herself was a light social drinker. But Ed's unusually heavy drinking seemed to accelerate his already dramatic mood swings and intensify the aggressive outbursts that were now beginning to embarrass his new bride. Never one to be inhibited by social convention, Ed Turner concentrated instead on a succession of career moves that led him away from automobiles, briefly into advertising, and then back to the billboard business. Florence was pleased that Ed seemed to have found himself and that he was prepared to settle down in Cincinnati near her mother. On November 19, 1938, as war clouds gathered across Europe and America was slowly trying to work itself out of the Great Depression, Florence was delivered of her firstborn. Bursting with pride and expectation, Ed decreed immediately that the boy would be named Robert Edward Turner III. Three years later Florence bore Ed a daughter. He was so thrilled that he let her name the baby Mary Jane. Yet when the Japanese launched their sneak attack on Pearl Harbor just three weeks later, Ed Turner did not think twice about walking away from his wife and children or the promising position he had just secured for himself with one of Cincinnati's largest outdoor advertising companies. Consumed by patriotism and a sense of adventure, he rushed to enlist in the navy. For the next four years Ed would trundle his wife and young daughter off with him to a long succession of Gulf coast posts. Curiously, however, he chose to leave his three-year-old son behind in Cincinnati. Ted lived there with his grandmother, Florence Sicking Rooney, until he was sent away to boarding school at the tender age of six.

Ted Turner has always had great difficulty talking about this period of his childhood. When he does, he usually manages to put a positive spin to the story. But he counts being left behind by his father as one of the saddest moments in his life—one that left an indelible scar on his psyche. The experience was clearly a significant defining moment. From that point on, Ted Turner's actions, if not his words, would mark him as a lonely, defiant outsider. This early abandonment also established a pattern of rejection by a father determined from the start to treat his son as harshly as he would treat his daughter kindly. It was only the first of many prolonged separations from his parents that would heavily influence the young Ted Turner. In fact, he would spend all but one of the next fifteen years away from his home and family. There is nothing mysterious about the origin of Turner's contradictory character. Deprived of his parents' love and affection, he sought approval wherever he could find it. This lost young soul became a dreamer because he had no other world quite so real as the one in his head. His enormous self-reliance was nothing more than a matter of survival. In fifty-five years Ted Turner hasn't changed. He is still the dreamer, the irascible, incorrigible outsider. He must still do it all himself, and he is still driven to seek out the approval of others in nearly everything he does.

After the war, Ed Turner brought his abbreviated family back to Cincinnati, where, with a little help from his mother-in-law, he set himself up in his own billboard company. Turner Advertising was hardly an overnight success, since Ed chose to locate the new business across the Ohio River in Covington, Kentucky, outside the lucrative but intensely competitive Cincinnati market. Once he signed up one of Cincinnati's bigger breweries, however, Turner Advertising was in business for real, and Ed never looked back.

Ed's early success, however, was nearly his undoing. His Cincinnati competitors were quick to follow him across the river to Covington and soon began to crowd him out of the market. He remembered a sleepy old billboard company in Georgia that had caught his eye during the war, and it took him just one visit to convince the retiring owner of Price & Mapes, Savannah's only billboard operator, to merge with Turner Advertising.

Once again Ed gathered up his wife and daughter and took them south. And once again he left young Ted behind. Noting that his boy, now nine years old, was in continuous hot water at his Cincinnati boarding school, Ed decided a little dose of military discipline might now be in order. Accordingly, Ted was packed off to spend the fourth grade at a stark, forbidding institution called Georgia Military Academy. Located about twenty miles southeast of Atlanta, Georgia Military sat on a lonely, isolated campus surrounded by tall Georgia pines and little else. The place would have done Parris Island proud and carried the unsavory reputation in those days as a haven of last resort for well-to-do young delinquents.

No one will ever know exactly what was in Ed Turner's mind

when he chose Georgia Military for his son. It is certain, however, that he never discussed the matter with Florence, who voiced her objection to the place, however feebly, years later and regretted not speaking out sooner.

It was inevitable that Cadet Turner would start off on the wrong foot at Georgia Military Academy. He arrived late, nearly six weeks after the beginning of term, since his father had been too preoccupied to arrange his transportation from Cincinnati. Ted's harsh midwest accent didn't help. Nothing, however, prevented his demanding obeisance from his three new fourth-grade room- mates the moment he unpacked. After taps, Ted quietly but firmly offered to take them on, one at a time or all together, whichever they preferred. It was all bluff and bravado, but none of the three was willing to accept this brash newcomer's invitation. Naturally Ted decided to push his luck. Talking after taps was strictly for- bidden. Undaunted, Ted shouted out the same challenge to the unknown occupants of the adjoining room. Unfortunately three strapping seventh-graders came barreling through the door and proceeded to pummel him to within an inch of his life.

Ted was beaten but hardly bowed; he had grown used to much worse at the hands of his father, and had learned to steel himself many times against beatings that were often without any real provocation. Ed Turner sometimes even stropped his son with a wire coat hanger. Anything these twelve-year-olds could wreak on him paled by comparison. "It was still pretty rough," Ted has recounted. "I was from Ohio. I was a northerner. I don't know what it was. Yes, I do know what it was. The other kids thought I was a show-off and a smart ass."

Georgia Military introduced Ted to the grand old southern con- cept of honor. His father spoke of *his* honor incessantly, and now Ted began to understand when he found himself having to defend his own, sometimes several times a day—whenever the rumor ricocheted around campus that Teddy Turner said Robert E. Lee was a traitor, prompting half a dozen outraged upperclassmen to chase him through the dorm, shouting, "Kill the Yankee bas- tard!"

Life at Georgia Military was not without its compensations, however. Founded in 1900, the school was run exactly like an army camp. Students woke to reveille at dawn, marched to classes, and spent their afternoons on the parade ground. Ted relished the tight structure of his life there and grew to love the military discipline. Introduced to close-order drill and the manual of arms, the young loner began to forge a connection between his own transient life and the careers of great Confederate military leaders, as well as the Greek and Roman generals they sometimes patterned themselves after. He loved the pomp of his Confederate gray uniform and began slowly to absorb all that it stood for. Soon even his alien accent began to soften, and before he was in the fifth grade Ted Turner could easily have been mistaken for a North Georgia native.

Since his parents never seemed to have room for him at home, Ted usually spent summer vacations with one set of grandparents or the other. There is little question that he preferred the bayou country of his grandfather Turner's Mississippi farm. It was here this self-reliant city boy first discovered the out-of-doors. Ted would lose himself for hours on end trudging up Sumner's old creek beds, catching hop toads and cow snakes, and exploring rabbit warrens along Cassidy Bayou. His grandfather taught him to trap snapping turtles with a piece of string and a little hunk of meat, a trick Ted would teach his own sons years later. He was fixated by the symbiotic relationship between his grandfather and his coonhounds and marveled at the way man, dogs, and quarry all seemed bound together in some private, mysterious world. Turner has carried on a lifelong love affair with his own hunting dogs and tries to make certain his favorites are nearby wherever he goes. Ted never forgot what he learned about nature during those Mississippi summers. When he began the fifth grade at Georgia Military, he sent away for a mail-order taxidermy course and actually taught himself the craft.

Ted came home the following summer to find his father riding the crest of an extended economic boom that had now spread throughout the Southeast. Ed Turner was on his way to becoming successful beyond even his wildest dreams. The "breathers" he used to enjoy with occasional lady friends down in the Bahamas had given way to lavish social outings on board the *Merry Jane*, the big motorized yacht that replaced his old Lakes schooner and was now Jimmy Brown's new responsibility. Ed entertained frequently, usually without Florence, and would often throw big parties for his customers and his friends on his boat or downtown at the old Savannah Hotel.

He took to having real Irish linen suits custom-tailored in New Orleans and would frequently disappear with Jimmy for days at a time to have a few new bespoke suits run up. Ed was also very particular about his Panama hats, always insisting on the genuine article, which he continued to wear long after they had gone out of style. Only a penchant for loud, expensive silk ties hinted that Ed Turner might be anything less than the prototypical Mississippi plantation owner he yearned to be.

By 1948, however, Ed Turner was ready to settle down in Savannah. He bought a large five-bedroom house at 3204 Abercorn Street, just a few blocks from the city's historic old Oglethorpe Square district. For the first time in his life, Ted would have a room under his parents' roof. Covered in ivy and shaded by one-hundred-year-old sycamores draped in Spanish moss, the red-brick colonial also had room for Jimmy Brown, who came in off the *Merry Jane* to live with the family.

By the early 1950s Ed Turner was proving to have a real genius for the billboard business. He now had virtual monopolies in Savannah, Macon, Columbus, and Charleston. Turner Advertising had become the largest outdoor advertising company in the Southeast. Despite this success, however, Ed continued to push himself to the limits of his physical endurance. He worked eighteen-hour days and then went on twenty-four-hour binges. His drinking was often out of control. Ed began spending less and less time at home. Jimmy Brown would usually drive him to the office in his massive new Lincoln Continental, but by noon Ed would already have drunk himself into a fog. Tall, handsome, and mustachioed in his twenties, he had put on considerable weight over the years and now looked far older than his thirty-nine years. He suffered from bleeding ulcers and frequent migraine attacks but believed his drinking was the cause of these ills. He also believed, fervently, that he could stop drinking whenever he chose. "I'd have more trouble giving up cigarettes than liquor," Ed once told his accountant, Irwin Mazo. And by exerting his enormous will, Ed would periodically endure extended dry spells, sometimes for as long as several months. But alcohol—and his philandering, which had now become embarrassingly obvious to nearly everyone in Savannah—provided his only relief from an inexorable pressure he felt mounting within him. A few weeks or months without a drink, and the furies deep inside would begin to stir once more. Then Ed would be off again.

Those same furies were responsible for the physical and emotional abuse Ed Turner often heaped upon his son. He would fly into rages at the slightest provocation, whipping Ted into submission over the most insignificant infraction. It was not unheard of, even in that relatively enlightened day, for a father to take his belt to a son. But Ed Turner's abuse went considerably further and often included the use of that wire coat hanger. The most painful punishment of all, however, may have been verbal, since his father's disapproval hurt Ted more than any beating. Courtly and courteous one moment, Ed Turner could suddenly turn violently abusive. Carl Helfrich, Sr., a Savannah architect whose son, Bunky, was a contemporary of Ted's, once noted that "Ed could turn on an old friend he felt had let him down." The most frequent victim of Ed Turner's unpredictable rage, however, was his own son.

Marshall Hartmann, Ted's stepbrother who came into the family when Ed Turner married Jane Dillard Hartmann, was an eyewitness to Ed's vehement outbursts. He saw firsthand the mounting tension between Ed and his son, which he believes may have contributed to their rapidly deteriorating relationship. Hartmann also believes Ed suffered from the volatility usually associated with a classic bipolar personality, which, says Hartmann, was, in all likelihood passed on to Ted. "Ed Turner was a wild man," he remembers. "He was very unconventional. His favorite comment was 'I'm a double-barreled, revolving son of a bitch,' and I guess he really was. Ed had a big mouth and a big car. He liked to drive fast, when Jimmy Brown wasn't chauffeuring him around, and he would tear up the roads between Savannah and Charleston. Naturally, he kept getting tickets. One time, though, he saw a cop speeding. Ed ran him down and made a 'citizen's arrest.' The guy told Ed he couldn't do that, and Ed told him, 'I'll see you in court.' The cop doesn't want that, so Ed says, 'Okay. You guys leave me alone . . . and I'll leave you alone.' He was like that. I don't think anybody else in the world ever had Ed's nerve."

Marshall Hartmann couldn't help noticing the sharp mood swings Ted seemed to share with his father. "I think both of them had an unusual ability," he says, "to deal with extreme highs and extreme lows. Ed saw all kinds of doctors, but it was always for his ulcers or his drinking or his smoking. I don't think any of them had even heard of manic depression in those days. Looking back, I'd say it was probably impossible for anybody to deal with Ed when he was on one of his extreme highs or lows. I guess the same could hold for Ted. He was just the mirror image of his father, and the two of them were always going at each other, tooth and nail.

"Ed was never abusive with me," Hartmann adds, "at least the way he was with Ted. He was tough. Made me pay for anything I broke around the house. But he never beat me, and I never had to pay rent the way Ted did. Because I was so much younger, I guess."

Some of the people who knew Ed Turner best are inclined to rationalize his treatment of Ted as strong discipline, the kind any father might dispense to a recalcitrant son. One close observer, Dr. Irving Victor, a Savannah urologist who was Ed Turner's friend and hunting companion for many years, realized Ed suffered from extreme mood swings but never connected those symptoms with the possibility that he might have been manic-depressive. "I saw him get very strict with my own children," Victor says. "He taught my son Kirk how to tie his shoelaces. But if Kirk didn't do it right, Ed would probably hit him. He was a disciplinarian, there's no question about that."

Florence Turner agreed. She felt powerless beside her husband and was unable to stay his hand. "Teddy was a little on the mischievous side," she admitted, "but he was never really bad. His daddy just ruled with an iron hand." Still, she added ruefully, "Ninety percent of the arguments I had with Ed were over his beating Ted too hard."

Young Ted was beginning to understand his father's ferocity could no more be averted than predicted. Ed Turner further confused his son with spontaneous bursts of generosity that often obscured the horror of his rage. As the summer of his tenth year drew to a close, Ted assumed he would be returning to Georgia Military for the sixth grade. Instead his father unexpectedly announced that Ted would be staying in Savannah, as his mother desired, and attending Charles Ellis grammar school. Then, out of the blue, Ed bought his son a new Penguin sailing dinghy. It was Jimmy Brown, however, and not Ed Turner who would first take Ted out on the Skidaway River and teach him how to read the wind and the water. "Our black houseman, Jimmy Brown, deserves all the credit for starting Ted in sailing," Florence Turner confirmed. "At first Teddy wasn't interested, but somehow Jimmy talked him into it."

When Ed Turner decided to join the elite Savannah Yacht Club, the evolving relationship between father and son underwent an almost imperceptible change. Still leaving the sailing lessons to Jimmy, Ed nevertheless enjoyed watching Ted compete in the club's junior regattas. Carl Helfrich was frequently among the spectators out on the yacht club veranda. He noted in passing that it was usually Ed Turner who towed those impossibly long strings of Penguin dinghies out to the races each Saturday morning behind the *Merry Jane.* One of Savannah's first citizens, Mills B. Lane, chairman of Citizens & Southern Bank, was also a frequent spectator, but his eye was on Ed Turner, the swaggering parvenu. "We have a long tradition of tolerating eccentricity in this town," Lane pontificated, "but Ed Turner was not somebody you'd ever put up for the Oglethorpe Club." Mr. Lane, who had once turned Ed down for a business loan, frequently wondered out loud how "a redneck cracker like Ed Turner ever got into a place like the Savannah Yacht Club." Ed hardly seemed to notice that he was frequently given a cold shoulder by Lane and most of Savannah's old-money establishment. Had he ever cared to respond, he might have suggested that Mr. Mills B. Lane take a good look at young Robert Edward Turner III. Still too young to show his real promise as a sailor, Ted capsized eleven times in his first year in the junior program but placed second two years later and won the junior championship the following year. Unaware of Mr. Lane's observations, Ted Turner was becoming convinced that winning sailboat races just might be a way to win his father's favor.

Ted's new success on the water, however, was not enough to prevent Ed Turner from declaring that one year at home was quite sufficient. Next semester Ted would enter McCallie, an exclusive boy's school in Chattanooga, Tennessee. "I don't think Ted was any great student," his mother observed. "He loved the outdoors, but he was not really too interested in schoolwork. It didn't move fast enough for him. His teachers said he was not working to the full extent of his ability." That may have been reason enough for his father's sudden decision to send him away once again.

"There was nothing I could do," Florence confessed. "I cried. It did no good. Ed told me he had the purse strings. I had to do what he said." Or perhaps, as Florence speculated, "Ed always insisted on sending Ted away to school because he was jealous of my love for the boy." Nevertheless, Ted entered McCallie in September 1950. He was about to turn twelve years old, and he would be the only seventh-grade boarder at the school.

Founded in 1905, the McCallie School is a highly regarded college preparatory school located on the slopes of Missionary Ridge just above Chattanooga. During World War I, McCallie, like many other independent schools at the time, instituted a military program as part of its regular curriculum. That program continued until the late 1960s, when military training was discontinued. Among the distinguished alumni of Ted Turner's era are such disparate overachievers as former Senate majority leader Howard Baker, Jr.; Ralph E. McGill, late Pulitzer Prize–winning editor of the *Atlanta Constitution;* Pat Robertson, president of Christian Broadcasting Network; former chairman of the Massachusetts Institute of Technology Dr. James R. Killian; and Charles Battle, vice-president of the 1996 Atlanta Olympic Committee. Ed Turner had selected one of the best and toughest schools in the South for Ted. He had also sent him off to McCallie two years earlier than the school usually accepted boarding students.

"I love McCallie," Ted Turner says now. "Probably no single thing or institution has influenced my life more." And indeed, he recently interrupted a talk he was giving at the John F. Kennedy School of Government at Harvard University to share his enthusiasm for the school with a young McCallie graduate in the audience.

"Ted hated McCallie," his mother attested. "He was a devil there. I had to buy him new shoes every time he came home. He wore them out walking punishment tours." According to Florence Turner, Ted would do everything in his power to avoid going back to McCallie after each school break.

Despite his earlier exposure to a military regimen at Georgia Military, it took Cadet Turner nearly three years to adjust to life at McCallie. "At first I was just a terrible cadet," Ted admitted. "I did everything I could to rebel against the system. I was always having animals in my room and stuff like that, and getting into trouble one way or another, and then having to take my punishment like a man." In fact, he once boasted, "I caused McCallie to completely review its whole disciplinary system. I had more demerits than anyone in the history of the school. They used to give demerits for dirty shoes and things like that. For every demerit, you had to walk a quarter of a mile. Well, there was only so much time you could walk on any weekend and anything left over was carried over.

"I wound up with more than one thousand demerits in my first year. Anyway, it was more miles than you could walk. So they had to devise a new system where you couldn't get a limitless supply of demerits. It got to the point where they just couldn't do any more with me."

"Ted was very much of a loner at McCallie," remembers classmate William Cook. "On the weekends, when the other guys would be going into town to movies and to record shops and things like that, Ted and his math professor, a gentleman by the name of Houston Patterson, would go out to Lake Chickamauga and sail. Because he'd come from Savannah, that was probably Ted's first love, and he spent a lot of time out there on the lake."

"Ted was a determined youngster," Professor Patterson recalls. "He wanted to prove to people you could sail year round, that weather made no dent in the sailing season. We never really had to break ice to go sailing, but Ted did sail in weather where no sane human being would ever set foot in a sailboat." What struck Patterson and others at McCallie about the tall, thin Ted Turner was his extraordinary persistence. "When he set his mind to something," says Patterson, "he always stuck to it until he eventually achieved it or got struck down trying."

Ted was not much of a leader, according to Patterson, and not even particularly popular. "He wasn't disliked. He just sort of went on his own little beacon."

"I wouldn't call him a loner," says James McCallie, a grandson of the school's founder and classmate during Ted's six years at McCallie. "He was really more self-contained than a loner. He had been away at boarding schools for most of his life, and that was very, very unusual in those days. He probably got all of his independence from having been on his own for so long. He could be pretty obnoxious, but he was tough. I think a lot of us admired him because he didn't seem to care a bit about what anybody else thought of him."

Ted left an indelible impression on a number of his seventh-grade classmates one autumn afternoon in 1951 when they piled into the locker room after football practice only to find a gaggle of other boys standing around, giggling and pointing. There, underneath a bank of showers turned on full tilt, was Cadet Turner sitting on a stool, singing at the top of his lungs, with the biggest erection most of those young innocents had ever seen.

Ted's classmates at McCallie were also impressed with his almost instinctive understanding of wildlife. He once won a five-dollar bet by catching a pillowcase full of squirrels. Ted won this unlikely wager by smoking the squirrels out of a tree with a tin of shoe polish he set on fire. "He created quite a problem," says his old dorm master, Elliott Schmidt, "when he tried to tame one of the squirrels and keep it in his room."

Ted gravitated easily toward mentors like Patterson and Schmidt, who was also head of McCallie's history department and coach of the debate team. He became particularly attached to Schmidt, who was clearly a substitute father figure. "I used to give him a lot of rope," Elliott Schmidt says. "I guess I was very, very unlike his father."

"He was never quite in danger of being asked to leave," says Spencer J. McCallie III, who graduated a year ahead of Ted and is now headmaster. "But he was always trying to see how far he could push the system, whether that included keeping live squirrels or even alligators in his room, setting all the school clocks on different times, or mocking his Latin instructor by organizing a group called Spastics Anonymous. Ted always seemed to know how far he could take things without going over the edge.

"And he questioned everything. The rules, the people. He was not a troublemaker. He just asked questions. 'Why are we doing this? Why is such and such a good idea?' He was an energetic kid. He stood out because he was so full of energy. Very intense. Not a contentious sort at all and certainly not hostile," says McCallie. "It was just 'Here comes Turner again. Let's see what he's up to this time.' "

Closemouthed about his life at home, Ted almost never mentioned his parents to his classmates or his masters. No one at McCallie ever met Ed or Florence Turner. Jimmy Brown would usually drive Ted up from Savannah at the beginning of each term and then pick him up again when school was out. "I got the feeling," Elliott Schmidt observes, "that what the father said went in that family and nobody ever questioned him. We didn't have to meet him to know that."

Ted remained several days after the end of his first year at McCallie, marching off demerits. When Jimmy Brown finally came to take him home, he brought the devastating news that Ted's sister, Mary Jane, had contracted a rare form of lupus, the chronic, inflammatory disease that causes the body to make antibodies against its own tissue. Mary Jane had fallen into a coma, Jimmy said, and the doctors were pretty certain she wasn't going to make it.

Rushed up to Baltimore's Johns Hopkins Hospital, ten-year-old Mary Jane hovered between life and death as Ed Turner frantically called in one specialist after another, trying desperately to save the young daughter he so cherished. Miraculously, Mary Jane emerged from the coma after nearly twelve weeks of unconsciousness. But she had sustained extensive brain damage and was now subject to frequent violent and uncontrollable seizures.

None of the doctors was prepared to say how long she might live. Mary Jane was brought back home to Savannah, where her condition deteriorated over a long and painful five-year period, during which she required almost constant and extensive medical attention.

"It is a terrible, terrible affliction, even today," says Dr. Robert Lahita, chairman of the Lupus Foundation of America. "It causes violent behavioral changes; angry, foul language; the inability to communicate. Everything totally out of character for the individual. It must have been pretty traumatic for Ted Turner to see his little sister in that condition. She would have been like a big rock around everybody's neck. With the advanced diagnostic techniques and new technology we have today, we can catch the disease early and keep it under control." Mary Jane Turner, however, contracted lupus in the early 1950s, before broad-spectrum antibiotics, CAT scans, and magnetic resonance imaging. In those days the disease was almost always fatal.

Ted was heartbroken at the sight of his sister in such agony. He seldom discusses Mary Jane's illness or the effect it had on him to watch her die a little bit each day. When he does, it is with unemotional detachment. "She came out of that coma," he once recalled, "with her brain totally destroyed. It was a horror show of major proportions. A padded room. Screaming day and night. It was something right out of 'Dark Shadows.'" Away at school, Ted had to live with the awful suffering he knew Mary Jane was enduring. When he was home he would lie awake at nights, listening to her screams through his bedroom wall and dying a little bit himself. His mother, however, devoted herself to around-the-clock ministrations to Mary Jane and had time for little else. This apparent withdrawal of her attention helped complete Ted's already strong sense of rejection by both his parents.

That first summer back from McCallie provided Ted with another rude shock. His father now expected him to put in a full forty-hour workweek at Turner Advertising. Whether it was to take his mind off Mary Jane or, more likely, to begin the arduous process of preparing his son for the day when he would take over the business, Ed Turner threw Ted into the deep end, paying him $50 a week to work on labor gangs that did everything from erecting new billboard sites to creosoting signboards and pasting up sixteen-sheet posters. Ed made it clear that he expected Ted to pull his own weight. He also began charging his son $25 per week, more than half of his take-home pay, for room and board. "Of course, that seemed harsh," Elliott Schmidt recalls, "but Ed apparently challenged Ted to stay somewhere else if he thought he could get a better deal. It was probably his father's way of teaching Ted that everything in this world has a price."

Despite the terms of his employment, Ted relished the discovery that he had a genuine capacity for hard work. He learned to concentrate on the job at hand and impressed his co-workers with his tremendous energy and endurance. "I used to fuss a lot when Ed would send Ted out to cut weeds around the signs that were in swampy places full of snakes," remembered Ted's mother. But there was precious little anyone was going to do about it. Ed Turner wanted his son to learn the business, from the bottom up. And young Ted wanted so to please his father. He understood implicitly that the harder he worked, the more likely his father was to take notice.

Saturdays, however, were for sailing and the junior program at the Savannah Yacht Club. Ted had already made the depressing discovery that he lacked the hand–eye coordination required for most sports. He had tried both football and baseball at McCallie but failed to make either team. He liked boxing well enough, but his long, gangly torso made him a perfect punching bag for most of his better-built opponents. Ted was very nearly resigned to becoming, much against his competitive instincts, a spectator rather than a participant. "I didn't have a lot of natural athletic ability," this most immodest of men now says modestly. Sailing, however, was a sport where brute strength and physical dexterity could be offset by intelligence and willpower. Sailing, his instructors assured him, could be learned. "This was a game that took nerves and brains and heart," Ted has noted with a certain satisfaction. "And I had a lot of heart." It was, moreover, a game his father had never really mastered. What further incentive could Ted have needed?

Pushing his eleven-foot Penguin to the limit every time out, he cut angles so sharply at the marker buoys that he invariably missed them (and disqualification) by a hairbreadth. He soon became known as "Hairbreadth Harry" around the club. He was also known as "Turnover Ted" and the "Capsize Kid" long before *Sports Illustrated* hung the sobriquets on him. A ferocious competitor who took crazy chances trying to ride out the fickle coastal winds off the Savannah shore, he frequently lost control and was swamped. "When he sailed," his mother remembered, "Ted would let his little Penguin turn over rather than put his sails down in rough water." It wasn't long, however, before Turnover Ted was the one everyone else had to beat. And Ted seemed to enjoy the attention almost as much as the trophies he began collecting.

"First thing you noticed about him when he got to a regatta," remembers Legarè VanNess, a Charleston sailor who often competed against Ted, "was his voice. Ted was one of the loudest mouths on the water. He would just be screaming and yelling about one thing or another, and he would get out on the race course and you heard nothing but Ted yapping. That was high profile."

Many of those who knew Ted in those years were inclined to write him off as a curious loner, an engaging oddball. In his own defense, Ted says, "I was interested in one thing, and that was finding out what you could accomplish if you really tried." If he lost himself in the classics—in C. S. Forester, Nordhoff and Hall, and Joseph Conrad—and later studied the exploits of Horatio Nelson and other heroes of the high seas, it was for a singular purpose. "My interest," Turner contended, "was always in why people did the things they did, and what causes people to rise to glorious heights."

"His father felt boys grew up better away from the house," speculates Houston Patterson, "and we were probably the only real family he had." The military regimen at McCallie, Patterson believes, "sort of channeled Ted's energies, of which he had an abundance. He was full of mischief and, at the same time, fairly well motivated."

By 1953, Ted's whole attitude suggested he was now determined to begin testing the limits of his own "glorious heights." A medal he had been awarded, somewhat surprisingly, as "neatest cadet" during the previous term at McCallie may have had something to do with this change. "I can still remember him," Spencer McCallie says. "A very intense young lad, tall for his age, standing out there on the parade ground receiving that medal. As proud as could be."

"I just wanted to be the best," is Ted's simple explanation for his turnaround. "And I saw that it could be done if you worked at it." Ted may also have been compensating for his sister's steadily worsening condition. At one point during his sophomore year, he stunned Houston Patterson by announcing his intention to become a missionary. Ted, who had been forced by his father to read at least two books a week during summer vacations, had become a heavy reader and under McCallie's strong Presbyterian influence had taken it upon himself to read the Bible, both the Old Testament and the New Testament, cover to cover, twice. Now he was ready to go out into the world and save some souls.

"I had the greatest difficulty imagining Ted as a missionary," says Patterson. But he admits, with his energy and persistence, Ted would probably have made a great one. Any spiritual aspirations Ted Turner may have harbored, however, as well as his abiding faith in the Almighty, were shattered when in his junior year he learned that Mary Jane had finally succumbed to the ravages of lupus cerebritis and died of systemic brain damage. She was just fifteen. "When his sister passed away, there was very little said about it," Patterson observes. "I didn't probe him for his feelings. Maybe I should have."

"Ted was distraught, utterly devastated," Elliott Schmidt adds. "He was extremely close to Mary Jane. But he never talked about her death." And Schmidt, reluctant to compound Ted's misery, never really discussed the situation with him, either.

Ted Turner eventually rose to the rank of captain at McCallie and served in his senior year as commander of Company E. At graduation he was awarded the Holton Harris Oratorical medal as McCallie's top debater. Having earned the respect of students and faculty alike, Ted was particularly pleased when his father gave him a new Lightning sailboat for graduation. Then Ed announced that Ted would have to pay for half with the money he'd earned over the past five summers. Ted accepted this "deduction," which he knew would wipe out his bank account, because he was lobbying hard for an appointment to Annapolis and hoped Ed would support him in this effort. Ed, of course, had his own ideas about college. He was determined to see his son at Harvard, where Ted could pick the best brains of the eastern establishment and bring something back home to the business. "He was always fighting with his father in those days," says Marshall Hartmann. "There was a lot of love, I think, but they were very much alike, and they were always locked in a power struggle over something, anything. Ed always wanted Ted to slow down, go into the business, and work his way up. I think Ted always had very different ideas about what he wanted to do with his life." In any case, Ted's gentleman's C-grade average at McCallie won immediate rejection at Harvard but proved enough to gain him admittance to Brown University in Providence, Rhode Island. He entered as a member of Brown's class of 1960, intending to major in classics.

Back home for one last summer before heading off to college, Ted proceeded to tear up the pea patch. "He was always up to something," Marshall Hartmann remembers. "He would drive Ed's big old Lincoln up to Charleston. He'd take it up to 120 or 130 miles an hour. There was one time when Ted came to some railroad tracks and a guy was waving like crazy, trying to flag him down. Ted just floored it and went on through. When he was over the tracks, he looked back and saw there was really a train coming through.

"He'd go to parties almost every night, debutante parties, I guess. Then bring his girlfriends back to Binden Hall. Then he'd go off hunting in the morning and leave them back at the house. And you'd wonder why he ever brought them over in the first place.

"Ted was also a terrific gin player," adds the younger Hartmann. "We would play all the time. We'd play six cards, and he'd lay his down and have me beat, every time. I never could figure out how he did it."

In addition to his good head for games, a thickening southern accent, and a deepening resentment of anything his father said or did, Ted went up to Providence that September with a kit bag full of untested ideas about himself. He also brought with him a distinct disinterest in anything academic and a burning desire to prove he could outparty, outdrink, and outscrew anybody else on campus. Included somewhere in all this baggage was a curious $5,000 pledge to be paid by his father if Ted could make it to his twenty-first birthday without having a drink. The story of this pledge was quickly embellished through constant retelling, mostly by Ted himself. The $5,000 soon grew to $1 million, to be paid by his grandmother, not his father, if Ted made it through Brown without drinking *or* smoking.

Alan Laymon, a Brown classmate, says Ted usually told the story of the pledge "with a bottle of bourbon in one hand and a huge, lit cigar in the other." Ted must have enjoyed the irony, since, like most self-respecting young Savannahans of his day, he started drinking in his early teens and had long since earned himself a name among his contemporaries (and not a few observant parents) as one of the town's more serious young debauchers. Ted began building on that reputation almost as soon as he arrived at Brown. "I think we were both on social probation," remembers Alan Laymon, "after the first three weeks of school."

"Basically, we all liked to get drunk and chase women," remembers Peter Dames, another of Ted's classmates. Like Ted, Dames was a military school graduate and, therefore, totally unprepared for the free-form social life at Brown. The preppies from Andover and Exeter had already done it all. "But for us," Dames says, "suddenly there was no 'lights out' at ten o'clock, no bed check, no inspection. You could drink and screw around all you wanted." And, Dames confirms, "they wanted."

Ted says he actually preferred McCallie's relatively strict, structured existence. "I didn't really like it," he has reflected on his time at Brown, "when there were no rules." But since there were rules, Ted quickly decided they were there to break.

This was Brown University of the Eisenhower era. Not yet coed, obsessed with outdated social requirements such as jackets and ties at meals, and governed by a vigilance committee, which, according to the Brown *Daily Herald*, "plagued the campus for short periods of time during the fall semester, orienting and indoctrinating freshmen." During Ted's freshman year, a senior was actually tried by the Brown Student Court for "taking a young lady's cigarette and blowing a stream of smoke in her face, causing a disturbance and generally reflecting extremely poor taste."

Fortunately, Brown's dean of students, Edward R. Durgin, took an early liking to Ted and some of his cohorts in crime. Otherwise their tenure there might not have lasted to midterm. A Naval Academy graduate and former submarine commander, Durgin saw Ted, particularly, as the Peck's bad boy of Brown's freshman class. "There was limited tolerance for most of our drunken shenanigans," says Alan Laymon. "Having a girl in your room, though, meant immediate expulsion. That was it. You were gone! There was no appeal from that sort of infraction." It was obviously only a matter of time before Ted would see how far Dean Durgin could be pushed. And push he did.

"Someone would find a car," says Laymon. "Usually it was Ted. And we'd take off every weekend to the women's colleges. Wheaton, mostly. Bill Kennedy, sometimes Peter Dames, Turner, and me. To drink, find girls, drink and raise hell, and make ourselves generally obnoxious." On one occasion, "Ted stole a schoolbus and stopped off at Wheaton to pick up a busload of girls. He got halfway to Hanover, New Hampshire, before being stopped."

Laymon also recalls that "Ted carried a pistol around for a while, and used to take pot shots with either a rifle or a pistol from his dorm window. He would also run around all over campus drunk out of his skull, flailing around in his Kappa Sigma fraternity robes, bellowing Nazi battle hymns outside the Jewish frat house." Laymon remembers Ted also put signs saying "Warning, from the Ku Klux Klan" on the doors of the few blacks then at Brown.

Not even his worst enemies, though, ever thought Ted was particularly bigoted. "He was certainly not vicious," asserts classmate Bill Kennedy. "He was just trying to be one of the boys. Trying to get some attention." Ted's own explanation for these insensitive lapses does not really help his case. "Hey, I didn't mean anything by those racial cracks," he would say years later. "You can't find any pictures of me with swastikas and a German army helmet. As for blacks, well, most of them are not black, anyway. They're brown. Well, aren't they? It's very seldom you see a really *black* black." This from the lad Jimmy Brown had taught to be color blind.

During one junket to Wheaton College, Ted decided to steal a portrait of Eliza Wheaton, the school's benefactrix, which hung in the administration building. "We stashed it in the car," recalls Alan Laymon, "and then decided to 'borrow' some bicycles and ride around the Wheaton campus, all the while being chased by the campus policemen. It was like the Keystone Cops. They said they were arresting us and took us to a police station on campus and put us all away in some back room. There was an unlocked door. Naturally we all escaped. And naturally it wasn't hard for them to track us down back at Brown."

"We were all called on the carpet by Durgin," says Bill Kennedy, "but somehow only Ted was suspended. Durgin said it was the culmination of many incidents, but you have to put it all in the context of Brown at that time. The 'incidents' involved rowdy, loud behavior on campus and walking through the quad with a can of beer." After Ted's suspension, Kennedy remembers, "I don't think any of us expected that he would ever amount to much of anything except a loudmouthed kid from the South."

Years later, when informed that Dean Durgin had passed away, Ted told friends he had always intended "to piss on the dean's grave." Preoccupied at the time with a world ocean-racing championship, he considered sending a bottle of "Turner's Best" up to Providence so someone else could take care of the deed for him. Like so many of Ted's whims, however, this one was forgotten almost as soon as the words had tumbled out of his ever-open mouth. That story, like many others to come, would soon begin to assume mythic proportions, and a sharp listener might even have begun to hear the first faint whispers of "folk hero" whenever Ted Turner's name crept into a conversation.

Ted marked time during his suspension by satisfying his military obligation with a six-month tour of duty in the Coast Guard reserve. Returning to Providence in the fall of 1957, he was hardly chastened, but he had also rediscovered sailing. Ted had shown early promise at Brown, winning nine intercollegiate races as a freshman. Now he applied himself in earnest and was selected to join three outstanding seniors—Bud Webster, Charlie Trammell, and Charlie Shumway—on the four-man team Brown sent to the national sailing championships in Newport Harbor, California. Brown finished a respectable fifth place overall, but Ted Turner proved he could hold his own with some of the best collegiate sailors in the country and was elected team captain as well as commodore of the Brown Yacht Club.

Roger Vaughan, a member of the yacht club during Ted's tenure as commodore, saw him as "too loud, too red in the neck, an on-stage drunk. He also won more races than anyone else on the team. None of which endeared him to me." Nevertheless, Vaughan joined Ted to help defend Brown's title at the 1958 Timme Angstrom regatta in Chicago. Brown had won the Timme Angstrom three consecutive times but in 1958 barely managed a second-place finish. It was at Timme Angstrom, however, that Ted was introduced to Judy Nye, the daughter of Sally Sollit and Harry G. Nye, Jr., a prosperous tool manufacturer and co-owner of Chicago's respected Murphy & Nye sail loft. Harry Nye was also a champion Star class sailor. His daughter was following in his footsteps and had been elected commodore of the Northwestern University sailing team. Roger Vaughan remembers warning Judy at the time, "You're crazy to get serious about Ted Turner."

"Looking back," Judy Nye admits, "he was probably right. I'm not sure any love was ever involved. Ted needed somebody to take care of him when Jimmy Brown wasn't around. And the fact that I was a pretty good sailor didn't hurt." Ted promised he would write once he was back in Providence. Judy remembers that it may have been as long as a year before she heard from him again.

To the students of the Silent Generation, Brown's faculty seemed distant and unapproachable. Classes were held each morning, and then the teachers disappeared into their comfortable quarters up on College Hill, away from the campus and the undergraduates. "There were probably a dozen top-flight faculty people at Brown in those days," observes Bill Kennedy. "John

Rowe Workman, who was an assistant professor of classics, may have been the best of the lot." A sophisticated scholar with a wry, contemporary sense of humor, Workman quickly won Ted over with his marvelously refined sense of the absurd. Painfully aware of the absurdity that had already become a hallmark of his own young life, Ted was drawn to this intriguing older man who also had a keen interest in disasters of any kind and had collected a library of several hundred volumes on the subject. Turner was quite taken by Workman's tales of the "social benefits" that could be derived from disasters like the *Titanic* and the *Hindenburg*. Ted's developing relationship with Workman also served to confirm his original inclination to major in the classics. Workman was one of the few Brown faculty members for whom Ted had any respect. For his part, Professor Workman was one of the first to see the humanist in Ted Turner. "He was a handful," Workman told the *Daily Herald* shortly before his death in 1987. "But, like a real humanist, he will go out of his way to be different. I gather," Workman added dryly, "that he also had quite a time with his father."

As if the good professor didn't know. No sooner had Ted informed his father of his choice of majors than Ed Turner fired off a letter that still reverberates through certain quarters of Brown University's classics department:

My dear son:

I am appalled, even horrified, that you have adopted classics as a major. As a matter of fact, I almost puked on the way home today. I suppose that I am old-fashioned enough to believe that the purpose of education is to enable one to develop a community of interest with his fellow men, to learn to know them, and to learn how to get along with them. In order to do this, of course, he must learn what motivates them, and how to impel them to be pleased with his objectives and desires.

I am a practical man, and for the life of me I cannot possibly understand why you should wish to speak Greek. With whom will you communicate in Greek? I have read, in recent years, the deliberations of Plato and Aristotle, and was interested to learn that the old bastards had minds which worked very similarly to the way our minds work today. I was amazed that they had so much time for deliberating and thinking and was interested in the kind of civilization that would permit such useless deliberation. Then I got to thinking that it wasn't so amazing after all. They thought like we did, because my Hereford cows today are very similar to those ten or twenty generations ago. I am amazed that you would adopt Plato and Aristotle as a vocation for several months when it might make pleasant and enjoyable reading to you in your leisure time as relaxation at a later date. For the life of me, I cannot understand why you should be vitally interested in informing yourself about the influence of the Classics or English literature. It is not necessary for you to know how to make a gun in order to know how to use it. It would seem to me that it would be enough to learn English literature without going into what influence this or that ancient mythology might have had upon it. As for Greek literature, the history of Roman and Greek churches and the art of those eras, it would seem to me that you would be much better off by learning something about contemporary literature and writings and things that may have some meaning to you with the people with whom you are to associate.

These subjects might give you a community of interest with an isolated few impractical dreamers and a select group of college professors. God forbid!

It would seem to me that what you wish to do is to establish a community of interest with as many people as you possibly can. With people who are moving, who are doing things and who have an interesting, not a decadent outlook.

I suppose everybody has to be a snob of some sort, and I suppose you will feel that you are distinguishing yourself from the herd by becoming a classical snob. I can see you drifting into a bar, belting down a few, turning around to the guy on the stool next to you—a contemporary billboard baron from Podunk, Iowa, and saying, "Well, what did you think of old Leonidas?" He will turn to you and say, "Leonidas who?" You will turn to him and say, "Why, Leonidas, the prominent Greek of the twelfth century. He will, in turn, say to you, "Well, who in the hell was he?" You will say, "Oh, you don't know anything about Leonidas?'' and dismiss him. And not discuss anything else with him for the rest of the evening. He will feel that you are a stupid snob and a flop and you will feel that he is a clodhopper from Podunk, Iowa. I suppose this will make you both happy and as a result of it, you will wind up buying his billboard plant.

There is no question but this type of useless information will distinguish you, set you apart from the doers of the world. If I leave you enough money, you can retire to an ivory tower and contemplate for the rest of your days the influence that the hieroglyphics of prehistoric man had upon the writings of William Faulkner. We speak the same language—whores, sluts, strong words, and strong deeds.

It isn't really important what I think. It's important what you wish to do with your life. I just wish I could see that the influence of those oddball professors and the ivory towers were developing you into the kind of man we can both be proud of. I am quite sure that we both will be pleased and delighted when I introduce you to some friend of mine and say, ''This is my son. He speaks Greek.''

I had dinner during the Christmas holidays with an efficiency expert, an economic adviser to the nation of India, on the Board of Regents at Harvard University, who owns some eighty thousand acres of valuable timber land down here, among his other assets. His son and his family were visiting him. He introduced me to his son, then apologetically said, ''He is a theoretical mathematician. I don't even know what he is talking about. He lives in a different world.'' After a little while I got to talking to his son, and the only thing he would talk to me about was his work. I didn't know what he was talking about either, so I left early.

If you are going to stay on at Brown, and be a professor of classics, the courses you have adapted will suit you for a lifetime association with Gale Noyes [Yale's noted professor of English literature]. Perhaps he will even teach you to make jelly. In my opinion, it won't do much to help you learn to get along with the real people in this world. I think you are rapidly becoming a jackass and the sooner you get out of that filthy atmosphere, the better it will suit me.

Oh, I know everybody says that a college education is a must. Well, I console myself by saying that everybody said the world was square, except Columbus. You go ahead and go with the world, and I'll go it alone.

I hope I am right. You are in the hands of Philistines, and dammit, I sent you there. I am sorry.

Devotedly,
DAD

Much has been made of Ted's arch response to this elegant but incoherent outpouring of a father's desperate love of a son he knew he was already losing. Fuming, Ted arranged for the letter to be published verbatim on the editorial page of the *Daily Herald* of April 15, 1957. But anonymously. With no mention of the Turner name anywhere. Nevertheless, the fallout was predictable. "Ed was beside himself," Florence Turner remembered. "Somebody sent Ed a copy of that newspaper, and he was furious. He felt betrayed, but I guess Ted was pretty mad, too." That "somebody" was almost certainly Ted himself, who had finally found a way to communicate with his father.

By majoring in classics, Ted may have won this skirmish with his father, but in the end he would lose the war at Brown. In part, the defeat was academic. Blessed with a selective, but almost photographic memory, Ted Turner could recite the *Rubaiyat* in its entirety and often would, drink in hand, given the slightest incentive. He could do equally well with Coleridge or Oliver Wendell Holmes or Shakespeare. What he had difficulty with were the lesser lights who might show up in such awkward situations as midterm examinations. According to Alan Laymon, who sat next to Ted, "He came into a classics final on Alexander the Great one day without ever having cracked a book. He drew this wonderful picture on his test paper and said Alexander was the greatest man who ever lived. And Bucephalus, Alexander's horse, was the greatest horse that ever lived. And Traveller, Robert E. Lee's famous mount, was the second greatest horse that ever lived. Then he just handed his paper in and walked out of the classroom."

It was not Ted's academic failings, however, that brought him back up before Dean Durgin halfway through his junior year. Twenty-one undergraduates had already been suspended that semester for violations of the rule against having women in dorm rooms. Ted Turner was, in all likelihood, responsible for one of those and is said to have informed—as a joke, mind you—on one of his Kappa Sigma fraternity brothers who dared keep a girl in his room overnight. Once word got out, Ted was forced to move out of the Kappa Sigma house into his own quarters off campus. He was later charged with destroying Kappa Sigma's homecoming display, a twenty-foot-tall papier-mâché statue of Paul Bunyan. "I don't know if Ted burned it down," says Alan Laymon, "destroyed it, chopped it down, or whatever. But that homecoming display was definitely gone in the morning."

There is no record at Brown of who might have blown the whistle on Ted. Nor does anyone even remember whether it was Gerda Dymza or Sally Nagel or some other young lovely who was in his room the night the campus police came knocking. But the rap sheet Dean Durgin pulled on Ted Turner the next day was more than enough to send him packing, this time for good.

Peter Dames and Alan Laymon were both expelled from Brown along with Ted, but for separate infractions. Dames and Turner hotfooted it straight down to Binden Hall, Ed Turner's comfortable old South Carolina plantation. Binden consisted of a thousand wild, mist-enshrouded acres, bordered on the west by the Edisto River, on the north by Calf Pen Swamp, and on the south by the Coosawatchie River. Tall Spanish oaks dripping with gray-green Spanish moss lined the long drive up to the main house. It was here that Ed Turner, visibly relieved that the folly of Ted's eastern education was now over and done with, welcomed the boys with open arms. He never so much as mentioned the infamous letter incident.

Ted planned to pick up his Lightning and, with Dames as crew, sail across the Atlantic. Speculating excitedly about the women who would throw themselves at their feet once they landed, he could already envisage their triumphant passage through Europe. Fortunately for Dames, who had substantial misgivings about this wild adventure, the pair arrived at Binden Hall only to find the Lightning in splinters under a sizable Spanish oak that had been felled during a recent hurricane. Much relieved, Dames was able to persuade Ted to rethink his plans and head south instead to Miami, where the pair holed up in a squalid room above the old White Horse Cafe in Little Cuba until their unused tuition money ran out.

The Coast Guard then came looking for Ted, perhaps at Ed Turner's prompting, and ordered him back into uniform for an obligatory "summer cruise," chipping paint and cleaning latrines on the *USS Tavis* out of Ft. Lauderdale. Dames went back home to New York City but soon returned to Charleston, where Ted's father gave him a job with Turner Advertising. Ten years later Peter Dames would be running the company.

When Ted completed his Coast Guard duty, his commanding officer, impressed by the young man's apparent inclination toward life in the military, offered him the prospect of an appointment to the Coast Guard Academy in New London, Connecticut. It wasn't McCallie, but it wasn't the loose, unstructured life of temptation he had led at Brown, either. Somewhat drolly, Ted declined the honor, saying he was "needed back home." Reminded a few years later that he might actually have risen to the very top had he opted for a career in the Coast Guard, Ted would respond, "But then I'd be retired by now and what would I do with the rest of my life?"

Of his return to Savannah, Ted said, "I wasn't sure how good I'd be at knuckling under. My father had brought me to my knees." He admitted his father might also have brought him to his senses when Ed sent him over to Charleston to join Dames for a little sales training with Hudson Edwards, one of Turner Advertising's best producers. Bringing in new customers was the one hurdle Ted still had to get over before he would be ready, at least in his father's eyes, to move up the management ladder.

"Ted traveled with me for about six months," says Edwards. "But you could tell he was a natural from the git go. Ted was one of the greatest salesmen in the world. Still is. Just like his father. Those two, they were so much alike they couldn't stay in the same room ten minutes together without starting to scream at each other, arguing over the best way to do this, or to do that. But either one of them could charm a rattlesnake." After hearing Edwards's glowing reports of his son's natural ability, Ed was convinced that Ted was ready to become a real part of the business. He announced that Macon would be Ted's next stop on the road to the top and made him general manager of the Macon operation. Before Ted could throw himself into this new challenge, however, there were still a few loose ends that had to be tied up.

Ever since their first meeting at the Timme Angstrom in 1958, Ted had been unable to forget Judy Nye. During his Coast Guard service, he sent out a stream of fervid love letters to her. When Judy responded favorably, he showed up in Chicago to ask for her help in the Y-Flyer Nationals and, almost as an afterthought, her hand in marriage. With Judy crewing, Ted won the nationals, his first significant sailing championship. Two weeks later, on June 23, 1960, Ted Turner and Julia Gale Nye were married at Chicago's St. Chrysostom Episcopal Church. They were both just twenty-one.

"Ted didn't want to go down to Macon and begin his career as a single person," Judy points out. "He was always thinking of his image, and I was somebody new. Not just one of the girls he'd been running around with down there." The newlyweds moved to Macon and immediately became one of the town's most popular young couples. Pleased that people seemed impressed with his new bride, Ted threw himself into his new job as Macon manager with a determination that must have surprised everyone except, perhaps, himself. Working fifteen hours a day, six and a half days a week, he doubled the Macon office's sales in less than twenty-four months, all the while networking himself into the local business establishment. He joined the Rotary Club. He chaired a local Red Cross fund-raising drive. He also made it a practice to play winning poker at least once a week with his Macon salesmen and a few of his best customers.

In keeping with his new status as branch manager and young man on the move, Ted also traded in his old Plymouth Valiant for a succession of exotic foreign makes, including a Porsche Speedster and then Judy's favorite, a Jaguar XKE. The couple joined the Macon fleet of Y-Flyers and were notoriously successful in weekend regattas, even after their first child, Laura Lee, was born on July 23, 1961.

"At the beginning I thought it was a really terrific relationship," says Legarè VanNess. "They sailed together, and they were very much a team. It always seemed to me that Ted and Judy were very much alike. They were a great young couple that a lot of us looked up to. There were always sparks flying around them."

Ted allowed Judy to indulge herself, providing she was frugal enough to save anything from the meager $500 allowance he handed her at the beginning of each month. This money had to cover the mortgage on the new house Ted had insisted on buying, as well as all the other household expenses. For a while Judy was forced to work as a part-time secretary just to make ends meet. Ted also insisted that she iron his shirts and boxer shorts, even shine his shoes. Judy taught herself to cook, after a fashion, since Ted announced that he expected her to prepare three meals a day, whether he was there or not. She was not allowed to serve anything that wasn't advertised on a Turner billboard. "I bring home the money," Ted told her, echoing his father. "You do what I say."

Ed Turner, according to Judy, had blessed their marriage and even found time to serve as Ted's best man. He had decreed it was good for the business. He even tried briefly to rein in Judy's independent streak, to see if she could be made to toe the line. "The provider must have his way," Ed told her when she came seeking his counsel after a particularly difficult period with Ted. "There is just no other way any marriage will work." It was also Ed who told his son, "Let it go," as soon as he saw the marriage begin to fail.

"After a while," Judy confided somewhat ruefully to Roger Vaughan, "I felt my entire ego had been robbed. Ted is the kind of person who will identify some feature on your face and shoot an arrow right into it." A quiet, uncombative person despite her notable success in sailing, Judy made halfhearted attempts to fight back. "I threw cold water on Ted a couple of times," she admits, "and once I think I threw a salt shaker at him when he started screaming. But I was really afraid of what might happen next."

During a series of frostbite races on Atlanta's Lake Allatoona one Sunday late in 1961, Judy was leading the fleet on points when she found herself between Ted and the finish line. "He got to leeward of me," she recalls, "and luffed me hard, hitting me. Suddenly I was out of the race." All very legal, Judy adds, "but really very dirty. Ted had brought his boat up into the wind and knocked me right out of the race. Because I was beating him. It was just something he felt he had to do. He couldn't have been very happy that I was beating him."

By the time the race was over, their marriage was as well. "We had a little fight. I went home, gathered up Laura Lee, and went back to my mother in Chicago. Ted came up to see me, to see if we could talk things out." Already pregnant with Robert Edward Turner IV, Judy relented and agreed to return to Macon, at least until the baby's arrival. Little Teddy was born on May 30, 1962, but this time it was Ted who took the initiative by moving out shortly thereafter.

With his marriage in ruins, Ted decamped to Atlanta, where Ed Turner was on the verge of a major expansion of his business. Those little black clouds—television and the "ban on billboards" movement—had not yet appeared on the horizon. With operations now in Savannah, Macon, Charleston, Columbus, and Cincinnati, Turner Advertising Company was throwing off more cash than Ed Turner could ever spend. But still he was not satisfied.

He had been devastated by Mary Jane's agonizing death. "I am strong!" Ed Turner's life once seemed to shout. "Get out of my way!" Here was a man who would work or drink until the sun came up, who would beat his son with a coat hanger and then double the punishment if the boy so much as whimpered. But Ed's young daughter had been something else—the brightest girl in her class until the lupus set in, a pretty little thing who worshiped the ground her father walked on and lit up his life with her smile.

Ed had tried every treatment, brought in every specialist that his now considerable resources could command. But once he realized Mary Jane's death was inevitable, he had turned his eyes away. "The Lord works in mysterious ways," a well-meaning friend consoled. "If that's the kind of God he is, I want nothing to do with Him," Ed Turner replied coldly.

Mary Jane may have been all that was holding his marriage to Florence together. They had approached the matter of divorce many times over the years but, like a couple of weary old warhorses, probably believed they were harnessed together for life. Although it was usually Florence who took the initiative, this time Ed went out to Reno on his own. When he returned that day in 1959 with divorce papers in hand, he walked in on Florence and told her to pack her bags, they were heading for Florida and a second honeymoon. Florence had heard all of this too many times to believe him anymore. "All right, then," Ed countered. "I'll get you that Chrysler Imperial you've been wanting so much. And we'll call it quits." He did, and they did, and shortly thereafter Ed invited his friend, Irving Victor, over to the house on Abercorn Street and handed him the title, which had only about $2,000 left owing. Victor protested his generosity, but Ed insisted that his friend take the house. He booked the mortgage as a loan that Victor understood he'd never have to pay and told his friend that a mere $25 a month interest would cover everything.

Old Savannah is broken into twenty-one city squares, each separated from another by two-block intervals. Laid out in 1733 by General James Oglethorpe, these stately squares make up an extraordinary historical district that includes some of the most remarkable examples anywhere of Colonial, Federal, Greek Revival, and Regency residential architecture. After his divorce from Florence, Ed Turner took a lavish bachelor apartment on top of one of these elegant landmark mansions, just a few blocks from the house he had given to Irving Victor. Ed continued carousing until all hours, but his periods of abstinence were growing longer and he even began checking himself into Silver Hill Hospital, an expensive drying-out refuge in New Canaan, Connecticut, whose clients at the time included people like Truman Capote and Rita Hayworth.

Ted's old classmate Alan Laymon recalls having lunch with Ed in Charleston during this period. "He wouldn't even let them put any sherry in his she-crab soup," Laymon says. "He was really trying to keep to his no-alcohol regime at the time."

Ed began spending more time at Binden Hall and even began to believe he could run his business from the plantation. Ted would come over from Macon or Atlanta on weekends when he wasn't sailing—he had graduated to Flying Dutchmen and Olympic 5.5's and would soon win national championships in both classes—but would go off hunting with Jimmy Brown rather than spend time with a father he perceived as increasingly distant. Ed was hardly offended, however, since he had become preoccupied with Jane Dillard Hartmann, an attractive middle-aged divorcée from Charleston. A little more than a year after his divorce from Florence, Ed surprised everyone by marrying Jane Dillard and moving into Binden Hall to stay.

Jane was a step up the social ladder for Ed Turner. Her father, William Dillard, was president of the Central Georgia Railroad and a prominent member of the Georgia establishment. Jane had a son, Marshall Hartmann, from her first marriage, and he came to live with his mother and Ed Turner until he graduated from McCallie in 1962, six years behind Ted. Marshall looked up to Ted as an older brother and was even a witness at Ted's marriage to Judy Nye. Once married, however, Ted seemed to slam the door on his stepbrother and has never publicly acknowledged their relationship. A quiet, dignified man now approaching fifty, Hartmann was mystified by Ted's sudden change of heart but has had almost no communication with his half-brother in nearly thirty years. As Ted's reputation grew, Marshall Hartmann chose to recede into anonymity, and a few years ago he asked McCallie to delete his address from the school records. In an effort to escape

Ted Turner's long shadow, Hartmann moved some years ago to the Virgin Islands, where he now lives on St. Thomas.

Jane Dillard helped him get back on track and Ed Turner now stood poised for his most ambitious leap. By 1962 General Outdoor Advertising, the country's largest billboard company, had grown into a bloated, undermanaged behemoth. Together with an old friend, Robert Naegele, who owned a sizable outdoor advertising company based in Minneapolis, and two friends of Naegele's—Curt Carlsson, owner of Gold Bond Trading Stamps and, today, owner as well of Radisson Hotels, and Dick Condon, a prominent advertising executive—Ed Turner planned to take over General Outdoor in a "bootstrap acquisition," the 1960s version of a leveraged buyout, where the buyer pays for his purchase with money borrowed against the assets of the acquired company.

Their plan worked, and since it had all been Ed's idea, he got his pick of General Outdoor's operations, acquiring Atlanta, Norfolk, Richmond, and Roanoke on extremely favorable terms. By giving the sellers a note secured by the assets he was acquiring, plus $750,000 that he had borrowed against his own business, Ed Turner acquired these plums, which together were worth well over $4 million, without spending a penny of his own cash. More important, the additional operations now made Turner Advertising the uncontested market leader in the South and one of the biggest billboard companies in the country. A very, very sweet deal, and one Ted Turner would dissect over and over and then incorporate into his own empire-building arsenal. Ted was ecstatic over the new acquisitions and even more pleased when his father made him assistant general manager of Atlanta, now Turner Advertising's biggest single operation.

"When Ed took over our firm in Atlanta," Dick McGinnis, one of General Outdoor's top salesmen, recounted, "he wanted to change everything right away." Always moving at high speed, Ed seemed to shift into overdrive once he began to realize the potential of his expanded business. He pushed his employees harder than ever, but nothing they did was ever enough. He seemed consumed by his need to control every aspect of the business, even poring over a salesman's expense accounts for hours, then telling the fellow to go out and get a new car on the company. Always a heavy smoker, Ed began to go through several packs of cigarettes a day. He also went back on the bottle in a big way. "Ted's father was a changing person," Dick McGinnis observed. "People who thought they'd known him for years maybe never really knew the whole man." Clouds were forming on the horizon, but neither McGinnis nor any of the others around Ed Turner could possibly have imagined the storm coming in behind them.

Ted sensed that his father was under tremendous stress, but he'd seen Ed like this before. He also realized there was precious little he could do to help. He had become consumed by his own ambition and was determined now to outshine even his father. He assumed that Ed's mercurial mood changes were merely a reaction to his own improving grasp of the business. "Ed liked to keep Ted on a short string," Houston Edwards recalls. "One minute he'd swear that he would never bring Ted up to Atlanta. The next thing you know, Ted is up there as his father's right-hand man." This ambivalence, which was shared by both father and son, made it difficult if not impossible for them ever to sit down together and discuss the future of Turner Advertising in any meaningful way.

Once his initial euphoria over the General Outdoor deal began to dissipate, however, Ed found himself sliding slowly, inexorably, into a prolonged and apparently irreversible depression. He was still running like sixty, but he had become concerned, he told Irwin Mazo, that he might have overextended himself. He worried that his financing might fall apart, jeopardizing everything he had worked so hard to build. "Ed had pulled off a terrific deal with General Outdoor," Mazo says, "but I wasn't sure what was coming next."

Others, including his personal secretary, Vera Guay, had similar apprehensions, but Ed went a long way toward dispelling them when he checked himself back into Silver Hill late in 1962. "He had just sold most of the company's Savannah operations," Guay remembered, "although nobody could figure out why. Right after that, he went back up to Connecticut."

Shortly after the New Year, and less than five months after he had closed on the General Outdoor acquisition, Ed Turner sat down at the drawing table in his room at Silver Hill and put in a long-distance call to Bob Naegele. "He was terribly upset," Naegele recalled. "Not making any sense at all. He told me he was having second thoughts about the properties he had just acquired. I'll never forget what he said: 'It's a long way, Bob, from the master bedroom to the basement.' "

Ed was unmoved. He was concerned about a slowdown in the economy, about increased competition from the newspapers, now that Turner Advertising had become such a visible target. But most of all he was deeply concerned that he might have bitten off more than he could chew, that the empire he had been building all these years was now suddenly too much for him to manage. His mind was made up, he said. He wanted to sell Naegele the Atlanta operation for a flat $1 million, the same price he had paid for that portion of the General Outdoor business. Not sure how to respond, Naegele agreed he would consider the offer, but only if Ed would let him sweeten the deal by $50,000, so Ed would earn at least a small profit for his troubles.

Ed checked himself out of Silver Hill and flew back to South Carolina, where he met with Bob Naegele's representatives, who had come down to Binden Hall to talk him out of the deal. Ed, however, had already drawn up a crude sales agreement, which he scribbled on a yellow legal pad. He was in no mood to discuss the matter further. He even demanded that one of Naegele's people write out a check for the $50,000 premium as a kind of good faith deposit, before they left.

When Ted got wind of the situation, he was mystified at first and then outraged by his father's sudden change of heart. He felt betrayed. He simply could not accept that his father would attempt to sell off the company's new crown jewel behind his back, without so much as a single word of explanation.

Irwin Mazo was equally dumbfounded when Ed told him about the proposed deal. "He said he'd made a big mistake, one that he was convinced would break him. I told him he was wrong. That this was the best acquisition he had ever made. Ed seemed pretty calm about the whole thing, but nothing he said added up." Mazo says Florence Turner even came to him, begging him to stop Ed from selling off Atlanta. "Florence and I had remained friends, and she asked me to intervene, but of course none of us knew what was really driving Ed."

Back in Savannah, Ed dropped in on his old friend, Irving Victor. They spent time reminiscing about a recent Canadian hunting trip they had taken together. Then Ed mentioned that he wanted to forgive the $2,000 mortgage still on the Turner Advertising books against the house he had given Victor. He began to rattle on about all the debt he had taken on in the General Outdoor deal. "Look, Ed," Victor finally told him. "I don't know very much about your business, but I do know that you'll never be able to spend all the money you've got, not in two lifetimes. So stop worrying."

"Ed then told me he was having trouble sleeping," Victor recalls. "He needed some sleeping pills and began to appear quite agitated. The way he explained it to me, his friend Bob Naegele had made him a nice offer for the Atlanta business, which he was inclined to accept. But apparently Ted was adamant and didn't want him to sell. Ed thought he would lose face with Ted if he went through with the deal. And lose an old friend in Bob Naegele if he didn't. He was very, very concerned that he might be seen as a man who couldn't keep his word, had gone against his honor. Then he started in about the new interstates that were coming and how billboards would be banned. There might have been a grain of truth in what he was saying," says Victor, "but essentially, his business appeared pretty sound." Then Ed got down to the real matter at hand.

"You're pretty concerned about me, aren't you, Irv? You want to put me into a hospital. I guess you think I'm going to kill myself. Well, you don't have to worry. I'm not going to do that." Victor knew that one of Ed's oldest friends had recently committed suicide and thought that might have put the idea in his head. But no, he told Ed, he wasn't worried about anything like that.

"I figured he was just trying to disarm me," Victor explains. "I'm a urologist, not a psychiatrist. And I told him to get himself some rest. Maybe in a hospital. Not a psychiatric hospital, just somewhere he could get some rest, so he could begin to think more clearly. And then Ed just picked up his hat and walked right out of my office. Said he had to get back to Binden Hall. It was late on a Friday afternoon. I remember because I was preparing for a hospital accreditation survey scheduled for Monday morning."

Earlier on that same Friday, Ed had called on his lawyer, Tom Adams, and spent an hour or so updating his will. Curiously, he mentioned nothing to Adams about his agreement with Bob Naegele and, in fact, took pains to ensure that Atlanta was included among the company's assets he intended leaving to Ted.

For Ed Turner, the end game had now become inevitable. His pride, overridden at first by concern for his son, for his wife, and for himself, could no longer be salvaged. He would lose face now, no matter what he did. Yet Ed felt he had no alternative. He must sell. At twenty-four Ted was still far too young to make a go of the expanded business—in Irving Victor's words, "too wet behind the ears for Ed to feel good about handing everything over to this boy."

"We argued bitterly," Ted remembers. "I offered to buy the business myself, all of it, including Atlanta." But his father remained silent and became increasingly calm in the face of Ted's volcanic eruptions.

"Ed thought Ted was just too young to run the business," Bob Naegele confirmed. "And if his son wasn't able to pay him off, Ed visualized losing everything. Their arguments were fierce. Ted called his father cowardly. He thought his father was insulting his intelligence."

After all these years, father and son were finally communicating on the same wavelength, but neither could live with what he was now hearing. In this test of implacable wills, it was Ed Turner who blinked. He had determined he was simply too tired, too worn out, to continue the struggle. In capitulating to a younger, stronger heir, he could not have known the surge of incandescent energy he would soon release within his son.

Ed Turner was a success by almost any man's measure. But Ted says his father failed by setting his sights too low. "My father always said to never set goals you can reach in your lifetime. After you accomplish them, there's nothing left." Ed had promised his mother when he had gone off to college more than thirty years earlier that someday he would be a millionaire. He had achieved that goal, several times over, and if his son was right, he had now left himself with nowhere else to go.

> *Father said clocks slay time. He*
> *said time is dead as long as it is*
> *being clicked off by little wheels;*
> *only when the clock stops does*
> *time come to life.*
>
> WILLIAM FAULKNER
> *The Sound and the Fury*

Chapter Two

The dawn broke clean and crisp over Binden Plantation on the morning of Tuesday, March 5, 1963. There was a damp chill in the air, and a layer of fog still clung close to the ground when Ed Turner finally came downstairs to breakfast. His wife, Jane, had seldom seen him in such good spirits and was relieved to note that the vacant, puzzled look he had worn throughout much of the previous week was gone. "He seemed his old self again," Jane later told Irving Victor. "He bounced in and didn't even bother with the newspaper that day, which was a little unusual."

Jimmy Brown had come over from his own quarters out behind the great house to fix breakfast, as he usually did when Ed was in residence, which, since he'd come back from Connecticut, now seemed like most of the time. Jimmy noticed that his employer polished off everything he had been served before pushing himself away from the table and stepping outside onto the veranda to savor what promised to be a magnificent late winter Carolina morning. Back inside, he asked Jimmy what he planned to serve for lunch. Then, wrapping himself in an enigmatic smile, Ed Turner began whistling a quiet little ditty, turned, and disappeared up the main stairway. He walked straight through the master bedroom and into the bath and without a moment's hesitation pulled out a small silver .38-caliber revolver, the same one

Ted had used when Jimmy Brown had taught him to shoot, calmly put the weapon to his right temple, and pulled the trigger.

Jimmy Brown was up the stairs as soon as he heard the shot, but there was little he could do. Ed Turner lay sprawled on the bathroom floor, life quickly draining from his body. The silver pistol and a single spent shell lay near his outstretched hand.

Jane Dillard was still downstairs, but she knew intuitively what had happened. She had been concerned about Ed's intention to sell off the Atlanta business and knew how painful his arguments with Ted had been. Jane had mentioned her concerns to Irwin Mazo but, not wanting to interfere, had done nothing further.

Now, with the pistol report still ringing in her ears, Jane Dillard picked up the telephone and called the Beaufort County Sheriff's Office. Then she phoned Irving Victor, who had just started his rounds at Canwood General Hospital in Savannah. Not even sure that Ed Turner was still alive, Dr. Victor told her to get Ed to the nearest hospital. "I'll meet you there," he shouted into the mouthpiece, and then, contradicting himself, said he'd drive over to Binden immediately.

"I must have broken every speed record in the book," Victor remembers. "The sheriff met me at the door and told me Ed Turner was already dead. That he had died about thirty minutes earlier, at nine-forty A.M. It was just the Beaufort sheriff, Jane, and Jimmy Brown when I got there, but all of a sudden the place seemed to be swarming with people."

Irwin Mazo and Tom Adams had covered the seventy-five miles from Savannah to Yemasee in well under an hour and pulled into the long drive that led to Binden's plantation house at about 11:00 A.M. Jane had gone into shock by the time they arrived, but her father, Bill Dillard, had already been called and was on his way down from the Central Georgia offices. Ted was away from the Atlanta office on business but was expected in Savannah the next morning.

Irving Victor remained at Binden Hall for the better part of the day, waiting until the coroner had come and gone and the sheriff's men had completed their work before he prepared to leave. He'd noticed Ed Turner's dogs outside baying their heads off all morning. When the sheriff's car roared off down the drive, sending gravel spraying in eighty-five directions, they began howling again, louder than ever. Irving Victor had hunted with Ed and those dogs more times than he could count. The thought sent a sudden shiver running down his spine as he started up his own car and slowly headed back to Savannah.

"We became friends," Victor says, "almost from the moment we met. Friends in every sense of the word. I really loved Ed, and I think it was mutual, like a brother."

Irving Victor may, in fact, have been as close to Ed Turner as anyone was ever allowed to get. Not only had Ed given Victor the house he now lived in, he had insisted that Victor buy some of his company's stock at book value, far less than it was actually worth. "If Ed Turner really liked you," Victor says, "he liked you real hard." The two friends even ended up purchasing adjacent plots in Savannah's Greenwich Cemetery, though neither ever expected he might have to bury the other.

Now, however, it fell to Irving Victor to make Ed Turner's funeral arrangements, and on the drive back to Savannah late that March afternoon, he thought again about Ed's visit to his office just four days earlier. Victor knew his friend had been under enormous pressure, but he could not believe that Ed might have been seriously worried about money. "Ed Turner was a very rich man," he recounts. "Even under the worst circumstances, it would be hard to see how money would ever be a problem for Ed. I could see that he was tired, physically exhausted. But I really thought he was just overstressed, maybe even worried about that whole 'Keep America Beautiful' thing. You know, the 'get rid of billboards' campaign? If I'd had an inkling of what he had in mind, I would have hamstrung him right then and there and carried him over to a hospital myself. Whether he liked it or not."

The *Atlanta Constitution* of Wednesday, March 6, 1963, carried a front-page story headlined BILLBOARDS RESTRICTED BY SENATE, detailing the passage by the Georgia State Legislature of a controversial new law limiting the number of billboards on interstate highways. The article appeared only a few columns away from the newspaper's announcement of Ed Turner's suicide.

His father's death hit Ted Turner like a tidal wave, washing over him, enveloping him, nearly drowning him in contradictory feelings. For twenty-four years Ted's own life had been tied inextricably to his father's. He had in many respects lived through his father. One day he'd expected not only to inherit his father's business, but to climb out of Ed Turner's long shadow as well. The two had never really discussed succession—that was not Ed's way. Ted had impressed his father with his performance in Macon, but praise from his father had never been part of the bargain. Intimations of his own developing ambition, however, had slipped into their relationship. Ted was no longer so intimidated standing toe to toe with his father whenever they squared off. Those little set-tos, which now came more and more frequently, were never over anything more important than the replacement of a billboard. Ted made certain, however, they always took place in front of Turner Advertising's most senior employees. Clearly he was testing the waters with his father, but he was also putting the rest of the troops on notice that he might be the only one among them equal to the old man. Privately, though, Ted still sought to please, to appease, to impress, and to placate his overbearing father in all his old, unspoken ways, until he came to realize that his father was actually dead serious about selling the Atlanta operation.

Ted was furious and fell, briefly, into a state of shock. He could not comprehend the obvious cowardice he detected in the man who had always been for him the absolute paragon of self-assurance. Ted had questioned his father, certainly, but never before had he dared challenge him directly over the future of the company. Now he was frustrated, confused, but also curiously energized by the prospect of doing battle at last with this man who had dominated him for so long. .

Ted knew the business intimately and had been running Turner Advertising during his father's absences at Silver Hill. Things had gone well on his watch, and he was ready to flex his muscles. He hounded Ed incessantly. Their arguments grew increasingly vitriolic, increasingly violent. Ted simply could not believe his father planned to give up what he had just won. He rejected his father's explanation that he might lose everything if the economy took an even modest downturn and then couldn't service the debt. "Ted called his father cowardly," observes Bob Naegele. "He thought his father was insulting his intelligence."

"Ted's first reaction," says Judy Nye, "was to blame the doctors. They had taken Ed off alcohol. Off cigarettes. Put him on all kinds of diets. He couldn't sleep. He was in terrible shape. Ted himself thought the doctors should have given Ed something to let him ease off his addictions. He said you don't just take everything away from a person all at once and not expect it to have some effect.

"Ed Turner was a wise man," Judy Nye adds. "He felt Ted was too young to take over the business on his own. He knew Ted was running around. He knew Ted was drinking too much. But what could he say? He knew he was also the pot calling the kettle black."

Bob Naegele agrees. "Ed thought Ted was too young to run the business," he says. "And if his son wasn't able to pay him off, Ed visualized losing everything."

The truth be told, however, Ted Turner had long demonstrated to his father and others that he could handle the business. Even some of the more dubious old Turner hands acknowledged that he had set the world on fire down in Macon. And when his father was away at Silver Hill, Ted had more than held his own in Atlanta. With the possible exception of Ed Turner, however, none of those observers ever imagined Ted was actually mounting a palace revolution. Yet that was exactly what he was planning. "Ted had always been on a crusade to please his father. That was pretty obvious from the start," Judy Nye points out. "But he was also on a crusade to outdo Ed. That's what was always in his mind. It's just that Ted certainly never expected his father to commit suicide. That really shook him more than anything." Ed Turner, Judy believes, could not have chosen a more devastating way to end the argument with his son. Now, Ted could never have the satisfaction of victory or ever gain the approval of the only person in the world whose approval he could not live without.

Ted stayed in the background at his father's funeral, letting others wring their hands, recite the homilies, deliver the eulogies. His mind was churning with the knowledge that his father had scoffed at his offer to buy the business. How could you ever come up with the money? his father had demanded. If the business goes under, who will bail you out?

Dressed for duck shooting and carrying his shotgun over his shoulder, Ed Turner had once showed up for dinner at the Rex, one of Savannah's most reserved eating establishments, asking for his friend Irving Victor. "That fellow over there," Ed had told the dumbfounded maître d'. "The one who makes every other urologist look like a nickel's worth of dog meat." Now it was Ted's turn to shock, as two days after Ed's funeral he dragged Irwin Mazo to dinner at the same restaurant, only to leave him open-mouthed as the young scion unveiled his plans for Turner Advertising.

"When they read out the will and Teddy got the company, I just assumed he would want to go forward and follow through with the sale to Bob Naegele," Mazo says. "Ted would have ended up with over a million dollars in the bank and still have the rest of the company after selling off Atlanta. He'd be set for life. It was no secret that he would know how to use that kind of money. Or about his great interest in sailing."

Ted, however, informed Mazo that he intended to sue Naegele, if it ever came to that, for taking advantage of his father when he wasn't in his right mind. Ted instructed the accountant to return Naegele's $50,000 good faith check immediately. When Ted discovered that Bob Naegele was sitting out the winter in Palm Springs, he decided to handle the situation himself and made plans to fly out to California.

Before leaving, however, Ted dropped the other shoe, revealing that he was indeed his father's son when it came to matters financial. Accosting Irving Victor shortly after the funeral, Ted mentioned the $2,000 mortgage on the Turner company books still owing against the house on Abercorn Street.

"That's right," Victor replied, "but your father said specifically that this obligation was to have been forgiven."

When asked about the incident, Victor says dispassionately, "Ted knew I didn't have anything in writing. He said he believed me. Then he said, 'But business is business,' and could I please take care of the two thousand dollars as soon as possible. There wasn't anything I was going to do under the circumstances except head right down to the bank and borrow two thousand dollars and pay him off."

Later, Ted asked Victor to return the Turner Advertising stock his father had sold him. He wanted the shares back, he told Victor, because he might have to sell parts of the company to finance the Atlanta operation. Ed Turner had allowed his friend to buy these shares for only $3,000, booking the purchase price as a loan. "Ted merely said he wasn't in a position to honor his father's commitment. That was enough justification for him. In the end," Victor relates, "I sold him back half the shares for the three thousand dollars which was on the books." Victor has held on to the balance and is pleased to tell anyone who asks that his Turner stock has increased more than a hundredfold over the years. He is also pleased to add that he wouldn't sell those shares to anybody, at any price. They are his last link to his old friend, Ed Turner, who managed to bestow an unusually lucrative and totally unexpected legacy on the good doctor.

Irwin Mazo offered to help Ted deal with Naegele, who was known as a sharp, sophisticated powerhouse in the billboard industry. Ted was having none of it. He jumped on a plane and the next day confronted Bob Naegele in his Palm Springs hacienda. Naegele was shocked to learn that Ted intended to run Ed's business. Completely misreading the younger man's intentions, Naegele felt Ted might be making a grandstand play to see if he could squeeze more out of Naegele's original (and reluctant) offer to buy back the Atlanta assets. Since agreeing to Ed's desperate request, Naegele had grown comfortable with the idea of adding Atlanta to his own holdings and quickly offered Ted $1.4 million, a whopping 40 percent premium over the price Ed had paid. Shocked when Ted turned him down on the spot, Naegele promised to keep the offer open for a year, in case Ted should run into any difficulties or change his mind.

There are many versions of what happened next, and even today the facts remain unclear. Ted seemed convinced Naegele intended doing him out of the company. Ted told Mazo and others within Turner Advertising that he would never let the sale go through. In fact, even before coming out to see Naegele, he made plans to transfer leases belonging to the newly acquired Atlanta operation to Turner's Macon unit. Threatening to erect billboards of his own in front of the ones already there, Ted intimated he would even torch the Atlanta boards if he had to. This literal, "scorched earth" threat and the subsequent "rescue" of Turner Advertising from the clutches of Bob Naegele may have existed almost exclusively in Ted Turner's overactive imagination, but the story has become embellished over the past thirty years, in great part by Ted himself, until it has now become a minor business epic.

True or not, the story served to give Ted Turner a big start down the road toward becoming a legitimate folk hero. "I was sad, pissed, and determined," he said nearly twenty years later, reminding any doubters that he was forced to go deeply into debt to hold on to the Atlanta business. "I was only a kid, but I had learned how to hustle. I went out and convinced the employees to buy stock in the company. I sold off all the real estate that I possibly could to raise cash. I sold my father's plantation. I borrowed against our accounts receivable. I squeezed the juice out of everything." What Ted conveniently overlooks is the fact that his father had left him a business that had plenty of juice left to squeeze.

Ted Turner has always operated on gut instinct, and his instinct must have confirmed one of the lessons he picked up from his early reading of military history. Manufacturing a crisis, he was convinced, might be the quickest way to rally the anxious troops at Turner Advertising. A crisis would focus attention on his strong leadership potential and help mute criticism of his youth and inexperience. Only Irwin Mazo, who was to work side by side with Ted over the next eight years as his financial adviser, accountant, and occasional father confessor, could see beyond the bravado. And the record will show that even old "Ozam," as Ted took to calling him, would sometimes read Ted Turner wrong.

"When Ted took over the business, Turner Advertising was in great shape," Mazo recalls. "No question we owed an awful lot of money, but the cash flow coming in each month was more than enough to cover debt service on the acquisitions. I think Ted understood that, even if nobody else did. And as soon as he came to see the light at the end of the tunnel, nothing was ever going to hold him back." Mazo, who is more than ten years Ted's senior, is a serious-minded, conservative professional. He had met Ed Turner during his divorce from Florence in 1959 and proved so effective in untangling Ed's convoluted finances that Ed brought him on board as Turner Advertising's chief financial officer. In addition to the business, Ted had inherited this quiet-spoken, highly capable financial expert and put him to work immediately, restructuring Turner Advertising's debt and opening up new lines of credit with the banks.

"But all that is getting ahead of the story," Mazo interjects. "First I had to adjust to the fact that Ted actually intended doing all this himself. And run the business. Not to mention spend as much time as he did sailing." That turned out to be quite an adjustment for Irwin Mazo.

"Right off, Ted created a sense of paranoia within the company, a sense that we were the little guys fighting for our lives against some unknown big guys. That made everything seem a lot more important than it probably was," says Mazo. "After all, we were not doing badly. And Turner Advertising was the biggest bill-board company in the South. One of the biggest in the country, actually." Ted compounded the sense of danger, though, with all kinds of subterfuge. "He even insisted on making his telephone calls to me on outside pay phones. He wanted people to believe our phones were tapped. Perhaps it would distract them from how well the business was doing."

Already well versed in the day-to-day operations of the business, Ted learned the financial end fast and insisted that Ozam keep him directly involved with the banks, with anything and anybody, in fact, who might seriously impact on the future of Turner Advertising. For his part, Irwin Mazo was often astonished at his young boss's crude but effective approach. "Ted rushed right into our lenders and bowled them over. More times than not, he came out with the new lines (of credit) he wanted.

"Loyalty is a big part of Ted," Mazo adds. "He expects unstinting loyalty from anyone he has to deal with. Banks, customers, employees. But he gives that loyalty back, in spades." Cross Ted Turner once, however, or even let him think he hasn't got your total support, and you may come to rue the day. As Jane Dillard soon discovered, much to her dismay.

Ed Turner had relished playing a game of wits each year with the tax man, a game Ed usually won. Ted discovered his father had sheltered a substantial amount of taxable income over the years by personally lending it back to the company. Jane Dillard now held all those old notes. In order to clean up his balance sheet, Ted went to her, proposing that she convert the notes into Turner stock. Somewhat skeptical that Ted could actually make a success of the business, Jane refused politely. As a result, Ted has not spoken to her since. This may also be the reason he has never recognized her son, Marshall Hartmann, as his stepbrother.

Insinuating himself into every aspect of Turner Advertising, Ted soon discovered that the billboard business could be a gold mine, a tax-depreciable revenue stream that threw off enormous amounts of cash with almost no capital investment and even less capital risk. Most outdoor advertising companies, Turner included, were de facto monopolies, especially in the South, and even in a soft economy growth could be sustained through mergers and acquisitions. The significant economies of scale achievable in outdoor advertising meant that the larger companies could generally operate at higher profit margins than smaller ones and could therefore price their competition out of business. Once that lesson was learned, Turner began adding to his little empire in a hurry.

Ted also continued to race virtually every chance he could. He still sailed Y-Flyers but was winning so consistently that he became impatient to step up in class. He wheeled around from race to race in a striking red Ferrari, making sure he was always parked where he and his new car would attract the most attention.

"Ted competed down in Savannah with a lot of very good sailors," says Saul Krawcheck, who sailed against him in the early 1960s and on occasion would also sail with him as crew. "He was so young, but he got to the top of the class very, very quickly. We sailed against each other in Y-Flyers, little flat sailboats, but fairly fast. He was a very, very tough competitor, and we really had some battles. Of course, we all regarded him at first as some sort of precocious kid, but there was something very refreshing about him. He was enthusiastic and willful and boyish," notes Krawcheck, who today operates a family haberdashery in Charleston. "But he was also charming. And not to be taken too seriously."

Krawcheck was describing a respected young friend and competitor. His words, however, could easily have been those of a young blonde Delta Airlines stewardess Ted encountered at a Young Republican gathering one autumn evening in 1963. It had been less than six months since Ed Turner's suicide, and Ted found himself in Atlanta without the kind of business connections he had so assiduously cultivated in Macon. He let Peter Dames serve as his pointman in opening up new contacts, and Dames had dragged him off that evening to meet some of Atlanta's up-and-coming young politicos. Ted was still unformed in his own political views, but he felt at ease among these budding conservatives and was merely following in Ed Turner's far-right footsteps. Politics was the last thing Ted Turner had on his mind those days. He was already twenty-five years old and had not yet even registered to vote.

Thinking he had shown up that evening for business, Dames kept trying to steer Ted into conversations with some of the young bankers and brokers at the party. But Ted seemed more interested in the ladies and kept his sharp weather eye peeled for pretty faces. Once he spied her, it didn't take him long to manage an introduction to Jane Shirley Smith, the proper young stewardess from Birmingham, Alabama. Ted Turner soon forgot all about business and began selling himself to Jane in earnest.

It was not going to be an easy sell, however, since this gaunt, gangling fellow pressing himself on her so diligently was hardly the kind of man Janie Smith had been brought up believing would carry her off into the sunset. He was cute, she admitted, and might even possess a bit of crude charm, but he kept it well hidden behind an exterior of egoistic self-absorption. On top of everything else, Janie learned the guy was already supporting two children from a failed first marriage. Her better judgment must have told her to run, not walk, away from this bluff young brag-gart who was now trying to fill up her calendar with dinner dates every night for the next six months.

Jane Smith had little intention of ever seeing Ted again after their first real date. He was nice, but hardly the kind of fellow you wanted to get serious about. But he was also the kind who simply wouldn't go away, and as Ted wheeled his Ferrari up to her front door night after night, Jane found herself looking forward to her evenings with this cocksure young man who was convinced he would someday be able to move mountains.

Jane Smith never thought of herself as having led a particularly sheltered life. At the University of Alabama, a school seldom noted for anything resembling a refined social life, she had en-joyed all the attention a pretty young blonde could expect. She'd had her pick of the lads along fraternity row and, after graduating with a degree in home economics, had even been courted by a couple of old McCallie boys. Jane Smith had never encountered anybody, however, quite like "Turner from Savannah." He didn't seem to know when to stop, and he certainly didn't bother to play by the rules. By the time she began devoting her weekends to watching him win sailboat races, Jane Smith was beginning to feel she might be hooked. And when she took him home to Bir-mingham to meet her parents, she began to fear it might all be over.

She was right. Her father took to Ted immediately. The most impressive young man, Tavis Smith told his daughter, he'd ever had the pleasure of meeting. This fellow's going to accomplish great things someday. Mr. Smith also told Jane he very much hoped that Ted would soon become a part of the family.

Two years after his divorce to Judy Nye and little more than a year after Ed Turner's death, Ted and Jane Shirley Smith were married in Birmingham. The date was June 2, 1964, but Ted has always confused it with his first wedding date, June 23. For years he believed he married both times on June 2, an error his assis-tant, Dee Woods, has helped to "confirm" every time she is asked.

The newlyweds set up house in Atlanta and were soon joined by the faithful Jimmy Brown, who moved up from Savannah to make sure Ted had everything he needed as he dashed off each weekend to sail. Within a few months, however, their little family grew again, as Janie suddenly found herself the caretaker of two toddlers, ages three and two. Ted had spirited his children, Laura Lee and Teddy, away from their mother in Chicago when Judy

Nye intimated that her new husband might be taking out his frustrations on them. Judy says today she was profoundly saddened at losing her babies. She made a halfhearted attempt to get them back, traveling to Atlanta, but once she got there she decided not even to call Ted or Jane and went back to Chicago without having even seen them or her children. It would be nearly twenty-five years, at Laura's wedding in 1990, before she would be reunited with them again.

It had taken Ted less than twelve months to have things sorted out at Turner Advertising to the point where he could devote himself to his real interest. He was racing Flying Dutchmen now, every chance he got. The Dutchman is a twenty-foot Olympic-class sailboat. Saul Krawcheck remembers a regatta at Charleston's Carolina Yacht Club during this period when Ted was having a rare off day. "Another sailor from Atlanta, Harold Gilroy, had beaten Ted pretty badly, and he was, well, very, very disappointed. Everyone retired to our house out on Sullivan's Island for dinner, and then we were planning to go back into town for a party. Ten minutes after we had all sat down, Ted simply up and bolted out the door."

"You can't leave now!" Jane shouted after him. "Ted, you can't just walk out of here like this. They're about to serve dinner."

Ted kept on walking. But before he was out of the house, he glared balefully over his shoulder at his young bride and shouted, "I've told you, Janie. Business comes first. My boat comes second. And you come third. See you later!"

About half an hour later, however, Ted came walking back through the front door. "I really think he came back," Krawcheck says, "simply because he didn't want to offend my wife, Blossom. I don't think it had anything to do with Jane. That's the kind of relationship they had, from the very beginning." Jane was learning that Ted not only did not play by other people's rules; he was often inclined to make up his own as he went along.

Ed Turner had seen his business as a way of life, as part of his very existence. He *was* Turner Advertising and never thought of himself as anything else. Ed could never have considered his business as a means to an end. Not so his son. Ted saw Ed's dedication as slavish devotion and once confronted his father on the subject. "You're not leaving the business to me," he charged. "You're leaving *me* to the business." Ted saw the billboard business as something less than a full-time job, and he was not about to let it consume his life. He spent the first few months after Ed Turner's suicide on Lake Allatoona and won the Atlanta Yacht Club championships in both the Y-Flyer and Flying Dutchman classes, a unique achievement that will never be equaled, since rule changes now make such a double win impossible.

Shortly after the Atlanta club championships, Ted became consumed with the prospect of competing in the Olympics. A fellow named Andy Green, a Ft. Worth, Texas, boat builder with a high-tech bent, showed up in Atlanta one day with several new custom-built Flying Dutchmen. They were obviously faster than anything else on the water. Ted was riveted and persuaded Green to let him race one of his new fiberglass Dutchmen.

Impressed with the design and spectacular performance of Green's boat, Turner talked him into teaming up, and together they won the 1965 North American Championships. Ted then suggested they formalize their relationship. "We could have a lot of fun," he told Green, who remained noncommittal. After a few more races together, and a few more victories, however, Ted simply announced they were now a partnership. He invested $100,000 in PlasTrend, Inc., Green's manufacturing company in Ft. Worth. Ted also insisted that his investment entitled him to a controlling interest. Looking back, Green professes no regrets but admits he may have given up control much too cheaply. "Like most everybody else," he admits, "I got caught up in Ted's unbelievable enthusiasm."

Once he had got his nose into Andy Green's tent, Ted threw himself into making further improvements on Green's already fast design. Together they came up with a breakthrough concept —a radical wooden hull covered with an aluminum skin only twelve mills thick. Their new Dutchman, however, was as fragile as it was fast. Aluminum deteriorates rapidly in salt water, and the PlasTrend hull would corrode right through if left in the water for more than a few hours. The partners were able to manufacture only a single prototype of this new boat, but bedazzled by gold medal visions, they set off anyway for the Olympic trials in Acapulco, Mexico. For Andy Green, the trials would be an acid test of his materials engineering. For Ted Turner, they were nothing short of the logical next step on his way to becoming the winningest sailor in the world.

"It was a good thing Ted was already rich and reasonably successful," Green says, trying to forget what happened next. Turner and Green had unquestionably built themselves a very fast Flying Dutchman. But the boat may have been too quick even for those two hotshots to handle. They managed to foul out in four of seven preliminary heats. They scraped buoys, hit other boats, even false-started twice. Absolutely nothing went right for the star-crossed partnership. Turner nevertheless proved himself a good loser. Even though he was known to gloat unmercifully over his victories, belittling the competition out loud and pointing out to the losers every mistake they'd made, he went out of his way in Acapulco to congratulate every single sailor who had beaten them. "As it turned out," says Green, "Ted is a much better loser than winner." But, Green adds, one would be missing the point not to realize that Ted's good sportsmanship was heavily influenced by his desire to understand why he had lost and what the winners had done to propel themselves across the finish line ahead of him.

Andy Green is now president of Composite Technology, Inc., an aerospace materials manufacturer. He is out of the boat business altogether, but he looks back on his experience with Ted Turner with a certain equanimity. "I know others have had their problems with him," Green observes. "As a matter of fact, I was probably very lucky. I understand he would fire his lawyer, Tench C. Coxe, in the morning and then hire him back in the afternoon. That never happened to me. In all the time we were together, I think there was only one time he ever really got sore. We were putting together a new Olympic-class boat, the Tempest. Just like always, Ted wanted to rush this one into competition, and we once again got ahead of ourselves and the boat really wasn't ready. We sailed it anyway, and once again we did very poorly. While we were still out on the water, he began hollering, bitching, complaining all over the place. I asked him what he wanted to do and he said, 'I want out!' "

By the time Green had brought the ill-prepared Tempest into the dock, Ted's mood had changed completely. "He tried to apologize for the way he had acted. He just wanted to concentrate on getting the Tempest to work. He would be very sincere when he'd say those things, but I figured it was time to buy him out, and eventually I did.

"I never knew his first wife," Green adds. "But one day he's telling me about what a good sailor she was, and he says she wanted one of our new Tempests. I knew he was married to Janie then, but he told me to get Judy squared away. We put a boat together for her. And then Ted starts telling me all the horror stories about their times together. How he'd come home exhausted, and he'd just taken her to bed, but she'd want more attention, and he would say, 'Leave me alone. I'm beat.' And how she would throw cold water on him to wake him up or come at him with scissors, things like that. I guess he just got tired of the whole program.''

Ted's sailing program, however, was another matter. Unlike his marriage to Judy Nye, it was deliberate and almost predetermined. From little eleven-foot Penguins, he had quickly moved up to the larger Lightnings, then Y-Flyers, and then to Flying Dutchmen. He was ready now, perhaps even compelled, to tackle something bigger. Inevitably it would be forty-, then sixty-foot ocean racers. And then the very top of the line—twelve-meter yachts that competed at the very pinnacle of ocean racing: the America's Cup.

Already moving at something close to warp speed, Turner would learn and master each of these new classes in less time than it took most men to correct a hook or develop a meaningful second serve. Plunge right in. Damn the torpedoes! If the wind and the gods were with you, you'd come out on top. Ever since Jimmy Brown had first introduced him to the vagaries of sailing on the Savannah River, Turner had eagerly sought out the next challenge, welcoming the opportunity to test himself against ever-increasing levels of competition. It was one trait that set him apart from his father, who preferred to consolidate his gains rather than continue to risk them for the sake of greater triumphs. Ted Turner never hesitated to risk everything—his money, his marriage, his company, his boat, or his own life—whenever he could roll the dice with Dame Fortune one more time.

"Life is a game," Ted is fond of saying, especially when the game gets serious. And Ted Turner is very, very good at games. Just ask anyone who has ever sat down and tried to beat him at gin rummy. Or backgammon. Or even Trivial Pursuit. But Ted always plays hardest when his back is against the wall, when the odds are so long he isn't given a chance. That's when Ted Turner's competitive juices really begin to flow.

Dennis Conner knows the consequences of going up against this ferocious competitor. Conner was on the receiving end of a roundhouse punch after he edged ahead of Turner to win the prestigious Congressional Cup in 1976. "Ted's strong point," Conner writes in his autobiography, *No Excuse to Lose*, "is neither innate ability nor attention to detail and preparation. It is his enthusiastic competitiveness and leadership ability. He drives himself and his crew as hard as any men can be pushed. . . . His kind of aggressive leadership works well when times are tough," Conner continues. "But it can be counterproductive when things are going well." Anyone who has ever known Ted Turner understands. Despite his indomitable competitive spirit, he is seldom able to let well enough alone.

Why hadn't Ted just taken the money and run when Bob Naegele offered to make him a millionaire at twenty-four? "My father had worked like hell all his life trying to make the big time. . . ." Ted has repeated the phrase over and over, as if it were a mantra that could somehow explain the fire that still burns in his belly. "He went as far as he could, and when he dropped the baton, it was for me to pick it up. Plus I am a fighter." Then he gets to the point: "I was raised that way. I could never be a dilettante living off the fat of the land. That business was really important to me. I don't know where I'd be without it. Off the deep end, I suppose."

Fortunately for Ted, and the several hundred others whose livelihood depended upon the survival of the Turner Advertising Company, he never had to go off the deep end. He was willing to learn the little he did not already know about the billboard business and more than ready to make the company even more successful than his father might ever have dreamed. "He is an aggressive, natural businessman," Irwin Mazo points out. "And there were very good managers in the company to help him over the hurdles. Ted got good advice in those days, and he generally followed it. Pretty soon, though, he figured out he could do it all himself if he wanted to."

Ted kept his father's longtime secretary, Vera Guay, in the company, where she continued as Ted's personal assistant for seven more years. Guay had witnessed the bitter arguments between father and son but, like most of the others, never really thought Ted could match his father. "But he has always been the best salesman in the company," Guay remembers. "And he sold himself to a lot of people—the bankers and the others—who had no idea what to expect from this twenty-four-year-old. What he did with that business really meant a lot to a great many people."

Once he took control of Turner Advertising, Ted moved quickly to expand into new markets. He bought out competitors in Knoxville and Chattanooga and began to consolidate his hold on the entire South. When he first tried to diversify into other businesses, however, he sometimes ran into difficulty. He lost money on a small silkscreen printing company and then had to fold a direct-marketing business he had acquired. When he stuck to billboards, however, Turner appeared to have no equal. A competitor from Greenville, North Carolina, once decided to move in on his operation in Charleston, thinking Ted was too preoccupied with his other interests to notice. Turner took the invasion as a personal insult, dispatched a battalion of his own people to Greenville, and leased every available billboard site in town. The poor fellow was soon completely overwhelmed in his home market. Within weeks he retreated from Charleston and then paid Turner a stiff premium to vacate Greenville.

"A lot of times back then," Turner's lawyer, Tench C. Coxe, himself the soul of sophisticated discretion, has recounted, "we sort of went to the edge. But Ted never wanted to be involved in anything that wasn't fair game." Coxe remembered Ted's attempt to acquire a billboard company that was being sold by sealed bid auction. "Ted was furious when one of the people involved offered to tell him the bid he had to beat. He will risk a lot," Coxe recalled, "but not his reputation."

Although he had been singularly unsuccessful in his bid to sail in the Olympics, Turner was already talking about moving up again, this time to ocean racing. In early 1962 he persuaded Legarè VanNess and a couple of other ne'er-do-wells from his Savannah small boat days to join him in his first season out in open water. Ted had chartered sail maker Charles Ulmer's *Scylla*, a Block Island forty-footer, intending to sail her in the series of winter races off the Florida coast known as the Southern Ocean Racing Circuit. The SORC at that time was one of the most difficult, competitive racing series in the world. *Scylla* was docked up north on Long Island, and Turner went to fetch her in the midst of the season's first snowstorm. He had brought Jimmy Brown and Irwin Mazo along to crew. Turner planned to sail the boat all the way south to Miami, in time for the start of the SORC series.

"The worst four days of my life," Mazo says unequivocally. "That was the first and last time I ever went sailing with Ted Turner. Everything went wrong on that trip, right from the start. The radio broke. Lines snapped. Gear went overboard. There was a fire in the galley that Jimmy Brown almost let get out of control. We were all ready to put in anywhere we could, but Ted wouldn't think of it. He knew we would all jump ship."

They survived a serious winter storm off Cape Hatteras and finally limped into Savannah by way of the inland waterway.

Mazo still smarts from Ted's explanation of his disastrous maiden ocean voyage. "I never crewed for anyone," Turner offered lamely. "How was I to know?"

Ted's modus vivendi, however, was now becoming evident to all who cared to notice. Keep looking for the next challenge. Try anything, if the odds against you are long enough. Keep moving. Fall down, get up, and fall down again, until you suddenly find yourself running with the wind. Blow over a few times, but then the finesse will come. It worked in Lightnings and had carried him to national championships in Y-Flyers and Flying Dutchmen.

Despite that unpromising beginning with *Scylla*, Turner was hooked on ocean racing right from the start. Nothing could have suited his temperament or his talents better. Alone against the elements, his fate in his own hands, a doughty crew ready to bend to his every command, Ted could finally realize the romantic vision he had of himself. He could sail away from the banalities of the business world, the petty demands of ordinary existence—out of time and into a place where he could join the company of his heroes.

Not unexpectedly, Turner's first season competing in the Southern Ocean Racing Circuit proved to be an unmitigated disaster. Ted and his Savannah stalwarts managed to complete most of the races they started, but it was usually touch and go all the way. When they finished an utterly improbable second on corrected time in the prestigious Lipton Cup, however, Ted began to think the gods might actually have smiled on him. Preparing for the 1965 season finale, a daunting six-hundred-mile run from the west coast of Florida to Montego Bay, Jamaica, Turner even began imagining he could win. But he almost blew out his mainsail rounding the Keys and then ran short of food and water before they'd completed even half the race. *Scylla* was blown so far off course that Ted finally confessed he had lost direction, then turned tail and headed back home. The problem, he concluded once they were all safely back on shore, must surely have been the boat. If he was going to succeed in ocean racing, Turner decided, he would have to buy his own.

The fastest of the new breed of ocean racers that year was the Cal 40. Ted ordered one of these swift new forty-footers, christening her *Vamp X*, the "Vamp of Savannah." He had to wait out the spring season for his new boat to be delivered, but he spent the time honing his small boat skills by continuing to race Flying

Dutchmen. He also began to take an interest in Olympic 5.5's, a new class of thirty-foot boats that resembled miniature twelve-meters.

Once he had her in the water, *Vamp X* began to run away from the competition almost immediately. And when Ted Turner won the 1966 Southern Ocean Racing Circuit series by the largest margin in history, it became painfully obvious to most of the ocean racing establishment that this brash young small boat sailor from Savannah might have to be taken seriously. In only his second year of ocean racing, against one of the largest and toughest fleets ever assembled, Ted Turner had achieved an almost unbelievable victory. "Winning the SORC," commented *The New York Times*, "in a stock boat like the Cal 40 is like driving a Buick Roadmaster out of the showroom and right into the winner's circle at Indianapolis."

"The elements of success in ocean racing are, in order of importance," Turner told the *Times* man in a gracious postrace interview, "a great crew and, in particular, great helmsmanship. You've got to be able to steer the boat right. Second is competent navigation. And third is good equipment." And then summing up his already well-defined competitive credo, Turner added, "You can't win races without working harder than the other guys."

A perceptive observer from *One Design and Offshore Yachtsman*, the highly regarded British magazine, sounded fair warning to ocean racers everywhere when he wrote that Robert Edward Turner III had not only arrived, but might even be around long enough to revolutionize the sport. "The way to win the SORC," he wrote, "is to be a Flying Dutchman skipper, fill out your crew roster with top small boat sailors, and then make a very loud noise. *Vamp X* and her stentorian skipper shook many a sedate offshore sailor more accustomed to racing against less dedicated competition. The reason she did it is Ted Turner."

Hoping his remarkable success in the SORC would carry over, Ted plunged into the 5.5-meter world championships, only to finish a distant twelfth out of fifty boats. Licking his wounds and still looking for momentum, he then finished an unspectacular ninth overall aboard *Vamp X* in the Newport to Bermuda race, but hunkered down to win first in class and fourth overall in his very first transatlantic race, the extremely difficult Bermuda to Denmark.

With two ocean-racing victories in three tries that year, Ted

Turner became compulsive, driven to compete, willing to race anything with sails. With noted boat builder Robert Derecktor crewing, Turner entered national championships for both 5.5's and Flying Dutchmen but finished far down in the field in both series. He used the occasion, however, to convince Derecktor to build him a new Cal 40 in time for the upcoming SORC. Turner admitted he was distracted now racing smaller boats and chalked up his poor performances that year to "fantasies" he said he was beginning to have about the America's Cup. Derecktor had come up with *Vamoose*, an aluminum forty-footer, which he designed and built for Ted in only three months. *Vamoose* was hardly ready to be raced, however, when Ted took her south for the beginning of the 1967 Southern Ocean Racing Circuit series. Now used to winning, he was a poor fourth going into the Montego Bay race, the last of the series. The winds reached gale force just as the starting gun went off, but Turner saw his chance. Risking total disaster, he kept his huge spinnaker sail flying from start to finish, determined to see if he could recoup everything in this final race. "We were either going to win or be dismasted," he told the *Miami Herald*. "The crew voted and we kept the chute up all night. They worked harder than any crew I've ever seen." *Vamoose* finished first overall, and a redeemed Ted Turner won his second straight SORC series. One unnamed crewman suggested the *Herald* forgot to mention the bullwhip Ted had used to keep everybody in line.

Turner was now not only obsessed, but fully committed to ocean racing. He entered every event he could, no matter where in the world it might take him. In his first five years of ocean racing he logged more hours at the helm than most sailors experience in a lifetime. He began leaving behind the pickup crews he brought up from Savannah and Charleston, assembling instead a group of inordinately talented, equally obsessive types like himself—men, and sometimes women, prepared to drop everything to race with Turner whenever they got the call. Ted also began having his boats delivered to the starting line so he could drop in out of the sky, sometimes only minutes before the start of a race.

Turner kept no less a demanding pace whenever he was back in the office, and by the late 1960s Turner Advertising was throwing off enough cash to provide him with both the time and the money to continue sailing almost full-time. He was coming to see outdoor advertising as a maturing industry, however, and was already looking for his next business challenge. "Ted's not like the rest of us," Legarè VanNess points out. "He's too much a competitor to sit back on his laurels." For Ted Turner, momentum had indeed become a way of life.

Irwin Mazo agrees. "I watched Ted put his father's business in order. He did that with his eyes closed, with plenty of time on the side for his sailing. He could have retired anytime during those early years and never looked back. But then we started making acquisitions, always trying to use the other guy's money. That was Ted's genius. He could charm the pants off anybody when he wanted to. Usually the fellow we acquired would turn right around and work twice as hard for Ted as he ever had for himself. That was the other part of Turner's genius, to get people as enthusiastic as he was. He could usually get them to believe anything. When Ted made his next move, into radio, it didn't make a lot of sense until you heard Ted explain it. Then, suddenly, we weren't Turner Advertising anymore, we were the Turner Communications Company."

Along with his appetite for new business, Turner also acquired a young man by the name of James C. Roddey, who became the first and last president of his company. He hired Jim Roddey away from the Rollins Company, where Roddey had been group executive in charge of Rollins's interests in radio, television, and the new business of cable television. Today Roddey is a multimillionaire private investor. Back then he was the smooth, sophisticated administrator Ted intuited he must have if Turner Communications was going to maintain its own momentum.

"Ted Turner is without doubt one of the very smartest people I had ever met," Jim Roddey says. "But it took me just two seconds to figure out that he was also completely wacko. He is a brilliant idea man, but he's been a plunger from the beginning. A plunger with extraordinary business judgment." With Roddey in tow, Ted heaved off to Chattanooga, where he intended to begin building his new empire in radio. "There was no stopping him," Jim Roddey asserts. "Ted had gone to school in Chattanooga, and he was determined to have a station there. We ended up buying the worst radio station in the country, and we still overpaid." But Ted had something else in mind: a quick change of format to "Top 40," a couple of hot young disc jockeys, and then the coup de grace.

Turner's outdoor billboards were consistently generating lucrative profits, but turnover among advertisers always left a number of his signs unsold. Rather than spend money maintaining those empty boards, Ted saw them as the perfect way to promote his radio station. "I know it doesn't sound very brilliant," Turner told Roddey, "but it's sure going to work." Over the next two years Turner Communications acquired a second station in Chattanooga, two in Charleston, and one in Jacksonville, Florida. With the promotional assistance made possible by Turner's billboards, every one of those underperforming stations was soon turning a handsome profit.

Ted Turner had gone bottom fishing in the radio business and, using his signboards for synergy, had succeeded in landing a few decent trophies. But radio proved to be no more interesting to him than the billboard business. Turner was moving into the major leagues in ocean racing and consorting now with kings and princes. Radio might be a good business—and the way Turner approached it, a very good business indeed. But deep down Ted Turner could feel the momentum beginning to slacken. And with the same sharp eye for a shift in the wind that served him so well on the water, he now began to scan the horizon for his next great business breakthrough.

Ted sold *Vamoose* less than a year after commissioning her and concentrated his efforts once again on sailing in the Olympics. That was a piece of unfinished business he was determined to resolve. Racing the new Olympic-class 5.5's wherever he could find any competition, he seldom finished first, but he was acquiring incredibly valuable experience under every kind of condition and was regularly going up against the best small boat sailors in the world. Rapidly he began to develop into an Olympic-caliber sailor himself, making believers of the few who watched him blow out time and time again, but then get everything right as he roared across the finish line ahead of the rest of the fleet. Few realized it wasn't just the Olympics he now had in his sights. Turnover Ted was preparing himself to become the best sailor in the world—as well as the most famous.

On the spur of the moment, he decided to enter the 1968 SORC and was able to arrange a last-minute charter of *Bolero*, the famous seventy-three-foot monster of an ocean racer berthed in Oyster Bay, New York. Turner and his crew arrived in the middle of December to pick up the boat and sail her south to Florida. Perhaps because of his earlier experience with *Scylla*, or maybe because of it, Ted was undaunted by subzero temperatures and the fact that Oyster Bay Harbor was frozen solid with ten inches of ice. Turner hired an icebreaker to open up a path out into Long Island Sound and began laying in stores for the trip. Once the ice had broken up, *Bolero* promptly went down at the dock. No matter: Turner ordered his crew to pump her out. The next morning they would head out into the Atlantic. Jimmy Brown, along as usual as cook and conscience, remembered the trip well.

"We nearly wound up on the rocks off Cape Hatteras," he recounted with great pride. "We were supposed to save ourselves anyhow we could. A couple of our 'greenies' had been washed overboard, only they were caught by their safety harnesses. Mr. Ted said, 'Hang on, we'll make it.' " And miraculously they did, only to be hauled into Moorehead City, North Carolina, where Ted allowed one day only for rest and repairs. With no allowance for having brought *Bolero* through an impossible winter ocean passage, Turner finished the SORC series that year in twenty-fifth place, which for him was nothing short of an embarrassing write-off.

Ted Turner has estimated that he spent well over $100,000 a year on racing during the 1960s, not to mention another $20,000 or so on air fares. Not much by today's standards, when a simple twelve-meter can cost more than $5 million just to build, and another $5 million or more to campaign. But Turner's expenditures were enough then to put him in the company of royalty and the red trouser reactionaries who dominated the international ocean-racing establishment. "A young upstart who sometimes offends old-timers," was the way *One Design and Offshore Yachtsman* described the irascible Turner among these elitists. "While he is not self-deprecative, he is not boastful. And he is quick to compliment worthy opponents. His boisterousness is the product of enthusiasm, not egocentrism."

Nevertheless, Turner succeeded in charming the pants off most people with his refreshing candor and utterly unpredictable style. He had also stopped sending Jimmy Brown out to drink his competitors under the table the night before a big race, gathering useful intelligence in the process ("Mr. Ted! Mr. Ted!" Jimmy once called out upon his return. "They got something called a boom vang to hold their boom. We got to get ourselves a boom vang.") Now that Turner was collecting new friends like Prince Harold of Norway and his father, King Olav, he could ill afford such stunts. "Harold sailed with Ted several times," recalls Legarè VanNess. "It was a thrill for me, but Teddy already knew all those guys. Spain's King Juan Carlos. King Constantine of Greece. He had met most of them already, and they loved him and thought he was the greatest thing in the world. To the crowned heads of Europe, Ted Turner was the quintessential American."

At one victory banquet in Stockholm, the after-dinner speaker found himself acknowledging so many titles at the head table that he let Ted Turner stand up and introduce himself.

"Well, there are sure a lot of kings in this room," Ted began, "but where I come from, every man is a king."

"Naturally," says VanNess, "Teddy brought the house down. They gave him a standing ovation. Then he went off in a corner and spent the rest of the evening debating constitutional monarchy with Juan Carlos." VanNess also remembers that Turner talked even then about the power of electronic media and how much good it could do for the world. "This was way before CNN and all that," he says. "Then Turner would go out with the rest of us and drink until dawn."

That Ted Turner loved to talk was a given. That he usually couldn't stop talking is an irrefutable fact. Fortunately Turner found no shortage of listeners among the stiff, straitlaced upper stratum of the international yachting fraternity. Here was a curious specimen, as full of wind as a Genoa jib on a downhill run; but, dammit, the fellow could sail. He seemed oblivious of the impression he created and was determined, whatever the cost, to have fun. Some of these nabobs no doubt hoped Ted Turner would trip on his own tongue. Others surely had little patience with the nonstop diatribes he would launch into on virtually any subject that struck his fancy. Turner's eclectic interests and encyclopedic knowledge have always been impressive, but his ability to marshal facts in support of his own positions can turn any dialogue with him into a vicarious experience.

"Ted always put himself in the middle of anything he talked about," says VanNess. "He somehow manages to make himself the focal point of any conversation. But, in all the time we've spent together, he has never once talked about his family, his father, his wife, or his marriages. It was always his ambitions, his dreams. Ted is all about dreaming."

Turner would have little time to dream in 1970. Rebounding from a mediocre racing season the previous year, he drove *American Eagle* to a first-place finish in the Southern Ocean Racing Circuit, his second title in five years. Sandwiched in between the first and second races in that series was a thirty-two-hour round-trip flight to Sydney, where Ted won Australia's prestigious Gold

Cup. Then he brought *Eagle* home second in the Newport to Bermuda race; finished second overall in the Chicago–Mackinac on Lake Michigan; and won the 5.5 U.S. nationals at Annapolis. Back in Australia less than two weeks later, he came in second in the 5.5 world championships, capping this extraordinary twelve-month campaign by being named 1970 Yachtsman of the Year. Turner beat out Californian Bill Ficker for the title, despite the fact that Ficker, a former Star-class world champion, skippered *Intrepid* that year to a stirring America's Cup victory over Australia's *Gretel II*.

The old guard may have laughed when Turner bought *American Eagle* and began racing Bill Lee's old America's Cup trial horse out in the open ocean, but by now he had logged more hours at the helm of a twelve-meter than any other sailor in history. And all the while he continued to prove he was also one of the world's very best small boat skippers. No wonder he began to dream again.

Turner was also beginning to attract attention beyond yachting circles. *Time* magazine wanted to put together a story on this hot young ocean racer now being touted as America's Cup material. Ken Danforth, *Time*'s man in Atlanta, wasn't sure about the assignment at first but, intrigued by the background material he began to unearth in researching his subject, finally decided there might be a pretty good story in Turner after all. Among other interesting tidbits, Danforth discovered that nearly every high-class hooker in Atlanta knew Ted Turner, and most of them made it sound as if they knew him pretty well.

"When I first walked into Turner's office," Danforth remembers, "I saw this imposing guy strutting back and forth, smacking a swagger stick into his palm. He said he'd take me out sailing, but first he wanted to give me some sort of test. He said he had a few questions that were designed to test my mental toughness. They were personal, and when I got a little heated and told him I was here to interview him, he just kept coming on. 'Well, answer the questions, dummy.' He said he wanted to see what kind of man I was. I thought he was way out of bounds, and I told him so, in no uncertain terms.

" 'Well, you passed,' Turner said, tickled silly with himself. 'I want real men around me, and you passed. We're sailing from Miami up to Tampa. Tomorrow morning. Now go get your bag packed and meet me at the airport.'

"There were a couple of other crew, old friends of Turners. Plus his wife, and a young, unmarried couple who handled the cooking and took care of his boat. Just as soon as we were out in the Atlantic, everybody started drinking pretty heavily. Turner never stopped talking, about anything and everything. Once it was dark, he began a whole monologue on war—quoting some of the Greek and Roman historians. It was pretty impressive. He's very keen on war, because, he told us, it has a 'cleansing effect' on the weaker members of society. Only the strong tend to survive, he said, and you didn't need two guesses to know which category Turner saw himself in. Then he began to sound pretty fascistic and began to run off at the mouth in a way that, even though I've heard talk like that all my life, was pretty shocking, coming from a guy with his background. Racist stuff, then all the details of some of the women he'd been with. And his wife just sitting there on the deck, cringing.

"Since I was there as a journalist, I didn't say much but concentrated on trying to get to know this guy. Then he started pushing the girl and the young guy who worked for him around like they were slaves. It was pretty good weather and we were making great time, so Turner just decides to strip buck naked, and so did the young couple and the other guys on the crew. He jumped up and down when I wouldn't. He called me a pussy. Said I wasn't the man he thought I was, something to that effect. I could only tell him I didn't want to become part of the story I was writing. I was an observer and didn't feel I had to apologize to anybody. After that he left me alone.

"As we were cutting through the Keys, rounding Key West, one of the men caught a king mackerel and pulled it on board. Everybody is still naked, except Turner's wife and me. She's still just sitting there, looking more mournful by the minute. Turner left the helm and grabbed a big winch handle and fell on his knees before this big fish and started beating the bejesus out of it. Still stark naked. He began really slashing at it, with blood and fish scales flying all over the place. All the time he kept shouting, 'Kill! Kill! Kill!' in that raspy, high-pitched voice he has. I had no idea what had come over the man. It was frightening, and if there had been any way I could have got off that boat, I would have. I couldn't figure out what his wife was doing on this trip. Then Turner comes up and starts pushing her around, shoving her and calling her every name in the book. The man was absolutely crazy. Manic. And, of course, I never got any kind of story at all."

Turner was thirty-two then and basking in the acclaim ocean

racing had brought him. He had already tired of the radio business—it was too easy, and not a little boring. He sensed that he might be losing that all-important momentum, just when he knew he was ready for something bigger. He had also decided that breaking into the big time would be infinitely easier if Turner Communications were a public company. All of which made him an obvious pigeon when the investment bankers came calling.

If you want some ham,
you gotta go into the smokehouse.

HUEY LONG
Campaign Speech (1931)

Chapter Three

On October 18, 1968, Robinson Humphrey Co., Inc., an Atlanta-based securities firm, unloaded 130,000 shares of Rice Broadcasting stock on an unsuspecting investing public. The net proceeds of this imprudent underwriting amounted to more than $650,000 but were immediately consumed by Rice Broadcasting's sole operating asset—WJRJ, a lackluster UHF (ultra-high-frequency) television station that had total revenues that year of only $411,000 and accumulated losses well in excess of $800,000. Despite brave pronouncements from Rice's management that profitability was just around the corner, the company's share price began to plummet immediately after the initial public offering. If Robinson Humphrey had not initiated an immediate, all-out effort to sell WJRJ-TV, they would almost certainly have risked watching the company go under.

What little Ted Turner knew about WJRJ he had learned from his own billboards. Rice Broadcasting had become a new customer that year, using the Turner signs to promote viewership through a desperate giveaway called the "Good Looks Sweepstakes." What Turner knew about ultra-high-frequency television, however, was exactly nothing. He couldn't even pick up Channel 17 (WJRJ) on his own TV. Not many could. In 1968 fewer than half the sets in the area were able to receive a UHF signal. WJRJ's own research showed that the station was viewed by fewer than

5 percent of the households in greater Atlanta. "I never watched any television in those days," Ted trumpeted, "but as soon as I heard that a television station in Atlanta was for sale, I got interested right away. Somebody told me it was an underground station, but I didn't even know what that meant."

For Robinson Humphrey, Rice Broadcasting was a serious local embarrassment. UHF television, these white-shoe bankers joked bitterly among themselves, seemed like nothing so much as a cynical plot perpetuated by the Federal Communications Commission to separate unsuspecting doctors and dentists from their wealth.

Still mindful of his maiden voyage with Ted on *Scylla*, Irwin Mazo was the first to realize that this time they might actually hit the rocks. "Tony Lott and those boys from Robinson Humphrey walked into Ted's office and knew right away they had found their man," Mazo recalls. "That station was within thirty days of going off the air, but Ted had already decided he was going to buy it." Turner knew television was growing faster than any other medium and assumed it wouldn't be long before TV started to cut into his outdoor advertising profits. The license to own a TV station, Ted was convinced, could be worth a fortune in a few years. In the meantime, billboards would continue to throw off enough profit to help him get the station into the black.

"I had already been through one big crisis with Ted when he took back the Atlanta billboard operation from Bob Naegele," Mazo says. "And here I was once again asking, 'Why are we doing this?' I just couldn't take it another time." Irwin Mazo felt obliged to save Ted from himself. He was supported by Tench C. Coxe, Jim Roddey, and most of the other Turner Communications board members. "If this deal doesn't work out," Mazo warned Ted, "everything will collapse. Everything you've got will be gone. We don't want to put it all on the line, because the result can't possibly be worth the risk."

Irwin Mazo might as well have been talking to a billboard. Or telling Turner he couldn't possibly win a transatlantic race in a fragile, five-year-old twelve-meter like *America Eagle*. The more his directors spoke out against the deal, the more convinced Turner became that he had to take the plunge. Turner, moreover, had concocted a way to buy WJRJ-TV for no cash and, at the same time, achieve his goal of making Turner Communications a publicly traded company.

On January 26, 1970, Jack M. Rice, a prosperous Atlanta coal merchant and chairman of Rice Broadcasting, announced the merger of his company into Turner Communications Corporation. The transaction consisted of a tax-free exchange of stock, with Rice shareholders swapping 3.6 shares of Rice Broadcasting for 1 share of Turner Communications stock. No cash was involved. Turner Communications became the surviving entity and a public company in the bargain, by virtue of having reverse-merged with Rice. Ted Turner wound up controlling the combined companies in a deal that valued WJRJ at about $2.5 million. For an additional $180,000 in Turner stock, Ted was able to acquire WJRJ's 1,093-foot broadcast tower in a separate transaction with a real estate partnership controlled by Rice's former owners. By the end of 1970, however, Turner Communications, which had never before been unprofitable, posted a net after-tax loss of over $700,000.

"We were certain Ted had gone crazy this time," declares Mazo. "That TV station was hemorrhaging, and we could see the whole company being pulled down with it." WJRJ was the weaker of two UHF independents in the Atlanta market. It had been losing more than $50,000 a month when Turner was handed the keys to the ramshackle concrete-block studios at 1018 West Peachtree Street. He ordered Jim Roddey to have the station's call letters changed to WTCG (Turner Communications Group) and then raced off to Miami and the start of the new SORC season—but not before informing his board that he had found another UHF, this one in Charlotte, North Carolina. And, Turner said, he could get it cheap.

Ted won the 1971 SORC, his third series win, but he lost the battle over Charlotte. He also lost Ozam, his father's friend and his own close adviser, when Irwin Mazo flat out refused to go along with the Charlotte acquisition and even considered mounting a palace revolution to have Ted thrown out as chief executive of his own company. "After that Irwin Mazo resigned," Turner explained. "And it's pretty tough when your own accountant quits because he thinks you're doomed." Even without Mazo, the board vetoed Charlotte. So Ted went right ahead and bought the station on his own.

"It was even more messed up than the one in Atlanta," he admitted later, "but it was only losing thirty-thousand-dollars a month." Borrowing $250,000 against his signature, Ted bought the bankrupt station on the Charlotte courthouse steps, just as the sheriff was about to begin liquidation proceedings. He assumed nearly $3 million in station liabilities in order to close the deal, securing the debt with his Turner Communications stock. Later he would have to borrow from his company to keep the Charlotte station on the air. He promptly renamed the station WRET, in honor, he said, of his father. To avoid an obvious conflict of interest, he also assigned Turner Communications an option to acquire the station in exchange for forgiving any funds it lent him.

Jim Roddey soon followed Mazo out the door, but not without a parting shot. "Ted would launch a new project and then disappear," Roddey says now with the affection that distance can sometimes provide. "Then he'd be back and start screaming at everybody to do it his way. He may be a genius," Roddey concludes, "but he's also the least sensitive person I've ever known." Irwin Mazo promptly appointed himself corresponding secretary of the Turner Alumni Association. It wouldn't be long before he and Roddey would be swamped with applications for membership.

WTCG's tatty little studio on West Peachtree looked like a Confederate supply depot that Sherman had somehow missed in his march to the sea. It had to sprayed at least once a week for fleas, but it became Ted's new command post and communications center as he hunkered down and prepared to pull his newly acquired television stations back from the brink. The problem was, he also planned to be on the water or in the air for most of the next eight months, since he was about to embark on his most challenging season of competitive sailing ever. Like his father, Ted did not make commitments lightly, but even those hardy souls who made up the Turner Communications Group were having difficulty seeing how he could pull this one off.

A bright young numbers man named William S. Sanders replaced Jim Roddey as Turner's de facto man in charge, when Ted wasn't around. Like most of Ted's new hires, Sanders had been brought in on instinct. This kind of decision usually turned on Ted's visceral response, whether the candidate was a prospective 5.5 crew member or a possible chief financial officer for Turner Communications. Ted's talent for picking the right individual for the job has always been vastly underrated and may, in fact, represent his greatest natural ability. He knew instinctively, right from the beginning, that he couldn't do it all alone, even though he has often given the impression he would like to. Ted is eminently approachable, so much so that he catches most people off guard. But he is almost impossible to delude and will seldom suffer a fool.

Turner has made some of his best hires across a back alley bar, from inside a bathroom toilet stall, and, too many times to count, from an adjoining tourist-class seat on one of the thousands of airline flights he has taken over the past thirty-odd years. He had to look no farther than his own backyard, however, to find Will Sanders, who was a sophisticated young accountant with Price, Waterhouse in Atlanta but who had also grown up a few years behind Ted in Savannah. Sanders's family had even been in the outdoor advertising business and, like Turner, he was a born entrepreneur. Four years at Yale had only whetted his appetite for risk. Sanders possessed a very cool head, a superb ability to negotiate, and an awesome talent for contract bridge. Since Ted's game was poker, usually with the accent on bluff, the two complemented each other perfectly and would spend the next nine years together building Turner Communications into a media powerhouse.

Will Sanders was also enthusiastic about the future of television. Advertising revenues were certain to increase, he believed. The Atlanta market was the tenth largest in the country. And UHF penetration was exploding. In the first two years Turner owned WTCG, his potential audience had grown from 5 percent of Atlanta's households to nearly 55 percent, and climbing. "Ted thought he could promote WTCG on his billboards," Sanders pointed out, "the way he had done with his radio stations. And he was right. It worked like a charm." But, Sanders continued, "WTCG could also have sunk our ass. There were times when we all thought he was crazy. But Ted is one incredible salesman." When he was there to sell.

By early 1971, however, even Will Sanders was willing to admit that Turner Communications was severely undercapitalized. "I could see the whole show was about to sink," he related, and prepared to begin selling off assets to keep the company afloat. Turner himself likes to dramatize the dire straits he says his company was in, and there is little question that WTCG was bleeding badly. There were two UHF independents in Atlanta, WTCG and WATL, both of which would post operating losses of nearly $1 million that year. But WATL didn't have its own billboards, and it didn't have the superb cost-cutting ingenuity of Ted Turner. The Federal Communications Commission reported that 99 of 146

UHF stations reporting in 1970 were operating in the red. Refusing to let R. T. Williams, his promotion manager, spend even $212.50 for new videotape to use in making commercials, Turner ordered him instead to erase old segments of "Divorce Court" that Ted had found in the cellar. But Will Sanders proved to be the genius behind the genius. Sanders kept things on a relatively even keel by effectively securing increased bank lines. He also got top dollar for a couple of unwanted businesses, raising more than $2 million through the sale of the Roanoke outdoor advertising operation and a radio station in Jacksonville, Florida. He even persuaded Ted, without so much as a whimper, to sell back his interest in PlasTrend to Andy Green.

More significant, Will Sanders was able to use the apparent fiscal crisis to buy back enough Turner shares to push Ted's ownership over 55 percent. A bit of financial legerdemain, to be sure, but Sanders succeeded in giving Turner the absolute control he had relinquished in the merger with Rice Broadcasting. Turner Communications stock had slid from $5 a share all the way down to $1, but Sanders was banking on an independent appraiser's estimate of the company's true market value. The appraisal confirmed Ted's belief that his company had doubled in value since the merger. Despite WTCG's operating loss, Turner Communications was now worth at least $12 million on the open market. And despite the fact that WTCG broadcast almost nothing but old black-and-white movies and stale reruns, the station continued to post impressive revenue gains. Turner even decided the station's call letters could now stand for "Watch This Channel Grow!"

On March 31, 1971, without any warning whatsoever, WATL's owners, United Broadcasting Corporation, decided to pull the plug on Atlanta, and their station went dark. Forever. Just like that. United was the second-largest group owner of independent television stations in the country, ranked just behind the Kaiser Broadcasting Group. United's corporate planners in Philadelphia had concluded that UHF television would never be viable in an industry dominated by the three major commercial networks and their affiliates. After watching Kaiser pour over $50 million down the apparent black hole of UHF, United decided to cut its losses and shut down WATL. It was an unexpected and almost unbelievably lucky break for Turner. His take on the situation, however, was somewhat different. Declaring this serendipitous event a well-deserved "victory over superior forces with bottomless pockets," Ted began dropping hints that he just might be invincible, even off the water.

In one brief moment WTCG went from fifth of five television stations to fourth of four in Atlanta. As the only remaining independent, Turner now had plenty of room to maneuver. As soon as WATL went off the air, he ordered R. T. Williams to prepare a "Thank you, Atlanta" broadcast, which aired that evening. The handful of viewers who tuned in may have wondered what in the world they had done to deserve Ted Turner's thanks.

Not only was UHF reception in Atlanta still terrible—WTCG's shaky signal would often fade away entirely behind the outlying hills—but Turner still had virtually no programming to counter the networks' popular lineups of new movies, professional sports, miniseries, and star-studded situation comedies. "The three other commercial stations in Atlanta all had network money behind them," Ted explained, "and they all programmed pretty much alike. I believe that people are tired of violence and psychological problems and all the negative things they see on TV every night. I felt the people of Atlanta were entitled to something different from a whole lot of police and crime shows with rape and murders going on all over the place." For the most part, however, "different" in the Turner lexicon proved to translate as "old and tired." And "cheap." And "black and white." The rest of the television industry had made the changeover to color, but without much cash Turner was forced to rely on ancient Hollywood warhorses, often choosing the old movies and sitcoms he had known as a boy.

"Ted didn't mind overpaying for the programs he bought," says Tom Ashley, whom Turner brought on board as WTCG's national sales manager. "He made a lot of friends in the industry by overpaying. People liked working with him. He would take the product," says Ashley, "and sometimes never even ask the price. That would drive Will Sanders crazy."

Most television stations, particularly financially strapped independents, typically licensed films for a limited number of showings. The rights then reverted back to the owners. Turner went against conventional wisdom and *bought* films outright whenever he could. That way he could run them as often as he wanted, prorating the purchase price over hundreds of airings. Few realized the significance of his approach, which necessarily limited him to the oldest, cheapest programs on the market; but by owning the product whenever possible, Turner gained the leverage that would ultimately make WTCG the single most profitable television station in the country. Sheer genius, or merely the inclination of a man with an aversion to chartering someone else's sailboat? No one was talking visionary yet when Ted Turner's name came up, but he was beginning to provide the wags with something to think about.

It may have been to Ted's advantage that not many Atlantans could pick up WTCG. Assume a dedicated UHF viewer could manipulate the complicated dial system most manufacturers then imposed upon anyone daring enough to venture beyond the conventional VHF channels 2 through 13. Then assume that viewer was able to divine the perfect angle for his delicate set-top rabbit-ears antenna, without which UHF reception was impossible. Then consider the acute case of déjà-vu he contracted once he saw, in living black and white, what all this effort had produced: "Lassie," "Leave It to Beaver," "I Love Lucy," "Father Knows Best," "Petticoat Junction." Turner called it "escapism," but out of these hoary reruns he was able to fashion a programming philosophy and an adroit advertising sales pitch. Promoting the innocent family values of these benign old chestnuts rather than the shows themselves, Ted would ignore ratings and sell around the competition.

Once he cornered the market on family values, Turner went after the news. Or, rather, the people who never watched the news. The networks fed their evening news shows to their local affiliates, but the ABC station in Atlanta chose instead to fatten its ratings by counterprogramming entertainment fare. When ABC finally came down hard on their affiliate and insisted it carry the network news, Turner rushed into the breach with old "Star Trek" reruns. It wasn't long before WTCG had captured a big portion of the evening audience for whom no news was the best news.

NBC's affiliate, WSB, was perpetually number one in the Atlanta market. When WSB declined to carry several network offerings in favor of more profitable locally produced shows, Turner pounced again and picked up a package of five NBC sitcoms from the network, eager to have any outlet in the growing Atlanta market. Soon Turner's billboards announced, with no little presumption, "The NBC Network has moved to Channel 17." Ted's ingenuous explanation: "We felt we could shake them up a little, let them know we're in the race."

All this television savvy from a guy who says he was too busy ever to watch. "Ted programmed the whole station, right from day one," recalled Gerry Hogan, who left a high-flying sales job in Chicago to throw in with Turner as general sales manager. "We never knew where he got his input. But he got it."

Connecting with the man in the street has always been one of Ted Turner's secret strengths. Despite his upper-middle-class background, he shares a visceral connection and has always identified with the little guys of this world. A living, breathing bundle of contradictions, Turner has spent his life trying to stand out from the crowd and at the same time blend in. He abhors artifice and has never had much taste for small talk. Yet his speech is riddled with the tired half-truths and schoolboy logic of a high school debater—which, from anyone else, would seem awkward and unnatural. Ted Turner, the voice of the people? One thing was becoming clear: he knew intuitively how to talk to them in television.

Since counterprogramming had worked so well for Turner, he couldn't resist throwing a little contra selling into the mix when he hit the streets with his gallant crew of advertising salesmen. You want to avoid clutter? he asked prospective advertisers, who watched, startled, when he began pounding on their desks. You want shock value? You want your message to stand out the way it never could on any other station? Then run your color commercials on WTCG, where all my programs are black and white! "Our audience may not be big," Ted told them, forgoing even the semblance of any supporting documentation, "but our viewers are way above the average viewer's mentality." How could he be so certain? "Because it takes a genius to figure out how to tune a UHF set, dummy!"

An old girlfriend helped Ted pull off his next programming coup. Married to one of Atlanta's top professional wrestling promoters, she persuaded her husband to move his matches from the local ABC affiliate to WTCG. Soon Channel 17's tiny little studio housed a full-size wrestling ring and rocked three nights a week to the cheers and jeers of at least a few dozen neighborhood kids who'd been asked to paper the house. Wrestling helped WTCG's anemic ratings begin to edge upward and first brought home to Turner the pulling power of professional sports.

The Atlanta Braves had arrived in Atlanta from Milwaukee in 1962. Their parent company, LaSalle-Atlanta Corporation, had lost nearly $1 million a year ever since, although part of that loss was defrayed by WSB, which paid LaSalle $200,000 a year for the right to telecast twenty Braves road games. The arrangement had not been particularly satisfactory for either party. When Ted Turner showed up and offered to pay LaSalle $600,000 a season for the next five years, the Braves decided not to renew their contract with WSB but to go ahead with this audacious young man with the big checkbook. Jack Carlin, the Braves' broadcast manager, didn't even blink at the fine print in the Turner contract, which allowed WTCG to broadcast *sixty* Braves games a season. It was a choice between overexposure, which might hurt the gate, and an immediate cash infusion, which according to Carlin, probably kept the Braves in Atlanta. Soon WTCG was the flagship station in a new "Braves Television Network." Turner copied Bill and Bob Wormington, who had strung together a two-state "network" from their little Kansas City UHF, and resold his Braves' broadcast rights to twenty-four other stations across six southern states. Almost without realizing it, Turner had created the largest "mininetwork" in the country. Considering WTCG's other offerings, Braves games also quickly became WTCG's highest-rated broadcasts. Paid attendance at Fulton County Stadium, however, plunged to the lowest in the major leagues.

Some in the Braves' management were concerned about the shift from WSB and voiced their concern. Bob Hope, the Braves' director of promotion, felt "the new television deal with WTCG was a major step backward in prestige, even though it was described as a significant financial gain. Money or no money," Hope felt, "it didn't seem right for a big-league team to be on a Mickey Mouse station with a reputation for showing only cartoons, old grade-D movies, and 1950s television reruns. We weren't even sure people could get the WTCG signal on their TV sets. No one will come in person to see our games. After all, sixty free games on television is a lot of baseball. Some of us thought the Braves might just be forgotten."

Of course, Hope was right on most counts. But at the time he had no way of estimating Ted Turner's determination to make a go of his new station or his desire to extend WTCG's audience beyond Atlanta to outlying cable systems throughout the Southeast. And he would find that once Turner began to apply his personal brand of promotional magic to the Braves' broadcasts, even sixty games would hardly be enough to satisfy the thousands of new baseball-hungry fans who, even though they lived hundreds of miles from Fulton County Stadium, would soon adopt the Braves as their home team.

Fourteen months after the merger, WTCG turned its first profit ever. And Ted's family could now watch him every Sunday morning, ensconced in a tattered leather wingback chair, introducing "Academy Award Theater." He wasn't Alastair Cooke, and the old movies seldom equaled "Masterpiece Theater." But it was another of Turner's successful counterprogramming efforts and went up against wall-to-wall religious broadcasts on each of the other Atlanta stations. That brief videotaped glimpse of their father was often the only one caught by the growing brood of Turner children, which now included Beauregard, Rhett, and Sarah Jean (Jennie) as well as Judy Nye's children, Teddy IV and Laura. Ted's absence was most keenly felt each Christmas, since December usually found him in Australia, competing in the Hobart to Sydney for the Gold Cup. No one has recorded whether Jane Turner ever sat through "Academy Award Theater," but she has admitted to dutifully lining up the kids in front of the TV on Sunday mornings to remind them what their father looked like. That show would be Ted Turner's only on-camera effort for nearly fifteen years. "It was kind of a joke," says Turner's production manager, R. T. Williams, "but Ted took it quite seriously and he was pretty good. Even if he hardly had the time to do it."

He couldn't have had a great deal of time for much beyond business and sailing, which for Turner was fast becoming more demanding than any business. Yet there was another, unacknowledged element in the equation, one Ted merely assumed as a given—the women. Like his father, Ted devoted considerable time and attention to the pursuit of "extracurricular interests," maintaining minimum discretion when he was away sailing but attempting to protect his family man's image when he was back in Atlanta. Turner's ocean crews often included serious female sailors like B. J. Beach and Patsy Bolling. But there were also innumerable racing groupies who often sailed with him as "unofficial" crew and more serious camp followers like Fréderique D'Arragon, the statuesque French blonde with the impressive exchequer. Turner's mental and physical equal, Fréderique could hold her own with him on virtually any subject, in any of four languages. And her checkbook gave her a confidence and independence he often found irresistible. Like his father, Ted was a good provider. He also needed the anchor of a family and, whenever the thought occurred to him, was deeply committed to his wife and children. But, like Ed Turner, Ted felt his role as provider entitled him to spend as much time away from home as he wished

—some of it, at least, dedicated to the challenge of the chase and the constant parade of leggy blondes who might find their way onto his arm or into his bed at every stop along the steep and slippery course he had chosen to follow.

Full of righteous piety, Ted could wax enthusiastic for hours on end about honor, loyalty, and integrity—the bedrock virtues of southern character and the values he holds most dear. He believes in God but has not regularly attended any church since his faith was shaken by his little sister's agonizing death. It's been nearly forty years since Ted has looked at a Bible, but he can still cite passages from memory that seem to contradict the double standard he practices. These contradictions, however, may be endemic to the South, which has ever turned a blind eye to the man's peregrinations while placing the acquiescent southern woman on a pedestal. And like many men of the sea, Ted Turner has always spent much of his life pondering the delights awaiting him in the next port. Judy Nye recognized Ted's weakness for a pretty face the first time she met him. "I think Roger Vaughan tried to warn me off Ted," she says. "Because he knew what a womanizer Ted was, even in college. He'd seen Ted with so many different ladies already that he didn't want me to end up being just another name added to the list."

Born and raised a strict Methodist fundamentalist, Ted's father was the first Turner in five generations to desert the church. Leaving his faith behind when he went north, Ed Turner set a formidable example for his only son, once telling him he had slept with over three hundred women by the time he was thirty, including every debutante in Cincinnati but one. "And I would have had her, too," he averred, "if there'd been more time." A tough act to follow. Ted Turner was driven, however, not just to emulate his father, but to exceed him in every way he could.

"Working with Ted was no bowl of cherries," recalls Tom Ashley, "but we all loved it. If you were producing, pulling your weight, he pretty much left you alone. You had to be in the office at eight-thirty every morning, but even if you got in a half hour early, he was already there. Nobody told us he slept at the office. But in all the years I've been in this business," says Ashley, "I've never seen a guy work harder." Turner would disappear sailing for weeks at a time, but then come back working harder and longer than anybody else in the company.

"At first, nobody took him seriously," recollects Ashley. "Big mistake. He is eccentric. Maybe even crazy. But Turner's bright, and he is driven. And he never gives up. I think Ted knew people were laughing at him back then. But he was never going to give up. And now he's the guy with the last laugh." Tom Ashley left the company and rejoined Turner twice over seven years, and today heads his own television distribution business. However, he is willing to concede that he has never had more fun than in those early days at WTCG. And he still gets mileage out of the story of Ted's most notorious advertising presentation—the pitch he made in the nude. "I never actually saw him do that," Ashley admits. "I always heard it was at some big presentation to Coca-Cola for his billboard company. But you still hear that story everywhere in Atlanta."

Few would deny the good times Turner provided. And most of his band of mavericks and merry men could put up with the temper tantrums and personal abuse—and with Ted's own peculiar brand of loyalty. R. T. Williams, always one of Turner's favorites, was returning with the boss from a very late, very liquid business dinner one evening. As they hove into the shadow of the station's imposing, 1,093-foot tower—which Ted liked to claim was the tallest of its kind in the country—Turner bet Williams he could beat his older colleague to the top. Taking the challenge seriously, Williams immediately stripped off his jacket and began climbing up the tower's framework. He kept going all the way to the top before looking down, expecting the always competitive Turner to be snatching at his heels. Of course, Ted had taken a longer, harder look at the tower and decided only a fool would attempt a climb like that. Williams got to the top in a little less than twenty minutes—something of a record that still stands—but he was stranded there for over seven hours until he got the nerve to make his way down in the cold light of dawn.

Ted had a slightly more difficult time trying to motivate his troops over at his Charlotte station. When the red ink there refused to dry up, Turner finally resorted to a desperate twenty-four-hour fund-raising "beg-a-thon." "It was amazing," Irwin Mazo recounts. "I left the company because I knew Ted would get in over his head. Now here he was, in over his head and on the air in Charlotte, asking people, if you please, to send in their money to save his television station." More than 35,000 viewers, however, responded, sending in contributions ranging from $.25 to as much as $100. Altogether Ted raised nearly $50,000 in less than one day.

"Naturally," says Mazo, "he turned around and used the money

to build a new parking garage at the station. But Ted also did
something that shows what kind of person he is. He kept the
names and addresses of every single person who sent in money.
When he sold the station eight years later, Turner sent every one
of them a check for every penny they contributed." Mazo adds
just a little wickedly, "Of course, I'm sure his legal advisers may
have had something to do with the refund. Still, he did manage
to pay everyone back. He never tried a 'beg-a-thon' again, but had
to keep borrowing from his company—I think the amount eventually was over two million dollars—just to keep that station
going. It was all secured by his Turner Company stock. There was
just no way Ted was ever going to admit he'd made a mistake
with that TV station."

Charlotte may have been a problem, but back at WTCG Turner
was quietly putting together a powerhouse of a television sports
package that would soon give him a virtual lock on the Atlanta
market. In addition to the Braves and his homegrown professional wrestling extravaganzas, Turner had acquired broadcast
rights to Atlanta Hawks basketball and Atlanta Flames hockey.
And he made it all look so easy—as easy as those impossible last-
to first-place finishes out on the ocean. Or the almost effortless
way he drew the pretty women to him the minute he walked into
a room.

The "escapist" combination of big-time sports and old movies
was soon enough to drive WTCG's ratings through the roof, and
soon the station was showing a remarkable 15-percent share of
audience, an almost unheard-of achievement for a UHF independent, anywhere. "At one point," Tom Ashley remembers proudly,
"we actually beat the local ABC affiliate for a full rating period.
And we were still having fun."

When it came to satisfying the FCC requirement that a station
broadcast at least seven hours of news and/or public affairs programming a week, Ted knew enough to stop experimenting and
let his instinct again be his guide. WTCG had little chance of
outgunning the three Atlanta network affiliates, so Turner scheduled his station's news hour at three o'clock each morning, following the "Late, Late Movie." Naturally WTCG's new show won the
time slot, since it was the only station in Atlanta still on the air at
that hour.

Turner installed Bill Tush, a weatherman he'd inherited when
he acquired WTCG, as the station's news director, anchor, and
incipient local celebrity. Tush would "rip and read" the news

from wire service dispatches and, sometimes, straight from the *Atlanta Constitution*. He occasionally livened things up by introducing a German shepherd as his coanchor and outdoor editor. He would also deliver the news from behind a mask of Walter Cronkite. During the Atlanta Braves' six-year sojourn in the National League cellar, Tush even delivered the scores with his head in a paper bag. Local insomniacs tuned in just to see what Tush would do next. One of his most loyal viewers was the boss himself. Nobody ever asked Ted Turner what he was doing up at that late hour, but he has nevertheless remained intensely loyal to Bill Tush, who is still with Turner Broadcasting more than twenty years after he became WTCG's first cult figure.

In 1971 WTCG lost more than $500,000. By 1972, however, the station was breaking even and would earn over $1 million the following year. Turner had not only found himself a new mother lode, he would soon turn the Atlanta and Charlotte stations into two of the most successful independents in the country. With a growing library of several thousand old movies and broadcast rights to Atlanta's major league baseball, basketball, and hockey teams, Ted Turner was ready to break out into a bigger market and saw the entire South as his natural audience, clamoring for WTCG's appetizing mix of sports, sitcoms, and familiar old movie classics.

In a new ruling intended to benefit struggling independent television stations, the FCC in 1972 allowed cable television operators to "import" distant signals from certain stations in the top one hundred markets across the country. Independent station owners like Ted Turner might now reasonably expect the heavens to open up and shower them with new profits. If only they were able to reach this huge new potential audience.

For I dipt into the future, far as human eye could see,
Saw the Vision of the world, and all the wonder
that would be;
Saw the heavens filled with commerce, argosies of
magic sails,
Pilots of the purple twilight, dropping down
with costly bales.

ALFRED LORD TENNYSON
Locksley Hall

Chapter Four

An enterprising appliance dealer in Latrobe, Pennsylvania, named John Walson looked out at the hills of western Pennsylvania that loomed in the distance and decided to take the plunge. It was 1949, and Walson had added a television set to the lineup of self-defrosting refrigerators, automatic washing machines, airflow dryers, wire recorders, and high-fidelity record players that crowded his shop floor. Introduced to the public at New York's 1938 World's Fair, television had been put on hold at the outbreak of World War II. Now TV was back and would soon capture the imaginations, if not the minds, of people everywhere. Even though the only signal being broadcast for much of the day was a fine-lined geometric test pattern, prospective television viewers would stand for hours in stores like Walson's, mesmerized by this new entertainment machine. Neighbor vied with neighbor to be the first on the block with a television. These video pioneers could always be identified by the jumble of outsize wire rods attached to their rooftops, signifying entry into this brave new world. Outside a few large metropolitan areas, however, would-be televiewers found it almost impossible to receive a signal of any clarity whatsoever without an impossibly tall antenna. And as John Walson soon discovered, if you happened to live behind the Allegheny Mountains, that antenna would have to be a full-fledged tower, several hundred feet high, to pick up television's line-of-sight signals.

Walson also discovered that his new televisions, with their boxy, furniturelike styling and eight-inch screens, did not sell themselves. Customers insisted on seeing working models with clear, sharp pictures. Being a practical man, Walson arranged to have a two-hundred-foot tower built on the top of Blue Mountain above Latrobe. He ran a wire coaxial cable from that new tower into his shop and could now pick up TV signals from Philadelphia that were as clear as if he were standing in the middle of Liberty Hall. Naturally anybody who bought one of Walson's televisions was allowed to hook into his tower on the mountain, which thus became the world's first community antenna television (CATV) system.

Ted Turner was eleven and a half years old in 1949 and preoccupied with Penguin races at the Savannah Yacht Club. Television was still a curiosity in Savannah and had just invaded the Turner household. Thirty-five years later, however, television would become the dominant influence on contemporary culture, and CATV, or cable television, would be an entrenched alternative delivery system reaching half of all the households in the country.

The growth of cable television was stalled in 1968, however, when CATV operators balked at paying copyright fees on the programs they retransmitted to subscribers for profit. Once the young industry agreed in 1972 to subject itself to a federally appointed copyright tribunal that would determine appropriate and affordable charges, the FCC issued the ruling that opened the door to the importation of distant signals. The actual mandate, which had been intended to benefit struggling independent television stations by allowing them exposure to cable households, was vague and contradictory and was seen as unworkable by most broadcasters. Even Ted Turner conceded shortcomings in the new FCC ruling but, in his 1972 report to shareholders, suggested that "stations like WTCG are the ones most likely to benefit from these new regulations." *Alea jacta est.* And the die *was* cast. From that moment on Ted Turner knew his real market was an ever-expanding audience beyond Atlanta. He began by coopting the television-starved citizens of Georgia's rural hill country, where television reception of any kind without cable was all but impossible. Turner managed to begin sending WTCG's signal via microwave into more than a hundred thousand new homes beyond the reach of the other Atlanta stations. Soon he would stretch his signal to Macon and Columbus and then down to Tallahassee. Through the good offices of the FCC, Ted Turner had taken a dog-eared independent UHF and turned it, in less than thirty-six months, into an invaluable regional franchise, the first "cable network" in television history. Perhaps more important, the signal he delivered proved uniquely popular with WTCG's newly expanded audience, which was in total sync with Turner's escapist programming. Ted Turner had crossed over the line from broadcaster to something else, but even he couldn't have foreseen how far this first step into the brave new world of cable television would take him.

Turner's troops had grown accustomed to seeing their leader desert the field of battle as the opposing armies were wheeling into position and then return just when his presence seemed most needed. This time, however, Turner took his leave before anyone realized there might even be hostilities in the offing. He had overcome the usual insurmountable odds in 1971 to capture the prestigious World Ocean Racing Cup, a series of eighteen insanely difficult races stretched out over a three-year period. After shipping *American Eagle* to Australia and finishing a disappointing thirty-fifth in the next-to-last qualifying race, (the Sydney to Hobart), Turner stole the cup by winning the very last race of the series. The victory had been expensive, and Turner could not afford to ship *Eagle* back home. But he had shown the ocean-racing world another side of his many-faceted character when he spellbound a roomful of well-heeled, world-class sailors merely by paraphrasing off the cuff from Joseph Conrad's *The Nigger of the "Narcissus"*: "Ah! The good old time—the good old time—the good old time. Youth and the sea. The good strong sea, the salt, bitter sea, that could whisper to you and roar at you and knock your breath out of you. The crew of the *American Eagle* drifted out of sight. I never saw them again. The sea took some, the steamers took others. The graveyards of the earth will account for the rest. So be it! Let the earth and sea each have its own." For the moment, the sea had Turner. But in due course he would belong to the world.

Turner continued to campaign hard in 1973. Before the start of the winter racing season, he acquired a new boat, *Lightning*, and drove her to ten first- or second-place finishes. He wound up out of the money only once all year, at the One-Ton World Championships in Costa Smerelda, Sardinia, where he finished sixth. It is difficult to exaggerate this remarkable record. Few amateurs have ever maintained such an extended schedule at such a high level of competition with such extraordinary success. Ted Turner managed the feat while overseeing his burgeoning communications company *and* planning to expand into the uncharted waters of cable television. Even the old fogeys at the New York Yacht Club were beginning to take notice—once they were able to forget that this was the same Ted Turner who had shown up at the 1970 America's Cup in Newport with *American Eagle*, flying the Confederate Stars and Bars and serving as "trial horse" to Australia's *Gretel II*. Roundly criticized at the time for "giving aid and comfort to the enemy," Turner could have reminded the NYCC that one of their own, the estimable Gerald Lambert, had been applauded forty years earlier when he lent his J-boat, *Vanitie*, to the British challenger for the same purpose. So much for amateur idealism and the New York Yacht Club's fabled "friendly competition."

"He had won big," Tench Coxe noted, "but he couldn't leave it alone. Ted kept seeing something else out there." For the moment, that something else was an unprecedented third victory in yet another Southern Ocean Racing Circuit series. That Turner still had his competitive edge became immediately apparent during the Lipton Cup, a coveted SORC trophy race. During his final spinnaker run into Palm Beach, Turner was leading the fleet, but a second boat was closing on him fast. Suddenly, three hundred yards from the finish, an ocean tug towing a huge barge appeared across his bow. The cable between the barge and the tugboat appeared ominously taut and was plenty high enough to sheer off *Lightning*'s mast.

The crew's eyes were all on Turner, who hadn't even considered changing course. "Damn the cable!" he finally shouted in that rasping high-pitched whine that was almost enough in itself to blow the barge out of the water. "We're going through!"

And through they went, when it became all too apparent to the tugboat captain that Turner had every intention of cutting between his boat and the barge. He slackened the cable, and Turner sailed on to victory, as he had known all along he would. "Ted is always winning, never losing," exulted Bunky Helfrich, who was part of that crew. "And he gives that same feeling to people sailing or working with him."

Turner was named Yachtsman of the Year again in 1973, and

when reporters asked him if anyone else had ever won the honor twice, Ted replied, "Yeah, a couple of guys. But no one has ever won it three times."

Turner's extraordinary effort in 1973 could be explained in part because this was the year the New York Yacht Club would select skippers for the 1974 America's Cup. Turner estimated he had spent well over $1 million in his ten years of ocean racing. Now he was waiting for the payoff call. It came from Commodore George Hinman, who headed the *Mariner* syndicate. *Mariner* was the new twelve-meter from controversial designer Britton Chance. Hinman had made two earlier calls before he got around to Turner. Robert "Bus" Mosbacher, an experienced America's Cup defender, and Buddy Melges, 1972 Soling Olympic gold medalist (and winner of nearly as many sailing trophies as Turner). Both turned him down because of business commitments or because they intuited *Mariner*'s supposed design shortcomings. Turner's record during 1973 had made him a logical first choice, but Hinman and his fellow syndicate members were concerned about Ted's "off-the-water indiscretions." There was one other slight problem. Ted had earlier applied for membership in the New York Yacht Club and been turned down, resoundingly. There was no actual rule that a defending America's Cup skipper had to be a member, but it would have been more than a little awkward to have the club's honor defended by a blackballed reject.

Reassuring themselves that Ted Turner was, indeed, "a hell of a sailor," Hinman persuaded Robert Bavier, who had been selected to skipper a rival twelve-meter, *Courageous*, to propose Turner for membership again. Hinman, a former NYYC commodore, then used all of his influence to push Turner's membership through just before year-end. Despite spirited opposition, Hinman's convincing argument that Turner could be better controlled inside the club than out apparently assured his election.

Britton Chance was determined that his radical, aluminum-hulled *Mariner* would be a design breakthrough. Working closely with Peter Desaix, chief of the ship yacht division of the Davidson Laboratory of the Stevens Institute of Technology in Hoboken, New Jersey, Chance had subjected *Mariner*'s daring "maxistep" aftersection to extensive, rigorous tank testing. Desaix personally supervised those tests and, like Chance, was convinced *Mariner* would sail away from anything else on the water.

Ted Turner had his doubts. He had never cared for Brit Chance or his derisive manner. Chance, moreover, was an entrenched member of the New York Yacht Club establishment. He had been involved in America's Cup projects for nearly sixteen years. Nearly ten years earlier Chance had tried to persuade Turner and Andy Green to coat the bottoms of their fiberglass Flying Dutchmen with "microbubbles," a Teflon-like skin that supposedly would allow a boat to "surf" over the water with greatly improved speed. Later Chance persuaded Green to drill hundreds of tiny holes in his boats, through which spaghettilike tubes would ooze polymers out into the water beneath the hull, greatly reducing friction and building boat speed. Both ideas had been quickly and summarily banned by race officials. A self-professed purist with respect to boat design, Turner had developed a profound distaste for Chance, whom he perceived as hellbent to win on technological gimcracks and gadgetry and not with Turner's preferred good old-fashioned guts and glory.

When the unfinished *Mariner* had first been put in the water, however, Turner showed up unexpectedly and, bursting with enthusiasm, took one look at the unusual twelve-meter and pronounced her the best boat Bob Derecktor had ever built. "Not by a damn sight," Derecktor replied ominously.

Turner's crew had been through the wars with him but included only two members, Rich duMoulin and Conn Finley, with previous America's Cup experience. They all had learned to win with Turner under generally impossible conditions, in all kinds of boats. But none of them had ever seen anything like those steps in *Mariner*'s stern section. Turner himself became uncharacteristically stoic when his eyes riveted on the "confused" wake off *Mariner*'s stern, an early warning that Chance's step design might be flawed. Jim Lipscomb and several other members of the film crew photographing the event for a CBS documentary also noticed the turbulent wake. Back on shore, Lipscomb tried to corner Chance for an explanation. "We kept asking him the same question seven different ways," he remembers, "and we kept getting the same answer: 'No comment.' "

Brit Chance himself was considerably more vocal and pleased to sound off at every opportunity on the subject of Ted Turner's sailing ability. He had done everything possible to block Turner's selection and told *Providence Journal*'s Doug Riggs that he "figured a breakthrough design was their only hope, with Turner at the helm."

Ted had promised himself he would toe the line in Newport, and his behavior during the first weeks of the June trials was exemplary. He insisted on using "Commodore" every time he addressed Hinman, but he did so with obvious respect. He broke out his trademark blue-and-white-striped engineer's hat, but otherwise he observed the syndicate's strict dress code, even down to out-of-fashion cuffs on the crew's white flannel trousers. Bunky Helfrich was struck by the enormous self-discipline Ted imposed upon himself, and when Turner banned drinking during work hours, he responded jokingly, "Listen, Turner, just because you can't handle it . . ." No drinking, Ted insisted, on the boat or anywhere in the vicinity, during working hours. And no laughing, either, until after the June trials.

Unhappily, *Mariner's* crew would have little to laugh about all summer. In Turner, Chance, and Bob Derecktor, syndicate manager Hinman had assembled an improbable supergroup of unusual talent and experience. Their combined résumés enabled him to accelerate the difficult task of raising the $1.1 million he would need to fund *Mariner's* America's Cup campaign. Putting Chance and Turner together, however, was like mixing gasoline and nitroglycerin. Adding the highly capable but irascible and outspoken Derecktor, who had also agreed to crew for Ted, meant that it was just a question of time before the *Mariner* team self-destructed.

The yachting establishment, most particularly at the exalted level of America's Cup competition, is comprised chiefly of powerful, wealthy individuals who either have inherited great fortunes or control large corporate empires that provide them with the time and the money to lavish millions of dollars and years of planning and preparation on one summer's worth of match racing. Twelve-meter boats, which became the new standard in 1958, are expensive, technological marvels and, since no one had yet succeeded in taking the cup away from the defending New York Yacht Club, were designed exclusively for match racing on specific 23.4-mile closed courses off Newport, Rhode Island. The competition was strictly amateur, meaning that it was difficult but not impossible to buy your way into the game. Even so, you still had to pass the scrutiny of the cup organizers.

The New York Yacht Club won possession of the original Hundred Guinea Cup, now venerated as the America's Cup, when the pleasure yacht *America* sailed across the Atlantic in June 1851, to beat the very best that Britain had to offer in a race against fourteen vessels of the Royal Yacht Squadron. Through twenty-three successful defenses over 123 years, the gentlemen of the club's cup selection committee had become as predictable as the tides. George Hinman had been officially involved with cup activities since 1958 and was twice a member of the selection committee. His choices of designer, builder, and helmsman for the 1974 campaign, not to mention his approval of *Mariner*'s unproven design, suggested to many of the wise old heads who gathered in the club's musty, oak-paneled taproom on West Forty-fourth Street that Hinman either must know something none of the other experts could fathom or else had taken temporary leave of his senses. Commodore Hinman, who had headed the *Valiant* syndicate in 1970, wasn't sure himself what the verdict would be.

Once she was in the water and under way in Newport, *Mariner*'s design flaws became immediately apparent to everyone but Chance, who kept insisting that Turner was the reason she performed so poorly. Turner contained himself, doing his best to stay in Hinman's good graces, until Chance decided to ship *Mariner* back to Bob Derecktor's boatyard for a major back-end overhaul. Then Turner blew. "Brit," he asked, making certain he was within earshot of several yachting writers, "do you know why there are no fish with square tails? Because all the pointy-tailed fish caught them and ate them." Then the coup de grace: "Damn, Brit. Even shit is tapered at both ends."

While *Mariner* was away, Turner was asked to take the helm of *Valiant*, the syndicate's "trial horse." Unused to this older boat or its young crew, Turner seemed erratic and uncertain. Hinman himself took over briefly, then asked Turner's tactician, a young West Coast hotshot named Dennis Conner, to try his hand. Nothing like this had ever happened to Turner, who found himself floundering without the control he usually enjoyed. He even fouled Conner several times when the two paired up after *Mariner*'s return. A few days later Hinman ordered the two skippers to exchange boats. Turner was devastated but had the presence to order his crew to remain on *Mariner* under Conner, promising that anyone who refused would never sail with him again. Conner went on to pummel him in several disastrous starting duels, and there was no place now for Ted to go but home. Even with a new "bustle" and a new skipper, *Mariner* still fared poorly. And on August 20, 1974, the selection committee "excused" her from further competition.

"Ted did a great job in many areas that summer," Commodore Hinman told Roger Vaughan in *The Grand Gesture*, his estimable account of the 1974 America's Cup. "But there was no question a change had to be made. His contribution was substantial. But he is an extrovert. He is temperamental. And he wasn't working out on the boat."

Ted had chartered *Kanaloa*, a seventy-foot luxury yacht, for Jane and the kids, whom he had brought up to Newport to watch him stand the establishment on its ear. Even his sixty-eight-year-old mother, Florence, was there. She hadn't seen him race since those early days at the Savannah Yacht Club. This handsome, regal lady with her long white hair done up in a bun, the way it had been forty years ago, was clearly responsible for most of Turner's good looks. But, she admitted, his competitive spirit had come from his father. "He certainly doesn't get it from me," she said in Newport. "I never cared if I won or lost."

Ted, however, did care a great deal, and there was one last offering to the gods of fortune he had to make before he left Rhode Island. Paying an unannounced call on Dennis Conner, who had surprised everyone by being asked to share the helm on the defending *Courageous*, Turner presented his rival with a small token, a photograph of himself, his famous mouth wide open, a gaping cavern of cacophony. The inscription, in Ted's ragged scrawl: "To Dennis, a good friend and a great helmsman." Conner responded blithely, telling reporters that "Ted Turner was the real hero of the summer." He said it with a straight face, perhaps intuiting that Turner might indeed be back in Newport someday soon.

Turner had leapt at the chance to compete in the America's Cup —it had been the realization of a lifelong dream—and, like the others in the *Mariner* syndicate, he'd thought at first that he might have a chance to win it all. On his very best behavior most of the summer, he could easily have won a McCallie medal as "Most Improved Cadet." But Turner chafed under the unyielding America's Cup protocol. He also found match racing far different from anything he'd ever known. Brit Chance's flawed design alone would probably have been enough to ensure *Mariner*'s elimination, but Turner had not helped his cause with his hell-for-leather approach and a crew that had virtually no cup experience. The next time, he vowed, things would be different. Sending Jane and the kids home, Ted kicked back to enjoy a few days of R & R on *Kanaloa* with pretty B. J. Beach, one of the ever-present daughters of the sea who always seemed to follow in Ted's wake.

Even before settling back into the cinder-block bunker that served as the headquarters of Turner Communications, Ted found himself dominating a CBS prime-time special on the America's Cup. His overpowering persona, if not his success driving *Mariner*, caused the public to sit up and take notice. Perhaps Conner was right, Turner mused. Perhaps he had been the real hero of 1974 after all.

The next cup defense was still three years away, but Turner was determined this time to be prepared. Although he mounted a serious bid to buy *Courageous*, he lost out to Ted Hood, the Marblehead, Massachusetts, sailmaker who had just beaten the Aussies to retain the cup. Hood was intent on organizing his own syndicate and had asked Alfred Lee Loomis, Jr., an old New York Yacht Club hand, to manage the operation. Together they planned to build a new aluminum twelve, using *Courageous* as a trial horse.

But who would drive *Courageous?* Hood favored Dennis Conner, who had handled the starts with him in their successful 1974 defense. Too aggressive for his own good, said Loomis, who was looking for a skipper who could also afford to make a hefty contribution to the syndicate. Money had always been a handicap for the self-made Conner, who still spent his time off the water as the salaried employee of a San Diego carpet company. Ted Turner was available, Loomis noted. And he could usually be counted on for a few hundred thousand. When no one else surfaced, Hood acquiesced, and the call went out to Atlanta.

Turner said "thanks, but no thanks" when Loomis explained the terms. Ted pointed out politely that he had just embarked on his busiest ocean-racing campaign ever and, with a third SORC victory already in hand, was anxious to see how far he could take his new yacht, *Tenacious*. Loomis persisted, however, and Ted then came back with his own set of terms: He would raise *all* of the necessary funds to sail *Courageous*, with part coming from his friend, Texas billionaire oilman Perry Bass. But he would sail *Courageous* as a full-fledged contender, not merely a trial horse. And Loomis couldn't fire him without Bass's approval.

Begrudgingly, Loomis agreed, but only on one condition: Turner would have to use Hood sails exclusively. "Then count me out, again," Turner retorted, adding insult to injury by pointing out that "it would be nice to have at least one amateur out there who wasn't part of a factory team. Who was doing it like it had always been done."

It has now been nearly twenty years since anyone could confuse the America's Cup with an amateur affair. But cup commercialism was just becoming apparent in 1977. The event that year was shaping up as a high-stakes duel between Ted Hood and the new *Enterprise* syndicate's Lowell North, the West Coast's leading sail maker. The winner stood to reap huge financial rewards, since his sails would then become the accepted standard around the world. But Ted Turner took his amateur status seriously and held to the high ground. Unable to find anyone else willing to sail on his restrictive terms, Loomis finally caved in and agreed to put Ted on *Courageous*. Just in case Turner got any ideas, however, Loomis made it perfectly clear that he and Hood had been close friends for over twenty years and, as Loomis announced to New York Yacht Club commodore Robert McCullough, "I'm backing Ted Hood, not a boat, and I'll stick with him to the finish."

Meanwhile Turner and *Tenacious* were taking ocean racing by storm. In less than eight months during the 1975 campaign, Turner finished either first, second, or third in eleven major events, including the Edlu Trophy (first), Block Island (second), Two-Ton World Championship (third), Larchmont Race Week (second), Britain's Admiral's Cup (third), Plymouth–La Rochelle, France (second), North American One-Ton Championship (third), Annapolis Skipper's Race (first), Australia's Southern Cross Cup (first), and the Sydney–Hobart (first).

Jimmy Brown would still show up down in the galley for some of these forays, and old friends like Bunky Helfrich and Legarè VanNess were still there standing their usual watches. Increasingly, however, Turner's crews were comprised of younger, battle-tested America's Cup veterans. Brit Chance had devastated Turner when he claimed it hadn't been *Mariner*'s "bustle" that slowed her down, but Ted Turner's "unreality and lack of planning—the bullshit, actually—that plagued Turner's whole operation from the start." Not a totally unfair accusation, as Ted himself might have admitted. But then Chance tried to nail the coffin shut on Turner by telling the papers, "I don't know if *Mariner* was good or not, but I do know one thing. If Turner and his crew had been sailing *Courageous*, they would have lost to *Intrepid*." Turner hardly needed any greater incentive, and over the next thirty months he set about organizing a cup effort second to none.

On his way back to Atlanta from another successful Australian campaign, Turner was also smitten with a new idea that would not only place him on an entirely new level of competition, but shower down upon Turner Communications enough new profit to push Ted Turner onto *Forbes* magazine's first list of the "400 Richest People in America."

While Will Sanders remained back in Atlanta to ponder the economic possibilities inherent in extending WTCG's increasingly popular signal, Ted Turner was gallivanting once again through the Tasmanian straits, this time powering his way in yet another new boat, *Pied Piper*, to yet another first-place victory in the Southern Cross Cup. There is no record of whether he recited any Tennyson or Coleridge as *Pied Piper* barreled through the unusually calm night seas, though he was known frequently to reel off hours of poetry at a time, all from memory. If Turner had looked up, however, he might have caught a glimpse of something streaking across the summer sky. RCA's newest communications satellite, SATCOM II, launched on December 2, 1975, was now in geosynchronous orbit 22,300 miles above the earth and clearly visible within much of the southern hemisphere. Even if he missed seeing its silent swath in the sky that night, Ted Turner would soon become obsessed with the potential he could realize from this fragile $50 million silicone sphere that had opened up the heavens and would change his life forever.

Communications satellites like RCA's are little more than orbiting antennas, which receive signals beamed up from earth and then rebroadcast them back across a "footprint" thousands of miles wide. A television signal makes the 44,600-mile round trip in less than a fifth of a second and can be received anywhere on earth within the satellite's footprint. Because the signal travels vertically through the atmosphere, reception is almost always crystal clear and generally unaffected by atmospheric conditions or weather. Even in 1975 a satellite cost only a fraction of the expense of stringing a terrestrial microwave system from mountaintop to mountaintop and offered significantly greater reliability and signal quality.

Despite the 1972 rule change allowing the importing of distant signals, cable television's growth continued to be something less than spectacular. Under chairman Richard Wiley, the FCC moved in 1975 to expand the rules even further in an attempt to jumpstart the cable industry yet again. Congress was enthusiastic about the possibilities of the "decentralization" of television distribution. President Richard Nixon's front man, Vice President

Spiro Agnew, saw this new impetus as a way to chastise and weaken the three major broadcast networks, which he described as the "nattering nabobs of the cultural establishment."

"Ted ran WTCG like a radio station," says Jim Roddey, "since that was a business he knew. He never really understood what independent television was supposed to be. Turner used his billboards to build an audience, instead of relying on expensive programming. And when cable offered him a chance to add several hundred thousand new households to his rate card, Turner plunged right in."

"He came into my office one day," Donald Andersson recollects, and said, 'Hi, I'm Ted Turner. I hear we think alike.' Within thirty minutes he was positive I would run a cable sales operation for him. He said he was going to Australia for an ocean race and would call me when he got back." Andersson was vice-president of research for the National Cable Television Association, a well-organized industry lobby. It was his specific job to ferret out ways the cable industry could capitalize on all the recent FCC rule changes.

Movies, Don Andersson knew, drove the cable business. The tremendous response of cable subscribers to Home Box Office, a new pay movie service, was evidence of that. And sports; Andersson knew sports were also very big with cable viewers. He had searched the country for independent televisions he could pipe into cable systems but found only a handful broadcasting both movies and sports. "Would it help if I bought the Braves?" Turner had asked Andersson, innocently enough. A few weeks later Turner had his answer, and Don Andersson had a new job—vice-president of cable for WTCG-TV.

"One night after about three beers," Ted recalls, making certain the spin works his way, "I went to Dan Donahue, who was running the Braves for LaSalle, and asked him what he and Bill Bartholemay planned to do. Donahue told me they had decided to sell the franchise. I asked, To whom? And he told me that they were going to sell it to me."

"I can remember the exact moment," Bob Hope says, "when I first heard that Ted Turner might buy the Braves. It was that kind of shock. I was walking down a staircase in the hotel lobby at the 1975 winter meeting in Hollywood, Florida, when a sportswriter approached me and asked if what he had heard was true. I asked Bill Bartholemay and Dan Donahue to deny it. When they wouldn't say yes or no, I knew a deal must be in the works." The

Braves' front office had been letting people go all summer, preparing for a sale. Dick Cecil, vice-president and point man in
bringing the Braves to Atlanta in the first place, had been the first
to go. Then John Riddle, the Braves' ticket director. Then Milo
Hamilton, their longtime broadcast announcer. Hope was certain
he was next and began an anxious dialogue with the sports desk
of the *Atlanta Constitution.*

"Dial-a-Prayer was busy," sports editor Lewis Grizzard wrote
in the *Constitution* one day, "so Bob Hope of the Atlanta Braves
called our sports department. When a sports publicity man starts
counting on sportswriters for friendly words, it's obvious absolutely nothing is going right in life. Indeed, Hope has to earn his
daily bread selling the Braves to a populace so hostile it seems
ready to storm the stadium to burn it down in protest—if anybody would ever go near the place. No wonder he's looking for a
soft shoulder to cry on."

Late in the morning of January 6, 1976, Bob Hope was summoned to meet with Dan Donahue, the Braves' president, in Donahue's office above the Stadium Club. Waved in by front-office
secretary Phyllis Collins, Hope was certain he himself was being
dismissed. When he opened the door to Donahue's office, he was
handed a single-page press release. Then he noticed Ted Turner
pacing back and forth in the far corner of the room. "Mr. Donahue
simply gave me a copy of the release and asked me to get it to the
media. Turner said he would be available to talk to anyone who
wanted to interview him. I took a moment to scan the release,
realized that I wasn't being fired—yet. And went to call the
media."

Ted Turner needed the blessing of the other National League
team owners and baseball commissioner Bowie Kuhn to buy the
Atlanta Braves. They were willing to overlook his glaring lack of
experience in major league baseball because Turner had been
introduced to them by Hall of Famer Stan Musial, who also happened to be Tom Ashley's father-in-law.

Despite his worldwide renown as a sailor, most Atlantans had
never heard of Ted Turner. And the news coverage of the Braves'
sale made it clear that even the media in Atlanta still knew very
little about this man who now owned the biggest sports franchise
in the South.

Without wasting even a day, however, Turner called Bob Hope
over to WTCG to help with a TV commercial he planned to make,
pitching Braves season tickets. Hope dashed off a script right

there in the studio, then was astounded when Turner took one look at it, mumbled, "Got it!" and proceeded to ad-lib his way through some on-camera nonsense with a ball, a bat, and an Atlanta Braves baseball cap. Turner babbled on about the virtues of baseball as a family event, then wound up the commercial with an unusual, unscripted offer: "Call me when you need anything from the Braves. If you can't reach me, call my pal Bob Hope at the stadium." Hope left WTCG's tiny studio heaving a sigh of relief. He knew his job was safe. There was no way, however, he could know that he'd just signed onto a ten-year roller-coaster ride.

When Home Box Office dug deep into the pockets of its parent, Time Inc., to come up with the $9 million required for a long-term lease on an RCA satellite, there were only two earth stations in the entire country that could receive its signal. "And no one," says Robbin Ahrold, HBO's former director of public relations, "could say when there would be more. HBO paved the way, but it wasn't clear when the earth stations were going to be out there." More than two years would pass before HBO would know its move to satellite had worked. "Until then," Ahrold comments dryly, "it was a question of survival." Where others saw intimidating risk, however, Turner saw the chance of a lifetime. And the cable industry was quick to see the satellite as its only means of survival.

Teleprompter Corporation, then the largest operator of cable systems in the country, endorsed satellite delivery at the outset and, by announcing in early 1976 that it would order earth stations for each one of its systems, provided the impetus satellite technology needed. Within weeks other large multiple-system owners (MSOs) followed suit. Their endorsement of satellite distribution helped push down the price of receive-only earth stations from $100,000 to $25,000 three years later.

The "uplink" facility needing to get a signal up to the satellite, however, was something else entirely. Uplinks still cost over $750,000. Turner approached RCA, hoping to pick up one off the shelf. He was told that satellites were not for "private" use and were intended to provide established networks like ABC, CBS, and NBC with an economic alternative to the expensive AT&T telephone lines they had been using to tie their network affiliates together. Turner tried AT&T, which by now had also entered the satellite business. Ma Bell, Turner soon learned, was in satellites simply to hedge against any possible loss of business on their terrestrial long lines. The telephone company had no interest in the kind of entrepreneurial flutter Turner was suggesting.

Picking his way through the rest of the telecommunications industry the way he sniffed out breezes that could fill his sails, Turner came upon an intense, wild-eyed believer who not only knew everything there was to know about satellites, but, once he understood what Ted had in mind, proved willing to throw in his lot with him as well. At forty-two Ed Taylor was Western Union's youngest vice-president. He had already spent nearly ten years in the satellite business. Taylor also served on the industry task force in 1967 that recommended satellite communication over any other system, most particularly AT&T's outmoded long-lines.

Turner had gone back to RCA and was finally able to induce them to grant him a long-term transponder lease on their newest satellite, on two conditions: Turner must provide his own earth station transmitter; and he would have to secure FCC approval. Calling on a few wealthy sailing friends in New York, Ted raised enough to cover the down payment on an earth station. He leaned on his friend, Sidney Topol, president of Scientific-Atlanta, Inc., to sell him a Series 8000 Satellite Earth Terminal. Then he took off again for Washington.

Communications technology had expanded so rapidly during the early 1970s that the FCC was hopelessly out of touch with the latest advances. Its rule book required immediate and extensive rewriting to cover the new uses and new users of satellites regularly being launched into space. When Turner finally got someone to give him a straight answer, he was told the FCC simply had no provision at the time for anything like his intended use. So he scooped up his application papers and returned to Atlanta with a problem that was now beginning to give him a bad case of the screaming meemies.

Backed into a corner, Ted Turner will unfailingly resort to direct action, simply because he cannot stand indecision. It makes little difference whether the issue at hand involves boats, business, or blondes. Turner will nearly always opt for instant gratification and the quick fix.

The likelihood is strong, therefore, that Turner merely picked up the telephone one Sunday evening in early 1976 and told Sid Topol to go ahead and deliver that earth station. Monday morning he sent one of his most trusted lieutenants, Terrance McGuirk, scouring the suburbs for a piece of land to put it on while he trudged over to the Citizens & Southern to see his banker, Richard Kattel, and work out some way to pay for the damned thing.

The legal intricacies of Turner's little million-dollar gambit into outer space were more than a little complicated and certainly innovative, at least by the letter of the law. What Turner was doing wasn't exactly illegal; he was just setting precedent—and setting the rest of the broadcast world on its ear. Putting up his own earth station didn't exactly make him an outlaw, but it didn't take away any of his appeal, either, as an incipient folk hero.

In less than a week a full-blown earth station transmitter/receiver some thirty feet tall had been installed at the bottom of a sparsely wooded hollow near Cobb Creek in Douglasville, Georgia. With its ten-meter dish pointed toward the heavens, its ten-ton white electronics trailer tethered nearby, its microwave antenna pulling in WTCG's signal loud and clear from the downtown Atlanta studios about ten miles away, and its high chain-link fence topped with three strands of double-edged barbed wire, Ted Turner's new earth station looked for all the world like some highly classified military installation, standing sentinel against an invisible enemy in the Georgia woods.

Ted had set up his earth station as a separate business, Southern Satellite Systems, Inc., only to be told by his attorneys that he probably wouldn't be allowed to own any part of the new company, since Southern Satellite would in all likelihood be construed by the FCC as a common carrier, and broadcast license holders could not own common carriers. Enter Ed Taylor. Ted offered to sell him Southern Satellite for one dollar, an offer Taylor found impossible to refuse. Then Taylor went to RCA, which now viewed Turner and his new earth station as a serious customer. RCA actually acquired Southern Satellite from Taylor, in exchange for Turner's agreement to a long-term lease on RCA's satellite. Ed Taylor then leased back the earth station from RCA and contracted with WTCG to uplink its signal. This financial fandango took all of six months, but on December 27, 1976, a little more than one year after Ted had read in *Broadcasting* magazine that HBO had opened up the heavens, the FCC finally approved Southern Satellite's application as a common carrier. Anticipating demand among cable operators, the FCC also halved the required size of satellite receiving dishes from thirty feet to fifteen feet, effectively cutting their cost by an additional 60 percent or more. Most commercial dishes today run between $1,000 and

$5,000, but Scientific-Atlanta's Topol still remembers that first price cut in 1976, which dropped the cost of a dish to $50,000. It was the beginning of the deluge, and within five years, thanks in no small part to Ted Turner, Topol's small electronics company would be a billion-dollar business.

Turner ordered up some fancy on-air graphics for the satellite launch and a new logo for the station, which he renamed once again. WTCG was now "the Superstation that Serves the Nation." That first day on the satellite, however, Turner's new Superstation was actually serving fewer than ten thousand households, all of them in thriving metropolises like Nome, Alaska; Nye, Oregon; Caribou, Maine; and Breeze Point, Washington—at the time the only cities with cable systems whose downlink facilities were capable of pulling in WTCG's satellite signal.

"What Ted was doing made a lot of sense," says Jeffrey Reisse, a cable executive who was running the Showtime pay movie channel. "But the guy certainly was a little crazy, pretty eccentric. Ted called me several times," Reisse recalls, "and I finally went down to Atlanta to see what he was all about. We had lunch and then he took me over to his office, where he got down all these big loose-leaf binders and began to read me the names of all the movies he had under license for WTCG. He knew I had been head of movies for ABC-TV, and he kept reading off these titles, somehow thinking he was impressing me."

Reisse, a thoughtful, sophisticated programmer who now runs his own pay television company, had been one of the first network television executives to jump into cable. "That's great, Ted. You've got quite a collection there," Reisse said, begging off as politely as he could.

"Wait, wait! Listen to this," Ted shouted when he saw Reisse heading for the door. Then Turner kicked off his shoes and, jumping onto his desk, began to act out *Charge of the Light Brigade*, one of the movies from his library.

"Ted, that's great," Reisse said as diplomatically as possible. "But I've got a speaking engagement and I've really got—"

Turner jumped down from his desk and grabbed Reisse by the shoulders. Then he put his nose right in the younger man's face. "How would you like to manage my station?"

"Uh, gee, Ted," Reisse said, backpedaling. "You know I just launched Showtime, and it's going pretty well—"

"I'll pay you twice what you make!"

Reisse was floored, but he still kept trying to make his way to the door. "That's very generous, Ted. But you don't even know what I make."

"I'll triple it, whatever it is. This is the greatest library of movies you're ever going to see. And they tell me you're the best movie programmer in the business. And I want you to be the guy to do it for me."

By now Reisse had inched his way out the door, but, not wanting to offend his host, he said, "Well, thank you, Ted. Very much. I've really got to go. I'll call you."

The offer was tempting, Reisse now admits, "but the thought of leaving New York to go to work for a guy who runs around his office in his socks . . . My whole life would be consumed by Ted Turner. Of course," he adds somewhat wistfully, "I'd probably be worth a whole lot more than I am today."

Turner was never able to persuade Jeff Reisse or anyone else, for that matter, to come in and run his Superstation. So he took on the job himself and readily admits that WTCG was saved by the satellite. Turner is quick to remind anyone who has forgotten that his Superstation may also have saved the cable television industry, just when it looked as though cable might be assigned to the backwaters of broadcast communications, bypassed by newer forms of wireless communications. A lesson driven home to Turner every time he passed WTCG's awesome old broadcast tower, instantly obsolete the day Turner turned the switch on his satellite Superstation.

Bob Hope, now in charge of promoting Ted Turner as well as the Braves, was still trying to find himself a permanent slot within the company when one morning early in 1977 Ted called him over to his new office at the Braves' Stadium Club. Co-conspirator of some of the wildest promotions ever seen in professional sports, Hope had grown into one of the brightest corporate communicators in the country. He was often an involuntary listener, however, when Turner would take off on one of his famous talking jags. "You think I'm crazy, don't you," Turner blurted out as Hope entered his office. "I just know you think I'm crazy." Hope had been told by Joe Shirley, head of security at Fulton County Stadium, that Ted kept a pistol in his upper right-hand desk drawer. "This can't be real," Hope thought, shifting awkwardly from foot to foot as he stood before his boss.

"I am crazy," Turner continued, "and I want to tell you why." After an interminable rendering of his life story, with none of the lurid details of his sister's death, his father's suicide, or his own anguish at having never been able to please him left out, Turner cupped his chin in his hands and staring straight through his promotion director, concluded, "Hope, I may be crazy, but I wanted you to know why."

Hope could not have known the irony implicit in Turner's words, or that they were an echo of Ed Turner's own lament at the height of *his* success. Then Turner got up and, without so much as a glance at Hope, stalked out into the corridor, where he began haranguing everybody he met.

"Of course I did," Turner told his reporters when asked if he'd ever had second thoughts about the satellite. "I'm not an idiot. I knew the risks. But I had to move fast, without a lot of people knowing what I was up to. I had to buy the Braves, and I also bought the Hawks for basketball. If the leagues realized what I was doing—broadcasting my sports far, far beyond Atlanta, where the franchise supposedly was—they would have stopped me cold."

Ted Turner was now able to give the people what he said they wanted: the chance to choose between the "least objectionable programming" of CBS, NBC, and ABC and something else. What Turner offered on his hyperbolic Superstation was appreciably the same fare he had been broadcasting all along. Proudly displayed among the Turner memorabilia shown to visitors on the tour of CNN Center in Atlanta is a typical program schedule from late 1976. This is the "alternative programming" Turner threw up on his satellite Superstation: 8:00–10:00 A.M., "Cartoon Cavalcade"; 10:30, "Steve Allen"; 11:00, "The Little Rascals"; 11:30, "Lassie"; 12 noon, "The Flintstones"; 12:30 P.M., "Mr. Ed"; 1:00, "The Munsters." Movies were saved for the evenings when the Atlanta Braves (now called "America's team") and Hawks were not scheduled. News continued to be relegated to the 3:00 A.M. time period, although Bill Tush's significant insomniac audience had grown to include devoted followers in Moose Jaw, Saskatchewan, and Goose Bay, Nova Scotia.

Viewers in the lower Forty-Eight, however, were somewhat slower to discover the Superstation. Advertisers avoided WTCG like the plague. During that first year on satellite, nobody was getting rich, with the singular exception of Ed Taylor. His Southern Satellite Systems received ten cents per month per subscriber from every cable system in the country which included the Superstation in its program package. Given the promotional appeal of major league sports and Turner's extensive library of popular "movie classics," many did. Ten cents a month per subscriber adds up, and Southern Satellite was soon generating revenues in the millions, with profits nearly as high, since there was very, very little operating overhead in a business that merely amounted to keeping all the electronic connections functioning properly.

Scientific-Atlanta and RCA were also immediate and significant beneficiaries of Turner's satellite breakthrough. Turner, however, was giving the Superstation away to cable systems for nothing, hoping to make a profit from advertising once he could document the size of the audience watching the Superstation.

Ted had sold advertising on the old earthbound WTCG by sheer force of his persuasive personality, without elaborate research or audience surveys—just as Ed Turner had sold billboards in the 1950s and 1960s. Turner had no Nielsen numbers, no acceptable ratings book to offer advertisers—not even anything resembling the accurate market and demographic data required by most advertisers. Much of the advertising he carried consisted of mail-order kitchen gadgets, "foolproof" fishing lures, and "bargain-priced" book and record deals "not available in any store." This kind of advertising paid on results only, so much per actual order, and didn't require the kind of market research Turner knew he eventually must have.

Stack the odds against Turner and he will usually prevail, not because he is necessarily the biggest, bravest, strongest, or smartest, but because he simply will not give up. Ted Turner does not know how to quit and will keep fighting until the tide has turned and the battle is won. Drawing solace from the fact that dinky little WTCG, which he had acquired for a few hundred thousand shares of his own stock, was now worth over $25 million (and was increasing in value by more than $1 million per month), Turner launched a promotional blitzkrieg to build the Superstation's audience as big as possible. He set aside more then $500,000 for advertising and promotion, then leveraged that amount several times over by persuading local cable operators to advertise his Superstation to build their own subscriber bases. It wasn't a difficult sell, since WTCG was about the only channel cable operators could offer viewers that didn't cost them anything.

Ted also realized that he could leverage his own increased exposure into promotion for the Superstation. Charming Harry Reasoner and a "60 Minutes" crew right out of their shoes, Turner shamelessly promoted his own interests through the good offices of CBS. He kept Reasoner and his crew waiting for over seven hours one afternoon but won him over with his on-air excuse. "I was late because I hadn't seen my boys," Ted told "60 Minutes," "for at least a couple of weeks and had to take them fishing. Hope you gentlemen don't mind." Reasoner's unexpected response: "He's one of the most refreshing, delightful people I've ever met." A few weeks later Ted appeared on Tom Snyder's late-night network talk show. He nonplussed Snyder on the air by offering him a job on the Superstation. When Johnny Carson threatened not to renew his contract with NBC, Turner rushed into the breach with his own offer. "When does Carson start?" the wire services wanted to know as they tied up the switchboard on West Peachtree.

Ted's Superstation strategy was built around low advertising rates. When he began to produce ratings, Turner underpriced his Superstation against the major networks. Looking for ways to expand its advertising reach, Toyota became the first national advertiser on the Superstation. To show his appreciation, Ted Turner would drive a little white 1976 Toyota for the next ten years. Soon other advertisers recognized the unique value Turner offered and began flocking to the Superstation. When *Time* magazine tested a new subscription offer, the publisher was so impressed with the results that *Time* increased its planned expenditure on the Superstation by over eightfold.

Six months after going up on the satellite, Turner's Superstation was adding more than 250,000 new households a month to its rapidly escalating audience. And Ted Turner was beginning to take bows for having "reinvented" television. He just smiled when people pointed out that he now seemed to have better name recognition than that other fellow from Georgia, Jimmy Carter. Turner, in fact, had toyed with the idea of running for office himself and was leaving the door wide open whenever anyone suggested he might be the perfect candidate. He was also taking care of business and missed three months of the 1977 ocean-racing season to concentrate on consolidating his Superstation's advertising sales program. But the battle to sell this new medium had not been easy. Some of his frontline troops were already beginning to burn out. Tom Ashley, elevated to president of Superstation sales in New York, had already left, and only four of the eight other national sales executives survived that first year. Turner himself, however, thrived on the pressure and began to worry the competition along New York's network row. Robert Wussler, then president of CBS Sports, remembers those early days of Ted Turner's "Superscam," as most Big Three network executives referred to the Superstation. "It wasn't just the networks who were concerned. Professional sports was upset as well. Turner was throwing his Braves up on the satellite and showing them in somebody else's territory." Wussler also remembers hearing the first rumblings from Hollywood, where movie producers and syndicators alike were waking up to the fact that Turner was paying to broadcast their films in Atlanta but sending them out all over North America. Hollywood was not happy about being shortchanged by Turner. It would not be long before the networks and the studios, as well as professional sports, began to strike back at this opportunistic adventurer who seemed to align himself with cable television but who now appeared, once again, to be playing by his own rules.

"Ted plunged us into the Superstation," recalls Don Andersson "and then cast us all adrift. No one had any idea where we were going."

No one, perhaps, but the captain himself, who was already packing his sea bag and heading back to Newport.

The way I get it, if you don't like the
way your team is going, you trade the
players. If you don't like your wife, you
trade her. But that gets a little expensive.

TED TURNER (1976)

Chapter Five

"I don't want to see any more 'Loserville' headlines in the Atlanta papers," Turner had told the large media turnout as he
stood blinking under the klieg lights of the press conference he
called to announce he had bought himself a baseball team. Turner
and his financial chief, Will Sanders, had found more than $1
million buried in the convoluted books of Atlanta-LaSalle Corporation, the group that had brought the Braves to Atlanta fifteen
years earlier. "I'm in Tap City," Turner told the media, but he
had bought the Braves with Atlanta-LaSalle's own cash and was
allowed to pay off the rest of the $12 million purchase price over
twelve years, an incredible bargain even in those days, despite the
Braves' lackluster record. "I'm a dedicated and hardworking
person," Ted told the media at that inaugural press conference.
"Getting into the World Series within the next five years is my
objective."

When the Braves opened their 1976 season in Atlanta a few
months later, Ted Turner became the first baseball owner in history to be given a standing ovation. After a totally unnecessary
speech introducing himself to a packed Fulton County Stadium,
Turner asked the crowd to join him in a rendition of "Take Me
Out to the Ball Game." After two false starts, Turner strode testily
out to home plate and took command. They were going to get it
right, dammit, Turner told the crowd, and with his help, they

finally did. Turner brought the house down in the bottom of the first inning when Atlanta's Ken Henderson blasted a towering home run over the right field fence to put the Braves ahead. Turner, who saw nothing wrong in congratulating his employee on the spot, soared over the box-seat barrier to shake Henderson's hand as he trotted around the bases.

"There's never been an owner like him," said Phil Niekro, the Braves' ageless knuckleballer. "He enjoys it more than anyone in the ball park. He'd really like to put on a uniform and play in the game. He ran with us and worked out in spring training. He communicates with the players, and I know his enthusiasm rubbed off on us. I think he'll have the same effect on the fans."

Some of Turner's fellow owners around the league, however, were less enthusiastic. Bob Howsam, for one. The Cincinnati Reds chairman made it known that Turner would be arrested if he ever tried going onto the field during a game in Cincinnati. "I don't care if he was born here," Howsam told the papers.

When he bought the team, Turner actually knew very little about the game of baseball. He soon learned, however, that motorized bathtubs, ostrich racing, and wet T-shirt contests—promotional gimmicks dreamed up by the Braves' hyper-imaginative publicity director, Bob Hope—for example, were even more important than understanding the rule governing infield flies. No matter how outrageous the idea, Bob Hope knew he could count on Turner's active and enthusiastic participation, if it would help fill the seats. Even if it meant the boss has to sweep the bases between innings or push a baseball around the diamond with his nose.

Not surprisingly, the seats did begin to fill up. Turner came close to doubling the Braves' admittedly anemic 1975 attendance by holding forth at virtually every home game in the owner's box alongside the Braves' dugout, personally directing proceedings over his new portable public address system. Introduced to chewing tobacco by his players, Ted would not show up without a large wad of Red Man tucked into his cheek, his Dixie spittin' cup close at hand.

"I bought the Braves," Turner told the people of Atlanta, "because I'm tired of seeing them kicked around. I'm the little guy's hero," he said, only half-joking since people were now starting to take this folk hero business to heart. "They love me. I run the team the way they think they would if they owned it. I come to all the games. Sit in the stands. Drink a few beers. Even take my shirt off. I'm Mr. Everyman to them. Their pal, Ted.''

Turner's sound and light show that summer went a long way toward easing the pain of losing for Atlanta. Unfortunately Mr. Everyman also had a pressing engagement coming up in Newport, Rhode Island, and wouldn't be around in 1977 to lead the Braves out of Loserville. Which may explain why Ted, having already consumed a bit more than a sailor's daily ration of rum, barged into the New York Yankee hospitality suite in the Waldorf Towers one autumn afternoon and began tacking his way across the room toward Robert Lurie, multimillionaire owner of the San Francisco Giants. The fourth game of the 1976 World Series had just been rained out, putting a damper on everyone's spirits, so the floor show that was about to begin was a welcome diversion, especially for the half dozen sportswriters who were there, never expecting they'd get a story anything like the one they were about to witness.

"Where's my ten thousand dollars?" Turner demanded when he finally succeeded in tying up next to Lurie. The Giants' owner assumed he was referring to the fine Turner had been assessed in midseason for talking to Gary Matthews, an erstwhile contract employee of the San Francisco Giants and the National League's leading home run hitter for the past three seasons. Turner was determined to have Matthews in a Braves uniform in 1977, although his too obvious approach was already the cause of considerable concern in the commissioner's office.

"It may cost you more," Lurie replied dryly, and then tried to brush Turner off by telling him what he already knew. "You're aware you can't make me an offer before November 4."

Warming to the possibilities of this little tête-à-tête, Turner began to dish out some southern hospitality and invited Lurie down to Atlanta for a surprise party he was throwing for Matthews a few days later at the Braves' new Stadium Club. "Everybody is going to be there to welcome Gary to Atlanta," Turner cooed. "The mayor, the governor, everybody. I'm putting a big message up on the signboard at the airport, 'Welcome to Atlanta, Gary Matthews.' "

Lurie asked if Ted had thought to send baseball commissioner Bowie Kuhn an invitation. "No," said Turner. "I've gone off Bowie ever since he fined me without even asking for my side of the story.

"There's no law against showing a player our fine city," Turner continued innocently. "You know I'm not going to make him an offer. That would be illegal, at least before the reentry draft deadline. I just want Gary to be aware of what a wonderful city he can play in. Then, when the time comes, I'm going to offer him more money than the Giants will take in next year. Of course, it may take much, much more than that."

Turner's comments made instant headlines. They also infuriated Bowie Kuhn, who, like most of the league's owners, was beginning to regret ever having allowed Ted Turner into organized baseball. Kuhn decided Turner's remarks to Lurie constituted "tampering" with a contract player.

When Turner actually signed Matthews to a Braves contract several weeks later, the commissioner announced he had to be punished. Kuhn would pass sentence, he said, at the owners' annual winter meeting, scheduled for early December in Los Angeles.

"I'll tell you what he's going to do," Turner told his front office managers, who had no idea why he had taken such liberties with the "tampering" rule. "He can give Matthews back to the Giants. But he won't do that because that's punishing Matthews. He could fine me, but that won't do him any good. I'd just pay and be perfectly happy. Or he could suspend me," he continued, his eyes catching fire, his arms flailing wildly. "Kick me out of the game for a whole season. Get me out of the way. He's been wanting to get rid of me. This is his chance."

When Bill Lucas, a former Braves player and, thanks to Turner, the first black general manager in baseball, entered the lobby of the Los Angeles Hilton a few weeks later, he stopped dead in his tracks. Ten feet in front of him, standing on top of the concierge desk, was the putative owner of the Atlanta baseball club, fulminating like one of the ornamental fountains that lined the hotel driveway outside.

"The commissioner of baseball is going to kill me!" Ted Turner was screaming at the top of his lungs. "Bowie Kuhn is out to kill me. My life is over."

Just as a phalanx of oversize hotel security men began closing in on him, Turner jumped down from his perch and rushed out of the lobby, without so much as a how-de-do to his friend Bill Lucas.

Three hours later Turner surfaced again, still speaking in tongues and holding forth, this time in the hotel dining room.

Ranting at the top of his voice, he could easily have been mistaken for some hyperactive Sunday morning television evangelist, prophesying, not the end of the world, but his own doom at the commissioner's hand.

The baseball owners tried to turn a blind eye to Turner's antics and get on with the business of their annual meeting. But Turner continued to bounce off the walls for the next three days, and before long the local media arrived to catch his act. "Kuhn's going to gun me down in this hotel like a dog!" he told the *Los Angeles Times*.

Coming out of an afternoon session on player contracts, Bill Lucas was collared by a Los Angeles radio reporter. "I don't know what to do with this," the reporter moaned, playing back a bizarre interview Turner had just given him. "I can't run it. But I don't want to give it to the police, either." Turner had told him in no uncertain terms he was going to get a gun and kill the commissioner before the commissioner got him first. "I can't run this," the reporter blubbered. "But what do I do?"

Lucas listened again to the playback. He agreed Ted sounded absolutely insane. He had to find Bob Hope, quick. "Ted's lost it, Bob!" he shouted as he spotted his colleague coming across the lobby. "He's lost his mind. Even if he *wanted* to get suspended, he's gone too far. We've got to stop him before they lock him up."

Hope, who'd seen Turner perform that morning, didn't disagree. Both men knew they might be risking their jobs, but believed now they had no choice but to try to save Turner from himself.

Turner was coming down the stairs when they caught sight of him again, an obvious West Hollywood professional hanging on his arm. Lucas rushed over and grabbed one of Ted's arms before he could get cranked up again. Hope brushed past the platinum blonde and grabbed the other. Together they pulled him on his heels into a small cocktail lounge off the main lobby where they dumped him unceremoniously into a booth at the rear of the bar.

Lucas looked his boss square in the eye, fully expecting Turner to lash out with his fists. It was Hope, though, who first summoned the nerve to speak. "You're absolutely out of your mind, Ted," he said, trying to lend as much authority to his shaky voice as possible. "You've gone over the line."

Turner's lady friend had followed them into the bar and began imploring Hope to back off, saying nobody could talk to Ted Turner that way. Turner just sat there calmly, somewhat blinded by a shaft of California sun that poured in through the window above his head. Without missing a beat, however, he looked straight at his two colleagues and asked calmly, "Do you think I should get on a plane and fly back to Atlanta?"

Stunned, Hope blurted out, "Yes, if you can't get your mind together and act right."

"Do you think I've convinced him I'm crazy?" Turner asked, still cool as you please, a hint of a smile curling up the corners of his mouth.

"Y-yes," Hope stammered. "And you convinced me!"

"Then I'm okay," he said. "I'll behave."

Turner proved as good as his word, remaining relatively normal for the last three days of the winter meeting and an uneventful flight back to Atlanta.

"I just can't believe it!" Ted cried out, failing to disguise his satisfaction two weeks later when he opened a curt, three-page notice of suspension from the commissioner. Under Kuhn's ruling he would not be allowed to "exercise any powers, duties, or authority in connection with the management of the Atlanta club; visit or be physically present in the Atlanta clubhouse or offices" for the entire 1977 season.

After considering his situation Turner told the papers, "I don't think the penalty fits the crime, but I'll be back. The last thing I guess I can say is, I hope to return soon."

He didn't have to say much more to rally all Atlanta to his cause. Governor George Busbee and Mayor Maynard Jackson headed a citizens' delegation to petition the commissioner. Delta Airlines flew them up to New York for free. They brought with them a citation passed by both houses of the Georgia legislature and signed by ten thousand Braves fans. Burger King's southeast regional marketing director, Dave Moody, distributed one hundred thousand postcards that would soon inundate Kuhn's office, calling for Turner's reinstatement. Ken's Tavern on Piedmont Street even came up with $1,000 toward a legal defense fund.

"The response was nothing less than overwhelming," observed Atlanta advertising executive Robert Green, who had turned his offices over to an adhoc Ted Turner Task Force. "It surpassed all expectations. Ted isn't your ordinary team owner. It wouldn't and couldn't happen with anybody else in sports. You just couldn't see this kind of response anywhere else." Atlanta Chamber of Commerce president Jesse Hill prepared a sobersided white paper on Turner's suspension and its economic impact on the city, declaring, "Atlantans are showing support for a team which has been out of contention for seven straight seasons. The improvement in this support is directly attributable to Mr. Ted Turner's enthusiasm and personal commitment to baseball in Atlanta. He has literally salvaged a sagging baseball franchise which serves 20 percent of the entire continental United States."

Turner himself kept an uncharacteristically low profile during all the tumult but did not overlook the opportunity to build a mailing list from the thousands of protest cards and letters that poured into Kuhn's office. Arranging "incentive compensation" for a couple of the commissioner's more comely office assistants, Turner had them send him the names and addresses of everyone who mailed in a protest on his behalf. The Braves management then sent them all season ticket applications.

Ted Turner was now bigger than ever in Atlanta. More important, he had the whole summer off to sail, without ever having to explain himself. Disappearing quietly up to Marblehead, Massachusetts, he set about fine-tuning his *Courageous* crew for the forthcoming festivities down in Newport. He still had one more card up his sleeve, however, and as 1976 was drawing to a close, he quietly closed on the acquisition of a 95 percent interest in the limited partnership that controlled the Atlanta Hawks basketball team. For just $400,000 and a $1 million note, he purchased a second major professional sports franchise for his brand-new Superstation. And still almost no one seemed to have noticed what he had actually accomplished.

Yachting is a gentleman's sport, and in dealing
with gentlemen, you can't be too careful.
                                    PETER FINLEY DUNNE
                                    Mr. Dooley

Chapter Six

Ted Turner's 1977 America's Cup campaign actually began on that foggy morning more than three years earlier when Commodore George Hinman replaced him as *Mariner*'s skipper. It had been a bitter moment for Turner, and, gathering his crew about him for one last drunken night together, he'd promised them they all would be back. "We were good sailors on a dog of a boat," observed Turner's perennial crew boss, Marty O'Meara. "We were desperate for a chance to prove how good we were on a good boat."

By the time he had arrived in Newport, however, most observers had already consigned Turner and *Courageous* to third place behind Ted Hood's *Independence* and Lowell North's new *Enterprise*. Hood looked on *Courageous* as little more than a worthy sparring partner for his new boat, which incorporated every technological and design improvement he could pack into her. As soon as *Independence* and *Courageous* were matched against each other off Marblehead, however, in wintry seas so cold both crews had to chip ice off their rigging, Hood began having second thoughts. "They thought it was my swan song," Turner said, warmed by the raging fire in his belly. "Now I wanted to prove it wasn't my fault that we lost." Hood might have questioned bringing this sly southern fox into his camp, but he could never have known that Turner would soon sail his second-hand *Courageous* straight into the record books.

Jimmy Brown had towed *Tenacious*, together with a $30,000 satellite dish, up all the way from Atlanta to Newport, unaware that Ted's three-legged cat, Tripod, was nestled in under the tarp and would soon emerge to join the crowd at Bannister's Wharf welcoming Hood and Turner into Newport. A large contingent of precise-minded Japanese has already spread the word about the unusually cold water temperatures which still hovered in the low fifties. Cold water in June usually meant stiffer than usual wind and water conditions in September, when the twenty-third defense of the America's Cup began in earnest. *Independence* and *Enterprise* had been designed to perform best in relatively gentle twelve- to fifteen-knot breezes, the kind experienced off Newport during the past several cup summers. A possible advantage for the reconfigured *Courageous*, which was now better able to handle a stiff blow, although few seemed to take note.

"Everything I do is a war," Turner proclaimed, diving into the subject of the cup trials mouth first. "And I'm doing everything right these days. When you're hot, you're hot." What about his suspension from baseball? "I thought it was a joke," he retorted. Turner's carefully engineered suspension allowed him to play the role of injured party to the hilt. "They wanted all this serious testimony under oath," he reminded the press indignantly. "I've been in protests involving kings, and nobody's ever forced me to take any oaths." Turner's pride had been piqued and his honor questioned. To this chivalrous son of the South, by way of Cincinnati, questioning his pride and his honor took all the fun out of the game.

"The commissioner says the game is too complicated," Turner recounted, after attempting to lead the Braves out of a sixteen-game losing streak by taking over for a day from manager Dave Bristol. "Skippering a twelve-meter is complicated," Turner declared. "Football is complicated. But my eight-year-old son plays baseball. How complicated can the game be? Let me tell you. The fans know how complicated this game is. One stood up in his seat and yelled at me, 'Hey, Turner! I can't stand this any longer.' I told him he only paid six dollars for his seat. I paid eleven million to sit two seats away and I'm not complaining." Turner was polishing his act at the expense of afternoon deadlines, but what, the assembled scribes wanted to know, did any of this have to do with the America's Cup?

* * *

Damon Runyon is reputed to have been the first to comment that watching a yacht race is a little like watching grass grow or paint dry. Had he ever squeezed himself into the cramped cockpit of a modern twelve-meter, exploding through the waves in twenty-five knots of wind—"taking the bone in her mouth," as they say—with all the force and fury of a runaway locomotive, Runyon might have revised his analogy. Viewed from a quarter mile away —which is about as close as most spectators ever get—twelve-meter ocean racers pairing off against each other in a match race look like large, graceful dancers performing an exotic, seaborne ballet as they converge and cross paths, then converge again, sometimes crossing so closely you might think their elaborate ten-coat paint jobs will peel off—provided, of course, that a lower spreader on one of them does not buckle first, sending a $100,000 mast and 1,800 square feet of Kevlar sailcloth crashing over the side and into the sea.

When a twelve-meter heels over in a hard blow, more than twenty tons of pull is brought to bear against her shrouds. The pressure at the base of the mast is nearly twice that. The offboard spectator never hears the earsplitting screech of steel cables on steel winding drums or the explosive smack of an aluminum hull against ten-foot seas. Sometimes not even the sharpest-eyed winch sailor will see the small handcrafted piece of Swedish steel hardware shatter under stress, sending a spar crashing down amidships. The eleven crewmen on each boat who stand up under this pressure are world-class athletes, trained to perform intricate team maneuvers with clockwork precision. They know differences in twelve-meter boat speeds are often ephemeral at best, and that misreading the wind or a single wave can often cost the race.

Not every yachtsman aspires to America's Cup competition. The twelve-meter rating, a complex formula in which various dimensions, including sail area, ballast, and beam, must all add up to exactly twelve meters, was not introduced until 1958. Once an intensely amateur affair, by 1977 the America's Cup was becoming big business. Turner's crew, which included eight hold-overs from 1974, would prove to be the last unpaid aggregation ever to compete. Turner himself strongly embraced this amateur ethic and was unstinting in his criticism of both Hood and North, each of whom stood to profit handsomely if the winning boat carried their respective sails. Despite his own perversely promotional bent, when it came to sailing, Ted Turner was a committed amateur. He even delighted in raising the already high anxiety

level of some of his well-heeled friends in the yachting fraternity
by calling for the elimination of tax-loss benefits as a requisite for
America's Cup syndicate members. No one was ever sure he was
just joking.

From the moment Turner arrived in Newport, his mouth was
usually working overtime. In 1977, however, he was determined
to prove he was something more than the flamboyant loser the
town had got to know three years earlier. Out on the water, too,
some changes were evident. Despite the fact that he was already
two-time "Yachtsman of the Year," the book on Turner had him
soft on starts and unable to sustain the kind of intense, intellectual concentration match racing demands. This time around,
however, Turner had already logged 20,000 miles sailing twelve-
meters, perhaps more than anyone in history. And this time, his
crew was capable and experienced, possibly, some observers
noted, the best such aggregation ever assembled. Turner's concentration, once sporadic and questionable, had become extraordinarily sharp and sustained. During the final race of the June
trials against Lowell North's *Enterprise*, he trailed at the final
mark by over seventeen seconds. Turner drove his crew furiously,
completing nineteen individual tacks on the last two-and-a-half-
mile leg to the finish. Each grueling change in direction and shift
in the set of the sails had been timed perfectly and executed mag-
nificently, and *Courageous* was able to convert that seventeen-
second deficit into an amazing forty-three-second victory.

By the time the July trials were under way, Turner had also
converted his four-year-old *Courageous* from a respectable underdog into the flatout favorite. *Courageous* had piled up a surprising
4–1 record against her newer stablemate, *Independence*, and an
even more impressive 6–0 mark over *Enterprise* and Lowell
North, whose reputation as a Star-class racer was legend. Hoping
some of this newfound success might be contagious, Ted invited
his Atlanta Braves up to Newport. "If I have to watch them lose,"
he said unapologetically, "they might as well see me try to win."

Not all his Braves made the trip. Andy Messersmith, Gary Matthews, and Willie Montanez, the three highest-paid players on the
team, telegraphed Ted a clear signal that despite all his honest
efforts to be one of the boys, his money couldn't buy their interest
or their loyalty. Despite the no-shows, Turner did his best to provide an example and ran up four more straight victories, something the Braves had not accomplished since late May. Hank
Aaron cornered Turner after *Courageous* had chalked up another

win in a picture-perfect tacking duel and, speaking for most of the Braves, said he had no idea what the maneuver was all about. "Tacks," Turner explained, cutting through the fog with perfect clarity, "are like snowflakes. They all look alike, but every one is different."

The Braves catcher, Vince Correll, seemed to understand, however, and whipped out a copy of Roger Vaughan's *The Grand Gesture* which he asked Turner to autograph. Clearly in need of no further inspiration, Correll returned to Atlanta the following night and led the Braves to an extra-inning victory over San Diego by parking a towering home run in the center-field seats.

Turner was himself swinging for the fences during the remainder of the July trials. *Enterprise* had begun to come together, and there were no more blowouts. Old cup hands noted the extremely honest weather and pointed out that there had been few extravagant wind shifts, and not so much as half a day of feinting, five-knot air with the kinds of holes a twelve-meter could fall right through. So far these 1977 trials had seen very steady going, and *Courageous* was making the most of it.

Back on land, however, things were turning a little stormy. Turner and his crew were quartered in Conley Hall, one of the converted twenty-room "cottages" along Newport's oceanfront. Ted had brought up Jane and the kids for the last two months of the summer. Jimmy Brown was there, too, in his usual capacity as general factotum to the Turner boys and the *Courageous* crew. Jimmy used the opportunity to take Beau and Rhett out into Newport Harbor and teach them a few of the fundamentals of dinghy sailing, as he had three years earlier in 1974 with Teddy IV and nearly thirty years before with Ted in Savannah.

Then came Bailey's Beach. Depending upon whose story you believe, Ted Turner (1) got himself tanked early in the evening and suggested to one or more of the local lovelies that what "these stiff old bitches needed was a good poking," implying he was just the fellow to do it. Or (2) he had merely been used by a social-climbing Atlanta arriviste who had never met Turner but delighted in showing him off to her friends at Bailey's Beach, one of Newport's most exclusive enclaves. Ted reportedly did a disappearing act with the decades-younger date of a very elderly gentleman guest. Whatever the facts, Turner felt compelled to write a letter of apology the next day to the president of The Spouting Rock Association, which oversees the posh beach club. As a result, Robert McCullough, commodore of the New York

Yacht Club and chairman, ex officio, of the America's Cup selection committee, was asked if Turner's selection might be jeopardized.

"We chuckled over that," McCullough replied. "If we had a problem with Turner, we would have told the syndicate to get themselves another man." Other yacht club members were somewhat less conciliatory. "If he's ever selected," predicted Don McNamara, a former America's Cup helmsman who voted against Turner's admission to the club, "he will be the first skipper in cup history to appear at the starting line wearing a muzzle." With Turner continuing to win, however, it was beginning to look like the NYYC might not have any real option. *Courageous* was now well out in front of both *Independence* and *Enterprise.* Then came the crisis of the sails.

The 1977 cup had originally looked to be a commercial shootout between Ted Hood and Lowell North, the world's two leading sail makers. Hood had initially expected to use *Courageous* not merely as a trial horse for his *Independence*, but as a floating test lab for a whole slew of experimental sails. When Turner insisted that he be given free rein as his price for skippering *Courageous*, he announced he would, peversely, be using North sails. Ted had the good fortune to have Robbie Doyle, Hood's talented young associate, on the *Courageous* crew and figured that way he would have the best of both worlds. Doyle was kept busy cutting and recutting all of *Courageous*'s older Hood sheets. That worked fine while Turner was waiting for North to deliver on his promise of new sails. But North's *Enterprise* syndicate was having second thoughts. North acknowledged his promise but told Turner his hands were now tied. Turner called North a "no-good liar" and set up a confrontation at the *Courageous-Independence* syndicate party at Conley Hall.

Turner arrived early and, as far as anyone could tell, was cold sober. He crossed into the yellow-and-white tent Lee Loomis had set up for the bar and, without breaking step, strode right up into Lowell North's face. Roger Vaughan, who was standing just a few feet away, noted that Ted started off cordially enough.

"I've been a good customer over the years, right?" North acknowledged as much but was unprepared for Turner's next shot.

"Well, I'm not going to be a good customer anymore. I want you to know I'm going to do everything I can to work against you for the rest of my life." Turner stood toe to toe with North, a big, burly man who may have been twenty or thirty pounds heavier than the wiry Turner. Ted was known to go after members of his crew occasionally out on the water but hadn't hit anybody on dry land since he had tried out for boxing at McCallie. No one doubted his intentions now, however, as he stood with fists clenched and shoulders squared. Crewmen from both *Enterprise* and *Courageous* started to square off for the battle royale. Luckily an ingenuous young female who had been waiting to introduce herself to North simply walked into the middle of the loose circle forming around the two men and defused the whole affair by asking Lowell North if he could get her a drink.

"I came down from my room," Turner admitted, "just to punch him in the nose." He kept up an incessant drumbeat of derogation against North for the rest of the trials, but never did get the sails he wanted. Lee Loomis, whose loyalty had been with Hood and *Independence* all along, made it all but impossible for Turner to count on new Hood sails, either. Still, Turner kept winning, and Lowell North was asked by his own syndicate to step down in mid-August as skipper of *Enterprise* in favor of Malin Burnham.

Following the Conley Hall confrontation Turner acquired a rather large shadow in the person of Conn Finley, his old friend and longtime mast man. At forty-seven, considerably older if not wiser than Ted, Finley is six feet seven and weighed over 240 pounds. Finley's job was to keep Turner out of trouble. Someone floated the rumor, later proved untrue, that Finley carried a set of police handcuffs in his pocket, just in case. With the August trials drawing to a close and Turner's selection more of a reality with each passing day, however, no one on *Courageous* wanted to see Turner denied the chance to defend the cup simply because he had let his pride get in the way of his judgment. Which is what nearly happened a few evenings later when Turner strode into the Castle Hill restaurant and spotted a New York Yacht Club member wearing a "Beat the Mouth" button.

"If you want to 'Beat the Mouth,'" Turner shouted across the room, "I'll give you a chance to do it right now if you want to follow me to the parking lot." Then he leapt across the table and ripped the button off the unsuspecting man's jacket with such ferocity that it looked as though he had torn off the poor fellow's lapel as well.

"It was obvious," the shaken member later admitted, "that Ted didn't like the sight of the pin. He has apologized to me twice now for the incident, saying he was sorry, pointing out to me that the pin just wasn't fair."

"Don't let Turner tell you they were all lined up against him," Lee Loomis declared. "He's got to be the underdog. That's all part of Ted Turner's act." Despite Loomis's wry observation, it seemed Hood and *Independence* were now the underdog, with Burnham and *Enterprise* a close second. Both boats had shuffled their crews throughout August, but Turner, who stayed with the same ten men throughout, kept winning and now looked nearly unbeatable.

On August 29, *Independence* was finally excused. Tears of empathy welled up in Turner's eyes as he watched the selection committee make its way to Hood's dock to deliver their verdict. That same day *Australia* completed a 4–0 sweep over *Sverige*, the sleek but badly sailed Swedish boat, automatically becoming challenger. Tossing good form to the winds and finally letting their real feelings show, Lowell North and his *Enterprise* syndicate, which would be excused the next day, broke tradition and threw in their lot behind the Aussie challengers. North even gave *Australia* the new sails he had held back from Turner, revealing the extent to which Turner's attacks had unnerved him. "At this point," the usually softspoken San Diego sail maker told reporters, reminding them he operated a small sail loft in Sydney, "I can't feel strongly about seeing Ted Turner win."

Newport had been awash in rumors all week that the selection committee was stalling and would somehow find a way to avoid picking Turner. But on the afternoon of August 30, at the very latest moment possible, Turner knew he was not to be denied. Beer in one hand, cigar in the other, he watched and waited as the launch carrying the seven committee members made its time-honored trip across the chop of Newport Harbor. Turner smiled when a late summer thunder boomer came up out of nowhere and caught the committee launch in its momentary deluge. Then, as if on cue, the heavens parted, the sun was shining again, and the committee chairman, Commodore George Hinman, was leaning over the launch rail to greet the man he had fired three years earlier as skipper of *Mariner*. Turner smiled again, graciously, doffed his trademark engineer's hat, and heard Hinman announce, "Gentlemen, congratulations. You have been selected to defend the America's Cup against Australia in the twenty-third Challenge Match."

Without waiting for Hinman to finish, the *Courageous* crew picked Turner up and sent him flying overboard for the traditional dunking in Newport Harbor. Turner climbed back on deck dripping wet, thanked the committee, and then told Hinman what the wise old sailor had known from the beginning. "We had a lot to show," he said deferentially. "Not necessarily that we were the best, but that we were a lot better than we looked last time out." Consumed by emotion, Turner almost swallowed those last few words. His voice was so stilted, his feelings so strong, he might have been addressing his own father after a comeback victory at the Savannah Yacht Club. The *Courageous* crew cheered, and, as the committee launch motored away, hoisted him up on their shoulders and marched down Bannister Wharf to face the assembled hordes of media people, well-wishers, friends, family, and other assorted camp followers.

Ted Turner had not only beaten the odds and outsailed two of the very best yachtsmen in the world, he'd done it with an amateur crew in a secondhand boat with tattered, three-year-old sails. He'd also managed to flirt with every girl in sight and even got to know a few who'd been caught in his wake. He'd crawled pubs with his crew, cheated at croquet, infuriated some of Newport's old guard. He'd gotten himself tossed out of some of the town's very best establishments and had even been banned for life from ever going back to the Black Pearl pub. He had stood the eastern establishment on its ear, taken on the professional sail makers, won over the New York Yacht Club, and now, as he stood within sight of sailing's ultimate achievement, Ted Turner knew he would be a hard man to beat. "If being against stuffiness and pompousness [sic] and bigotry is bad behavior," he admitted ingenuously, "then I plead guilty.

"There will never be a time in my life as good as this time," he continued, putting his modesty in his pocket. "I can't believe all this is happening to me. I'm so hot I just tell my guys to stand by me with their umbrellas turned upside down to catch the stuff that falls off me. Savoring his new role as defender of the America's Cup, Turner then added, "And I can't think of anything I could do to be any better. My biggest problem now is to keep from getting a big head. You guys don't think I have one, do you?"

Heady stuff, even for a self-proclaimed folk hero. Yet Turner was already the anointed hero of this America's Cup, and had been, almost from the moment he'd arrived in Newport. The "people's hero," the media called him, and then began climbing all over themselves to stick him with new monickers like "Captain Outrageous" (*Newsweek*); "Captain Comeback" (*BusinessWeek*); "Terrible Ted" (*People*); "The Pirate from Peachtree" (*Time*); and the ubiquitous "Mouth," which the *Enterprise* syndicate had first made up into buttons and then into T-shirts and pennants. Turner's recognition as owner of the Atlanta Braves and Hawks, together with the notoriety of his widely publicized contretemps with the commissioner of baseball, had kept him on the sports pages for most of the past year. People who had never been on a sailboat, never even seen a twelve-meter, showed up in Newport at the start of the June trials. The crowds kept building right through September. The largest media contingent in the history of the cup had accommodated itself to Turner's daily dockside briefings after each race and then to the more formal post-race press conferences at the National Guard Armory up on Thames Street. Turner's Superstation followed his progress all summer, inserting announcements of each victory in the middle of the Braves games. Most of the poor media wretches assigned to Newport that summer assumed they would be faced with an arcane and eminently unreportable three-month-long event. Ted Turner had changed all that and kept everyone on red alert. Asked to assess Turner's impact on the America's Cup, Commodore Robert "Bus" Mosbacher, once Richard Nixon's chief of protocol, was nothing if not diplomatic. "I'm not sure I should comment on that. Certainly he brought a lot of color to it. He was quotable, good source material for the morning headlines, so in that way he brought color and a certain, uh, attention. His Braves fans got interested in the America's Cup."

Bob Bavier was equally reserved but relentlessly honest. Like Mosbacher, Bavier is a former cup skipper and past commodore of the New York Yacht Club. He readily admitted, "No one else has ever gotten the public so involved, no one else was such a sentimental favorite. In his inimitable way Ted has made more people aware and care about the America's Cup than anyone else in the event's long history."

"One Sunday in July," *Courageous* tactician Gary Jobson remembered, "we stopped at three newsstands on the way to the boat to get *Time* and *Newsweek*. Turner read about himself in *Newsweek*, then asked me to read the coverage in *Time* to him. We were ten minutes late getting to the dock."

Turner's insatiable appetite for publicity was, in fact, beginning to take its toll on Jobson and threatened to undermine the hugely successful, symbiotic relationship between skipper and tactician, which even uninitiated observers had come to see as an integral factor in *Courageous*'s success. Gary Jobson had not been Turner's first choice as tactician, and it had taken many months of working together before the two developed into a winning team. Turner had originally asked his friend and former America's Cup tactician, Graham Hall, director of sailing at the U.S. Naval Academy in Annapolis, to join him on *Courageous*. Hall had been unable to arrange leave from the academy and recommended Jobson, a three-year collegiate all-American. Jobson worked well with Turner in two early tune-up races and then was instrumental in Turner's breathtaking victories in the SORC and the even more coveted 1976 Congressional Cup. Now, after four months of close, constant contact, these two polar opposites had developed sufficient trust and respect to compensate for their boat's outdated design and overused sails.

The tactician's role on any ocean racer is important. On a twelve-meter it is crucial, the skipper's sine qua non that can provide the measure of difference, as it had all summer for *Courageous*, between otherwise evenly matched boats. One of Ted Turner's greatest strengths had always been his uncanny ability to come up with the right man for the job. Case in point is his selection of Dennis Conner, the only member of the *Mariner* crew in 1974 Turner didn't know well. Conner was nevertheless already recognized as one of the best small-boat skippers in the world. And Turner wanted the best. Like Conner, Gary Jobson was an extremely skilled small-boat sailor.

"Ted's personality swings were extreme," Dennis Conner warned. "He could be a confident leader ashore, but so hyper and nervous on the boat that he could upset the entire crew by the start of a race. You can't emulate a personality like that. Turner listened to me and followed my advice until the pressure started to build up, and then he did whatever he wanted, even if it was the wrong thing."

Turner himself came up with the idea of the walks, which cemented his relationship with Jobson. Every morning, and then again in the afternoon after they'd come off the water, he and Jobson walked together, from Conley Hall down to Bannister Wharf and then back again—alone, away from the gathering tumult that enveloped the cup and most of its participants. As Jobson later pointed out, "It was real communication of real information—of the sort that should be exchanged between skipper and tactician." They discussed crew performance, sails, starting techniques, their own interaction. That Turner should have suggested such a regimen and then adhered to it so rigidly revealed the potential he had so seldom explored for introspection and self-analysis. But over the weeks and months of those walks, Ted also began to meander into territory well beyond Jobson's comfort zone.

Turner began talking about his family, his childhood—subjects he had never really discussed with anyone, not even his wives. He talked about his father's suicide, the satellite business, his own political ambitions. He even began asking Jobson which Braves he should consider trading and how he could make the Hawks into a winning team.

Turner talked incessantly, Jobson recalls, day after day, week after week. He talked more about himself than he probably ever had to anyone. He talked about death, about the difficulty he sometimes had relating to other people. Turner poured out everything, giving it all to Jobson so his tactician could use it later when he had to inspire his skipper to victory. At his captain's initiative and invitation, Gary Jobson pried open the lid on Ted Turner's psyche, hardly aware that Turner would stop at nothing, even if it meant crossing into the murky realm of the id and the ego, if the effort could help propel him across the finish line a winner.

Turner had been known to become so keyed up before a big race that he would vomit as the starting gun went off. In the lull before the start of the America's Cup challenge round against the *Australia*, the pressure had become almost unbearable, so he decided to blow off a little steam in the Demitasse Derby, a media event which pitted the skippers and tacticians of cup contenders against each other in little single-handed Dyer Dhow dinghies. Gary Jobson had built up what looked like an insurmountable lead as they approached the finish line off Goat Island. Out of nowhere, Turner breezed across his bow and won the race. "Yeah, well, there was a really bad wind shift on that last leg and I lost seven boats," Jobson explained. "Now tell me, don't you think Ted Turner needed to win that little regatta?"

In a rare unguarded moment just before the Cup Finals began, Turner confessed to *Newsweek* that the pace that summer had nearly drained him dry. "There have even been a few bad moments," he told the startled reporter, "when I've been too exhausted to make love." But such times were rare and Ted was tickled pink when George Hinman told him not to change a hair on his head. After a rough start in 1974, Hinman had been genuinely taken with Ted's ingenuous challenge to an establishment the respected old sailor had now come to see as atavistic and out of tune with the times.

Some of those closest to Turner, however, knew that he himself had undergone a sea change of sorts and was discarding his old guts-and-glory, win-at-any-cost approach in favor of a more careful, considered demeanor. Deep inside he may have been as anxious as ever, but his dry heaves and hurtful little insults were no longer quite so obvious. It may have been the cathartic effect of his daily sessions with Gary Jobson or merely the fact that he was now a white-hot media property, on stage twenty-four hours a day. The change that had come over Ted Turner was ever so slight, but the eleven men who would now go out to sail with him against *Australia* had become increasingly aware of it and heaved a collective, if silent, sigh of relief.

The New York Yacht Club expected the 1977 spectator fleet to be twice as big as 1974. No one, however, expected anything like the more than one thousand boats that showed up for the first race on September 13. Everything from Baron Marcel Bich's magnificent 139-foot schooner, *Shenandoah*, to worn-out commercial fishing boats and tiny one-man dinghies that could barely stay afloat in the wash created by this motley armada. One man even drove a motorized bathtub out past Seal Rock in honor of Turner's bathtub victory, he said, at a Braves game. A flotilla of over twenty different aircraft, including seven news helicopters, a couple of Coast Guard A-40s, and the Goodyear blimp *America*, hovered over the starting line, which coincidentally paralleled an old World War II torpedo practice range about five miles outside Newport Harbor.

"Brown lost. The Braves lost, too," Turner told the *Providence Journal*, exuding confidence as he stepped aboard *Courageous* for the long tow out. "But it's all right. They thought this was my swan song. Now they all think I'm going to be the first to lose the cup. That's not possible, is it?" As Doug Riggs points out in *Keelhauled*, his excellent examination of amateurism in the America's Cup, "It was that outrageously uninhibited, almost naive, childlike adoration of self, followed by the quick phrase that lets you know he can recognize his folly, but can't help himself, that either charmed or repelled people about Ted Turner."

Courageous was a good boat, and that is all Turner and his crew felt they would need. Forget the Aussie's newfangled keel, their new low-riding hull design, and their new Lowell North sails. Boat speed not withstanding, the cup figured to turn on sailors and their execution. Gary Jobson summed up the Americans' approach. "Turner's been sailing almost every day against great sailors like Ted Hood and Lowell North. There's no way the Australians can match the competitive edge of our crew."

"But we've still got to fight the pressure of being the first to ever lose the cup," Turner added judiciously. "If that ever happens, the New York Yacht Club will replace the cup in their trophy case with the head of the losing skipper."

The Australians were led by Alan Bond and his Sun City Yacht Club, surely one of the most inexclusive institutions in the world and, in fact, a blatant attempt on Bond's part to promote his Sun City real estate development in the arid wasteland that is western Australia. Bond was already an America's Cup veteran, however, and had gone down in a game effort with *Gretel* in 1974. He was here now with a sleek new boat and, Noel Robins, a new skipper. Robins was an accomplished sailor, but he lacked the fire and finesse of *Gretel*'s John Bertrand, who would make yachting history in 1983 by beating Dennis Conner for the cup.

As it turned out, the challenge round was very, very close, despite Turner's carefully considered game plan. "Ted loves to be ahead and to leeward, working the boat up to windward," Gary Jobson thoughtfully explained to the handful of reporters brave enough to attempt a technical explanation of Turner's strategy. "On the first windward leg, you'll probably see a few token tacks thrown in, and one boat will develop a twenty-five- to fifty-second lead at the mark. The reaching legs will be standard—reach-reach, and *Courageous* will gain on the reaches, whether she is ahead or behind. She will make better roundings because she doesn't have a detached trim tab. If *Courageous* is ahead on windward legs, she will sit right on *Australia*'s air, and *Australia* will probably eat too much of it. If *Courageous* is behind, she will tack off immediately, and the boats will split, with *Courageous* covering a lot from behind. At the end of the leeward leg, if *Courageous* is ahead, she will be at least twenty seconds farther ahead at the finish. If *Australia* is ahead by no more than thirty seconds, *Courageous* may catch up. It's as simple as that."

If there were any media people left in the room when Jobson had finished, they would have realized he had just written their stories for them. The first three races, in fact, unfolded almost exactly as Jobson had predicted.

Turner and *Courageous* took the first race in moderate air by one minute forty-eight seconds, a slim enough margin to give the

Aussies a glimmer of hope. Once back on land and in front of the hundreds of whirring cameras and bright lights of the television crews, however, Turner won the first day's post race press conference by a Georgia mile. "Fame," he said, diplomatically thanking Lee Loomis, Ted Hood, and Robbie Doyle, "is like love. You can never have too much of it."

Courageous led *Australia* by a wide margin in the second race, which was abandoned with Turner just a quarter mile from the finish after *Australia* had exceeded the five-hour time limit. The official *Courageous* press statement amounted to all of one sentence: "If you have ever heard eleven grown men cry, it was when the gun on the committee's boat went off," signaling that the race would not count.

The wind remained moderate for the next race but Turner continued to be the eye of a growing storm of media attention. As *Courageous* was being towed into port after her second straight victory, Turner complained to Jobson that the spectator fleet seemed slightly diminished from the first day. Turner instructed his tender driver to bring him in closer along the docks so he could acknowledge the cheers of the several thousand people who had begun to gather there each afternoon to welcome him back.

The crowds waited all afternoon each day, in the rain, in the dark, just to traverse the six blocks with Turner from Bannister's Wharf, past the Black Pearl, down Thames Street, up America's Cup Avenue, and right to the door of his daily press conference. "All riiight!" Turner said as the crowd swarmed around him, shaking his hand and shouting their congratulations. The cheering swelled as Turner's parade passed Clarke Cooke House. Beer in hand, he doffed his Greek fisherman's hat in acknowledgment. He lit a cigar as three women threw their arms around him and planted kisses on both cheeks. "All riiight!" intoned Turner, to no one in particular, after each kiss.

"Ted, all these girls," cried his wife, who had now joined the procession.

"I can't help it," he pleaded, grabbing a kiss from yet another young woman who was hanging on his arm. Horns were honking, the cheering was getting louder. Someone handed Turner a can of Foster's, the Australian beer. "That's all right," Turner shouted, chugging the one liter can without coming up for air. "Some of my best friends are Australians."

One disbelieving reporter from California was worried. "I'm not sure I ought to wait here," he said. "Suppose he takes a car?"

"Ted Turner won't take a car," replied a knowing hand from the *Atlanta Constitution*, as certain that Turner would stay on foot as he was the sun would rise on the morrow. "He loves this walk too much. It's like his goddamn army."

"Yeah," said Turner, recognizing the reporter as he swept by. "It's crazy, isn't it?"

After a third straight victory, Turner took over the post-race press conferences from the cup committee's Bill Ficker, another former winning America's Cup skipper, and began serving as master of ceremonies, interlocutor, and host of television's newest, wildest talk show. Two minutes and thirty-two seconds had been the margin of victory in this third race, prompting speculation over what the results might have been if the two crews simply changed boats. "We're used to our boat, our sails, our rig," Turner replied with a straight face. "Noel is used to his. It's like asking Noel Robins or me what would happen if we switched wives. Noel is used to his wife and he likes her better than mine. And I like mine better than his." Before the assembled scribes could stifle their laughter, he put the inimitable Turner touch to his comment, adding, "She ain't much, but she's all I got."

Both boats were dead even across the starting line in the fourth race, but as Jobson had forecast, *Australia* was left sucking backwind at the first mark. *Courageous* kept improving her lead and went on to win by two minutes and twenty-five seconds. Despite a spirited effort by the Aussies, their boat seemed burdened by an inability to point high, which may have been the result of Lowell North's inferior sails and Noel Robin's inability to set his new sheets properly.

As *Courageous* crossed the finish line, the New York Yacht Club committee boat hoisted its orange and blue pennant, to which both twelves signaled "Affirmative." Then bedlam broke out off Brenton Reef. A thousand boat horns let loose at once as *Courageous* lowered her sails and was lashed to her tender for the tow back into Newport.

Escorted by two Coast Guard cutters, sirens blaring, blue lights flashing, *Courageous* sluiced through the ocean into Newport Harbor as hundreds of other vessels attempted to follow as close as possible in her wake. Fireboats sent streams of water hundreds of feet in the air, arcing over Turner and his crew. Roman candles, boat flares, and fireworks went off, fog horns bleated. Even the bells of Newport's churches began clanging in welcome. The Goodyear blimp swept in low over *Courageous*'s mast, giving

the camera crew on board their first look at the conquering heroes. "Now you've got your crowds," a jubilant Gary Jobson
shouted over the din to his captain.

Ted Turner stood alone on the bow, his feet spread wide apart,
his cigar cocked sharply upward. He was already beginning to
look a little unsteady. His fisherman's hat was askew, his yellow
slicker pants at half-mast. But all Newport was his, and Ted
Turner knew it.

Puffed up like a peacock, Turner stood ready to welcome Commodore Hinman and the rest of the New York Yacht Club contingent on board *Courageous*. His crew began tossing everybody
within arm's reach into Newport Harbor. When they ran out of
cup officials, they started in with their own wives and girlfriends.
Turner continued to swagger and strut on deck, his arms raised
in triumph, his voice reduced to a hoarse whisper, and his narrow
eyes beginning to look like tiny slits. Hundreds had clambered
onto the roof of the Aquidneck Lobster Company next to Bannister's Wharf. They cheered when Ted guzzled another beer or
swigged from the dozens of bottles of champagne and rum being
thrust into his hands. And they cheered when Turner grabbed a
hose and ran up and down the dock, spraying everybody in sight.
But they cheered the loudest when he turned on the staid old farts
still sitting in the NYYC committee boat and gave them a soaking
they'd never forget. Ted Turner had preserved America's honor,
retained the Auld Mug, and reverted to a ten-year-old brat. The
cheers grew even louder and Ted smiled his gap-toothed smile,
savoring every second of it. He grabbed at his shirt and pulled it
up over his neck. "Show me your tits," he yelled to the gaggle of
women now clinging to his arms. Some actually accepted his
invitation.

There was to be no victory walk this day. His swagger had
turned into a stagger, and the crowd had already swept Ted up
on its shoulders. Turner's feet would not touch ground as the mob
surged out into Thames Street and began the trek up the hill to
the armory. He was embraced, kissed, pawed, kissed again. And
again. Some women tried to tear the green *Courageous* shirt off
his back. He loved it, and took another long pull at yet another
bottle of champagne.

Gently deposited at the armory's front door by two of Newport's finest who had moved in to protect him from the crowd,
Turner stared blankly at the *Providence Journal*'s Doug Riggs, who
said later he was astounded Ted was still on his feet. Turner stum-

bled through the entrance amid clamorous cheers and began picking his way unsteadily across the armory's floor, tripping over the dozens of lighting and television cables stretched around the room. *Australia*'s crew did their best to cheer him on with a creditable chorus or two of "Dixie." Once he had finally struggled up to the rostrum, Turner recognized Alan Bond but very nearly fell into the stout syndicate leader's lap. After righting himself, he proceeded to barge straight into Bill Ficker, who was still earnestly attempting to maintain a semblance of decorum in the midst of such chaos.

"It's your boat, Ted," Ficker declared gamely, "but it's my press conference."

Still on his feet after finishing off the better part of a bottle of aquavit the Swedish crew had pressed on him, Turner was already groping for the microphone in Ficker's hand. "I—I never loved sailing against good friends any more than the French, or the Aussies," he stammered, now clutching a bottle of Mount Gay rum that had appeared out of nowhere. "I love them. They are the best of the best. I love everybody in this room. You are all the best of the best." Then he plumped himself down on an empty chair as Alan Bond stood up to speak.

R. T. Williams and Sid Pike were on the floor right in front of the rostrum table. These two production executives from Turner's WTCG had been setting up all afternoon to make sure the Superstation was right on top of the media blitz they knew would follow Turner's triumph. Concerned when he saw a CBS camera zoom in on his slumping boss, Pike reached under the table and tried to pull the rum bottle out of sight. When he felt the bottle slipping out of his grasp. Turner immediately began yelling like a stuck pig. "Pike, you dumb fuck! Give me that back." Attempting to retrieve the bottle, Ted slowly slid all the way under the table until he was stretched out flat on the floor. Three television cameras sent the image out live, and a short time later the entire episode became a part of media history when it was replayed on "60 Minutes." Bill Ficker reached down to help pull Turner back onto his seat but nearly dropped him when Ted began fondling Ficker's shiny bald pate. Then Captain Courageous finally stood up, shakily, and, clearing his throat, began what was to be the most memorable victory speech in the 126-year history of the America's Cup.

"I love everybody in this room," Turner repeated over and over, his words as thick as the demerara rum he continued to swig.

"The best . . . the . . ." Gary Jobson touched his elbow and shoved a hastily scrawled note under his nose, but Turner plowed on. "I, uh, I want to thank my crew. They busted their behinds. And I want to thank George Hinman and the New York Yacht Club for the opportunity—" Jobson nudged him again, hard, but could not stop his skipper, who was now on a roll. "We worked hard, we busted our behinds. I like Ficker. And I want Bob McCullough, Commodore McCullough, and the crew of *Courageous*, my crew—" With a long, guttural glissando, Turner began to sink to the floor. As one, the *Courageous* crew surged forward toward the rostrum. With a thunderous cheer they swept up their skipper and carried him aloft right through the cheering crowd and out the door at the rear of the armory.

"We, too," a vastly relieved Bill Ficker finally was able to utter once all the commotion died down, "would also like to thank the crew of the *Courageous*."

It was still not yet seven-thirty on the most memorable night yet of Ted Turner's thirty-nine years on this planet. Coming to life outside in the street, he broke away from his crew and took off cross-country, somehow making his way back to his room at Conley Hall, where he passed out cold, oblivious of the pandemonium that continued through the night in his honor.

Ted Turner's heroic collapse may have amused the media and helped add to the stature of this popular folk hero, whose exploits were now threatening to become legend. But as he slid under the table that night at the Newport Armory, Turner took with him the last semblance of amateurism that the America's Cup would ever see. This rash, impulsive, gloriously uninhibited cross between Huck Finn and Horatio Nelson had, against all odds, remained true to himself and, *mirabile dictu*, had even dared to have fun while he was accomplishing the impossible. With refreshing candor, the Aussie's John Bertrand seriously suggested "The New York Yacht Club should have installed a brass commemorative plaque on the spot where Turner fell, an appropriate memorial for this last great gesture of carefree amateur recklessness."

Once he was back on his feet the next day, Turner proved not only resilient, but resoundingly positive about returning to Newport to do it all over again. At the first of many, many post–America's Cup press conferences, he had difficulty constraining himself. The four races he had just won had lasted a total of 1,041 minutes, and the difference separating *Courageous* and *Australia* at the end amounted to less than 240 seconds. "When I come back," Turner announced, not a little immodestly, "I won't change anything on *Courageous* or the crew. We're fast. We're perfect. She's the most perfect twelve-meter that ever sailed, and I can't think of anything I could do to be any better."

Australia's skipper, Noel Robins, confessed he had made a poor choice of sails several times during the early races and felt that could have made the difference. Alan Bond was somewhat more gracious in declaring that Turner had sailed what amounted to a flawless series, "with a huge assist from his tactician, Gary Jobson, who played the wind shifts to perfection." But when they come to write the history of this glorious twenty-third defense of the America's Cup, it's most likely that Ted Turner will be remembered less for the way he won his victory than for the way he celebrated it.

De dog hab four feet, but him trabble only one path.
OLD GULLAH PROVERB

Chapter Seven

Turner's triumphant return to Atlanta was sweet but short-lived. Mayor Maynard Jackson declared September 23 "Ted Turner Day," and after nearly eighteen hours of accolades, speechifying, and enough champagne to float *Courageous*, he came back down to earth and put his feat in the kind of perspective most Georgians had been waiting to hear. "After all," he burbled to a cheering crowd outside Peachtree Plaza, "winning the America's Cup isn't as important as winning the World Series!"

The Braves were still mired in last place, but attendance had nearly doubled since Turner bought the team, thanks in no small part to the owner's penchant for personal publicity. The Atlanta Hawks had already turned around and looked like contenders for the 1978 playoffs. Both teams were fueling the Superstation's growth by over one hundred thousand new cable households a month. Soon WTCG's national audience would exceed two million, twice its Georgia viewership. In documents filed with the Securities and Exchange Commission, Turner Communications Corporation now estimated the fair market value of its assets at over $50 million. With 87 percent ownership of his company, Ted Turner's own personal net worth had nearly doubled in less than twelve months. And he had spent less than fifteen days in the office all year.

Not even Ted Turner, however, was immune to the inevitable

letdown after having devoted himself so completely to an effort most of his newfound public had trouble even understanding. His high spirits plummeted once he was back in the office and he realized that in his absence his business had not only been running, but running itself quite well. He began receiving lots of letters from women he'd never met. "Suggestive letters," his personal assistant, Dee Woods, recalled. "They tell him they like the way he walks, things like that." Woods remembered what some of the male executives had said when she first came to work for Turner in 1971. "So, you're the one," they warned her, "who's coming to work for that son of a bitch?" The women in the company, Woods added, had a slightly different perspective. "It was all, Oohh, Dee. Can I come and help you?" When Ted was named *Playgirl* magazine's Sexiest Man of the Year, he had been tickled pink. But when he went around showing the magazine to Woods and everybody else in the office, he impressed upon them that what he liked most about the piece was the magazine's emphasis on "Turner's unquenchable desire to win." He was even more pleased when the *Constitution* named him Sexiest Man in Atlanta, over Falcons quarterback Steve Bartkowski and Turner's pal, city councilman Wyche Fowler. "Ted has five kids," the newspaper noted. "He must be sexy."

Turner's usual sixteen-hour workdays were not easy to fill up after a summer of such intensity, even though he continued to wear half a dozen hats and could glide seamlessly from billboards to broadcast, from the Braves or Hawks to a serious and informed discussion of pending broadcast legislation—not to mention an occasional rumination on the imminent duck-shooting season. With his momentum winding down, Turner began to reach out for some new challenge. He toyed with the idea of a race around the world but settled for putting together another winning campaign on the Southern Ocean Racing Circuit. Somehow he also found time to take the entire Atlanta Braves baseball team to lunch at the New York Yacht Club, partly, he admitted, so they could ogle the original America's Cup in the club's *sanctum sanctorum* and partly because it made awfully good copy along Madison Avenue.

While he was in New York, Ted also taped a now notorious "Dick Cavett Show" and, unexpectedly, came close to blows for the first time since his confrontation in Newport with Lowell North. Tired from a trying day leading his troops into the breach on behalf of his Superstation, Turner showed up early for the taping, only to learn that Cavett was still finishing up another show. When they finally got under way, Cavett expected the bumptious, off-the-wall character Turner often seemed to be. Instead it was Cavett who began to look like the inarticulate bumpkin once he opened up on Turner. After a bit of verbal fencing over the despised "Mouth of the South" business, a frustrated Cavett dove right in and asked, "Let's not leave viewers with a false impression. You are a colorful, boisterous, sometimes inebriated playboy type. Maybe it's an act or it's created by the press, but that is your image. You wouldn't deny that, would you?"

"I have heard that you are a little twinkle-toed TV announcer," Ted responded with utter insouciance. "Would you deny that?"

Dredging up some old news about Donald Davidson, the Braves' erstwhile traveling secretary, Cavett asked Ted if he had actually fired Davidson over his personal expense accounts, which regularly included limousines and lavish hotel suites.

"Yes."

"Wasn't he a midget?"

"Yes. He's the only midget I've fired in my twenty years in business."

"Didn't you have a good line about that?"

"I said, 'Put him up on a desk so I can look him in the eye and fire him.' But it wasn't my line. If so, I'd have your job and you'd have mine." Blinded by the bright studio lights, Cavett couldn't see whether Turner had actually begun to clench his fists. But the look on his guest's face told him instantly the interview was now over and the show would never air.

"Everybody wants to be a star," Ted announced to the world not long after his America's Cup victory. "But has anyone transcended his profession," *Sports Illustrated* wanted to know, "grown bigger than life, become more important, become a star, any faster than Robert Edward Turner III?"

"I'm not a fire-eating, maniacal madman who beats his kids and deserves to be thrown out of our national pastime," Turner replied.

Apart from his ability to talk the hind leg off a mule and still not take himself or anybody else too seriously, Ted Turner was an almost instant favorite of the media for one simple reason—he was that rarest of birds, an honest man. He was also likable as all get-out, most of the time. Despite his run-in with Cavett, he could charm infinitely more difficult interlocutors like Tom Snyder, who kept inviting Ted back after grilling him for almost an hour and a half on his NBC talk show. "You were terrific," Snyder told him with genuine enthusiasm.

"You ain't such a bad boy yourself, Snyder," Turner replied. And he then offered Snyder a job on his Superstation. "Just name your price."

On his thirty-ninth birthday Ted let a team of *People* magazine photographers wedge him into a tiny Minifish sailboat, load him up with a baseball bat, a Braves cap, and a basketball, and then shove him out into the middle of some pond in suburban Marietta —all by way of illustrating why he had been chosen one of the publication's Twenty-Five Most Interesting People of the Year. Then he was off with his wife to celebrate at—where else?—an Atlanta Hawks basketball game. They brought a cake out at half-time, a round mound of chocolate with long vanilla fingers reaching around the birthday cake/ball. After the crowd gave forth with a hearty and heartfelt chorus of "Happy Birthday," Turner went back to his seat, his fingers awfully sticky and his eyes a little moist.

Sid Pike, WTCG's general manager and the fellow whose arms appeared on "60 Minutes" when he was filmed grabbing the rum bottle off the rostrum up in Newport, has no regrets about trying to save his boss. "One of my responsibilities," he said, "if I know he is doing something wrong, is to try to stop him. But did you ever try to stop a speeding train? He has a tremendous desire to win. He doesn't like to lose. And if he does, he is one of the few people I have ever known who benefits from the loss. Ted asks himself, 'Why did I lose?' I don't know why he has to win so much. It's a compulsion with him."

Turner himself sees it somewhat differently, and the distinction, at least to him, makes all the difference in the world. "I don't think winning is everything," he explains. "It's a big mistake when you say that. I think *trying* to win is what counts."

He wasn't sure whether he was winning or simply trying to win when he answered the call of the National Cable Television Association to appear in Washington to testify against something called the "retransmission consent provision." Hurrying up to Washington to do battle against this new chimera, Turner found himself face to face at a House communications subcommittee hearing with his old adversary, Bowie Kuhn. Lined up behind the baseball commissioner were Larry O'Brien, National Basketball Association commissioner; John Zeigler, National Hockey League president; and Tom Hansen, National Collegiate Athletic Association executive director. Each of these gentlemen glowered across the witness table at Turner and then proceeded to swear on a stack of Bibles that current FCC regulations, which allowed cable television operators across the country to pick most broadcast program signals out of the air and retransmit them to their paying customers via coaxial cable, were outrageously unfair. The sports officials were there to lobby for a change in these regulations that would require cable operators to obtain the consent of a broadcasting station or programmer before "pirating" its signal.

Kuhn was quietly eloquent in suggesting that a disastrous undercutting of hometown loyalty, not to mention box office receipts and local television revenues, would result if retransmission consent were not required. Following long, well-documented testimony from each of the other witnesses, Ted Turner finally stood and faced the committee. "I am appearing here as a broadcaster," he said. "As president of Turner Communications Corporation and WTCG, and not as owner of either the Atlanta Braves or the Atlanta Hawks.

"While voicing support for retransmission consent," Turner continued, "these monopolistic sports interests know full well that they have absolutely no intention of granting consent. This new law, if passed, will result in the smaller cities and towns across America being deprived of the same variety and high quality of sports broadcasts available in major cities like New York, Chicago, and Los Angeles. The open and competitive market we see today will become totally noncompetitive if restrictive retransmission consent becomes law. And I don't think any of you gentlemen here today would stand up and say you are in favor of a monopoly."

Round one to Turner, defender of the oppressed, protector of the free market, and, by slight coincidence, principal target of the proposed new legislation. But as Ted and his troops would soon discover, this was merely the opening skirmish in an all-out war of attrition. Lined up against Turner's Superstation were all the forces of darkness, namely professional sports, Hollywood, the entire television broadcasting industry, and most especially the three large commercial television networks, which had not yet decided to unfurl their colors but were well aware of the potential threat to the profitable stranglehold they and their colleagues had on the distribution and dissemination of virtually all news, sports, and entertainment programming in the country. Turner had caused these interests to line up against him very simply because he was now airing, for anyone who cared to hook up to WTCG, over one hundred Atlanta Braves games; twenty-six Atlanta Hawks games; eight NBA "Game of the Week" broadcasts; the NBA playoffs; ten major college basketball games; the entire NCCA playoffs; twenty-six Atlanta Flames hockey games, plus the Stanley Cup; six Atlanta Falcons football games; and five North American Soccer League games. Interspersed with all of this were the movies in Turner's growing library of over thirty-five hundred Hollywood films. No wonder some of the brass at CBS, NBC, and ABC thought they might already be looking at the dreaded Fourth Network.

In 1978, Turner laid out over $2 million for historic old Hope Plantation, a magnificent five-thousand-acre preserve near Jacksonboro, South Carolina. Back in Cincinnati, Ted's mother broke out in an awful rash when she heard the news. She shuddered to think that her son, with all his promise, might be living out the fate of his father. Ed Turner's acquisition of Binden Hall, coming as it had just before their divorce, seemed to signal for both of them not only the end of their marriage, but an end as well to Ed's own effort to save himself. Ted laughed off the comparison, as he was inclined to do whenever his father was mentioned, and joked to Peter Dames about releasing five hundred naked women on his new plantation so he and his friends could hunt them down. Obviously he was outdistancing the Furies and may even have thrown them off the scent for a while.

"I used to worry about him ending up like his father," Jane Shirley Smith Turner observed. "But Ted's more stable now than when I first met him." And, she might have added, a good deal more contradictory. During their marriage Ted looked to Jane to maintain their home, keep him supplied with clean shirts and socks just as Judy Nye had, and look after the children. It was a marriage of convenience held together by a certain amount of genuine affection. As Judy Nye firmly believes, Ted is the kind of man who has to be married to someone. Love might enter the picture, but it hardly ranked then near the top of his criteria for marriage. As he'd had with Judy, Ted had an implicit understanding with Jane that his public persona would always be that of a married man. Privately, however, he would act as he pleased. "I was reared by a mother who was a mother, and I think my children deserve the same," Jane explains, attempting to rationalize the more than twenty years she spent as a virtual single parent to their own three children and the two stepchildren she had inherited from Ted's first marriage. "It's the role of every housewife, a role played by millions of women all over this country. I guess I wouldn't be human if I didn't harbor a little resentment."

"Jane Smith knew all the right people in Atlanta," says Geraldine Moore, an old Atlanta friend and neighbor. "She introduced Ted into the Atlanta gentry. And here he was, some kind of upstart from Savannah, marrying this darling little girl and bringing along these two kids. We thought he was some kind of nouveau riche, you know. She brought him into our crowd, but he never really became a part of it. I think Ted always felt he was very different. I don't think he was ever what you'd call a social animal, probably even when he was a child. Nobody ever got close to him. We all played bridge once or twice a week for years, but I still can't say that I ever really knew the man. I don't know if he ever really carried on what you could call a conversation with anyone."

Jane thought Ted had been kidding when he told her he was going to buy the Atlanta Braves. She's not shy about telling people she still wishes he had been. "He was talking about it for a long time, but I just blotted it out of my mind. Ted was forever bringing up one thing or another he wanted to do," she said. "For a long while, it was saving the old Fox Theater in Atlanta. Another time he had just come back from a sailboat race in Australia and he talked about moving the whole family down there and starting over. It was not until he actually did it that I realized he was serious about the Braves. That's just Ted's way.

"We both used to be so conservative," she continues, reaching way beyond any political context, "and I guess we both still are. You can tell by the children's names. Ted named them. Yes, Rhett is named for Rhett Butler. Beauregard, or Beau, as we call him, is named for General Beauregard. He wanted to name Jennie Scarlett, after Scarlett O'Hara. But I wouldn't let him—I thought that would be a little too much for her to live up to. Then he decided to name her Jeannie, after Stephen Foster's song 'Jeannie with the Light Brown Hair.' But I changed it to 'Jennie.' "

Jane almost never went sailing with Ted. "I used to, when we were first married. But being on a ship is worse than camping now. It's crowded and uncomfortable." Then she adds paradoxically, "I'm not the kind to stay home and clean up all the time." Jane and the kids did travel, when Ted wanted them, to Newport, to Miami, and once all the way to Sydney, Australia. But most of the time the longest trips she took were back home to visit her family in Birmingham. Despite what she says, Jane Turner spent most of her time at home with Ted's five kids. Jimmy Brown, who moved in the day they were married, was all the help she ever had and, according to Jane, all she ever really wanted.

"I'm used to hiding out, and I think it has been better to be anonymous," she says somewhat more accurately. With the exception of making formal appearances with Ted at business or sporting events like the America's Cup or Braves games, her life revolved around church, friends, her neighbors, and her children. "It's been good raising my family without being involved in the social life," she adds. "All our social life was involved with Ted's business, and that was fine with me. It's been a relief that I haven't had to fool around with social demands." When Ted was at home they often enjoyed a game of backgammon together. "But Ted said I didn't play too well. He always won and said he was just winning his own money, so what was the point?"

Jane Turner never talks directly about the abuse she endured during her twenty-five-year marriage. "Ted demanded one hundred percent from me and from the children. When he wanted something, it had better be at the top of my agenda." Jane admits Turner would explode if even one of his orders was not carried out. "Ted has a temper," she acknowledges, "and when he gets angry and starts yelling, somebody is bound to end up crying, or worse.

"When Ted was home, if he said everybody had better be in bed at nine, they were. If he was home for breakfast, he demanded that all the children be seated at the table at eight A.M., when he came in. If they weren't, it would be the kind of scene everyone liked to avoid. So we would naturally all be there, waiting for him."

"After a few years, they just seemed to go in different directions," says Gerri Moore. "Janie and I continued to be friends, and I still see her from time to time. But Ted was different. He didn't seem to fit in or even want to fit in, and he left her with all those kids to raise. Janie immersed herself in being a kind of wife-mother. Savannah is even more close-knit than Atlanta," Moore adds, "and I don't know that the Turners were ever accepted there by the so-called Savannah gentry. Ted was never someone you went out of your way to know, although everybody knows who he is and knows all about him. He's not a really nice person, the way he played around on his wife. He was very raw, very crude about it, but I don't think Janie put up with it for the money or the easy life. I really don't think she ever cared about the money. I think she really loved him. Or thought she did."

Jane Turner learned to live with a part-time husband and the almost overwhelming responsibilities of rearing five very independent children by convincing herself that having Ted away all the time might actually have been an improvement over having him at home. "Sometimes it was boring that Ted wasn't here. But we'd have gotten on each other's nerves," she said, "and probably have driven each other crazy if he had been home." Jane never tried to compete with Ted the way Judy Nye did. She seldom let her own self-esteem get in the way of this accommodation of a marriage. She certainly never thought of fighting back and sometimes went overboard the other way, occasionally retreating into too many cocktails, ignoring the dozens of attractive female companions she knew Ted was squiring wherever he went, even in Atlanta, right under her nose. But, like so many silent, long-suffering southern women before her, Jane remained true to her tradition, if not to herself. Roger Vaughan understood precisely when he observed, "Ted Turner is the anachronism; Jane is responding to him with reflex, in kind."

"I've seen them, the groupies. They're always there," Jane would repeat over and over in reply to the endless queries put to her about Ted's flagrant infidelities. "It's kind of pathetic, frankly, because they're young and that's all they can get. That's why it doesn't really bother me. He always comes back. I trust him. No matter what anyone says," she would assert with a brave face, "I always know he's faithful to me."

Despite the unusual aspects of his marriage to Jane Smith, Turner's almost infallible sense of timing, whether in the bedroom or the boardroom, is sometimes intimidating and very often overwhelming. He was right, of course, about UHF television and even more right about satellite distribution. He picked up both the Braves and the Hawks at their respective nadirs and for fractions of their respective fair market values. He arrived on the ocean-racing scene when it was just waiting for somebody to blow open the doors to a newly democratized America's Cup. A born contrarian, Turner makes his best moves when all the cards are stacked against him, when even his closest advisers are predicting all but certain disaster or defeat. Turner does fail. He will even walk away if he doesn't feel right about a situation. Without hesitation. Without explanation. But more times than not, he has been right, and until the record begins to turn against him, he must be accorded the benefit of the doubt.

His chief financial officer, Will Sanders, tells of the time Turner, with no apparent prior knowledge of the precious metals market, decided one day he would buy some Krugerrands, the one-ounce South African gold coins popular in the late 1970s. Ted bought $2 million worth of the coins, which took virtually all the cash he had at the time. Sanders tried to talk him out of this rash investment, urging him to keep his money in guaranteed, interest-paying government securities. Naturally Turner plunged right ahead, purchased the Krugerrands, and made over $3.6 million profit when the price of gold proceeded to go right through the roof. For years afterward Turner always carried a Krugerrand in his pocket, coolly flipping one solid gold coin until he lost it and had to ask Sanders to draw down another. What Sanders sometimes fails to mention is that Turner forgot the combination to the safe where he kept his Kruggerands and had to blow off the door before he could cash in the coins.

At the 1979 Six Meter World Championships in Seattle, Turner was seated at dinner one night next to Tom Blackaller, the former race car driver, sail maker, and America's Cup sailor from San Francisco. Blackaller's flamboyant style and great charm with the ladies appealed to Turner, and the two had been friendly rivals for years. Blackaller, in fact, had just defeated Ted in the Australia/America Six-Meter Challenge Cup and was running ahead of him in the world championships. Bored with the dinner table conversation and exhausted from nearly fourteen hours of sailing, Turner took out his Kruggerand and began passing it around. When Tom Blackaller handed him back a quarter, Ted exploded in mock anger, "Blackaller, come on. Give me a break. You're beating me, so give me a break."

"Nothing personal, Ted. I've been beating you all week. I want to beat everybody," Blackaller responded.

Turner stopped short for just a moment, mindful of the forth-coming 1980 America's Cup now less than a year away. "You're right, Blackaller. Beating everybody. That's a worthy goal. Dennis Conner says he doesn't care about the rest. As long as he beats me, he's happy. But you got to try to beat everybody. That's what makes it fun."

Modern ocean racing traces its history back to 1812 and the founding of Britain's Royal Yacht Squadron in the tiny village of Cowes on the Isle of Wight. Just off Portsmouth and the south-western coast of England, Cowes had a year-round population of only 2,500. Each August that number swells to include several hundred of the best international ocean racers in the world, as well as another 25,000 spectators. Cowes Week consists of five different races of varying distances and degrees of difficulty, lead-ing up to the four-day Fastnet, which begins in the Solent, the turbulent body of water that separates Cowes from Portsmouth, and then runs 605 nautical miles around Fastnet Rock off the Irish coast and back to Plymouth.

"Your Majesty, I regret to report, there is no second," Queen Victoria's equerry had responded when asked which yacht fol-lowed the schooner *America* across the finish line in the historic 1851 race through these same waters. Ted Turner's approach to the 1979 Fastnet was equally absolute. He had set the race record in 1971 with his old twelve-meter, *American Eagle*, and was the big winner thus far in the week-long buildup to Fastnet. Gary Jobson had helped put together a mixed crew of young stalwarts and seasoned veterans, including Robert H. "Bobby" Symonette, a fifty-year-old Bahamian, and Peter Bowker, a fifty-two-year-old English navigator. Also on board was Robert Edward "Teddy" Turner IV, Ted's sixteen-year-old son, who had worked on *Tena-cious* all summer as paid hand to Ted's professional captain, Bud Sutherland.

Weather reports at the start of the race on the final Saturday of Cowes Week forecast force seven winds—between 32 and 38 MPH —which might begin to kick up sometime on the following Tues-day. This kind of a blow was welcomed as a decent sporting chal-lenge by the experienced Fastnet ocean sailors, since most of the fleet would be on a pell-mell downhill run to the finish line by then.

When *Tenacious* rounded bleak Fastnet Rock at 6:30 P.M. on the third day out, she was running strong, holding her place well up among the leaders. Peter Bowker was in his cabin trying to pick up the BBC evening weather report. Suddenly his radio crackled to life with an urgent warning: "Finistere, Sole, Fastnet. Severe winds. Force nine. Increasing, strong force ten. Imminent." Bowker didn't need to hear any more and immediately reported to Turner, "We're going to have a lot of breeze!"

The skies around *Tenacious* had already turned a sodden gray and the air temperature was dropping fast. Still, running for shelter seemed unnecessary, perhaps even impossible. "I felt a little bit like Noah," Turner later recounted in *Motorboat & Sailing* magazine. "I knew the flood was coming. And I had a boat ready that would get me through it."

Then the cyclone hit, slamming into the fleet with force ten winds exceeding 70 MPH. Huge, towering waves fifty feet high picked up the sleek ocean racers and tossed them about like toothpicks. Boats were capsized, righted, and swamped again, their crews dangling from their safety harnesses like helpless marionettes. Less fortunate yachtsmen were flung against their wire railings or washed overboard. Arthur Moss, skipper of the British yacht *Camargue*, recalled with typical British understatement, "Our steering wheel, complete with a man attached, just went soaring out into the sea."

Staring straight into the mouth of the storm, Ted Turner was in his element. Here was an enemy, a challenge like no other he had ever faced. He spun the wheel furiously, trying to plane the waves like a surfer, rising up thirty or forty feet at the crest and then slamming down when they broke, with a force strong enough to shake his keel bolts loose. Turner knew that he had to keep going to survive, but he also knew that plowing on meant having to sail straight through the rest of the fleet that had not yet reached Fastnet Rock.

"Waves were like cliffs instead of hills. And when one of them hit," Turner noted, "it was like getting hit by a Mack truck." The adrenaline was pumping. Lives were at stake, including his own. "You all right, boy?" Turner shouted to his son, lashed to the gangway railing and so sick he could barely mutter a faint "Yessir." "It was a matter of self-preservation. You let your boat go over and you're lost. We kept up a little sail and raced like mad. There wasn't much else we could do." Except come through unscathed and—the idea forming in his head had a delicious ring to it—maybe even win this damn race and break his own course record.

Fastnet would go down in yachting annals as the worst catastrophe in ocean-racing history. Of the 302 boats that set out from Cowes that sunny August afternoon, only ninety-two ever crossed the finish line at Plymouth. Eighteen men were drowned, and four others died on shore. Scores were injured, including Peter Bowker, who was hurled against *Tenacious*'s wheel, bruising two ribs and nearly bending the wheel out of shape. Twenty-five yachts were abandoned or sunk. Dozens of others were disabled and left to drift in the Irish Sea. The Royal Air Force and Royal Navy, mounting their biggest rescue operation since World War II, kept the death toll as low as it was. For eighty-four straight hours eight helicopters, six light destroyers, and nearly two hundred volunteer commercial ships ranged over ten thousand square miles, pulling 160 sailors out of the sea. Tall masts on some of the larger yachts made it impossible to pluck men from the decks.

"The idea of jumping into those huge seas was appalling," said Frank Worley, a crewman on *Camargue*. "In the end, we were all pushed in by the skipper. When it was his turn, it took him a good long time to make the jump. An RAF chopper found the abandoned shell of the thirty-five foot *Ariadne*, one of thirteen American yachts in the race. The pilot at first reported there were no signs of life, but minutes later spotted a man bobbing in a life jacket in the boiling waves and winched him up. Frank Ferris, skipper of *Ariadne*, died four hours later in a shoreside hospital."

Once the terrible winds had blown themselves out, however, *Tenacious* found herself in open ocean with a clear shot past the Scilly Islands straight into Plymouth harbor. It was dark when she finally slid across the finish line at 10:22 P.M., and the little port was enshrouded in a thick fog. The tension evaporated, however, as the jubilant crew stepped back onto dry land and headed for hot showers and warm, dry clothes—all except Turner, who looked dog-tired but still seemed in top form, sounding off on life, women, and sailboat racing. Looking around the quay in vain for other finishers, he surmised that *Tenacious* must have won the race.

Turner and his men heard continuing reports on the BBC about damage to some of the fleet, but they were still unaware of the immensity of the tragedy or that Plymouth was in chaos. It was not until he got to his room at the Holiday Inn that Ted realized he had just taken part in a world-class yachting disaster. "Do you realize they all think we're dead back there?" he reported to his crew. "They had us listed as missing yesterday. The whole world's gone crazy over this thing."

Early the next morning reporters began tracking him down, looking for an eyewitness account, hoping for a sound byte that would put a human touch to this immense, impersonal tragedy. Ted Turner didn't let them down. He will always speak his mind and is sometimes oblivious of the consequences. His abiding candor makes it all but impossible for him to respond in any other way. In contrast to Edward Heath, former British prime minister, who limped into Plymouth harbor and pronounced the experience "the worst I have ever been through" before offering his condolences for those lost at sea, Ted Turner appeared thoughtless, even callous, when he cracked to a reporter from *The New York Times*, "It was rough! Rough! We never slowed once. In fact, they forgot to put the checkered flag out for us and we just kept coming in, full speed." Not sure that sounded entirely right, he kept plowing on. "Everyone had a ball. Once it was over. Like any experience, whenever you come through it, you feel better. We're not talking about the other people who died, but to be able to face it all and come through, that is exhilarating."

The British were stunned, and when *Tenacious* was named overall winner of the race, Turner attempted to smooth things over by putting Fastnet into his own unique historical perspective. "It was a storm precisely like this," he began, posturing for the television cameras with an American flag draped over his shoulder, "that saved England from the Spanish Armada. You ought to be thankful there are storms like that, or you'd all be speaking Spanish. Whenever you sail the English Channel, you've got to be prepared for that kind of storm." Realizing he had done it again, Turner tried quoting a few snatches from "Horatius at the Bridge" and then undid himself all over again. "Aw, it—it's hard to be real happy today," he stammered, "because so many people have gone up to that great yacht race in the sky. But at least they won't have to worry about setting the storm trysail anymore. In a way, I'll be happy when my turn comes, too."

After the *Tenacious* crew joined a crowded memorial service at St. Andrew's Church, Turner packed his bags, collected his son, and caught the night train back to London. He took with him another suitcase full of silver, the lion's share of the trophies awarded during Cowes Week, viscerally aware that once again he had rolled the dice and won. His mind was already churning with thoughts of the next challenge, but first he had to call Dee Woods in Atlanta and make sure the world knew Ted Turner was still alive and kicking.

> *If you want it to be unique, it has*
> *to be at least a little unusual.*
>
> WILLIAM S. PALEY (1951)

Chapter Eight

By 1980 nearly two-thirds of all Americans looked to television, specifically network television, according to a Gallup poll, as the source for most or all of their news and information. The network news departments, once habitual loss leaders but also dedicated defenders of the public's right to know, were evolving into bloated money machines with a bottom-line mentality symptomatic of the era when no one stopped to think that double-digit growth might not continue forever.

By 1980, however, so much money was flowing into the news coffers that no one blinked when news department budgets began soaring out of sight. In Washington, for example, the combined bureaus of CBS, NBC, and ABC totaled more than two thousand full-time employees. Even the lowliest grip on a network news camera team traveled first class, by contractual agreement. Salaries for on-camera talent shot up into the high six figures, and superstar anchors like Walter Cronkite, Chet Huntley, and David Brinkley began commanding multimillion-dollar compensation packages.

Operating out of cavernous new studios and employing the latest technical devices money could buy, the network news departments redefined the state of the art each evening with twenty-two minutes of smooth, seamless programming. Each of the major networks was now spending nearly $150 million a year just to produce the evening news. Despite all this money and high-ticket manpower, a typical network news operation still transmitted fewer words in a year than a relatively modest nontelevision news service like Knight-Ridder would crank out every twenty-four hours. In the rush for higher ratings and greater profits, few noticed the slow but inexorable erosion of public confidence upon which the networks' news franchises had been built.

Network executives often found it convenient to downplay the new profitability of their news operations as an excuse to forgo the expense of covering less appealing, more complex, serious stories. CBS president Frank Stanton could have been speaking for all three networks in 1975 when he testified before a Senate investigating committee: "Since CBS News cannot be self-supporting," he said with unnerving conviction, "we must pay attention to the economics of broadcasting in making decisions involving great costs."

No longer a loss leader, television news had become a vital marketing tool and an important contributor to a network's bottom line. No one on that Senate committee in 1975 ever even questioned why CBS News could not be "self-supporting," yet by 1980 the "CBS Evening News" alone was generating an operating profit of over $100 million a year.

Along with this new profitability, the networks found themselves with an embarrassing conflict regarding their responsibility to inform the public and their desire to attract advertisers with ever improved ratings. In *Making News*, his excellent dissection of the television news business, Martin Mayer makes the case that the network news divisions, even in the so-called golden era of Elmer Davis and Ed Murrow, in fact eschewed any social responsibility and were reluctant to admit that their real audience was the great unwashed, the illiterate and marginally literate who had no other access to news or information and were therefore dependent upon television news.

Mayer says he has been booed in public only once, at a CBS-sponsored forum on news and public affairs programming, when he pointed out to an outraged audience that, contrary to popular opinion, "the average viewer of TV news shows was considerably older than, and educationally and economically downscale from, the average viewer of entertainment shows." Television news executives had long derived a certain satisfaction, not to mention status and inflated advertising rates, from thinking otherwise. Now transformed into such an important new source of profit, however, television news, like the lowliest sitcom, was forced to abandon even the pretense of a responsibility to inform in its scramble to boost ratings. The result was less news, but more increasingly slick, selectively programmed "infotainment."

None of this, of course, escaped the attention of Ted Turner, who could read an income statement with the best of them and had to be impressed by the new profitability of television news. Despite all the bombast he used as a smoke screen to disguise the fact that he was too smart to compete in a local news war he could never win, Turner liked the idea that he could own the product and would not have to license news from a network or a Hollywood studio.

"I came up with the concept for a news channel even before my Superstation was up on the satellite," Turner says now with remarkable hindsight, "because business is like a chess game and you have to look several moves ahead. Most people don't. They only think one move at a time. But any good chess player knows when you're playing against a one-move opponent, you'll beat him every time." Turner was still not yet ready to make his move, but Harold Rice, vice-president of operations for RCA Americom, confirms that Turner had, indeed, described his idea for an all-news network in 1976, when he was arranging for satellite distribution of the new Superstation.

"Successful entrepreneurs," says management theorist Peter Drucker, "find innovative ways to seize unoccupied niches or carve out new niches of their own. Combine this ability with a contrarian nature," Drucker says, "and you have a powerful force for change. True entrepreneurs learn as much from their failures as their successes. But when they finally prevail, it is the conventional wisdom which is most often proven wrong."

Ted Turner has never met Peter Drucker and, despite a voraciously eclectic reading habit, has never admitted any familiarity with Drucker's writings. When he was just a teenager, however, Turner learned many of the same basic business principles from his father, an equally astute, if considerably less well-known, management theoretician. And he has been able to turn these tenets to great advantage ever since.

Ed Turner built his business around the simple truths he read in *Success*, the magazine for entrepreneurs, and imparted them to his son on the long drives they would take together to the far corners of Ed's rapidly expanding outdoor advertising empire. He instilled in his son the need to build value into everything he owned, to use common sense rather than the crutch of market research, and to use somebody else's money whenever possible. He also taught Ted to set targets but to keep redefining his goals as he advanced up the ladder of success. To Ed Turner's simplistic business philosophy, Ted himself added the old marine corps cliché, "Lead, follow, or get out of the way." He had built his business, as well as his life, around such basic bromides, and they have seldom failed him.

Once Turner had successfully exploited satellite distribution, common sense suggested that he continue to develop this unique franchise before the rest of the world beat him out of it. Ever since his successful defense of the America's Cup in 1977, Turner had known his Superstation would come under increasing pressure. He also assumed that someday soon he would have to backstop his money spinner with another satellite-delivered cable channel. He optioned a second transponder from RCA before he was even certain he would have anything to put on it. By 1978, however, Turner was close to knowing what that next channel would be.

Holed up in a dusty little office high above New York's *Daily News*, far removed from the world of international ocean racing, was another idea-a-minute man who was giving considerable thought to the concept of an all-news channel. Reese Schonfeld, in fact, had devoted most of his adult life to the news business, becoming notorious, if not exactly well known, for his forays into "alternative news."

A tall, perpetually rumpled individual, Maurice Wolfe Schonfeld is the consummate news junkie. His disdain for anyone who does not share his passion for the news shows immediately in distracted gazes and vague, distant responses. But get Reese Schonfeld on his subject and his eyes begin to light up, his voice takes on an urgent new timbre, and he becomes as animated as a computer graphic.

Schonfeld had honed his reportorial skills at Dartmouth and Columbia, where he earned both a master's in government and a law degree. He still possesses the disarming manner of a courteous country lawyer, which he might easily have become had he not been seduced early into the news business. He began as a gofer at UPI Movietone, one of the last of the old theatrical newsreel producers trying to make the transition into television. Schonfeld was exposed early to the visceral business of putting news on film, but doing it at absolute rock-bottom cost. He rose quickly at UPI, first to reporter, then producer, and then went outside to sell the product in a market where customers were disappearing faster than yesterday's headlines. Along the way he met another veteran of the independent news wars, Burt Reinhardt, who had been a Movietone cameraman in World War II and won a measure of fame as the man who photographed Gen. Douglas MacArthur's famous return to the Philippines in 1944. Reinhardt and Schonfeld became inseparable and also interchangeable as they traded jobs and hired each other, depending on who had the bigger annual budget. The experience for both men proved invaluable and turned Schonfeld into one of the most innovative contrarians in the news business.

Bankrolled by the Colorado conservative, brewer Joseph Coors, Schonfeld founded TVN, the first independent news service available to any television station in the country. The expense of providing enough timely news to attract a sufficient number of subscribers, as well as questions about Coors's objectivity, hampered TVN from the start. Despite Schonfeld's ingenious efforts to save money and still put out a credible product, profits remained elusive and TVN was soon out of business. Schonfeld, however, gained some minor place for himself in the pantheon of television news when he managed to scoop all three major television networks on Premier Nikita Khrushchev's 1961 appearance at the United Nations. Forgoing remote coverage, Schonfeld simply photographed TVN's reporter taking the story off the telephone.

Determined to make an independent news operation work, Schonfeld next sold a group of five large independent stations on funding a cooperative effort to distribute ninety-second news clips to each other by satellite. Under the aegis of Independent Television News Association (ITNA), Schonfeld succeeded in signing up sixteen other independent stations that became ITNA's only paying customers. He called on WTCG-TV in Atlanta and made a nuisance of himself trying to sell news to the one independent in the country who could have cared less. Once Turner launched his Superstation, Schonfeld was back, trying to interest this new cable innovator in joining ITNA. His path would frequently cross with Ted Turner's at various industry get-togethers. Due principally to Schonfeld's prodigious efforts, ITNA finally began to make some headway. When he met Turner again at a 1977 cable television convention, Reese Schonfeld was determined to try one more time to sell him a few minutes of news feed for the Superstation.

Turner had been swaggering around the convention hall for hours, sandwiched between two leggy blondes, when Schonfeld was finally able to collar him and begin his pitch. It was obvious that Turner had been drinking and was hardly in a state to talk business, but Schonfeld plowed ahead doggedly. He was spouting discounts, ratings, and a whole laundry list of other minutiae when Turner cut him off in midsentence.

"News? I can't do news," he slurred as the startled Schonfeld began to backpedal. "Who wants news, anyway?" Turner's voice was now ricocheting off the rafters as a crowd began to gather. "Don't it make you sick, after watching all that news? Listen," he said, pausing to make sure none of the bystanders missed his punch line. "You know what my motto is? 'No news is good news.' "

Though Turner was almost certainly thinking about his own all-news service in 1977, he was not yet ready to discuss it openly. And Reese Schonfeld is convinced that his own persistent advocacy of an independent all-news network made a lasting impression on Ted Turner, all appearances to the contrary. "He was having a good laugh at my expense," Schonfeld explains, "but there's little doubt Turner was giving news his serious attention."

By now Schonfeld had become known as the "godfather of electronic news," and his ideas were beginning to attract attention throughout the media industry. Still at ITNA, Schonfeld drafted his own business plan for a start-up news operation and trooped the package around to venture capitalists and investment bankers. Despite the appeal of his ideas, however, the jury was still out on whether a cable television news service could actually turn a profit.

Enter Gerald Levin, the man who had put Home Box Office up on the bird. Levin didn't have to be sold on the potential of satellite distribution or cable. He was looking for a way to parlay Time Inc.'s strong name and immense editorial resources into electronic media and asked Schonfeld to work with him to develop a plan for a cable news channel, albeit an eight-hour service that could be repeated two or three times every twenty-four hours. Levin hired Schonfeld as a consultant, and the two were absolutely certain they had a winner. Their project died a-borning, however, when it was shelved in mid-1978 by Time Inc.'s board of directors, who were concerned that a cable news channel might somehow compromise HBO's own obviously lucrative potential.

Earlier that same year Scripps-Howard also began planning an all-news cable channel. So did Kay Graham's Washington Post Company. Both called Reese Schonfeld for his input but were slow to decide how they wanted to proceed. Joel Chaseman, head of Graham's Post-Newsweek television stations, was particularly anxious to repeat his success with all-news radio and was chafing at Mrs. Graham's hesitation. He tried to keep Schonfeld on the line, repeatedly promising that Reese would have a major role in anything the Washington Post Company did.

Admitting that he shelved any ideas he might have had about a news service until mid-1978, when threats to the Superstation's continued growth became real enough to get him thinking again, Turner now began exploring all-news in earnest.

One night before a Hawks game, he called a group of his top managers together for dinner at the Omni. He just wanted to bounce a few ideas around, he told them, get their input, and see what they should be doing next.

Bob Hope, the man who now handled Ted's own personal public relations, as well as promotion for the Braves and the Hawks, thought Ted might be planning a new all-sports network. That idea died when everybody realized it would kill the Superstation, which was now throwing off rapidly growing profits, if they ever had to find a replacement for the Braves and the Hawks.

Turner then suggested pulling the plug on WTCG's Atlanta over-the-air broadcast signal, making it the first major cable-only network. Too radical, the salespeople said. They'd lose half their national advertisers and all the station's local sponsors.

Turner kept throwing out ideas, his antennae tuned to pick up every response, sifting the reactions and then feeding the information into his cerebral data bank. One of his managers mentioned an all-music network that would play hit songs like the radio. Impractical. Who would ever watch music? An HBO clone was considered briefly, then discarded. With dinner almost over Turner then unveiled the real reason he had called everyone together that evening.

What about an all-news cable network? Hope and the others could hardly believe their ears. Was this the same man who was on record stating, "I hate the news. News is evil. It makes people

feel bad. I don't want anything to do with the news"? Bob Hope
suggests that Turner seemed serious but had a different slant on
the idea. "If we do the news on cable only and don't have a broadcast signal, the FCC can't tell us what we can and can't show,
right?" Right, his minions conceded dutifully.

"Then we can show the most gory murder, like when a man
kills his wife or girlfriend and chops her up in little bitty pieces
and puts her in the freezer, right?" Right, again, they chorused,
and began drifting away from the table, not at all sure what
Turner had up his sleeve this time, but dead certain they didn't
want to miss the start of the Hawks game.

Terry McGuirk remembers that first evening in 1978 and says
Turner never let up on the channel, even when he took the company's senior managers out sailing. Turner talked up the venture
whenever he went, to McGuirk, Will Sanders, Bob Hope, several
of his advertisers, even some of his ball players.

Turner estimated it would cost at least $20 million to get an all-
news operation off the ground. A sports service would have been
infinitely more difficult to budget, he contends, since broadcast
rights to some events could be open-ended. By the end of the
summer, however, Turner had done such an efficient job of selling
everyone else on the all-news idea that he now seemed to have
sold himself.

With so many others looking at a news project, Turner may
have felt time was running out. In December 1978 he and Mc-
Guirk went out to the Western Cable Television Convention to
present his plan to the cable industry. Turner made an impassioned pitch based on the importance of all news as a public
service and a drawing card for new cable subscribers. Then he
presented the cable operators with a virtually risk-free proposition: Turner would spend his own $20 million to put an all-news
channel on the air. The cable operators would then pay him $.20
a month per subscriber ($.15 if they took the Superstation as well)
once the service was up and running. A mere pittance, Turner
took pains to point out, compared to the immense value a news
service would add to their systems. When McGuirk circulated the
agreements they had brought with them, Turner was dumbfounded as the operators, to a man, smiled, stood up and filed out,
leaving him standing there alone with McGuirk and a pile of un-
signed documents.

It wasn't competitive pressure, however, but an expiring option
that helped make Turner's all-news network a reality. He had

conveniently acquired rights to the last available cable transponder on RCA's yet-to-be-launched satellite, SATCOM III, and was now under pressure to exercise his option or lose access to RCA's new bird.

Reese Schonfeld hadn't heard from Ted Turner since their embarrassing encounter at that cable convention in 1977. Turner had kept tabs on Schonfeld, however, and knew all about ITNA's new low-cost television service. Banking on Schonfeld's frustration at running what amounted to a nonprofit cooperative effort, he put in a call to New York. "Hey Reese!" he shouted. "You want to do this thing? Okay, then get down here and let's do it!"

Reese Schonfeld had committed himself to ITNA and happened to be in the midst of contract negotiations with ITNA's five station owners. He had also given his personal commitment to Joel Chaseman, whom he knew and liked, but feared might never be able to rally Kay Graham or her board to his all-news cause. Determined to realize his dream of an all-news network, and opportunistic enough to take the first real offer that came over the transom, Schonfeld hesitated just a beat or two before agreeing to meet with Turner in Atlanta.

"Ted planned to give me the whole treatment," he recalls. "Take me down to the plantation, bring on the broads, do everything he could to bring me on board." It was hardly necessary, since Schonfeld had worked all his life for the chance to build his own all-news operation. As soon as he hung up with Schonfeld, however, Ted Turner had placed two more fateful telephone calls —to Russel Karp, head of Teleprompter, then the largest cable company in the country, and to Gerry Levin of Time Inc. Turner offered both equal shares in his news project, provided they agreed to share the investment. Each listened respectfully and then declined to join what each assumed was a seriously underbudgeted $20 million boondoggle. He might need at least two or three times that much, and neither man was prepared to take that risk. Their quick turndowns would later cost each company several hundred million dollars in lost opportunity.

Ironically, Time Inc. would pass up another chance five years later to acquire half of CNN for $350 million. Nicholas J. Nicholas, the Time Inc. executive who turned this offer down, calls it "the single biggest mistake of my career." Levin, of course, as chief executive officer of Time-Warner, today controls approximately 19 percent of Turner Broadcasting, an investment that may now be worth as much as $1 billion.

Reese Schonfeld was already sold on the idea of throwing in his lot with Ted Turner, but he contained his enthusiasm as he stepped off the plane in Atlanta and let Turner whisk him over to a long lunch at the Stadium Club. How serious, Schonfeld wanted to know, was Turner, and what kind of commitment was he prepared to make to his all-news project?

"Anybody who thinks I'm not serious," Turner exclaimed, "just doesn't know me. Am I a miracle worker, or what? I bought the Hawks three years ago. I had, you know, just two days to make up my mind. They were moving out of town. I saved them."

Turner saves them all. He saved WTCG because he understood the future and was able to act on it. And WTCG, in turn, saved the Braves. "If it wasn't for Channel 17," Turner likes to remind anyone within earshot, "we wouldn't have a basketball team here in Atlanta. We wouldn't have a soccer team. And we might not even have a baseball team. When I do something, I try to do it the best way I know how and," he adds, resting his case, "I think my life has been a reflection of that."

Turner told Schonfeld he considered this new venture so important, he would even refrain from giving it his own name. He planned instead to call it the Cable News Network. Schonfeld's whole demeanor changes when he talks news. Turner understood the fire he could see in the other man's eyes. These two had more in common than either might have cared to admit. Both possessed towering egos and volatile tempers. Both were fiercely competitive, risk-taking opportunists, though Schonfeld was really risking only his reputation while Turner would be putting at least $20 million on the line. Each in his way was an impossible taskmaster, passionately loyal to those who stayed the course. Both were also exceptionally volatile personalities, subject to frequent, unpredictable mood swings. They were destined to travel a long, long way together over the next two and a half years. Yet Turner and Schonfeld would never really come to know each other any better than two strangers seated together on a crosstown bus.

Lunch dragged on into the late afternoon, but when Turner finally got around to the business at hand, the formalities didn't take long. Pulling out a single sheet of blue paper that would serve as their basic agreement, he said he was prepared to offer Schonfeld an initial two-year contract as Cable News Network's president and chief operating officer. Base salary would be $100,000, the highest Schonfeld had ever earned. Turner even sweetened the deal with a generous allocation of TBS stock options. Schonfeld talked about the problems they might have in attracting people to Atlanta. He mentioned that his wife, Pat O'Gorman, an experienced television editor, could handle that side of the operation. Then they began delving into each other's ideas on program formats. Schonfeld expressed serious concern about the integrity of the news product. He would have a free hand, Turner assured him, although it was apparent the two had somewhat different perspectives on how to build and keep an audience. Turner saw the format divided into news, sports, business, and soft news features, something like twenty-four hours of the "Today" show or "Good Morning, America."

"We've got to have more breaking news," Schonfeld asserted, "and a format that will let us go live whenever we can. We want to get to the news first, put it on the air while it's happening. We'll be the only ones in the world who can do that."

Turner appeared convinced. "Just keep me in the picture," he said, reassuring Schonfeld once again that he would have a free hand in developing CNN's organization and programming. He pushed the blue paper across the table, beaming as Schonfeld signed it on the spot. "Hey, Reese, let's do this thing!"

Turner finally had the man who could make his news project a reality, and it didn't matter now if the whole world knew about it. Waving the blue paper Schonfeld had signed, Turner trotted him around the Turner Broadcasting headquarters, shouting, "Y'all come meet Reese Schonfeld here. He's gonna be the president of CNN. And I'm gonna be the most powerful man in America!" Catching Schonfeld's eye, he decided he'd better add, "The two of us. We're both going to be the most powerful men in America." Schonfeld attempted a wan smile, but he was beginning to understand what Ted Turner was all about.

Anybody but a man like Reese Schonfeld might have had serious second thoughts as they climbed the steps together up to Turner's cramped second-floor office. "You've got to line up some names, quick," Turner explained. "We're going public with this thing at the National Cable Television Convention. In Las Vegas. In three weeks. And we'll need names, some big names." Now that CNN had a president, Turner expected the whole project would simply fall into place. "I'm going to have a press conference and we'll tell the whole world. We'll need names, Reese. Some big names. This time we're going to make it official. CNN will go on the air on June first, next year. Come hell or high water!"

Schonfeld looked around at all the sailing trophies, the model boats, and the framed pictures of Turner on his boats, in a Braves uniform, on a *Sports Illustrated* cover. He knew Turner was serious about the news project and believed he might even be serious about committing everything he had—Reese had heard he was worth more than $50 million—to see the idea through. But Turner hadn't even asked to look at the business plan Schonfeld brought with him. And the only discussion they'd had about a budget was Ted's directive that development costs be kept under $20 million. Okay, Schonfeld thought, I can play that way. After all, I've been shooting from the hip most of my life, performing minor miracles in the news business on shoestring budgets, always keeping one jump ahead of the demanding people who signed the checks. But here was Turner, telling him they were going public with CNN in just three weeks. And then announcing that he was going sailing. That afternoon. Leaving Schonfeld to get CNN on the air in twelve months.

"We need names," Schonfeld shouted into the telephone once he was back in his New York office. His first call had been to his old friend Burt Reinhardt, who was working on the development of home video products for Paramount Pictures. "We need names, Burt. And by the way, I need you." Within the week Reinhardt had signed on as CNN's new operations manager. Then Schonfeld went after two other veterans of "alternative" news, Ed Turner and Ted Kavanau. Both men listened attentively as Schonfeld described the situation and then responded simultaneously. Forget CNN, they said. They both wanted the job he would be vacating at ITNA.

When Schonfeld heard Dan Rather was unhappy over Walter Cronkite's apparently endless valedictory at CBS, he bounced the idea off Turner. "I think we can get Rather for $1 million a year plus stock and the chance to build our network around him," Schonfeld speculated.

"Who's Dan Rather?" Turner replied with a straight face.

Working his Rolodex hard, Schonfeld decided to go after Douglas Edwards. Then David Frost. Even Geraldo Rivera, whose favorable response was enough to give Schonfeld second thoughts. Meanwhile Turner had forged ahead on his own and approached Cronkite himself, whom he knew from his America's Cup forays. Television's most respected newsman responded with consum-

mate civility, saying he would love to go sailing with Ted, anytime. Then Schonfeld hit on a terrific idea.

Daniel Schorr was a three-time Emmy Award–winning newsman and former member of Ed Murrow's famed CBS news team.
Schonfeld knew him from occasional free-lance assignments they
had worked on together. He was pleased that Turner seemed to
recognize Schorr's name and agreed to see if he could persuade
the legendary journalist to join them at the cable show in Vegas.
Schorr, who was teaching at UCLA, said he knew nothing at all
about cable and even less about Ted Turner. He was headed west
on a lecture date, however, and agreed to stop off on his way to
meet Turner and hear about his new Cable News Network.

"I only knew what I'd read in *Time* magazine," Schorr recalls.
"But I had been told that one of the things Turner did was a kind
of lampoon of the news in the middle of the night. So naturally I
was a little bothered about why Reese would think I might want
to join this guy's operation." It was with some misgiving that Dan
Schorr walked into the hotel suite in Las Vegas, only to be met by
an effusive, utterly gracious Ted Turner. Caught off guard, Schorr
quickly saw that Turner, despite his gestures of hospitality, was
in a desperate state. Downstairs in the ballroom twelve hundred
cable operators were waiting anxiously to see whether Turner
could deliver on all the hype he had been putting behind CNN.
Upstairs Turner Broadcasting personnel were working the corridors like political professionals, buttonholing key delegates, securing commitments from as many operators as they could,
aware that Turner's four o'clock press conference was now less
than an hour away.

"I started in asking a lot of questions, naturally," Schorr says,
looking back on the experience with a sense of irony. "It was
obvious Turner wanted to hire me, but he hadn't given even the
slightest thought to any of the details. Would I have to read commercials? Would I have a free hand in making editorial judg-
ments? What kind of backup support would I have?" Turner was
a moving target, pacing back and forth like a caged tiger. He
would dart into one of the adjoining rooms for a momentary conference and then reappear and resume his pacing. Schorr looked
over at Schonfeld, who was sitting in the corner, nervously drum-
ming his fingers on a table. Schorr wasn't used to not getting
answers, and he felt his own temper beginning a slow boil. In a
career that spanned over forty years, Dan Schorr had earned a
reputation as one of the toughest reporters in the business. He

was a veteran of Watergate, the State Department, and the White House. He was on Nixon's "enemies list." He'd been arrested by the KGB and thrown out of Russia for defying Soviet censorship. But never in his life had Schorr seen anything like Ted Turner. "This guy was wound up, really wound up. He never stopped moving. He had a feral, animallike quality. He was never not in motion. And he was distracted, only half there. Lots of phone calls, lots of ducking in and out of the suite. He obviously had an awful lot of balls in the air."

Finally Turner stopped dodging the bullet. He wheeled around, threw his hands up in the air, and blurted out, "Look, I have a press conference in less than twenty minutes and I'm going to announce the start of the Cable News Network next June first. If you will appear with me, if you want to work with me, let's sign something. Anything!"

Dan Schorr had just turned sixty-three. Finally settled into a new house in Washington, he was looking forward to spending time with his young wife and children, something he never really had time to do when he was at CBS. Like Turner, he was a born contrarian, but without Turner's finely developed sense of the absurd. Schorr could feel the old urge to break new ground, to challenge the system, surfacing once again. But he wasn't really sure why he was even sitting there, he would later recall, listening to a man who appeared to be in an advanced state of lunacy. "Then Turner started shouting," Schorr remembers. "He said he would pay a lot of money, a very substantial amount of money. Just for the use of my name."

In 1976 Schorr had resigned from CBS when the network failed to support him in an historic confrontation over freedom of the press. He had refused to reveal his sources at the CIA in the Pentagon papers case. Cited for perjury, Schorr stood his ground and won. "I absolutely will not do anything I don't want to do," he told Turner. "Nothing I feel might compromise my professional standards." He looked Turner straight in the eye, fully expecting him to blink.

"Write that down and I'll sign it," Turner exclaimed, shoving a piece of hotel stationery into Schorr's hand.

"I wrote my own protection into the agreement right there, in my own hand," Schorr says. "I have never before or since had that kind of protection in any contract I've ever signed. Of course, when Turner's lawyers saw what he'd agreed to, they were pretty upset. And that clause, which as far as I know is unique in the annals of broadcasting, probably cost me in the long run. But it gave me complete editorial control. I became CNN's first editorial employee, with an ironclad, five-year contract. Probably the tightest anybody had ever seen. Just so Ted could go ahead with that press conference.

"When Turner signed that agreement with me," Schorr continues, "there was no CNN, no structure, no organization, no office, no anything. This guy had the reputation of a buccaneer, but later on I came to understand that he was really serious about doing something worthwhile. He was very, very different from the kinds of professionals I was used to at CBS. But now that there's some distance between us, I can say with conviction that Ted Turner is very probably the closest thing there is to Bill Paley today.

"Paley, of course, had three great qualities—a knowledge of programming, superb entrepreneurial skills, and an awareness of where the communications business in his day was headed. Turner has that same kind of programming sense. He's also a terrific entrepreneur, maybe even better than Paley. And he understands cable and its potential. I could see that he was starting to do in 1980 what Bill Paley had done fifty years earlier. And frankly, I was happy to be along for the ride."

An incandescent Ted Turner waltzed around that hotel suite for several minutes before scooping up Schorr and Schonfeld and sweeping downstairs to meet the press. There were no blondes on his arm this time. Instead he was flanked by Dan Schorr, CNN's new senior Washington correspondent, and the network's newly minted president, the redoubtable Reese Schonfeld. Turner was two feet off the ground as he stood before the packed room, grinning like a young buck at his first debutante ball. After introducing his two colleagues, he began to waffle on and on about some of the "names" Schonfeld had brought into the fold, commentators like Roland Evans and Robert Novak, astrologer Jean Dixon, pop psychologist Joyce Brothers, medical columnist Neil Solomon, and a host of other lesser lights. Schorr winced noticeably, but Turner rushed right on. The June 1 launch date? Absolutely goddamn firm! Turner reiterated. And what would CNN actually look like? Mr. Schonfeld will answer that question, thank you very much."

That was on May 21, 1979, and with a little more than eleven months before sign-on, Ted Turner's Cable News Network was anything but real. Turner knew he could not afford to have any doubts if this idea was going to work. He also knew that he would

have to carry it forward with his own momentum. Full speed
ahead. He was on the threshold of hitting it big, bigger than he
had ever dreamed he might. But with the 1979 summer ocean-
racing season about to begin, he had to hope he'd picked the right
man in Reese Schonfeld to make it all happen.

"It wasn't just the money. It wasn't even his conviction. I was
convinced Ted was really ready to roll the dice," Schonfeld says
today. "It was also the fact that he was willing to lose everything
—his television stations, his sports teams, his plantation, his
yachts, everything—if Cable News Network didn't work. By personally guaranteeing every nickel he would need to get CNN off
the ground, Turner clearly stood to lose a lot. As if he still had
something to prove," Schonfeld avers. "As if he still needed some
justification for having made all that money."

"Reese walked around forever with his idea for an all-news
channel," recalls anchorman Dave Walker, who with his wife,
Lois Hart, would soon inaugurate CNN. "But he hit pay dirt when
he ran into Ted Turner. There had been talk for some time about
Ted's running for president, and I think that could have been a
big factor in Ted's decision finally to get into the news business.
We had heard he was approached about the Senate, either from
Georgia or South Carolina, where he has his plantations." But the
Senate was not the White House, and once CNN was off the
ground, Turner would begin to raise his sights.

Turner wasn't thinking politics, however, as he headed back up
to Newport in August 1979. He had some serious sailing still
ahead of him during the late summer and would be out on the
ocean again in the spring. The 1980s America's Cup Trials would
begin, coincidentally, on June 2nd, the day after he had committed to launch CNN, and he was determined to attempt a repeat
victory with *Courageous*. Turner would surface from time to time
during the next several months, making certain that visible progress on the news channel was being made, and then disappear out
to sea again. Reese Schonfeld had the mountainous task of building Cable News Network from the ground up, in just eleven
months.

Les Brown, then television editor of *The New York Times*, had
been in Las Vegas for Turner's press conference. "Once he actually announced CNN," Brown says, "we invited him into the
Times for lunch to meet the editors." Turner showed up fifteen
minutes late, with Schonfeld in tow and immediately went on the
offensive.

"Who the hell set this up, Reese? I want him fired," Turner began, ignoring the assembled *Times* editors.

"Ted Turner came in there very, very manic," Brown recounts. "Almost out of control. We chalked it up to eccentricity. He was trying to break into the big leagues in the news business, and I guess we threw some pretty tough questions at him. He got very defensive. He says things that would destroy anybody else. But he comes on so strong that there's not much you can do but just sit back and wait for him to finish."

The *Times* editors probed the extent of Turner's commitment to his all-news channel and then, turning on Schonfeld, questioned the benefit of live, unedited news coverage. Won't you find yourself forced to chase a lot of ambulances and cover a lot of two-alarm fires? they asked. "Yes," admitted the new president of Cable News Network. "But if we don't, we'll never know which two-alarm fire will be the one that burns down Chicago."

"Awwriiight!" exclaimed Turner, ending the luncheon, now certain he had once again picked the right man for the job.

By late summer Reese Schonfeld had moved into high gear. In addition to Burt Reinhardt, now on board as his backup and overall operations manager, Schonfeld signed up Ted Kavanau, as CNN's senior producer. A legend among television newsmen, Mad Dog Kavanau had established himself as one of the most aggressive production executives in television. Known to carry a small revolver strapped to his ankle, Kavanau was sometimes too aggressive but would stop at nothing to get a story. He was reputed to have once held a union official out an office window by his ankles until he admitted he was behind a shake-down of station personnel. Kavanau had been fired from virtually every important position he'd ever held but one—he quit as news director of KTVU in Oakland, California, when he was pressured against his better judgment into firing someone else. Kavanau was considered a monumental liability by most broadcast companies. He was also considered one of the best newsmen in the business. And he would walk across hot coals for his old friend Reese Schonfeld.

The CNN senior management team was now set: Schonfeld, Reinhardt, and Kavanau, three renegades from independent television. News junkies all, but not one of them burdened with five-year plans, quarterly earnings reports, or $100,000 market studies —the kind of corporate baggage that could sink a start-up operation like CNN. Schonfeld and Co. were setting out together to return the television news business to what it used to be thirty years earlier, propelling themselves at the same time straight into the twenty-first century. It wasn't long before they were dubbed Reese's Pieces, a term that stuck and would later come to include most of CNN's rapidly expanding young management team.

Setting up shop in an old abandoned white-columned bawdy house at 1044 West Peachtree, across the street from the concrete bunker that served as headquarters for Turner Broadcasting, Schonfeld began reviewing the hundreds of résumés and personnel reels that had been flooding in ever since the CNN press conference in Las Vegas.

Schonfeld led a raid on his old ITNA, where he found Jane Maxwell and Rick Brown, two resourceful young practitioners of his low-rent approach to the news business. Next Schonfeld and Sam Zelman, a retired CBS news executive, hit the networks. They picked off ABC's George Watson, an experienced Washington bureau chief who signed on at $100,000 a year, and promptly became CNN's highest-paid editorial employee.

Schonfeld made a pass at CBS anchorman Douglas Edwards, offering him a reported $250,000 a year to make the jump to CNN, but lost out when CBS matched his bid and gave Edwards a new five-year contract. Schonfeld was successful, however, in signing Jim Kitchell, an NBC News veteran, who had directed everything from Huntley-Brinkley to the Olympics, the Kennedy assassination, the *Apollo* moon landing, and countless national political conventions. Kitchell had been enticed on board with the title of senior vice-president of operations. Another NBC veteran, Bill MacPhail, signed on as CNN's new sports director. A handful of seasoned professionals with several lifetimes of experience, tossing their hats into the ring without any idea how Ted Turner could come even close to meeting his June 1 launch date or avoid bankrupting himself if he were ever unlucky enough to get CNN on the air.

Nothing, however, was going to stop him. Turner seduced his old Savannah friend and sailing companion, Bunky Helfrich, into supervising the design and construction of CNN's new headquarters. With neither time nor money enough to consider building anything from scratch, he dragged Helfrich and Schonfeld all over Atlanta, combing the town for an appropriate site they could make over inside the six months still left before sign-on.

After they had seen several broken-down hotels and a couple of decrepit old office buildings, the winds of fortune suddenly shifted in Turner's favor once again. They were blowing, in fact, down a little rise not more than a few thousand yards east of his existing Superstation studio. Straight toward twenty-one acres of rolling greensward, hard by the Georgia Tech campus. These attractively landscaped grounds along Techwood Drive once housed the Progressive Country Club, a "social and athletic institution organized," says a past president, "to take the Jewish boy off Atlanta's streets." Built in 1938 to resemble a poor man's Tara, the club's three-story red-brick headquarters came replete with Doric columns and a long, wide drive that led up to the front portico. The place had been home for the last several years to a tribe of itinerant drifters who had taken up residence in the Progressive's old men's locker room.

When he was told that the little rise just behind the crumbling old clubhouse was reputed to have been the scene of the last Confederate stand against General Sherman as he marched into Atlanta, Turner determined to close the deal on the spot, settling on a purchase price of only $4.2 million.

Reese Schonfeld's dream of an all-news operation was built around something he called an "open newsroom." The idea had been playing in his head for years, but now he found himself having difficulty communicating the concept to Helfrich and his associate, Michael Briles. He saw the space, he said, more like a 1930s newspaper city room than a television studio. He imagined the whole business exposed—the announcers, the director, the cameras, even the writers and editors handling the stories. Schonfeld desperately wanted the viewer to become involved in the process, to understand and feel the immediacy of what live news was all about. Impossible, he was told by experts who said the ambient noise would be intolerable, the lighting necessary to light up such a set would fry everybody to a crisp, the visual confusion of several dozen people on screen simultaneously enough to send viewers reaching for their dials.

Almost ready to concede that what he wanted might, in fact, be unworkable, Schonfeld heard about an out-of-the-way station up in Vancouver that boasted what appeared to be the only operational open-plan television newsroom in North America. With Bunky Helfrich in tow, Schonfeld headed for Vancouver, pronto.

The trip came close to being the last either man would ever make for CNN. After a long plane ride from Atlanta they walked into the Vancouver studio, only to be met by an anxious young receptionist who told Schonfeld he must call Atlanta immediately. Apparently, one of the Canadians told them, Ted Turner had been lost at sea, off Fastnet, during a race off the coast of Ireland. It was the worst disaster in yachting history. When Dee Woods confirmed the tragic news, Schonfeld could not believe his ears. Dumbfounded, he looked at Helfrich, who had been staring at one of the BBC monitors in the reception area. Without Turner CNN would never happen. It was his money, his momentum, but most of all his commitment that had given life to Schonfeld's dream. Schonfeld was completely devastated; Helfrich no less so. Standing in the center of the little broadcast studio, the two men began slowly to collect themselves, trying to make some sense out of an utterly incoherent situation. Their Canadian hosts understood and gently tried to console them. Suddenly Helfrich let out a shout of recognition. There was Turner, dockside in Plymouth, England, his unmistakable gap-toothed grin flashing across a row of studio monitors as he was interviewed by the BBC. Ted Turner appeared very, very much alive. And so, too, was Reese Schonfeld's dream, as well as his newly reconfirmed faith in the power of live television.

Bunky Helfrich had seen enough of the Vancouver studio to understand Schonfeld's concept of a total news environment and he went straight to work drafting a physical plan that would involve the viewers by drawing them into the complex activities of the newsroom without overwhelming the news itself. Turner liked the idea and, once he saw Helfrich's plans, gave his immediate approval for the open-plan newsroom. CNN, however, would not be on the main floor, as Schonfeld had envisioned. That was to be reserved for the money-making Superstation. CNN would fit nicely down in the basement, Turner suggested, but would still look "as good as anything at Black Rock."

Schonfeld estimated that it would take at least $30 million to get CNN on the air and through the first twelve months of operation. Few others in the industry believed that even twice that amount would be sufficient, but since CNN was sailing into uncharted waters, no one, not even Schonfeld or Turner, could possibly say with any certainty what an all-news network might actually cost. Turner made much about the high-risk game he was playing. In fact, he had sold his Charlotte television station, WRET-TV, to Westinghouse for $20 million cash, a very handsome profit over the less than $1 million he'd dug out of his own pocket to pay ten years earlier. Will Sanders had been able to float an additional $20 million line of credit with First National Bank of Chicago, although the bank required Ted's real estate and

other personal assets, including his remaining cache of Krugerrands, as collateral. The risks of launching CNN were well within
the means of an entrepreneur like Ted Turner since he signed all
the checks and could decide when and if he ever wanted to fold
his hand. "There is risk," he liked to say, "in everything you do.
The sky could fall, the roof cave in. Who knows what's going to
happen? I'm going to do news like the world has never seen news
done before." But with a personal fortune now approaching $100
million, Turner obviously considered the risk manageable. More
surprising, perhaps even to Turner, was the hesitation of so many
larger media companies, most with ten times the financial resources of Turner Broadcasting, which decided to remain on the
sidelines and let somebody else prove how lucrative an all-news
operation could be.

On December 10, 1979, however, just when everything else
seemed to be falling neatly into place, Turner saw the risk he had
assumed was not entirely financial. On a clear, cold winter morning off Cape Canaveral, RCA launched SATCOM III, the communications satellite intended to be the new prime carrier of cable
television programming, including Turner's Cable News Network. Four days later, RCA engineers suddenly lost the tracking
beacon on their new satellite. "We are searching the heavens,"
RCA vice-president Robert Shortal told the media. "Other companies with satellites are searching the heavens. The U.S. Air
Force is searching the heavens. We honestly don't know what
happened. It could have descended into some weird orbit and we
can't find it. Or for all we know, it's on its way to Mars."

Ted Turner was in Anaheim, California, at the Western Cable
Television Convention when he heard about the satellite's disappearance. He was about to announce CNN's first advertiser, Bris-
tol-Myers, a breakthrough $25 million account. Turner knew that
his contract with RCA provided for a backup transponder and he
wasn't about to let anything jeopardize this major advertising
coup. He was also about to give Reese Schonfeld an object lesson
in momentum theory. Without missing a beat, Schonfeld says,
Turner told him to carry on. Everything would work itself out, he
said, once he got back to Atlanta.

Instead, things started unraveling rather rapidly. Turner discovered that RCA had made similar backup commitments to five
other new cable programmers but had only two available transponders on their backup satellite. He was enraged and flew with
Schonfeld, Reinhardt, and Tench Coxe to confront the RCA exec-

utives at their New York corporate headquarters. Turner demanded to meet with RCA's chairman and for the better part of an afternoon, rocketed around RCA's legal library in Rockefeller Center, demanding, cajoling, insisting, threatening, and ultimately intimidating the corporate types sufficiently to draw Andrew Inglis, president of RCA's Americom satellite subsidiary, into the fray. Inglis tried to explain his company's predicament, arguing that Turner's backup guarantee was exercisable only in the event of a successful launch. He suggested that Turner could sue RCA. If the courts agreed the backup clause was binding, Inglis agreed RCA would have little choice but to award one of the two precious backup transponders to Cable News Network.

"Turner called us all into his office when he got back," recalls Ted Kavanau, "and we figured it was all over. He is a terrific fighter, but he knew this time he was really backed into a corner. With everything on the line, he brought us over there to tell us he wasn't giving up. We all filed into his office half expecting some kind of funeral oration, and there he was, strutting around, pounding his fist, and telling us not to give up the fight. He made it seem almost like a crusade, only the enemy wasn't RCA. It was the networks. He was waving this huge broadsword he kept in his office, swinging it around over his head, shouting, 'We will not be stopped! No matter what it costs, we're going on!' After that there wasn't one of us in that room who wouldn't lie down and die for the guy."

It took nearly sixty days, but on March 5, 1980, U.S. District Court Judge Ernest Tidwell in Atlanta issued a preliminary consent decree, giving Turner his critical backup. "This order puts us back on the satellite," Turner told a hastily assembled press conference convened amid the piles of bricks and plasterboard at the half-completed Techwood Drive facility. "I am absolutely confident that once up there, we'll stay up there. I think the people of America need this in-depth news service, and I'm willing to risk everything I have to provide that service, come hell or high water. I said we'll sign on June first, and we will sign on June first," he admonished the small group of reporters standing around in bright yellow hardhats. "We won't sign off until the end of the world—and we'll cover that live!"

Turner didn't bother to tell the press he had won the day in court and gotten CNN back up on the satellite by brazenly claiming a conspiracy, accusing RCA of attempting to keep his all-news network off the air to protect its NBC subsidiary. He also neglected to mention that the court had awarded him only a preliminary decree, stipulating that "in no event shall Turner's right to retain use of the transponder extend beyond December 1, 1980." As part of the consent order, Turner had also been required to drop his demands for financial damages in his suit against RCA, an amount Turner claimed now exceeded $34 million.

Determined to create a state-of-the-art news operation but still blissfully unaware of what that might actually mean in terms of dollars and cents, Reese Schonfeld planned to capitalize on new technology by abandoning the traditional one-inch "broadcast quality" videotape system in favor of more portable and infinitely cheaper new three-quarter-inch equipment. He also envisioned the world's first paperless, computer-driven news operation, with each of the network's various functions tied together in one contiguous cybernetic network. Of course, no such system yet existed, anywhere.

A few months earlier Schonfeld had met two young computer whizzes, Peter Kolstad and Ed Grudzian, who had built a little California software business called BASYS around a computer system they developed for all-news radio. Schonfeld gathered them under his wing, and the two young engineers were now ensconced in the bowels of the old white house in Atlanta, creating the same kind of system for CNN.

Along with nearly one hundred new employees, tons of equipment began arriving almost daily at the new Techwood studios, only to be left crated in the middle of the new concrete floors poured over the old Progressive Club's once lavish ballroom. Each week the contractors were falling farther behind schedule while still promising to have the place finished by sign-on. A Caterpillar tractor had already filled in the old swimming pool, on top of which were now planted six shiny new ten-meter satellite earth stations, the largest such nonmilitary array in the country. The old stone fountain out front still didn't work and wouldn't for at least another year. But Techwood Drive was coming together fast enough for some of the newer staff to begin referring to the place, affectionately, as Kosher Kolumns. This precipitated an almost instant response from Turner, who issued his first official CNN staff memo insisting on the term *headquarters*, effective immediately. Or else.

"There was no precedent for this kind of building," Bunky Helfrich points out, "simply because technology in the broadcast field was advancing so quickly. While we were still upstairs build-

ing, they were downstairs in the basement beginning rehearsals."
Technology notwithstanding, Helfrich had neglected to include
any rest rooms in the CNN floor plan, and the proud people who
were to make history on June 1 were forced to resort to the dozen
or so Porta-John units that were hastily installed out back.

With his master plan finally beginning to take shape, Bunky
Helfrich found himself forced to walk off the job, leaving his partner, Mike Briles, to see Techwood through to the finish. Helfrich
had a pressing engagement with Turner and the rest of the *Courageous* crew in Newport. The America's Cup trials were less than
a month away, and they had yet to put their boat in the water.
"CNN was basically a three-year project," Briles noted, "done in
less than eleven months." Who else, Schonfeld wondered, would
be imaginative, industrious, and insane enough to have accepted
this challenge? On a budget that was laughable. And in Atlanta,
Georgia, for crissakes!

Now when Ted Turner walked into the Dallas Convention Center in late May and took his seat at the 1980 National Cable
Television Association's annual meeting he was greeted with a
five-minute standing ovation. His Superstation had already elevated the industry above a limited pay service. Now Turner was
about to provide a genuine cable-exclusive programming service
to rival, he said, anything the networks might deliver. The mood
within the industry had clearly changed from skepticism to supercharged excitement. The real excitement, however, was playing
right out there on the convention floor. Splashed across four huge
CNN monitors was a continuous feed from Atlanta of the Cable
News Network live, in dress rehearsal.

"We think it will fly," pronounced cable pioneer Irving Kahn,
president of Broadband Communications. "Cable operators will
make room for it. This kind of programming will give a big boost
to the industry."

"There's little question there will be an audience for CNN,"
confirmed Paul Kagan, one of the industry's most highly regarded
analysts. "All Turner has to do now is get it on the air. And once
it's on, it will be very hard for anybody to drop the news. They
will expand channel capacity before they drop CNN."

System owners crowded around the CNN display, gleefully
mugging for cameras with Turner as they signed up for CNN.
Warner Communications and a few of the other large MSOs saw
CNN as a threat to their own programming plans, but William
Pitney, senior vice-president of Atlanta's Cox Broadcasting, the

first cable system to contract for CNN, spoke for a majority of those hovering around Turner in Dallas. "You hear a lot about him," Pitney acknowledged. "He's a maverick, he's outspoken, and all that. But he generally accomplishes what he sets out to do. In our book, he's a winner."

Turner boldly predicted, somewhat optimistically, that CNN would reach more than 2.5 million cable households at launch. "The largest opening paid circulation of any service since the beginning of the cable industry," he announced proudly. "I am the right man, in the right place, at the right time. Not me alone, but all the people who think the world can be brought together by telecommunications."

The only skeptics left in the convention hall when Turner had finished seemed to be potential competitors, companies like the Washington Post Company and Time Inc., which had looked into all-news television and rejected the idea as unfeasible. The Post's J. Christopher Burns's comments revealed his company's anxieties. "Turner is trying too hard," Burns suggested, blissfully unaware of the irony of his remarks, "to produce a conventional newscast. There is little question he will be judged unfavorably when he is compared to the network products. The way for Turner to make CNN work is for him to do the show he really wants to do—a spontaneous, personal, interesting news show. It will get flagellated in the press," Burns predicted, "but it will be popular. I think the way to make it work is for Ted Turner to anchor the evening news himself."

That idea might have appealed to Turner back in the days of his Sunday morning stints on WTCG. But working with news professionals like Schonfeld and Schorr, Ted Turner had come to intuit, if not fully understand, the importance and the responsibility of the public trust he was assuming with CNN. "By the end of our first month," Turner promised, "we'll have over three million viewers—that's more than the circulation of *The New York Times*, the *Chicago Tribune*, and *The Washington Post* put together." A little overwhelmed with the immense potential of his undertaking, Turner puffed himself up and proclaimed that "CNN will be one of the truly great accomplishments in the history of communications." Not many who were with him in Dallas were prepared to argue the point.

Sometime in the early spring, however, with CNN's launch less than ninety days away, it dawned on Reese Schonfeld that the gradually expanding budget he had been working from for almost a year would fall far short of providing enough technical and production personnel to keep his around-the-clock news operation on the air twenty-four hours a day. Even a nonunion shop, Schonfeld admitted, couldn't make people work more than fourteen or fifteen hours at a stretch. Schonfeld figured he may have underbudgeted by as many as a hundred people.

Necessity, the mother of so many other diabolical ideas, smiled on Reese Schonfeld one bright spring morning and showed him how he could afford most of the people he needed: simply fold several jobs into one, creating a kind of one-man television band —cameraman/soundman/writer/producer—and give the job a snappy new title, something like "video journalist" or "veejay."

Pat O'Gorman and a handful of other CNN worthies fanned out across the nation's campuses, offering graduating journalism students this chance of a lifetime, at $3.50 an hour. Nearly one hundred wildly enthusiastic, totally inexperienced young collegians soon descended on Atlanta to be converted by Ted Kavanau and Jim Kitchell into overnight videojournalists. "We aren't just starting up a new network," an exhausted Kavanau told *The Wall Street Journal* after one particularly grueling eighteen-hour training session. "We're running a television school, too. And we have less than sixty days to turn those people into broadcast professionals.

"We threw those kids into hotels and motels," Kavanau remembers. "Reese even thought about buying a place we could convert into a veejay dorm. We stashed them in places like the Rodeway, the Admiral Benbow, and Master Host. This is the big untold story of CNN. With less than two months to sign on, we brought these kids into Atlanta and started teaching them how to use the equipment, just so we could get on the air. We had an army of college kids on our hands. But it was beginning to look like the whole project would depend on them." Classes at CNN College were about to begin and would last less than six weeks. Graduation day was June 1. Guaranteed.

"That early crop of veejays," recalls Fran Heaney, CNN's first graphics director, "were some of the most beautiful kids you'd ever see, anywhere. They were just gorgeous people. The girls were pretty. The guys all handsome. They were all adrenaline junkies, just like the rest of us.

"It was just like a 'news kibbutz,' " Heaney says, "with all these young people thrown together. They would end up working fourteen, sixteen hours a day, and then they all just moved over to one of the motels and stayed up all night drinking, screwing, laying out lines of coke, and snorting together. It all got pretty wild. All these news maniacs living so intensely. It was such a scene," adds Heaney, "that Hollywood has now got hold of the story. There's a producer, Sandy Perlman, who's putting together a movie about the veejays, a kind of *Breakfast Club* Meets *M*A*S*H*, that sort of thing. Some of those kids brought marijuana into CNN and sold pot all over the place. It was the start, I guess, of the go-go 1980s, at least for Atlanta."

James Christy was a typical veejay. He had been studying film part-time at New York University, selling insurance in his free time to pay tuition. When Pat O'Gorman showed up in Washington Square, her pitch was irresistible. Figuring he'd never have a better chance to break into television, Christy left immediately for Atlanta. Six weeks later he found himself manning a camera on the set with Don Farmer and Chris Curle, two of CNN's early anchors.

Chris Pula gave up waiting on tables to become a veejay. Now a senior executive at New Line Films, Pula says, "CNN was probably the best job I've ever had. Also one of the toughest. I think we redefined what 'deadline pressure' was all about. We had so much to learn. All that equipment, the computers, what the news business was all about. When we started, there was no tape file, nothing anybody could draw upon. So the veejays had to come up with graphics all the time, sometimes twenty or thirty each hour. Versus maybe five or six on the 'CBS Evening News.' The networks took all day to put together five or six graphics. We had less than an hour to get ready for the next hour's twenty or thirty. We had state-of-the-art equipment. All you had to do was learn how to use it.

"We got good real quick," Pula says, "and when the Grass Valley people or the Adda people, the ones who manufactured our computer graphics equipment, started bringing people from the networks down to see what we were doing, you felt pretty good. We made plenty of mistakes in those early days and I remember thinking, I'll never learn all this. Then, a year later, I would have ten graphics to do and look up at the clock and see that it was two minutes to the top of the hour and say, 'God, I can go out and get a cup of coffee. I've got two whole minutes.' "

"No matter how difficult it seems," Professor Kavanau told his charges, "you're going to make mistakes. But remember, you'll also be making history. You people will be in the textbooks. We're setting the standard," he said, sounding just a little bit like Ted Turner. "We're running a graduate school, a twenty-four-hour news service, and an electronic experiment. All at the same time."

Mad Dog Kavanau delivered the valedictory two days before sign-on and sent his veejays out to do battle with the invisible forces of A. C. Nielsen. "We're not going to be the Cronkite news —a beautiful package that takes twelve hours to prepare," he told his charges. "But we will keep the show interesting. We'll tell the viewer what we're going to do, and then we'll show him the re- porter in action. But listen up, people," Kavanau warned. "We will have absolutely rigid standards of journalism. There will be no ad-libbing, no editorializing, nothing anywhere that's going to debase our product." Looking out over his young troops, Kavanau could see that many of the veejays were dangerously close to physical exhaustion, and CNN had not even gone on the air. "We're tight," Kavanau told *The Wall Street Journal*, "but you have to maximize your people and keep the metabolism high."

Turner had been caught off guard that spring when the sale of his Charlotte television station to Westinghouse had been blocked by the challenge of a group of local black activists. Hank Aaron, now a director of Turner Broadcasting, helped resolve this difficult situation by arranging for the Reverend James Barnett, leader of the protest group, to be retained as consultant for the company's affirmative action program. Turner also agreed to donate nearly $500,000 to Johnson C. Smith University in Charlotte. The $20 million Turner needed for CNN's launch came through when the sale was finally concluded a few days before sign-on.

Turner knew he should be in Newport with *Courageous*, but as the countdown to CNN's launch began, he found himself spending most of his time in Atlanta. A month-long baseball players' strike allowed him to devote nearly all of his time to CNN, where he watched the network's dry runs well into the late evening hours. On a midnight stroll around CNN's new chrome, glass, and suede studio, Turner stopped next to the site of the Progressive's old swimming pool. Sweeping his hand toward the six large satellite dishes now planted there, he told John Huey of *The Wall Street Journal*, "When I was a kid, I was really upset that there weren't any more new worlds left to discover." Pausing to tuck a handful of chewing tobacco into his cheek, Turner stared up at the stars, and continued. "But this world is better than anything Captain

Cook ever dreamed of. I'm so proud of all this, I can't stand it."
Directing a well-aimed stream of tobacco into his little Dixie
paper cup, he began to reveal to Huey a glimpse of the whirling
dervish that is Turner's truest self. "I've got at least five lives to
lead," he proclaimed. "I've got so many lives to lead, there just
isn't enough time to do it all. That's why I work so hard and spend
so much time on my business. I've got so much to do I can't
believe it. But, damn, it's all so much fun!"

Workmen were still putting a last-minute coat of paint on the
old Progressive Club on the humid Sunday afternoon of June 1,
1980, as more than seven hundred invited guests began gathering
on the newly sodded lawn outside Ted Turner's Tara on Techwood. The atmosphere was down home, relaxed, almost like a big
southern family wedding, with lots of hugging and cheek kissing
and back slapping, despite the fact that nearly half of those in
attendance appeared to be working press. Turner himself arrived
early, just after one o'clock, and came in talking nonstop, swaggering around the frantic newsroom with his hands stuffed in his
pockets. He had attracted an unusually eclectic crowd that fine
afternoon, including NFL commissioner Pete Rozelle, Congressman Wyche Fowler, Dr. Joyce Brothers, and Phyllis Schlaffly,
along with a mixed bag of local celebrities, politicians, television
executives, and advertisers. Diplomats and broadcast officials
from several foreign governments mingled with a slew of Turner
Broadcasting managers and their families. Jane Turner and the
kids were there, of course, but she just smiled and kept to herself
most of the afternoon. This was Ted's show, and she had long
since learned how to play hostess without taking any of the spotlight away from her husband.

"Ted considers himself a devoted husband and father," Jane
told a man from *Time* magazine, "but we are probably the ones
who are paying the real price of his ambition."

Nothing could diminish the excitement, however, as the big
moment drew near. Half a dozen tables of food and drink had
been laid out under a huge yellow and white tent. Some of the
more adventurous guests wandered around the newly landscaped
grounds, gawking at the gleaming white satellite dishes out back
and marveling at the physical transformation Turner had effected
on the old Progressive Club. A dead squirrel was floating on the
fountain out front, but most of the locals were too impressed with
the handful of celebrities Turner managed to attract to notice.
Four military bands, representing each of the individual service

branches, kept things lively. There was even a crew from Turner's Superstation covering the event live, with Turner's favorite on-air personality, Bill Tush, serving as master of ceremonies.

Down inside the bowels of the old Progressive Club itself, the atmosphere was considerably less relaxed. Nearly a hundred haggard individuals were bouncing off each other like balls in a huge, high-tech pinball machine. The tension was almost unbearable. They knew the countdown had begun. In just a few moments they would be expected to make television history. Alec Nagle, Ted Kavanau's stalwart young assistant, had long since assumed the role of spark plug firing the CNN engine. Now he was moving from desk to desk, shouting, "Let's rock and roll, everybody! Six minutes to sign-on!"

Glitches in the new BASYS computer system caused rented typewriters to sprout up everywhere in Reese Schonfeld's paper-less newsroom. Once it was working, News Fury would spit out a torrent of copy that could be sorted and selected at any video terminal in the newsroom. Unfortunately CNN would have to get off the ground the old-fashioned way. Ted Kavanau called every employment agency in Atlanta and booked a few dozen typists around the clock in a frantic effort to stay ahead of the news flow he knew was about to begin. These very proper temps, sitting wide-eyed and alert, contrasted sharply with the haggard-looking young newsies in perpetual motion whirling around them. Schonfeld later confessed that without "those wonderful black ladies of a certain age who never stopped typing," CNN would never have gone on the air.

Stepping up to a microphone and gazing blankly up into the heavens, Turner cleared his throat, thanked everybody for coming, and quickly introduced Tom Wheeler, president of the National Cable Television Association. After a few perfunctory words of praise, Wheeler put forth his bid for rhetorician of the year by pronouncing CNN "a telepublishing event marking a watershed in information provision."

Reese Schonfeld was up next. Hobbling toward the microphone, his face broke out in a twisted grimace. Somebody must have screwed up downstairs, everybody figured, and Reese was unhappy again. In fact, Schonfeld had been suffering from a serious hernia but resolved to get CNN on the air before he did anything about it. This was his moment, he knew, even though the day belonged to Ted Turner. So Schonfeld stood at the microphone nearly bent over double and noted briefly that it had been "just one year, twenty-two days, and seven hours since I received that fateful telephone call from Turner." Now he was ready for the world to decide how well he'd responded.

After a brief benediction by the Reverend William Borders of the Wheat Street Baptist Church, Turner was back at the mike, looking at his watch again and preening in front of a live CNN camera. He ordered three flags, representing the state of Georgia, the United States, and the United Nations, raised over CNN headquarters and then lapsed into a long-winded piece of poetry dedicating the news channel for America—the Cable News Network. The massed military bands launched into a stirring rendition of the "Star Spangled Banner." Turner stretched up to his full six feet two inches and placed his hand over his heart. Then he let loose with his own updated rebel yell, "*Awww*riiight!!" CNN was on the air.

"At least I think we're on the air," Ted Turner declared, as if to reassure himself. "At least I hope so."

Dave Walker and Lois Hart, one of the ten anchor teams that would rotate in two-hour shifts around the clock, were doing their best to remain calm while Ted Kavanau and Sam Zelman, standing just a few feet away, stood screaming at each other about the best way to introduce the newborn network.

"We need an opening statement, goddammit!" Kavanau insisted.

"No, they should define the mission!"

"Let 'em just open with the news."

They were interrupted by an earshattering drumroll coming over the studio speakers. A camera cut from the three flags outside and was now zooming in on CNN's six giant earth stations. Another cut, this time a slow panning shot of the chaotic but immensely impressive CNN newsroom. Schonfeld rushed downstairs, where he felt he belonged, and was trying to separate Kavanau and Zelman when all three were caught by the camera and suddenly realized they were about to appear live, from Alaska to Hawaii. A graphic appeared on screen, announcing "CNN, the News Channel."

Another drumroll. Dave Walker stared straight into the camera and without waiting for a director's cue, intoned calmly, "Good evening. I'm David Walker."

"And I'm Lois Hart. Now here's the news."

The news spigot had been turned on, as Turner had promised, and it would not be turned off until the end of the world. Turner said he was prepared even for that, and had ordered a tape of the massed army, navy, and marine bands playing "Nearer My God to Thee," programmed to kick in automatically at Armageddon.

CNN's inaugural evening of news was carefully planned to showcase the network's impressive technical capabilities. The top breaking story that day was President Jimmy Carter's visit to the bedside of Vernon Jordan, the black leader who had been shot in Ft. Wayne, Indiana. "God sent us that story," Schonfeld said as he penciled in the piece as CNN's lead and first "live cutaway." Dave Walker read a brief follow-up on the state and federal investigations. Lois Hart followed with a short piece on reactions to the shooting among citizens of the Indiana steel town. Cut to Jordan's hospital room, where Carter was holding a press conference. When he suddenly realized ABC, NBC, and CBS were there as well, Schonfeld began praying quietly. If one of the networks denied CNN access to the AT&T transmission feed, he would lose his signal. Suddenly Jimmy Carter's face filled the CNN screen. "Thanks, God, for staying with us," Schonfeld shouted, realizing that the networks had not usurped his line after all and would hold the story for their evening newscasts. "That's what going live is all about," he added, congratulating his troops on CNN's first scoop.

A few minutes later CNN displayed more of its new technological razzle-dazzle. In one monumental round of satellite switches, CNN went to Jerusalem for a live report from correspondent Jay Bushinsky, then to Los Angeles and anchorman Bill Zimmerman for an update on the California primary, then across to New York and Mary Alice Williams for the latest on Yankee hero Reggie Jackson—who had gone out celebrating after slugging an eleventh-inning home run against the Toronto Blue Jays, only to become involved in a barroom incident that found him dodging bullets—then back down to Key West, where Mike Boettcher stood on a dock to welcome the latest wave of Cuban boat people, although the nearest boat person was still fifty miles offshore and would not make landfall for at least another ten hours.

Never in television history had anyone put together so many live remotes, all stitched seamlessly by satellite and wrapped up neatly by CNN's Atlanta anchors. The news was fed into Atlanta by twenty full-time reporters from bureaus in six U.S. cities, plus London and Paris. CNN augmented this limited overseas coverage with satellite feeds from a number of independent sources, including UPI Foreign, ITN, and Viznews.

CNN carried seven national advertisers at sign-on and at rates that averaged $102 for each thirty-second spot. The network's very first commercial, a Maalox spot with E. G. Marshall, was interrupted after only six seconds when CNN suddenly broke away for President Carter's Ft. Wayne press conference. Reese Schonfeld noticed Turner wander onto the newsroom floor just as he gave the signal to cut live to Ft. Wayne. "Ted," he called out, forgetting that the live mikes picked up everything in the newsroom, "how did you like the way we just cut away from our first commercial?"

"That'll show them we don't bow down to advertisers," Turner shouted back, grinning from ear to ear. "We're a real news operation, aren't we, Reese?" Then he turned and was off, roaming through the bustling newsroom, congratulating everyone but forgoing the usual quick little kisses and fresh squeezes most of the female staff had come to expect. Now that CNN was safely off the ground, Turner's attention was clearly somewhere else. Working his way across the floor, almost oblivious of the stream of congratulations and occasional cheers that broke out whenever another television first was recorded on this inaugural evening, Turner kept walking. He looked right through Kathleen Sullivan, who was standing by for her ten o'clock shift with coanchor Bill Zimmerman, as if she were invisible. Turner himself had recruited Sullivan, a local anchor at Salt Lake's KTVX-TV when they'd met in Deer Valley, an exclusive enclave above Salt Lake City. It wasn't long before Sullivan got herself hired as CNN's first foreign correspondent. Even before there was a network, Turner had packed her off to El Salvador. She'd managed to get back in one piece, though without much in the way of usable footage. Once CNN was on the air, however, Sullivan's appeal became quickly apparent and she soon developed into the new network's closest semblance of a star.

Flushed and still high on the day's excitement, Turner finally found his way into Sam Zelman's empty office and plumped himself down in front of a TV set. Since CNN's own building was not yet wired for cable, he sat there alone in the dark, twirling the UHF dial until he finally found WTBS. He leaned back contentedly, relaxing for the first time all day as he watched his Braves take a close one from the Dodgers. Several veejays passing in front of Zelman's open door heard a loud, rasping "Awwriiight!" None of them could have known what a truly satisfying day this had been for Ted Turner.

Only about 1.7 million cable households, however—far short of the 2.5 million Turner predicted—could even receive CNN at sign-on. A significantly smaller number actually tuned in. In the Atlanta area, where interest in Turner's new venture was understandably running very high, fewer than twelve thousand subscribers were able to see what the all-news channel looked like. Basing his projections on the rapid increases in audience size his Superstation was chalking up, Turner and his team simply oversold themselves on the number of cable systems with enough channel capacity to take on his new service. Now Turner would have to wait for cable to catch up with his aggressive projections or sustain the kinds of losses that could put him out of business within the year.

Turner had hoped all along to hit break-even sometime during CNN's first twelve to eighteen months of operation. "I am scared," he confessed, with his usual candor, to a reporter from *Panorama* magazine, which reported the shortfall in his audience projections and commented at length on the interest several of the larger media companies had suddenly developed in the all-news business. "The boss may be a rich man in his circles," *Panorama* concluded somewhat disconcertingly, "but the $100 million Turner says he has to lose on CNN is less than one-sixth of what the Washington Post Company took in last year, and there are several other even bigger vultures circling in the sky. No wonder Ted Turner is nervous."

Most impartial observers, however, were slightly more sanguine about CNN's chances. Turner, they pointed out, had already overcome enormous odds just getting his news channel on the air. His Superstation was now throwing off more cash than even Turner had predicted. While the rest of the world focused on CNN, the Superstation had quietly become one of a handful of powerful programming engines, perhaps the most powerful, since it came free to both cable system operators and consumers, driving the rapidly growing cable industry. CNN would soon become another important stimulus to cable's growth, but first the fledgling news service had to prove it could stay in business.

When he took over WTCG, Ted Turner had not been shy about voicing his disdain for the news. But Ted Turner contradicts himself with regularity. If he discovers a weakness in his own position or has been shown to be wrong, count on him to change sides immediately and argue against his original position with equal, if not greater, force and furor. When he launched CNN, Turner deftly executed just such an about-face. News was no longer an afterthought but had become, conversely, Turner's new raison d'être. The dedicated professionals who helped put CNN on the air had opened his eyes to the power and the possibilities inherent in the news. The more Turner learned about this side of the broadcast business, the more intrigued he became. Ted Turner was beginning to understand why the major networks valued their own news operations so highly and soon found himself, somewhat unexpectedly, becoming a champion of broadcast journalism.

At CNN's inaugural Turner told several reporters in the crowd that he hoped his new network might help bring peace to the world. "I'm going to travel around to every foreign country and get the head of the country to show me the things he's proudest of about his country. And send it all back by satellite," he boasted, sounding like some space age Colonel McCormick.

When Turner starts in on his larger agenda interests, most reporters put down their pencils and stop taking notes. "Nobody believed him, did they?" observes Reese Schonfeld. "With anybody else, you would say that kind of talk is ridiculous. But Ted will find a way to do it. He was already discussing with me the possibility of getting a feed from Russian television in 1981. I told him I doubted their government would permit it, but who was going to tell Ted it was impossible."

We come by the water and we will go by the water.
OLD GULLAH PROVERB

Chapter Nine

Win or lose against *Australia* in 1977, Ted Turner never had any doubts that he would return to Newport. And he was determined that *Courageous* would again be his to command. In 1979, Turner finally acquired his favorite twelve-meter for $510,000. He also bought *Independence*, Ted Hood's old twelve, and put her out on a charter option to Russell Long, a hot young helmsman just out of Harvard. When he returned from Fastnet, Ted outfitted *Courageous* for a series of fall tune-ups against Long, who had been sailing off Newport all summer.

"This is the first time I've sailed the boat in two years—two years and a month," Turner observed, his bleary eyes hidden by dark green sunglasses, his striped engineer's hat back on top of his rapidly graying head. "The last time I stepped off *Courageous* was when we sailed the fourth race in the America's Cup—it was the America's Cup, not the World Series. But I'm going to be in the World Series soon, too."

It was obvious after only a few races, however, that *Independence* was not much of a trial horse and was never going to match *Courageous* in boat speed. Long decided to exercise his option and bought *Independence* from Turner. Then, he sent her in for a massive redesign.

Long's impressive rebuild placed *Independence*, which he re-christened *Clipper*, on the cutting edge of twelve-meter technology. He saw himself now as a legitimate America's Cup contender, the youngest in history. Most observers, however, expected the 1980 cup trials to be a spectacular match-racing duel, perhaps the best ever, between Ted Turner and Dennis Conner in his new twelve-meter *Freedom*.

His words notwithstanding, Turner took *Courageous* out for a spring tune-up in May and declared himself "ninety percent of where I want to be in September." Despite all of his bluster, Turner said he would be there to defend his honor and the cup, approximately in that order of priority. "We're going to be there and we're going to race. I'm up for it," he asserted. "The whole crew is up for it. I've got an awful lot more on my mind than I had in 1977, but we want to prove something."

In the twelve months leading up to the 1980 trials, Turner put in only fifty days of sailing, including the miraculous four-day Fastnet. "Dennis Conner should be our major competition," Ted concluded. "He brags that he sailed 340 out of the last 365 days." Easing an ash off the end of his cigar, Turner added, "That doesn't necessarily mean too much."

Turner had raised only $650,000 to campaign *Courageous*. Conner would spend more than $3 million on *Freedom*. Even Russell Long's budget, at $1.2 million, was nearly twice as much. Ted Turner, the last true champion of amateurism, continued to rail at the commercialism he saw creeping into cup activities and arrived in Newport with the last unpaid crew in America's Cup history. Yet he allowed himself to be photographed for a Tiparillo cigar advertisement in the *Courageous* cockpit, thereby undermining his own amateur status and introducing the first instance of on-board advertising to the cup.

The psych war continued, however, when Turner announced at the New York Yacht Club's annual spring banquet, "No matter who wins this summer, I will retain the America's Cup." Then he unveiled what looked suspiciously like the same ungainly ewer that had resided under bullet-proof glass in the club's trophy room since 1855. Once the uproar died down, Turner explained calmly that he had outbid the club for a "sister casting" of the original One Hundred Guinea Queen Victoria Cup the schooner *America* had won 125 years ago. The existence of this twin cup had been rumored for decades, but when a reputable London dealer had come to the club with what he'd said was the real thing, the wise old heads on West Forty-fourth Street told him to come up with a proper provenance before they would even consider the purchase. Not one to sit on his hands, Turner picked up the trail, offered the dealer $5,000 cash, and come away with his personal America's Cup. Naturally, his trophy has proved to be authentic.

Mind games aside, when Turner finally made his formal entrance into Newport that June, it was with a noticeable lack of glint in his eye or fire in his belly. His adoring public expected him to do it all over again—derring-do on the high seas and just plain daredeviltry on shore. David Ray, owner of Newport's notorious Candy Store pub, set the tone by providing Turner and the entire *Courageous* crew "lifetime gold cards," allowing them to drink for free, forever.

"We own Newport," Turner declared bravely as the *Courageous* crew settled into their quarters at Salve Regina Hall, a converted convent that had been turned over to his syndicate for the summer. Sadly, Ted Turner's lease on the America's Cup was just about to expire. Not even David Ray's gold cards could not change the course of sailing history.

Dennis Conner did not coin the phrase *endless campaign*—that was the handiwork of the yachting press. But his more than 1,300 hours of intense preparation for 1980 added up to more time than all the other American and foreign contenders lumped together had invested in their collective cup efforts. Conner's lavishly funded Ft. Schuyler Foundation syndicate had cornered every top sail maker in the world, including John Marshall (North), Tom Whidden (Sobstad), and Jack Sutphen (Ratsey & Lapthorn), and made them a part of *Freedom*'s crew. Conner had even hired Ted Hood to trim sails for *Freedom* during the Trials. He had the benefit of two full years' competitive sailing against *Enterprise*, a trial horse that had almost proved the boatspeed equal of *Courageous* in 1977. Conner also had a professional trainer exercising his crew every morning before they hit the docks. Employing his "no excuse to lose" philosophy, Dennis Conner made sure that absolutely no one on the *Freedom* team had a lifetime gold card to the Candy Store.

Each day, before leaving Bannister Wharf for Judith Point and another day of racing, Conner would go down to the docks to survey yet another set of new sails for his boat. Ted Turner would be there, too, but he was manning a dockside pay phone, shouting instructions for a new advertising sales campaign to someone in

Atlanta. And when he wasn't on the phone, he'd be busy signing autographs or holding forth to yet another wave of reporters. Turner was also getting a kick posing for Barbara Pyle, the pretty brunette *Time* magazine had sent up to photograph the trials. "Why don't you come down to Atlanta and work for me?" Turner asked, throwing out one of his most overworked invitations.

"Maybe I will," Pyle replied without looking up from her camera.

Veteran America's Cup writer Norris Hoyt had been watching Turner all month and felt he was greatly underestimating Conner's enormous preparation and sophisticated operational support. Hoyt also saw Dennis Conner as the arch manipulator. "I have a feeling Dennis can get people to do things they don't want to without knowing they're doing it until it's too late. You really don't know whether he's living a life of quiet desperation, or whether he's enjoying himself."

Russell Long found his fast new *Clipper* at least the equal of the older *Courageous* and was beginning to give Turner a run for his money during the pretrial tune-up races. His smooth patrician manner and long flowing blond hair created an immediate sensation with Newport's younger set, piquing Turner even more than his improving chances on the water. Long's only saving grace, as far as Ted was concerned, was the good judgment he had shown in making Tommy Blackaller *Clipper*'s assistant helmsman. The two old rivals bounced off each other like a couple of dodge-'em cars at a country carnival, trying always to dent each other's egos but never inflicting any real damage. Turner became hopelessly intrigued, however, when he caught sight of the smashing twenty-three-year-old blonde Blackaller had brought with him to Newport. Congratulating his friend on his usual good taste, Turner decided he'd better file this one away for future reference.

The long-awaited duel between Turner and Conner, which had preoccupied the international yachting world for the past year and a half, turned out to be a nonevent. Turner and *Courageous* took the first race by a slim margin and then proceeded to lose the next eighteen straight to *Freedom*. Ted didn't fare much better against Russell Long's *Clipper*. Plagued by equipment failures, crew miscues, and just plain bad racing luck, Turner was finally forced out of the last of the June trials when *Courageous* lost her mast in a freak accident with *Clipper*. He then proceeded to break the rules by engaging in an unauthorized race over the Fourth of

July break with Alan Bond's new *Australia*. The NYYC had warned Turner against such breaches in 1977, but he found the prospect of an impromptu street fight against his old adversary as irresistible as an open microphone. Ted Turner has never been known to walk away from either.

"It was very light air, and you really couldn't tell anything," a member of the *Australia* crew said later. "But I think Turner'd be the only one ever to come over like that. Ted Turner is a true sportsman. The America's Cup is really a race of nation against nation, but Turner treats it like a true sporting event."

Two days later, however, Turner ran afoul of the selection committee once again, this time for bringing *Australia*'s tactician and designer, Ben Lexcen, on board *Courageous* during a trial heat against *Freedom*. Conner was outraged when he discovered the infraction and filed a protest, which the committee had no choice but to honor.

"I think Ted sails best if he feels his back is up against the wall," Conner commented even before the dust had settled. "He sails best if he can harbor some ill feeling toward the other person. Ted has always been good at this. It's made him a tremendous competitor, but this time he's taken it too far." The committee decreed that Turner be set down for the remainder of the July trials. Since the rules breach occurred during the last week of the month, however, that amounted to the loss of just one day's racing.

Turner may have sailed more miles in a twelve meter than anyone in history, but those miles were already beginning to recede into the past. By the beginning of August 1980 he and his crew had put in fewer than 20 days on the water together since they'd sailed to victory three years earlier. "When we talked about coming back two and a half years ago," Gary Jobson attempted to explain, "Ted told us this was all the time he felt he could put into it. We knew that, and we were still willing to give it a shot. Maybe it will turn out we were a little overconfident. Ted is someone who has lots on his mind at any given time," offers Jobson, ever the apologist. "It's normal. This summer was no exception."

Dennis Conner, however, knew that Turner was at his best when everyone else had counted him out. "Ted's charisma," Conner admits grudgingly, "often leads people to underestimate his sailing ability. He is a good upwind helmsman, but he may be the very best at downwind sailing."

What most of the yachting fraternity already knew, however, the rest of the country would soon discover. "Ted was totally outclassed by *Freedom*," Russell Long noted dispassionately, since he and *Clipper* were also on the brink of elimination. "Besides, Dennis is proving this year to be a much better sailor. It's time," Long then added, somewhat uncharitably, "Ted realized that he's a middle-aged man chasing a dream. The level of the game has become higher than anything he's ever seen."

Turner's impossible dream of repeating his 1977 triumph had become a haunting nightmare. For several days during mid-August, he had been trying to signal the selection committee's blue launch, *Hatferascal*, as if he were beckoning the Grim Reaper. "Whenever they come, we'll be glad to see them," he told reporters. And soon enough Commodore Robert McCullough arrived to extend the committee's thanks. "We do appreciate," McCullough intoned solemnly, "what you've done to help defend the cup."

With those words Captain Courageous was excused from further competition without a whimper. In an unusual gesture, however, McCullough and the entire seven-man selection committee, all wearing the same somber black blazers and Panama straws emblazoned with the NYYC orange and blue ribbon band, clambered on board *Courageous*. They shook each hand and had warm words for every single member of her crew, including the young reserves who served aboard her tender, *Fire Three*.

That night Turner and his crew made good on their gold cards and closed down the Candy Store one last time. Everybody stood up on the bar and had his say. There were rounds and rounds of toasts to *Courageous*, a noble lady, even in defeat. She had proved herself, and so, in the eyes of the world beyond Newport, had Turner and his crew. "It hurts worse than he'll tell you," volunteered Marty O'Meara, one of Turner's old lieutenants. "We came in here assuming we'd go all the way. Our pride was on the line. There was a lot of time, a lot of money, a lot of hopes that went down the tube today." Afterward Turner and Jobson took one more long walk together, just as the dawn began to break over Aquidneck Island. "Well," said Jobson, "I think that's it."

"I think so," Turner replied, his mind preoccupied with the crushing responsibilities that awaited him in Atlanta. And with that intriguing young blonde he had met with Tom Blackaller.

* * *

Reese Schonfeld always said God had smiled on CNN on opening night. His proof was the deluge of major, fast-breaking headline stories that the heavens rained down upon CNN almost from sign-on. Schonfeld wanted stories CNN could "own," continuous, breaking news events that might be difficult for the networks to capture in brief sound bites on the evening news. What he got that first year CNN was on the air was Mount St. Helens, a month-long saga of the volcano that refused to die. Then Hurricane Alan, the worst storm out of the Caribbean in over twenty years. Then, in rapid succession, the Republican and Democratic conventions. By the time the 1980 presidential campaign had begun, CNN had found its rhythm and was even beginning to make headlines of its own.

Reese Schonfeld had been careful not to draw too much attention away from Turner during CNN's early days, but now, his hernia taken care of, he was beaming like the Fastnet light as he stormed around the CNN studios, justifiably bursting with the proud knowledge that his news operation really did work. "Reese Schonfeld was the guy who really made CNN," says Lois Hart. "He's a journalist at heart, even though he was trained as a lawyer and seemed to spend most of his time as an administrator. Reese is also crazy, wild, with a monumental temper. None of us had any idea how we were going to fill up twenty-four hours, but to Reese that was never the problem. He worried about what it was all going to look like on the screen—what kind of format CNN would ultimately have. This may sound ridiculous, but I don't think any of them—not Reese, not Turner, not Kavanau or any of the others who were responsible for getting this incredible thing off the ground—I don't think any one of them really knew what CNN would look like. The one mantra that everybody chanted during those early days was 'Nobody's a star. The news is the star.' Well, that was fine," Hart adds pointedly, "but we all knew the real star was Ted Turner."

CNN was news without stars, news without end, and news virtually without editing. With the exception of a number of married couples like Hart and her husband, Dave Walker, most of the on-air talent were unused to the kinds of deadline pressures Turner's all-news channel now imposed on them around the clock. CNN was one of the few broadcast organizations in the entire industry that encouraged husbands and wives to work together, and the network benefited mightily from this policy, which, of course, started at the top, since Schonfeld brought in his own wife, Pat

O'Gorman, right from the beginning. Don Farmer and Chris Curle, Bill Zimmerman and Deenie Diskin, and Donna Kelly and Mike Michaels were only a few of the more than a dozen married couples working for CNN at sign-on. "It made good sense," says Hart, "and frankly, CNN got a damned good deal all the way round. Plus they rewrote the rules. Now you see husbands and wives working together almost anywhere in the industry."

And there was Ted Turner's own example. Once back in Atlanta, Turner plunged right into his businesses—more intensely, some thought, than ever before. He told the world up in Newport that he was through sailing, that he would not compete again on the international ocean-racing circuit, and that he intended to sell his boats. It was still too early to see how serious he was—the new SORC was still four months away. But there was little question he was intent now on seeing CNN through to profitability. Rumors of trouble at home were rife in the newsroom. Turner began spending most of his time at Techwood. He would sleep on the couch in his third-floor office, then wander down in the middle of the night to get some coffee. Of course, being Ted, he couldn't resist sounding like the man in charge, giving orders, asking questions, checking into everything, even at three in the morning. "You'd be sitting there in the middle of the night," says Heaney, "trying to put together a weather map. You'd look up and there would be Ted Turner, standing right in front of you in his bare feet, nothing on but a rumpled old bathrobe."

"He would generally come down and get two cups of coffee," Dave Walker remembers. "He had a shower and everything up in his office, and in those early days you'd see him running around in that bathrobe, saying, 'Hi, how you all.' He was a sight, chewing tobacco all the time, spitting in that little Dixie cup he carried around, and juggling those two cups of coffee back upstairs."

Turner had a string of lady friends he brought around to the office. Some of them would even be there for those early morning coffee breaks. Fran Heaney remembers the time he trooped Raquel Welch through the newsroom. "I don't know whether he was dating her," Heaney says, "or she was suing him. He always had lots of dates coming around." Some of the female anchors were sometimes less than flattered to receive an invitation to come up and chat with the boss. Marcia Landendorff was sure her job was in jeopardy when she responded to one such invitation by asking if her boyfriend could come meet Ted, too. More and more frequently, however, the lady coming down mornings from the third floor was Turner's new pilot, the pretty blonde with the crooked smile he'd met in Newport. Her silver-colored DeLorean was becoming a fixture in the company parking lot.

A flood of big news stories had helped get CNN off to a fast start that first summer, and the network's willingness to take its technology to the limit usually made up for its thin coverage. Schonfeld's extreme low-rent approach kept CNN's losses manageable but sometimes caused serious strains on CNN's human resources. Bernard Shaw and Mary Alice Williams, covering the Democratic convention from an inhuman perch above Madison Square Garden, almost walked off the job when they were left high and dry for several hours with no link to their floor reporters and no soundproofing. "We just let the music play," says Williams, a particular favorite of Turner's and today host of her own show on NBC. "There was simply no way we could ever talk over it." The CNN "skybox" was not much bigger than a Porta-John, and guests couldn't be interviewed unless one or the other of the anchors moved out of the booth.

Schonfeld spent his budget on getting the news, not accommodating anchors or anyone else at CNN. "He overspent on videotape machines," Gene Wright reported, "and bought seventy-two for the launch. We probably could have got by with half that number, since we didn't have enough trained editors to work all seventy-two machines for at least a year." But Schonfeld also worked without backup equipment, so-called redundant hardware, assuming nothing CNN used would ever break down. Most of the staff knew Schonfeld had never actually run an operation of this size, much less any news operation that broadcast live from a studio. And soon, not even Schonfeld himself could keep light bulbs he never allowed to dim from bursting or overheated cameras from catching fire. The entire CNN studio operation looked as if it might melt down from equipment failure during those early months, making Schonfeld a belated believer in redundancy.

Mad Dog Kavanau would occasionally cause a glitch or two that helped break the tension of those early days. Dave Walker was in the anchor seat one such afternoon when Kavanau signaled him to begin narrating the live feed coming up on Walker's monitor. With no idea what the story was about, Walker gave a brilliant off-the-cuff performance, narrating what appeared to be an ordinary fender bender coming in live from Rome's Via Venezia. "What we are seeing," Walker reported gallantly, "is actual raw video. What we are seeing is . . . ah . . . apparently an auto accident . . . Oh, yes, an automobile accident. . . . The police appear to be arriving." Kavanau was just off camera, flailing his arms and frantically signaling for the news copy, which would explain the story. "It appears . . . uh, as though the occupants of the two cars are . . . uh . . . are angry at one another. . . ." Mad Dog just hid his head in his hands and wondered if CNN could last through the end of the hour.

On the day Nicaragua's General Somoza was assassinated, two young veejays were screaming at Lois Hart, who was already exhausted from over two hours in the anchor chair. "Pick up the phone! Pick it up!" they shouted in unison. "Talk to her. Margaret's on the phone from Managua with the Somoza assassination."

"So I picked up the phone," Hart recalls, "and I knew immediately we've gotten this poor girl out of bed. 'What? Hello?' I tell her that the dictator, that Somoza has been shot, and she goes, 'Oh, wow! Really? What happened?' This kind of thing happened almost every day during the first year or so. With all those college kids behind the cameras," Hart says with a smile, "it's a miracle anything ever got on the air at all."

"If you liked doing newsies' news," senior producer Ed "No Relation" Turner recounted, "this was the place to be. If a reporter standing in front of a building had a good story, we would use it. I didn't care if she was pretty or not, so long as she was believable. I got there at six in the morning, every day. We'd have our assignments meeting at eight. For me, this was the place to be, and it's still a joy, every day I'm here."

Impatient with CNN's fitful progress, Turner couldn't resist going on the air himself, as he had once done to raise money for his Charlotte station. He offered "I like CNN" bumper stickers at $5 a pop over his Superstation. The idea was somewhat less than successful, but it led to his next brainstorm. Preempting WTBS altogether one day, he gave viewers around the country a full twenty-four-hour sample of CNN's nonstop news. The deluge of subscribers he predicted never materialized, but CNN's audience continued to build, due in great measure to an unexpected lift in the economy that allowed system operators to finance expanded channel capacity. His Superstation experiment, however, prompted Turner to add the "TBS Evening News" to the Superstation's daily program schedule in late 1980.

"This is not going to be a diversion from what the Superstation is," announced Joy Sterling, WTBS's proud new twenty-six-year-old news director. "We're going to produce the hell out of the CNN material we run. We're making phone calls, doing research. We're doing the work of real journalists." Hired on the spot by Turner himself when she interviewed him during the 1979 One-Ton Championships in San Francisco, Sterling came to Atlanta aspiring to an anchor slot at CNN. "Ted asked me to produce the TBS newscast," Sterling says, "beginning the day after CNN signed on. "I told him that was impossible. All he said was it was the first time in the history of the Superstation that anybody had ever used the word *impossible.*" Naturally Sterling somehow got her "Evening News" on the air, even though she and her program were replaced six months later by a direct feed from CNN, proving that Turner had never actually taken his eye off the bottom line, even if he had, momentarily, been distracted by Sterling's pretty face.

Reese Schonfeld and Ted Turner happen to share the same November 19 birthdate, although Schonfeld is older by seven years. Turner suggested they celebrate their 1980 birthdays together over dinner. Neither mentioned the strain each felt was beginning to develop in their relationship, and putting business aside, they proceeded to enjoy themselves thoroughly that evening. Toward the end of the meal, however, Turner looked up and out of the blue asked Schonfeld to imagine he were a competitor. What would you do, he asked, his voice suddenly serious, if you wanted to put CNN out of business?

Schonfeld took the question in stride. He and Turner both knew there were several large companies watching CNN closely, waiting for any sign that Turner might be in over his head. Some of these companies were even ready with fully developed business plans. Schonfeld knew, because he had helped draw them up over two years earlier. He told Turner that the easiest way to hurt CNN would be with a "headline service," a simple repeating wheel of news stories, patterned along the lines of all-news radio. Schonfeld and Turner, in fact, had discarded the headline concept in favor of CNN's more complex format, which they felt would hold viewers' attention for several hours, not just one turn of the wheel. "The headline format—drive-time television," Schonfeld declared, "has tremendous appeal and won't cost much to produce. But why let people think they can get all the news in fifteen or twenty minutes when you want to keep them tuned in for two or three hours?"

Turner agreed. "But since we are likely to have competition, shouldn't we beat them to the mark and do it ourselves?" A few days later Schonfeld presented him with a hastily updated plan detailing a headline news service for cable television. Turner promptly shoved it into his desk drawer without even cracking the cover.

Outside Turner Broadcasting, speculation was running high that CNN's escalating expenses were beginning to drain the company coffers. The company, the rumors suggested, might soon be facing a liquidity crisis. Development costs at the news network had run over $18 million, and although monthly losses appeared to be coming down, TBS had already borrowed over $27 million to finance CNN. Cash was tight. The company's new finance vice-president, Bill Bevins, took pains to deny stories that he was meeting CNN's payroll from concession receipts at Braves and Hawks games. But Terry McGuirk acknowledged that he had raised a little cash by extracting prepayments from several large advertisers and his admission set the tongues wagging again. With the Superstation throwing off more than enough cash to cover all of CNN's operating costs, these maneuvers seemed unnecessary, but were typical of Turner's cautious approach, a lesson he had obviously impressed upon the rest of his Turner Broadcasting management. Cox Cable's Walter Pirey spoke for many in the cable industry when he told the *Atlanta Constitution*, "I don't think Turner is in the sort of trouble some people say he is. He knew CNN was going to lose money for a while. He may have a money crunch, but it's temporary. The cable industry is exploding, and with that explosion, he'll be saved."

Nevertheless, when Time Inc. sent Gerry Levin down to explore Turner's interest in selling CNN, Turner was persuaded to begin building a war chest. He decided to go forward with a planned sale of $15 million of Turner Broadcasting stock. The new equity would value his company at close to $200 million and allow TBS to increase its bank lines by at least another $50 million. SEC rules, however, prevented Turner from talking about the company or its financial situation until the planned stock registration was completed. During this so-called quiet period Sandi Freeman booked Turner as a guest on her CNN interview show. "There are just two subjects you absolutely cannot mention,"

Schonfeld warned Freeman. "His father's suicide. And the company's stock offering."

Schonfeld had discovered Freeman, a popular Chicago talk show host, and brought her into CNN with mixed emotions. She was an appealing interviewer, and Turner seemed to like her a lot. But Schonfeld considered Freeman's show "soft" and most of her interview subjects "inappropriate" for an all-news network. For her part, Freeman was afraid she had become a pawn in the developing power struggle between Schonfeld and Turner. So she decided to go for broke.

Freeman began her Turner interview with an indelicate question about Ed Turner's death and then segued straight into a discussion of the Turner Broadcasting stock offering. Dan Schechter, Freeman's producer, remembers how the lawyers and bankers who had come into the studio to watch the show began falling out of their chairs. "Freeman led with the only two questions Schonfeld had warned her not to use. Despite Turner's incoherent responses, the lawyers and bankers agreed we had probably ruined any chances of going forward with the underwriting."

Dan Schechter can't say for sure, but he believes that what happened between Turner and Freeman was probably premeditated. "Without telling either his bankers or his lawyers, Ted simply decided Turner Broadcasting was worth a good deal more than the underwriting valuation. He decided, then and there, to kill it. I don't know if he let Sandi in on his plan, but she was having enough trouble with Reese and probably would have done the opposite of anything he told her." Schechter thinks Turner may also have had second thoughts about giving up any equity— he was now back up to 87 percent of the outstanding shares— regardless of the price.

Toward the end of 1980 Westinghouse Broadcasting confirmed its long-rumored merger with Teleprompter Corp. The merger would create one of the largest multiple-systems operators in the cable industry. More significant, Westinghouse's Group W broadcast unit had created all-news radio and would now almost certainly make a move into cable. It might be time to dust off Reese Schonfeld's proposal for a headline news service, but since he had proven so adept at the intricacies of legal infighting, Turner decided to slow Westinghouse just a bit for now by filing a formal writ with the FCC. He protested government approval of the proposed Westinghouse-Teleprompter merger on the grounds of "unfair competition." At the same time he asked Bob Wussler to put out feelers to CBS and a couple of other media giants, "just in case." He also released the results of a new Nielsen audience survey, a study billed by Turner as the most extensive ever conducted on the national cable television audience. The Nielsen survey showed that cable viewers rated CNN "equal to or better than network news coverage." The battle lines were being drawn.

CNN, meanwhile, was involved in skirmishes on another front. During the presidential campaign and the early days of the Reagan administration, CNN had generally been included as a "fourth network" and allowed the same access to the president and the White House as the three major networks. The majors were now becoming increasingly critical of CNN's shoestring approach, and CBS used its influence with the White House to have CNN excluded from the official press pool.

"We don't think there should be pools," Schonfeld complained. "We can beat them one on one. We do it all the time. But we can't compete when all three networks get together and decide to freeze us out. The networks are refusing to recognize there's another player in the game."

Network officials pointed out that participating in a pool with CNN was something of a one-way street. "We don't want them in the pool," said CBS, "because they can't contribute to it." While CNN was more than happy to use material shot by the pool, the networks were usually prevented from using CNN material because it was shot with nonunion crews. Money was another problem. CNN balked at paying an equal share of pool costs, because, Schonfeld reasoned, its audience was proportionately smaller. Being cut out of the pool ruled out live coverage of the president. It also diminished CNN's importance in the eyes of Washington newsmakers, and that rankled Ted Turner. On May 11, 1981, he filed a federal lawsuit in Atlanta, naming as defendants CBS, NBC, and ABC, as well as the president of the United States, White House chief of staff James Baker, deputy press secretary Larry Speakes, and, for good measure, Secretary of State Alexander Haig. Demanding a jury trial and unspecified monetary damages, Turner said that "the networks and the White House conspired and combined to violate the U.S. Constitution by denying CNN due process of law and freedom of speech." Turner also claimed the networks violated antitrust laws guaranteeing CNN's right to free trade. "For over fifteen years," Turner charged, "CBS,

ABC, and NBC have been the principal participants in the market for the production of TV news programming. They have enjoyed a monopoly in this market. Our efforts to break this monopoly outside the legal process have been fruitless, and we are now forced to take this action, both for the good of the news business and for the good of the American people."

Turner had raised a valid and long overdue challenge. Broadcast lawyers across the country were gearing up for a protracted and lucrative constitutional battle. "From the beginning of Washington journalism, some news organizations have been given preferential treatment," admitted former director of CBS News Fred Friendly. "What's surprising is that no one until CNN ever challenged the rules."

Adding more fuel to the fire, Turner flew to Washington and told a raucous news conference that he was also calling for an immediate congressional investigation into network programming "to determine whether it has a detrimental effect on the morals, attitudes, and habits of the people of this country." He found himself aligned with the Reverend Jerry Falwell and the Reverend Donald Wildmon in demanding that the three major networks return to "More wholesome programming like 'Leave It to Beaver' and 'Father Knows Best.'" Both programs happened to be superannuated staples of Turner's Superstation, but he was not, he emphasized, a member of the Moral Majority. "I generally support their efforts," he added, "and anybody else who is working within the free enterprise system to clean this mess up." He had been careful to keep his distance from the radical Right. Not everyone, however, was convinced.

Turner said he planned to rent a theater in Washington to show members of Congress a special CNN program, "Television: The Moral Battleground." He then proceeded to show reporters a forty-five-minute preview, adding that current network programming was as dangerous to the security of the nation as oil pricing by the Organization of Petroleum Exporting Countries (OPEC). "All three networks are operating in lock-step, in cartellike fashion," he charged. "They are totally irresponsible, and consciously or unconsciously they are tearing this nation down and tearing it apart."

In launching such a broad, frontal assault on the networks, Turner risked being bitten by a snake in his own swamp. Congress was already overdue in looking into the almost free rebroadcast of programs by satellite. Turner's payment of Atlanta-size fees for what amounted to nationwide broadcast rights was rapidly becoming a serious concern among the Hollywood studios who continued to sell him product, as well as the actors, writers, and producers who created the shows, which made his Superstation so profitable.

"We're at war with everybody," Turner observed accurately. "Now we have lawsuits against the three networks, the White House, and Westinghouse. And we're winning—or at least we haven't lost yet."

Clearly an unequal combatant in the capital wars, CNN's Washington bureau was not only frozen out of the White House pools, but was forced to fill up an almost unconscionable amount of air time. CNN began with ten bureaus around the world, but the heart of its struggle for news credibility lay in Washington, where most of the national news stories originate. With only a handful of personnel, the bureau was expected to produce live reports every half hour, plus longer segments for CNN's two-hour prime-time newscast, plus weekend interview shows and spot live coverage as needed. This was more air time than the major networks' three Washington bureaus combined. Furthermore, the capital still had not been cabled, so newsmakers and legislators could not see themselves on CNN and had little idea of the new network's impact.

Turner quickly resolved that situation by contributing a $13,000 satellite dish to the House of Representatives and then wiring each congressman's office. He also arranged for his senior Washington correspondent, Dan Schorr, to have a dish of his own, the first residential satellite receiving station in the District of Columbia. During an appearance together at the Washington Press Club, Turner learned that Schorr's two preteen children couldn't see their father on CNN. "I'll give you a dish," he promised Schorr, and sure enough, two weeks later a crew from Scientific-Atlanta showed up and began sinking a huge white satellite dish into a foundation of newly poured concrete.

Schorr was pleased, even though the dish seemed able to pull down just one signal—CNN—from the satellite. Sid Topol, Scientific-Atlanta's chief executive, later told Schorr that Turner had specifically ordered the dish tuned to receive CNN only. "Don't worry," Topol promised impishly, "I'll get it fixed." And he did, Schorr reports, opening up a panorama of free programs from space at Schorr's house on Woodley Drive.

George Watson, the respected ABC veteran who launched

CNN's Washington bureau, became the young network's first defector. His leaving had nothing to do with a satellite dish. "It was," he said, "Atlanta's preference for features over hard news." Dan Schorr said it was simply "a matter of volume. There was no problem of hard news versus soft news. There was just an unbelievable, constant pressure for more news." CNN had difficulty, however, providing adequate coverage of the myriad hearings, speeches, press conferences, and other quasi-news events with what amounted to an absolutely bare-bones staff. Schonfeld would castigate the bureau people for wasting their resources on "hack hearings" and ordered CNN reporters to cover the less essential events alone, forgoing camera coverage in favor of a reporter's studio summary. Anything to get the story on the air, Schonfeld rationalized, mindful that the networks were hoping to win a war of attrition.

At that same Washington press conference he used to fire his opening legal shot against the networks and the president, Ted Turner sent a jolt through the international ocean-racing world by capitulating completely on another front. Angus Phillips of *The Washington Post* caught him pacing backstage restlessly, brooding in the dark wings before going out to bash the big boys. Phillips had never met Turner and, hoping to ease into an exclusive interview, tossed out a soft opening query about Turner's plans for the upcoming ocean-racing season. Turner exploded and, wheeling around to look Phillips square in the face, shouted, "I'm through with sailing. I don't even want to talk about it. I'm sick of sailing. I'm sick of the professionalism, the downright cheating. Did you read about the SORC last winter? All three winners were disqualified! They broke the rules. I'm through with all that."

Three weeks earlier Turner had called Jim Mattingly, his long-time crew chief and offshore boat boss. "Look," he'd told Mattingly, "what do you think about scrapping all of our racing plans for the summer?" Mattingly knew that Turner was devoting more time than ever to CNN and his other broadcast interests and assumed he was simply too busy to race that season.

"A day later," Mattingly recalled, "Ted called back and said, 'Scrap the plans and sell the boat." Mattingly was stunned. Several months earlier Turner had sold *Courageous* to a private foundation for $300,000. Her new owners planned to use the famous America's Cup twelve meter to foster interest in the cup, sponsor sailing clinics, and raise money for a new state-of-the-art ocean racer. But now Turner wanted to sell *Tenacious* as well. "It's the winningest boat in the world," Mattingly said. "You know he's serious when he puts *Tenacious* on the block. He told me he had no plans ever to return to ocean racing. If he does any competitive sailing at all, it's going to be day racing his Hobie Cat."

"We probably sailed in three hundred races," Turner's former cup tactician Gary Jobson commented nostalgically when *Tenacious* changed hands about a week later, "and I bet we won half of them. There will never be another record like that put together."

Turner Broadcasting System's annual stockholders meetings tended to be a lot like Turner Broadcasting's majority shareholder: casual, quick, and unorthodox to a fault. In fact, since Turner himself owned 87 percent of the outstanding shares, the meeting could have been held in a telephone booth. As it was, some forty curious souls, including press and TBS management, ventured up to the Stadium Club to hear what the man who had just opted out of competitive sailing, declared war on the White House, and aligned himself with the Moral Majority would say next.

They weren't disappointed. Exuding his characteristic self-confidence, Turner ran through the meeting in racehorse fashion, announcing, "It is possible the company will break even in fiscal 1982 and return to profitability in 1983." He also announced he was "close to agreement" with Citibank on a new $50 million line of credit—the principal reason, it turns out, Turner decided to abort the previous winter's stock offering on the Sandi Freeman show. Saving the best for last, he calmly declared it was his intention to make "Atlanta the major motion picture production center in the United States" and announced a new one-hundred-thousand-square-foot film and television studio on Techwood Drive, contingent, as always, on "available financing."

Turner also mentioned he was seriously considering selling a CNN feed to local television stations. He felt certain most of them, including many network affiliates, would jump at the opportunity to subscribe to a twenty-four-hour news service and relished the prospect of needling the network news departments once again.

And, oh, yes, about all those offers from companies seeking to acquire or merge with CNN? Turner would say only that "one major company has, in fact, offered me the key to the corporation. But there is no reason why we would want to merge with anyone.

We're the fastest growing company in the nation, I believe . . . er, certainly in the communications industry. I don't feel I'd be a good division head in anybody else's company."

Nevertheless, big media companies were continuing to keep a close eye on Turner and CNN—and badly misreading most of the signs. Turner was canny enough to give the impression he was anxious to talk to anyone. Most interpreted that as a sign of desperation. Like the good poker play he is, Turner was merely checking everybody's hand, to see how high he should up the ante. As CNN monitors began to appear in network executive offices, speculation over Turner's likely fate became a major preoccupation in the broadcast industry. Bill Leonard, outgoing director of CBS News, was concerned enough about the implications of an outside source like CNN providing CBS affiliates with a twenty-four-hour news service that he commissioned a study to see what such a venture might cost. Leonard had concluded that "CNN made us all wonder whether we should not take steps of our own to offer viewers the same service or something close to it." And when Leonard reported to Gene F. Jankowski, president of the CBS Broadcast Group, that "it would probably be a hell of a lot cheaper just to buy CNN" than to build such a service, Jankowski immediately telephoned his old colleague Bob Wussler and told him to set up a supersecret meeting with Turner.

"We went down in the CBS plane," Leonard recalls. "Just Jankowski and me. Turner met us at the hangar and drove us over to an airport motel. I had met him a couple of times, but never on business. Never for something like this." Turner brought Wussler and Bill Bevins along and, after sending out for something to eat, went into his pacing routine, trying to wear out the thin carpet in the cramped motel suite. Finally he couldn't stand any more of the small talk and blurted out, "Well, what do you guys have in mind?"

"Gene and I had discussed what we'd say on the way down," Leonard recalls, "and it was decided I'd do most of the talking. I told Turner we'd be very interested in buying CNN, or the whole company, whichever he wanted to discuss. I also said that we would have to have at least fifty-one percent."

When he heard that, Turner smiled a Cheshire cat smile and replied, "We'd be very interested in selling you CNN or the whole company, whichever you prefer, but you can only buy forty-nine percent or less." That was the end of the conversation. The meeting, according to Leonard, didn't last another five minutes.

Despite a distinguished career as one of the most respected news executives in television, Bill Leonard never quite got the hang of dealing with an entrepreneur like Ted Turner. "We were pretty arrogant in those days," Leonard admits. "There wasn't even any question in our minds. We had to have editorial control. The idea of an all-news operation on cable was certainly a good idea. CNN wasn't much in those days, but with an infusion of CBS News talent and savvy, yes, I think we could have made something of it.

"Looking back, I would have to admit we were probably a little too hasty. I think we were much too hasty in not trying harder to put a deal together. It would have been good for Turner and it would have been good for CBS. I'm not sure Mr. Paley would ever have agreed to anything except editorial control, but Turner knew it was going to take him some time—three or four years, he told us—before he could break even."

If Turner had any misgivings about the meetings, they were not evident. He drove Jankowski and Leonard back to their plane himself and seemed in high spirits. "I'm sorry we can't do business," he told Jankowski, and then added, "But it's really no problem. One day I'm going to buy your whole network anyway." Everybody laughed, but as the two CBS executives were clambering back on board their private jet, Turner asked innocently, "Is this plane for sale? If I can't buy the network, can I buy the plane?"

"He was a very fresh guy," Leonard says, "but you had to like him. Looking back, I can say now I absolutely wish we'd told him we could live with forty-nine percent. We could have had a joint venture, and it probably would have been a terrific deal for both of us."

Bob Wussler kept the wires hot for several days after that meeting, but the prospects of any deal with CBS for the moment would take a backseat to the considerably more pressing matter of Westinghouse Broadcasting's not unexpected announcement of their plans to launch Satellite News Channel, a competing twenty-four-hour-all-news service. What sent the Turner troops scurrying to their battle stations was the surprising news that the project would be a joint venture between Westinghouse and ABC Video Enterprises, a division of ABC Network. Prophetically, Westinghouse said SNC would be a "headline news service" and would launch on April 1, 1982, with a second "in-depth" news channel to follow sometime later in the year.

Ted Turner didn't have to think twice before making his own pronouncement. "They're in for the fight of their lives," he said, and then announced that CNN II, currently residing between the covers of Reese Schonfeld's business plan, would be on the air on January 1, three months before Satellite News Channel was to sign on.

We have seen the [news] and it is us.

WALT KELLY

Pogo

Chapter Ten

"Ted's happy—we're at war again," Reese Schonfeld declared as he and other CNN senior managers filed out of a rare early Monday morning meeting in Techwood's third-floor conference room. "Ted's reaction to competition is to go on the offensive. It's the only way he knows how to respond. He feeds on risk, and his appetite is insatiable."

Turner had come roaring back from the solitude of a three-day weekend at Hope, his 5,100-acre plantation in Colleton County, South Carolina, where he had gone to cogitate on the ABC-Westinghouse situation. He was in one of his moods, that was obvious, but he also seemed focused, resolute as to how he would address what was fast becoming CNN's day of reckoning. He had announced that CNN II would preempt Satellite News Channel. In a speech he likened to Franklin Roosevelt's declaration of war after the Japanese bombed Pearl Harbor, Turner announced he was not only going head to head with Satellite News Channel, but he would launch his new CNN II in just ninety days, beating the competition by three full months.

"It's a preemptive first strike!" he shouted, brandishing his favorite Confederate saber high over his head. "I don't know exactly how long we can last, but I figure our only chance is to split the market." Turner kept repeating that he was prepared to spend every cent he had to beat back the enemy, and it was not long before he had whipped most of the room into a whooping frenzy. Schonfeld, Reinhardt, and one or two others had mixed feelings about Turner's maximum-risk strategy, but they kept their feelings to themselves. This was, after all, Turner's show.

CNN was now sixteen months old and going very strong. Revenues were beginning to exceed $3 million a month, and break-even was well within sight. Remarkably, Turner had built a ground-zero, twenty-four-hour news operation for just a little more than $35 million. The service was now sent into 13.9 million cable households and, according to Nielsen, was attracting nearly 6.0 million viewers a week. Without the ABC-Westinghouse threat, CNN would soon become a profit spinner to rival the Superstation.

Editorially CNN was scooping all three major networks on a regular basis and had even won the grudging respect of Richard Wald, ABC's senior news executive, who was compelled to proffer a backhanded compliment when asked by *Time* magazine to rate Turner's new network. "CNN does a nice, straightforward basic rendition of the news," Wald admitted, "very competently."

Westinghouse had surprised the industry by announcing it would give away Satellite News Channel free to cable operators and in some cases even pay them to carry the new service. Schonfeld was concerned that the expense of launching CNN II, which Turner estimated at about $15 million, would mean cutbacks in CNN's own expanding budget, which was now approaching $50 million a year. With Turner's limited cash resources, why not reduce or eliminate the operator fees? Wouldn't that remedy CNN's biggest handicap and at the same time prevent systems from dropping a proven service for Satellite News Channel's new, untested product?

Turner was adamant. Hunkering down and reinforcing Cable News Network would not be enough. He had kept to his word about reinvesting in CNN and plowed every available dollar he could back into the news operation. The results had clearly been worth it, but now even he was forced to admit that he had no idea how long the company could hold out against a competitor with relatively unlimited resources. "I know," he told Schonfeld and the others, "we can never win a war of attrition."

Westinghouse owned the largest group of radio and television stations in the country. With its recent acquisition of the Tele-PrompTer systems, it was now also one of the largest cable system operators. Satellite News Channel could draw on its highly successful Group W all-news radio network, as well as on a newly expanded ABC News operation, now headed by the aggressive and imaginative Roone Arledge. ABC also held a 15 percent interest in ESPN, an all-sports cable channel, giving the network a popular and increasingly profitable cable programming franchise as well as significant leverage with cable operators.

The only defense against ABC Westinghouse, Turner felt, would be a daring frontal attack. He would head them off before they got even a foothold in his market. Already concerned about the mounting legal expenses of his White House pool suit, Turner was worried that Congress might now finally pass new copyright legislation that would require his Superstation to pay significantly increased royalties or be locked out of certain markets altogether. Either way the vital cash flow he had been depending on would be reduced.

The battle was shaping up as a defining moment in cable history. For ABC and Westinghouse, Satellite News Channel represented a timely, worthwhile strategic investment. Turner hoped that by dividing the market he could diminish his competitors' appetite for risk. He also hoped to benefit from their divided leadership, which he believed would make it difficult to get quick decisions through two large corporate hierarchies. He wanted to make sure Westinghouse and ABC, both of which were public companies, knew they were in for a long and very expensive battle. Turner realized he was in the fight of his life and intended to take no prisoners. He would have it no other way. "After all," he announced to the broadcast media in his opening salvo, "we can never lose if we never give up."

Mad Dog Kavanau was assigned to structure a fast-paced "headline" service that would leave Satellite News Channel in the dust. "We're going to preempt 'em by moving very quickly," Kavanau promised the 150 producers, directors, anchors, and technicians posted to CNN II. "And grabbing every single cable system we can find with a short-form network of our own." Kavanau relished the opportunity of building a whole new operation according to his own vision. Out of work and almost ready to quit the business two years before, Ted Kavanau now had the opportunity to prove himself to the industry against two powerhouse competitors. "We're going to do everything they say they're going to do. Except ours will be first and ours will be better. They have only money to lose," he told his new recruits. "But we have everything to lose."

Cable operators from across the country assembled in Boston for their annual convention a week later, anxious to hear what Ted Turner promised would be a major announcement, as well as further details about his new Cable News Network II. What they got was nothing less than an old-fashioned revival meeting, with Turner in the pulpit at his messianic best. After a concessionary statement that CNN II would be distributed free to any operator carrying CNN, Turner indicated he was otherwise holding his ground on fees and not caving in to ABC-Westinghouse. "When I cast my lot with the cable industry ten years ago, I dreamed all these things would happen. It's not unexpected that the second-wave companies, the three major networks, would figure out a way to get control of the news on your cable systems." Then he threw away the microphone and began his real pitch, a feverish fifty-minute tirade on the time and money he had spent in Washington lobbying on behalf of the cable industry. "Your battles have been my battles," he told the cable operators, "ever since I joined the industry." His voice bouncing off the back walls of the Copley Plaza ballroom, Turner then reminded his audience, "Timing is everything, and the good Lord and destiny are looking after both of us. If we had lost the retransmission-consent battle, we'd all be a lot poorer. But we've won every important battle we've needed to win against those no-good SOBs who are trying to sneak in the door now."

Despite Turner's heroic rejoinder to the ABC-Westinghouse challenge, most industry observers felt it was just a matter of time before the larger entry with the deeper pockets won the day. Conceding that Turner had "done things no one else could do," *Forbes* magazine wondered what Turner could now do against such seemingly insurmountable odds. *Forbes* took little note, however, of the indecision and turmoil within the corporate ranks of both Westinghouse and ABC. Nor did *Forbes* or anyone else bother to mention that Satellite News Channel's new president, William S. Scott, lacked any experience whatsoever in dealing with the cable industry. Fewer still appreciated the ferocity with which Ted Turner would fight to save CNN as well as his company.

ABC's Roone Arledge was circumspect at best in describing how he would respond to Satellite News Channel's request for network news material. "Raw footage only," he mandated, "and no ABC correspondents on camera." Arledge also ordered ABC News producers to hold back any possible footage from SNC that might later be deemed usable by the network. "Our first priority," an Arledge spokesman told *Broadcasting* magazine, "remains the ABC network news operation. Our facilities will just supply extra footage for the cable service that won't be in competition with broadcast news." And if there was still any misunderstanding, Arledge himself added bluntly, "If Barbara Walters were to interview the Ayatollah Khomeini, obviously we would consider that an exclusive for 'ABC World News Tonight,' and not something for Satellite News Channel."

Turner was elated at Arledge's position and quickly began to see that this battle was not so one-sided after all. "Anybody who goes with them," Ted Turner responded, "is going with a second-rate horseshit operation. Are there any questions?"

Dozens of calls were beginning to come in from cable operators around the country worried that Turner's new broadcast news feed would affect their existing agreements with CNN.

One call to Atlanta, however, offered more than nervous questions and proved, ultimately, to be not a little premonitory. Warner-Amex Satellite Entertainment, the cable partnership between Warner Communications and American Express, was looking for a way to amortize its sales and marketing costs. Warner-Amex had called to inquire whether Turner might be interested in farming out advertising sales of both CNN and CNN II. The deal made sense on all sides, and when Turner was also able to secure Warner-Amex's transponder on RCA's main cable satellite for his new CNN II, he felt the odds suddenly shift in his favor. Like ABC-Westinghouse, Turner thought he had little choice but to put CNN II up on one of the Western Union satellites, which could be received by fewer than 20 percent of all cable systems. He had never expected to find a slot on the RCA bird. Now it was Westinghouse that would be left out on the same limb Turner had found himself dangling from two years ago when RCA's newest satellite began its one-way tour of the cosmos.

And Mad Dog Kavanau was proving, Turner noted, to have been an inspired choice to run CNN II, which he decided on the spur of the moment to rename Headline News. "Kavanau was a fabulous character," says Fran Heaney, "a kind of Ninja newsman. He figured out the whole thirty-minute wheel in two seconds and then organized an entire editorial organization even before they had finished putting up our new building."

With Turner's blessing, Kavanau pushed up his development

budget from $15 million to $20 million. He badgered Reese Schonfeld for more talent, more equipment, more space. In less time than it had taken for him to forget the bathrooms at CNN, Bunky Helfrich had purpose-built a glossy new studio and production facility for Headline News next door to CNN's basement newsroom. Kavanau had huge sliding steel doors installed outside his new control room. Necessary protection, he said, from terrorists who might try to knock his new service off the air. Never exactly thrilled about having to oversee an in-house "competitor" to CNN, Schonfeld became increasingly difficult, in Kavanau's eyes, and began turning down his requests for new expenditures. Soon the two old friends were barely speaking. Some even said the steel doors at Headline News were there to keep Schonfeld, not any unlikely terrorists, off the board and out of the studio. "Working with Reese was no bed of roses," Kavanau acknowledges. "He was a kind of genius, what he did with CNN, but he was never easy to work with. You can check that out with anybody who was there."

Turner himself had become uncomfortable with Schonfeld's towering ego and frequent tests of authority but was even more concerned about the growing threat of unionization at CNN. Noting with intense interest Turner's plan to sell CNN footage to broadcast television stations, most of which were unionized, the National Association of Broadcast Engineers and Technicians (NABET) had sent a team to Atlanta to lay the groundwork for a vote to make Turner Broadcasting a union shop. Turner now had over 450 staffers in a dozen domestic and international bureaus, with others about to open in Philadelphia, Detroit, and even Moscow. He made it clear he expected Reese Schonfeld to resolve the union situation in the company's favor.

Everyone acknowledged that compensation at CNN was low and benefits practically nonexistent. Schonfeld had set up many of the technical jobs, particularly in the bureaus, as arm's-length contractors for hire, thereby avoiding direct conflict with the broadcast unions and allowing CNN to control its costs by expanding and contracting free-lance technical personnel as needed. NABET was also fighting a rearguard action of its own against IATSE, the larger motion picture union that used the decline in feature film production as an excuse to move into the broadcast industry and unionizing CNN had become a high-profile priority. For Turner unionization would mean critical new costs that he would probably not have been able to meet. It would

Sent away to boarding school first at the age of six, Turner entered Chattanooga's elite McCallie School in the seventh grade. After a rocky start, he was honored as "Neatest Cadet," won the Tennessee debating championship, and graduated with a Gentleman's C grade average. "Ted hated McCallie," attested his mother. "He was a devil there." "I love McCallie," Turner says now. "Probably no single thing or institution has influenced my life more." (Photo: The McCallie School.)

Despite years of beatings and abuse, no father ever looked more fondly on his son. Beaming at Ted's 1960 wedding to Judy Nye, Ed Turner told the twenty-one-year-old bride, "The provider must have his way. There is just no other way any marriage will work." Less than three years later, Ted's first marriage fell apart when he rammed Judy, then pregnant with their second child, Robert Edward (Teddy) Turner IV, in a sailboat race to keep her from beating him. (Photo: Julia Nye Hallisy.)

"There were always sparks flying around them," says Turner family friend and former crewmate, Legarè VanNess. Even as they were leaving the reception *(top)*, however, it was obvious to first wife, Judy Nye, the honeymoon might already be over. In 1964, Ted married his second wife, Jane Shirley Smith *(above left)*, an airline stewardess from Birmingham, Alabama, who bore him three more children *(above right)*. "Business comes first," he told her. "My boat comes second. And you come third." Incredibly, that marriage lasted 24 years. (Photos, clockwise, from top: Julia Nye Hallisy; Jay Leviton; *Atlanta Journal and Constitution*.)

Turner took time out in June 1985 from his ferocious assault on CBS, Inc., to attend Teddy's graduation *(above top)* from The Citadel. With him there were (left to right) his second wife, Janie; son Rhett; daughter Jennie; and Ted's seventy-six-year-old mother, Florence Rooney Turner Carter. Less than two weeks later, he would change course and begin negotiations to acquire MGM from Kirk Kerkorian. (Photo: Wade Spees/Picture Group.)

Five years later, Turner had discarded his role of proud family man and taken his romance with Jane Fonda public. There was no mistaking Hollywood's newest power couple, when a newly svelte Ted Turner showed up at the 1990 Academy Awards with Fonda *(right)*. (Photo: Reuters/Bettmann.)

CNN provides Turner with extraordinary access. He dines frequently at the White House, whether its occupant is Ronald Reagan *(left)*, George Bush, or Bill Clinton, and sees himself as a kind of ambassador without portfolio when he visits everyone from Fidel Castro to Saddam Hussein. (Photo: Courtesy Ronald Reagan Library.)

Expelled from Brown University in 1959, Turner has accumulated nearly a dozen honorary degrees, including an LLD from Emory University, which he received with former UN ambassador Andrew Young *(above)*. In 1993, Brown made him a Doctor of Humane Letters to complement the strictly honorary Bachelor of Philosophy degree conferred in 1989. (Photo: *Atlanta Constitution*.) Still sporting his "Gettysburg" beard, Turner accepts the 1992 EMMY *(right)* for CNN's historic Gulf War coverage. (Photo: James Smeal/Ron Galella Ltd.)

Turner used the occasion of CNN's tenth-anniversary blow-out *(left)* on June 1, 1990 to introduce Jane Fonda to Larry King, the news network's first $1 million-a-year anchor and CNN's only real on-air celebrity. "This is a happy—this is a getting along thing, right?" the twice-married King asked his boss. "The two of you are—in . . . ?" Later, the notorious puff-ball interviewer asked Jane, "Did you two recently—is this true—release six lizards in your Santa Monica house, to hunt down bugs because they're more ecological?" A flabbergasted Fonda replied, "No. No. I have rabbits and things that do that." (Photo: Rob Nelson/Black Star.)

Time magazine made Turner its 1991 Man of the Year *(above right)* for rewriting the very meaning of news from something that *has* happened to something that *is happening*. That same year, he paid $320 million for Hanna-Barbera (Yogi Bear, the Flintstones, the Jetsons, et al). Turner now owns nearly half of all the animated cartoons in the country, more than enough to make his new twenty-four-hour Cartoon Channel an instant worldwide success. (Photo: David Tulis/*Atlanta Journal and Constitution*.)

Reese Schonfeld *(above left)*, CNN's first president and chief operating officer until Turner fired him in 1982, was known as "the godfather of electronic news" and is generally credited as the real genius behind Cable News Network. Today, Turner takes most of the credit for CNN's extraordinary success. Often compared to William S. Paley *(above right)*, Turner, in fact, has played an even more influential role in reshaping the global broadcast industry. "I'm sorry we can't do business," Turner told one of Paley's senior executives in 1982, "but it's really no problem. One day I'm going to buy your whole network anyway." Enamored of the 1950s sitcoms he grew up watching, Turner was all smiles when he met with MCA's Sidney Sheinberg *(below left)* and the original "Beaver," Jerry Mathers, to announce his relaunch of "Leave It to Beaver." (Photos, clockwise, from top left: Cotten Alston; Michael A. Marcotte/Crain Communications; and AP/Wide World.)

Ted Turner has continued to reinvent himself over the past forty years, but he has seldom let his feet leave the ground or forgotten his lifetime love affair with the Great Outdoors. A Confederate Yankee born in Cincinnati, Ohio, Turner is the very epitome of a contemporary Southern country gentleman and still owns impressive antebellum plantations in both South Carolina and Florida. He is also one of the largest landowners in the West, with major ranches in both Montana and New Mexico. He and Fonda both list CNN's Atlanta headquarters as their official residence, but they spend less than a week a month in their new $3 million penthouse atop CNN Center. Turner has traded his old white Toyota *(top right)* in for a limousine, but he still enjoys an occasional turkey shoot in Florida *(bottom right)*. His million-dollar "mansionette" in Roswell, Georgia *(bottom left)* was once JJ Ebaugh's hideaway. (Photos: clockwise, from top left: Kenneth Jarecke/Contact; David Burnett/Contact; Michael Pugh/*Sports Illustrated;* George Lange/ Outline; and Rob Nelson.)

Reese Schonfeld and his "Reese's Pieces" created CNN from ground zero in just eleven months. A group of early employees, including current chief operating officer Ed "No Relation" Turner (*center*, sitting on step at front), posed proudly in front of CNN's first home, the old white-columned former bawdy house at 1044 West Peachtree Street, Atlanta.

"We aren't just starting up a new network," Ted "Mad Dog" Kavanau deadpanned. "We're running a television school, too. It was beginning to look like the whole project would depend on an army of college kids" *(top)*. CNN's non-union "veejays" learned enough to get CNN on the air and revolutionized traditional broadcast production procedures in the bargain. Today CNN's huge Atlanta newsroom *(bottom)* is the vortex of the world's largest news gathering organization (Photos: Cotten Alston; Cotten Alston; and Ted Thai/*Time* magazine.)

Turner's extraordinary libido often led him into odd extramarital liaisons, like his two-year affair with *Playboy* covergirl Liz Wickersham. A few of Turner's female friends, however, like Barbara Pyle *(top center)*, helped crystalize Turner's diverse interests. Pyle met Turner in 1980 and has served ever since as TBS' conscience on environmental issues. Yue-Sai Kan *(top left)* was one of China's most popular television stars and admired Ted's "lovely children." Kathleen Sullivan *(top right)*, was a Salt Lake City newscaster when she met Turner and became CNN's first foreign correspondent, before there was an all-news network. Gabrielle (Gay) Manigault *(center left)* is the daughter of one of Turner's best friends, Charleston publisher Peter Manigault. Mary Alice Williams *(center bottom)* was CNN's first New York bureau chief and one of CNN's most prominent anchors until she left to join NBC. Katherine Leach (bottom, left), a spunky Atlanta interior decorator, may be one of the few ever to silence "The Mouth of the South." (Photos, clockwise, from top left: Fred Conrad/*New York Times; Atlanta Business Chronicle;* AP/Wide World; Ron Galella Ltd.; Ron Galella Ltd.; *Atlanta Journal and Constitution.*)

Turner left Liz Wickersham *(top)* for JJ Ebaugh; their eight-year romance ended when *Atlanta* magazine called her "The Woman Who Tamed Ted Turner." (Photos: Ron Galella Ltd.; Ralph Daniel/*Atlanta* magazine.)

A man's man and also a man of the people, the same Ted Turner who could bask shirtless at a Braves' baseball game, beer in hand and "chaw" of tobacco in his cheek, would also show up at the Elysée Palace with second wife, Jane Smith, to meet French premier François Mitterrand *(top)*. Campaigning harder than most political candidates, Turner isn't running for any political office, yet. He travels incessantly, often giving several speeches a week, and usually arranges to meet the man in charge of whatever country he happens to be in at the moment. He met kings, princes, and multimillionaires during his ocean racing days. Now, with Fonda at his side, Turner is on a first-name basis with most world leaders. Mikhail Gorbachev *(bottom)* credits Turner's CNN with helping save his life and quashing the coup that threatened to return the Soviet Union to a dictatorship. (Photos: AP/Wide World.)

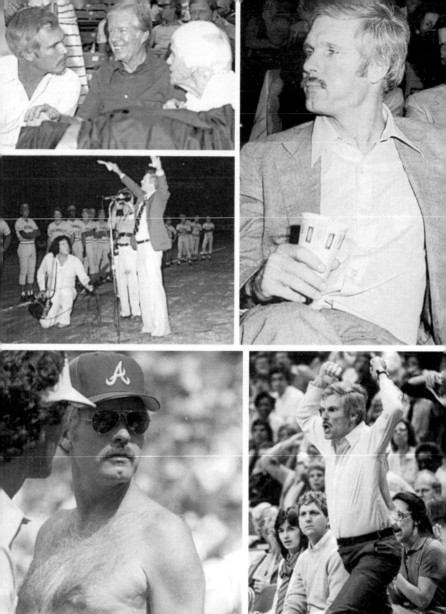

Turner *(top right)* once pushed a baseball around the bases with his nose, while Fonda *(bottom right)* was hired to shape up the Los Angeles Dodgers. When Turner acquired the Braves in 1976, he discovered a new mentor in Bill Bartholemay *(bottom left)*. (Photos, clockwise from top right: UPI/Bettman; AP/Wide World; *Atlanta Journal and Constitution.*)

Opposite: Jimmy Carter and Miss Lillian *(upper left)* often joined Turner in the owner's box. Taught to chew tobacco at spring training, Ted would show up everywhere with a plug of Red Man in his cheek, his spittin' cup in hand *(upper right)*. Turner never hesitated to go shirtless in his pre-Fonda days *(bottom left)*. He led the crowd *(center left)* in singing "Take Me Out to the Ball Game" but forced 40,000 opening-day fans to sing the song three times, until, he said, they got the words right. Ted took his frustrations indoors when he bought the Atlanta Hawks in 1977, but despite his trademark histrionics *(bottom right)*, the Hawks have yet to make it to the NBA championship round. (Photos: Walter Victor; except for bottom right, Randy Taylor/Sygma.)

Ted Turner won more ocean races than anyone else in history, was named "Yachtsman of the Year" an unprecedented four times, successfully defended the America's Cup in 1977 with an outdated, secondhand *Courageous (top)*, then went home to ponder his enormous store of silver trophies *(bottom left)*. "We were the best sailboat crew in the history of the planet," he observed, modestly, "and we knew it." Turner may have needed assistance from his tactician, Gary Jobson, to win the singlehanded Demitasse Derby *(center right)*, but he brought Jobson and his entire *Courageous* crew, including sixteen-year-old Teddy, home first in the disastrous 1979 Fastnet. (Photos, clockwise from top: Bob Dollard; AP/ Wide World; AP/Wide World; *Atlanta Constitution*.)

Although Turner kept his victorious 1977 crew together for the 1980 America's Cup, the pressures of repeating as defender and launching CNN proved too much. Turner tried every trick in the book but was beaten badly by the infinitely better prepared Dennis Conner. Turner barely had time even for the daily strategy walks with Gary Jobson *(bottom right)*, which had proved so useful in 1977. Nothing could make up for his lack of boat time and when he was finally "excused" by the selection committee in early August, Turner would shake hands with commodore Robert Mc-Cullough *(bottom left)*, but never sail again. A few months later he even sold *Courageous*. (Photos: Bob Dollard; UPI/Bettmann.)

When they finally married after a whirlwind two-year romance, Fonda and Turner chose to be surrounded by their close friends and family. Jimmy Brown *(bottom, far left, partially hidden)*, Ted's lifelong companion, teacher, surrogate father, and general Turner factotum, arranged the private affair and made certain everything at Avalon plantation was just the way his Mr. Ted wanted it that day. Later, Fonda exercised her wifely prerogative, when Ted fell asleep *(top right)* during the Braves' 1992 National League championship playoffs. (Photos, clockwise, from top left: Gamma Liaison; *Atlanta Constitution;* R. N. Owen/Black Star.)

also almost certainly mean the end of the popular veejay system, which allowed entry-level personnel an opportunity to learn on the job while performing the multiple tasks of writer, camera operator, editor, and producer—an opportunity not available under union rules.

The union, however, may have been the least of Schonfeld's growing list of problems. Everyone at CNN knew his distaste for matters financial but assumed that, as the network's chief executive, Reese Schonfeld had at least a handle on the numbers. Turner Broadcasting's chief financial officer, Bill Bevins, was beginning to suspect otherwise. Schonfeld had an amazing ability, Kavanau recalls, to keep a running count in his head of all the expenses he was incurring and then make sure he came in under budget at the. end of the year. CNN had earned particular praise during 1981 among news professionals everywhere for its interminable but riveting live coverage of the Falklands war. The network may have overstayed in Beirut, but it had been able to capture startling live images of the street fighting there after the major networks packed up and went home. Through Schonfeld's legerdemain, CNN was able to overcome a government blackout and broadcast live pictures from Poland of the incipient Solidarity uprising. Schonfeld simply arranged for a CNN stringer offshore on an island in the Baltic Sea to pirate the official Polish television signal and then retransmit live to Atlanta. These expensive editorial "stunts" made front-page headlines for CNN but, as Bevins feared, also were making a shambles of Schonfeld's CNN budget.

Schonfeld's innovative, ad hoc approach, however, was beginning to unravel. He sent Dan Schorr to Berlin on the strong "hunch" that the Shiite Muslims were about to release several American hostages. Schorr could not confirm the rumor, even through his usually impeccable White House and CIA sources, but went anyway when Schonfeld told him CBS had already dispatched Dan Rather. The only unusual sight Schorr witnessed during five lonely days at Frankfurt am Main was a badly disappointed ABC News crew, which finally showed up, certain that CNN would never allow Dan Schorr to spend several days at a U.S. Air Force base in Germany if a major story was not about to break. With cash still tight and NABET knocking on the door, Schonfeld's often exciting and sometimes productive seat-of-the-pants management style was beginning to lose favor up on Techwood's third floor.

When the day of the union vote finally arrived, NABET organizers were certain they had made sufficient inroads among the younger, politically motivated CNN staffers to ensure victory. Turner called in Schonfeld and the other managers as the votes were counted. Schonfeld was certain he knew and understood the people who worked for him and could depend on their support. Turner and Bevins were considerably less confident. When the final count was in and it became obvious that the employees had endorsed management and rejected the union by an overwhelming three-to-one majority, Turner's congratulations struck Schonfeld as perfunctory, perhaps even a little sour. Unable to savor what should have been a triumphant moment, Schonfeld left the Techwood studios that night knowing "Turner was prepared to fire me on the spot and name Jim Kitchell as CNN's new president if we had ever lost that vote."

"Reese was pretty aggressive and, in those days, kind of a maniac," recalls Fran Heaney. "The TBS people didn't like him at all. But he got what he needed, and without him, there never would have been any CNN." Like Turner, Schonfeld was a supreme risk taker, and like Turner, he may also have been a fatalist. The difference between the two, however, was that Schonfeld's fate was now in Ted Turner's hands.

Still not entirely certain of his own destiny, Turner had become preoccupied with the ABC-Westinghouse challenge and spent an increasing amount of his time touring the country making speeches against the networks and against ABC in particular. Brandishing purloined copies of internal ABC memos, Turner produced evidence that the network had done its best to stifle cable's remarkable growth. He had a field day with the trade press, castigating ABC's bloated network budgets and heavy emphasis on T & A with "jiggle shows" like "Charlie's Angels," playing up his own pioneer role and unceasing lobbying efforts on behalf of the cable industry.

With just six weeks to go before Headline News' scheduled New Year's Eve launch, ABC struck back unexpectedly and announced that it was expanding its own evening network news program from thirty to sixty minutes. Despite serious objections from their affiliates, both CBS and NBC announced that they would soon follow suit. "Watching all of this with a certain bemusement," *The New York Times* commented wryly, "are the folks at Cable News Network, which provides twenty-four hours of news daily, including a two-hour evening program from eight to ten o'clock each weeknight. Indeed, on breaking stories, CNN is sometimes the only live show in town. And now CNN is about to launch a new service, Headline News, which will offer yet another twenty-four hours of news programming each day. Does Ted Turner know something," the *Times* asked, "that the networks don't?"

Not everyone was as sanguine as *The New York Times*. A highly regarded media research study commissioned by Compton Advertising reflected the prevailing opinion that "Turner will enjoy a short-term advantage, but the ABC-Westinghouse venture will dominate by 1990." The Compton study predicted Turner might even have the edge for as long as four or five years, but then "a merger or outright sale will be necessary." Even Turner's old friends at *Forbes* were moved to comment, "Most men might then sell out and go away, rather than crash in flames, which is increasingly likely to be Ted Turner's ultimate fate."

By December 31, 1981, Headline News was ready to burst forth upon the world. The new service had enlisted fewer than one million cable subscribers, but that had not deterred Ted Turner from laying on an impressive midnight fireworks display that would light up most of downtown Atlanta. Turner was upstairs with Schonfeld and a host of media and advertising dignitaries in the third-floor conference room at Techwood, uncorking the champagne. "Mad Dog Kavanau had created a news network that wasn't for old people, or the hard of hearing, or substance abusers," recalls Fran Heaney, whose graphics wizardry helped accelerate Headline News' already frantic pace. "We were simply too fast."

At 11:59 P.M. the fireworks began exploding outside, spelling out a giant "CNN #2—1982" against the darkened Atlanta sky. Kavanau himself was behind the control board, going berserk as the seconds ticked off to midnight. Suddenly Headline News was on the air. Anchorman Chuck Roberts quietly intoned, "Hello again, and Happy New Year. In the news, Poland's military regime will force the unemployed into compulsory labor in an effort to put Poland's economy back on its feet. . . ."

Kavanau had promised his people, "I will not let you fail." He was as good as his word, cramming twenty-two stories into the first eight minutes of Headline News' air time. Turner came into the studio," Fran Heaney remembers, "shouting and shaking everybody's hand. 'I knew we could do it,' he kept saying. 'I knew we could do it. Happy New Year, everybody!' Then he came over and kissed me. Fortunately Ted watched only a few minutes of the news and then gathered up his crowd and took them all back upstairs." Just in time, since Paul Amos, Kavanau's stalwart assistant and the new general manager of Headline News, was still reshuffling several late-breaking stories he had just pulled off the wire as the service switched on. Kavanau was beside himself, certain that Turner would return to the control room and discover they had been forced to run a rehearsal tape to fill up the remaining minutes of Headline News' first half hour on the air. "When they left," Heaney says, "we were finally able to regroup. We got the service restarted at the beginning of hour two, never again to stop."

Mad Dog Kavanau's "If it bleeds, it leads" editorial philosophy was clearly reflected in his new service's disproportionate number of death and disaster stories. One critic counted nine such pieces—the kind that could be told quickly, with arresting visuals —in less than twenty minutes of air time, including a Galveston, Texas, barge accident; an Amtrack derailment; an attempted cave rescue in England; a natural-gas fire in Oklahoma; a man left dangling in California from a high-tension electric wire after being electrocuted; a father who died trying to save his drowning son; and a mine disaster in Ohio. "So much for Ted Turner's complaints," wrote *Atlanta Constitution* TV editor Richard Zoglin, "about blood and gore on television news."

In early 1982, Judge Orinda Evans of the U.S. District Court in Georgia gave CNN a much needed boost, decreeing in a landmark decision that exclusion from the White House television pool "denies the public and the press their limited right of access" guaranteed by the First Amendment. Suddenly CNN had been elevated to parity with the three major networks. In an out-of-court settlement, all parties accepted CNN's inclusion in the White House pool, acknowledging "no inequality of personnel, equipment, or competence as among CNN, ABC, CBS, and NBC."

As Martin Mayer points out in *Making News,* his thoughtful dissection of the television news business, the news service Reese Schonfeld and Ten Turner had built "with Dan Schorr and Charles Bierbauer, as well as Tom Braden and Patrick Buchanan, and Evans and Novak . . . was quite decently balanced—and what with Bob Wussler in the front office and Ed ('No Relation') Turner down in the basement, CNN could lay at least as strong a claim to the spirit of the old CBS News as Van Gordon Sauter and Ed Joyce ever could in the CBS building itself."

The pool victory, however sweet, came at a high price. Legal fees and expenses ran nearly $2 million. Under the ruling, CNN would also be obligated, moreover, to purchase at least $1 million in new technical apparatus to handle overseas pool assignments. CNN would also be expected to share a minimum of one-sixth of total pool costs, expenses the cash-tight Turner organization could ill afford, as it cinched in its belt and battened down for a long struggle against SNC. Turner abhorred the new drain on his cash flow but savored the irony that it was Westinghouse, after all, that had provided him with the funds to launch CNN in the first place, by acquiring his Charlotte station in 1980 for $20 million.

Calling him "one of the nation's most celebrated entrepreneurs," New York District Court judge John M. Canella handed Turner a curious personal defeat just as the Georgia courts were confirming his momentous victory in the landmark suit. Judge Canella made short shrift of a move to dismiss a breach of contract suit levied against Turner by publishers Simon & Schuster. Ted had committed to write his autobiography and then retained his friend and Fastnet crew member, Christian Williams, to ghost the book. Simon & Schuster rejected the manuscript and sought to recover their embarrassingly modest $25,000 advance. The book, later published by Times Books under the title *Lead, Follow, or Get Out of the Way*, was written off by the *Atlanta Constitution*, which said "most of it is nothing more than ingratiating. It is full of heroics, but excruciatingly bereft of real people or real feelings." Ted Turner himself bought up most of the modest print run and distributed autographed copies to his friends and business associates. In 1986 Simon & Schuster would again contract for Turner's life story, this time paying him the considerably larger advance of $1.2 million. S&S group president Jack Romanos said at the time, "Turner's life has many aspects that echo the Iacocca phenomenon. It's a surefire number one best-seller." After a heroic effort by the magazine writer Joe Klein to capture Turner in print, Ted himself decided he had not yet found the author who could do him justice and finally returned the advance, although the publisher had to send an aide to Atlanta to collect it. Ted Turner's autobiography, if it is ever written at all, will almost inevitably be a very long one-character book.

When Turner decided to substitute Headline News for the CNN news feed he had begun selling to local broadcast stations, he knew he might open himself up to severe criticism from the cable industry. But Turner felt he needed the extra revenue stream and also felt that increasing the new service's audience would help legitimize Headline News against the heavy promotional onslaught he expected from SNC. "When I make a decision," Turner told the BBC, trying to explain the logic of his move, "I go ahead and make it. If I'm wrong, I admit it and change. It's just like sailing a boat. It doesn't always work out. But with a boat, there can only be one captain, or you won't get anywhere. Nelson manned the fleet, didn't he?" As susceptible to Turner-speak as anyone else, the BBC nodded politely and broadcast that inimitable statement of management philosophy, verbatim, in a fascinatingly uninformative profile of Ted Turner titled *The Man from Atlanta*. Turner, of course, not only rebroadcast the program on his Superstation, but kept tapes handy for anyone wishing a quick refresher course in how to build a media empire.

More than two hundred broadcast television news directors, a third of them from network affiliates, showed up in Atlanta to hear Turner's syndication pitch for Headline News. They soon warmed to his proposal when he exclaimed, "We symbolize the end of network news as you have known it. Before we entered the picture, a station that wanted to include national or international stories on its own news shows was stuck with whatever the networks chose to feed you from their reject pile." He quoted CBS's Richard Salant, who admitted, "When we first began, I told our affiliates [CBS' news feed] will be our 'overset matter,' our outtakes, not our best stuff." Well, Turner boomed, now the "best stuff" was available to everybody.

"The response was fantastic," exclaimed Henry Gillespie, chairman of Turner Program Services, the unit designated to handle distribution of Headline News to the television industry. Gillespie's view was generally confirmed by the enthusiastic reaction of most of the broadcasters in attendance. "My impression is that a lot of stations are definitely interested," said Fred Barber, general manager of Atlanta's NBC affiliate, WSB-TV. "That would include us."

"We're very interested for all seven of the Gannett stations," said Jeff Davidson, vice-president of Gannett Broadcasting, adding, "We've asked all of our station managers to propose time periods when they could fit Headline News into their daily schedules." Gillespie admitted that it would "take some explaining to dissolve fears on the part of the cable operators, who might resent 'their' news service being peddled to TV stations, which they see, in many cases, as their direct competitors." Turner had already provoked one unexpected response, from outside the cable industry, when CBS announced it was planning to offer its affiliates a "night-owl news service" between the hours of 2:00 A.M. and 5:00 A.M. ABC and NBC were quick to follow with similar overnight services, all in direct response to Turner's decision to sell Headline News to their affiliates.

Inside Black Rock, a few farsighted CBS executives were still politicking furiously in favor of a direct entry into cable news. Ernest Leiser, a senior vice-president in the news division, had been requested by no less than Bill Paley himself to develop a business plan for CBS's own twenty-four-hour all-news cable channel. Paley had recently given up operating control of his company to his hand-picked successor, Thomas Wyman, but he retained nominal authority as chairman of the CBS board. Leiser's thoughtful, voluminous report could easily have been written by Reese Schonfeld and, in fact, followed CNN's format and cost structure almost to the letter. Leiser calculated that the project would require an investment of about $50 million to reach breakeven, or just about $15 million more than CNN had cost two years earlier—the principal cost differential being an additional $10– $12 million Leiser estimated in unavoidable union compensation and benefits.

Word of Leiser's business plan leaked out to Turner, who redoubled his efforts to sign up as many CBS affiliates for his new Headline News syndication program as possible, hoping to distract this new enemy and keep CBS off-balance. Ernie Leiser was a respected veteran news manager, near the end of a distinguished career when Bill Paley singled him out to champion the cable news project. Unfortunately both Paley and Leiser were far removed from the treacherous political currents swirling through Black Rock during those unsettled days. Paley had stacked the CBS board with independent outside directors, most of whom were content to let Wyman run the company as Paley's anointed heir. Paley had used up most of his own waning influence by persuading Wyman to go forward with a disastrous cultural channel, an ill-fated $30 million leap into cable that the company had just written off.

When Paley brought Leiser to the board with yet another cable venture, at a time when network revenues were down significantly in the soft early 1980s economy and expenses in every division were skyrocketing through the roof, the outcome was almost preordained. Leiser made his presentation and then watched Paley fuss and fume when Wyman refused even to call a vote on the matter.

"Is that what we've become?" Paley shouted. "A bunch of idiots who don't know how to say anything but no?" Gathering up his papers, he threw a withering look at Wyman and stormed out of the meeting, leaving Ernie Leiser to beat his own diplomatic retreat. Within weeks CBS had, once again, forgotten all about its natural and obvious interest in cable news. Ernest Leiser took early retirement shortly thereafter, assuming a senior teaching post at the Columbia School of Journalism. Tom Wyman had trouble even remembering Leiser's project until a few years later, when Ted Turner would refresh his memory and come calling on CBS.

Not yet privy to the outcome of Leiser's presentation to the CBS board, Turner wanted to throw yet another obstacle in the path of any potential competitors. "CNN Radio was all Turner's idea," says Ted Kavanau. "None of the rest of us would have thought you could recycle the same material yet again. He's the genius behind all this, even if we were the people who put it all together. Turner knows how to capture every market, even if there isn't even a market there."

Turner was ready to throw everything he had at ABC-Westinghouse, and even then he wasn't certain it would be enough. He knew he had the advantage of being on the right satellite, and he felt he could count on a certain amount of loyalty from cable operators. To make absolutely sure, however, he had himself photographed in workingman's jeans and slightly muddied boots, guitar in hand, looking for all the world like a small-town Marlboro Man. "I Was Cable When Cable Wasn't Cool," the shot was captioned, a takeoff on a Tom T. Hall country hit. Blown up even bigger than life-size on twenty-four-sheeters and plastered on billboards outside every cable industry gathering in the country, the poster would "remind people," explained Arthur Sando, TBS's new publicity chief, "what a pioneer Ted Turner really was. He had fought their battles and built their programming, and now it was time the cable industry showed Ted Turner they were behind him. That poster was just a reminder he'd been behind cable ever since he joined the industry."

Opening up an all-fronts attack, Turner not only played on the loyalty of the cable industry, but began to foment suspicion of

ABC's underlying motives in entering the field. He charged that ABC was working to destroy the cable industry even as it vied for a piece of the action. Citing the network's quick move to cut its losses in its failed Cable Arts Channel, Turner accused ABC of flooding the market with "loss leaders," blocking out legitimate cable program prospects and then collapsing them when it became clear they could never make money. In an open letter to cable operators, Turner proved how devious the network could be by quoting the chairman of the ABC affiliates' committee, who urged local stations to help the network's anticable cause by airing every possible news story, talk show, and documentary detailing the threat of cable to "free, over-the-air television broadcasting."

"With one hand," Turner charged, "ABC embraces cable with its proposed Satellite News Channel. In the other is a dagger to put us away." Hammering his point home, he added, "ABC has said all along that broadcasting is their first love and their first commitment. That's why I don't think they are going to get any clearances in the cable industry. And if they don't get clearances, they're not going to be able to stay in business." And just to make sure that the ABC and Westinghouse shareholders got the message, Turner repeated his charge in *Broadcasting* magazine and then said it all one more time for *The Wall Street Journal*.

Turner found it convenient to wage his war of words against all three networks, not just ABC. He brought down the house at a standing-room-only National League of Cities convention session attended by mayors and city councilmen from around the country. "Network television's staple of sleazy sex and violence," he decried, "are contributing to the moral decay of our cities . . . Network news focuses on the bad news that depresses our people . . . They only mention public officials when there's a scandal . . . Their newsmen are bigger than the news . . . Who elected Walter Cronkite president, anyway?" Turner urged the municipal managers to "franchise and franchise quickly. Modern cable television, that's the modern way to communicate with your constituents.

"The future must be different in the communication field if we are to survive as a free nation. When we were boys," he added to reverential applause, "I volunteered for military service. I figured I owed two years to my country." Of course, Turner didn't say he'd never actually served two years, but who would ever bother to check that he had enlisted in the Coast Guard's six-month reserve program to *avoid* being drafted for a full two years? Later, at a Milwaukee Advertising Club meeting, he shamelessly quoted an "anonymous source" when he announced, "Network television is responsible for a documented four-hundred-percent increase in crime over the past twenty years." His audience cheered enthusiastically, despite the fact that it was their investment of hundreds of millions of advertising dollars each year that kept the networks in business.

That Turner could so blithely and blatantly mouth such statements never seemed to bother his audiences; in fact, his poetic license helped pack the house wherever he appeared. Even when he stepped over the line, as he often did, his message and his passionate delivery usually won his audience over. "American television network executives," he charged before a Veterans of Foreign Wars convention in Philadelphia, "should be tried as traitors." This time he named Hollywood's studio executives as co-conspirators. "They are all traitors to this country," he said, "and deserve to be tried as such." After urging the veterans to join him in his quest for a congressional investigation of network television, he gracefully accepted the VFW's annual "News Media Award" as the man who had done the most that year to promote "traditional American values."

When he found himself addressing a House subcommittee convened to look into violence on television, Turner began his remarks by exclaiming, "A large part of our populace is sick." Pounding his fist on the witness table and then standing to repeat his comment for the television cameras (including his own, which carried his testimony live over the Superstation), Turner rambled on for several minutes and then brought the proceedings to a standstill by demanding, "The network's own television licenses should be revoked immediately and given to responsible citizens who will do good." He was followed in the witness chair by the Reverend Donald Wildmon of the Coalition for Better Television and then by Dr. Thomas Radacki of the National Coalition on Television Violence. Observers might have been forgiven for assuming that Turner considered these archconservative spokesmen his intended "responsible citizens." And any doubt that Turner had crossed over into the lunatic fringe should have evaporated when he called for a cigarettelike "caution statement" to be run at the bottom of the screen on all network television broadcasts, alerting viewers—"Warning: Too much television can be damaging to your mental health." But it was only Ted Turner, warming up to the real battle at hand, against ABC-Westinghouse and anybody else who sought to invade his TV turf.

"It was a little hard to take this guy seriously," says Les Brown, then television editor of *The New York Times*. "His manners were, to say the least, a little unusual. Most of the time he sounded almost as if he were drunk. When I first met him, I just assumed he was some kind of redneck on the loose. But right from the beginning there was something about the guy that was engaging, almost endearing. No question, he's a man's man, but back then he was also refreshing, candid, and very, very likable. He would say anything, but you got the feeling that he believed most of it. He was," says Brown, "unlike anybody else I'd ever seen in television.

"There was one situation," Brown recalls, "where I was interviewing him for a cover piece in *Channels* magazine. I was using a recorder, and when he'd launch into another one of his famous tirades—'The networks are destroying the nation,' that sort of thing—I'd switch it off. He would slow down. We'd chat for a few minutes, and then I'd start taping again. Off he'd go, on another of those tirades, almost as if I were switching him on and off. I think he knows exactly what he's doing. He was always the greatest interview in the world. And his personality serves him well. I have never met anyone else who could get away with the things Ted Turner does, the things he says, and not have the wrath of God come down on them instantly."

Richard Zoglin, TV editor of the *Atlanta Constitution* during the early 1980s and the media writer with the most frequent access to Turner in those days, agrees. "He made a lot of noise," Zoglin remembers, "that made him seem like a dyed-in-the-wool right-winger, a radical conservative just like Jesse Helms or Don Wildmon. But I never thought he really had anything in common with those people. I think he discovered he could get all the attention he wanted by running the networks into the ground. It made good business sense, but I also think he tapped a real southern vein and knew people were becoming uncomfortable with some of the things they saw on TV. Turner," adds Zoglin, "preferred the old programs himself, and he preferred the old movies. Like *Gone With the Wind, Citizen Kane*. If anything, he was an 'America first' type, a cold war type, very patriotic. Then he began to change."

* * *

For several months Turner had been rebuffing calls coming into his Atlanta office from an unsuspected fan of CNN well known for his own unquenchable rhetoric. Although he'd been too busy to respond to the first few inquiries, Turner finally was able to accept Fidel Castro's invitation to visit Cuba in early February 1982. "Fidel says he's been watching CNN," Turner explained, "and thinks it's great. Now he wants to meet the guy who started it. He's also a baseball fan, and he knows I own the Braves.

"I'm a very curious person," Turner said, unaware that he might be taking his first step toward the education of Citizen Ted. "I had never been in a Communist country, and I was just interested in learning a little bit about how it all worked."

Traveling with a CNN crew of three, Turner took a commercial flight from Miami to Havana and spent four days with Castro. "It's not somber like Russia is somber," he said excitedly. "I've never been to Russia, but I hear it's somber. Cuba is tropical, and the people are like the weather. They still cha-cha-cha and all that." He spent two days with Castro on the south coast of Cuba, first fishing and then duck shooting. "He's an exceptionally good shot," Turner commented, "and I ain't bad myself." In spite of a broken finger he had sustained in a game of basketball, Castro managed one duck per one and a half shells. "I don't really know how many he got," Turner added, "but he chooses his shots carefully. He gave me an award—best ratio of ducks per shot of any guest he'd ever had." Back in Havana they toured the city, visiting several factories and schools as well as the capital's broadcast facilities. Then Castro took the owner of the Atlanta Braves to his first Cuban League baseball game.

Turner was enthralled and, seizing the opportunity, suggested his Superstation televise the Cuban All-Star Game. "They're going to play it at night for us because the Braves play a televised afternoon game that day, May 9. I don't know how we'll do with advertisers, but I think it will be interesting. People are always asking what kind of baseball they play down there. Now they can see for themselves." Turner also attempted to arrange through his host an international all-star game between Cuba and the United States. "But I'll have to go to Bowie Kuhn about that," he said, "and who knows?"

During a late night soiree at Havana's famed old Tropicana nightclub, Turner was able to persuade Castro to tape a promotional spot for CNN. The next morning, Turner's last in Cuba, they cut a four-minute testimonial in which Castro offered a good-natured apology for "smuggling" the CNN signal into Cuba. "Space is universal," theorized the foremost Communist leader in the Western Hemisphere, "and news is universal, also. One cannot, therefore, smuggle news, since it belongs to everyone." He had become addicted to CNN's twenty-four-hour schedule, he said, and watched the news network "quite often" when he was working very late into the night.

Back in Atlanta, Turner was surprised at the rash of criticism his trip received. After a debriefing in Washington by the National Security Council, he decided to hold a press conference in his Techwood offices to set the record straight. "People only complain when they don't like something," he theorized, waving one of the long, dark, hand-rolled Havana cigars Castro had given him and looking statesmanlike in a new Oleg Cassini gray pinstriped suit, part of the booty he received for endorsing the designer in a magazine advertisement. "Nobody ever calls when they like what you are doing. They figure that's what you should have done anyway."

Even his mother expressed concern about his trip to Cuba, however, and Turner interrupted the interview for his ritual Wednesday telephone call to Cincinnati. "You've got the wrong impression, Mom," he tried to explain. "It wasn't illegal. I went down there as a newsman. I've already talked to the people at the White House and told them everything I learned down there. I just went down there as Citizen Turner. Everything's okay, Mom. Yes, I love you. Everybody's fine. I'll see you soon."

Turner took his feet off the desk, walked to a window overlooking the old Progressive Club golf course, and, assuming his version of a statesmanlike pose, put down his Havana and stuffed his hands in his pockets. "I told the president," he said somberly of Castro, "to ease up a bit. I told him, 'You're a little too harsh in what you say about us.' He's a very interesting, very colorful man. It's hard to understand," he concluded, any shred of diplomacy now eluding him completely, "how we can trade with Russia and not with him. After all, Castro's just a knothole on the log."

Knothole or not, Castro had made a profound impression. He and Turner talked for hours about the land, about the environment, about ways they could improve relations between their countries. It wasn't political, Turner said later; more personal, one on one. "I realized I was just ambling through life." He had been moved to find a kindred spirit in Castro, who not only grappled with the larger issues that were beginning to bedevil Turner, but seemed undaunted by the immense challenges they presented. And, like Turner, Castro also seemed to know how to have fun.

"I interviewed Turner right after his first trip to Cuba," Richard Zoglin recalls. "He showed me pictures of the two of them posing like a couple of body builders at Muscle Beach. It was obvious that trip got him thinking about his own future. Turner's not deep —he has instant opinions, and when something shakes those opinions, to his credit, he's willing to change. I don't think Turner ever gave much serious thought to anything. He tended to operate on instinct. But his instincts are incredibly good."

During his visit with Castro, Turner had arranged to counter the April 1 launch of Satellite News Channel with a remarkable fifteen hours of live television broadcasting from Cuba, ending a twenty-three-year blackout between the two countries. Turner aired his Cuban broadcasts in April, but SNC postponed its launch until May 1. May 1 then became June 1. Three weeks later, on June 21, 1982, ABC-Westinghouse finally pushed the button and put an abbreviated all-news service on the air. Not only was SNC on the wrong satellite and without any significant input from ABC News, but fewer than half of the twenty-four local stations contracted to provide regional feeds actually went on line. The others were apparently still mulling Turner's offer of twenty-four hours of national and international news and would, ultimately, opt out of their arrangements with ABC-Westinghouse. Turner had guessed right once again. Executive indecision and turmoil at the operating level had nearly doubled SNC's estimated start-up costs. ABC corporate executives admitted publicly that the cable news operation would "sustain heavy financial losses at first, with a break-even point now probably four or five years out."

The cable operators had not let their pocketbooks outweigh their loyalty to one of the industry's most important pioneers, and once they saw the actual ABC-Westinghouse news product, they lined up behind Turner and CNN. Speaking for many in the industry, Marc Nathanson, who represented more than forty California cable systems, told *Time* magazine, "I'm supporting old Ted and sticking by his service. He's here now and he's sticking. There's no telling how long we can count on SNC."

Just a little over twelve months, as it turned out. After slightly more than one year of bitter infighting against CNN and Headline News, ABC-Westinghouse openly admitted having already lost more than $60 million, twice their original estimated investment.

Industry insiders placed the actual figure significantly higher, perhaps as much as $80–$100 million.

The stock market intuited the outcome, even before the war was over. By mid-1983, Turner Broadcasting shares had soared by over 40 percent. Flush with $150 million in new paper profits from the rapid run-up in the market value of his 87 percent holding in TBS, Turner hastened the demise of the Satellite News Channel by offering to pay ABC-Westinghouse $25 million for SNC's 7.5 million subscribers. The offer was accepted immediately, sending TBS stock climbing higher and giving Turner an even sweeter victory over the awesome economic power of the American Broadcasting Companies and Westinghouse Electric Corporation.

"It's a great deal for Turner no matter how you cut it," proclaimed Bonnie Cook, a veteran stock analyst for J. C. Bradford & Co. "He picks up more than seven million SNC subscribers, which now gives Headline News more than ten million unduplicated households. CNN already reaches more than twenty-one million. Turner has a terrific new audience to sell to advertisers, at rates which he will inevitably increase. But the real gain comes from the fees he is collecting from cable operators. Now they have no place else to go." Significant new profits at no increase in operating expenses, a textbook operation, and the envy of everyone else in the broadcast industry.

If there was any question that CNN had now arrived, Professor Andrew Stern, director of the Graduate School of Journalism at the University of California at Berkeley, spoke for many when he decreed, "CNN's reporters are not million-dollar names, but very often what is reported is identical to the network news. The rest of it is pretty much a headline service. It's not as good, but it is not that bad. If Dan Rather weren't a recognizable star, it would be amazing how similar CBS and CNN would appear."

"The one thing everybody feared when Turner started CNN," Richard Zoglin points out, "was his getting involved on the editorial side. With one or two exceptions, that simply never happened." Reese Schonfeld knew that better than most, since Turner had, for the most part, honored their agreement that Schonfeld would have exclusive operational control of CNN. Turner had used his position to influence one or two personnel decisions, but he usually backed off from interference on the editorial side until one of his favorites, the striking Marcia Landendorff, had her contract come up for renewal. Landendorff and her husband joined CNN together in 1980, but the marriage dissolved under the tremendous stress of their round-the-clock schedules. Landendorff then caught Turner's eye and was made prime-time anchor on CNN as well as TBS News anchor on the Superstation. Schonfeld had every intention of renewing her contract until Landendorff's agent, Alfred Geller, demanded a 100 percent increase in salary, confident that Turner would support the raise.

Geller also happened to represent Sandi Freeman, still host of CNN's prime-time interview show. Schonfeld never felt Freeman was appropriate for the slot and had grown convinced that someone like Lou Dobbs would boost the show's soft ratings Freeman usually commanded. Although married at the time, Geller had taken a strong personal interest in Freeman and was soon clashing openly with Schonfeld over the production of her show. Sandi Freeman was another favorite of Turner's, and Geller, who had also been negotiating new positions outside CNN for both his clients, was nevertheless shocked when Schonfeld informed him that neither her contract nor Landendorff's would be renewed.

"I was in the midst of closing a deal for Marcia with WCBS in New York," Geller says, "and was way down the road with Sandi on several other situations when I get a call early one Sunday morning. It's Ted Turner and he says, 'Well, Alfred. You won. We've fired Reese.' " Geller, who later divorced his wife and married Sandi Freeman, jumped on a plane and spent the next ten days negotiating new contracts at CNN for both Landendorff and Freeman. "Bob Wussler handled the first round," Geller recalls, "but we weren't getting anywhere. Finally they brought in Bill Bevins, Turner's chief financial officer. Very smart guy, from East Tennessee State. But since Turner wanted both women back, it wasn't that difficult to cut new deals for each of them. The Atlanta papers all said I was the one who got Reese Schonfeld fired, but Bevins is the guy. He was fed up going around begging for information from Schonfeld on how he was spending Ted Turner's money."

Schonfeld himself does not contest Geller's assessment, other than to say his agreement with Turner allowed him complete operating control of the network. The records show that Schonfeld had always managed to stay within budget. However, it was his aggravating habit of never informing anyone else before he went forward with what were often construed as serious financial commitments that may have set Bevins and, ultimately, Turner against him. Although his fate appeared to have been sealed by the Sandi Freeman affair, Schonfeld plowed right ahead and proceeded to hire Mike Douglas, just as Geller was attempting to get his two clients back on the CNN payroll. Douglas would replace Lee Leonard on CNN's Los Angeles–based entertainment interview show at a reported salary of $1 million—without Turner's prior knowledge or approval.

Schonfeld's friend and ally Ed Turner was astounded when he found out about Douglas. "Ted felt he should have been talked to, not so much to overrule Reese, but if nothing else, as a courtesy. Reese, on the other hand, felt he had absolute authority to do what he wished." The two men were destined to come unstuck, if only because their operating styles were so similar. Both flew by the seat of their pants, and both were tempestuous, explosive leaders with unusual abilities to recruit and retain highly capable, enormously loyal, immensely dedicated followers. Turner had presented Schonfeld with a copy of Dale Carnegie's book *How to Win Friends and Influence People*, suggesting that it might prove useful. Schonfeld says he never cracked the cover, but as Dee Woods pointed out, Reese kept forgetting it was "Turner's name on the door and Turner's name on the checks."

Schonfeld's departure as president was a wrenching blow to most of CNN's three hundred staffers. The way it had all happened left many with the distinct feeling that his place could never be filled. "A lot of us felt it was all over," recalls New York bureau chief Mary Alice Williams. "Reese had a professional commitment, a commitment to the news that was probably irreplaceable."

"He made it the most exciting time," agrees Dan Schorr. "It was an age of experimentation. Reese would try anything, go anywhere. Sometimes he'd fall on his face, but it was glorious, what the news business is all about."

Turner immediately appointed Schonfeld's old administrative sidekick, Burt Reinhardt, as CNN's new president. Ed Turner, who began calling himself "ET" to avoid having to deny any relationship with Ted, was elevated to executive vice-president and became CNN's principal spokesman to the outside world. "Burt Reinhardt was a much more cautious, stodgy person," relates Schorr. "When Turner fired Reese, you really had a bookkeeper running the place."

Turner tried to minimize the damage to CNN's operations and morale and persuaded Schonfeld to remain for a time on the network's board of directors. He also almost immediately began to rewrite the history of their relationship, taking as much credit for the creation of CNN as he dared and suggesting that Schonfeld had come close to "bankrupting the company." Sometime later, when it appeared Schonfeld might actually have talked NBC into funding a competitive all-news cable channel, Turner would remark, "I never should have fired Reese. I should have killed him."

Shortly after he was fired, Reese Schonfeld was invited to lunch by CBS chairman Bill Paley. "He wanted me to put together a cable news operation for CBS, to go head to head with Turner. But the timing was all wrong. ABC-Westinghouse was about to leave the market after losing more than eighty million dollars. Maybe after they go down, I told him." Paley persisted and wanted Schonfeld to come to work for CBS, to bide his time until CBS could put together its own cable news project. "But I'd learned," Schonfeld says. "I wasn't a corporate type, and I couldn't take his money. He said he'd get back to me when they were ready to go, but of course they never, ever got that far.

"With all that money, and all that talent," Schonfeld muses, "CBS probably would still never have gotten clearance on more than a handful of cable systems. They were the enemy, the most hated network. CBS had led the charge in Washington against the cable industry. Anytime cable went to the FCC and asked for anything, CBS would file a violent objection. If CBS were to go out into the cable industry and say 'Now we're going to be your friends' to the same guys they'd been lambasting all these years, nobody would ever have believed them. Just look what happened to ABC when they tried it."

Shortly after Schonfeld's departure, some CNN staffers thought they saw the heavy hand of Turner's writing on the wall. Ted Turner had never attempted directly to influence CNN's editorial content, but here he was in the studio one morning preparing to deliver a personal editorial against the makers of the movie *Taxi Driver*, which Turner felt strongly had incited John Hinckley, Jr., in his attempt on Ronald Reagan's life. "I am very, very concerned," Turner intoned on the air, "that this movie was an inspiration to Hinckley and was partially to blame for his attempted assassination of our president." Turner also criticized *The Deer Hunter* and *The Warriors*, declaring, "These sorts of movies must be stopped! And if you're as concerned as I am, you should write your congressman right away and tell him you want something done about these destructive motion pictures. Thank you very much."

Turner's comments aired eleven times on CNN and three more times on the Superstation over Memorial Day weekend before Dan Schorr, the network's "conscience," demanded the right to offer a rebuttal. "They were furious," says Schorr. "There were very scared people between Ted Turner and me who had to go to him and say, 'Guess what Schorr wants to do now.' They were worried that he would go berserk and blame them." Schorr's "air-tight" contract guaranteed him editorial freedom, and he went on the air to tell CNN viewers, "I must respectfully disagree with any suggestion advocating legislation against movie or television companies. . . . Such legislation would clearly be a violation of their constitutional right of free expression." Schorr's editorial reply was broadcast just once. A scheduled repeat was canceled, although Turner swore he was blameless. "The next time I saw Ted," Schorr recollects, "he came up to me and said, 'Dan, I've learned a lesson. I will never do another editorial.' He explained he hadn't realized what he was getting into." Ted Turner has never since attempted to air his personal views on CNN or any of his other networks.

Schorr doesn't believe the decision was difficult. "Turner was developing a philosophy," he says, "a calculated policy of avoiding controversy on CNN. Critics conceded the network was terrific on breaking stories and live coverage, but seldom provided any meaningful analysis or commentary. You never got a sense of what you saw on CNN actually meant." Even Reese Schonfeld, Schorr adds, "used to say CNN was a mile wide and an inch deep." Turner, however, was beginning to see the international potential of CNN and, in Schorr's opinion, made a conscious decision from that point on to stay away from controversy. "You can't air a Japan-bashing commentary," he points out, "when Turner's just trying to get started in Japan. And he knew my contract guaranteed my right of reply to anything he said on the air. I was important to them at the outset," Schorr says, "but Turner's developing global aspirations made it easy for him. Aside from the fact that I insisted on total editorial independence, I think they were eventually willing to let me go because Turner really wanted to begin to play down commentary and analysis altogether."

When Burt Reinhardt presented him with a renewal contract, minus the editorial independence clause, Schorr was disappointed but hardly surprised. His previous contract had been honored, if sometimes only in the letter, not the spirit, of the agreement. Turner had kept the pressure on his senior Washington correspondent in other ways. Schorr was asked to share anchor duties with former governor John Connally during the 1984 Republican convention but created a big stir over the matter. "Reinhardt was furious," Schorr says, "that I threw my weight around." Schorr believed Connally wanted to help Turner finance a run at one of the networks and didn't much like being used as a chip in somebody else's high-stakes poker game.

On New Year's Day 1985 the picture Schorr had been picking up on the satellite dish Turner had given him five years earlier suddenly went blank. CNN had shifted to a new satellite and neglected to inform its senior correspondent. "Turner may have been sending me a message," Schorr says. Two months later he was told to begin taking three months of accumulated overtime as terminal leave. "Turner had no intention of extending that contract he had dashed off in Las Vegas, and I had no intention," says Schorr, "of accepting any other.

"Bill Headline, CNN's Washington bureau chief, called to say arrangements were being made with the Potomac Satellite Company," Schorr recalls, "to remove my satellite dish on June 3, the first business day after the expiration of my contract." More amused than incensed, since his children had begun to find rented movies preferable to free pictures from space, Schorr reminded Headline that Ted Turner himself had given him the dish and he would need Turner's own written request before he would give it up. And, oh, yes, Schorr added: "I will need the concrete used to anchor the dish removed and my land restored to its original condition. I also pointed out to Mr. Headline that the arrival of the dish had occasioned a certain amount of media attention and that it might be expected that its removal would not go unnoted."

Several weeks passed before Headline finally relayed word to Schorr that "Atlanta" had decided he could keep his dish. "A useless monument," Schorr says, now that Washington has finally been wired for cable, "to six exceedingly interesting years with Ted Turner."

In 1981 Turner secretly approached financier Kirk Kerkorian, who controlled MGM/United Artists, and made preliminary in quiries about buying the company. Turner was already finding it difficult to acquire motion pictures for his Superstation at the same low rates he had once enjoyed in the 1970s and had begun to explore new sources for programming. Kerkorian took Turner no more seriously than most of the New York network executives who continued to laugh him off, but he was solicitous to a fault, as was his style, when Ted came calling. MGM's crown jewel was its unique film library, but Kerkorian and most of Hollywood misread Turner's interest and assumed he was hell-bent on owning a studio. Kerkorian also assumed that Turner would never be able to meet anything close to his asking price, which he pegged at an astronomical $2 billion. After that cordial but unproductive first meeting, the two parted on friendly terms. Kerkorian, however, made a mental note to keep the lines open, just in case.

With ABC-Westinghouse now dispatched and CBS's cable news project caught in corporate limbo, Turner felt comfortable enough in late 1982 to relaunch his exploration of the tantalizing possibilities to be found in talking to other large media companies. Wussler continued to be his pipeline into CBS, but Bill Paley's influence had now deteriorated almost completely and Tom Wyman appeared to have put any expansion into cable on permanent hold. NBC professed interest in sitting down with Turner, but that network's management seemed preoccupied with one internal crisis after another. According to M. S. "Bud" Ruykeyser, NBC's longtime spokesman, the network regularly "disparaged Turner as a lunatic," making any substantive talks difficult, if not impossible.

Turner continued to talk takeover and was frustrated that no one at the networks wanted to play his game. Reese Schonfeld, however, was not unaware of the possibilities and had been developing a close relationship with Lawrence Grossman, a former advertising and public relations executive, who was now head of NBC News. "If you guys ever want to get into the cable news business," Schonfeld told Grossman and some of the network's other senior managers, "you've got to do it now! ABC is still hurting from SNC, and CBS is never going to get off their duffs." This was Schonfeld's grandstand play, and it was working. Grossman and the other NBC managers liked what they were hearing and agreed to fund the $35 million Schonfeld estimated an NBC cable news network might cost. Providing, they added, Schonfeld could talk enough cable operators into giving him upfront clearance.

Congress had recently passed yet another Cable Television Act, which worked heavily in Schonfeld's favor. The new law prohibited cable operators from dropping an existing service unless it was replaced with something "comparable." Schonfeld was certain that with NBC's support, he could put together something more than a little "comparable," and he believed he might be able to clear as many as thirteen million cable households right off the bat. "Let us get our own operation going," he would tell the cable operators. "We'll go head to head with Ted Turner. And we'll beat him because we'll get better ratings."

John Malone is an imposing, steely-eyed Yale graduate with two master's degrees and a doctorate in operations research from Johns Hopkins University. He was very clear in his personal view that the networks had made "the classic error of fighting a new technology rather than trying to own it." He is also president of Telecommunications, Inc., the largest group of cable systems in the country and he leapt at the opportunity to throw in his lot with Schonfeld and NBC, even offering to put up $2 million or $3 million in development money. And Malone added, true to his style, "We'll also take two seats on the board."

Elated, Schonfeld next went to Bill Daniels, one of the very first cable operators and a recognized godfather in the industry. "You're not doing this just to get even?" Daniels asked Schonfeld pointedly. But he liked the idea. "We'll put you in business," he said, "and we'll make sure you stay in business. Why don't you call it KTHN?" Schonfeld was caught off guard, but he relaxed when he saw the smile creep across Daniels's face. "Promise me you'll call it KTHN," Daniels said, almost cracking up. "The Keep Ted Honest Network."

Schonfeld practically flew out of Daniels's office back to Denver's Stapleton Airport. More certain than ever that he would soon be heading a cable news operation again, this time as a major shareholder, he called Lawrence Grossman to give him the good news. When he awoke in New York the next morning, however, Schonfeld was shocked to see a story about his new venture splashed all across *The Wall Street Journal*. "Turner had been on the phone with Grossman and then with Grant Tinker, NBC's chairman. When I saw that story, I knew it was all over."

" 'Why do you guys want to compete with me?' Turner had asked NBC. 'Why don't you just buy into CNN, which you've wanted to do for years?' Naturally," recalls a crestfallen Schonfeld, "the idiots at NBC bought it." Turner proceeded to tie up

Grossman and the NBC lawyers for months. They kept flying down to Atlanta and coming back empty-handed. And of course Turner never sold NBC one share of CNN. "Turner was spectacular at keeping these corporate types on the hook," says Schonfeld. "He actually sold his company four or five times and just never signed the deal."

Turner, in fact, had now talked himself into seriously considering buying a network, not selling. He felt NBC was probably the most vulnerable of the Big Three. What he didn't know was that Thornton Bradshaw, chairman of RCA, NBC's parent, had already decided to seek a buyer for the whole company. Bradshaw had been meeting with MCA's Lew Wasserman for more than two years trying to work out a deal. When T. Boone Pickens, the Texas corporate raider, acquired nearly 5 percent of RCA's outstanding shares, Turner decided to join forces. Pickens was clearly interested in RCA, he assured Turner. More important, he was capable of marshaling enough Wall Street money to complete the deal, leaving Turner with the NBC network. Pickens, however, had spread himself too thin and, with several other balls in the air, told Turner he would just have to mark time for a while. Forced to fume on the sidelines, Turner watched as Jack Welch, chairman of General Electric, swooped in and put together a deal with Bradshaw almost overnight, edging out both Wasserman and Michael Eisner of Disney, who also coveted NBC and had entered the picture once Pickens's bid seemed to bog down. The sale brought RCA and NBC back inside General Electric, where both had been until 1933 when a government decree had forced GE to divest the two companies.

Meanwhile TCI's John Malone watched and waited. He was not about to miss any opportunity to leverage a better deal from Turner. Malone called Turner out to a "cable summit" in Phoenix and convinced him he would resurrect Schonfeld's NBC cable news project unless TCI and several other large operators got "favored nation" rates from CNN. "The threat was enough," Schonfeld reports, "for TCI, ATC, and one or two other cable giants to leverage very low fees from Turner. And then it was really all over." Schonfeld went on to devise a local all-news operation for Joseph Albritton in Washington and continues to develop news, feature, and infotainment programs for broadcast and cable. But he would never again return to the idea of mounting a cable news competitor to CNN.

While he had been sweet-talking NBC, Turner also approached

Al Neuharth, chairman of Gannett, who was in the midst of launching *USA Today*, a new national daily newspaper. We could be interested in doing something with you, Neuharth told Turner, but we've got to see what happens to our new paper first. Neuharth was not the only one interested in CNN. Turner continued talking to Time Inc., Hearst, and the Washington Post Company. He played them all to a fare-thee-well, always listening, always tossing out higher and higher values to test their reactions, but never making anything close to a commitment. "If any of those corporate chiefs had understood how Turner operates," says Tom Ashley, "they would have figured out that he was just shopping, just trolling for information, seeing if he could catch himself a big fish. Ted makes decisions in a millisecond. He hasn't got the patience to sit around and talk a deal to death like these corporate types. Unless it serves his own interest."

Having spent the better part of the last twenty years on the road, Turner was not about to settle down and vegetate in an office. CNN was in Burt Reinhardt's capable if conservative hands. The Superstation continued to surge right along, tracking the rapid expansion of the cable industry. Bill Bevins was gaining stature inside the company and out with his cool command of the numbers and no-nonsense negotiating style. Turner's impressive numbers man was proving himself a uniquely capable and invaluable financial manager, but his frequent successes were the result of weeks', sometimes months' worth of complicated negotiations. There was little enough of interest for Turner in these matters, so he figured it was time to take another trip to see his "Commie buddy, Fidel Castro."

Once again he brought along a CNN crew. Castro took him duck shooting again, and then they hit all of Havana's hot spots. Turner probed Castro's apparent interest in restoring relations between Cuba and the United States, and it was easy for the American to believe he might have been making progress where twenty-five years of international diplomacy had failed. On his return this time, however, Turner did not speak to the press (or even his mother) about the trip. He merely placed two large mounted ducks on a shelf in his office (claiming they had been shot by Castro). He also put several photographs of the voluptuous, bikini-clad blonde he had taken on the trip into his office photo album (to be pulled out whenever he needed a break from a particularly inquisitive interview). Then he settled back to watch what his minions at CNN would do with all the footage they had shot in the largest Communist country in the Western Hemisphere. The CNN camera crew had, indeed, brought back several hours of footage, but according to one of the producers assigned to edit the tape, barely a frame was usable. It seems Turner's immensely photogenic young lady had caught the cameraman's eye and managed to appear in virtually every shot.

"Do you think I'm crazy?" Jane Turner asked a startled reporter from the *Atlanta Constitution* one evening during a reception at Atlanta's Peachtree Hotel. "Do you think I'm crazy to stay married to Ted?"

The question begged an answer, but the reporter, who had never even met her, could only shrug and beat a hasty retreat toward the bar. Turner himself had taken up virtually full-time residence on Techwood's third floor. Any semblance of a home life was evaporating rapidly, despite his need to have Jimmy Brown gather everybody for weekends at Hope or at his historic Kinloch plantation near Georgetown, South Carolina. Turner had acquired Kinloch in 1983 from Eugene DuPont for $2.9 million and reveled in digging for bits of old china crockery, Civil War musket balls, and the occasional arrowhead found on its magnificent grounds. Curiously, Turner would often invite his lady friends to join the family on these weekend excursions. Mary Ann Loughlin, a CNN anchor who gained international notoriety by staying on the air for over thirteen hours straight during the *Challenger* space shuttle tragedy, remembers visiting Hope Plantation several times as well as St. Phillips, Turner's private island off the South Carolina coast near Beaufort. "They weren't exactly vacations," Loughlin recalls. "Ted had everybody programmed virtually every minute. The places are pretty spartan, and naturally, he never would allow air-conditioning. But the land was beautiful, and you were never going to get bored with Ted Turner. He loved the history of the land and was always digging around for things or talking about the battles that had been fought on his land. He was in his element on those plantations, even though I don't think I ever really saw him relax."

"It's the only thing that lasts," Turner once said of his abiding urge to acquire property. "Land and the video business," he said, "will last forever." Sinking his roots in centuries-old southern landholdings may also have helped obliterate the sense of rejection he once felt as a Yankee in the South. With houses in and around Atlanta and several farms scattered throughout central Georgia, Turner was rapidly becoming one of the largest land-owners in the Southeast and had made up in spades what his grandfather lost on his cotton farm in Mississippi.

"If you close your eyes," Peter Dames once said, "you can almost hear the Confederate soldiers breaking camp on the land around Kinloch." It was an image that was more real for Ted Turner than many of his own actual heroics.

There was little that was heroic, or otherwise notable, about the buxom blonde who graced the April 1981 cover of *Playboy* magazine. Unlike most *Playboy* cover girls, however, who seem to disappear somewhere into talk show heaven, this one watched her career take an unusual turn once Ted Turner saw the magazine. A former Miss Universe contestant from Riverdale, Georgia, Liz Wickersham had the good fortune to catch Ted Turner's eye almost as soon as *Playboy* hit the newsstands. In less time than it took him to wink, Wickersham was installed as an announcer on his Superstation. Soon she began showing up at cable conventions on the boss's arm. When Reese Schonfeld hired Mike Douglas, Wickersham and Turner journeyed out to Los Angeles together for his inaugural show on CNN. Since they knew they might be recognized, Turner was careful to bring Terry McGuirk along as his beard. As Douglas's cameras zoomed in on Wickersham's incredibly perfect teeth, McGuirk, a happily married man, was seen dutifully slipping his arm around her waist, smiling bravely into the lens.

For a while Liz Wickersham showed up everywhere with Turner, and he returned the favor by bringing her over to CNN, where she was installed in Dan Schorr's old 6:30 P.M. time slot. "The idea that Ted would take away a news program to put on somebody like Liz," says Schorr, "was precisely the kind of thing I had been worried about when I first joined CNN. She was more than just friends with Ted, so there really wasn't much anybody was going to do."

Wickersham herself, however, is an unusually cheerful sort and soon won over most of the CNN staff. Anchor Lois Hart remembers her fondly but will never forget the Las Vegas cable convention where Ted was bouncing around with Liz on his arm, showing her off like a door prize. Suddenly he spotted another bombshell at one of the tables. "I mean," Hart recalls, "this one had to be a pro, all done up in leopard-skin pants, with enough makeup to cover a battleship. Ted takes one look at this babe and his eyes pop out of his head. Bye-bye, Liz! That's one of the things that made him so appealing. He had a capacity for work," Hart adds, "beyond anything I'd ever seen, but he also had a capacity for play like nobody on this earth has ever seen. You did have to feel a little sorry for Wickersham. She really had no idea what she'd gotten into."

A change was coming over Turner, however, in spite of his penchant for working hard and playing harder. Like his father, he sent his sons off to military school, although McCallie was changing and no longer even required uniforms. Like his father, Turner let months slip by without ever seeing his children and then would come down on them like a drill sergeant whenever they cried or complained. "No," he once told a writer from *Sports Illustrated*, "I don't wish I had more time to reflect. I'm involved in such an intensive series of negotiations and business deals, none of my mental powers can be spent reflecting." But he awoke each morning to the same relentless imperative, the same gnawing, cursed anxiety he could dispel only with action, with accomplishment. He continued to talk, too, of suicide, despairing of ever finding any real purpose in his life. Certainly he had not found it in the trophies, the millions he had already made, or the women he pursued (and whom he counted almost as another kind of currency to be banked).

He had come to understand that being in the news business, being honored as the creator of Cable News Network, could provide access to a world whose doors had previously not been open to him. Turner was still caught up in the hustle, and he was secure in the knowledge that he was already one of the best at buying, selling, and building businesses. But he was now finding himself with people whose interests extended far beyond business, with people who rarely found his endless iterations of schoolboy classics compelling.

"When I was younger," Turner told *The New Yorker*, "racing all over the world and having a ball, I didn't think about the world situation. I used to think everything was fine. So then, here I was in 1980, starting CNN—this global, twenty-four-hour-a-day network—and I decided I needed to find out what was happening in the world. You know, what was really happening."

Turner wasn't sure he could make anybody understand. But he knew there was work that remained undone, new challenges for him to take up, something that could soak up his ravenous, restless energy. Ted Turner sought purpose, not power. Hell, he would say, I get so many Man of the Year awards, they're running out of parchment. I can get an honorary degree from some matchbook college anytime I want. And indeed, Ted Turner had already accumulated half a dozen. According to Alan Laymon, his old college classmate, Brown University even offered him an honorary degree.

"He turned it down, of course, since he was thrown out before he was able to graduate." Brown eventually rectified that slight on February 5, 1989, by conferring on Turner at a private ceremony something Brown president Vartan Gregorian calls "a 'bachelor of philosophy' degree, a degree for those who did not complete, for whatever reason, their undergraduate studies. It's a very special degree. Only fifteen or twenty have been awarded to Brown men, people like I. F. Stone, who also never graduated. Ted Turner is one of our outstanding nonfinishing students. For us not to recognize him," Gregorian says, "would have been amiss." Turner's unique "bachelor of philosophy" certificate, replete with Latin inscription, hangs in his office today.

Turner met Jacques Yves Cousteau sailing and in 1983 ventured to the Amazon, where his eyes were opened by Captain Cousteau's unflagging commitment to the environment. Turner came away so impressed that he arranged to help fund Cousteau's work by contracting with the Cousteau Society to produce for the Superstation an initial $6.5 million series of documentaries on Cousteau's expeditions. The relationship would evolve into one of TBS's most extensive, long-term programming endeavors.

Slowly, the idea was taking shape. Men like Castro and Cousteau provided the catalyst. The challenge, the purpose, seemed to be seeking him out. He could build on what he already had, make Turner Broadcasting the largest, most powerful communications complex on earth, not as an end in itself, but as a means of educating the ignorant, of ending the devastation and the poverty on this planet—maybe even of saving the planet itself.

"Ted had always been a 'closet environmentalist,' " says Barbara Pyle. "He'd just never had anyone to listen to his concerns." Turner had installed Pyle at the Superstation to make documentary films. "But I don't know anything about making documentar-

ies," she cried. Teach yourself, Turner had told her, and then set
off to follow his own advice.

A self-described "wild-eyed do-gooder," Ted Turner knew he
seemed always to put reporters to sleep when he got around to
the "message" part of any interview. He was finally beginning to
understand why his listeners' eyes would roll up into their heads
and their feet begin to tap nervously whenever he launched into
one of his doomsday diatribes. He still could not see the dichot-
omy between his words and much of his life, but he did know that
he must appease his conscience. He had come to view his networks as potential global soapboxes and, however naively, ex-
horted Pyle to address her documentaries to the most serious
subjects—nuclear destruction, overpopulation, the environment
—almost impossible prospects for an entertainment-oriented Superstation. Just go out and do it, Turner said, promising not only
the air time, but the critical financial support as well.

"I started studying the world," Turner asserted, "and I began
to seek out the experts and the politicians who understand the
planet better than I do. It's a crazy idea, I know, but I decided we
had to take better care of our planet, because in taking care of our
planet," he continued, unaware of the irony of his words, "we
might even be able to save ourselves." Ted Turner could devote
himself to saving the planet and save Ted Turner from himself in
the bargain. Perhaps he had finally found a way to keep his personal furies at bay.

Reese Schonfeld knows all about Turner's anxious quest.
Schonfeld lived a lifetime dreaming about CNN. He had been
determined to show the network newsies, who had given him
nothing but the backs of their hands all those years, that he could
not only do it, but bury them at the same time. The beginning of
the end of the glory days of network news can be traced to this
rumpled-faced man who made order out of chaos in the basement
of a mock antebellum mansion off the expressway a few miles
from downtown Atlanta. The success he savored was dry and bitter, but Schonfeld blamed himself, not Turner. He had set his
sights too low, or perhaps he'd never been able to raise them high
enough. "Nobody believes him, do they?" he says when asked
about Citizen Turner's larger agenda. "My own inclination is that
it's impossible. With anybody else, you'd say it's ridiculous. But
Ted will find a way to do it. To save the world. There's no telling
where he can take this thing now."

Begin with the individual, and before you know it,
you have created a type; begin with a type and
you have created nothing.

F. SCOTT FITZGERALD
The Rich Boy

Chapter Eleven

Ted Turner has long seen himself as the pious actor in a series of self-scripted morality plays. So long as the adversary was big enough, Turner would zero in, like a heat-seeking missile, on its weaknesses, its inherent vulnerability. Then with his mouth instead of a slingshot, he would demolish his target more certainly than little David ever put away old Goliath. It had worked with the nabobs of the New York Yachting Club. It worked with ABC-Westinghouse. And it was beginning to work against the three major television networks, who were now giving Turner lip service, but still considered him little more than an eccentric burr under their respective corporate saddles. It had even (sometimes) worked when Turner took on the White House and Congress.

Sometimes, however, the magic simply failed to work at all. Like the morning in Washington, D.C., when he came down to breakfast with his lawyer, Tench Coxe. Coxe had suggested, in view of the importance of their first appointment that day that a quick change of shirts might be in order, "You're missing the third button, Ted. And you want to make a good impression." No time. They were already late for their 8:30 A.M. meeting with Senator Slade Gorton, Republican from Washington and member of the Commerce, Science, and Transportation Committee. Hearings on new legislation which could significantly increase cable television copyright royalties were scheduled to begin the next day. Gorton represented a vital swing vote which would keep the critical, and to Turner, potentially disastrous, legislation in committee forever.

Breezing past an aide who tried to intercept him in the reception area, Turner burst into Gorton's office, mumbled a weak apology, and then plunked himself down on a leather couch opposite the senator. Puffing furiously on the cigar he had brought in with him, Turner launched abruptly into an inexplicable, incomprehensible fulmination against the legal profession. Then he stopped as suddenly as he had begun. His head now wreathed in a cloud of smoke, he leaned over to Gorton and asked, "You're not a lawyer, are you, Senator?"

Tench Coxe, who had been looking around desperately for a hole to crawl into, interjected as calmly as he could, considering the circumstances, "He was the attorney general, Ted, of the State of Washington for ten years."

"Guess that's the same thing," Turner opined, and launched right back into his tirade. After another fifteen minutes of nonstop filibuster, Turner suddenly slumped over and put his head in Coxe's lap. Then, without raising his head, he addressed Gorton: "Okay, your turn now, Senator."

Nonplussed, Gorton was asking for an explanation when Turner bolted up off the couch and stormed out of the office, leaving the senator fuming in midsentence.

In order to further press his case against the proposed new copyright fees, which he said "could put me out of business," Turner had been invited to testify the following morning before the full Commerce committee. Without even acknowledging Gorton's presence on the committee, Turner rushed right into his pitch, spicing his melodramatic appearance with outrageous non sequiturs and unfounded facts. Suddenly he fell to the committee room floor, exclaiming, "I am dead! Dead! Dead!"

He had already drawn everybody's ire by withdrawing his support from an intensively negotiated compromise bill intended to reconcile the interests of program originators and the cable industry. Despite his antics, however, Turner now appeared to have been working hard behind the scenes with Georgia's Senator Mack Mattingly, a Republican, to fashion an amendment to the proposed legislation that would throw the copyright issue right back into the courts. Calling Turner's surprise maneuver an "end run around the whole compromising process," John B. Summers, executive vice-president of the National Association of Broadcasters, said it showed what a travesty the legislative process had become when "one guy with a lot of charisma can just sweep through the Senate, captivating people to vote his way." Turner would lose the battle when the new copyright legislation finally became law in 1983, but eventually he would win the war.

Licking his wounds from this latest roughing up at the hands of the legislators, Turner decided to take his act on the road. He was open for business now, to any and all comers, making speeches, accepting awards, granting interviews, and making headlines every time he opened his mouth. And always, always keeping his eyes peeled for the next deal. *Playboy* magazine contributing editor Peter Ross Range had caught Turner on the cusp of his 1977 America's Cup success. "How do you figure a guy who thinks he was once Christopher Columbus? Or John F. Kennedy? Or Sir Francis Drake, bearing down on the Spanish Armada? Do you figure him nuts or not?" Range asked.

In a wild, uninhibited, no-holds-barred interview, Turner had advocated "lots of sex for everybody. That's a solution to the world's problems. Violence in sports. That's what men really enjoy. Getting together and beating the shit out of each other. Politics. I could win a presidential election easier than any living man except Jimmy Carter. I'm the only white man who could get every black vote in Atlanta. They love me here because I don't go around acting like a millionaire. And sailing. I'll keep sailing for the same reason I always did: I enjoy it. Sailing is like screwing—you can never get enough.

"Wow! *Playboy!* That's big time!" Turner exclaimed when he saw that interview in print. Five years later, as Cable News Network began to change the very nature of the news business, *Playboy* decided it was time to revisit the man Peter Range had called "a fanatically positive thinker, a blithe spirit who skates along on the smooth ice of his own self-confidence." They sent Range out to determine if there was any reason now to alter that assessment. The man Range found, after many wasted trips, canceled appointments, and aborted interview sessions, had become "at least a partial victim of his own celebrity." Range also noted that Turner had changed in other ways as well.

"He is no longer the laugh-a-minute, expository motor-mouth who sees a classic metaphor behind every man's maneuvers. He still relishes the role of underdog but views his competitors not merely as bigger, but as part of a dark conspiracy threatening him, his company, and, for that matter, the whole of American civilization."

Range followed Turner from his Hope Plantation to Atlanta and then on to Washington, enduring one violent outburst from his interview subject after another. Turner threatened to call off the whole interview several times, but when Range asked him what he had been doing walking around the back lot of MGM in 1980, Turner was intrigued. He wanted to know how Range had learned about that first off-the-record visit to Kirk Kerkorian.

With his usual candor Turner also admitted he had been disappointed that chairman Bill Paley hadn't shown up at his latest attempt to explore a merger with CBS. "I didn't get to meet Paley," Turner told the reporter. "I'd like to someday." But, Range countered, you're on record in *Broadcasting* magazine calling Paley a "failure," and you called "CBS a cheap whorehouse run by sleaze artists."

"I'm up some days," Turner replied decisively, "and down others. If I'm feeling a little down, I'll let it all hang out. I do have a slight propensity to put my foot in my mouth." Such introspection was rare for Turner, and catching himself, he decided he had better shut down the interview right there. Range was struck by Turner's violent mood changes. He could be the voluble, charming, self-infatuated Turner of his public image one minute and then suddenly turn dark, hostile, threatening. Turner described his life as "a living hell"; he seemed a "driven, ravaged man, and yet," according to Range, "a man who continually sought more of the same punishment." After several more failed attempts to complete his interview, Range was finally invited to join Turner on a cross-country flight he was taking to Las Vegas with Liz Wickersham.

Seated comfortably in the first-class cabin, next to the old, co-operative Turner, Range was confident he had caught his subject at last on one of his "up" days. He decided to attempt a penetrating question or two about Turner's now very substantial personal wealth. "I give away a tremendous amount," Turner replied without emotion. "I contribute to a number of charities. I make tremendous amounts of political donations. I fly tourist on airplanes." This trip, he explained, was an exception, to please Liz. "I cut my own hair. I live without air-conditioning. I drive a small car."

"Wait a minute," Range interrupted, "that's your old PR. You drive one of the most expensive cars made in Japan."

"That's right," Turner replied, his mood suddenly beginning to change. "But I *used* to drive a small one." Toyota was a big advertiser, he pointed out, and they had given him a bigger model. Their biggest, in fact. Suddenly bored with the whole business, he got up and began wandering around the cabin, talking to passengers about his Braves' chances for a pennant in 1983. While he was out of his seat, Wickersham slid over next to Range and, only half-jokingly, suggested that she might be an appropriate *Playboy* cover for the Turner interview issue. "After all," she reminded the reporter unnecessarily, "I was on the cover a couple of years ago."

After returning to his seat, Turner agreed to continue the interview, but it was obvious to Range that his mood had darkened considerably. He attempted a question comparing television morality with personal behavior. Turner nearly went berserk. "I never said I was perfect," he shouted. "I don't just have my own personal standards that run my network! I don't feel like I'm really compromising my principles." Then he paused. "I am one second away from never asking [*sic*] you another question! I'm sick as hell of you!" Suddenly Turner reached over and grabbed Range's tape recorder and smashed it on the cabin floor.

Oh, my God, Eastern Airlines stewardess Chris Mink remembers thinking. What's happened now? Turner had flown into a blind rage and was in the aisle, grinding Range's tape recorder into the cabin floor. Swearing at the top of his lungs, he snatched Range's camera bag full of tapes and kicked it past Mink, bruising her thigh, into the cockpit door. He picked the bag up off the floor and hurled it straight at Range's head as the other first-class passengers looked on, stunned. Turner then slumped back down on the seat next to Wickersham. Spotting several tape cassettes on the cabin floor, he bolted out of his seat again, picked up the tapes, and lurched past the forward galley into the lavatory.

Less shocked than anyone else in the cabin, Wickersham leaned over to Range and, attempting to offer some reassurance, confided, "Don't worry. He's under a lot of pressure. He did the same thing to me once, getting on a boat in Greece. He got mad and kicked me right in the shin."

Turner returned from the lavatory, apparently oblivious of the sensation he'd caused. "It's the same thing I did on the 'Tom Cottle Show,' " he said to no one in particular, referring to the time a television talk show host had been on the receiving end of a similar, unexpected outburst. Turner then turned to Range and, with an utterly bland expression on his face, said, "I'll replace your tape recorder." Then he took his seat and remained there for the uneventful last leg of the flight into Las Vegas.

When the interview appeared a few weeks later, replete with witnesses' names and specifics of the damage he'd inflicted on the aircraft, Turner remained silent and chose not to challenge the details. During a flamboyant appearance at the National Press Club in Washington a few weeks later, however, he dismissed the *Playboy* piece as the "distortions of a vindictive reporter." Free-wheeling and free-associating his way through a fifty-minute appearance that had the room full of media people alternating between uproarious laughter and breathtaking gasps, Turner admitted that he had been worn out, almost totally exhausted. "But I'm still carrying on," he added, puffing up to his full height and sticking his perfectly cleft chin straight up in the air, "about as well as I can."

Back in Atlanta, Georgia governor Joe Frank Harris declined Turner's invitation to sit in the owner's box on the Braves' opening day, despite what finally looked like the beginning of a promising season. Recalling his predecessor's experience, Harris said he'd be happy to throw out the first ball but would rather sit somewhere up in the stands, not in Ted Turner's box seat. Governor Busbee, it seemed, had been victimized by Turner's habit of vigorous tobacco spitting. Harris vowed he wasn't going through the same ordeal. "Poor George," Harris told the papers as opening day approached, "would have to take his hot dog back home to the governor's mansion so he could eat it in peace."

"Ted has always been fanatic about the thing he's doing at the moment," says Bob Hope, Turner's former publicity chief. "He was like nobody else I have ever seen. He would work himself into a frenzy or whatever it was that had his attention. Then crash, totally. And walk right away from it if it didn't work. He's more open than anyone I know about admitting defeat. Sometimes, though, he would just work himself into the sickbed. Trying to lead too many lives at once sometimes came close to doing him in."

That Turner was able to maintain his frenetic schedule, jammed solid with business meetings and public appearances, did not seem unusual to those who had watched him lead for years what Bob Hope calls his "multiple lives." For nearly twenty years Ted Turner managed to maintain an alternate existence among the dedicated group of ocean racers who got caught in his slipstream and hung on long enough to play a part in the unequaled record of victories he accumulated from 1964 to 1980. "He would drop out of the sky, just as the boat was pulling away from the dock," remembers Patsy Bolling, who sailed with him in the early 1960s. "But the second Turner would take the helm, you knew he was going to squeeze out every knot of speed that was in her." There was nothing easy about ocean racing Turner style, Bolling points out. "You could stay up all night partying the way Ted did, but you still had to be fit to sail across the Atlantic at dawn."

That Turner could also find time for all the women in his life amazed even those who thought they knew him well. No prude, Bob Hope admits he was astounded at the "incredible numbers of women Turner ran through. And such a variety of types." Hope calls Turner's incessant womanizing a "comic-book life-style. He didn't waste a lot of time wooing any woman. He was brash, chauvinistic, right to the point. He'd win 'em over and shack 'em up. Then move right on to the next one." Turner may have been disappointed at not having been born Christopher Columbus or Captain Cook, but he was successful in making his own unique history exploring the female of the species.

Ted moved so fast, Hope remembers, that he would sometimes have to leave one lady behind as he rushed to take up with another. He would bring his girls to the ball games all the time, Hope says, and park them a few rows behind the box where he'd be sitting with his wife. "You had to feel for that lady. She knew what was going on every minute. He once dished off Fréderique D'Arragon to Pete van Wieren, the Braves' traveling secretary, simply saying, 'Take care of her.' " It was van Wieren, not Turner, who got chewed out when the hotel manager caught D'Arragon sunbathing nude by the hotel pool. "Then Jane Turner would show up," Hope says, "and we'd all try to hush everything up. But she'd come right out and say, 'I know you're talking about Ted's French whore.' She knew and she suffered."

The girls had come easy for Turner once he hit his late teens. He had grown into a darkly handsome, smooth-talking young rake whose own inflated estimates of his appeal could perhaps be excused in light of his tremendous popularity, even notoriety, among Savannah's debutante set. "When I was seventeen I had written a suicide note and I was standing on the fifth-floor ledge of the Read House Hotel in Chattanooga ready to jump. It was over a girl. Then I thought 'If I jump now, it's all over. Maybe I should jump tomorrow.' " Over the years, Turner's high opinion of himself hadn't changed, but neither had his almost magnetic attraction, which had proved irresistible to a succession of alluring members of the opposite sex. Barbara Pyle, the *Time* magazine photographer who had caught his eye in Newport, turned out to have a mind of her own, and over dinner one evening Turner pressed upon the pretty brunette a copy of Jimmy Carter's *Global 2000* environmental report. When Pyle revealed she shared his interest in the environment, Turner hired her on the spot. "He shoved the report in my hand," Pyle recalled, "and said, 'Okay, kiddo. This is your job description.' "

Barbara Pyle was very different from Turner's usual women friends. Born in Oklahoma thirty-three years earlier and educated at Tulane, she held advanced degrees in both logic and philosophy. Turner was immediately attracted by her sophistication and her spunk. He made her Turner Broadcasting's first full-time executive in charge of environmental affairs.

It was through Barbara Pyle that Turner met Jeanette H. (Dusty or JJ) Ebaugh, the tall, striking twenty-three-year-old who had come to Newport in 1980 with Tom Blackaller. Turner hardly failed to notice JJ as she rocketed around town on a tiny moped, "terrorizing," as Pyle once told *Atlanta* magazine, "the other America's Cup syndicates."

At five eight, with straight, shoulder-length blond hair and a body as trim as an ocean sloop, "JJ was the best-looking thing on the dock that summer," said Pyle. "The most outstanding woman." And it did not take Ted Turner long, once he had been excused from further Cup competition, to separate Ebaugh from her long relationship with his old friend Blackaller. That part was easy. Turner simply called and asked her to sail with him in what turned out to be his last Southern Ocean Racing Circuit series. A passionate and experienced sailor herself, JJ rushed to join him in St. Petersburg. "My relationship with Tom was over," she said, "so it wasn't a conflict. It was a wonderful invitation—to be on *Tenacious* with one of the greatest helmsmen of all time!"

Ebaugh was very aware that Turner was married. She also clearly understood what she later said was the personal nature of his invitation. "Him platonic?" she once told a reporter. "With Ted Turner? You've got to be kidding." Back in Buckhead, the family values and temperate morality that Ted made so much of in his public posturing were taking a hard beating.

Jane Smith Turner had long been able to live with Ted's double standard. She suffered in silence when he embarrassed her in public and wrote off his blatant affairs as trivial, meaningless flings. "I've seen them . . . the groupies," she kept telling reporters bold enough to confront her with the obvious. "They are always there. Ted knows I will always be here. He needs me and he loves me. That's why none of that ever really bothers me."

That was before early 1981, when Ebaugh moved to Atlanta, bag and baggage—which included her Olympic-class sailboat, a $15,000 Formula Ford racing car, several trunkloads of books, and all her personal belongings. Moving in with her friend Barbara Pyle, JJ soon became inextricably entwined in Ted Turner's life. A licensed commercial pilot as well as a sailor and race car driver, Ebaugh bought a secondhand plane, since Turner had put her on the payroll as his personal pilot.

It became clear almost from the outset that JJ Ebaugh was no dockside dolly, no seafaring groupie to be tossed overboard with yesterday's chum. Although handicapped with eyesight barely sufficient to get her past her pilot's test, Ebaugh was a lean, lanky blond bundle of kinetic energy unlike anything Turner had ever encountered. She had sailed with the best, could drive rings around his tinny little Toyota, and, of course, could fly. She also had brains to spare and a curiosity that rivaled his own. And as her friend, British race car driver Philip Creighton said. "She was, ah, packaged right."

Shuttling Turner back and forth to an ever-expanding schedule of speaking engagements and business meetings, Ebaugh would pick up Jane and the kids at the end of each week and ferry the whole family down to one of their South Carolina plantations. After deadheading back to Atlanta for the weekend, she'd return each Monday morning, in a routine that could have made sense only to Turner himself and almost certainly must have eroded whatever vestiges of self-esteem Jane had left.

"I remember being in the ladies' room at Techwood once," recalls Fran Heaney, "when Jane Turner came in. She'd had a few cocktails, and she just went on talking and talking about Ted. I was embarrassed, but it was obvious she wanted to talk to somebody. She just went on about his girlfriends, about how could he do this to her. She was so very, very sad. She looked like she was going to burst out crying."

Heaney also recalls a story that made the rounds at CNN not long after Ebaugh's arrival: "Mrs. Turner had been drinking quite a bit down at their beach house on St. Phillips Island. She took a sailboat out by herself and capsized—nobody knows what really happened. She was missing for quite some time, and when she finally made it back to shore, she was all cut up and bruised. Ted didn't go down to take care of her. Bunky Helfrich did."

Jane Turner continued to smile through it all, but she once confided to a few friends her own apocryphal tale of social survival when Ted sent her off to the Ashram, a very exclusive California fat farm. Not that her weight, she says, was the issue. "It was Ted's fear that I might get soft, you know, flabby. Out of shape." After four days of intensive exercise and a near starvation diet, Jane was on the verge of checking out of the place when she met a kindred soul at the end of her own tether. When Jane mentioned she was from Atlanta, the woman asked if she knew "Teddy Turner." Jane nodded dolefully, and her new friend motored right on, never expecting where she was headed. Well, what did they think of Mr. Teddy Turner down in Atlanta, Georgia? she asked innocently.

"Oh, they think he's some sort of folk hero," Jane responded with an utterly straight face. "What do they think of him in California?"

Her friend suggested that the word on Turner in Malibu was that he got away with quite a lot. But what's his family like? she wanted to know.

"Oh, he loves his family a lot. He goes hiking and fishing with them and loves spending time with his kids."

That's not what she meant, the woman responded. What she really wanted to know was, what could his wife be like? Why wasn't she ever with him?

"Oh," said Jane, "but she is. It's just that the press never writes about it." Then she felt compelled to let her hair down. "It's me. I'm his wife," she blurted out tearfully.

The other woman let out an anguished cry and began pouring out her own unexpected confession. Her husband was away from home a lot, too, she said, and she knew all too well what it was like to bear such a cross.

"Well, who's your husband?" Jane asked, wiping away her tears.

"Sly Stallone," the other woman answered.

"We met everybody from Dr. Seuss to the chairman of Time Inc.," Ebaugh says of those busy days shuttling between cable conventions, advertising sessions, and the surreptitious meetings with big media companies that Bob Wussler kept arranging, principally to bolster Ted's ego and reassure him that Turner Broadcasting's value continued to spiral upward. Wussler also succeeded in keeping CBS's interest in a cable news operation sufficiently alive to promote two further meetings after that short-lived first attempt outside the Atlanta airport. Turner let the rumors run rampant, so that even his advertising negotiations with Warner-Amex were at first construed as merger talks by the industry and the media. And after each meeting Turner would come away reassured that, despite appearances, he was on an escalator going straight up.

JJ Ebaugh soon tired of shuttling Turner around the country, however. As headstrong and independent as he was, she resented playing pilot during the week and then being told to disappear while he played family man on weekends. With so much free time on her hands, she would round up crew chief Phil Creighton and head back out to the race track with her Formula Ford. "JJ had real potential," Creighton says. "She was very competitive, very precise. She ran a couple of tremendous races."

It was JJ's close friend, Barbara Pyle, who first opened her eyes to the problems of the environment and overpopulation. Mankind, she soon came to believe, was rapidly trashing the planet. "Suddenly my life was directed," JJ recalled. "Technology was in a holding pattern waiting to be used." The technology she had in mind was the satellite, and as Ebaugh pointed out exuberantly, "I'm flying for the man with all the satellites."

Immersing herself in a bookstore of literature on global concerns—*The Fate of the Earth, The Global Possible, Limits to Growth, New Genesis, The Aquarian Conspiracy*—she discovered hundreds of organizations around the world struggling to address the same critical issues with which she was now consumed. As he had with Barbara Pyle, Turner responded to JJ's new interests and was pleasantly surprised to find in Ebaugh a sympathetic sounding board for some of the ideas he himself had harbored for years. In 1982 Ebaugh was inspired to begin a book project, detailing her vision of satellite-transmitted television broadcasts that would help to foster international awareness and cooperation. Turner encouraged her, as he had Pyle, but JJ's book project blossomed instead into a weekly TBS series called "Planet Alive," which one critic termed "a kind of ecological 'Entertainment Tonight.'" Ebaugh's "energies" also helped catalyze Turner's own thoughts for his Better World Society, the nonprofit foundation he established in 1985 to develop and underwrite documentary and environmental programs that could be programmed by Turner Broadcasting System.

It took more than her own television series to satisfy Ebaugh, however; she grew increasingly frustrated by Turner, who avoided anything remotely resembling a commitment. "It was okay for him to go home to his wife," JJ complained, and she promptly retaliated by seeing other men.

Turner had difficulty understanding that Ebaugh could not accept his double standard. He had sworn he would never, ever leave Jane. Everybody, including Ebaugh, knew that. But Jane Turner herself had long since realized there was little left in their marriage and continued to accept the abuse Ted heaped upon her regularly and publicly. With uncommon resolution she tried instead to salvage her self-esteem, although her attempts were peculiarly rooted in the culture of southern womanhood. She tried modeling. She opened a boutique. And then she discovered therapy. Something clicked, and she found new resolve and a hundred reasons not to give up on her marriage, at least not without a fight. It wasn't easy, but eventually she even induced Ted to see an Atlanta psychiatrist, Dr. Frank Pittman. Dr. Pittman just happened to be a specialist in male self-esteem.

That introduction proved to be one of the most fateful moments in Ted Turner's life. "What I do is help men," Pittman says, "who don't have a very good image of their own masculinity because of a failure in their relationship with their father." What Pittman got when Ted Turner walked into his office at Atlanta's Northside Hospital was the challenge of a lifetime—a classic manic-depressive, bipolar personality who was also not only a functioning adult, but an individual of monumental personal accomplishment.

For more than forty years Ted Turner had been able to sublimate the cruel and damaging physical and emotional abuse that constituted much of his relationship with his father. A classic bipolar personality profile himself, Ed had been incapable of returning the love and attention his son so desperately sought. Pursued for most of his life by personal demons not entirely of his own making, Ed Turner suffered the same biochemical imbalance he passed on to Ted and found it all but impossible to sustain anything resembling a real relationship. He was never an affectionate man, even with Florence, and he placed Ted in the hands of his surrogate, Jimmy Brown, leaving this loyal, understanding black man to give his son what he himself could not provide. Mary Jane's awful, extended battle with lupus destroyed what little faith and hope remained in Ed Turner and helped drive him even farther apart from his son and his wife, who dedicated her life to making their daughter's tragic end as painless as possible. Ed fell back on his drinking to mask his almost unbearable pain. Though he would become increasingly dependent on her approval and made many attempts to reestablish communication with her, even up to the very day before his suicide, Ed and Florence Turner separated almost as soon as Mary Jane was gone and then divorced after twenty years of a nearly soulless marriage.

Despite Ed Turner's gregarious and often appealing demeanor, he endured a lonely, private hell on earth, often erupting with seismic force at the slightest provocation. According to Irving Victor, Ted idolized his father and poured out his heart to a man who could not return his love or affection but instead beat him unmercifully—with his fists, with wire coat hangers, razor straps, and belts—anything he could grab whenever he waded into Ted's world after a hard night away from home. Ed Turner once even ordered his son to beat *him*. "He lay down on the bed," Ted has recounted, "and gave me the razor strap, and said, 'Hit me harder.' That hurt more than getting beat myself. I couldn't do it. I just broke down and cried."

"Ed once told me," says Ted's first wife, Judy Nye, "that he wanted Ted to fear him. He wanted to breed insecurity into his son. He believed insecurity bred greatness." Ed must have known it also helped kill any love that might ever have existed between father and son.

Irving Victor was one of the few to whom Ed Turner tried always to show his best side. However, even Victor admits that he was often shocked by Ed's treatment of his son. "He was tremendously difficult with Ted," Victor recalls, "although Teddy looked up to him as if he had hung the moon. It's hard to know what really goes on in that kind of situation, but I think Ed took out an awful lot of his hostility on the boy."

When he wasn't being beaten, Ted was being rejected, sent away to military school, or handed over for safekeeping to Jimmy Brown, who would teach him what his father could not, even instructing Ted to address his elders as "sir." Ted Turner was as insulated and intolerant a father as Ed had been and, like his father, handed over his own children to Jimmy Brown whenever he could. Ted Turner likes to imagine himself as a family man and has been incredibly adept at dropping into that role whenever it suited him. But Ted Turner is also an impossible taskmaster whose three sons and two daughters always feared the consequences of stepping even one inch out of line.

"When he did spend time with the family," says his eldest son, Teddy IV, "he acted like kids were a necessary evil."

The Turner children were not allowed to cry in Ted's presence. They were punished for the slightest impropriety. They were forced to follow a militaristic regimen whenever they spent weekends on one of his plantations. After one particularly painful canoe trip on the Chattahoochee River with his father, young Teddy, then about eleven, remembers saying "no" when asked if he had enjoyed himself. "Boy," says Teddy. "He smacked me hard!"

It was Dee Woods, Turner's capable and often compassionate assistant, who would remember the birthdays and anniversaries, buy and wrap the presents, and then make sure that everything got home on time, whether Ted himself did or not. And it was Jimmy Brown who took young Teddy up to McCallie in the late 1970s, just as he had taken Ted up from Savannah to Chattanooga at the beginning of each term.

Ted Turner had made it perfectly clear to Jane when he married her that he had no intention of remaining monogamous. He might therefore have been unable to appreciate the irony of Jane's having led him to Dr. Pittman's door in a last-ditch effort to salvage their twenty-year marriage. "The patient's goal," Pittman said in describing what he hoped Ted could achieve through therapy, "is to learn to have a partnership with a woman he can see as his equal." The goal thus defined, Turner was induced again to pick up the gauntlet, as he had always done when the risk was sufficiently challenging. This time, however, the challenge was nothing less than the search for himself. He knew of no other way to respond than to throw himself into Dr. Pittman's treatment with his characteristic ferocious determination.

"Mood disorders," writes Dr. Demitri Papolos in his definitive treatise, *Overcoming Depression*, "are the 'common cold' of major psychiatric illnesses. More than twenty million Americans will suffer an episode of depression or mania during their lifetimes. Those who have manic depression will veer from periods of superactivity, manic elation, and grandiose schemes to periods of despondency, immobility, guilt, and the inability to experience pleasure or even to think normally." Psychiatrists term these highs and lows "bipolar disorder." Also referred to as manic-depressive illness, recurrent mood disorders, or bipolar depression, mania and depression have affected mankind since biblical times. King Saul exhibited bipolar characteristics, as did King George III, Abraham Lincoln, Winston Churchill, and Theodore Roosevelt. Many psychiatric experts today believe the disorder fuels a certain kind of drive and creativity, citing manic-depressive writers and poets like Johann von Goethe, Honoré de Balzac, Leo Tolstoy, Virginia Woolf, Ernest Hemingway, Robert Lowell, and Anne Sexton. The composers George Frederic Handel, Robert Schumann, Hugo Wolf, Hector Berlioz, and Gustav Mahler were all subjected to violent mood swings and were likely manic-depressives. More recently, towering creative talents like Joshua Logan and Alfred Hitchcock, as well as *The Washington Post's* brilliant publisher Phil Graham, were diagnosed bipolar personalities. The constant thread in their lives is a history of searing anguish, shattered relationships, psychosis, and frequently suicide.

Manic depression is known to concentrate in families, suggesting a genetic transmission. Family studies consistently show that vulnerability to bipolar disorders is inherited. Current research has focused on the search for a gene as a possible mode of transmission, or a genetic marker, which would identify those at risk. The exact cause of the condition remains unknown, but researchers have implicated the limbic-diencephalic system near the center of the brain. This system regulates information of an emotional nature and governs an individual's "fight or flight" response mechanism. Studies show this system may hold the clue to a relationship between stressful events and the development and spontaneous cycling of mood disorders.

Lithium, usually in the form of lithium carbonate tablets or lithium citrate liquid, is the medication of choice in treating manic depression. When used preventively, lithium can protect against or radically reduce the possibility of future episodes of both mania and depression. No one yet is quite certain why it works, however, or how lithium can be so effective against both mania and depression. Miraculously, it somehow changes chaos and disruption into stability and productivity.

Ted Turner's violent mood swings, his voracious sexual appetite, his inability to sustain personal relationships, and his frequent but irregular cycles of depression and hypomania are typical manifestations of a manic-depressive illness known as cyclothymia. Episodes are not of sufficient duration or severity to qualify cyclothymia as a major affective disorder, since the cycles typically last for only a few hours rather than days or weeks. Cycles often begin in late childhood or adolescence. Mood states can change so frequently that patients often exhibit extremely short attention spans, are frequently bored, and even find holding two-way conversations next to impossible.

Ted Turner's behavioral patterns, which exhibit nearly all of the traits of the classic bipolar personality, may provide an explanation for his lifelong obsession with his own death. He talked openly of suicide for years, especially, say his top executives, during moments of depression. And he characterizes his life as a struggle to master his "greatest fear—the fear of death." For many years, a lethal reminder of this struggle lay in Turner's desk drawer—his father's silver .38 revolver, the same weapon Ed Turner used to blow his brains out. Many of those who worked most closely with Turner were certain he would someday act on this lethal impulse. "He saw himself," confirms Jim Roddey, "as part of a tragedy played out on stage. Everyone else kept interrupting the show with applause. Only Ted knew how it was all meant to end."

Diagnosis and treatment of Ed Turner's disorder had not been possible in the early 1960s, but by 1985 Dr. Pittman was able to recognize Ted's obvious symptoms, make a proper diagnosis, and place him on a sustained program of preventive lithium treatment.

Within just a few weeks the lithium began to take effect. What the people around him were seeing now was an unmistakable change in Ted Turner's behavior. When several of his senior managers commented on the apparent change, Turner proceeded to bring them right into therapy with him, so they could better appreciate what he was going through.

"Before, it was sometimes pretty scary to be around the guy," admitted JJ Ebaugh. "You never knew what in the world was going to happen next. You just never knew if he was about to fly off the handle. That's why the whole world was on pins and needles around him. With lithium," said Ebaugh, "Ted became very even-tempered. He's just one of those miracle cases. I mean, lithium is great stuff. But in Ted's particular case, lithium is a miracle."

Turner himself agrees the lithium has put him on a relatively even keel. But at what cost? "Many patients incorrectly look on lithium as a 'mind control' drug," says Dr. Donald F. Klein of Columbia University College of Physicians and Surgeons. "They miss the exhilarating rush of wild, kinetic energy which they believe was once the source of their brilliance and creativity. That idea," says Dr. Klein, "couldn't be farther from reality." Lithium does not change a person's personality.

Dr. Hagip Akiskal, director of the University of Tennessee's Affective Disorders Clinic, agrees. "Lithium interacts to correct a pathological imbalance in the brain, letting the true personality emerge, the personality once overshadowed by the bipolar disorder. Lithium restores the imbalance and helps reduce or eliminate altogether the wild mood swings of manic depression."

Dr. Mogens Schou, a Danish psychiatrist who spent more than thirty years attempting to educate the world on the values as well as the dangers of lithium, has written voluminously on the relationship between bipolar disorder and creativity. "He has seen more manic depressives," suggests Dr. Akiskal, "than perhaps anyone else in the world." Dr. Schou believes most of the artists and other creative personalities he has treated have become more, not less, creative as a result of lithium medication.

"The aspect of manic-depressive behavior that is usually most noticeably altered by lithium," Dr. Klein explains, "is the characteristic hypersexuality of many bipolar personalities. Bipolar disorder tends to heighten the libido, enhancing an individual's perception of his own sexuality, and provides him with the energy to pursue sometimes unlimited opportunities for sexual encounters. The bipolar may also see himself as sexually irresistible, and be consumed with a desire to disrobe, no matter what the circumstances.

"The predatory pleasure of the hunt," Klein adds, "is self-reinforcing—chasing, chasing, chasing faster, faster, faster. The individual is often bored once the conquest has been made and, unable or unwilling to attempt a sustaining relationship, anxious to move on to the next challenge. The result is often empty, hollow self-gratification.

"The pleasure of the feast, on the other hand, is consummation. A bipolar disorder can create very heightened degrees of anticipation, which in turn produces very acute and powerful sexual responses."

What happens if a patient undergoing lithium therapy suspends or suddenly terminates treatment? Extensive studies at Centro Lucio Bini in Cagliari, Italy, have determined that rapid withdrawal of lithium—over a period of less than two weeks, for example—can be associated with early recurrence of mania in some patients and both mania and depression in the vast majority. Once begun, lithium treatment can last a lifetime.

Ed Turner's suicide left Ted with his own self-imposed deadline. "He felt his father had died tragically," Dee Woods recalls, "and that it was his duty to die tragically." It was also the only way he knew to complete the hand fate and his father had dealt him. "I had counted on him," Ted Turner admits, "to make the judgment of whether or not I was a success." Ted had taken no part in the arrangements at Stipple's Funeral Parlor in Savannah and kept his emotions to himself as he stood at the rear of the little chapel and listened to the eulogies for his father. But the silence emanating from Ed Turner's lifeless form was deafening and would haunt him throughout his life.

Ted Turner has always placed a high premium on loyalty. He relies upon the men with whom he has chosen to surround himself, whether in world-class ocean-racing competition or in business. He learned early the value in being able to choose good men and true and give them free rein—as long, of course, as they always understood who was in charge, who remained the captain with his steady hand at the helm. Now that Ted Turner was placing himself in another man's hands, letting someone else guide him through the rocky shoals of his own life, he was prepared to exercise the same visceral trust he had always asked of his crew. Dr. Pittman rose to the challenge and, with Ted's enthusiastic cooperation, helped him begin to exorcise the specter of his father. And once he put himself in Dr. Pittman's hands, Turner the supreme pragmatist was able to begin the emotionally strenuous effort, finally, to grow up.

Folks, there's going to be a leetle mite of
trouble back in town.

ROBERT PENN WARREN
All the King's Men

Chapter Twelve

"It's a pretty crazy company," said financial analyst and Turner specialist Bonnie Cook. "In fact, they have a deficit net worth. Turner is a company where the crystal ball gets very hazy. I like the company, but it is a risk investment."

The risk was still there, but the mid-1980s brought something new to Turner Broadcasting: profits. And with profits came renewed interest in the company on Wall Street. In 1984 Turner made net after-tax income of $10.1 million on total revenues of $281.7 million. The flagship of the system, WTBS, was now the most profitable television station in the country, earning over $43.3 million in operating profits. Bankers began falling all over themselves to lend the company money. A consortium headed by New York's Chemical Bank opened up a new line for over $190 million, much of it stretched out well past 1995. First Boston then raised $50 million in new equity, reducing Turner's personal holding from 87 to 80 percent, but placing an imputed market value of over $500 million on the company. Interest alone on the new bank debt would amount to nearly $26 million a year. Still, the investment community was beginning to believe.

"Turner will earn its way out of debt," Bonnie Cook said with a sigh, "providing Ted doesn't come up with another of his wonderful ideas."

Of course, it was Ted Turner's "wonderful ideas" that had

caused Turner Broadcasting's market value to increase nearly one hundredfold in the little more than ten years since he'd swapped $2.5 million of his stock for Atlanta's WTCG, the broken-down UHF outlet that grew into the "Superstation that Serves the Nation." John S. Reidy, Drexel Burnham's highly regarded media analyst, bought TBS shares for his personal portfolio and called the company a "conceptual investment." "The question is, do you want to run with this guy or not. Personally I think he's brilliant."

Turner dutifully notified his shareholders of his assiduous efforts to merge TBS with another, larger media company—any larger media company. It didn't seem to matter. "In recent months," he said, "your management has conducted preliminary discussions with a number of major companies in the entertainment industry to explore potential areas of combination of business interests." Acknowledging the latest in a series of meetings with CBS that had stretched out over three years, Turner reported meetings with CBS chairman Tom Wyman, as well as with heads of several other CBS divisions. "While these discussions were conceptually wide-ranging and demonstrated long-range possibilities for enhancing our operating structure, we have concluded," Turner admitted, not surprisingly, in his 1983 shareholders letter, "that our interests are best served by continuing on our present course."

When Getty Oil was acquired by Texaco in February 1984, however, the transaction signaled the opening round in a rash of staggering, multibillion-dollar takeovers that were soon to become a hallmark of the 1980s. Turner immediately registered his interest to Texaco in acquiring ESPN (Entertainment and Sports Programming), the twenty-four-hour, advertiser-supported cable sports channel Getty controlled. The American Broadcasting Companies already held a 15 percent interest in ESPN, however, and ABC quietly acquired the remaining 85 percent for $202 million before anyone else could even bid on the network. Turner was furious and wailed like a stuck pig. "The sale of ESPN," he complained, "was completed while we and a number of other parties were waiting for the financial information necessary to prepare a bid."

Riled that he had not even been given a chance to make an offer for ESPN, Turner decided to corner the cable sports market for himself. Pump in some money, buy up all the action, force ESPN and the others out of business. Turner and Bill Bevins had gone up to New York and sufficiently impressed the people at Pru-

Capital, the investment arm of Prudential Life, to cause them to offer him $200 million to fund his new effort. "I suppose, in a strictly emotional sense," said Alan Cole Ford, sports specialist for Kagan, Inc., a cable consulting organization, "it's easy for Ted because it's ABC. He's beaten them once, with Satellite News Channel. And he is probably convinced he can do it again."

Turner immediately went out and signed a $20 million deal with the National Basketball Association, giving up the right to broadcast all but twenty of his own Atlanta Hawks' games in exchange for a full season's worth of exclusive NBA coverage on cable. He then offered the new United States Football League $62 million for three years' exclusive cable rights, forcing ESPN to raise its own bid to $70 million to secure a package it had acquired one year earlier for only $11 million. Turner then began direct negotiations with Notre Dame for the right to broadcast all of their games. He also paid an undisclosed amount for cable rights to the Southeastern Football Conference. "We're going after everything—basketball, baseball, football, auto racing, wrestling," said Bob Wussler. "You name it. We want it."

The approach was hardly calculated to win friends in the industry. Soon critics began suggesting WTBS's call letters now stood for "Where the Bidding Starts." Turner was upping the ante for everyone in cable sports, sometimes bidding three or four times the amount on the table. But the real impact, once again, would be felt by ABC. By making a quantum leap in sports coverage, Turner not only gained a competitive advantage over ESPN, but strengthened his Superstation, which now reached more than 35 percent of all U.S. households and was cable television's leading program network.

A few months earlier Turner had traveled to Russia for the first time, hoping to establish the exchange of news footage between CNN and Intervision, the official Soviet international television agency. He also discussed selling to Soviet TV such TBS shows as Jacques Cousteau's "Amazon" series. When the Soviet bloc pulled out of the 1984 Los Angeles Olympics and scheduled its own Friendship Games, Intervision immediately contacted Turner and asked if WTBS might be interested in broadcasting an "alternative Olympics," which would be held in Budapest and would include athletes from the Soviet Union, East Germany, Cuba, Mongolia, Vietnam, Hungary, Bulgaria, Czechoslovakia, Poland, and several other Communist nations. ABC had paid a record $225 million for the rights to the Los Angeles Olympics. Turner would get these new Friendship Games for free, paying only for the satellite feed to Atlanta, where he could edit and add English-language narration before sending the games back out again on the Superstation. Intervision even invited Turner to send his own team of sports commentators to Budapest. "I'm quite aware that it will be controversial," Turner said, acknowledging the resistance he expected from some advertisers. "That's not always a bad thing." It didn't hurt that this windfall also came at ABC's expense, since the Soviet boycott of Los Angeles would force the network to make advertiser rebates for its own Olympic programming.

Turner's strong push into sports was not due entirely to ESPN. Nor was it entirely voluntary. In 1983 federal courts had upheld the steep rise in copyright royalty fees. By mid-1984 WTBS had lost over three hundred thousand households as cable operators cut off the Superstation rather than pay the new copyright fees, which in some cases had risen by more than 1,400 percent. Gill Cable, a big operator in northern California, wanted to drop WTBS but retain CNN. When Turner said no, Gill went to court, claiming Turner Broadcasting violated antitrust laws. "Let's say Turner's image in the cable industry was not what it once was," said Robert Hosfeldt, Gill's general manager. "I think his halo has tilted a bit."

Local television stations had never liked Turner, even the ones who bought Headline News. His Superstation, they complained, took money out of their pockets by broadcasting reruns of programs to which they had bought exclusive local rights. Stanley Hubbard, head of Hubbard Broadcasting in St. Paul, Minnesota, took Turner to court but lost when Turner was able to argue that new technologies such as satellite transmission were not covered by the old copyright laws, since they hadn't existed when the original legislation was drawn up. Hubbard appealed, and as long as the case lingered in the courts, an air of uncertainty would hang over the Superstation.

Hollywood's movie producers and program syndicators didn't bother litigating, and simply refused to deal any longer with Turner unless he paid significantly higher prices for their shows. Turner's sources of programming were quickly drying up. Sports, even at the inflated prices Turner now seemed willing to pay, was a logical alternative.

"There is no doubt we admire Ted Turner in this industry," said Ed Allen, chairman of the National Cable Television Association, "but he has to realize, as we do, that there is no such thing as a free lunch. Someone has to pay for his crazy bidding. He drives the prices up for ESPN, for the USA Network. And in the end, he forces the cable industry to pay more and more for programming. It's money we can't pass on to the customers."

With his usual impeccable sense of timing, Turner drove the wedge a little deeper and announced he would launch a music-video channel to compete with the wildly successful MTV, a joint venture between Warner Communications and American Express. Turner made his surprise move known just one day before MTV Networks issued 5.1 million shares of stock in its initial public offering. He may have cost MTV as much as $11 million, since the threat of new competition from Turner caused the underwriters to make an eleventh-hour reduction in the stock's share price. Later the same day, Turner made certain there was no confusion about who had done the damage. At a New York cocktail party for cable operators, he railed on about Warner and called the company "sleazy," vowing to have his competing music-video channel on the air within ninety days. Naturally his remarks found their way into the papers, forcing MTV to announce VH-1, a new music channel designed primarily to compete with Turner's "middle of the road" effort.

Once the damage was done, Turner dropped his plans (and nearly $2 million) to get into the music business, but he knew he had to control the product and began casting about for other network concepts. He had always seen himself as a programmer, whether of broadcast or cable or some new technology. Few understood that it was economics, not ego, that lay behind his grandiose ambition to control one of the major networks. "If you add up all the advertising dollars spent on television in the United States," said Greg Blaine, a media specialist at Foote, Cone & Belding in Chicago, the "three major broadcast networks garner ninety-six percent of those dollars and yet possess about eighty percent of the viewing audience. Commercial cable, on the other hand, has twenty percent of the national audience but accounts for only about four percent of the advertising dollars." Turner realized the differential in those percentages could be worth billions.

Turner had continued to call on Kirk Kerkorian five years after their first meeting in 1980, "to see if I could acquire MGM through merger. Where we would have been partners. And every year, Kerkorian kept saying, 'No, no, no.' He never took us seriously."

Frustrated in his desire to own product, Turner redoubled his efforts to control a distribution channel. In a rousing speech before Washington's National Conservative Foundation, he vowed he would soon take over one of the Big Three. "Those networks," he said, repeating his favorite refrain, "need to be gotten into the hands of people who care about this country. If we are to survive as a nation," Turner added darkly, "we'll look back at this time in history and say we were misusing our communications systems so terribly." Alluding to a recent meeting with CBS chairman Tom Wyman, Turner said he had tried to take over CBS on a "friendly basis" in 1983, "but they turned me down because I would have too much say in the corporation."

Wyman had his hands full in those days, defending CBS's lackluster performance to an increasingly disenchanted board of directors. He denies the meetings with Turner ever passed beyond the exploratory stage and suggests that Turner would have controlled, at best, less than 25 percent of any possible combination of CBS and TBS. Undeterred, Turner continued to meet with other distributor prospects, including Time Inc. and Gannett, although he was unaware that Time and Gannett were also talking to each other and, in fact, were in the final stages of merger negotiations. The corporate politicking was almost too much for Turner, and, growing bored, he turned his attention away from a merger with CBS toward another more likely and, in his eyes, significantly more vulnerable network target.

Despite formidable success at the Los Angeles Olympics, ABC had been shaken by Wall Street's growing criticism of the network's uncertain management, particularly in regard to its failure, after pouring over $330 million into ABC Video Enterprises, to stop mounting operating losses, which now exceeded some $200 million. ABC's total assets were estimated at about $3.8 billion. With 74 percent of the network's stock in institutional hands, Wall Street was suddenly thinking the unthinkable: a hostile takeover was now possible, maybe even plausible. When Jefferies & Company, a Los Angeles broker often used by raiders to accumulate stock quietly, confirmed that one of its customers had been buying shares, ABC earned the dubious distinction of becoming the first television network ever to be put into play.

Central to any unfriendly network takeover, however, would be the approval of the Federal Communications Commission. All radio and TV stations operate under FCC licenses, and under the Communications Act of 1934, a broadcast license can change hands only with the prior approval of the FCC, which generally recognizes 51 percent ownership as the threshold for defining control. Networks themselves aren't licensed, but since each of the Big Three owned the maximum allowed five television stations, FCC approval was requisite to any change of control, even if the new owner planned later to divest the licensed stations.

Broadcasters and communications lawyers had always assumed the FCC would block an unfriendly takeover, but the issue had never been tested. H. L. Hunt, the late Texas oilman, began accumulating CBS shares in 1965 and talked openly about acquiring the whole company, although he eventually lost interest and liquidated his CBS holdings. In 1968 conglomerator Harold Geneen actually received FCC permission to acquire ABC, but that deal collapsed when the Justice Department threatened to intervene on antitrust grounds. Later that same year Howard Hughes's unsolicited offer for ABC was ended when the reclusive billionaire refused to testify on his own behalf before the FCC.

Despite these failed attempts, most industry observers were coming to believe that the free-market philosophy espoused by FCC's chairman, Mark S. Fowler, now made a broadcast network takeover possible. Meanwhile ABC's stock began a noticeable run-up in price, with most analysts still valuing its assets at more than double its current market price of $70 per share.

Insiders on both sides have acknowledged that Turner was in touch with Nelson and Bunker Hunt, but the two Texas wildcatters had hit a major financial dry hole in their effort to corner the world silver market and were busy making the rounds on Wall Street, trying to bail themselves out of the crisis they had created for themselves. Turner also met with North Carolina's Senator Jesse Helms and Fairness in Media, a conservative advocacy group, although Turner's outside counsel, Tench Coxe, told *The Wall Street Journal* that both of those conversations had been "inconsequential." Coxe, however, arranged for former FCC chairman Charles Ferris to meet in mid-February on Turner's behalf with members of the commission to explore procedures for the precedent-setting acquisition of a broadcast network. After learning of the meeting, *The Wall Street Journal* published a denial by Turner that he was planning a bid for CBS. Financial analysts, watching CBS stock begin to climb, concluded that *somebody* must be after the company; if not Turner, they wondered, who might the buyer be?

Dennis Levine, a thirty-one-year-old mergers and acquisitions professional at Shearson Lehman Brothers, the investment banking arm of American Express, had seen Turner come into Shearson seeking the investment advice and fund-raising ability of this powerful arm of American Express. Levine was rapidly building himself a lucrative network somewhat different from anything Turner knew. A product of Bayside, Queens, and the son of an aluminum siding salesman, Levine had gravitated upward through the banking business from Citibank to Smith Barney, and now to Shearson, where he carried the mainly honorific title of senior vice-president. A pompous, self-deprecating man riddled with insecurity but determined to rise above his background and join the new breed of "players" on Wall Street, Levine was earning nearly $600,000 a year at Shearson. Despite his position and his compensation, Levine possessed few of the basic technical financial skills necessary to succeed in the investment banking business. Levine skated right over these deficiencies, however, because he proved to be a master at acquiring insider information and he was hardly burdened with any of the requisite ethical inhibitions that might have prevented his using this information for his own benefit.

For over five years Dennis Levine had been operating an ever-expanding information network of young insiders planted deep within Lazard; Smith, Barney; Goldman Sachs; Shearson; and Wachtel, Lipton, a leading takeover law firm. By the time Turner walked into Shearson Lehman, Levine had already determined he would leave. He had his eye on Drexel Burnham and the junk bond money machine Michael Milken had created there. The growth of the merger business had begun to accelerate at such a furious rate that an M&A specialist like Levine, despite his lackluster résumé, was in demand. Levine not only seemed to know much of what was going on in the takeover business; he was also close to the notorious arbitrageur/deal maker Ivan Boesky.

Spurning offers from Morgan Stanley and First Boston, Levine got what he wanted at Drexel—a managing director title and minimum guaranteed compensation of $1 million a year. Boesky had invited him to a secret meeting at the Harvard Club months earlier and Levine, confident he had cut himself a tremendous deal—5 percent of the profits from any information he provided —had been feeding Boesky information for months. Levine was finally in the big leagues and when he passed along to his friend information about Turner's plans to take over CBS, the news was too good to pass up. Soon, Ivan Boesky was accumulating CBS stock as if it were going out of style.

ABC was still his number-one target, but Ted Turner had no inkling Leonard Goldenson, ABC's aging chairman, had been negotiating secretly for weeks with both IBM and Capital Cities Broadcasting. When he approached his Atlanta banker, Robinson-Humphries, which itself had been acquired by Shearson Lehman, Turner was sent to see Richard Bingham, head of Shearson's mergers and acquisitions department. Bingham and his team listened politely as Turner and Bill Bevins outlined their intention to take over ABC. "The arithmetic's simply not there, Ted," one of the Lehman bankers volunteered. "You don't go after a billion-dollar company like ABC with fifty million in cash." Bingham posited that it would take at least $2.5 billion to acquire American Broadcasting Companies, and at least $3.5 billion for CBS, the other network Turner mentioned as a potential target. That's why we're here, Turner responded. We're looking to you guys for the best way to put a deal together.

Several days later, on March 1, 1985, ABC rejected Capital Cities' offer of $110 per share but indicated that an all-cash offer of $120 would be acceptable. Cap Cities had brought in the legendary "value investor" Warren Buffet, whose Berkshire Hathaway company would contribute more than $500 million to the transaction. Incredibly, no word leaked of the pending deal, partly, Turner would later learn, because Cap Cities had been negotiating directly with ABC and the network's bankers at First Boston. On March 13, however, a deal was struck. *The New York Times* proclaimed the $3.5 billion sale of ABC to a "little-known media company" as "one of the biggest business stories of the decade."

The news caught Turner off guard, but he immediately switched gears and reset his sights on CBS. Reacting instantly, the Tiffany Network subpoenaed five brokerage firms—Dillon, Reed & Co., Goldman Sachs & Co., J. Streicher & Co., Jefferies & Co., and Goetz, Batcchker & Co.—in an effort, according to a CBS spokesman, "to discover the nature and extent of Ted Turner's trading in CBS stock." Turner, meanwhile, was cooling his heels at Shearson, wondering why Richard Bingham had suddenly done a disappearing act. What Turner couldn't have known was the panic that struck CBS once news of the Cap Cities takeover of ABC became public. CBS founder Bill Paley, together with fellow CBS director and financier James Wolfensohn, had appealed to James Robinson, chairman of Shearson Lehman's parent, American Express. You don't want this redneck Turner taking over CBS, do you? Paley complained. Find some conflict and tell him Shearson can't represent him. Wolfensohn, who had close business ties with both Jim Robinson and American Express, echoed Paley's directive, pointing out the danger a man like Turner could represent to the entire broadcast industry. Wolfensohn also reminded his friend that this was the same Ted Turner who had once been blackballed by the New York Yacht Club.

Jim Robinson is the silky-smooth, well-born son of a Georgia banker, the kind of fellow who would never have lent Turner a dime even if he had come, cap in hand, looking for ways to finance his acquisition of a money-losing Atlanta UHF station. A calculating sophisticate who was attempting to turn American Express into a world-class financial services empire, Robinson was only too pleased to accommodate his old friends at CBS, passing the word to Shearson to plead a conflict of interest and send Turner packing. Shearson managing director Sherman Lewis apologized to Turner on behalf of his firm, explained the putative conflict of interest, and then innocently suggested that he might try the good folks at E. F. Hutton. Lewis even agreed to provide Turner with an introduction through Hutton's chairman, Robert Foman.

With his own next choice, First Boston, also apparently conflicted out, Turner had been inclined to go, instead, to Drexel Burnham. He discovered that CBS had already covered that base, however, and had paid Drexel a significant retainer to ensure they would be unavailable to anyone else. Which is why Drexel and Mike Milken were forced to sit on the sidelines during the lucrative changes in control of all three television networks that were to occur over the next nine months. *Business Week* quoted Drexel's Fred Joseph's pious explanation in a comment that left most of Wall Street laughing out loud. "Even under new, liberalized ground rules," Joseph pontificated, "the regulatory hassle would still be a pretty serious constraint. And," he continued in a most uncharacteristic tone, "attacking a major part of the media may be ill advised in its own right."

Turner was anxious to move. With both First Boston, Drexel, and now Shearson out of the picture, he decided to accept Lewis's suggestion and go with E. F. Hutton. Any further delay would only give CBS more time to set up its defenses.

One of the few old independent white-shoe firms left on Wall

Street, Hutton had suffered a precipitous decline in both profits and prestige during the early 1980s and was eager to get back into the game. A high-profile takeover like CBS would quickly reestablish the firm's fading reputation. Consequently, Bob Foman welcomed Turner with open arms and quickly negotiated a $2 million initial retainer, plus various stepped "success fees" that could eventually exceed $30 million. Hutton's new merger chief, Daniel J. Good, viewed the takeover of CBS as a deal that would put Hutton back on the map, despite the fact that no one at the firm had any real experience in FCC-regulated transactions.

On March 5, 1985, FCC chairman Fowler testified before a House subcommittee that the commission was seriously considering a procedure that would remove a key obstacle to a hostile network takeover. Under Fowler's proposal, an acquirer could park his newly acquired shares in a trust while attempting to gain control of his target. During that time the commission would not even consider a petition to deny the takeover. If the acquirer's tender succeeded, he would then have to file a standard transfer application for the network's broadcast licenses and secure FCC approval in the normal manner. "This new proposal," said Howard F. Roycroft, an FCC specialist at the law firm of Hogan & Hartson, "is very significant. There is no doubt it would facilitate a network takeover."

Breaking up a great communications empire like CBS was such a radical concept at the time, however, that most financial analysts consistently undervalued the individual assets of the company. Hadn't CBS chairman Tom Wyman spent the last five years diversifying CBS into a broad-gauged media and communications conglomerate? Hadn't he just spent more than a third of a billion dollars for twelve hot Ziff-Davis magazines while divesting less profitable businesses like toys and musical instruments? CBS shares were undervalued in the marketplace, most analysts agreed, simply because the Street assigned no "takeover value" to the company. Both Wyman and CBS founder Bill Paley, despite their differences on other matters, were intransigent and extremely public in their determination to keep CBS independent. The tangle of regulatory and legislative considerations alone seemed certain to ensure that CBS was, in fact, takeover proof.

Undeterred, Dan Good began pulling together a team of over thirty Hutton professionals to work with Turner. With Hutton less than six months, Good was pleased to be leading the firm's attack on this high profile takeover. He also saw the CBS deal as a way to vault over an old Hutton insider, James Lopp, and take control of Hutton's entire corporate finance group. When Turner, Bill Bevins, and George Vandeman, Turner's legal adviser from Latham & Watkins, showed up for their first strategy session, Good was ready with a battle plan. Unlike the bankers at Shearson and most industry analysts, Good had not been deterred by Turner's anemic balance sheet. How would a minnow like Turner Broadcasting, with maximum borrowing power of perhaps $400 million, swallow a whale like CBS, which Good estimated might now cost as much as $4–$5 billion? Simple, he suggested. By letting CBS's own shareholders finance the acquisition.

Multibillion-dollar leveraged buyouts were still a relatively rare phenomenon, but, Good reasoned, Turner's acquisition could probably be financed with the sale proceeds of CBS assets like the company's radio and television stations, as well as its music and magazine publishing divisions, leaving Turner with his real target, the CBS network. With a little luck, Good suggested, Turner might even wind up making a profit on the transaction, in effect paying nothing for the network. Ted Turner had built his business empire on his father's dictum: Never use your own money when somebody else's is available. The simple logic of Good's proposal had enormous appeal, and when Good suggested a two-step transaction, with the first step consisting of a no-cash exchange offer of notes, bonds, and TBS stock for CBS stock, Turner gave Hutton the go-ahead.

Turner had noted the steady rise in CBS's share price, from $72 in early February when he had first showed up in Shearson Lehman's offices to over $100 in mid-March, but he was unaware that it was Ivan Boesky who was running the price up with his heavy buying. He realized that eventually he would need not just cash but additional credibility, and after an inconclusive dialogue with Boesky, who had made it his business to seek Turner out, Turner began meeting with a laundry list of other prospective partners. One who indicated interest was financier William Simon, the former treasury secretary who had recently lost out in his $1 billion effort to acquire Multi/Media, a substantial regional broadcast group. Another was MCI, William McGowan's long-distance telephone company. Neither, however, was willing to commit more than a modest $50 million in cash, hardly enough to provide Turner with the kind of credibility Warren Buffet and his $500 million had given Cap Cities' successful takeover bid for ABC.

Traditionally a power in raising capital for established businesses, Hutton had never been a factor in the rapidly developing high-yield junk bond market dominated by Drexel and Milken. With its elitist, "old boy" approach to investment banking, Hutton had relied far too long on the sanctity of long-standing client relationships and had consistently lost business to the new breed of ambitious, deal-oriented young investment bankers now emerging as the new powers on Wall Street. Bob Foman recruited Dan Good and his colleagues Jim Dwyer and John DeRosier from A. G. Becker, hoping they could help to put Hutton back in the front ranks of investment banking. "While Hutton wouldn't be considered the usual firm to handle a transaction like Turner's," *The Wall Street Journal* reported, "it won't take a great deal of talent to contact the usual players in junk bond financing."

Raising a few hundred million dollars in new capital for a blue-chip client like AT&T or General Motors would not have been much of a challenge for Hutton or anybody on Wall Street. Locating $5 billion to finance a hostile takeover of a formidable target like CBS was something else. Hutton's credibility, and Turner's, however, took a nosedive some ten days later when Hutton pleaded guilty to more than two hundred counts of mail and wire fraud, an indication, at the very least, of the firm's lackadaisical management.

With widespread speculation now beginning to link him with a bid for CBS, Turner suddenly became unavailable to the media. Congenitally incapable of keeping a secret, Turner was showing such admirable constraint that *The Wall Street Journal* was moved to announce, "The Mouth of the South Is Closed." His newfound silence, however, was driving Tom Wyman and CBS to distraction. At the company's regular meeting with financial analysts, Wyman publicly excoriated Turner as "extremist" and "without proper conscience." There was "utterly no financial substance," he added, "behind reports that Ted Turner was trying to take over CBS." Nevertheless, some of the more astute listeners at the CBS meeting thought they might have heard the slightest hint of panic beneath the chairman's generally upbeat presentation. They were pleased to hear that CBS had asked a consortium of five United States banks to open a new $1.5 billion line of credit, with a second line for $750 million coming from a group of nine foreign banks, funds that analysts assumed could be used to buy other companies or repurchase CBS stock, making it harder for Turner or anybody else to swallow the company. "We are in a position," Wyman said, "to react promptly, should anything of real sub-

stance develop." Wyman uncorked even stronger language at a
cocktail party following the meeting, claiming, "Mr. Turner simply does not have sufficient moral character to run a network."

A few of the investment bankers present, however, wondered
whether Wyman and CBS weren't seriously underestimating
Turner. His financial acumen, they suggested, was generally overshadowed by his brash public persona. His reputation for abra-
siveness blurred his considerable abilities to add significant
incremental value to anything he touched. "Labels like 'Turbulent Ted' and 'Captain Outrageous' just don't apply, at least not
anymore," said Richard MacDonald, media analyst for First Boston Corporation. "No one sees the substance. He's a damned good
businessman. The man knows how to make money."

Without admitting he was taking Turner seriously, Wyman
began an attempt to link him with Jesse Helms' Fairness in
Media, and Donald Wildmon's Coalition for Better Television.
Wyman was even able to have Turner subpoenaed in late March,
demanding that he describe under oath his ties to any fundamentalist or conservative organizations. At the same time CBS
reached an out-of-court settlement with Fairness in Media to provide them with the CBS shareholder list, although the settlement
was (intentionally) too late to allow a proxy mailing before CBS's
upcoming annual shareholders meeting. The CBS board also
rammed through a quiet change in the company bylaws, elimi-
nating the right of any shareholder holding 10 percent or more of
the common stock to call special shareholder meetings.

On March 30, Ivan Boesky filed Securities and Exchange Commission documents disclosing that he owned an 8.7 percent stake
in CBS and was now the company's single largest shareholder.
Bill Paley's beneficial holdings amounted to less than 6.5 percent.
CBS immediately went on the offensive, charging in a federal
lawsuit that Boesky had not only financed his $247.1 million pur-
chases of CBS stock illegally, but had also failed to disclose in his
filings "conversations" CBS said Boesky had with Turner. CBS
also indicated it would reject Boesky's demand that it buy back
his stock at a premium to the average $92 price per share he had
reportedly paid. Indicating it intended to play hardball with anybody who attempted to move on the company, CBS also lodged
formal complaints against Boesky at the New York Stock Exchange, charging him with violating margin requirements and
failing to disclose his "attempted greenmail" of CBS in his SEC
filings.

Suddenly, however, Wyman's aggressive strategy seemed to backfire. Rumors of impending mergers with a "white knight" like Time Inc. or General Electric filled the financial press. CBS stock quickly climbed well beyond the $110 per share Boesky was demanding. Analysts were rethinking their valuations, and *Business Week* reported that estimates of the CBS radio and TV stations alone ran as high as $2.7 billion or $90 per share. Boesky told *The Wall Street Journal*, "Buying CBS stock is like buying a dollar for fifty cents." CBS founder Bill Paley was rumored ready to lead an investment group to take the company private if a hostile takeover showed any sign of succeeding. Despite Wyman's statement at the CBS annual shareholders meeting that "to the best of our knowledge, there is no financial substance to rumors that Ted Turner will be taking over this or any other network," CBS suddenly found itself in the awkward and unusual position of being in play for the first time in its corporate history.

On Thursday, April 18, 1985, Ted Turner walked onto the stage of the grand ballroom of New York's Plaza Hotel. Facing a ballroom packed with over two hundred reporters, financial analysts, and investment bankers, he stared straight into the live television cameras and, with an appropriately somber mien, declared war on CBS. Speaking in an unnatural, dull monotone, Turner read a terse two-minute statement his lawyers had prepared, sticking to a script for the first time in his life. The room exploded in pandemonium, but Turner, following instructions, turned on his heel and walked off the stage, explaining, "I'm not allowed to comment on this proposal, but my investment banker, Dan Good, will try to answer your questions."

Good was immediately backed up against a wall and, as the TV cameras closed in, did his best to explain that Turner Broadcasting had filed an unsolicited offer with the Securities and Exchange Commission to acquire all of CBS's common stock in exchange for high-yield notes, debentures, and TBS shares. The complicated package, Good said, had an estimated face value of at least $175 a share, or $5.41 billion. "We tried to design a security package," he said, "to appeal to a wide variety of investors, both retail and institutional." The Turner proposal, Good claimed, was "the first leveraged buyout ever directed to shareholders" and ultimately might change many times before anyone signed on the dotted line.

Reaction was instant. And overwhelmingly unfavorable. CBS's intensive public relations effort to discredit Turner and any bid he might make was proving effective. "This offer frankly borders on the ludicrous," commented Smith Barney's media analyst Edward Atorino, speaking for many of his colleagues. "Turner was, in effect, asking CBS's public shareholders, over 70 percent of which are institutions with presumably some fiduciary responsibility toward their holdings, to become his creditors. He expects them to swap highly liquid equity in a profitable business to become lenders to an overwhelmingly leveraged company. To meet interest and principal on the exchange package he offered, Turner admitted he would have to sell off most of CBS's nonbroadcast assets, as well as certain of the CBS-owned radio and television stations."

"Given this scenario," asked money manager Mario Gabelli, "could Turner's deal possibly succeed? In theory it shouldn't, if only because there's absolutely no cash flow to support the paper, other than the company's own assets."

"It's great press, and it's something that sells newspapers," said former CBS programming chief Fred Silverman, who spoke for Hollywood, "but if it ever did go through, I'd have to take a look at what's happening to this country."

Despite his differences with Turner, Dan Schorr offered a somewhat different perspective when the *Los Angeles Times* asked him to comment on Turner's bid for Schorr's old network. "There are two points to remember," Schorr cautioned. "One, I'm told by people better informed than I that it's impossible for Turner's bid to succeed. Two, everything he has ever done has been impossible."

As CBS unlimbered its legal guns and prepared for battle with Turner, Ivan Boesky decided to take his profit and quietly left the field, selling off his CBS shares in the open market for a tidy $32 million profit and disappearing into the woodwork. Boesky did not want to get caught up in litigation that might disturb his cozy new arrangement with Dennis Levine, now happily ensconced at Drexel Burnham. Four years later, however, Levine would blow the whistle on his friend, "the Russian," who in turn would trade his own testimony against junk bond king Michael Milken for a reduced prison sentence. Court transcripts confirm that Levine's tip on Turner constituted the beginning of his new arrangement with Boesky, although no charges regarding the Turner/CBS situation have ever been lodged against either individual.

Morgan Stanley, the CBS investment adviser, responded immediately, publicly terming the proposed takeover "grossly inadequate and financially imprudent." The CBS board met three days later and opened up a full frontal attack. Wyman continued to cast aspersions on Turner's "moral fitness to run a network" and was sounding more like Ted Turner than Turner himself as he reiterated his concerns about Turner's "close ties with un-named ideological groups." "Those who seek to gain control of CBS News," Wyman added for good measure, "threaten its inde-pendence and its integrity—and this country."

CBS then made its own filing with the Securities and Exchange Commission, urging the commission to void Turner's registration as fiscally unsound. The network also claimed that TBS had never actually been profitable, had kept improper books for more than ten years, and had "misstated earnings for 1983 and 1984—the basis for a major TBS debenture upon which at least some of the current exchange offer was based." The network also unveiled a report prepared by its auditors, Coopers & Lybrand, predicting that a combined CBS and Turner Broadcasting operation would be bankrupt by 1987. CBS also claimed that Turner had im-properly amortized $25 million used to buy out the now defunct Satellite News Channel and also failed to account for certain losses by the Atlanta Hawks basketball team. In its filing CBS declared it had "no plans for an extraordinary transaction, such as a merger or reorganization"; "no plans to take the company private or invite in a 'white knight' in a purchase, sale, or transfer of any of its assets"; "no plans to make a material change in the present capitalization or dividend policy of the company"; and "no poison pill through a tender offer or other acquisition."

The poison pill, Wall Street concluded, would be CBS itself. "The minute Turner takes over CBS," a network spokesman told *The Wall Street Journal*, "its value will drop by at least 20 per-cent." Then, parroting the network's party line, he added, "Any-one who buys a media company for ideological reasons must be prepared to pay dearly for that conviction."

CBS next filed actions in both New York state and federal courts, accusing TBS of a litany of additional securities viola-tions, as well as conspiracy to defraud; then, without waiting for Turner to petition the FCC for its approval of the takeover, CBS filed lengthy and well-documented objections to any change of control, citing Turner's fiscal irresponsibility and immoral char-acter. "We intend to challenge his fitness, not just to operate a network, but to be a broadcast licensee at all," one member of the CBS legal team told *Business Week*.

The network's army of Washington lobbyists also went to work on Capitol Hill, pressuring every congressman and federal agency in sight to investigate Turner's proposed "rape" of one of the country's broadcast treasures. Their efforts bore fruit at the Justice Department, which indicated it would render an evaluation of any antitrust or other regulatory violation within thirty days.

Variety reported that Tom Wyman personally called the heads of each of the fourteen U.S. and overseas banks with whom he had just opened up new credit lines, as well as the several investment banking firms with which CBS did business, making certain each understood clearly that dealing with Turner would be a "serious conflict of interest," subject to legal damages if breached. Wyman also hinted darkly that he might even change the contracts of top CBS talents Dan Rather and Michael Jackson, among others, so that they would be abrogated in the event of a takeover or change of control.

Caught off guard by the ferocity and apparent effectiveness of CBS's counterattack, Turner and his team attempted to regroup, directing Dan Good to rethink the merits of Hutton's no-cash proposal. It was clear, despite increasing criticism of Tom Wyman's management, that Turner was up against a formidable opponent. Wyman had taken off the gloves and was using Turner's own words to destroy any credibility he might have had as a network owner. "In light of the long list of pejorative statements he is on record as having made," Wyman trumpeted, "about various minority, religious, and ethnic groups, we believe TBS's acquisition of CBS would seriously undermine the network's present broad acceptance by the American public. We also believe that control of CBS by TBS," he continued, "would also jeopardize important relationships with our affiliated stations, the creative community, advertisers, and our employees."

Despite credible new estimates of CBS's liquidation value ranging upward to more than $8 billion, or nearly $3 billion more than Turner's offer, Wall Street was succumbing to the network's anti-Turner public relations blitz and began to laugh off his bid. CBS stock dropped from a high of $117 on the day of Turner's offer to $102 two weeks later and would have fallen further if the Street had not expected another CBS suitor to emerge. Even *The Wall Street Journal* was convinced by CBS's punishing attacks on Turner's character. It dismissed his bid with the front-page headline OUTLANDISH, FITS IN WITH HIS IMAGE and belittled his effort as "Terrible Ted's Network Obsession." Turner knew now he could not succeed without a healthy cash component to his offer and began an almost desperate round of meetings to find a strong equity partner. Hampered by Hutton's relative inexperience in hostile takeovers and with so many obvious sources of equity already sealed off by CBS, he turned to strategic partners like Gannett's Al Neuharth, who expressed some interest but was still in the middle of secret merger talks himself with Time Inc. Even PruCapital, which had so enthusiastically offered to invest $200 million in TBS just a few months earlier, began to back off, pointing out that its parent, Prudential Life, might be in conflict since the insurance giant was currently in negotiations that could make it the largest holder of CBS preferred stock. Of course, Prudential would later see no such conflict in being on both sides of other contentious megabuck takeovers like Macmillan and RJR, but neither Turner nor his investment advisers at Hutton seemed able to overcome the pressures CBS had obviously brought to bear on the Pru.

An exceedingly private person, CBS's Tom Wyman had been reluctantly drawn out into the limelight by Turner's takeover attempt. Wyman was facing his toughest challenge in five years as head of the network, but he proved to be a cool, confident, and immensely sophisticated strategist, always at least one jump ahead of an uncharacteristically muzzled Turner, who was kept silent by SEC disclosure rules and could no longer fall back on his usual overheated rhetoric to keep the opposition off-balance.

"What Tom's doing now?" asked his former boss, William Spoor, chief executive of Pillsbury. "Fighting off anyone who tries to take over CBS. That fits his personality. Wyman's a tough competitor, a terrific fighter, and anyone underestimating him is making a serious mistake."

Determined to show both Turner and Wall Street it was business as usual at CBS, Tom Wyman took just enough time off from his Turner-bashing campaign to close an all-cash $100 million acquisition of five Taft Broadcasting radio stations in early May, making the CBS Broadcast Group the country's largest. Wyman admitted to the media, however, that battling Turner now consumed more than half his waking hours. He was a professional manager who liked his job and felt he was more than earning his $1 million–plus annual compensation. Wyman's tough "damn the torpedoes" attacks on Turner were lauded in the business press (CBS TAKEOVER DEFENSE: IT'S TOP-RATED, headlined *Fortune* magazine in a May cover story), and his antitakeover strategy was deemed an elaborate, elegant construction of intimidation and delay. Savvy arbitrageur Salim B. Lewis was effusive in his praise of the barricades Wyman had erected around the network. He predicted, "Anyone who tries an unfriendly takeover of CBS can be sure of only one thing—he won't win." Still, the CBS board seemed not only unsympathetic, but at times almost ungrateful, as if Wyman himself and not Turner might have put the company in its present predicament.

Nor was Wyman particularly heartened when Bill Paley, hospitalized briefly when Turner's bid had first been announced, finally broke his silence with a public statement on the takeover. "CBS is more than a business," Paley said soberly. "It is a public trust. And for more than a half century, CBS has been my life. What this company means to me cannot be measured in monetary terms. To risk its loss now would be to trifle recklessly with the company's future and with the public interest."

Inside CBS, Wyman and Paley had grown increasingly critical of each other, and the network founder's unusually candid comments in the press did nothing to help heal the rift. Paley could not forgive Wyman for unseating him as chairman in 1983 or for killing Paley's determined efforts to move CBS into cable. Wyman, for his part, could not help noticing the omission of any direct reference in Paley's remarks to his success thus far in protecting CBS. He was not at all certain that Paley had been referring to him when he called for CBS to be led by "reliable, responsible people with the skill, the talent, and the courage—and, when necessary, the self-discipline and forbearance—to meet the public responsibility that is inherent in the management of this company." Could Paley be planning to take CBS private himself? Wyman began to wonder in response to the intimations of many of his friends on Wall Street.

Ted Turner was hardly concerned with such speculation. The ineffable logic behind his bid for CBS escaped most observers. While Wall Street was writing him off as a megalomaniacal, egotistical dreamer, Turner was, in fact, digging in for the fight of his life. He knew taking over a network was possible, even before Cap Cities had succeeded with ABC. He understood the complex, multidimensional effort it would take, and for nearly five months he proved he could hold his own against ABC/Westinghouse, one of the most formidable combines in corporate America. Leaving George Vandeman, his principal outside legal adviser, and Bill Bevins to go it alone in New York, where they directed the three-front attack on Wall Street, in Albany, and in Washington, Turner withdrew from the field to assess his chances and try to understand why, when the numbers made such good sense, the marketplace had responded so poorly to his offer.

"Bill Bevins and I practically lived together for four or five months during CBS," Vandeman says. "We were like Siamese twins. Ted had the vision. Bill's job was to run the numbers and figure out how to make it work. I oversaw our quite sizable legal team and directed the legal effort. There was just no way, zero, that CBS was ever going to make it easy. Wyman was tough; he told us in the one meeting we had that Turner was wasting his breath. And, of course, everyone laughed us off the Street."

Just when it looked as if Turner's CBS bid might die a-borning, however, the TBS registration statement won SEC approval, and one week later Turner's combative, detailed filing with the FCC was received so positively by the investment community that CBS stock climbed back up to $118 per share. Now aware of the asset values Turner had been touting all along, investors pored over Bill Bevins's detailed projections of the combined companies and gave a passing grade to his prediction of positive year-end cash balances despite debt service of over $3.6 billion through 1994. Michael Arends, an investment analyst with Kemper Financial Services, echoed Wall Street's suddenly positive response. "Now that Turner's proved the numbers work, all he has got to do is sweeten the deal. If you are Ted Turner, you certainly haven't opened with your top bid."

Not everybody was cheering, however. The run-up in CBS's share price reduced the premium of Turner's $150 face value package. And in Washington, Missouri Democrat Senator Thomas Eagleton moved to require the FCC to hold evidentiary hearings on hostile takeovers of any network. Eagleton's proposal omitted any mention of his long-standing personal ties to Tom Wyman. Both were from St. Louis, born two months apart in 1929. Both attended St. Louis Country Day School. And both then went together to Amherst College.

"Once we began to show investors what the combined companies would look like," Vandeman says, "once we showed them how those notes would be repaid—who would buy the CBS divisions, what they would sell for, and what kind of a company would be left—the financial community slowly came to respect the Turner offer. Obviously," he added, "CBS respected it from the outset, knew it was entirely possible. Or they would not have launched the massive attack we were up against."

"CBS will never be the same again. We intend to go right to the shareholders and let them decide who is offering more value. From this point forward, CBS lives by different rules." The speaker was Turner's Washington lawyer, former FCC chairman Charles Ferris, his white hair and rumpled seersucker suit in keeping with the unpretentious tastes of his client. He was buoyant after leaving a preliminary FCC hearing at which he had been told that Ted Turner was "apparently fit to operate a network, whether it's in Atlanta or New York." Turner was now prepared to hit the road, taking his proposal personally to large institutional holders of CBS stock. Meanwhile Dan Good and his team at Hutton had been calling on prospective buyers of the nonbroadcast assets Turner intended to sell, although some would say later that Hutton had got the cart before the horse. "We had already been offered several billion for some of the assets," Good revealed, "and we hadn't even solicited formal offers yet."

Wall Street had taken a closer look at the pieces of CBS Turner could divest, and suddenly his proposal looked considerably more interesting. "We intended putting all the various assets to be sold in a liquidation trust," explains Good. "We'd appoint independent trustees, and the assets would be sold in an orderly manner over a two-year period, with the proceeds distributed to the CBS shareholders. We had planned all along—it was a kind of hidden agenda—to pay cash for the broadcast assets and exchange paper for the nonbroadcast assets, with the shareholders getting about five times the current CBS dividend through the trust until full cash payment was generated through asset sales. It was a technique I used effectively in the Dillingham Corporation liquidation in the 1970s. We planned to use the same structure, a liquidating trust, with CBS. A trust has a market value and trades on its own, separately, and the proceeds are then distributed to the shareholders."

By early July it became clear that Turner's bid for CBS was developing legs, but most investors still expected a new bidder to emerge, someone with real cash who could drive the price up closer to the kind of value Turner had demonstrated was there. Ironically for CBS, the worst that could happen now would be for

Turner to withdraw his bid and walk away. With CBS shares
hovering near $120 and buoyed by the expectation that Turner
was about to sweeten his offer with a cash component, the Street
expected sharks like Carl Icahn or Boesky to move in again if, in
reaction to a Turner retreat, the price plummeted fifteen or
twenty points.

To stay free of a takeover, CBS was now down to two options:
either tender for a large amount of its own stock, loading the
company with so much debt that a raider like Turner would be
unable to pile on any more; or sell off a large chunk of itself, either
directly or through the issuance of some of the seventy million
authorized but unissued shares in its treasury, making it difficult
if not impossible for Turner to acquire the two-thirds ownership
necessary for change of control under New York's tough new takeover laws.

"Sure, you need a 67 percent shareholder approval in New
York," Ferris pointed out, "but what people don't realize is that
Ted can always make a second bid to meet a CBS attempt to
recapture its shares or sell off new stock. The company is controlled by institutions, which are interested strictly in getting the
best value for their investment in CBS."

In early June, Turner interrupted his search for equity partners
to attend Teddy's graduation from The Citadel. Then he retreated
to Avalon, his classic turn-of-the-century hunting plantation near
Tallahassee, Florida. He had purchased the 8,100-acre estate in
1984 for $8 million from Alexandra McKay, widow of the founder
of Benjamin Moore Paints, and moved his family into the sprawling green-and-white lattice-trimmed plantation house. Dan Good
visited Avalon during the CBS takeover attempt and marveled at
the unspoiled beauty of this north Florida paradise.

"We spent a lot of time with Turner down there," Good said,
"and I got to know him pretty well over the three months or so
we worked together. I think he knew he might be out of his element, but he listened carefully and was a very quick learner."

Good also remembers meeting Jimmy Brown at Avalon and
noted the unusual rapport that seemed to exist between the amiable black man and Turner. "Just watching the way the two of
them were with the dogs and the horses gave you the feeling," the
investment banker comments, "that business wasn't the most important thing in Turner's life, even though he was right in the
midst of trying to take over the biggest television network in the
world."

On July 3, however, just as Turner was feeling confident that his bid for CBS would be successful, the network finally played its trump card. In a move Tom Wyman said offered "creative protection for his shareholders," CBS announced plans to repurchase 6.4 million shares (21 percent of its outstanding stock) for $150 each—$40 cash, plus $110 face value of a new ten-year investment-grade note paying 10⅞ percent interest. The market responded favorably, and CBS stock rocketed upward on Wyman's announcement, rising from $112 to over $125 per share. Turner still believed his new $175 package of debt and equity could prevail, particularly since he was now planning to put nearly $100 cash into his offer, more than twice the cash component of CBS's buy-back proposal.

Over the long Fourth of July weekend, however, Turner and his team had a chance to read the fine print in CBS's offering circular and began to understand what Wyman meant by "creative protection." The key defensive element in the CBS package lay in the way the company planned to raise $125 million of the total $880 million the buy-back would cost. CBS would issue preference stock to five major institutional investors—Prudential Insurance, Raytheon Financial, Northwestern Mutual, American General, and American International Group. The preference shares would be convertible into CBS common at a price not less than $110 and not greater than $150. These institutions would have the right to convert their preferred shares into securities of any company acquiring CBS, but without the typical "poison pill" premium. The other provisions of the issue, however, were very poisonous and limited CBS to a very low debt-to-equity ratio, far below anything Turner could attain unless he were to put forward an all-cash offer. Nor would Turner be allowed to buy out the preferred shareholders even if he could, since CBS was given first rights of refusal. "We can't even offer Prudential two hundred cents on the dollar," one of the Hutton advisers moaned. And if Turner were somehow to overcome these hurdles and gain control of CBS, he would have to live with the preferred shareholders for at least ten years, when the securities would become redeemable. The CBS defense, moreover, did not hinge entirely on the preferential shares. The notes CBS shareholders would receive contained provisions barring the company from disposing of major assets or from exceeding a debt-to-combined-capital ratio even more strict than the preferred stock limitations. These rules could be waived only by a majority of CBS's independent directors. The catch for

Turner was that the right to waive the rules would be abolished if CBS were acquired.

Turner's immediate response was a "vigorous legal challenge." Seeking an injunction against the CBS tender, TBS filed suit in the U.S. District Court in Atlanta, charging that CBS directors had violated their fiduciary responsibility to shareholders. TBS also asked the FCC to rule on whether the CBS plan constituted a change of control, an event requiring FCC approval. Despite all the legal Sturm und Drang, however, Turner realized his best hope lay in the possibility that a judge would conclude there was no legal justification for the tough provisions of the CBS tender and throw out the offer.

"You have to look at it as part of the whole," Dan Good explained confidently, defining the approach TBS would take in court. "This is nothing more than an illegal attempt to entrench CBS management. They are doing everything they can to keep the CBS shareholders from getting our offer." A court date was set for July 24, but Turner was determined to launch his own counteroffensive and told his advisers he might not be able to maintain his silence much longer.

Addressing the National Press Club in Washington a few days later, Turner said at the outset that he would not discuss the CBS situation, but then he plunged right into a scathing comparison of the two proposals. Claiming to have spent more than $15 million so far in his pursuit of CBS, Turner called the CBS plan "a partial recapitalization, a partial cutback, and a partial liquidation of nonbroadcast assets. It is," he said, "only a portion of what needs to be done." Accusing Tom Wyman and CBS management of misrepresentation in their SEC filings, Turner detailed his charges point by point. He also castigated CBS for its intention to offer Bill Paley a cash price of $150 each for 434,489 of his shares rather than the $110 note other selling shareholders would receive. "A sweetheart deal," Turner called the arrangement, which CBS said had been designed "to limit shareholder tax liability and was made in view of Paley's commitment to and long identification with CBS."

"Turner seemed as confident as ever," reported *Broadcasting* magazine, "and certain that he now had CBS on the defensive. ' "If we fail," ' he told the National Press Club, 'is still not in my vocabulary.' "

Without waiting for the legal proceedings to begin, Turner, Bevins, and Vandeman hit the road in a hurry, flying all over the country to meet with prospective investor/partners, while Dan Good and his team now concentrated on winning over the institutional investors who controlled nearly 70 percent of the CBS shares. "We had meetings everywhere," Vandeman recounts. "With companies, wealthy individuals, pension funds, wherever we thought we could find partners who would bring cash to the table or who might be interested in acquiring some of the CBS assets we planned to sell."

The tide seemed clearly to have shifted in Turner's favor, and the Turner team met with genuine interest wherever they went. "Turner was absolutely magnificent," says Vandeman. "He's one of the great genius salesmen. He's flamboyant, obviously, but he can also have an audience eating out of his hand as soon as he walks in a room. Turner opened their eyes to the real values that could be achieved from media properties. He was a challenge to work with, but exciting at the same time. And sometimes a little frustrating—remember, we still had a live SEC filing and had to be very careful about what we said and didn't say. That sometimes caused problems. But," Vandeman adds, "when you see what Larry Tisch did with CBS, he followed our script almost to the letter—it was all spelled out in our registration statement."

In between stops on their hectic turns around the country, Turner found time to drop in on his Atlanta Braves, who were mired in the National League cellar once again despite a whole generation of new young ball players whom manager Bobby Cox had slowly been developing down in the Braves' farm system. Often, when flying back from Avalon Plantation in his six-seater Merlin IIB, Turner would keep going right on up to Washington and the new offices of the Better World Society. There he would change hats briefly and put in a few hours of nonprofit fundraising.

"Ted approached me in late 1984," says Tom Belford, then head of Vanguard Communications, a Washington-based, issues-oriented consulting firm. "I was already working for the Audubon Society and a number of other groups, and Turner Broadcasting retained me to develop what became the Better World Society. I remember our first meeting in February 1985," says Belford. "By then Ted had put up nearly $500,000 and brought me on board full-time as the first director. Russ Peterson was there for that first board meeting. We also had Jacques Cousteau's son, Jean Michel, who was also a director, at the meeting by telephone from Paris. Ted felt the so-called larger agenda issues were being underreported in the media, and he set up Better World to provide a vehicle to fund television documentaries that would never get made any other way. He wanted it to be strictly nonprofit, with a majority of non-U.S. directors. My job was to bring in foundation money, matching funds, grants, that sort of thing. Turner Broadcasting would provide air time for these documentaries and help fund the organization."

According to Belford, Turner played an active, hands-on role right from the beginning and was instrumental in bringing into Better World such dignitaries as Jimmy Carter, Lester Brown, the Aga Khan, Norway's Grottarlem Brundtlandt, China's Zhou Boping, Nigeria's Olusegun Obasanjo, Maurice Strong, Roderick Corazo from Costa Rica, and Cousteau. "We knew about the CBS situation," Belford says, "but Turner was always very involved in this organization, and he kept his other interests completely separate. Essentially the whole Better World thing was his idea."

"It was a mystery," says Reed Irvine of Accuracy in Media, one of the conservative advocacy groups that had been coming down hard on CBS News and Dan Rather because of Rather's supposed leftist/liberal bias. "Turner was always very patriotic—even outrageously so. But he was changing, rather suddenly, some people thought. Some of us wondered why."

"No mystery at all," volunteers Bob Wussler, conspicuous in his absence from the battle to take over the network he once ran. "Ted's gotten stronger, and he has become a lot more credible. It's not that he always reinvents himself. I think he's just a lot more comfortable these days letting the world see him the way he sees himself. I've been with him for more than five years," Wussler said, "and I've seen him go through a couple of major changes."

Twelve months earlier Turner had been sitting in his Atlanta office watching the Los Angeles Olympics. "What's wrong?" Wussler asked him when Turner walked into his adjoining office.

"Wussler, that's what's wrong," he said, pointing to a TV monitor tuned to the same Olympics broadcast. "We never should have boycotted the Olympics in 1980. And the Soviets should never have boycotted this one. Where's the next one?"

"It's in Seoul," Wussler replied, not sure what he was driving at.

"You know the guys in Moscow," Turner said. "They'll never go to South Korea. I want you to go over there," he told the former president of CBS Television. "Tell them we're going to buy all the rights to the next Olympics and make sure nobody boycotts them."

One week later Wussler was in Moscow proposing that the Russians buy all the rights to the 1988 Olympics with Turner Broadcasting. "I thought I'd get blown out of the water," Wussler recalls. "Never in my wildest dreams did I think anything would ever come of it." The Russians seemed reluctant to tamper with the Olympic Games and wanted to know why Turner had in the end not been able to broadcast their counter-Olympic Friendship Games in 1984. "Timing," Wussler lied, not wanting to admit that politics had been the real stumbling block.

And after nearly three weeks of amiable but endlessly frustrating negotiations in Moscow, timing again appeared to be a factor. Looking for a showcase for Mikhail Gorbachev's new *glasnost* policies, the Soviets proposed a new in-between Olympics, which they would produce with Turner in 1986. These "Goodwill Games," they said, would match Soviet and U.S. athletes against each other for the first time since the 1976 Montreal Olympics. Wussler wasn't sure. The Soviets had just shot down a South Korean airliner off Kamchatka. The timing, he mused, this time would be more difficult than ever.

Turner's reaction, however, was immediate and overwhelmingly affirmative. "Let's do it!" he told Wussler when he heard the proposal, and to all intents and purposes the Goodwill Games were a done deal. The Russians would provide the facilities and the athletes. Assuming Wussler could overcome the objections of the International Olympic Committee and Ronald Reagan, whom Turner had called "the worst president in American history," all Turner had to supply was a little hard cash, his TBS cameras, and some English-language commentators. Now, with less than ten months before the first-ever Goodwill Games were to begin, Wussler had absented himself from the CBS takeover team and was working around the clock to bring off what would turn out to be the most expensive private Olympic games in history.

On July 29, 1985, Cable News Network broadcast a brief item noting that "the chairman of Turner Broadcasting was in Los Angeles for talks with MGM/UA Entertainment Company executives." A Turner source immediately issued a denial to the *Atlanta Constitution*, saying that Turner had been in Los Angeles talking to a group of different film companies about his proposed takeover of CBS. "We could see a shift in the wind," says George

Vandeman, "long before the CBS situation was played out. Ted had been talking to Kirk Kerkorian since 1980, and in early July Kirk called him and said he was ready to sell. Ted, Bevins, and I had been out in California talking to MGM for nearly three weeks —we had already totally forgotten CBS and were letting the Hutton team play out that hand. But we were in very serious negotiations with Kerkorian well before the end of July. Turner knew he couldn't do both deals, and he felt MGM made much more sense."

According to Dan Good, "Hutton was just days away from announcing a new, cash-heavy package" to offer CBS shareholders when Bill Bevins called and said, "We're pretty far along on MGM now and Ted wants everything else on hold until we know how this one works out." Good and his team were crestfallen. So was Hutton chairman, Bob Foman, who saw his dream of vaulting his firm back into the front ranks of Wall Street's powerhouse investment banks evaporate overnight.

Meanwhile, Turner had been hooked nicely by Kirk Kerkorian, who had brought him rushing out to Hollywood with the news that Egypt's wealthy Fayad family was about to make an offer for MGM/UA. CBS could wait, Turner decided. "Without MGM, there was a question mark about the long-term viability of the Superstation. I mean, every time we signed a new movie contract, it cost us more," adding that some studios, including MGM, now refused to license films to WTBS at any price. The Superstation accounted for over 80 percent of TBS's profits, and Turner felt he had to act quickly to protect his core business.

"I'm in a business where the big are getting bigger," he rationalized, "and the small are disappearing. I want to be one of the survivors. This makes us more of a major player. It gets people's attention. I mean, we are in show biz, aren't we?"

A mystifying master deal maker whose quiet stare and wide toothy grin belied his scorpion's sting, Kerkorian was much more comfortable out in the desert than cooped up with Hollywood's power brokers in the Beverly Hills Hotel's Polo Lounge. He had not been able to make much of a success of MGM/UA as a film company, but that was hardly the point. With a personal fortune now approaching $1 billion, Kirk Kerkorian was about to pull off another of his revolving-door deals and would practically double his net worth in the bargain.

Kerkorian had also loaded MGM up with over $700 million in

long-term debt and other liabilities, the result of two recent restructurings that allowed him to take out virtually all of his original investment while still retaining control of both MGM and United Artists. When Turner showed up on the MGM back lot in Culver City, he had a chip on his shoulder the size of a boulder and quickly succumbed to Kerkorian's promise that he would hold off the auction he was planning if they could reach a quick agreement. Turner, whose own penchant for making instant deals was well known, took the bait. If he wasn't going to be William S. Paley, Turner may have figured, at least he could be Louis B. Mayer.

Unintentionally, Tom Wyman played to Turner's weakness by adopting a time-consuming strategy of drawing him out in the courts and at the regulatory agencies. Turner's threshold of boredom was lower than a storm cellar, and he had been able to sustain his interest in CBS only because he had so many other balls in the air at the same time. At exactly the same moment he announced his initial exchange offer for the network, Turner was also concluding negotiations for the acquisition of Omni International, a fourteen-story "megastructure" with hotel, retail, office, and other facilities in downtown Atlanta that would soon become the new home of Turner Broadcasting and CNN. The $39-million transaction with Tom Cousins, an Atlanta real estate developer who had earlier sold Turner the Atlanta Hawks basketball franchise, would quickly appreciate to nearly double its cost under Turner's effective stewardship.

"The game I'm in is building assets," Turner said, "and I've never minded overpaying if I know the values are there." Walking into the MGM offices in Culver City that July afternoon in 1985, Ted Turner was about to put that dictum to its sternest test.

Kerkorian was more than a little certain of his buyer and played Turner perfectly. There would be no investment bankers or other advisers—just Kerkorian and MGM president Frank Rothman on one side and Turner, Bill Bevins, and George Vandeman on the other. Pleased to go head to head with the famed deal maker, Turner was two feet off the ground and as manic as ever. He had just begun seeing Dr. Pittman in Atlanta but there was no evidence yet that the lithium had kicked in. Turner felt the adrenaline pumping, the blood rushing into his brain. He was out there to buy a movie studio, and damned if he would come away empty-handed.

"We're getting more than a third of the greatest films ever made," he gushed to Bevins and Vandeman. "We're getting Spencer Tracy and Jimmy Cagney working for us from the grave."

Despite broad hints from Kerkorian, nobody from the Turner camp even bothered to check whether there might actually have been any other interested bidders for MGM. A quick call to Al Fayad in London would have called Kerkorian's bluff, but Turner couldn't have been less interested. And he didn't bat an eye when Kerkorian announced coolly that his price of $29 per share, or $1.6 billion, was "firm and not negotiable." Then Kerkorian dropped the other shoe. For that price he was keeping not only United Artists, but the 1,457 films in the old Warner library and the rights to RKO's old films as well.

Turner had heard that Charles W. Knapp, the flamboyant former chairman of Financial Corporation of America, had recently offered Kerkorian $22 a share for MGM/UA and been turned down cold. Now Kerkorian was asking nearly one-third more for only half the company. "If you'll throw in those other old movies, I'll pay the price," Turner said, not missing a beat.

When Bill Bevins heard Turner's response, the chain-smoking accountant almost choked on his ever-present Salem cigarette. He had valued MGM at a price somewhere between $24 and $26 per share. Most financial analysts, using traditional discounted cash flow estimates of MGM's principal asset, its library, placed the value substantially lower, in the vicinity of $22 per share. "Looking back," Bevins explains, "we knew $29 was high. Maybe the business at auction would have brought $25 or $26. Suppose we had bid slightly less. We could have lost the one thing we had always wanted for a lousy $25 million." Bevins's level-headed financial engineering had kept TBS solvent despite Turner's inclination to keep spending. Now Bevins was beginning to catch Turner's buyer's fever. "The probability," he told *Fortune* magazine, "that we would have been able to save a great deal at auction was not great." If in fact, Bevins forgot to mention, any other bidders even showed up.

Negotiations began on Thursday, July 25. "We went right around the clock," George Vandeman remembers. "Ted saw things in the deal that nobody else could. He was already talking about colorizing. But it was up to Bill Bevins and me to work out the actual details. We'd meet with Ted at breakfast, then regroup for lunch and maybe at the end of the day. Bevins and I lived together for nearly ten days, then Ted came in on the last weekend to lock up the deal."

After a full forty-eight hours of around-the-clock negotiations, a preliminary agreement was reached at six A.M. on Monday morning, August 5. Two or three new sticking points kept everybody at the table until late that afternoon. Finally MGM/UA corporate vice-president Art Rockwell called in the press to announce, "It appears that a definitive agreement has been reached. For $29 a share, approximately $1.6 billion cash, MGM/UA will merge with Turner Broadcasting System, becoming a wholly owned subsidiary of TBS."

It was to be the first acquisition of a major movie studio by a broadcaster since General Tire & Rubber acquired RKO Pictures over thirty years earlier. Turner, however, didn't even stick around for the congratulations but headed straight back to New York that same day for a press conference kicking off the first Goodwill Games, now set for the following summer in Moscow.

The deal had been put together so fast that Turner's team had not even had a chance to scrutinize MGM's books. "Normally you have from the time you sign the deal to the time you close," recalls Vandeman, "to perform appropriate due diligence, to verify the accuracy of financial statements related to the condition of the business." Kerkorian was hardly accommodating. "I don't want to sit here forever wondering whether I have a deal," he told Turner. "You've got one week to tell me whether you're in or out."

A task force of forty lawyers and accountants immediately descended on MGM and began dissecting the company's financial materials. Another team of legal experts from Ziffren, Brittenham, and Branca, a top Los Angeles law firm, was brought in to help analyze and verify the thousands of individual licensing agreements that constituted the MGM library. The Turner teams found the data badly organized but without any significant surprises that might have killed the deal. Ziffren, Brittenham concluded the library would produce a minimum of $100 million in revenues for 1985. There were at least a half dozen new films already in the can and awaiting release, but with Kerkorian's deadline almost upon them, no one had a chance to look at the product MGM had in its pipeline. Nor did they have any way of assessing the production operations on the back lot itself. "In twenty-twenty hindsight," Bevins would say later, "the fact that the studio was in free fall was not all that clear at the time."

"Mr. Kerkorian is no dummy," Turner added. "He knew what he wanted to sell, and what he sold was the troubled part of the company. And I bought it. Normally things aren't for sale if they are in great shape. Right?" With the due diligence now out of the way, however, Kerkorian was insisting on a "bulletproof" agreement that would lock Turner into the deal. He was also insisting on all cash, which posed a bit of a problem—until Kerkorian offered to take Turner over to Beverly Hills and introduce him to his friend Mike Milken.

With penetrating insight, fifteen-hour workdays, and almost unbelievable powers of concentration, Michael Milken had turned Drexel-Firestone, a medium-size Philadelphia stockbroker, into Drexel Burnham Lambert, the new terror of Wall Street. Along the way Milken had begun to do business with some very doubtful characters, among them Victor Posner, Meshulam Riklis, and Ivan Boesky. But working from his trading desk in Drexel's Beverly Hills office, Milken had also raised billions of dollars for underfinanced companies like McCaw Cellular, Telecommunications, Inc., Rupert Murdoch's 20th Century–Fox, and, not incidentally, Kirk Kerkorian's MGM/UA. Milken had put together over $400 million in junk bond financing for Kerkorian in early 1984, allowing him to stretch out a major portion of the company's debt for another ten years. Now, just a little more than a year later, Kerkorian had retained Drexel once again, this time to assist in the sale of MGM. Michael D. Brown, one of Milken's colleagues from Drexel's corporate finance group, had been assigned to work with Kerkorian on the project but was involved only peripherally in the Turner negotiations, which Kerkorian handled himself.

Bill Bevins had come out earlier in the spring to solicit Milken's help in financing Turner's bid for CBS, only to find out that Tom Wyman had beaten him to the punch by retaining Drexel's corporate finance group in New York. Milken himself had just completed financing for Rupert Murdoch's $1.9 billion buyout of Metromedia, the largest independent broadcast deal in history and later the cornerstone of Murdoch's Fox Broadcasting Network. Milken liked to consider himself more of a social scientist than a financier, and for years had been predicting the decline of the Big Three television networks.

"I began telling clients in 1981," he told *Forbes*, that NBC, CBS, and ABC would be left at the post. The parallel is the earlier explosion of special-interest magazines which put big broad mass magazines like *Look* and the old *Life* and the *Saturday Evening Post* out of business. The same thing was inevitable in TV. Cable was junk from an investment ratings point of view. But cable was the future. Proving he believed what he said, Milken had raised several hundred million dollars to keep John Malone's incipient cable empire growing when the banks refused to lend him any more.

By the time Kerkorian walked Ted Turner into Drexel's West Coast offices on Wilshire Boulevard, Ivan Boesky had already become an integral cog of Milken's vaunted junk bond machine. That spring, at Drexel's annual client conference, the first of the notorious "predator's balls," Boesky boasted about the tens of millions in profits he was making on CBS stock and suggested to several of Drexel's better-heeled clients that if they joined him, they could push up the price even farther. We won't file the requisite SEC disclosures, Boesky proposed, and no one will know your position. According to Jesse Kornbluth's *Highly Confident*, an unusually informed Milken biography, one of these investors immediately reported Boesky's blatantly criminal proposition to Milken, who suggested, oddly, that the informer must have misunderstood his sometime friend.

In February 1985 Leon Black, the thirty-year-old co-head of Drexel's merger and acquisitions group, had come up with a concept that made tangible Milken's awesome power to raise capital and secured the almost messianic influence he would exert over his universe of high-yield bond buyers. Milken was known to be fanatic about keeping his promise to raise money for any client. Black turned these promises into de facto currency—Drexel's infamous "highly confident" letters. Even though Mike Milken never, ever put his name on one, a Drexel highly confident letter was almost as good as money in the bank.

Turner was exactly the kind of client Milken most liked—bold, brash, not afraid to go up against the establishment. The two of them hit it off right away. After having been forced to watch Turner's foray against CBS from the sidelines, Milken was pleased to be working with him and assured Turner that as inflated as the MGM deal had become, Drexel could finance it. As MGM's banker, he already knew the company's balance sheet inside out and would not have to spend any time learning the business. Michael Brown would continue representing Kerkorian's interest. Milken would take on Turner as his own client and, despite the obvious and extraordinary conflict, gave his word that Drexel would respect the confidentiality of any information Turner Broadcasting shared with the firm.

Not even a highly confident letter, however, was enough to quiet the skepticism that had been building ever since Turner's MGM deal had been announced. On August 16 *The Wall Street Journal* commented dourly, "Despite the Drexel letter, it remains unclear whether Milken can raise the funds and, if he does, whether Turner can ever support the huge amount of debt which the deal will heap upon Turner Broadcasting." As MGM's summer film releases bombed out, one after another, and the studio's production expenses were revealed to be rocketing out of control, Milken's usually reliable bond buyers began balking at the deal. "Highly confident" became a relative term, and even Mike Milken soon realized that to be completed, the deal would in all likelihood have to be restructured.

"In 1970, Lorimar had a library of old TV films which it was carrying on its books for zero," Milken recalled later. "We used this zero book-value asset for financing, based on the earning potential of the Lorimar library in syndication. No one had ever done that before, and with Turner we used the MGM library as collateral, even though Kerkorian had written the value of those old movies down to zero. Actually they were appreciating assets," Milken pointed out, "not depreciating assets, since each time they were put out for rental, the rental rates went up. And for Turner, they were also a guaranteed source of future programming." Still, it took a call from Milken to Ivan Boesky to get the deal moving. According to court records, Milken directed Boesky to make aggressive buys of MGM stock, which would not only support the MGM share price, but help Milken unload the Turner bonds, since the market would gain confidence in the MGM deal once it became apparent an important arbitrageur like Boesky was betting Turner would be able to close. Government prosecutors were never able to prove Milken offered Boesky any inside information regarding the Turner/MGM transaction, despite Boesky's testimony that Milken had promised he would make up any losses incurred on the MGM trades, in exchange for half of the profits. Confident in the knowledge that the MGM deal would go through, but also would be reconfigured at least once before closing, Boesky plunged heavily and wound up splitting a reported $3 million gain on his MGM shares with Michael Milken.

Those lucrative trading profits, however, were incidental to the extraordinary $68.4 million placement fee Drexel and Milken stood to earn once Turner's $1.4 billion junk bond financing was completed. To collect that fee, Milken had to find some way to offset MGM's rapidly deteriorating financial condition. No small task since MGM's next four pictures—*Year of the Dragon, Code Name Emerald, Marie,* and *Fever Pitch*—had cost well over $100 million. They were to earn, cumulatively, less than $5 million in rentals. "Dogs, hell," said Bevins. "You couldn't feed these films to dogs. Things really got bad when the studio went into free fall."

An even more serious problem, however, threatened to jeopardize the entire transaction. Two days before Turner signed his August 6 agreement with Kerkorian in Los Angeles, MGM/UA had sold the MGM library's pay television rights to Rainbow Service Company, a small cable program distributor on Long Island. The Turner people had known about the deal but were never shown the contract, which gave Rainbow permission to prohibit MGM films from being shown on certain cable networks, among them WTBS. "Rainbow was able to sucker MGM into granting them exclusive basic cable rights," recalls George Vandeman, "and that would have killed the deal for us."

Kerkorian sued Rainbow, trying to break the contract. Rainbow countersued. Milken could see the whole transaction unraveling and interceded, urging Kerkorian and Turner to find some way to resolve the problem. Six weeks later Rainbow agreed to tear up the contract for $50 million, with Kerkorian paying the lion's share of the out-of-court settlement. If Turner had any second thoughts about buying MGM, the Rainbow contract would clearly have given him reason to walk away from Kerkorian's "bulletproof" agreement. In fact, the setback hardly dampened Turner's enthusiasm for the deal, and he was already in deep discussion with Richard Frank, president of Walt Disney Studios, about coming in to head the MGM operation.

Milken, however, was running into unusual resistance in the marketplace. Prospective bond buyers were sitting on their wallets, seriously skeptical that the new combination of Turner Broadcasting and MGM, with less than $200 million in projected free cash flow, could possibly service the debt on $1.5 billion in pricey junk bonds. The continued hemorrhaging at MGM didn't help. "MGM was a deteriorating asset," noted Bevins, who was trying to keep a cool head among all the overheated egos that were on the line. "We simply weren't getting what we thought we paid for." Many of Milken's prospective bond buyers agreed, and some even began to worry that Congress might shove through new legislation regulating retransmission of television signals, which could put Turner's Superstation out of business.

In early October Kerkorian and Turner finally agreed to a re-structuring that kept the purchase price for MGM at $1.6 billion but reduced the cash component in the deal from $26 to $20 a share. The difference was to be paid in TBS preferred stock. Kerkorian and the other MGM shareholders would receive 53 million shares of TBS preferred. Turner's agreement to assume $578 million in MGM debt pushed up the total cost of the deal to $2.1 billion—less some $480 million he would receive from the sale of United Artists back to Kerkorian.

Even these reduced cash terms, however, were not much of an inducement to Milken's usually malleable bond buyers. Losses continued to mount at the studio, and partly as the result of immediate write-downs of the summer flops, MGM reported a $26 million net loss for the quarter ending November 30. "When you suffer the kinds of losses we suffered at the studio," Bill Bevins commented dryly, "the financing becomes a nightmare." Turner had originally hoped to keep control of MGM's production facilities as a means to create new product for the Superstation, but now it was rapidly becoming obvious that not even another highly confident letter from Mike Milken was going to close this deal. Reluctantly Turner decided he would have to sell the studio he had not yet actually acquired.

He knew that Terrence A. Elkes, president of Viacom International, Inc., a diversified cable programmer that owned Showtime and MTV, was seeking acquisitions, and soon Turner was back in New York, involved once again in serious negotiations. He had learned a thing or two about high finance from Messrs. Milken & Co., and had picked up a few pointers on deal making from his friend Kirk Kerkorian. But Elkes was a shrewd and calculating survivor of the network wars. "We thought Kerkorian was a tough negotiator," recounts George Vandeman, who had made the trip back east along with Turner and Bevins. "But we hadn't seen anything until we saw Terry Elkes."

Even so, Turner was eventually able to persuade Elkes to pay $225 million for a half interest in the MGM studio and surrounding Culver City real estate, plus a half interest in MGM's videocassette operation. By early January they seemed to have reached an agreement that also included a commitment by each partner to coinvest in a series of movies over the next five years. But after an intensive examination of MGM's assets, particularly the films that were still in the production pipeline—the same movies MGM/UA executives had touted to Turner as box office sizzlers—Elkes was certain he had Turner on the ropes and decided to cut back his investment in the venture to $175 million. "They kept trying to squeeze more blood out of the turnip," recalled Drexel's Michael Brown, who suggests the Viacom deal may actually have fallen through, ironically, because Turner became nervous about the five-year commitment to make new films.

Whatever the reason, Milken now saw the whole MGM/UA transaction beginning to unravel. He called in every favor he could to sell off the last of the $1.2 billion in Turner bonds. To make the paper as palatable as possible and reassure nervous investors, he also extracted Turner's agreement to include an incendiary new condition in the bond covenants, compelling Turner to pay off $600 million of 14 percent notes, half of the total issue, within just six months!

Turner might have been better off if Milken had failed to sell the bonds, but on March 25, 1986, Turner Broadcasting System finally became the proud owner of Metro-Goldwyn-Mayer. Ted Turner had come out to California six months earlier thinking he was buying the most famous film library in the world. He wound up buying a nearly bankrupt movie studio, warmed briefly to the idea of becoming a movie mogul, then realized he was about to sink lower than the Savannah tidal flats under a mountain of almost unimaginable debt. Recalling the tiny little porcelain figure of Jiminy Cricket that sits on his desk back in Atlanta, Turner decided the only thing to do was "accentuate the positive."

By acquiescing to Kerkorian's byzantine deal structure, he had been forced to pay for MGM assets he didn't need, including MGM's production and distribution operations, its film processing lab, and its studio lot in Culver City. His only real negotiating triumph had been in getting Kerkorian to throw in 1,450 more films that United Artists owned, bringing to 3,650 the total number of titles he had acquired. Turner got the library he wanted, and according to his seat-of-the-pants projections, at least a thousand of these titles would have enduring commercial value, since he planned to air them forever on WTBS. The majority of the films, however, were already licensed to other broadcasters and wouldn't even be available to Turner for several years. "It's a good thing," one of the Drexel wags commented, "that Turner's mind is always five or ten years ahead of everybody else. He can now begin planning how he's going to use these movies in 1995."

As he worked through the complexities of the drastically re-structured transaction, Turner might well have begun to wonder whose side Drexel had been on. Milken had written a second oner-ous condition into the junk bond covenants which prevented Turner's paying cash dividends on the 53 preferred stock issued to Kerkorian as compensation for the reduced cash component in the purchase price. Beginning in June 1987, those preferred shares would earn annual dividends of $1.45 each. Turner could not buy back one of Kerkorian's $220 million of preferred shares without the bondholders' approval. Nor could he pay Kerkorian preferred dividends in cash until he had repaid at least two-thirds of the junk debt, including the $600 million Turner had agreed to repay by September 1986. This new arm twister meant Kerkorian would be paid dividends in new shares of Turner Broadcasting common stock. And, Milken had insisted, if the market price of TBS common fell below $15 a share, those common stock divi-dends would have to be enriched with additional shares of pre-ferred, creating the potential for virtually limitless dilution. Thanks to Michael Milken, Kerkorian stood a fair chance of even-tually gaining control of TBS, and having the opportunity to sell MGM all over again.

"I'm not an accountant," Turner explained, when asked if he had bothered to read the fine print. But he understood the di-lemma he had created for himself. And he vowed to liquidate the preferred long before Kerkorian could regain control of MGM. Turner spent $85 million to jump-start the studio's production program and then hit the road again to raise new capital to pay off the $600 million of notes, which would come due in six months.

Drexel went into the market and began soliciting bids for all of MGM's assets except the film library. The asking price—surprise, $600 million! When bids started coming in during the first week of June, Turner was finally, reluctantly, convinced that selling assets was really the only way he was ever going to find the capi-tal he needed. Mike Milken's old client, Lorimar Telepictures, now a rapidly expanding television producer best known for "Dal-las," already occupied over a third of the MGM lot. Needing more room, Lorimar agreed to pay Turner $190 million for the MGM real estate and film lab.

Who stepped up to pay $300 million for MGM's legendary roaring lion logo; its movie, television, and videocassette production operations; and its distribution network? With Turner's permission, Drexel's Michael Brown had given Kirk Kerkorian an overview of the bidding situation. When he saw the other bids coming in on the low side, Kerkorian himself reacquired the rest of MGM, which, thanks to Turner's capital infusion, now included a newly debt free United Artists. Kerkorian pocketed a cool $100 million profit on this elegant maneuver and Michael Brown won himself a short-term seat on the Turner Broadcasting board of directors. Kerkorian, of course, would find Giancarlo Paretti, a parvenu Italian of seriously questionable credentials, who somehow cobbled together $1.3 billion in 1990 and bought control of Kerkorian's MGM assets—but not before Kerkorian took one more pass at Turner, attempting to hook him again in 1989 by suggesting he might be interested in an exchange of the studio for Turner Broadcasting stock. For "tax reasons," Kerkorian explained. The deal never got beyond the talking stage, however, and both Kerkorian and Paretti, as well as Credit Lyonnaise, the French bank that financed the Paretti acquisition and ultimately took control of MGM, have been locked in international litigation that threatens to last through the turn of the century.

On June 6, 1986, however, Ted Turner announced the completion of the MGM asset sales and was able to breathe a long sigh of relief. He wound up having paid a net purchase price of $1.1 billion for MGM's library of 2,110 classic films, plus rights to an additional 1,450 Warner and RKO titles. To complete the transaction, though, he had been forced to sell off every other part of MGM except the dozens of golden Oscar statuettes, which now line the executive corridors of Turner Broadcasting.

Included among the valuable titles Turner now owned were his personal favorite, *Citizen Kane*, which he has watched over a hundred times, and *Gone With the Wind*, the motion picture with which Turner himself has always most closely identified. The library also included *Casablanca*, *The Wizard of Oz*, *Grand Hotel*, *Singing in the Rain*—many of the greatest films ever made, as well as evergreens like *It's a Wonderful Life* and *Miracle on 34th Street*. Most of the films were black and white; some seven hundred were relics of the silent era. At an average cost of slightly over $300,000 per title, Turner agreed that you'd have to like old movies an awful lot to consider his purchase anything close to a bargain. With a network sitcom costing anywhere from $300,000–$450,000 per half-hour episode, however, analysts were now revising their assessment of the price he had paid. Even some of Turner's most vociferous critics, after years of watching the major television networks battle each other to see who could produce the "least offensive programming," were beginning to understand that a lot of people would rather watch a great old movie anytime than the forgettable fare the networks continued to serve up.

"How can you go broke," Turner asked at the time, "buying the Rembrandts of the programming business, when you are a programmer? The studio and the library would have sold for at least $1 billion or $1.2 billion to somebody, so I might have paid $300 million more than anybody else." In the next breath Turner insisted it was worth it. "I paid full value," he said, "and value to me was greater than to anybody else because I had a distribution system that wants old movies, and I like old movies. I've never done anything like this before. It's like sailboat racing in a hurricane. It's like being in an airplane in a storm. You buckle your seat belt and hope for the best."

Shortly after he had completed his takeover of MGM, Hollywood thought it would take a new look at this brash interloper from the hinterlands and see what he was made of. "They asked Ted to be the featured speaker," says George Vandeman, "at the kind of affair that attracted all the studio heads, all the television network programming chiefs, everybody who was anybody in the business. They all wanted to see this fellow who had just bought MGM. I was up in the hotel room with Ted before that speech, and I can tell you he had no clue as to what he was going to say to these people, not a clue. He hadn't given it a thought."

Twenty minutes later Turner was leading Vandeman downstairs, still with no idea of what he was going to say. "I was a little anxious," Vandeman recalls, "and I told him, 'This isn't going to be easy. You're a maverick in this town, Ted. You may not be welcomed with open arms.'" Turner himself could feel the electricity as he walked into the crowded ballroom and stepped up to the speaker's stand. Hollywood was holding its breath, waiting to hear what Ted Turner had to say for himself.

"In three minutes," Vandeman recounts, "Turner had the entire audience eating out of his hand. He had the entire *industry* eating out of his hand. I don't think even one person in the room knew what he said. He just absolutely won everybody over with his charm. The guy is incredible, really incredible!"

Alan Ladd, Jr., was one of those Hollywood movers and shakers who quickly came under Turner's spell. Ladd had been vice-chairman at MGM/UA under Kerkorian and Frank Rothman. He agreed to stay on after the deal closed and found Turner the most unusual boss he'd ever worked for. "He was very charismatic," says Ladd. "And on top of everything else, he turned out to be a very decent person. Everybody thought he was out of his mind making the kind of deal he did with Kerkorian. Including me. He had no eye for the movie business, no experience whatsoever. Well, everyone else was wrong. And he was right."

Most analysts at the time, however, thought Turner had over-paid for MGM by at least $300–$500 million. One Hollywood veteran was even quoted in *Fortune* magazine as saying, "Turner got the worst screwing in the history of American business." Based on the assumption that the MGM library should have been valued at about ten times its 1985 cash flow of $80 million, a full price might have been in the neighborhood of $800 million. "No one has ever lost money owning a film library," media analyst Paul Kagan remarked at the time. But no one had ever paid so much for one, either. Turner always liked operating right out on the edge where the stakes were the highest, the drama the most intense, and the competition the toughest. He may have met his match in Kirk Kerkorian, but he still managed to avoid going over the brink.

Just two months before Turner had signed his "bulletproof" agreement with Kerkorian, Rupert Murdoch's News Corporation agreed to pay John Kluge and Metromedia $1.9 billion for seven (mostly underperforming) independent television stations with an aggregate cash flow of less than $95 million. Murdoch had been praised for his vision in understanding the "opportunity cost" of what later became the Fox Broadcasting Network. Yet Turner was generally assumed to have been taken to the cleaners over the MGM deal. It may have been Turner's bad fortune to have fallen into the hands of Milken and Drexel Burnham, partic-ularly in view of Milken's admitted conflict of interest, but where else was he to turn? Drexel's dominance in the junk bond market in 1985 was nearly exclusionary, and Turner realized he had no choice but to place himself in Milken's hands. Turner became part of Michael Milken's very crowded calendar that year, which in addition to Murdoch's Metromedia deal, included a host of other egregiously overpriced transactions—William Farley's Fruit of the Loom, Nelson Peltz's National Can, and Ronald Perlman's Revlon—all hugely problematic transactions at the time and all generating huge fees (as well as immensely lucrative direct or indirect incentives) to Milken and his Drexel colleagues. That Milken got the MGM deal done was certainly to his credit. That he persuaded Turner it could get done only on such onerous terms may have been open to question.

Part of Turner, obviously, needed to make grand acquisitions like MGM, not just for the strategic reasons he stated, but so he could keep toting up his personal worth on napkins for everyone to see while asking the waiter for one more round—not for the sake of the deals or the money involved, but as mile markers, proof positive that he was really getting somewhere in his tumultuous life. If that part had been all there was to him, however, he'd have been just another multimillionaire on his way to the top of the *Forbes* "Four Hundred." It was the other part of him— the part that needed to show his strength, to be the guy who comes out on top in even the most impossible situation—that produced the crackling cage of friction the world was now coming to know as Ted Turner.

*When Brer Rabbit takes a notion to go anywhere
right quick, he jes' picks up the miles wid his feet
and drops 'em off again, like a dog sheds fleas.*

JOEL CHANDLER HARRIS
Tales of Uncle Remus

Chapter Thirteen

From the start of Ted Turner's little sortie against CBS, his life
had consisted of fourteen- and fifteen-hour workdays, punctuated
by almost perpetual travel, sometimes as many as two or three
coast-to-coast trips a week. That kind of schedule had once been
a breeze for him. But he was wearying of investment bankers,
lawyers, and all the money managers he had wooed so incessantly
over the past fourteen months, and now welcomed even one- or
two-day respites back in Atlanta. The effort of completing the
difficult MGM transaction had taken an obvious toll on the usually inexhaustible Turner. He had lost at least ten pounds. He had
forgone the at-home trims Jane had been giving him for years,
and his hair, now growing stylishly down over his ears, was turning snowy white. At forty-seven Turner was beginning to have
difficulty passing himself off as a wunderkind. He had, moreover,
contracted an incommodious low-grade virus that he couldn't
seem to shake and had taken to spending more and more time on
his convertible couch up on the third floor of Techwood Drive.

Despite nearly a year's worth of Dr. Pittman's counseling,
Turner still seemed as irritable as ever and perhaps even a tad
more moody, if that were possible. The heavy lithium treatments
that probably saw him through the tough days of the MGM deal
hardly slowed him down. He would still ramble on in endless
stream-of-consciousness monologues, usually pacing so insis-

tently around his trophy-crammed office that his associates would often keep count of the circles he made, wondering what new vision might be festering just underneath the surface, ready to bubble up into their next great adventure. "I'm not concerned any longer about myself," Turner kept insisting. And money ceased to have any interest for him at all. "I'm concentrating on the biggest problems the world has. I'm trying to get bigger so I'll have more influence. It's almost like a religious fever." He envisioned Turner Broadcasting educating the world about the dangers of nuclear weapons, environmental abuse, and over-population. TBS had produced a recent special on Martin Luther King, which Turner called "heavy stuff, man. You won't see that on CBS."

Turner once said, "Everything I do is a war. It's a war between the forces of good and evil, hatred and stupidity, greed and mate-rialism versus the forces of light."

And it was true that, on this particular morning in late 1986, padding around his Techwood office in an old bathrobe as the sun came up over Atlanta, Turner hardly looked like the monied rake-hell who had sent CBS into a crippling $1 billion buy-back of its own stock and then stood Hollywood on its ear by confounding conventional wisdom and making a go of his on-the-cuff acquisi-tion of MGM. In a room littered with sophisticated electronic gear, Turner paused to glance around him—at the stuffed ducks he'd shot with Fidel Castro, the mounted fish, the coiled rattle-snake, the Civil War swords, the Nazi regalia, the silver sailing trophies, the oil paintings of *Courageous, American Eagle,* and *Te-nacious* hanging from the walls. "I want to be successful in busi-ness so I can communicate with people," he said. "I'm putting on a full-court press now—to stop the arms race, control the popu-lation, protect the environment."

Like Turner, CNN was beginning to grow up. The network cele-brated its fifth birthday on June 1, 1985, with an informal bash at Harrison's, the house watering hole on Peachtree Road. Never known for his loquacity or his loose grip on the purse strings, CNN's nearly invisible president, Burt Reinhardt, gave the short-est anniversary speech on record: "Let's party!" And party the several hundred Atlanta-based CNNers did, for they were no longer the Chicken Noodle Network, as the Big Three network news departments had dubbed them, but full-fledged members of the media establishment, standing on the very frontier of the new global news business.

CNN's live coverage of the hijacking of TWA Flight #847 was prelude to a succession of even more impressive coups—Mexico City's devastating earthquake, which set viewing records and helped CNN secure the highest daily cable audience rating in history; and CNN's fifty-three hours of continuous coverage of the Geneva summit between President Reagan and Soviet leader Mikhail Gorbachev, which included close to one hundred interviews with experts in U.S./Soviet relations and brought home a slew of prizes, including CNN's first Award for Cable Excellence (ACE).

CNN had also launched the first twenty-four-hour news service in Europe and broadened its coverage to include Canada, Japan, and Australia, as well as parts of Central and South America. Larry King, a celebrated but congenitally soft radio interviewer, replaced Sandi Freeman with a one-hour prime-time call-in show that quickly became CNN's highest-rated program. Recognizing the young network's rapidly accumulating achievements, the *Los Angeles Times* said, "There is no way to be fully and immediately informed without CNN. Ted Turner's scruffy little all-news network has grown up to become indispensable." Apparently the U.S. State Department was in full agreement. Alexander Haig had installed a large television monitor in the State Department crisis room, tuned permanently to Cable News Network.

Throughout 1985 and 1986, CNN did more than report the news—it sometimes made headlines. The escape of the network's Beirut bureau chief, Jerry Levin, after eleven months of captivity led news broadcasts worldwide, even though the poignant story of Ed Turner's ceaseless efforts to free his colleague remained in large part untold. Turner, now CNN's executive vice-president yet still unable to go anywhere without having to explain that he was unrelated to his boss, took personal responsibility for Levin and spent eleven harrowing weeks on his own in Lebanon tracking down every lead personally until his bureau chief was finally free.

At 11:38 on the morning of January 28, 1986, Nancy Reagan was upstairs in the Executive Mansion getting ready to leave for lunch with a group of friends from Beverly Hills when she suddenly gasped and screamed: "Oh, my God! No!" She had been riveted to a television screen watching CNN, as the *Challenger* spacecraft rose majestically from the gantry, slowly began its climb, then rolled over and burst into a horrifying fireball. Thirteen hours later, Mary Ann Loughlin and Tom Minter, the CNN anchors who had been broadcasting the fatal lift-off, finally handed over the microphone to their replacements after the longest on-camera stint in television history. Loughlin remembers the *Challenger* coverage as the most unforgettable experience in her life and a defining moment for CNN. "Suddenly every news editor in the world was tuning in to our broadcast. We became a global news service at that moment. I still get stopped when I walk through airports in Europe by people who remember that broadcast."

Atlanta television columnist Dick Williams found himself marveling "at the incredible creation of Ted Turner and Reese Schonfeld" and announced in mid-1986, "CNN has come of age, without question or reservation." A few months later Ed Turner introduced a new technological innovation that gave CNN even greater ubiquity: suitcase-size "flyaway" satellite uplinks—collapsible dishes that could be carried on board commercial aircraft. CNN could now cover breaking stories live, anywhere in the world, in just the time it took to get a reporter on site. The revolutionary $250,000 flyaway dishes, Ed Turner promised, "would change the face of TV journalism."

Now that his MGM purchase was behind him, Ted Turner was doing his best to reenergize in time for the Moscow Goodwill Games. "MGM is absolute history with him now," declared Taylor Glover, Turner's Atlanta stockbroker and occasional hunting companion. "He's gone on to no telling what else. He's in a hurry now to get something else going. Ted Turner won't rest until he's dead."

Soyuzsport and Gostelradio, the Soviet sports and broadcast agencies, agreed to put up $70 million to Turner's $35 million for the inaugural Goodwill Games, a fifteen-day affair staged in Moscow's Lenin Stadium that brought together 3,500 world-class athletes from over fifty countries. Turner succeeded in laying off some $10 million of his investment on Pepsi-Cola ("Official Drink of the Goodwill Games") and several other advertisers. He broadcast over 125 hours of the games on WTBS and an ad hoc syndicated network of over-the-air broadcast stations he put together around the world. A *succès d'estime* despite low audience ratings, the Goodwill Games won Turner a measure of respect among international athletics organizers, who agreed he had the beginnings of a pretty good idea: a regular quadrennial off-year Olympics. He would continue to lose money on the venture through 1990, but Turner owned the television rights lock, stock, and barrel and when the 1994 Games kick off in St. Petersburg, Russia, he will begin to reap millions in profits from this extraordinarily unlikely gambit into international athletics. It was without even a sideways glance at his bankers, therefore, that Turner showed up back in Atlanta after the 1986 Games, flashing photos of himself and his son Teddy on a shooting party with several senior Soviet officials.

His children had grown up right in front of his eyes—young Teddy was already twenty-three, out of college, and working as a veejay at CNN. Laura and Rhett were both about to graduate and head out into the world, with Beau and Jennie only a couple of years behind. But Turner, despite his genuine concern for their well-being, hardly had time to notice that the lakefront house in Roswell, one of Atlanta's choice bedroom communities, was becoming an empty nest. Even Jane now spent the majority of her time at Avalon Plantation, coming into town only a few days a month. Ironically, what had been a last-ditch effort to save her marriage by getting Ted to see Dr. Pittman was instead proving a spur to its demise.

Turner's relationship with his company also appeared to be undergoing a seachange. In late 1986 it was announced that a five-member executive committee had assumed responsibility for day-to-day operations of Turner Broadcasting System. "Ted Turner still runs the show," Arthur Sando told financial reporters anxious to know what might be behind the move. "With the global expansion of CNN and the acquisition of MGM on the West Coast, Ted's travel schedule has been rather hectic." The new committee included executive vice-president Bob Wussler; Jack Petrik, vice-president/programming; Gerry Hogan, vice-president/broadcast sales; Terry McGuirk, vice-president/special projects; and Bill Bevins, vice-president/finance. "With the work load increasing," Sando added, "Ted felt he wanted to put a structure in place that would help out with the day-to-day operations. He wanted fewer people reporting to him, and he wanted the day-to-day operations taken off his back.

"This is not a reorganization," Sando stressed. "This is basically formalizing what has been an informal structure. I repeat, Ted still runs the show. Ted Turner still runs the show, is involved in the decision making, and retains the titles of president and chairman of the board." The new arrangement would not affect

Cable News Network, which remained an independent operation
of the company. CNN's president, Burt Reinhardt, continued to
report directly to Turner. But TBS, once the quintessential one-
man media company, the chairman's vehicle of expression in the
material world, was evidently reflecting some of the changes
Turner himself was undergoing.

Turner ran his business the way he captained his boats. Former
crew member Roger Vaughan calls the technique "dangerously
mounting hysteria." Turner relied on creative tension to bring out
the best in his workers. He pitted crew member against crew
member, manager against manager, stretching their limits by un-
derhiring, underbudgeting, and underplanning. The tension
could be palpable, but the results were often extraordinary.
Turner attracted and retained a remarkable number of highly
productive, intensely loyal managers, many of whom joined him
early in their careers with little intention of staying more than a
year or two, until the fun wore off. Suddenly they found themselves running a billion-dollar business. Turner's new management structure was merely an acknowledgment that he had
hardly been running the company out of his back pocket. With
the exception of Jack Petrik, all of the members of the new executive committee were under fifty years of age. Average tenure with
the company was slightly over ten years.

Turner's real involvement with his company, however, hardly
changed at all. He still spent the majority of his days on the road,
as he had for the last fifteen years—although his audience now
included advocacy groups as well as advertisers and their agencies, cable organizations, top news and media executives, and
government and political leaders around the world. He always
found time as well to speak to college and university groups at
least once or twice a month.

Lisa Blackaller, the daughter of Turner's old friend and sailing
competitor Tom Blackaller, happened to be a member of the
Stanford University student speaker's bureau. In late 1986, she
used her father's name to attract Turner to Palo Alto. Turner
accepted the invitation, and since JJ's father was now associate
dean at Stanford, he brought her along as well.

"I told my dad that Turner was coming to Stanford and invited
him up for the lecture," Lisa Blackaller recalls. "I thought he'd
get a kick hearing his old pal. The two of them were practically
living legends. We were sitting in one of the front rows together

when Ted came on stage. He was rambling on for the longest time about world peace and the environment. It was a pretty windy speech, but everybody was taking it all pretty seriously. Then, all of a sudden, Turner spotted my father in the audience and he started laughing so hard he couldn't continue.

"JJ and her father were there, too, right there in the audience. And Ted stops in the middle of his speech and shouts, 'Hey, Tommy Blackaller, right? Hey, everybody, I stole this guy's girlfriend. There she is, right back there.' " The entire audience gaped at Blackaller and his daughter and then swiveled around to ogle JJ and her father. Turner was strutting around the stage, laughing his head off. "It was all done in jest," Lisa Blackaller says. "It was a very funny situation. Ted even made my father stand up and take a bow. He stood up and waved at the crowd. Dad was on to his next girlfriend by then, and she was only eighteen. So he kind of tossed the ball back to Turner. The two of them were really like peas from the same pod."

"Ted had told Janie over and over that he would never divorce her," recalls JJ Ebaugh's older sister, Sandy. "He never really planned to, even when Jeanette was pretty much his number one." Nor was JJ herself under any illusions regarding Turner's intentions. "My sister," says Sandy, "never, *never* expected that Ted would ever become a one-woman man."

Still, Turner knew by now that his marriage was as good as over. He had been reluctant to confront Jane with the reality of their situation, but she beat him to the punch and asked for a trial separation. Once she took the initiative, Turner felt free to discuss the subject and openly admitted that his life was beginning to change. "I mean, when you leave your wife of twenty-three years and run off with a thirty-year-old woman, that changes things, doesn't it? I've been hopping a little more." Until then, Turner had ensconced JJ in a pleasant little farmhouse down in Clayton County, about an hour outside of Atlanta; but now he was willing to bring things out in the open. They moved into a historic, hundred-year-old log cabin "mansionette" just outside Roswell and not more than a stone's throw and a half from the Turner residence.

The MGM situation meant that Turner was spending more time than ever on the West Coast, and that was fine with Ebaugh, who found the physical, free-thinking California life-style very much to her liking. She traded in her flying suit and racing helmet for

the cerebral pursuit of new age thinking and began to see that she
and Turner had the potential of being a computer-matched couple capable of saving the world.

Ted bought a house for the two of them in Big Sur, an unpretentious, rustic lodge that had once belonged to actor Ryan O'Neal
and was perched high on the edge of a bluff overlooking the Pa-
cific. Not counting the palatial new aerie he would soon start
building on top of the new CNN Center in downtown Atlanta,
Turner and JJ would soon share eight different residences. But it
was the house in Big Sur they found themselves returning to most
often, and it was there that a mutual friend, Alice Acres, introduced JJ to her new mentor, an "evolutionary scholar" named
Riane Eisler.

Employing a potpourri of literature, legend, mythology, history, and research from a dozen different scientific disciplines,
Eisler had begun to fuse a startling new philosophy of human
cultural evolution. "Our earliest societies were based on cooperation, not conflict," she points out in her best-known work, *The
Chalice and the Blade*, challenging the view held by most anthro-
pologists and historians that human development was character-
ized by internecine rivalries. "The Earth was a mother nourishing
its gentle children. Women were revered as givers of life." This,
according to Eisler, is the "partnership model," dating back to
about 20,000 B.C. Its counterpoint, the "dominator model," is em-
bodied in Genghis Khan, who swept out of the East, bringing
death and discord and establishing the "dominator" state as the
predominant social structure. Eisler includes Stalin's Russia, Hit-
ler's Germany, Khomeini's Iran, and Saddam's Iraq as examples
of modern "dominator" states. Eisler also categorizes American
fundamentalists, toxic polluters, and male chauvinists as part of
the same "dominator" species.

Eisler emphasizes that true partnership must flow upward from
the individual man and woman to national and global levels.
"[Turner and Ebaugh] are in a position to play a major role in
changing our basic premises. The images they project through his
[television] networks are of enormous importance. We've got to
replace the dominator image. We have idealized the killer as hero
all the way from Ulysses to Rambo."

JJ brought Turner together with Eisler, and their paths crossed
again at a peace conference in Atlanta, where both were speakers.
"Like all of us," Eisler notes, "Ted carries a tremendous amount

of dominator programming, and that's a struggle for him, not just against external institutions and power structures. It's internal."

Eisler and her husband, Dr. David Loyle, had set up the Center for Partnership Studies, and JJ was soon asked to become a director. "Ted is growing up by leaps and bounds," Eisler noted one evening when she was a dinner guest at the house in Big Sur. "JJ tells me Ted will often say to her, 'I don't want to do it that way. That's the dominator way.' " Turner later became a member of the center's advisory council, though taming the quintessential dominator in himself had not been easy. "When I met him, I felt that yearning for connection," says Eisler, "for a caring connection. And a profound desire to make things better. He's childlike, not in the sense of childish, but in still having a sense of hope, a sense of the possible. There's goodness in Ted Turner," Eisler notes, "in this wonderfully gifted, precocious boy who is still saying, 'Look at me! I'm doing it well, aren't I?' "

"He had no partners his whole life," JJ points out. "Not in business, in sailing, or in his family." In fact, in nearly three decades of sailing, Turner never crewed for anybody else. He was the skipper, and the thought of accepting any other role never even occurred to him. He walked over people the same way he ran roughshod over conversations. He made up all the rules and then threw them away if things weren't going his way. Ted Turner was the man who changed things, who molded people and institutions to suit his needs and meet his demands. Had Ebaugh succeeded in changing him? Was he no longer the warrior trapped in an age of antiheroes? Was Ted Turner, in fact, on his way to becoming, as many were now beginning to believe, a new man—more relaxed, more self-assured, happier—at peace with himself? Or was he burning out, the raging fires of his ego banking as he approached his fiftieth year?

"There's no question I've changed quite a bit since meeting JJ," Turner told *Atlanta* magazine. "You can't have a very close relationship with someone without both of you being altered."

The perception outside of Big Sur, however, was that any changes Ted Turner might have been experiencing were not entirely voluntary. "He came to town fully clothed," said Art Murphy, a University of Southern California economist and respected Hollywood analyst, "and left in a barrel. He took a bath."

Murphy might not have been right, but he wasn't alone in believing that Captain Courageous was about to get his comeuppance. "His reputation in Hollywood," *Newsweek* prophesied, "may already be beyond repair. There had been talk of a new breed of Hollywood mogul, a visionary, a showman. But since his purchase of MGM, Turner's image in Hollywood has gone from swashbuckling new man in town to the philistine from the South." Still burdened with nearly half a billion dollars of debt, Turner was perceived by most outsiders to be in fairly desperate need of a bailout.

In early 1987, just as his eldest son, Teddy, was recovering from a near fatal automobile accident in Moscow, where he had been working as a CNN cameraman, Turner began to consider his alternatives. He had been among the first to explore the feasibility of boosting the revenue potential of his new library of classic films by using computers to tint old black-and-white films. Colorization was still in its infancy and the process was extraordinarily expensive—about $1,800 per minute, or $180,000 for an average film—and very time consuming. "Even if Turner had access to the entire colorization industry in the United States today," predicted entertainment analyst Anthony Hoffman of Los Angeles' Union Bank, "he'd be able to do only about two films a month. That's not going to make a dent in his problems."

Turner paid an average of slightly over $300,000 each for the 3,560 films he had acquired. He figured the investment of an additional 50 percent of their cost would just about double the value of the films. But in championing "colorization," he hit a raw nerve in Hollywood and further offended the motion picture establishment. Hollywood, in fact, fought his efforts to colorize some of MGM's classics—all the way to the floor of Congress. Representative Robert Mrazak, a New York Democrat, even proposed federal legislation that would prohibit the "destruction of America's cinema masterpieces." Woody Allen, Steven Spielberg, and a host of other Hollywood luminaries all showed up in Washington to testify against Turner. And when he mentioned that one of the first films he would tint would be his favorite, *Citizen Kane*, Orson Welles spoke from the grave, via a deathbed agreement he had extracted from RKO, ensuring that *Kane* would forever remain untouched.

Perceived initially as an aesthetic folly on Turner's part, colorization has actually proved to be a bonanza for his company, increasing the value of black-and-white classics like *It's a Wonderful Life* and *Miracle on 34th Street* at least ten times over. Colorization even improved some films like *Gone With the Wind*, which has already been retinted twice to preserve the magnificent original colors that had begun to fade on the master negative.

"In the first six months after we colorize a film," Turner has pointed out, "we more than pay for it." Turner's leap into colorization helped put a young computer company, Color Systems Technology, Inc., on the map when he gave them an initial contract for $18 million to colorize one hundred films from the MGM library. Three were completed in 1986 and another fifteen in 1987. Despite his plan to show some of the MGM classics only in color on television, Turner defends colorization by explaining that the original black-and-white prints and negative remain intact and will always be available to purists.

Colorization had not endeared Ted Turner to Hollywood, and now Wall Street seemed to have turned against him as well. Ignoring the evidence, the financial press continued to castigate him for having plunged irresponsibly on MGM. Disappointed that the TBS stock price seemed to be going nowhere, analysts began falling over themselves to be the first to predict the collapse of the company. "Turner saw stars in his eyes and felt MGM was the answer to his dreams," said Anthony Hoffman, "but the answer to his dreams has turned out to be a nightmare." The financial community, fickle in the extreme, was now nearly unanimous in its assessment that Turner had finally rolled the dice one time too many.

Surprisingly, however, Turner Broadcasting posted an impressively strong performance for 1986. Revenues were up significantly, with the MGM library alone producing over $125 million. Turner's confidence in the value of the library proved to be justified, but few financial analysts fixated on the $121 million net loss his company reported for the year, and almost no one gave him credit for having paid out over $200 million in interest during 1986.

Without the $15 price fuse tied to Kerkorian's preferred dividends, Turner might well have limped through the next several years until he was able to restructure his entire debt. Despite a roaring bull market, however, Wall Street's generally pessimistic perception of the company continued to depress Turner Broadcasting's stock. The share price flirted dangerously with the lethal $15 price throughout most of 1986 and early 1987. Once TBS shares dipped below that level, Turner would be forced under the agreement Mike Milken had structured to issue enough preferred stock to Kerkorian to make up the difference. The preferred would, in turn, multiply like crazed amoebas as additional dividends, which could only be paid in more common stock, came due. Cynics even began to speculate that Kerkorian might have sold Turner MGM simply to gain control of Turner Broadcasting System. All too aware of that possibility, Turner decided to open his doors to offers of assistance from outside interests—and, ironically, this time it was CBS that came knocking.

On September 16, 1986, Tom Wyman had sought out and invited Lawrence Tisch into CBS—through the back door. In his role as "white knight," Tisch was now closeted at Black Rock with Wyman and the CBS board. Van Gordon Sauter was lunching a few blocks away at Alfredo's Restaurant where the CBS news division president was seated across the table from an old associate, Turner Broadcasting's Bob Wussler. After a few wry comments about Tisch's efforts to sell off CBS's nonbroadcast assets —exactly the plan Turner had proposed when he'd made his own aborted run at CBS a little over eighteen months earlier—Sauter got right to the point.

"I've been authorized by Gene Jankowski [CBS Broadcast Group president] to discuss our acquiring an ownership position in CNN." CBS was now prepared to take a minority position, Sauter volunteered, but wanted a first option to buy the network if Turner ever put it up for sale.

"I was very encouraged," Sauter recalls. "We had a good, substantive discussion and agreed to get back together in a day or two." Sauter was, in fact, elated as he left the restaurant, certain he had finally found the way to put CBS into cable and, at the same time, reduce some of CBS News' high operating costs. Sauter called Jankowski on his car phone and told him the good news, only to learn that Tom Wyman had just been forced out of the company by Tisch. All bets were off. "My meeting with Wussler was consequential—could have been very consequential," Sauter says today. "Unfortunately I was fired from CBS the next day."

Turner had now been around the track so many times he could almost make his way blindfolded through the boardrooms of New York's media conglomerates. Leaving Bob Wussler back in Atlanta with time, he came calling himself, cap in hand, on Time Inc.'s chairman and chief executive officer, J. Richard Munro. An ex-Marine who should have been enamored of Turner's visceral, hands-on management style, Munro was atrophying in the Time, Inc., culture and much too concerned about the rumors of a hostile raid on his own company to give serious consideration to a man his advisors had warned him "drinks too much, spends money like a madman, and chases women."

Turner made several attempts to meet with Munro and at last simply showed up at the Time-Life building unannounced. Incredibly, the Time chairman hid out on the thirty-second floor for several hours before appearing to face Turner, only to hand him over to Nick Nicholas, Jr., Time's cold-blooded chief financial officer. Nicholas was "amused by Turner, but just didn't like the numbers." Turner had offered Time a half interest in CNN for $300 million. Nicholas was aware of Turner's earlier discussions with Time Inc., going all the way back to 1979, when Gerry Levin could have secured a half ownership at Cable News Network for an investment of only $50 million. This time, Turner offered Time Inc. a half interest in CNN for $300 million. Ignoring Turner's new proposal, as well as the synergies that had prompted Time Inc.'s continued interest in CNN, Nicholas offered Turner $225 million, plus another $75 million if and when CNN ever met certain revenue and profit projections. Turner needed every bit of the $300 million, in cash however, to take out Kerkorian and extinguish the $15 share price fuse. When he found Nicholas haughtily intransigent and unwilling to negotiate, he walked.

"It may have been the biggest business mistake of my life," Nicholas would say many times afterward. But the numbers just didn't compute. The return on investment, he rationalized, however inaccurately, would have been zero or less. Nick Nicholas never had any illusions, however, regarding CNN's intrinsic value to Time Inc. He promised himself he would someday take another shot at Turner.

Meanwhile Turner could feel Kerkorian closing in on him. He looked to Bill Bevins, but his financial Houdini seemed to have run out of the tricks that had made him a darling of the investment community. Having worn out his welcome on Wall Street, Turner decided to pay a visit to his old friend and cable mentor, Bill Daniels. It was Daniels who helped him bridge a $3 million cash flow shortfall when the Charlotte station sale bogged down just before the CNN launch. And it was Daniels who had been instrumental in arranging Turner's buyout of Satellite News Channel from ABC-Westinghouse. Now Daniels feared that Turner's company would fall into the wrong hands. Of course, "wrong" to Daniels and his fellow operators meant anyone not already in the cable business. Daniels knew Turner had been talking to the networks again, and he knew about Turner's visit to Time Inc. He also knew Rupert Murdoch also had his eye on TBS. And everyone in the world seemed to know about the $15 share price that could trigger Kirk Kerkorian's control of Turner Broadcasting. Daniels was concerned enough to call a "cable summit" in Las Vegas, where Turner could present his case before a dozen or more of the largest operators in the country.

The meeting was held on March 25, 1987, one year to the day after Turner had finally closed on the MGM/UA transaction. Bill Daniels had assembled a group of the most powerful and influential cable executives in the country. TCI's John Malone served as chair. Nick Nicholas, still hoping to have CNN for himself, sent Trygve Myhren, head of Time Inc.'s American Television and Communications subsidiary.

Bill Bevins opened the meeting with a brief but convincing financial presentation of TBS's projected growth and development. Malone expressed the group's concern that Turner might fall into "alien hands." Turner then proposed a $550 million package of equity and debt he had devised with Malone and Stuart Blair, who ran TCI's subsidiary, United Artists Communications. The new investment, Turner said, would enable him to renegotiate the junk bond debt and redeem Kerkorian's preferred stock, making any further discussions with the broadcast networks unnecessary. "With this investment," Turner declared, "Turner broadcasting will remain safely within the hands of the cable industry."

The genial Bill Daniels attempted to jolly several of the more recalcitrant cable operators into line behind Turner's idea. The group huddled briefly without Turner and then came back with several conditions, the most important calling for the TBS board to be enlarged to fifteen members. The cable operators would have seven seats. Turner and the other common stock shareholders would have eight, but the cable operators would have special voting rights, entitling them to require a supermajority (80 percent or more) on any matter not defined as "being in the ordinary course of the company's business." Approval of twelve of the fifteen directors on the enlarged board would now be required on any expense in excess of $2 million—an effective pocket veto by the cable operators of any significant expansion plans Turner might have. Although Turner would still retain slightly more than 50 percent of his company's equity and over 60 percent voting control, he would no longer be free to make the kind of offhand investment decisions that had proved so successful in the past.

"I like to think that we're Brer Rabbit," Turner said, explaining his situation. "When he got caught, he was hoping he'd get thrown right into that briar patch. Well, that's what happened to us. We got thrown right where we wanted to be. Sure, I've got negative covenants, but the negative covenants I have with the cable operators are not significantly different than they were with the banks, the banks being the junk bonds. Now there's so much supposition and conjecture. It's great. We create more ink, even though we're not saying anything. And everybody says, 'Well, he's finished this time.'"

Fourteen cable television companies, including Malone's Tele-Communications, Inc.; United Artists Communications; American Television and Communications and Home Box Office, another Time Inc. subsidiary; Warner Cable Communications; Continental Cablevision; and United Cable Television agreed to invest approximately $550 million for about one-third of Turner Broadcasting. Trygve Myhren insisted that Time Inc. be allowed to operate Cable News Network if Turner ever decided to step down. The new investors insisted on the right of first refusal if Turner ever decided to sell out altogether. Time Inc. and Tele-Communications, the two largest cable operators and arch-enemies, negotiated a mutual buy-sell agreement between themselves, effectively neutralizing each other and, at the same time, leaving Turner in control of his own company.

The new investment valued Turner Broadcasting at over $1.5 billion and gave the company sufficient cash not only to take out Kerkorian, but allowed Turner to bid for a piece of the NFL football schedule in 1988. Wall Street, however, saw the deal as a "bailout" and continued to excoriate Turner for having paid too steep a price for MGM. Other critics were kinder. As *Broadcasting* magazine pointed out, "That's step one in Turner's recovery plan. He's now in an incredibly strong position to take step two, which is to use the leverage his new partners can provide to launch new programming."

"People assumed it was a bailout," complained Turner. "I've seen it a dozen times, but I never said that. There were several other entities sitting there willing to do the same thing, maybe even on more favorable terms. We were not desperate in any way, like CBS was, with its massive layoffs in the news department and huge buy-back of its own stock. We may have looked like we were in financial trouble, but you didn't hear any crying on the part of anybody at Turner Broadcasting. We had oodles of alternatives, and we picked the one that made the most strategic sense for us."

"We felt that a financially healthy TBS," confirms Tim Neher, president of Continental Cablevision, "would benefit the entire cable industry. If we hadn't stepped in when we did, someone else would have, and they might not have shared our interests in continuing the same quality of programs."

Why turn CNN over to a broadcaster, who would distribute it free over the air? John Malone couldn't have been more blunt. "If we hadn't rescued Ted Turner," he said, "TBS would have been bought by Rupert Murdoch and CNN now would be running *Murder of the Week*."

"All of a sudden," says JJ Ebaugh, "he had twenty-seven new partners and he had me. He had more partnership thrust on him than he had ever known." Reports soon began circulating, however, that John Malone, recognized as one of the toughest but most efficient managers in the industry, was already applying pressure and attempting to coerce Turner to give up his "one-man-band" approach to management. All sides have acknowledged that the early meetings between Turner and his new board were long, tense affairs. Turner continued to believe he had been right on MGM and was, moreover, still captain of his own ship, but he freely admitted, "My power is somewhat diminished." He had remained the last amateur in ocean racing until the fun had gone out of the sport and he could no longer control his own destiny. Now he saw the broadcast industry changing in much the same way, becoming capital-intensive, with power narrowing into the hands of the few large players who had the cash and controlled the distribution.

All Turner had was the programming. He figured he didn't need much more. He already held title to more film and television programming than any other broadcaster in the world. He believed, not unrealistically, that his company's assets, *excluding* the MGM library, were now worth at least $50–$60 per share, not the $15–$20 price at which his shares then traded. Turner estimated he could get $600 million or more for his two news channels and perhaps another $600 million for the Superstation. He had often confused Wall Street and consternated his investors, but he had shown an uncanny constancy in his ability to add value to his assets. "Ted has been on the edge financially with MGM," Nick Nicholas observed somewhat ruefully. "But I would never bet against him. Maybe he wins so much because he knows where the edge is."

By aligning himself with the cash-rich powers of cable television—and then playing them off against one another—Turner believed he was assuring his own future and the future of Turner Broadcasting. He acknowledged the constraints, which would keep him from freewheeling into any new venture that caught his fancy. But he also flexed his muscles, just to let his new partners know he wasn't about to roll over and play dead. When Michael Fuchs, one of his new board members, told him he could not "take millions of this company's dollars and squander them away on an ideology that's out there in the wild somewhere," Turner responded by doubling TBS's support of the Better World Society. At the same time he delivered issue-oriented programming to the Superstation at a quarter of the usual cost and, to drive home his point, proudly nominated several of the Better World–financed projects for broadcast industry awards, winning big. When he wanted to acquire 750 RKO films that had not been included in the earlier MGM package, he demanded board approval to spend $30 million and quickly got it.

"These are smart guys," *Broadcasting*'s Don West explained. "They wouldn't have made this kind of investment in Turner if they didn't think he could pull it off in the long run."

Bill Daniels agrees and is pleased he had been able to help put together Turner's cable consortium. Daniels became a TBS investor himself, winding up as the company's largest individual shareholder behind Turner. "The cable industry," Daniels says, "is faced with what might be called 'the Turner dilemma.' The only thing worse for the industry than having Ted Turner as the most important person in cable is not having Ted Turner as the most important person in cable."

With new capital from the cable operators, Turner was able to get back to the serious business of building his business. He was ready to launch yet another programming venture, to be called, shamelessly, Turner Network Television, or TNT. The new network would have the same two revenue streams as his news channels—advertising and subscriber fees. Three-quarters of its programming would come from the MGM library, which he had renamed Turner Entertainment Company. Turner had first floated the idea of TNT in 1982. Now the unique leverage of his new cable consortium quickly became apparent. With their co-operation, he was able to secure sufficient clearance to ensure that TNT would be the most successful network launch in cable history.

In *Three Blind Mice*, his otherwise perceptive analysis of the decline of the three major television networks, Ken Auletta makes a cavalier assessment of Ted Turner's attempt to acquire CBS in 1985. Had Turner succeeded, Auletta concludes without supporting his contention, "he might be dismissed today as a buffoon." In retrospect Turner came closer than anyone realized in his attempt to control CBS and in all likelihood would have succeeded had Kerkorian not stepped in and offered him an even more attractive acquisition, one he had already been chasing for over four years. Turner's CBS strategy—selling off most of CBS's nonbroadcast assets and then combining the network with his own programming businesses—made solid business sense and would also have provided significantly greater returns to CBS shareholders, who sat back and watched Lawrence Tisch and his Loew's Corporation acquire control of CBS at a zero premium to the depressed market price of the company and then proceed to execute Turner's planned asset sales almost to the letter. Yet Tisch, whose reputation as a shrewd investor and tough trader obscured the fact that he had absolutely no experience running a broadcast network, underpriced the CBS assets he sold by hundreds of millions of dollars. He even erred in allowing Peter Diamandis and the management of CBS Publishing to buy the magazine group and then "flip" it less than ninety days later for a quick $300 million profit.

With the success of Turner Network Television, Turner would soon emerge as one of the most resourceful programmers in broadcasting. That this success was built upon the presumed financial quicksand of his MGM deal is all the more remarkable. Turner was mining his new archive so astutely—syndicating MGM films for television in both the United States and Europe and using his library as the cornerstone of the highly profitable TNT—that once again the revisionists on Wall Street were beginning to take another look at the MGM/UA transaction. Apply a little hindsight, and the $1.2 billion net price Turner ended up paying no longer seemed outlandish. Some analysts were even willing to admit that MGM might prove to have actually been a bargain. In 1990 *Institutional Investor* called Turner's MGM acquisition one of the "deals of the decade." The MGM deal's ultimate value, however, may prove less important than its unintended consequence. The price of Turner's getting Kerkorian out was allowing the cable operators into his company. As an insurance policy, which guaranteed Turner the programming he needed, MGM by any measure was expensive. But Turner now owned the product, just as he has always owned as much of the product as he could afford. He knew no other way to run his business and could not resist taking potshots at programmers like his new partner, Time's Michael Fuchs, for not following his lead. "They must feel like bozos," he said. "Time sat there with HBO paying out $500 million, $600 million a year for ten years for programming. They spent $6 billion. And they licensed that programming from the producers and own almost no negatives. I showed everyone," Turner added. "It made a lot of sense to buy MGM. I showed 'em!"

Having gotten his cable partners inside the tent, Turner could now expect them to help him prop it up. There would be disagreements, to be sure, and continuous, unresolved conflicts of interest, but Turner Broadcasting was fast regaining its reputation as a money machine, and having virtually every important player in the cable industry on his board lent Turner considerable cachet and enormous new clout. "If we hadn't been undercapitalized," Turner declared, "we could have grown a lot faster."

But if he hadn't been undercapitalized and then had the insight and good fortune to bring such a powerful and influential group of partners into his company, it's unlikely Turner would be chairman of Turner Broadcasting System today.

> The supple, well-adjusted man is the
> one who has learned to hop into the meat
> grinder while humming a hit parade tune.
>
> MARSHALL McLUHAN
> *The Mechanical Bride*

Chapter Fourteen

The huge gray concrete monolith that now houses Ted Turner's empire also encompasses much of what is left of Atlanta's old railroad yards, once the hub of one of the busiest land transportation networks in the country and, in fact, the city's original raison d'être. Within the confines of this real estate complex reside the corporate headquarters of Turner Broadcasting System, the Omni Hotel, Arena, and Music Center (all owned and managed by Turner), a movie theater, a radio station, and the usual ubiquitous panoply of restaurants, bars, and ice-cream shops. Once home to Sid and Marty Krofft's indoor 'toon theme park, the principal building is now called CNN Center and dominates Atlanta's impressive skyline. A $3 million penthouse apartment has been built into the top floor of this sprawling structure and is now Ted Turner's legal residence.

Steady streams of tourists wend their way up the "world's longest free-standing escalator" from the center's atrium lobby on hourly tours through the studios of Cable News Network and Headline News. The most popular stop along the way is the life-size cardboard cutout of Ted Turner himself, standing sentinel beside a surprisingly unimpressive collection of Turner memorabilia. Tour takers inevitably line up to pose for snapshots with the chairman of Turner Broadcasting, who is content to stand there forever, arms crossed, his face frozen in a permanently triumphant smile. After the tour, which lasts about forty-five minutes and rivals the equally impressive yet equally ramshackle Civil War Cyclorama in Grant Park as one of Atlanta's top tourist attractions, tour visitors are deposited back in the CNN Center lobby, smack in front of Turner: The Store, a sprawling souvenir shop that traffics in everything from *Wizard of Oz* beach towels and Superstation T-shirts to Scarlett O'Hara chocolates and *The CNN Cookbook* (featuring Ted Turner's favorite recipe for chile con carne).

Turner's own fourteenth-floor executive inner sanctum is manned by a phalanx of security guards and secretaries. The corridors leading to his corner office suite are lined with Turner memorabilia, somewhat more personal and considerably more revealing than anything the public ever sees on a CNN tour: Civil War swords and rifles, movie stills from *Gigi* and *An American in Paris*, an oil painting of Clark Gable as Rhett Butler, cigar in hand at a gaming table, several dozen (reproduction) Oscar statuettes, and two mounted mallard ducks, shot by Fidel Castro in 1982. A huge Native American war bonnet hangs in an alcove next to several Civil War paintings and an oversize "family portrait" of Louis B. Mayer's impressive 1948 stable of stars. Interspersed among this excessively eclectic collection are blown-up photographs of Turner, recording his various triumphs, business and personal, on land and at sea.

The corner office itself houses a bank of Sony television monitors along one whole wall. Enough silver trophies to stock the Atlanta branch of Tiffany's refract their silent images and create constant, colorful reflections that give the large room a nervous, kinetic energy. Turner's desk is dominated by two gold Emmy award statues and his personal mantra, "Lead, Follow, or Get out of the Way," which appears on a miniature billboard and is also engraved on a curious, burnished-bronze sculpture. The picture of his father, which resided on Turner's desk for nearly thirty years, is no longer in evidence, and nearly a decade has passed since anyone has seen that silver .38-caliber revolver.

Turner acquired this $39 million "megastructure" in 1985, in the middle of his run against CBS. The strain of holding his business together during that monumental street fight and then his long, extended campaign to acquire MGM had taken its toll but did not prevent his completing the purchase of these new quarters on his usual advantageous terms. Turner had felt so run-down at the time, and appeared so uncharacteristically lethargic to his colleagues, that Dee Woods thought he might have contracted Epstein-Barr, a debilitating virus sometimes called "the writer's disease." It turned out he had altitude sickness, the result of the incessant takeoffs and landings required by an impossible itinerary. By 1987, however, Turner had considerably altered his unrelentingly high-pressure life-style.

"Ted's become much more reflective," says his old confidant Bill Daniels. "He stayed nineteen until about two or three years ago. Then he went to thirty-four. He's a man with a lot of scars from the discovery that there were consequences to pay for his actions."

"When I was a young man," Turner himself reflected, "I was a good man. I worked hard. I was always honest and a good patriotic citizen, paid my taxes, had never been indicted for anything. But," he continued, "I was more interested in my own pleasure, in making money. I was interested in winning sailboat races, primarily. Gradually, over a period of time, I would see what was happening."

Could it be that the lithium and the counseling were finally having an effect? At JJ Ebaugh's enthusiastic urging, Turner had begun seeing several new therapists, including one who specialized in what JJ termed "high-performance couples." The more he learned about himself, however, the less he seemed to want to explore their own unusual "partnership."

After seven years of her on-and-off relationship with Turner, JJ Ebaugh decided to "cross learning curves" with someone new. "It was a friendship," she said, "that just crept up on me. I never discussed it with Ted. He'd be jealous."

In 1987, shortly after Turner took off for Africa with his family in one final attempt at a reconciliation with Jane, JJ packed her bags and moved in with an empathetic California doctor. Turner was devastated. He cut short his trip and flew straight back to Atlanta. For weeks he pressured Barbara Pyle and JJ's other friends to arrange a reconciliation.

"He put up the most aggressive campaign to get me back," Ebaugh recounted, "that I have ever heard about or read about in my entire life."

No less susceptible to a broken heart than any of the dozens of ladies he had walked out on over the years, Turner was indeed desperate to have Ebaugh back. "Ted was so insistent," JJ says, "telling me all the things he would do. Frankly, I wasn't as committed as he was. I thought I'd be back for a few months, but his commitment inspired me."

"It took her a while," added Ebaugh's sister, Sandy, "even after Ted said 'I can't live without you,' to really believe it."

JJ finally agreed to give the romance another chance, and together they moved back into the log cabin in Roswell. Turner swore off other women and immediately instructed his lawyers to begin formal divorce proceedings. He also acceded to Ebaugh's desire to spend more time in California and, at her urging, remained in therapy, this time with a considerably more open and receptive attitude. "I started to listen," says Turner, the man with the untamed mouth, "and not be judgmental, to wait until someone was through rather than interrupting them. And then think about what they said before I prepared an answer." Impassioned, and blindly devoted to winning Ebaugh back, he began to unbend and put himself increasingly in her hands. "I learned to give and take," he says, "better than I ever had previously."

It would take two years, a cash settlement of over $40 million, and Turner's Kinloch Plantation before his divorce from Jane would be final, but the struggle to change himself was already well under way. Already some ten pounds thinner and in better shape than he had been for years, Turner promised Ebaugh he would stop drinking. He also began working out on a regular basis and even had an exercise bicycle installed in his office. He believed now that he and JJ could go out to conquer the world, together. At first, JJ admitted, he sometimes screamed like a stuck pig. "He determined all the schedules. And tried to second-guess me. I wasn't given the responsibility I should have. He had his business. He wanted all of his and some of mine, too.

"I knew I would never have an equal share because of who he is and who I am," Ebaugh reflected, fondling the gold dolphin earrings Turner had given her. "Dolphins don't dominate each other," she explained. "It was an outstanding, probing battle."

But Ebaugh persevered and, as unwilling as Turner to acknowledge the possibility of defeat, eventually prevailed. "He gave up $40 million," she noted with particular satisfaction, "and a whole harem of women. That's a hell of a lot." Noting that Turner had "developed a lot of trust and confidence" in her, Ebaugh added that he had even "left the door open" to starting a second family. "He said we'll do whatever I want."

As his trust in Ebaugh grew, Turner saw that she could help him reestablish communication with his children, who had grown even farther away from him, in part because of the bitter divorce he had thrust upon their mother. He and Ebaugh took all five kids, together with Teddy's new bride, Genie, for a week-long family vacation to Alaska. Since that seemed to work out so well for everybody, they began spending weekends and holidays together. The Turner offspring were "kind and respectful to me," Ebaugh notes. "There's a certain amount of natural resentment. But I can't tolerate negativity. I think the best about everybody, expect the best, plan for the best."

Turner also took JJ out on the road with him whenever he traveled on business, which was incessantly. Ebaugh seemed to thrive on the exposure. In one ninety-day period they visited Boston, Washington, Denver, Montana, Los Angeles, San Francisco, England, France, Germany, Italy, Greece, Sweden, and the Soviet Union, almost nonstop. Despite the demanding itinerary, they traveled in a relatively simple, unpretentious style. "We don't do limos," Ebaugh said. "None of that stuff. We're country people." Turner still drove his little white Toyota when they were in Atlanta, and he kept the old six-seater Merlin IIB, because, JJ pointed out, "a jet uses three hundred gallons of fuel just to take off. That's disgusting."

JJ taught Turner how to fly-fish, and he fell in love with the sport. When they were at home she did most of the cooking herself, leaving Jimmy Brown with nothing more to do than rustle around on one or the other of Ted's plantations. Most of the time she was decked out in blue jeans and a loose-fitting man's shirt, although in public she favored simple, stylish clothes. She wore almost no makeup, and her hands, rough and rarely manicured, were a badge of honor—the hands of an active, outdoor, working woman. Turner radiated happiness when he was with JJ and seemed supercharged with energy and a sense of mission. Riane Eisler remembers that he "seemed profoundly changed." How much of a transformation had he undergone? "He's the only one who can really make that kind of assessment," she says, but it was obvious that Ebaugh had indeed tapped a whole new reservoir of self-esteem within Turner. JJ referred to their new crusading partnership as an ongoing, living process.

"He's taken to it with real enthusiasm and commitment," she would say. "He's been magnificent."

Turner and Ebaugh turned their attention to the Better World Society which their earlier conversations had originally inspired. The Better World Society and soon all it represented had become an impressive demonstration of Turner's newfound commitment to their partnership.

"When you have critical issues like nuclear arms, ecological devastation, and a global population explosion putting man in the category of an endangered species—that's Captain Cousteau and a lot of other futurists talking—broadcasting has a responsibility to point these things out to people," Turner declared. "That's what Better World is trying to do."

"Harnessing the Power of Television to Make a Better World" became the organization's slogan, a heart-shaped globe its logo. Half of the Better World Society's annual budget of approximately $2 million went toward the production of issue-oriented television programs. Between 1985 and 1989 Better World funded over forty documentaries, most of which were broadcast on CNN, Turner's Superstation, or other cable networks. Better World also distributed its program free to China and the Soviet Union.

Better World held two large meetings a year—one in the United States and one in some designated flashpoint overseas. In 1988 it was decided to hold the overseas meeting in Baghdad, although Iraq at the time was involved in a shooting war with Iran. Turner personally led the negotiations with Iraqi authorities and, although the meeting never happened, was able to establish personal contacts with a number of government ministers that would later prove invaluable.

"I remember the meeting in Costa Rica," says Better World executive director Tom Belford. "Jean-Michel Cousteau screened a film there on some children of poverty. When the lights came back up, we were all surprised to see Ted wiping his eyes—he'd been sobbing all through the screening, but we thought it must have been one of the Costa Ricans.

"Working with someone like Turner," says Belford, "was the best experience of my life. He's not the easiest guy in the world to get along with, but if you want someone with vision, who is passionate about things, who puts his money where his mouth is, who is willing to take a lot of risk, and who will give you, personally, a lot of room to do your thing, you couldn't ask for a better situation.

"Ted's philosophy," Belford adds, "is 'Do well by doing good.' The basic idea of Better World was his. He gave more than $2 million in personal contributions and services. But he pushed us all to leverage the society's budget into many times that amount. It's true his interest in Better World fluctuated, but I think that was more because of business pressures than any lack of interest in the project. In the end I think Ted felt our priorities had got turned upside down. Better World seemed to be spending more time raising funds than doing anything else, and he felt he could use his resources more effectively in some other way."

Turner's infatuation with Ebaugh, and her own fascination with the almost cosmic potential she felt they possessed as partners, could sometimes result in occasional sightings of Turner's newly submerged superego. No one was quite certain how seriously to take him when he demanded one day that two well-known Hollywood screenwriters, as well as several high-profile movie producers, be flown into Atlanta for a top-secret story meeting at which he personally pitched the idea for what he called the "ultimate movie"—a "peace epic" he had conceived with JJ in which he himself would act as go-between for Gorbachev and Reagan. All three principals would star as themselves, naturally. Once Turner convinced the two superpowers to lay down their weapons and walk with the lambs, he would, according to his script, assume his natural role as leader of the free world. Fade-out. Which is exactly what the visitors from Hollywood did.

Many of Turner's less cosmic ideas, however, sometimes proved highly imaginative and often challenged conventional wisdom. Sometimes they were also so obvious as to be almost incomprehensible. He originally conceived TNT in 1982, for example, as a broadcast (not cable) network to compete directly against CBS, NBC, and ABC. To finance the idea, he had come up with a radically simple concept. Rather than paying producers up front for their programming, he proposed to "deficit-finance" his network's shows, paying producers nothing up front but then dividing with them prorated shares of TNT's advertising revenue. As an extra incentive, Turner offered producers nearly total creative control over their shows. Only the producer, moreover, could cancel a show. Devilishly clever and maddeningly logical, the concept offered a producer guaranteed compensation proportionate to his show's actual audience appeal. Obviously, Turner theorized, producers would be highly motivated to produce only those programs that could command the highest ratings. And similarly, they would voluntarily cancel those shows that were poorly received.

It sounded terrific the way Turner explained it and he was stunned when Hollywood rejected the idea without a second thought. "You cannot expect producers to produce programming purely on speculation," rationalized Alvin Rush, president of MCA-TV, which produced more network television shows than any other studio.

"If I make a program for a million dollars, who's going to guarantee me that million dollars?" asked Lorimar's Lee Rich.

And if producers took over total creative control of their programming, Madison Avenue wanted to know, how could Turner guarantee advertisers the sort of uplifting, profamily moral entertainment he berated the networks for abandoning?

"We haven't really gotten into that," Turner replied, realizing that once again he might be way ahead of his time. He beat a hasty retreat from Hollywood, toward a more accommodating audience at the Edinburgh Television Festival, where, as keynote speaker, he delivered a promise to expand CNN into Europe. "I intend to conquer the world," he declared, "but instead of conquering with bombs, I intend to conquer with good ideas."

His good idea for Turner Network Television, however, finally found a responsive audience when his newly expanded board of directors put its stamp of approval on the project. Turner had projected seven million TNT subscribers at launch. Malone, Time-Warner, and Turner's other cable partners actually delivered more than twice that number—seventeen million—assuring TNT the most successful network launch in television history.

"We'll have to crawl before we walk," said TNT's new president, Gerald Hogan. For the first year TNT would air only one "major event" show a month. The remainder of the schedule would be reruns of shows like "The Muppets" and "Fraggle Rock" and lots of old movies from the MGM library. Later Turner would introduce impressive new made-for-TNT motion pictures like *A Man for All Seasons*, *The Rachel Carson Story*, and *The Jackie Robinson Story*. And soon TNT would be spending more than $150 million a year for new programs, almost twice the budget of any other cable service. Turner had succeeded in cloning Headline News from CNN. Now he proved he could replicate his Superstation with a newer, flashier TNT. "It's just like Procter and Gamble or General Foods," he says. "That's the problem with CBS, NBC, and ABC. They've only got one channel apiece in a fifty-channel environment. I have four." With another on the way.

Armed with "high concept" programming and Turner's enormous film library, TNT went head to head with the three major broadcast networks, as well as Rupert Murdoch's new Fox Broadcasting in an effort to win their viewers over to cable. "You've still got that twenty-seven-million household disparity," TNT's Scott Sassa pointed out, "between the number of homes that can now receive cable and those that actually do. That's $54 billion worth of untapped assets the cable industry has out there."

"The fat days of the Big Three are over," Turner proclaimed, and TNT proceeded to prove him right by exceeding every projection he made.

Despite the new network's astounding success, however, Turner was feeling new pressures from his cable partners. TNT's success had less to do, they said, with Turner's shrewd judgment than with their material support, which guaranteed TNT's impressive audience of more than thirty-five million subscribers after just one year on the air. "That kind of success," said Standard & Poor's Jeffrey Evans, "is unprecedented." This was quickly reflected in the price of TBS common stock, which went from a low of $8 in the wake of the 1987 stock market crash to a high of $58.25 in late 1989, following TNT's impressive debut.

The company's return to Wall Street's favor, however, had taken its toll on Turner's financial chief, Bill Bevins, who had suffered two mild strokes and the indignity of having continuously to take each new financing innovation, every new investment decision, back to the new board for approval. Finally he decided to step down. His replacement, Randy Booth, proved adept at dealing with both the banks and the board and was able to capitalize on TNT's smashing success by lining up the company's first new financing since the MGM deal. Eight banks, led by Chase Manhattan, anted up nearly $1 billion in new credit, an unusual endorsement of a company that less than twenty-four months earlier had been written off by virtually the entire financial community. Like the U.S. Cavalry in one of Turner's TNT epics, this new financing arrived just in time.

Restrictive covenants in the MGM junk bonds prevented Turner from paying his new cable partners cash dividends and forced him to issue them stock instead, with the likely prospect that Turner might eventually be forced to yield control of his company to Time Inc. and Tele-Communications. Randy Booth's new bank financing, however, allowed Turner to complete a restructuring of Turner Broadcasting's total debt, retiring $1.6 billion in junk bonds and preferred stock and replacing the remaining obligations with much lower-interest bank loans, debentures, and convertible stock. "Turner is now viewed," said Anne Lorsung, a senior bond analyst with money manager McCarthy, Crisanti & Maffei, "as a very strong credit within the high-yield universe. The cable operators' ownership position has actually helped to stabilize the credit. And Turner has proven he can run the company in a responsible manner."

"Turner Broadcasting has a great one-two combination," added Merrill Lynch's Igor Fuksman, who underwrote $200 million of Turner's new debt. "It combines the top creative programming team and the most financially astute operators in the cable TV business. That is quite a powerful alliance!"

Although Michael Milken was no longer involved, Drexel Burnham also participated in Turner's restructuring, replacing nearly $550 million of their old junk bonds with lower-interest senior subordinated debentures. "It's a synergy that sells," said a Drexel manager, who noted that the new Turner issue had been oversubscribed by more than three to one. This was quite a change from 1986, when Michael Milken had been forced to pawn off several hundred million dollars' worth of Turner preferred to Ivan Boesky because he couldn't find another buyer. Now one of Milken's greatest success stories, Turner remained intensely loyal, even after the discredited former king of junk had been indicted for insider trading. "If this guy ever goes to jail," Turner announced at the last predators' ball in 1988, "then I want to be right there in the cell next to him."

Without question Turner was once more on a roll. In 1988 TBS revenues approached $1 billion, and the company at last began generating surplus cash again. Turner continued to insist that the cable consortium's investment in his company had not been a bailout and pointed to TNT's explosive financial success, as well as the company's recent financial restructuring, as evidence that Turner Broadcasting was hardly dependent upon these operators.

In fact, the conflicting interests and Machiavellian maneuvers of his cable partners, who themselves were often at odds, sometimes prevented Turner from capitalizing on significant opportunities. When the chance arose to gain control of the troubled Financial News Network, Turner saw it as a natural complement to his two other news services. "Ted is impulsive," decreed Michael Fuchs, who had his own agenda as head of HBO. "Ted had only one speed—full speed ahead. But the board slows decisions down at the right times. It lends a balance. That is the reason Turner Broadcasting is in such terrific shape today." Fuchs and the other cable operators on Turner's board hinted they would invoke their power to veto any expenditure over $2 million. The Financial News Network acquisition never even came to a vote.

Turner chafed under these constraints but could brush off such rebuffs because he believed that ultimately he will either regain control of his board or convince the cable operators to go along with his ideas. He was no longer the unpredictable outsider, despite Michael Fuchs's observation, but an unquestioned industry leader who was learning the value of corporate governance. "I knew a lot of my partners pretty well before we came together," Turner says, containing his frustration admirably. "We may be moving a little bit slowly, but I'll guarantee you we're not going to make any major mistakes."

"In 1980," observed White House correspondent Bernard Shaw, "the politicians acted like they were meeting their commitment to charity by coming to the CNN booth and giving interviews." By 1984 things had begun to improve, and CNN had attained a measure of respectability, if not quite parity, with the three major broadcast networks. When the Democrats came to Atlanta in 1988, however, it was the major networks who began wringing their hands.

"We are the host hotel. The convention is being held in our building," said Ted Turner, barely able to contain himself, "and we will be the news network of record for the political process. We knew the convention was probably coming here when we bought the place."

In early July blue-and-white banners sprouted everywhere in downtown Atlanta. CNN's evolution from "Chicken Noodle Network" to rapidly expanding international news organization was nearly complete. An *American Politics* magazine poll in late 1987 showed that the publication's readers, mostly political professionals, preferred CNN over the broadcast networks by nearly two to one. Nancy Reagan admitted the only television she watched was CNN. Once banned from Number 10 Downing Street because Margaret Thatcher thought anything on cable must by definition be pornographic, CNN was now given regular, exclusive access to the British prime minister, who asked personally to be wired for the service.

"Normally we don't go around throwing a lot of big parties," Turner explained, "but since this is the first time a convention has been in Atlanta and since we are so involved, we thought it would be appropriate." He sounded almost casual describing the titanic CNN reception that would kick off the 1988 Democratic convention. To make certain nothing was left to chance, Turner hired Susan O'Neill, a professional events coordinator and daughter of House Speaker Tip O'Neill. As it turned out, CNN was the only news organization not covering the party, which drew the heads of all three broadcast networks, Governor Michael Dukakis and Senator Lloyd Bentsen, a slew of Hollywood celebrities, and every professional Democrat in the country. Turner and Ebaugh were evident everywhere that evening, but once he had performed his official duties as host, he and his lady shyly disappeared upstairs to his private quarters.

Unlike his father, who enjoyed playing host drunk or sober and was renowned for his generous and expansive hospitality, Ted Turner has always preferred either to monopolize the spotlight or make himself invisible. He will push a baseball around the bases with his nose in front of fifty-five thousand screaming fans at Fulton County Stadium, but he froze when Tom Belford asked him to host a Better World Society dinner. JJ Ebaugh was no more comfortable in such situations, although she had taught herself, with the help of Riane Eisler's "practical as well as theoretical caring," to speak publicly "at the drop of a handkerchief."

Forever on the road, Turner and Ebaugh managed to visit another twelve countries in less than six weeks during 1988 and then returned home only to find themselves gracing the cover of the November 1988 issue of *Atlanta* magazine. The photograph showed a radiant, smiling couple, but the magazine's cover line, THE WOMAN WHO TAMED TED TURNER, proved as fatal to JJ as a knife through her big heart. Turner had walked away from his marriage of twenty-three years, paid out more than $40 million in a staggering divorce settlement, the largest in Georgia's history, and even submitted himself to sometimes excruciatingly painful self-analysis, all because of JJ Ebaugh. Now he felt betrayed and disillusioned. Was this how JJ saw their partnership? Was this the way the world saw Ted Turner?

Not knowing whom to blame, Turner erupted in silent, smoldering anger. He did know, though, that nobody could ever tame Ted Turner. Two months after the *Atlanta* magazine had appeared, Turner and Ebaugh's relationship was, for all intents and purposes, over once again, and although they would continue to see each other, there would be no more mention of a "cosmic partnership." Turner indicated that he was ready now to throw himself headlong into a new commitment, any kind of new commitment—but clearly one that he would now undertake on his own. The contacts he had made through the Better World Society, as well as the access CNN provided him around the world, had begun to convince him that he might be uniquely qualified to assume the role of communicator/diplomat. Without portfolio, of course.

"I had a lot to do with Nicaragua," he declares. "I went down to Central America with the Better World Society. We met with the regional leaders and with [Costa Rica's president, Oscar] Arias, who was coordinating peace efforts. And we met with [Sandinista leader Daniel] Ortega. And we met with all the ambassadors. And sixty days later the war was over."

Turner's shoot-from-the-lip brand of diplomacy—short on discussions of superpower hegemony and the intricacies of missile throw-weights and long on an optimism bred of repeated successes in the business world—was not always so effective. Stepping into the middle of a shooting war between Iran and Iraq, Turner told his Iraqi friends, "Hey, guys. The rest of us are really concerned about you all, about people being killed over there. We think you've suffered enough. Sooner or later the war will be over. Why not just end it now?"

Undeterred by failure, Turner found it easy to state that "politics reacts to what people want, at least in democratic countries. Governments do not lead, they follow." And, of course, governments could always opt for Turner's third choice: Get out of the way!

"Governments are reactionary, all of them," he proclaimed. "If you're part of the government, then you've got to be loyal to the government. It's wonderful to have far-thinking, futuristic leaders. But they very, very seldom get elected—because you've got those who have a vested interest in continuation of the system, which is almost everyone in power. For everybody in business— almost everybody—the big thing is protecting the status quo. So, someone's got to be out there leading. In television, you can lead. You can initiate things. There's no way the U.S. government could have initiated, for example, the Goodwill Games."

Demonstrating the sort of initiative he believed a government incapable of, Turner introduced *World Report,* a weekly two-hour series that broadcast uncensored news and documentaries from all over the world. "Over one hundred countries participate in the news network in some form," Turner said. "We think of Maggie Thatcher and Gorbachev, but we never think that there's anything else going on in the world. The average American," he added, defining the problem, "doesn't know from squat."

The arch-conservative *National Review* called him a "Soviet apologist" and blasted *World Report* as blatant agit-prop. The liberal *Nation* castigated him as "a tool of right-wing fascists." But Turner persevered and began chairing communications seminars in Atlanta for all of the countries participating in his *World Report* projects, which proved to be a unique, uncensored window on Third World television programming. *World Report* also forged effective and invaluable relationships between Turner/CNN and local broadcast authorities around the world. While the major U.S. networks were cutting back international coverage, attempting frantically to hold on to their dwindling share of the American television news audience, Turner was busy arranging news feeds and distribution outlets for CNN wherever he could, laying the groundwork for the world's first truly global television network.

"I'm fifty," Turner said with a loud, melancholy moan when a reporter from *The Washington Post* reminded him of his birthday. "It's amazing how it sneaks up on you, isn't it? Seems like only yesterday I was younger." Ted Turner was acknowledging the passage of his first half century, somewhat ironically, in a hotel elevator going down, down, down. Fifty is a pretty good age, he was told by the reporter. "I'd rather be forty-two," Turner bellowed in his more southern-than-southern drawl. Crow's feet spread out now from the corners of his steel blue eyes. He hadn't lost a hair on his head, but it had gone snowy white, almost overnight.

"I did a lot of racing years ago," Turner reflected, "but I was always a hard worker and I wasn't just out on some yacht with a bunch of women. I was racing with men and racing across oceans and things. I was competing at the very highest levels of a very competitive and difficult sport. But racing is something you do on weekends. And I worked like the devil the rest of the time. If I were just dabbling, I would not be around now," said the man who was still very much around and feistier than ever. "The golden age of cable is dawning," Turner promised. "The golden age of the networks is already over, and they're struggling to try to hang on. If I have my way, I intend to kick their ass. That's what I want to do. I don't play to lose, and I'm not complacent."

The man who had already launched more television networks than anyone in history celebrated his fiftieth birthday by inviting the reporter back up to his hotel room, where they shared a box of chocolates the manager had sent up and watched *Indiana Jones and the Temple of Doom* on television. When the reporter jokingly suggested that this spartan celebration might be in keeping with the parsimonious paychecks Turner doled out to his hardworking CNN staffers, Turner replied, "I obviously must be paying them fairly well or nobody would be there." Then, to prove the years had not taken any of the sting out of his sharp tongue, he added, "We probably pay more than *The Washington Post* does. Newspapers are notoriously poor payers."

There was no limousine waiting downstairs when Turner dashed through the lobby the next morning and headed out into the street. There seldom was. Turner preferred to walk and, after twice asking directions, leaned into a brisk November wind and struck off toward the new Washington headquarters of the Better World Society. With the breeze blowing his raincoat up over the back of his head, Ted Turner looked as though he might actually be flying by the seat of his pants.

Although he had broken up with JJ Ebaugh after the *Atlanta* magazine cover story, their relationship was not entirely over. Ebaugh continued to divide her time between Atlanta and Big Sur and even today holds down a sinecure job at CNN. Turner still enjoyed JJ's company and appeared reluctant to plunge back into his old free-form bachelor existence. At a 1988 Better World Society awards dinner, however, his eye fell on Yue-Sai Kan, an exotic thirty-nine-year-old Chinese-born broadcaster whose weekly documentary series, "One World," presented a glimpse of Western life-styles to more than four hundred million viewers in mainland China. That was an audience, Turner noted enviously, at least ten times greater than CNN's. Kan was something of a celebrity throughout Asia and had appeared on hundreds of magazine covers before breaking into television in the early 1970s. She produced and starred in her own show for Central China Television. As Turner presented Kan with a Global Communications award, he asked with his characteristic indiscretion if she'd be interested in joining him after the dinner. Thus began what Kan says diplomatically was a "very nice, very pleasant relationship."

Kan, who had been born to a wealthy family in Guilin, China, worked eighteen hours a day and shared Turner's global sensibilities. They began dating almost immediately. "He was warm and sweet and childlike," Kan says. "There is something so endearing about the man." Turner would pick her up in his plane and fly down to one of his plantations. "Ted's all about what he's interested in," Kan notes objectively. "Not what anyone else is interested in. He's very passionate about his environment projects. But," she adds, "Ted is Ted. He's very self-centered. He adored his mother, probably more than anyone else. I don't think he was ever very devoted to his wife." Kan met all of Turner's children at one time or another and was immensely impressed by their southern manners. "I don't think," she adds, "Ted was all that close to any of them."

Yue-Sai Kan still has an affectionate spot in her heart for Turner, whom she considers "a visionary—what geniuses are made of." But two months after they met, she was swept off her feet by James McManus, a wealthy industrialist she married in 1990. Turner consoled himself by wringing time from his hectic schedule for Katherine Leach, a leggy, thirty-something interior designer whom he had brought in to redecorate his penthouse atop CNN Center. Not that Turner was considering tying himself down to one woman again any time soon. He asked Lori Henry, Better World Society's well-connected development director, to pull out her West Coast Rolodex. "I'll be in Los Angeles all next week," he told her, "and I'd like you to line up these ladies for me." Then he reeled off the names: Cybill Shepherd, Raquel Welch, and Jane Fonda.

Having spent years raising funds for advocacy organizations like Turner's Better World Society, Henry had unique access to an impressive range of Hollywood celebrities. But she was unable to elicit any interest from either Shepherd or Welch (who was a plaintiff in a breach of contract lawsuit against Turner and MGM/

UA). When Henry got Jane Fonda on the phone, however, the response was somewhat unexpected. "I'm sure Mr. Turner is a very nice man," Fonda told her, "and I would like to meet him. But I'm going through a terrible, terrible divorce right now and don't really want to see anyone. Perhaps he could call me back in about six months?"

Turner was not about to be dateless in Los Angeles and handed the ball to his assistant, Dee Woods, who immediately called Fonda back. Woods's great strength was gentle persuasion, and after nearly twenty years with Turner, she had learned never to come up empty-handed. It wasn't long before she was able to confirm to her boss that Jane Fonda would indeed be joining him. She had turned down dinner but agreed to be his guest at a fund-raising breakfast in Beverly Hills.

"He lives for romance," JJ Ebaugh once said of Turner. "But it's always *'C'est moi. C'est moi.'*"

As he flew west to meet the next great challenge in his life, Ted Turner might have wondered whether the truth of that assessment would ever really change.

Man came by to hook up my cable TV.
We settled in for the night, my baby and me.
We switched 'round and 'round 'til half-past dawn.
There were fifty-seven channels and nothing on.

Bruce Springsteen
57 Channels (And Nothin' On)

Chapter Fifteen

A Secret Service man put the radio telephone back in its holster, told the president to pull in his fishing line and buckle up, then slammed the Cigarette into high gear, sending the huge monohull racing boat slashing through the Atlantic back toward Walker's Point. Agents gathered around the television set at Surf Lodge, George Bush's magnificent old shingled mansion in Kennebunkport, Maine, had broadcast a "red alert." Over a million Chinese demonstrators were pouring into Beijing, and the whole damned thing was coming in live on CNN!

In his New York office, independent media consultant Reese Schonfeld was telling a reporter he felt CNN had the potential to become "the most important instrument of communication in the world." The thought of the network he had helped launch becoming so powerful, Schonfeld said, "was not a little frightening." Wistfully he added, "I didn't want to stay there forever, but I felt that for CNN to really work, I probably should have done one more three-year contract." The network's immediacy, Schonfeld believed strongly, was its heart and soul, and he longed for CNN to assume a more influential, even "dangerous," role in world affairs.

In Beijing four CNN correspondents, led by anchor Bernard Shaw, were broadcasting from a makeshift set in the midst of the formal Chinese garden behind Sheraton's Great Wall Hotel. The "flyaway" satellite earth station sending Shaw's image to CNN headquarters in Atlanta was positioned unobtrusively just a few feet away, out of sight of two Chinese "minders," who were arguing with Shaw on camera as one of the most dramatic news stories in television history began to unfold. It was Saturday morning in Beijing, early Friday evening in the United States. Most of Shaw's commentary was heard by Bush and his aides in Kennebunkport and White House and Pentagon officials in Washington, as well as senior Politburo members in the Kremlin and much of the rest of the Western world.

> Shaw: Overnight the capital of this great country did not sleep. People were in the streets throughout the night, as we were. . . . The troops just stood there as the people moved in. . . . I am being told that the Chinese government has closed the city of Beijing and no journalists are being allowed in. Unbelievably, we all came here to cover a summit and we walked into a revolution. We're being told that if we don't stop transmitting, the Chinese government will take our equipment. . . . President Bush is being quoted by reporters covering him in Maine, and it's being relayed to us. He is saying, "Word of the news blackout is very disturbing."

CNN cameras up on the hotel roof continued to pan across Tiananmen Square, teeming now with nearly 1.5 million student protesters, as hundreds of armed police and soldiers began to take up positions on the perimeters of the great space. Suddenly the television picture froze and Lou Walters, CNN's anchor in Atlanta, appeared on screen, blurting out a quick wrap-up of the situation, which he ended by concluding that the appearance of troops pouring into Tiananmen "does signal some sort of government movement on the students."

Then, just as suddenly, Bernard Shaw reappeared from Beijing. The blackout had been caused by a technical glitch in Atlanta, not by the Chinese censors. Alec Miran, CNN's field producer, was holding off the Chinese, telling them he was "powerless" to shut down Mr. Turner's network without "written authorization." One of the Chinese officials quickly collected his wits, produced a yellow legal pad, and scratched out in Chinese: "As an observer of the Ministry of Telecommunications of China, and according to the directive from the superiors . . . I am hereby announcing that CNN should stop the movable earth station and its transmitting frequencies right away. (Signed) Mr. Chou Ying Juing, 11:02, 20 May, 1989, Beijing Summer Time." Then the Chinese pulled the plug on CNN, ending the network's riveting coverage of its own reporters being thrown off the air.

"Karl Marx, Meet Marshall McLuhan," trumpeted *Newsweek*.

"An historic piece of television," said the *Orange County* (California) *Register*.

"CNN performed a great national and even international service," said former CBS News executive Fred Friendly.

With the whole world no longer watching, several thousand more riot police moved into Tiananmen behind hundreds of Russian-built M5 tanks and massacred hundreds, perhaps thousands, of unarmed citizen protesters. "A big, continuing story is the best thing that can happen for CNN," said Turner. "The China story was great. What we need is for the students here to riot." Then, after a pause, he decided he'd better add, "Of course, I'm just kidding."

A few months later Ted Turner was parading around the results of a new *Times Mirror* poll that showed CNN had become the "most believable" of any television network and ranked second only to *The Wall Street Journal* in terms of overall public confidence. Writing in the *Washington Journalism Review*, William Small, former NBC News president, said, "The three major broadcast networks' monopoly on national and world news is now a shattered memory."

"CNN has opened up a whole new communications system between governments," Marlin Fitzwater, White House press secretary, told *The New York Times*. "In many cases," he added, confirming the reality of Tiananmen, "it's the first line of communication we have." The CIA, embarrassed that their own intelligence continually lagged hours, and sometimes days, behind CNN's broadcasts, was forced to begin around-the-clock monitoring of the network and summarily junked plans initiated during the Reagan administration to develop its own private all-news/intelligence network. CNN, *The New York Times* reported, had become de rigueur for many heads of state, including King Hussein of Jordan, Margaret Thatcher of Great Britain, and Saudi

Arabia's King Fahd (who not only watched CNN incessantly, but often place middle-of-the-night calls to his Washington ambassador to discuss stories the network was covering).

A few months after Tiananmen, Turner became the first "entrepreneur" ever to win the Paul White Award of the Radio-Television News Directors Association, the highest honor in broadcast journalism. Paul White was the CBS News director who assembled the famous Ed Murrow team. The award would be only the first in the continuing series of honors Turner and CNN would soon be accorded. CNN's critics, led by Dick Salant of CBS News, had once wondered out loud how Turner could possibly find enough material to fill twenty-four hours. Now, the only empty table at the Paul White Awards presentation belonged to CBS News. "I was standing right next to Ted when he launched CNN," recalls Bill Daniels. "He turned to me and said, 'The day the world comes to an end, CNN will be there to cover it.' Now he's found so much news that he may not be able to make room for that story."

Once derided as "the little network that couldn't," CNN turned ten years old on June 1, 1990. In an incredibly short time, Turner's all-news network had become one of the most pervasive influences in U.S. television, reaching nearly sixty million homes across the country. CNN was also gaining considerable influence around the world. With 1,600 staffers and twenty-one bureaus stretching from Chicago to Cairo, from Moscow to Managua, CNN now aired in over one hundred countries. The network was daily enhancing its ability to play out the drama of breaking news anywhere. Some viewers were even beginning to receive a slightly customized CNN International broadcast originating in Europe, which mixed local news and weather reports with CNN's domestic feed from Atlanta. CNN was monitored in embassies and government ministries, and was now available in nearly two hundred thousand hotel rooms around the world. With over six million regular cable subscribers on the Continent, Turner was preparing an abbreviated version of CNN designed for local pickup by broadcasters in Greece, Spain, and Italy. A CNN test signal now beamed down on Korea, Taiwan, and most of Southeast Asia. CNN was also available in Japan, Australia, and New Zealand, giving Turner coverage on six continents and making CNN the first truly global network in history. In 1990, Turner arranged for an over-the-air CNN subscription service in Moscow. He considered CNN's international success especially important, since the news network would soon open the door to entertainment programming as well.

Despite all the accolades, however, CNN continued to cause controversy. Its success seemed to draw increasing critical fire, and too often much of the criticism may have been deserved. During CNN's live coverage of the U.S. invasion of Panama, for example, the network broadcast a 900 number so viewers could cast their votes, at $1.75 per ballot, regarding General Noriega's future prospects. Lack of firm direction at the top began to look like lack of vision when CNN paired a blond, breezy, and utterly inexperienced Texas judge, Catherine Crier, with the highly regarded Bernard Shaw to coanchor the network's prime-time evening news. Crier did nothing for CNN's ratings but wreaked havoc among staffers who still subscribed to Reese Schonfeld's old mantra "The News Is the Star." Crier eventually proved herself on the air, but was hardly missed in 1992 when she jumped to ABC as Diane Sawyer's backup.

A struggle was already under way, however, for the very soul of Ted Turner's indomitable news machine. As the network began its second decade, it was transition time at CNN. Burt Reinhardt had judiciously taken the reins from Reese Schonfeld in 1982 and guided the operation well into the black. But Reinhardt was now seventy years old and near retirement. Speculation was rife regarding his successor, and Turner did little to quiet the rumors. Four senior CNN executives—Paul Amos, Ed Turner, Jon Petrovich, and Lou Dobbs—lobbied hard for Reinhardt's job and, with it, the opportunity to implement their personal visions of what CNN should look like in the 1990s. Bob Wussler might also have been in the running, but he used up most of his chips with Turner when he became involved in a nasty punch-out with Bill Bevins. Wussler later resigned to become president of the ill-fated COMSAT Video Enterprises.

Turner knew CNN was well positioned for the coming age of information, but he was equally aware of rapidly intensifying competition for CNN's audience. Solidly profitable by 1985, CNN was now generating more than $350 million in annual revenues and nearly $150 million in operating profits. When Turner talked about CNN's future, he did not suggest great changes in either format or operations. "Five years from now," he said, "I don't anticipate CNN will look appreciably different on screen than it does now." His primary focus was on enhancing CNN's ability to go live anywhere in the world, and this he expected to accomplish

344

simply by adding more bureaus and staffing up such key branches
as Washington and London.

If that was what Turner wanted, insiders knew, that was very
probably what would be. Cable consortium or no, Ted Turner was
still running the show. The drive over the past few years to take
CNN international and the formation of the network's new inves-
tigative team had come straight from the top. "Ted Turner *is* the
CNN strategic planning department. Period," declared Lou
Dobbs.

NBC's Bob Wright was smarting from embarrassment after
CNN severely trounced NBC News with superior coverage of the
early hours of the San Francisco earthquake. CNN's outstanding
coverage of Hurricane Hugo, the invasion of Panama, the fall of
the Berlin Wall, and Tiananmen Square all sent tremors rippling
throughout the television news industry. But the attention CNN
was beginning to attract helped blur the network's immediate
future. Ratings had stagnated at around .7, and Turner knew
CNN would require continued investment and new leadership if
the network was going to realize its potential as a world-class
news machine.

In London, Rupert Murdoch's new satellite-delivered Sky News
offered CNN the sincerest form of flattery—an out-and-out imita-
tion of Turner's around-the-clock news operation, with graphics,
studio design, and anchor personalities clearly inspired by the
CNN originals. Launched in 1990, Sky News represented a serious
potential competitor to CNN. Drawing on its formidable global
newsgathering resources, the British Broadcasting Corporation
soon joined Turner and Murdoch with its own international television news service.

"The perception abroad," suggested Peter Vesey, managing director of CNN International, "had always been that CNN was
very American." Vesey attempted to make CNN more "European" by greenlighting extended coverage of events with particular relevance overseas, employing more European anchors, and
building up a specialized staff in Atlanta to package international
stories. Vesey introduced an evening business news segment prepared in conjunction with London's *Financial Times* and, on
Turner's instructions, implemented a policy of providing CNN
gratis to any head of state requesting the service. Over one
hundred governments took advantage of the offer. Most had CNN
installed in their intelligence service offices as well. By 1990, more

than 150 foreign broadcast systems had also become paying subscribers, extending CNN's reach to more than forty million additional viewers outside the United States.

With one Gucci-clad foot resting delicately on a large glass globe
that sat in the middle of the floor, Turner welcomed yet another
bevy of reporters into his Atlanta offices for the obligatory interview on CNN's tenth anniversary. Emulating Charlie Chaplin in
The Great Dictator, Turner flipped his dark-blue-and-red Atlanta
Braves tie back and forth and spun the globe around with such
nervous energy that he himself appeared to be in perpetual motion. "I've said this a million times," he began almost without
exaggeration. "I felt a responsibility to find out what's going on
in the world. That's why I started CNN. Prior to that, I wasn't
really into the news. I followed it in a cursory fashion, but I was
into winning sailboat races and," he added, cracking a barely
perceptible smile, "into raising my five small children." Not one
of the reporters blinked, so he kept right on. "Then I started looking into what was going on. Any questions?"

He had staged the same show at least a hundred times and was
aware that it was his remarkable delivery and not necessarily
what he had to say that made these little sessions such compelling
theater. Several months earlier he had turned this same stump
speech into a veritable second coming when he wooed and won
once again some of Hollywood's most powerful TV and film executives. Turner had used the occasion of a Bel-Air Hotel breakfast
meeting to announce his intention of becoming a major Hollywood producer. Again. Everyone in the room knew in intimate
detail how he had been taken apart and put together again by
Kirk Kerkorian and Michael Milken. "The last time you saw me,"
Turner admitted, "I came out here with a load of cash and left in
a barrel."

But this time Turner was making Hollywood an offer it couldn't
refuse: a free ticket for frustrated talent to make the movies most
of the majors wouldn't touch. "Ted's Better World Society," explained TNT executive Linda Berman, "dealt with the environment, nuclear waste, homelessness, and hunger. We are going to
translate some of those concerns into dramatic ideas. We intend
to establish our niche as an alternative programmer."

Two years later, Turner Pictures was hardly a major studio, but

Turner had become one of the most active producers in Hollywood, even if his studio happens to be in Atlanta, and was churning out nearly two pictures a month.

Turner's movies were made for television on budgets that were considered miserly against an average negative cost of over $22 million for theatrical features. But he began to invest more than $150 million a year in production, augmenting that total with elaborate (and expensive) coproduction deals with partners like Italy's RAI Television. He also financed pet projects like Isabella Rossalini's long-delayed documentary about her mother, Ingrid Bergman. And when production head, Scott Sassa, arranged for Jane and Peter Fonda to narrate a retrospective on their father, Turner himself showed up at a breakfast meeting to negotiate a final contract with the famous actor's daughter.

Bob Wussler believes Turner "had been captivated right from their first meeting at Pat Medavoy's benefit breakfast in Beverly Hills." But the Jane Fonda he met that day at breakfast was all business and oblivious to the attention he directed her way. Hardly the kind of impression Turner was used to making. And now, at their second meeting, Jane merely wanted to ensure that the film on her father was actually going to be made.

When he asked for a real date, Turner came up empty. Even the prospect of meeting again to discuss her father's film yielded only a couple of impersonal business dinners. If Turner was smitten, he kept his feelings well hidden and went about his business, which those days continued to include Kathy Leach, his Atlanta decorator.

Fonda had been stunned by the discovery that her husband had fallen in love with Vickie Rideout, a thirty-one-year-old Harvard-educated speech writer for presidential candidate Michael Dukakis. She had been so preoccupied with the breakup of her marriage that she barely even remembers those first few meetings with Ted Turner.

The prospect of divorce had been enough to send Fonda back into therapy. "I never thought I'd see the day," she said, thinking of the years she had already spent in counseling. "It's so Hollywood." She also visited Dr. Frank Kramer, the Beverly Hills plastic surgeon who had lifted several years off her face in 1987. This time, she spent another $5,000 having her upper and lower eyelids lifted. She went next to Dr. Norman Leaf for two small C-cup silicone implants, emerging with renewed self-esteem and an impressive new bustline. Then Jane Fonda did what she could to jump-start her life. Indulging in a brief fling with a blond Hollywood hairdresser named Baron Matalon, she next became involved with Lorenzo Caccialonza, a strapping Italian muscleman in his mid-thirties. Lorenzo turned out to be exactly what the doctor ordered. Since Turner continued to be preoccupied elsewhere, Fonda allowed him to spirit her off to the Caribbean, where she was able to unveil her impressive new figure at a topless beach on St. Bart's.

In 1979 Jane Fonda won an Academy Award nomination as Best Actress for her role in *The China Syndrome* as the crusading television reporter investigating the meltdown of a nuclear power station. Less than a month after the movie opened, life imitated art when one of the reactors on Three Mile Island blew, triggering a national debate about nuclear safety. Nearly ten years later, a two-man TBS camera team huddled on the shoulder of a two-lane highway about a mile south of Middletown, Pennsylvania. Denied access to the nearby Three Mile Island nuclear power facility, they could shoot only from outside while TBS reporter/producer Sharon Collins toured the plant.

"Ted Turner came up with the idea for 'Network Earth,' a weekly half-hour TBS series." The TBS team talked to residents in a low-income neighborhood in nearby Harrisburg, then interviewed Jane Lee, whose farm near Middletown had been in her family for two hundred years and provided a clear sightline to the Three Mile Island cooling towers. They also taped local veterinarian Robert Webber, who reported the birth of a horse with five legs shortly after the 1979 blowout.

"Man needs to make peace both with himself and with the other inhabitants on this planet," Ted Turner had said. "It's a matter of survival. And it's a matter of good business." In 1970 WTCG had just fifty employees. By 1990 Turner Broadcasting employed more than four thousand people in twenty-five cities throughout the world. Turner's little Atlanta UHF television station had already spawned four major broadcast networks, reaching tens of millions of viewers on six continents. By 1989 Turner Broadcasting revenues had increased nearly one hundred–fold, to just over $1 billion. With success now measured in hundreds of millions of profit dollars, and his company on solid financial footing for perhaps the first time in twenty years, Turner could set about redefining his company's mission. Henceforth, he declared, Turner

Broadcasting would inform, educate, and entertain. The order of priority was hardly incidental and represented a policy Turner had been following informally for nearly a decade.

Long considered a zealot without a cause, Turner was described by Dan Schorr as a "bundle of contradictions who does not fit any ideological stereotype and who speaks in generally conservative terms about the economy and domestic affairs." This was the Turner who could declare ominously during his bid for CBS that "the greatest enemies America has ever had—posing a greater threat to our way of life than Nazi Germany or Tojo's Japan—are the three major television networks and the people who run them, who are living amongst us and constantly tearing down everything that has made this country great." By 1990, Turner was ready to announce a new personal political philosophy: "I'm a conservative liberal," he declared. "I'm liberally conservative. Like Jesus, I've made my peace with the Soviets. They're not my enemies."

Speaking in Colorado before John Denver's Windstar Foundation, Turner offered his listeners a new epiphany: "It was a terrible realization for me to come to," Turner admitted, "because no one loves our country more than I. But I have come to the conclusion from studying it, from a global circumstance, that *we* are the greatest problem in the world." He still considered himself "a great patriotic American," but Ted Turner said he was now ready to concede that "the national interest today is subservient to the international interest."

The far right, once enamored of Turner's attacks on the networks and Hollywood, was left speechless. *The National Review* called Turner "a poor man's Armand Hammer, who has absorbed too many ideas from friends, including Castro and Gorbachev." Fairness in Media spokesman James Cain could only add: "Turner's no Jesse Helms and he's certainly not a Ronald Reagan conservative."

Turner confused even his new admirers on the left, however, when he decided to hold a Better World Society meeting in Beijing, China. Bringing along Katherine Leach, Turner indicated this meeting might be Better World's last hurrah. Nevertheless, Glenn Olds, the society's new director general, and his executive director, Vicki Martell, planned an itinerary that would take them out in style.

The somber Better World delegation trekked from the Great Wall to the China Family Planning Institute to the Economics

Ministry and then on to a whirlwind round of official dinners, each punctuated by endless toasts of lethal Chinese cognac. Turner remained on his best behavior until a final luncheon at Beijing's Foreign Press Association, when he suddenly reverted to form. It had been just a little over a year since Tiananmen, and the two hundred or so members of the Beijing-based Western media were suffering under one of the tightest news blackouts in recent memory. As Turner rose to speak, they were more than a little ready to kick back and enjoy some fireworks.

"The first thing I want to tell you guys," he began, "is that you can call yourselves foreign correspondents. Well, none of my bureau people here and none of my people in Atlanta are allowed to use the word *foreign.* 'Foreign' means alien, like ET. You guys should call yourselves the International Press Club, or international correspondents, or something. Anything but 'foreign.' My own people bet me five dollars I wouldn't tell you what a horrible name you have. So there, I've said it. And now I'm five dollars richer.

"I also want to tell you I'm not speaking as chairman of the Better World Society. And I'm not speaking as chairman of CNN, either. I talk as 'Citizen Ted' here, so you can ask me anything you want. I just might not give you any answers."

The roomful of reporters kept him going for over an hour, jotting down quotable quotes from Turner on everything from the Braves' latest losing streak to world peace, the environment, and the population explosion. Then, inadvertently, Turner dropped the bomb. In reply to a question about the tragedy of Tiananmen Square, he said, "Beijing's students were breaking the law. We bleed in our hearts for the students. We also bleed for the government and the soldiers who felt like they were forced to take that action." Two hundred mouths fell open, all at once. Someone asked if he could repeat what he had just said. Turner plunged in again: "The students should have known better, don't you think? They had been warned."

"Tiananmen Ted" made headlines all over the world the next day. And after several rounds of apologies to Chinese exiles and students residing in the United States, Turner Broadcasting people in Atlanta and Better World people in Washington and New York simply gave up, waiting for Turner himself to come home and explain what he had meant. Of course, he did explain. And explain. And explain. He'd been misunderstood, misinterpreted, misquoted. He met with delegations of outraged Chinese exchange students. And then, because he was Ted Turner, it all seemed to blow over. "When you travel with Ted," explained Vicki Martell, "you get used to that kind of thing. It's just part of the package. He certainly doesn't mean to offend anyone."

No one who has spent much time with Turner can fault his sincerity; the worst he can be accused of is an occasional and often abominable lack of tact. His words sometimes get so far ahead of his mouth, they seem to have a will of their own. "On the surface, there's still the same bluster," *Forbes* magazine was moved to report, "the same habit of getting your attention with seemingly outrageous statements. But you sense also that success has strengthened [Ted Turner's] confidence and his destiny as a man who will help change the world."

This man's destiny, sad to say, includes inflicting the Wild Samoans, two of Ted Turner's less lofty idealists, on an unsuspecting world. The Samoans are a professional wrestling tag team that fosters the notion that Samoans, every last one of whom is a U.S. citizen, are large, inherently violent Neanderthals. The Wild Samoans, together with the Cuban Assassin, Norman the Lunatic, and Abdullah the Butcher, perform for Turner under the aegis of World Champion Wrestling, an entity he acquired in 1989. WCW matches appear four hours weekly on TBS, another three hours weekly in syndication, and on several pay-per-view extravaganzas each year. The one woman featured on World Champion Wrestling is a professional manager known only as "Woman." She's not too bright, but she's got a body that doesn't quit and a costume that quits a little too soon. Woman heralds a show that is long on graphic and gratuitous violence, ethnic and racial stereotyping, sexist titillation, and naked hostility—brought to you by the man who believes in "doing well by doing good.

"I am desperately trying to hook the world together as quickly as possible, so we can share all the information and wisdom of our brilliant scientists and businessmen," Turner will say with an absolutely straight face. "I want to help the people who are working hard to improve relations between the nations of this earth so the world can come together. We want to look to the future—not the past. We need more cultural exchanges, scientific exchanges, satellite exchanges. And," he adds, "athletic events." But don't confuse Turner with Hearst, McCormick, Beaverbrook, or even Murdoch, exploiters all, who sought the lowest common denominator. Turner is sincere in his efforts to raise the level of broadcast quality. But, hey, Ted Turner would remind you, "rassling fans are humans, too!"

Turner makes three or four speeches a month and sometimes books that many in a single week. The American Speakers Bureau ranks him right behind Ted Koppel of "Nightline" as the speaker college audiences most want to hear. He commands a lofty $25,000–$35,000 per appearance but often foregos his fee or makes sure it ends up in some charitable coffer. His personal appearances are much like those of a man running for office, except that Turner doesn't have to run for anything. He just wants to spread the word. If he didn't, he might actually have to spend time writing memos or reading business plans, or worse, dealing with the byzantine machinations of his cable partners on the Turner board.

Turner continued trying again to hook up with Jane Fonda throughout the spring of 1989. But she was oblivious and had taken herself on the road. Having cavorted her way across Europe with Lorenzo Caccialonza, she was now, in fact, standing face to face with his mother in Milan. As much as Fonda might have wanted something to happen, however, it was simply not to be. Mama Caccialonza put her foot down, telling Lorenzo that the fifteen-year age difference between them was simply too much. *Finito la musica!*

Upon her return to Los Angeles, Fonda was finally able to wrap up a bitter $10 million divorce settlement with Tom Hayden. Turner continued to press himself upon her but was growing impatient when Fonda failed to respond to his repeated overtures. As a result, he found himself spending time with Gabrielle (Gay) Manigault, the daughter of his South Carolina friend and neighbor, newspaper publisher Peter Manigault. A pretty brunette easily young enough to be his daughter, Manigault was considerably more sophisticated and unquestionably less inhibited than most of his previous ladies. When Gay Manigault turned up on Ted's arm at a Better World Society dinner in Boston, the tabloids had a field day.

While Turner consoled himself with Ms. Manigault, it was Fonda who remained aloof, attempting to wean herself from public involvement with her ex-husband by reclaiming her persona as a political crusader. She took over Hayden's Campaign for

Economic Democracy, renamed it the Campaign California, and began making fund-raising appearances as a member of its executive committee. "I was a political woman before I met Tom," she explained. "I think I will be a political woman the rest of my life. I am much more interested in issues than in candidates."

Eventually she began work again with her production partner, Lois Bonfiglio, on two important film projects—Neil Sheehan's Pulitzer Prize–winning Vietnam chronicle, *A Bright Shining Lie*, and an American version of Pedro Almodóvar's *Women on the Verge of a Nervous Breakdown*. First, however, Fonda had to deal with a more immediate issue—the presence, once again, of a very persistent, very interested Ted Turner. On this particular occasion the impatient media mogul had broken off a business meeting in downtown Los Angeles to cool his heels out front in the office of her Beverly Hills exercise studio, waiting for her to finish a workout session.

"The idea of Ted ever waiting for anyone," says Bob Wussler, "is absolutely preposterous. Ted is the kind of guy where if you flew into the airport with him and you had a bag checked and he didn't, he wouldn't wait for you. He'd go ahead and take a taxi."

But after two failed marriages Ted Turner was finally determined to get it right. From his point of view, says one of Fonda's close friends, "Jane was serious and smart and beautiful and passionate, and that's a very powerful energy when it comes together." Turner was also clearly attracted, as Vadim and Hayden before him had been, by Fonda's unique Hollywood star power.

"Turner knows how to treat a lady," a longtime friend of Fonda's told the *Los Angeles Times*. "It's that old-fashioned southern kind of stuff—gifts and caring. Tom was not good at all that. Turner acknowledges her in public. Jane responds to all that chivalry. Tom couldn't acknowledge her. I remember Jane would sit next to Tom sometimes and place his arms around her so it would look like they were together. Turner's one of the most interesting, fascinating, globally thinking people she's ever encountered."

"I think what intrigues everyone about them," adds another Fonda associate, "is that they're equals. Given who they are, the probability of them each being with an equal is pretty unlikely."

"If you're a strong, famous woman," says Fonda herself, "it's not easy to find a man who doesn't feel threatened."

Turner was not only not threatened, he happened also to be the younger man Fonda had apparently been looking for, although the age difference between them amounted only to eleven months.

Turner and Fonda also shared strikingly similar backgrounds. Both suffered the loss of a parent by suicide, and both were certified overachievers, driven by fathers who never seemed satisfied. Turner often described himself as growing up in a family that "thought Roosevelt and Truman were communists." As a young woman Fonda had been an active America Firster and actually served as Miss Army Recruiting in 1962. Now both were on the cutting edge of a new liberal humanism.

Jane Seymour Fonda was second-generation Hollywood aristocracy, born into wealth and fame but fated to spend much of her life searching for an identity she could call her own. Named after King Henry VIII's third wife, Lady Jane Seymour, and called "Lady" by her coolly dispassionate father, Fonda was destined to be a high-strung thoroughbred. Her father's Italian ancestors had emigrated to America early in the nineteenth century and founded the town of Fonda, New York, before heading west to Omaha, Nebraska, where Henry Fonda was born. Her mother, Frances Seymour Brokaw, was descended from Horatio Seymour, a New York governor who lost in his bid for the White House in 1872 to General Ulysses S. Grant. When she was twenty-one, Frances married George T. Brokaw, an immensely wealthy New York lawyer who proceeded to drink himself to death four years later. Within twelve months, however, Frances was back at the altar; in the most spectacular society wedding of the 1935 season she married Henry Fonda "of motion pictures," as *The New York Times* delicately put it.

With a four-year-old daughter from her marriage to George Brokaw, Frances desperately wanted a son and did little to conceal her disappointment when Jane was born on December 21, 1937. Jane was handed over at birth to a stiffly proper governess who followed Frances's orders that anyone coming into physical contact with the infant must wear a surgical mask. Holding the baby was discouraged, kissing strictly forbidden. Rejected by her mother, Jane turned for love and affection to a father who had become almost wholly consumed by his own burgeoning career. Henry Fonda would prove as unresponsive to his own daughter as Ed Turner was toward his son and namesake. Neither Fonda nor Turner ever graduated from college, although both possess relatively high IQs (his is 128; hers is 132) and both attended a succession of expensive private boarding schools.

"As a young girl," Jane Fonda recalls, "most of my dreams evolved from the basic need of being loved." When Jane's brother,

Peter, was born, Frances smothered him with the affection she'd never given her daughter. Jane tried to win her mother over by dressing like a boy, in boots and jeans. She was even sent home once from the exclusive Greenwich Academy in Connecticut when she fractured her arm fighting with a boy who had made fun of her prepubescent figure.

When Jane was twelve, Henry Fonda announced he was leaving Frances for Susan Blanchard, the twenty-one-year-old stepdaughter of Oscar Hammerstein. Her mother wished Henry well in his new marriage, checked herself in and out of several private sanitariums, and finally locked herself in her bathroom at Craig House in Beacon, New York, where she slit her throat from ear to ear.

It was at Emma Willard, an elite but austere girls school near Troy, New York, that Jane first began the daily ritual of binge-and-purge eating known as bulimia. After every meal she would routinely induce vomiting by sticking her finger down her throat in a dangerous routine she continued almost daily until she was thirty-seven years old.

Fonda somehow made it through her freshman year at Vassar, but her classroom attendance suffered when she began spending long periods in New Haven with a handsome Yale senior named James Franciscus. At the end of her sophomore year Jane left Vassar for Paris, where she fell in with the expatriate American crowd hanging out in the offices of the *Paris Review*. Summoned back to New York for her father's fourth wedding, Fonda studied piano at the famed Mannes School, painting at the Art Students League, and, at the suggestion of her friend Susan Strasberg, acting at the famed Actors Studio. "Lee Strasberg stopped me and said he saw a tremendous amount of talent. Nobody had ever told me that I was good at anything. That absolutely changed my life."

Fonda also signed on as a Ford model and almost immediately became one of New York's top cover girls. While she was still studying at Actors Studio, producer-director Josh Logan signed her to a five-year, five-picture contract, and paired her with Tony Perkins in her first movie, Warner Brothers' *Tall Story*.

The Eisenhower era was still in full flower, and Fonda's appealing natural beauty was out of favor in the age of plastic. "Jack Warner, the head of the studio, sent a message to the set," Fonda recalls, "that I had to wear falsies because you couldn't become a movie star unless you were full-breasted." Hardly mincing words, Warner had added: "She's got a good future if you dye her hair blond, break her jaw and reshape it, and get her some silicone shots or falsies."

"I just assumed these men were the experts," Fonda later admitted, "so I allowed myself to be changed. That was the standard being laid out for you as a woman, as to what you were supposed to look like all the time."

Warner's publicity machine worked overtime to establish Jane Fonda as their most promising newcomer. They needn't have bothered, since the media were instantly enthralled by this implicitly sensual, articulate, and outspoken young actress.

By the end of 1960 Fonda had been on the cover of *Look* and *Life* and profiled in *Time*. Offered the lead in Arthur Laurents's *Invitation to a March* on Broadway, Fonda was still not committed to an acting career. She was, however, fiercely determined to prove herself to her father. But when the sister of a close friend committed suicide during the out of town tryouts for *Invitation*, Fonda was devastated and unable to continue. She admitted to frequent thoughts of her own suicide. "I always think about it," she revealed later. "But I never would do it. I'm telling you I value my life too much. I think I'm too important."

Roger Vladimir Plemiannikov, better known as Roger Vadim, the sexual Svengali who first bedded Brigitte Bardot, Annette Stroyberg, and Catherine Deneuve, had spotted Jane Fonda in 1958 during her first visit in Paris. Five years later she was back in Paris again, preparing to star in Vadim's new film, *La Ronde*. He was thirty-five, ten years older than Fonda and with two children. But Fonda saw Vadim as a mentor who might convince her of her talent.

Once they had wrapped *La Ronde*, Fonda and Vadim moved in together. Fonda found herself in Russia twenty years before Ted Turner would make his first trip, but their initial reactions were almost identical. "I couldn't believe it," she said. "All my life I'd been brought up to believe the Russians were some alien, hostile people sitting over there just waiting to swallow up America. Nothing could be further from the truth."

Ironically, Henry was the only Fonda who seemed even remotely aware of politics. He campaigned hard and long for John Kennedy in 1960. Like Turner, Jane slept through the civil rights movement, the Cuban missile crisis, the assassinations of John and Robert Kennedy, and America's growing involvement in Vietnam. Parisians were taking to the streets almost every day, but "la BB Americaine" was hard-pressed to defend her country among Vadim's coterie of French intellectual friends, many of whom were socialists and communists or left-wing sympathizers like Jean-Luc Godard, Yves Montand, and Simone Signoret. In their view the United States was not much more than an imperial aggressor. It would be another four years before her own political awakening, but already Jane was rapidly becoming aware of how little she knew about her own country. When she began to articulate her doubts about the sincerity of Lyndon Johnson's motives in Southeast Asia, her comments were picked up by *The Los Angeles Times*. "Daughter?" Henry Fonda responded. "I don't have a daughter."

A decade of therapy brought Fonda to the realization that she must compete with her father, become an even greater star, and thus win him over. Out of the blue she announced that she was going to marry Vadim. "I guess because of my father. I knew I was hurting him." The news came as a surprise to Vadim, but he took it in stride and somewhat reluctantly agreed to go along with her whim.

"No one ever walks out on a Fonda," her father had always told her.

"She will leave you," Vadim's mother predicted.

Jane signed the bridal register "Lady Jane Seymour Brokaw Fonda Plemiannikov," the name she would proudly use for the next eight years on her passport, contracts, and all other official documents. Henry Fonda had not been invited to the bizarre Las Vegas ceremony and had to read the next day's *Los Angeles Times* to discover that his daughter had finally made an honest woman of herself.

Fonda and Vadim quickly retreated back to France, where they converted a quiet old farmhouse in the little village of Saint Ouen-Marchefrois, some forty miles west of Paris, into a center of serious filmmaking and a hotbed of radical political discussion. Two of Vadim's closest friends, novelist Roger Vailland and his wife, Elisabeth, came to exert a profound influence on Fonda, both sexually and politically. The Vaillands had emerged from World War II devout communists, and both were also in the front lines of a new sexual revolution. The Vaillands felt that extramarital sex was part of a husband's marital duty, and Fonda did not object when Vadim began bringing home his own lovers. On the contrary, "Jane eagerly complied, seeming to understand and, as always, went all out—all the way," he said.

Fonda has never denied this. And, no longer frightened of hav-

ing a child, she began to hear her biological clock ticking. Thus it was, as she neared her thirtieth birthday, that she announced to Vadim she was three months pregnant with a baby girl.

Awaiting the birth of her daughter, Fonda found her social conscience heightened and began to take an active interest in world affairs for perhaps the first time in her life. "I began to love people," Fonda says. "To understand we don't give life to a human being only to have it killed by a B-52's bombs, or jailed by fascists, or destroyed by social injustice." The Vaillands introduced her to their friend Vanessa Redgrave, who had evolved from an English Socialist into a vehemently anti-American Trotskyite. The two young second-generation film stars quickly became close friends, with Redgrave an enthusiastic catalyst in Fonda's conversion to radical politics.

Politics couldn't have been further from his mind at the time, but Ted Turner was in the process of changing his own life forever. He had set out two years earlier aboard *Vamp X*, his thirty-eight-foot sloop, to compete in his first transatlantic ocean race. He had never crossed an ocean before, but he had assembled a ragtag crew that included Jimmy Brown and John Tuzo, a clubfooted retired ship's captain, and he was determined to win the 3,600-mile race to Copenhagen. "Mr. Ted likes to win," Jimmy Brown said in the understatement of his life. "No way he likes being a loser."

"The first night out," remembers Skip Ryder, another crew member, "gigantic waves broke, submerging the whole boat under three feet of water. For a minute I thought we were sunk. Everybody's eyes got real wide, including Turner's."

Heading north along the Great Circle route, Turner tried to skirt the iceberg lanes but soon ran into cold, heavy weather. Ryder suffered a concussion while changing a spinnaker and went into convulsions. Jimmy Brown began to radio for help, but Turner shouted him down and kept going. "Don't bother," Turner yelled over the storm. "We're going to bury him at sea." Jimmy Brown wasn't sure the boss was joking.

"There was ice forming everywhere," Jimmy recalled, "and we had to chip it off. It was really chilly down below, because a fiberglass boat doesn't hold any heat. Everything got real hectic —know what I'm talking about? Mr. Ted kept having to go up the mast all the time to fix things. We had this conference in the cockpit, and there was quite a debate about who would go up. Everybody said, 'Not me, not me.' "

Radio reports had *Vamp X* leading the entire fleet at the halfway point. Turner was ecstatic and began pushing even harder. "After it looked like we would have a lot of wind all through the race," Jimmy Brown related, "Mr. Ted ordered everybody to take a shower to lighten the boat. That left us with only a gallon of water, and I had to mix the dehydrated food with seawater— know what I'm talking about? It tasted horrible. Mr. Ted made everybody eat it, but it just made you thirstier still."

The main boom broke and had to be jury-rigged. Jimmy Brown was kept busy mending torn sails and repairing other broken gear. Ryder was still weakened by his concussion, and the rest of the crew was almost too seasick to work. Turner took most of the watches by himself and, for twenty more days, hauled himself up the mast to fix broken lines. He changed sails singlehandedly, remained at the helm for day-long stretches, and finally, against all odds and obvious common sense, blew into Copenhagen nearly forty-eight hours ahead of his nearest competitor.

When Jane Fonda sought her brother's opinions about Vietnam, the industry's newest leather-jacketed antihero had nothing to say in his country's defense. Espousing the new credo of sex, drugs, and rock 'n' roll, Peter Fonda's role in *Easy Rider* was about to make him the idol of America's alienated youth. Jane continued her binge-and-purge routine, augmented by diet pills and Valium to calm her nerves, but Peter was tripping daily on some of the same chemical substances. His, however, were hardly the prescription variety. Reflecting his generation's general distrust of the establishment and violent opposition to the Vietnam War, Peter left Jane convinced that her French critics might be right about America.

On July 28, 1968, Jane Fonda gave birth to her first child, named after her friend Vanessa Redgrave. "When Vanessa was born," Fonda related, "it was as if the sun had opened up for me. I felt whole, I became free." Less than six months later, however, she would announce, "I wasted the first thirty-two years of my life," and began making up for that lost time with a vengeance. Introducing Vadim to Andy Warhol's Factory and the even more uninhibited Hollywood crowd orbiting around Roman Polanski, Sharon Tate, and millionaire hairstylist Jay Sebring, Fonda experimented with mind-bending hallucinogens for the first time and became mildly addicted to marijuana. She began expanding her sexual horizons, testing Vadim's commitment to sexual equality, sometimes even bringing home servicemen fresh from tours of duty in Vietnam. She also cut off her hair. "I always had a deep-rooted psychological need to be a boy," she explained. "Now I am one."

On New Year's Eve 1969, Jane Fonda stepped off a plane at New York's JFK and was told she had just won the New York Film Critics award as Best Actress for *They Shoot Horses, Don't They?* A little before ten that evening she sat down with Rex Reed in her father's brownstone on East Seventy-fourth Street and began a long, rambling interview for *The New York Times* that would presage a new Jane Fonda. "You don't mind if I turn on?" she asked Reed, opening a little silver snuff box and expertly finger-rolling a joint with the fine gray hash she brought back from—where? India, Morocco, Nepal? Fonda really couldn't remember.

"We were the sloth generation," she told Reed, describing her 1950s contemporaries. "Now the kids are active. Take a simple thing like turning on. Doctors, lawyers, politicians—I don't know anyone who doesn't turn on. Except maybe in the South. I guess the South is still fifty years behind."

For nearly ninety minutes, according to Reed, she talked nonstop, about the speed-reading courses she was taking, the auto-hypnosis classes she hoped would help her end her three-pack-a-day cigarette habit, and her relationship with Vadim. "We are very friendly," she said, "with all my husband's wives and mistresses. He has taught me how to live, and if anything ever happens to our marriage, he'll always be my friend. Forever," she added ominously, "is a very difficult word." About her father she said, "I don't understand him, but I love him. You must admit my father, with the kind of image he had, produced peculiar offshoots. He's always been the all-American liberal Democratic good solid citizen—look at all the presidents and senators he's played—and here his son is, a pot-smoking hippie, whatever that means. And his daughter—I don't know what she is!"

As fireworks began exploding over Central Park, Fonda heard her father and his new young bride, his fifth, Shirlee Mae Adams, coming up the stairs. She leapt up and began waving her arms frantically to dissipate the pot smoke, then helped her father welcome in the New Year with a cold bottle of Dom Pérignon.

On March 8, 1970, Jane Fonda was arrested by military police at a Native American protest rally inside Fort Lawson, near Seattle, Washington. Thus began a decade of militant protest that threatened not only her popularity, but her film career. While in Seattle she become acquainted with Fred Gardner's antiwar GI coffeehouses. Since she knew little about the war, or the Black Panthers, or the feminist movement, or the farm workers, or welfare mothers, or any of the other grass-roots causes that were beginning to boil to the surface of American politics, Fonda decided to reacquaint herself with the country she had emotionally abandoned twenty years earlier when she had married Vadim.

With the redoubtable Elisabeth Vailland at her side, Fonda set off on a two-and-a-half-month tour across the nation, stopping at Native American reservations, army bases, GI coffeehouses, and college campuses—anywhere she could soak up information and commune with like-minded thinkers. "I took off on that trip a liberal," Fonda noted, "and I ended up a radical. What that means is this: I ended up understanding that there are many forms of starvation and that the struggle is my struggle. The same system in this wealthy, vast, rich country that makes it so there are people starving and illiterate and people who can't get medical care and who are being framed and shot and put into prison for political reasons is the same system that has messed me over as an upper-class white person."

When Henry Fonda read Jane's new personal "manifesto," he told *The New York Times* she had become "my erstwhile, my alleged daughter." Back in Los Angeles, where he had gone with Vanessa to work on a Rock Hudson film for MGM, Roger Vadim shrugged off inquiries about his wife by telling reporters, "I feel as if I were baby-sitting for Lenin."

Yes, Fonda said, there would be a revolution. "And yes, I'm afraid it will be a bloody one." She admitted that "the hardest thing for me is to take the subway instead of taxis. It's very hard," she said, "for someone who has all the luxuries to understand people who are less fortunate. The fact that I have a governess means I can't relate to people who don't." By the end of 1970, a Gallup poll showed that Jane Fonda had already become one of the "Ten Most Unpopular People in America."

John Frook of *Life* magazine captured the poignancy of the new role Fonda had created for herself: "She walks around with a solemn Red Guard face. It is as if she thought a show of cheerfulness might betray her. Jane Fonda really wants to be Vanessa

Redgrave. She would like to go Vanessa one better and be burned at the stake. You cannot help but be impressed by how college students regard her with something approaching reverence. Standing there, dealing out radical verities and political catch phrases, many of them as naive as they are sincere, she has students hanging on every word. If Jane Fonda only had a sense of humor, a sense of history, and a power base," Frook concluded, "she could cause a real commotion."

During the 1970s, Fonda led a double life. She was committed to both the movement and motion pictures, and even won an Oscar for her moving portrayal of a call girl in *Klute*. But she had grown far apart from Vadim, feeling desperately alone and in need of a new mentor, another substitute for her father. Tom Hayden, whom she had met at an anti-war rally in Ann Arbor, was available and answered the call.

"To understand Tom and Jane," wrote Christopher Anderson in *Citizen Jane*, "all you have to know is that they are both very, very ambitious people. Tom was a big hero to the people who mattered most to Jane. She still had lingering doubts about herself, and he could dispel them. This great intellectual was taking her seriously, so she figured everyone else would have to. When they got together, he was broke and she was worth millions. Jane was also a powerful force—a hundred times more famous. Hayden had been out of the spotlight for a while. He wanted the access to Middle America she gave him."

At Hayden's suggestion, Fonda took a step in July, 1972, that would change her life once again and move her quickly from the front ranks of Hollywood's most bankable talent to the top of Richard Nixon's infamous "enemies list." Dressed in the black pajama uniform of the Viet Cong, Fonda spent fourteen days in North Vietnam, being led on a meticulously orchestrated tour of bombed-out hospitals, schools, factories, villages, and reservoirs. In carefully staged photo ops she met U.S. servicemen from the notorious "Hanoi Hilton" prisoner of war camp. She was shattered by the suffering and devastation she saw throughout the countryside. Filmed cheerfully taking a tour in the gunner's seat of a North Vietnamese antiaircraft battery, Fonda was undone by the very medium that had created her. She also recorded ten radio broadcasts in Hanoi which would haunt her for years to come.

"Fonda and Hayden have become the Mork and Mindy of the New Left," the *Hollywood Reporter* noted. They were married on

January 19, 1974. Jane was four months pregnant, and in addition to the free-form vows ("Will you, Jane, marry Tom, and will you try in this marriage to grow together, to be honest, to share responsibility for your children, and to maintain a sense of humor?"), Jane finally swore off her twenty-three-year addiction to bulimia. "The choice," she noted, "was between being a good mother and wife and being a bulimic." Despite this courageous effort to regain control of her life, however, Fonda continued the almost daily use of diuretics to relieve her body of excess water—another dangerous habit she had practiced since she was nineteen. She also still found it impossible to stop chain-smoking.

"Overnight," her lawyer Richard Rosenthal recalls, "money became the driving impulse. Power was the objective." The Haydens were looking for "some high-minded purpose to make themselves rich." Following the birth of her son, Troy, Jane signed up for classes at a Los Angeles exercise studio run by Gilda Marx. Inspired to go into the exercise business Fonda decided she was "enough like other women to be able to give them what they—and I—want."

She opened the first Jane Fonda Workout Studio in 1979. It was an immediate success. Jane Fonda's *Workout Book* followed three years later and quickly shot to the top of *The New York Times* bestseller list. Then Fonda made a videocassette of the book, creating the first best-selling nonmovie video. By the mid-1980s her fitness empire was generating more than $20 million a year, much of which was consumed by Hayden's quixotic political ambitions. "Tom," Fonda announced proudly, "is going to be president."

In 1982 Henry Fonda finally won his first Oscar—for *On Golden Pond*, the brilliant screen adaptation of Ernest Thompson's off-Broadway play, which IPC, Jane Fonda's own film company, had produced. He was seventy-seven and too ill to accept the award for himself. "It was very, very touching," recalls Hayden. "Fonda was so overwhelmed when Jane handed the Oscar to him, he couldn't say a word. He was just sitting there in a state of bemused shock with the Oscar resting on his lap." Four months later Henry Fonda woke up in a hospital bed and simply stopped breathing.

The complicated love-hate relationship with her father that had shaped so much of Jane Fonda's life and provided her with the incentive to strike out and succeed on her own was now ended. She still needed the affection and approval Henry Fonda had never been able to provide, but she knew now she would not get it from a surrogate father figure. She had long assumed responsibility for her political activities, films, and other business interests. Now she began to wonder what life could be like with someone who might be prepared to treat her as an equal.

"Don't forget," she told biographer Christopher Anderson, "I am the number-one major late starter—living proof that it's never too late."

> *All I can say I've done is agitate the air ten or*
> *fifteen minutes a day and then—boom—it's gone!*
> EDWARD R. MURROW (1955)

Chapter Sixteen

"She's decathecting from Hollywood," said an old friend as she watched Fonda's relationship with Turner begin to blossom. Late in 1989 Turner reemerged and would not let Fonda out of his sight until she was his. He took her everywhere—to award dinners, to CNN's gala tenth anniversary celebration, to his daughter Jennie's wedding, to his plantations and his ranches, even to the White House, the Kremlin, and the Élysée Palace, where the couple dined with Bush, Gorbachev, and Mitterrand. He showered her with flowers and sentimental little presents. This most public of courtships was documented step by step for an adoring public with some of the most intensive media coverage ever extended to a pair of middle-aged lovers trying to make up for lost time. Cynics began to speculate how long it would be before their torrid affair would burn itself out, postulating that they were simply in love with the possibility of being twice as famous as each had been on his own. The tabloid press, of course, was feasting on reports that it was already over and began pairing Ted and Jane with new partners as outrageous as Fergie and Robert Redford. Through it all, however, Ted and Jane maintained a discreet silence—so much so that the *London Daily Mail* even confused its Turners when it included a photo of CNN's Ed Turner in a front-page story headlined TV TYCOON MENDS FONDA'S BROKEN HEART. I sent them a note," commented ET, "saying, 'It's not true I'm dating Jane. I'm dating Peter Fonda, her brother.' "

"I knew she was a protester in Vietnam, against the Vietnam War," Turner noted. "I knew she was in the movies, and I knew she did exercise videos. And I thought she was cute." But he told Fonda, "If you're going to be with me, you're going to have to cut back your work unless you could ever win an Oscar," blissfully unaware that she was already a two-time Academy Award winner.

When the helicopter settled down next to CNN Center in downtown Atlanta, bug-eyed staffers got their first sign the courtship had turned serious as Fonda materialized for an overnight visit to company headquarters. Turner himself lugged her bags into the building. After a quick tour of the CNN studios, the couple disappeared upstairs to his new rooftop digs, reappearing the next morning for breakfast at the Hard Copy, CNN's in-house cafeteria. Then Fonda dragged Turner down Peachtree Street to the City Athletic Club for an introduction to the Fonda workout regime. They appeared a few days later holding hands on national television at the People's Choice Awards. Turner took her to a glamorous Volunteers of America benefit dinner at the Beverly Wilshire Hotel. Then the couple went prime time at the 1990 Academy Awards. Fonda stole the show, of course, dazzling photographers and a worldwide television audience with her daring décolleté blue-sequined Versace. They were both starry-eyed and nuzzled each other so incessantly that many in the audience thought they might have been stuck together with Krazy Glue.

"The relationship is a natural," Fonda declared. A natural for mutual exploitation, replied the cynics, who couldn't help noticing the contradiction between the couple's pleas for privacy and their easy accessibility for absolutely any photo opportunity. "Did it ever occur to people that we are human beings with hearts and emotions?" rejoined Fonda.

"It's hard to have your life dissected," Turner added, saying he would leave it to Fonda to explain why she thought the couple clicked.

"Ted can keep up with me," Fonda declared flatly. "He's a very, very funny, lovable, complicated person. More than anybody, he has changed the world into a global culture. He has tremendous vision."

A charitable JJ Ebaugh, who has become a born-again Christian but still lives on one of Turner's Georgia farms and reports in occasionally at CNN, says succinctly, "He's serious about this —very serious. They have a lot in common, and they're crazy about each other. Still, she *is* twenty years older than I am."

"Fortunately I have a fair amount of business in L.A.," Turner said, beaming. "We've been doing a lot of different things—going to the movies, bicycling, working out. Yeah, I've been working out some since I've been seeing Jane. It's true, the more vigorously you exercise, the better you feel." At Fonda's request Turner, who was looking a bit older than his fifty-two years, had also again promised to give up tobacco, both smoking and chewing. Under her rigorous physical regimen, he would soon shrink by almost eighteen pounds. Turner applied himself with his usual fierce determination, hoping, perhaps, that all the healthy living wouldn't kill him.

"I think they're appropriate for each other," Laura Turner, Ted's eldest, observed when she finally met Jane. "They might even end up in the White House someday. My father and Jane would make a great president and first lady."

Over the next several months Fonda began to understand what life with the peripatetic Turner could be like as he led her on a dizzying odyssey. They flew to Washington, where Ted accepted a Georgetown University diplomatic journalism award for CNN and made several appearances before various congressional subcommittees exploring reregulation of the cable television industry; went to Orlando so Ted could accept another Humanist of the Year award; hopped to New York, where Ted spoke at the Brown University Club; and on to Spokane and Seattle to promote Ted's 1990 Goodwill Games. Then the couple rushed back to Atlanta for CNN's tenth anniversary blowout on June 1 and continued on to Los Angeles the next day, where they showed up at a Dodgers-Braves baseball game. "Where are we?" he asked Braves manager Bobby Cox. "Three or four games better than last season?" When he learned the club was actually behind last year's pace, Turner responded irrepressibly, "Oh, well, the team seems to be more exciting to watch. They *look* like they're playing better." Then he swept Fonda back up to the stadium clubhouse for dinner, promising to catch another game or two later in the season.

Back in Atlanta, the sportswriters were having a field day. "Instead of hanging out with Jane at the Academy Awards," the Atlanta *Constitution*'s Furman Bisher noted, "Turner should be back home trying to figure out how to unload André Thomas for a real relief pitcher. Cool it with your queen of sweat, Ted, and do something about your miserable excuse for a baseball team."

Admitting he had "mellowed so damned much since he met Fonda," Turner became agitated by rumors that he was now planning to step down sometime soon from Turner Broadcasting and bliss out, enjoying his billions and life ever after with Jane. His name was still on the door, his memento-laden office suite still had the best view in the place, but the industry's most explosive growth company seemed almost overnight to have matured into a conventional, bottom line–driven corporation that answered only to directors more consumed with divvying up Turner's enormous assets than continuing to build on the unique global franchise he had already created. Turner bristled at any suggestion that he was ready to step down. "I'll be here as long as I live," he snapped, full of vintage Turner bluster. "There are a lot of people who would like to own this company. But I haven't decided to retire."

He knew Time's Nick Nicholas, among many others, still coveted CNN and resented the stories Nicholas would plant from time to time in the trade media hinting at Turner's imminent retirement. Turner acknowledged these barbs by sending Nicholas two dozen red roses the day Time Inc. was swallowed up in its supposed "acquisition" of Warner Communications.

A triumphant TBS annual shareholders meeting in Turner's Omni Hotel that June was interrupted when one stockholder moved that Jane Fonda be nominated for election to the company's board of directors. "Do whatever you want," Turner responded solicitously, but no one seconded the nomination. Reed Irvine, a perpetually dissident shareholder, demanded that Fonda apologize for an antiwar speech she had made at the University of Michigan fifteen years earlier. Turner parried by suggesting politely that he would speak to her about it at the appropriate time. Despite obvious synergies—he was one of the world's biggest broadcasters, and she owned her own motion picture production company—Turner told his stockholders, "Our relationship is not about work. We have no plans to do anything together." Then the two of them packed their bags once again and headed off for a week's cruise in the Greek islands, where, Turner told Peter Dames, he was going to do "a little courting."

Watching carefully as the couple held hands over moonlit dinners, strolled among the ruins of the Temple of Poseidon at Cape Sonunion, and lolled about for days under the warm Aegean sun,

Dames got the impression that this kind of courtship might be a new experience for Fonda. "She's not used to being treated like a lady," he concluded as Turner continued to shower her with little presents and twenty-four-hour attention. "She's used to picking up the tab. She was very receptive. I could see it on the trip. She was thinking, God damn!"

Committed to a California environmental initiative which she helped place on the ballet in 1990, Fonda persuaded Turner to join her for a weekend in the Hamptons. She had arranged an important political fund-raising benefit at the Amagansett, Long Island, oceanfront estate of "Saturday Night Live" producer Lorne Michaels. This kind of thing had never been Turner's cup of tea, and he offered to write her a check for $100,000 if Fonda would call off the trip. When she insisted, he went along dutifully, showing up in boots and jeans. Sucking on one beer after another, he kept to the perimeter of the party, prowling around the magnificently landscaped grounds and distancing himself from the impressive crowd, which included Billy Joel and Christie Brinkley, Calvin and Kelly Klein, Jann Wenner, Barry Diller, Chris Whittle and Priscilla Ratazzi, Julian Schnabel, and Kathleen Turner. When Fonda stepped up on the porch stairs and began her pitch, Turner suddenly came to life. "Listen up!" he demanded over the quiet roar of the ocean only a few yards away. And the desultory Hamptonites listened up. When Fonda finished and the couple had worked their way through the long buffet line, Turner picked over his food, then suggested they beat a hasty retreat back home. He was certain there was a better way to save the world.

"Isn't it funny," mused former CNN anchor Don Farmer, capturing the irony of Turner's situation with no more subtlety than Turner deserved, "that the woman they used to call 'Hanoi Jane' and Ted Turner, who used to be a right-wing nut, have wound up together?"

No private enterprise in history has ever created a sporting event anywhere near so grand as Turner's Goodwill Games. Seventeen days of competition, more than ten thousand of the world's best athletes, and 160 hours of cable-exclusive television. If the concept had bubbled up from almost any other source, it might have died a-borning. Although Turner had the foresight to guarantee advertisers a 5 percent share of the television audience, only a handful had signed up. Nevertheless, he convinced his board to finance his Goodwill gamble by selling them on the idea of extracting $1 per subscriber from every cable operator in the country. It helped that Turner's cable partners controlled more than a quarter of the industry and, collectively, represented nearly twenty million subscribers.

Today, Turner Broadcasting officials speak of the Goodwill Games as "a franchise" or "an investment with escalating value." Despite accumulated losses of nearly $60 million, Turner's *succès d'estime* now looks as if it will pay off big. The well-produced Seattle games won him the critical endorsement of every important international athletic organization, including the International Olympic Committee, and the athletes themselves, who were delighted to have an off-year opportunity to see how they stacked up against the world's best. The next Goodwill Games begin on July 23, 1994, in St. Petersburg, Russia. PepsiCo and Reebok International lead an impressive array of advertisers who have already signed on. Turner has announced a unique joint airing of the weekend events over ABC-TV and TBS. He is assured of a profit for 1994 and can expect the 1998 games, which are to be held in New York City, to produce the television sports bonanza he predicted all along.

On a warm, wet morning in August 1990, CNN's Washington bureau chief Bill Headline found himself in the living room of the imposing northern Virginia residence of His Royal Highness, Prince Bandar Bin Sultan Bin Abdul Aziz, Saudi Arabia's ambassador to the United States. Eight days earlier, Iraqi forces had swept across the border and invaded Kuwait. Headline and his counterparts, George Watson of ABC, Timothy Russert of NBC, and Barbara Cohen of CBS, were there to firm up arrangements with the ambassador for on-site news coverage of this new Middle East conflagration that many believed would soon involve the rest of the world. On August 23, CNN producer Robert Wiener landed at Saddam International Airport. The arduous trip from Cairo, normally an hour's flying time, had taken Wiener eight days, thanks to cancellations, interminable security checks, and the failure of Iraqi broadcast authorities to decide whether they would ever allow the Western media into Baghdad. The long haul from Atlanta to Baghdad had taken Turner's Cable News Network a bit longer—ten years to be exact—but now the former "Chicken Noodle Network" was in place and ready to make media history.

An internal power struggle which threatened CNN had to be

settled first, however, before the network could go out and win over the world. "I'm not going to go out and hire Michael Gartner, a newspaperman," Ted Turner had sworn, promising everyone that CNN's new president would come from within the organization. Naturally, he appointed a newspaperman, Wyatt Thomas Johnson, Jr., the forty-nine-year-old vice-chairman of the Times-Mirror Company and former publisher of the *Los Angeles Times*. His choice shocked everyone, causing consternation and confusion among the CNN staff and doing little to improve rapidly deteriorating morale just as the network was about to go to war.

Once again, however, Turner relied on instinct and was certain he had made the right choice. Tom Johnson is a native Bibb County Georgian, born into a working-class family from Macon. He'd landed his first job, at the age of fourteen, as copy boy on the *Macon Telegraph*, worked his way through the University of Georgia and then Harvard Business School, and won a White House fellowship. Still in his early twenties, Johnson was appointed special assistant to President Lyndon Johnson and soon came to the attention of Otis Chandler, who named him editor and then publisher of the *Dallas Times Herald*. Chandler took note of the job Johnson did in Dallas, and of the young man's enormous potential for leadership, and brought him to Los Angeles as publisher of the company's flagship paper. When Chandler retired in 1989, he promoted Johnson once again, this time to vice-chairman of the parent Times-Mirror Company. It had taken Turner all of fifteen minutes at their first meeting to know that Johnson was the right man for CNN. Surprisingly, Johnson accepted Turner's offer and was so eager to get back into the news business that he took a significant cut in compensation, even agreeing to work without a contract.

Tom Johnson's first day on the job at CNN amounted to a baptism under fire. Less than twenty-four hours after he walked onto the newsroom floor in cavernous CNN Center, Saddam Hussein launched his anschluss against Kuwait. Fortunately Johnson is a very, very fast learner, with a Rolodex second to none. During the early days of Desert Shield, he was able to stay above the frenzy, playing the role of "servant leader" and lending vital support to his other managers, as CNN put ten years of experience to the test and began a massive mobilization for a war most staffers felt had now become a dead certainty. "If we could somehow pull it off," speculated Robert Wiener from Baghdad, "it would be the journalistic equivalent of walking on the moon. To cover a war live in real time, from behind enemy lines in the enemy's capital! Not even Murrow," Wiener gushed, "has done that, but I could easily imagine old Edward R. lickin' his lips at the prospect."

CNN, which prided itself on its objectivity, fell prey to the mounting jingoism then sweeping the country. "It's as though we were in training all this time for just this story," Ed Turner recalled. "We worked harder to put the necessary technology in place," he said, "to get the news out of the Middle East quicker than ABC, NBC, or CBS." Ted Turner had spent a decade courting broadcasters in hot spots like Iraq, making CNN available in government offices and inviting government participation in his "World Report" projects. That investment was now about to pay dividends, in spades. Iraqi Television's director general had visited CNN headquarters in 1990 for a "World Report" conference.

"You have a meeting like that," commented Eason Jordan, CNN's vice-president for international affairs, "and relationships are cemented." Even so, Jordan had to send more than one hundred letters and telegrams to various Iraqi government officials in the Foreign Ministry, Information Ministry, and broadcast authority, as well as to the Iraqi ambassador in Washington, before CNN received permission to broadcast live from Baghdad. Jordan supplied his Baghdad crew with two INMARSAT suitcase-size satellite telephones. Less than forty-eight hours before the war actually commenced, Jordan finally received word that CNN would also be allowed to bring in one of its new $400,000 portable flyaway satellite transmitters. In Atlanta, Jordan, Tom Johnson, Ed Turner, and the other CNN managers were elated. They knew, when and if war broke out, CNN would have the only live broadcast coming from behind enemy lines. Ed Murrow may have been lickin' his lips, but Ted Turner was bustin' his britches—his boys had done him real proud and were showing the kind of enterprise he had used ten years earlier to get CNN off the ground.

Robert Wiener's CNN Baghdad crew included Bernard Shaw, John Holliman, and Peter Arnett, plus a small team of cameramen, engineers, and support personnel. Shaw had been in the middle of a swing through the Middle East and was to be flown out of Iraq on January 16 after a scheduled interview with Saddam Hussein. Arnett had been called in at the last minute to replace Richard Blystone, who had unexpectedly been called back to London. Holliman was the agricultural expert who had come to CNN in 1980 as a farm reporter, planted crops in the old Techwood swimming pool, and was now completing his second tour in Iraq.

In early January Tom Johnson ordered a chartered jet, at $10,000 a day, to remain on standby in Amman, just in case he had to get his Baghdad team out fast. Johnson had also authorized Robert Wiener to draw several hundred thousand dollars to use if they had to buy their way out of a tight spot. Peter Arnett, remembering his experience during the American evacuation of Saigon, immediately sewed $100,000 into the lining of his leather jacket, which he would not take off again for the next six weeks.

When the United Nations Coalition drew its "line in the sand" on January 15, 1991, forty-five Western news correspondents and television technicians—including representatives of CNN, ABC, NBC, CBS, and the BBC, as well as several major U.S. and European newspapers and news magazines, and three international wire services—were on standby at Baghdad's Al-Rasheed Hotel. Presidential press secretary Marlin Fitzwater had issued a warning a few days earlier, urging all Western media to leave Baghdad immediately. However, his warning, and subsequent warnings from the U.S. embassy in Baghdad, were largely ignored, since most of the press there anticipated something less than a massive UN military response and didn't want to miss out on the story. Few anticipated the Iraqis' preemptive "media strike," which meant they were all now virtual house prisoners in the Al-Rasheed, a crumbling old relic of Baghdad's better days whose century-old wine cellars were being hastily converted into a makeshift bomb shelter.

On January 16 Fitzwater waltzed into the White House press room and once again warned the American media to get its people out of Iraq. This time he sounded serious. And when the secret invasion code—"Everything's fine at home, except the kids have the sniffles"—was relayed to the Al-Rasheed, all hell broke loose.

"Listen, guys," Peter Arnett counseled, "absolutely nothing's changed between yesterday and today except for Fitzwater's announcement. It's obvious the White House doesn't want us here. They don't want any reporters here, but that doesn't mean we should panic. I say we stay and that's that."

Fortunately Tom Johnson is possessed of enormous self-confidence, because he had one hell of a decision to make. He had let colleagues remain in place in Nicaragua and Tehran when he was running the *Los Angeles Times*. Two of them never made it back. Now he had less than twenty-four hours to decide whether to keep the eight-person CNN team in Baghdad or bring them home. Press secretary Fitzwater called from the White House and virtually ordered Johnson to recall his people. Johnson huddled with Ted Turner. *The New York Times, The Washington Post, The Wall Street Journal, Time, Newsweek*, and even the BBC and Britain's ITV were already out. Turner was adamant. The decision, he insisted, should be left up to each individual. Johnson agreed and was about to place the call to Robert Wiener when the CNN switchboard interrupted him to say the president was on the line. It was George Bush, working the phones personally, imploring Johnson to shut down CNN's Baghdad operation. Baghdad was going to be very dangerous, the president warned. The lives of Johnson's people would soon be in grave danger. After implying an attack was imminent, Bush expressed the hope that at least his "good friend Bernard Shaw would get out quickly." Bush's direct intercession served only to stiffen Johnson's resolve. When Turner said he was in solid agreement, they put the call back in to Baghdad.

"Robert, I am not, repeat, not going to order you out. Anyone who wants to leave is free to leave, but I am not going to order you out. Do you understand?"

"I assume this call is monitored," Johnson continued solemnly, "so I'm going to be as circumspect as I can. You know there are a lot of, um, inviting, well, there are areas all around the hotel that the coalition is very interested in. Is there any possibility of moving to another location?"

Anticipating the war's outbreak, Wiener had installed a special four-wire telephone line in the Al-Rasheed, which allowed him to avoid going through the hotel switchboard. The Al-Rasheed wine cellar, it turned out, was one of the few safe spots in the city. Wiener was also reluctant to give up the unbeatable camera position he had secured on the balcony outside CNN's suite, overlooking most of downtown Baghdad. "I know what you're driving at, Tom," he told his new boss, "but it's simply not a viable option."

Wiener, Arnett, Shaw, and Holliman, as well as the CNN production team (Nic Robertson, Ingrid Formanek, Mark Biello, and Kris Krizmanich), all elected to stay. Less than twelve hours later, on January 16, 1991, the first fighter-bombers came screaming in over Baghdad, signaling the beginning of what the *Washington*

Journalism Review would later call "Global Village War I." ABC, CBS, and NBC managed sporadic telephone connections out of Baghdad, but that first day of Desert Storm really belonged to CNN. When the Iraqis shut down the Al-Rasheed switchboard, Robert Wiener's "independent" four-line telephone hookup became the outside world's only link with Baghdad.

ABC was actually the first to report that the bombing had begun. During the *"ABC Evening News"* broadcast, Peter Jennings spoke by phone to Gary Shepherd from Baghdad and was assured that "absolutely nothing is happening here." Moments later Shepherd reported "flashes in the sky" and calmly told Jennings, "There's obviously an air raid under way right now." Then his line went dead. ABC got the scoop, but CNN was able to take over the story and dominated coverage through the rest of the night with little real competition from any other news medium anywhere.

CBS News lost contact with its Baghdad correspondent, Al Pizzey, just before the "CBS Evening News" signed on. The CBS producer asked CNN to help locate their man. Bernard Shaw reported on the air that Pizzey was safe, sipping tea downstairs in the Al-Rasheed's basement bomb shelter. Ignoring the obvious danger to themselves, Shaw and the other CNN reporters even joked about their situation on camera. Viewers around the world saw Bernie Shaw duck for cover when he heard a loud noise outside the door of CNN's Baghdad "studio" on the sixth floor of the old hotel. "We've got to run," Shaw said coyly. "Somebody's coming in the door. We're going to hide." Crouched down on the floor between rooms, Shaw continued the broadcast despite the Iraqi intelligence team out in the corridor.

When Secretary of Defense Dick Cheney held an unusual nine P.M. press conference at the Pentagon that night, he volunteered, "The best reporting that I've seen so far on what is transpiring in Baghdad was on CNN."

With his own network knocked off the air, Tom Brokaw was forced to interview CNN's Shaw to give NBC viewers a late evening update. Closing out the interview, Brokaw was moved to praise Shaw, Holliman, and Arnett for being very enterprising and brave indeed. "CNN," Brokaw told his viewers, "used to be called the 'little network that could.' It's no longer a little network."

"Within minutes of that first bomb burst," reported *Entertainment Weekly*, "the Cable News Network achieved total air superiority over the broadcast networks and held it until Iraq temporarily shut down their news operation some sixteen hours later. Ten-year-old CNN ordinarily scores less than one-tenth the ratings of either CBS, NBC, or ABC. But on January 16, the first day of the Gulf War, 10.8 million households tuned in to CNN." CNN's actual audience was considerably larger, since hundreds of stations around the country took the liberty of tapping in to its coverage. Even network affiliates switched from their own network news to pirated CNN satellite feeds. As Dick Aiken of Britain's ITV Channel put it, "They cut to Bernie Shaw because it was clear that they were getting their heads handed to them."

On January 17 Tom Johnson received a somber call from NBC News, indicating the Al-Rasheed was on the coalition's bombing target list for that night. Without missing a beat, Johnson placed a call directly to General Colin Powell in the Pentagon. Johnson knew he was way out of bounds, calling the chairman of the joint chiefs of staff, but somehow his call was put through. Was it true, Johnson demanded of Powell, that the Rasheed was about to be bombed? Powell was incensed. The hotel was filled with civilians, the chairman responded angrily, including Bernie Shaw, one of Powell's closest friends. The coalition, Powell insisted, had no intention of bombing the Al-Rasheed. The hotel, of course, remained unscathed throughout the war, although buildings all around it were leveled with pinpoint bombing.

"The reason I stayed in Baghdad," Peter Arnett says, speaking for the entire CNN crew, "is quite simple. Reporting is what I do for a living. I made the full commitment to journalism years ago. If you ask are some stories worth the risk of dying for, my answer is yes. Many of my journalist friends have died believing that." Four days after the war began, however, just seventeen journalists remained of the hundreds who had been covering Baghdad. Nine of those were CNN personnel.

Eventually there were only Arnett, Robert Wiener, and CNN cameraman Nic Robertson. The Iraqis finally expelled even Weiner and Robertson. Arnett continued to broadcast over his gaspowered INMARSAT satellite telephone until the Iraqis let him use the flyaway again. Bob Furnaud, CNN's executive producer in Atlanta, devised the question-and-answer format that helped Arnett go beyond the censored reports he was forced to file. At first Arnett was almost universally praised for his extraordinary coverage, and he appeared well on his way to another Pulitzer Prize. He seemed the perfect choice for this tremendously difficult assignment until he gave a heavily censored report about coalition prisoners of war. Then a firestorm erupted over his "milk factory" story, which suggested that coalition bombers had intentionally demolished a factory making infant formula. Thousands of letters poured into CNN's Atlanta headquarters, criticizing Arnett and calling for CNN to end its "propaganda broadcasts." CNN's Washington bureau received repeated bomb threats. Administration hawks lined themselves up against Arnett and CNN. Senator Alan Simpson of Wyoming called Arnett a "sympathizer." NBC military analyst Harry Summers even suggested he might be guilty of treason. White House chief of staff John Sununu, who would become a CNN commentator less than a year later, took up the cry and began applying heavy pressure on both Turner and Tom Johnson to get Arnett out of Baghdad and off the air. Protesters outside CNN headquarters took up the chant "Baghdad Ted and Hanoi Jane" in an attempt to persuade the country that Fonda had somehow influenced Turner sufficiently for him to become a propaganda tool for Saddam Hussein.

Brookings Institution's Stephen Hess, an expert on the relationship between the press and government, lined up against CNN's critics and observed that Arnett's reports served a purpose by telling Westerners what the Iraqi government wanted its own citizens to know about the war. "It's different," he acknowledged, "but it's a service. There's no reason to believe we're being misinformed."

"What is new in this war," Hess concluded, "is not censorship —Vietnam was the exception, a noncensored war. What is totally different is an instantaneous, continuous, and international network. CNN really is the story. And it's clear that we all have a lot to learn about this new phenomenon."

Tom Johnson and Ed Turner had worked overtime to establish balanced coverage and provide an informed perspective on Arnett's reporting. Johnson made certain CNN producers made it absolutely clear to viewers through the use of on-screen graphics inserted in Atlanta that Arnett was subject to Iraqi censorship. Johnson brought in seventy-five high-level military experts, including former defense secretaries Casper Weinberger, Alexander M. Haig, Jr., Harold S. Brown, James Schlesinger, and Donald Rumsfeld, as well as experts on specific Iraqi weaponry, desert warfare, and Middle East intelligence, to amplify Arnett's reports and explain developments as the war unfolded. In fact, during Desert Storm CNN broadcast over four hundred individual analyses, more than ten new commentaries a day, nearly four times as many as any of the major broadcast networks.

"CNN has been ground zero for critics, for colleagues, for viewers, for families, for the military, for the news makers and the news haters," observed Johnson. "I think we were fortunate to have on site, in the most difficult of circumstances, a seasoned combat correspondent like Peter Arnett, who was tested time and again. He was there so that all the viewers could be there, and see as much as we could see.

"The people here," he continued, "have made news policies and decisions never before faced by journalists. There were no guidebooks, few rules, and a lot of professional land mines. CNN has written a new book," Johnson added proudly, "and I feel CNN served its profession and its viewers with distinction."

Ted Turner reported that the Gulf War coverage was costing his company about $1.5 million a day, but he had given Tom Johnson and CNN a blank check to spend whatever it took to get the story. On the air twenty-four hours a day, CNN leased more satellite transponder time than all the other U.S. networks put together. "What CBS did during the Gulf War," commented retired U.S. Air Force general Michael Dugan, a CBS military analyst, "was watch CNN."

Until January 16, 1991, CNN had rarely drawn more than a million viewers in the United States during any given program period. During Desert Storm, as many as fifty or sixty million viewers at a time saw Scud Missiles soaring live over Tel Aviv and Saudi Arabia, Peter Arnett interview American prisoners of war, and Saddam Hussein himself watching CNN. Ted Turner made every attempt to keep CNN impartial, but when the network broadcast pictures of Saddam gloating over his American hostages, CNN drew bitter condemnation from critics who feared Turner might have converted CNN into a propaganda machine for a madman. "There is no 'enemy,'" Bernard Shaw said, attempting to justify Turner's policy of impartiality. "There is no 'friendly.' I can't take sides when my work is seen and heard in one hundred and five different countries. As an American, how I feel privately, that's personal. But professionally I do not take sides. As a reporter, I'm neutral."

It works both ways, CNN's John Holliman decided, citing Dick Cheney's on-camera praise of CNN's coverage, as well as Colin Powell's gratuitous references to the innocuous information he said he received over the air from his good friend "Bernie," information that might easily have angered Saddam and cost the CNN reporters their lives.

When Ted Turner revealed to members of the Overseas Press Club in Washington shortly after the end of the Gulf War that he received death threats over his decision to let Peter Arnett remain in Baghdad, he attempted to downplay the situation. "Everybody dies sooner or later," he said calmly, not sounding at all like the old Ted Turner who once welcomed the assassin's bullet. "We decided if we were going to get blown away, we're going to get blown away. There wasn't any way we weren't going to leave him there, as long as he wanted to stay."

During most of the Gulf War, Ted Turner kept in close, daily contact with Tom Johnson and Ed Turner, who had gravitated upward after Johnson's arrival to become CNN's second in command. When the war expanded to several fronts—Riyadh, Jerusalem, Kuwait City, and Geneva—Turner reconfirmed his commitment to spend whatever it took to keep CNN out in front. Turner did, however, sign up MCI, CNN's first ever "global advertiser," who paid a special "worldwide" rate to sell its long distance service on the world's first global network. And he would materialize in the CNN studio from time to time, graciously thanking employees who were working eighteen- and twenty-hour days, some with little or no time off once the bombing began. He refrained from attempting to second-guess Johnson or Ed Turner on the constant daily decisions they were forced to make in juggling CNN's enormous new logistical, reportorial, and political responsibilities. He refrained from making the kind of controversial public statements that had once caused CNN professionals such discomfort, and he was also sensitive enough to keep Jane Fonda a million miles away from CNN while controversy still raged around Arnett's broadcasts from Baghdad.

"I saw him only once—in the cafeteria," recalls Major General Perry Smith, retired USAF, one of the two principal military analysts among the dozens used by CNN during the six weeks of Desert Storm. Smith had signed on for the duration after being asked, in typical CNN fashion, to drive from his home in Augusta, Georgia, to Atlanta late one afternoon just before the January 15 United Nations deadline, to offer an informed opinion—gratis—on the direction a possible air war might take. Like the good trooper General Smith obviously is, he remained at his CNN post for the next six weeks, often supplying as many as ten different commentaries during a single twenty-four-hour period. In the middle of the war, CNN agreed with his suggestion that he be paid "a small honorarium." When he ran into Ted Turner in the Hard Copy, the CNN cafeteria, Smith recalls, "He shook my hand, told me I was doing a good job, and was gone in less than a minute."

Once the cease-fire was struck on February 28, 1991, however, Turner reemerged with a vengeance, determined to capitalize on the momentum CNN had earned during the Gulf War and aware that his network's success had already spawned half a dozen competitors.

He quickly opened up a dozen new CNN bureaus, at a cost of over $1 million each, and could soon boast on-the-spot coverage from New Delhi to Johannesburg to Buenos Aires. But, commented Tom Johnson, "CNN will continue to be what has been described many times as a lean and mean news machine. My mission is to balance editorial growth with revenue growth. We're not going overboard on expenses, and we are not about to begin paying megabuck anchor salaries."

CNN collected a trunkful of awards for its Gulf War coverage, including a National Headliner Award and the George Foster Peabody Award. Ted Turner accepted the kudos, graciously acknowledging the efforts of CNN's management and editorial teams. Turner also showed the competition he had not lost his knack for reselling what he already owned, creating new profits out of whole cloth. During the war Turner had proposed tapping CNN's audio feed and turning it into a satellite radio service. "Once the bombing started," recounts Len King, now general manager of CNN Radio, "we signed up over a hundred stations." Dozens of other station managers discovered they could get Gulf War coverage for free simply by pirating CNN's signal. "Some station managers called to confess," says King. "A lot wouldn't even tell you who they were—guilt tripping, I guess." Overnight Turner had created another new business that not only helped swell his coffers, but was succeeding where his competitors, like General Electric, which sold its NBC Radio Network to Westwood One, had failed.

When all the smoke from Desert Storm had cleared, it became obvious that the CNN the world had been watching was not just an extension of American domestic television news, but a genuinely global network with a truly international mission whose anchors just happened to live and work in Atlanta, Georgia, U.S.A. The political and journalistic consequences of what Ted

Turner had created were becoming apparent. But they were also unpredictable, and perhaps uncontrollable, even in the context of CNN's new global village.

"Welcome to 'Larry King Live,' " the announcer intoned, leaving viewers from New York to New Delhi not a little nonplussed. "Tonight, males turning to their plastic surgeons to be all they can be. Plus, lovely Jane Fonda makes the best with what she's got." Fonda had been booked on King's show, CNN's highest-rated program, to promote her newest video, *Jane Fonda's Lean Routine*, when Turner decided unexpectedly to appear with her. "Jane," King asked ingenuously, "before we talk about the video —how's everything going with you and Ted, America's most famous couple?"

"As far as I can see, it's going great," Turner interjected. "Not a very long answer, but you know I'm not used to really talking too much about my personal life."

King, who pulled down a cool $1 million per year as Turner's highest-paid employee, wasn't about to press the point. "What, Ted, could you tell us about Jane? Anything that surprised you the most? I mean, Jane Fonda has been in front of the public for a long time, a lot of people have different perspectives on her as an actress, an activist. What about her surprised you?"

"I would say that she's a sweet, kind, down-to-earth person, in spite of all the tremendous success she's had. She hasn't stopped being a regular girl. Right?"

"And Jane," King plowed on gamely, "what surprised you the most about Ted?"

"How funny he is," she blurted out, breaking into a little laugh at the lunacy of this media moment. "And how romantic." Turner didn't bat an eye. "Another thing is that he knows so much about birds and the wildlife and fishing and things like that, it's just amazing. You drive around with him and if he sees a bird flying, even at a distance, he'll know what it is."

Then King popped the big question. "Did you two recently—is this true? Did you release six lizards in your Santa Monica home, Jane, to hunt down bugs because they're more ecological than insecticides? Is that true?"

"No."

"I've got it written here," King continued, undeterred, "that you—you didn't release those six lizards? Where did that come from?"

"I have rabbits and things that do that."

*Dey wuz always layin' traps for Brer Rabbit
and getting kotched in dem deyselves and dey
was always a pursuin' after him, day in and day out.*

JOEL CHANDLER HARRIS
Nights with Uncle Remus

Chapter Seventeen

"You are all my neighbors now, whether you like it or not," Ted Turner announced shortly after he bought Texas oilman William Carr's historic old Sixteen Mile Ranch, near Toston, Montana.

Midway between Helena and Bozeman, Sixteen Mile was approximately that distance from the headwaters of the Missouri River, where Lewis and Clark began their trailblazing trek across the Rockies. Sixteen Mile is also adjacent to Mineral Springs Confederate State Park, although Turner was unaware of this coincidence when he first arrived in Montana. Soon after he had closed on the purchase and renamed his ranch the Bar None, Turner added an additional 2,080 acres of adjacent land to the 18,695-acre spread, making it one of the larger working ranches in the area. Local hunters, well aware of Turner's reputation as a sportsman and crack shot, were disappointed to learn that he intended to return the property to its natural state and would continue Carr's limited-access policy. Still, Turner was generally considered a welcome contrast to the wealthy bicoastals who flocked to the Big Sky country throughout the 1980s, buying up every "celebrity ranchette" in sight.

"Turner is a conscientious neighbor," says Bill Don Brainard, a local rancher who dined frequently with him during Turner's first days in Montana. "He brought his kids up here and took the trouble to introduce himself around to the area people."

In fact, Turner had found an appealing new soapbox as well as a new home in Montana, and he quickly became one of the state's most visible part-time residents, as well as a lightning rod for local controversy. He took up fly-fishing again, this time with a vengeance. Determined to master the sport, he joined the local Madison-Gallatin chapter of Trout Unlimited. He joked that after only a year or two of trying, he was proficient enough at dry fly casting not to hook himself in the back of the head. "I find it to be my second most favorite thing to do," he said, the Turner tongue planted firmly in cheek, "but a reasonably close second."

It took him less than a year to decide to extend his Montana holdings. Early in 1989 he offered to buy the Climbing Arrow, second largest ranch property in Gallatin County. When co-owner Marcia Anderson turned down his unsolicited offer, he went back to Jim Taylor, the Hall & Hall broker who had sold him the Bar None. Taylor knew his customer and suggested that Turner might appreciate the Flying D, one of the premier ranch properties in the West. One look at this unique property and Turner was sold —so sold, in fact, that he almost forgot to ask the price, which was $22 million and change for 110,000 deeded and 20,000 leased acres. The purchase brought Turner's Montana holdings to over 150,000 acres and certified him as one of the largest landowners in the state.

The Flying D lies about twenty miles southwest of Bozeman, in Gallatin Gateway, Montana. As the traveler heads south through the tiny town on Highway 191, past the Gallatin Gateway Inn, past the old railroad station, the walls of Gallatin Canyon rise up suddenly and form a dramatic natural stone gateway to Yellowstone Park. The whitewater Gallatin River separates the Gallatin and Madison mountain ranges, and here, at the spot where Spanish Creek pours into the Gallatin River, lies the entrance to the Flying D. A stately carved wood sign arches high over the rough washboard road leading into Turner's huge ranch, which stretches west farther than the eye can see, across broad, rolling hills to the northernmost reaches of the Madison range and the famed Spanish Peaks. Surrounding the northern borders of the spectacular Lee Metcalf Wilderness and large sections of the Beaverhead National Forest, the Flying D is crossed by the Great North Trail, a prehistoric highway that extends along the entire eastern face of the Rockies. Evidence of a large post-Pleistocene settlement, consisting of more than 250 tipi rings, has been unearthed on the Flying D. Enough artifacts have been found on the property to suggest the existence of an ancient trading center, active centuries before the arrival of the white man. The old Cherry Creek Trail which runs across the Flying D is actually one of a network of preexisting pathways that led to these centers. When the late afternoon sun begins to slip down behind the Continental Divide, the hundred twilight hues that enthralled earlier inhabitants ten thousand years ago still envelop this land. Evening shadows play against the Flying D's undulating rangelands the way a setting sun plays off the open ocean.

The Flying D is as full of natural charm and mystery as it is of history. Ted Turner was enthralled by the sheer size and magnificence of this property, which was quite unlike anything he had ever seen. Once he learned more about the ranch's history, Turner became convinced that he had found, at last, an appropriate place to sink his roots. A week after closing on the Flying D, however, he revealed that something more than mere emotion had caused him to pick up one of the largest commercial cattle ranches in Montana. As usual, he had seen something most others couldn't. He announced that he intended to sell off all of the more than four thousand head of cattle that had come with the Flying D and was then assured of a full house when he agreed to reveal his plans for the ranch at an open forum in Bozeman on land management and ecology.

Nearly 1,000 people turned up to hear what Turner would say, although only 250 could squeeze inside the auditorium at Bozeman's tiny Museum of the Rockies. With his usual off-the-cuff candor, he held the audience spellbound for nearly an hour as he unveiled his intentions. He was going to turn the clock back at the Flying D, he said, nearly two hundred years. He was returning the land to its natural state, the way it was before the white man came to Montana. He would manage the land for wildlife instead of sheep or cattle. Then he threw real fat on the fire by announcing that he was going to reintroduce buffalo to his land. Not only that, said Turner, he was going to turn the Flying D into the biggest buffalo breeding ground in the world.

"That's what everyone wants. Get a great idea and hit the big time," he explained to the openmouthed Montanans. "It's like Edison with the light bulb. Or Henry Ford with the Model T. Everyone wants to come up with the new thing. The great new idea that let's 'em hit the big one. At least, that's what I've always wanted to do," said the man who had already hit more than a few big ones himself. "Try something different than what's been done before. Create a new thing and make a killing.

"I just never liked cattle," he confessed, laying his cards on the table, "even though my dad had them. They trampled down all the grass, and that ruined the cover for quail, which I loved to hunt." Most of his listeners couldn't believe Ted Turner, the king of global communications, the man who owned the biggest news business in the world, standing here in Bozeman, Montana, telling a couple of hundred cattle ranchers he was dead serious about buffalo. Perhaps they would have understood him better if they'd heard his pitch about peat some fifteen years earlier. Turner's South Carolina plantations sit on top of some of the richest peat deposits in the country. During the energy crisis of the early 1970s, Turner voiced serious plans to mine and market peat as an alternative to fossil fuels. Was buffalo another boondoggle like peat? Or was he once again riding a wave no one else could catch? Was Ted Turner, in fact, about to become the new Baron of Bison?

It didn't much matter what they called him. Turner was dead serious. He said he was going to build an initial herd of six thousand buffalo as soon as he could sell off all the Flying D's cattle. Then he ticked off for his audience the reasons why he was certain his buffalo project was going to work. Lower fat and lower cholesterol, of course. Less labor intensive. Significantly higher profit margins. "Unlike cattle, bison don't just eat the best grass. They'll eat the weeds and plants. Unlike cattle, bison don't need hay in winter, except for the buffalo calves, and then only when the bison cow is carrying a second calf. Bison have a higher tolerance for cold weather," Turner added, sounding for all the world like the state's newest 4H Club inductee. "Their metabolism rate slows, and they require less forage. Their thicker coats better insulate them. They don't ruin rivers and stream banks like cattle. They don't wreck tree stands. They stick to the plains, grazing in the fiercest sun, not sheltering in shade. And they're cleaner," he added knowledgeably. "They wipe their bums."

Old-timers in Bozeman were consternated. Some, like ninety-year-old Malcolm Story, whose grandfather brought the first Texas longhorns into Montana, were more than a little put out at the thought of Turner running buffalo on the Flying D. "For Turner to tell us how to ranch," said Mr. Story, "I find that entertaining, and I don't think I'm alone in saying that."

Already under pressure from the declining beef market and constant threats to grazing rights, cattlemen feared the worst if any of Turner's bison ever got off the Flying D. Some, like Congressman Vernon Westlake, whose cattle ranch abuts Turner's property, expressed concern that his bison would carry brucellosis, a highly contagious disease that causes cattle to abort their calves. "That is potentially quite a problem," Westlake said. "Some of us feel that it will have to be very rigidly controlled so there won't be any chance of the buffalo mingling with other people's cattle." Turner said he was planning to inoculate all his buffalo against brucellosis and had already begun putting solar-powered electric fences around the borders of the Flying D. "If they get out," he added like the good neighbor he intended to become, "naturally I'll be responsible."

Dennis Rowe, one of the few small buffalo ranchers in the area, tried to rationalize his own involvement without aggravating his neighbors the way Turner had done. "It takes less hired help, but Turner will have to pay the same livestock tax as he would on cattle. It'll have an impact short term, but there's a good market for buffalo, and his timing couldn't be better."

Ted Turner said he wanted to raise buffalo "because I always was fascinated by them and I just like watching them. They were also extinct, and I want to make sure that doesn't happen. I also intend," he added pointedly, "making twice as much from bison as you would make from cattle."

Turner also said he hoped the herd of eighteen hundred trophy elk roaming the Flying D would double, although he planned to let that happen naturally. "The only reason those elk are there at all is that they aren't massacred. Without the cattle, there will be enough grass left for them to eat." The increased elk, he added, would spill out to surrounding private and Forest Service land, where they could be hunted. Turner said he planned at least one annual charity trophy elk hunt but dashed the hopes of local hunters again when he said he would continue the previous owner's no-access policy toward hunters. "I bought the place to get away from people. If I wanted to be around people, I would have stayed in Atlanta. The only way to get access is to do like I did and work forty or fifty years and make twenty-two million dollars and then go buy it for yourselves.

"Me, I want to live as far away as I can from everybody," he added. "I am becoming a hermit. There is nothing wrong with that."

In addition to elk, the Flying D abounds in mule deer, moose, black bears, coyotes, and other indigenous wildlife, although few in Bozeman believe the *People* magazine story that Turner is nurturing six pairs of bald eagles on his property. He was open, he admitted, to the controversial reintroduction of wolves to the land, however, and suggested, "If the Fish and Game Commission wanted to put grizzly bear down there, and nobody objected, I wouldn't have any problem with that, either."

Bud Griffith has managed the Flying D under various owners for more than thirty years. When Turner ordered the ranch returned to its natural state, it fell to Griffith to oversee the removal of all the outbuildings, corrals, cattle pens, and barbed-wire fencing that he himself had put up over the past three decades. Griffith was also asked to eliminate all the overhead power lines and utility poles on the property and then bury the thousands of rock cairns that previous owners had laboriously heaped together to open up fields for alfalfa planting. "Ol' Bud got pretty worried," Turner said with only a slight hint of sympathy in his voice, "that I was going to make them cart all those rocks away. I compromised, since he sweated so much to make those piles years ago. I told him we'd just dig holes and toss them in."

A few months later Turner announced that he had placed the Flying D in a conservation easement, the largest such commitment in Montana's history. This unusual move would allow Montana's Nature Conservancy to protect in perpetuity about 128,000 acres of Turner's property from development of any kind, including new buildings, roads, trails, mining, timber harvest, and waste dumping. The easement, which was similar to others he had entered into earlier covering Hope Plantation in South Carolina and Avalon Plantation as well as St. Phillips Island off the South Carolina coast, is so restrictive that even the Flying D's fencing would be removed to ensure natural wildlife migration. Local critics hooted that Turner had either lost his mind or figured out a new way to beat the taxman. He would benefit, they pointed out, through a charitable tax deduction based on the reduced value of his land. Montana property taxes, to be sure, are among the country's lowest, but the tax benefits which accrued to Turner were, in fact, insignificant and hardly covered the expense of returning his land to its natural state.

Nature Conservancy groups, on the other hand, have benefited enormously from Turner's conservation easements. Linda Haseltine, secretary of the South Carolina unit, calls Turner "an extreme conservationist. You can't rely on the state or federal government, and he knows this. But," she added, "in every area of dealing with Ted Turner, he has his own ideas. Conservation is no exception."

"The Flying D is a handsome, high-quality place and deserving of Turner's conservation intentions," said Bob Keisling, director of special projects for the Helena office of the Nature Conservancy. "He has demonstrated in both word and deed he is a strong conservationist." Turner is a member of the Nature Conservancy's national corporate relations committee and, says Keisling, "he will make a good neighbor and a nice addition to the Montana community. Bozeman is extremely lucky Ted Turner's the one who's coming in."

"I'm spending more time in Montana than I should," Turner says, "and a lot less than I'd like to." He has also ended up spending a lot more money in Montana than he may ever have planned. "I've invested plenty of bucks turning this land back to the way it used to be. More than I thought I would. But it's worth it."

Late in the summer of 1989 Jane Fonda began showing up in Bozeman with Turner. She stayed at the Gallatin Gateway Inn, just a few miles from the entrance to the Flying D. They went to fly-fishing school together and shared candlelit dinners at the somewhat self-conscious inn or at Sir Scott's Oasis in nearby Manhattan. Peter Fonda, who lives a half hour away in Livingston on the eastern slopes of the Gallatin range in Paradise Valley, arranged for his friend Jack Horner, curator of the dinosaur collection at the Museum of the Rockies, to give the couple a paleontological tour of Turner's properties. Horner is a specialist in dinosaur behavior, discoverer of the famed Egg Mountain site in eastern Montana and dinosaur consultant to Steven Spielberg on the film *Jurassic Park.* Horner calls Turner's Bar None ranch "one of the most complete geological examples I have ever seen." Sixteen Mile Creek, which runs across the property, has laid bare geological layers from almost every major epoch, from Precambrian through Neocene, and has provided sufficient evidence to suggest the possibility of further exceptional finds. The Turner Family Foundation, a philanthropic trust set up by Turner in 1991, provided Horner with a $25,000 preliminary study and excavation grant. In the summer of 1992 Horner hit pay dirt—the fossilized remains of three juvenile brontosaurs, the first ever found in Montana. He is certain there are more major discoveries still in the ground under the Bar None and lauds Turner as the only Montana landowner ever to fund a dinosaur dig on his own land.

"Turner is very interested in our efforts," Horner says, "and visits the dig sites whenever he's in town. He even brought Jimmy and Rosalynn Carter over for a look last summer." Despite the rich potential of the Bar None, however, Horner doesn't expect to discover much in the way of paleontological finds on the Flying D. The rock there, he says, is predominantly Precambrian gneiss, older than any fungus or mitochondria, and therefore not likely to harbor many fossils. Horner has identified one section of tertiary rock on the ranch, however, which he believes could yield up the remains of mammals like the saber-toothed tiger and woolly mammoth.

With a population of less than eight hundred thousand, Montana is now America's second largest congressional district. Montana is also the battleground in a ferocious struggle between the lanky, gaunt-faced locals and the deep-pocketed newcomers who continue to migrate from both coasts to this last, best place. A new wave of post-1980s pioneers has created a land boom in Bozeman (elevation: 4,793 feet) while real estate elsewhere is still seeking bottom. The town never experienced the mining or metal booms of places like Butte and as a consequence remains much the same solid community it was seventy-five or even a hundred years ago. Today, though, the new cooperative store in town stocks Love brand body oil; Life & Tree laundry liquid; fourteen types of dried hops; liquid dispensers of molasses, safflower, and shoyu; nine different trail mixes; and nineteen types of granola— hardly the staples the good citizens of Bozeman might have found on their shelves even ten years ago.

Ron Marlenee is a vigorous conservative Republican congressman and fierce defender of gun rights who once made his position clear by brandishing an Uzi on the congressional firing range. Out on the stump Marlenee loves nothing better than railing against liberal reformers like Ted Turner and Jane Fonda, "who want to come in and tell us how to run our state, how to regulate land use and dietary policy." Marlenee warns of the "two-headed spotted alleywalker, mascot of the 'hot-tub liberals.' This is not a skirmish," he cautions the locals. "This is an all-out war."

It's difficult finding anyone in Gallatin County who doesn't have an opinion about Ted Turner or Jane Fonda, one way or the other. A few even find the Japanese real estate investors who snapped up ranch properties with such abandon in the early 1980s preferable. One Montana state official went on record recently in *Outside* magazine, chafing at Turner's "take charge" attitude. "Ted Turner owns more of Montana than all of the Japanese put together," he wrote. "But the Japanese have come over and tried to adapt to our culture. Turner has come in and, right from the beginning, tried to tell us how to do things."

Turner is sensitive to such criticism and made certain one of his first stops after he bought the Flying D was Stacey's Old Faithful, a rough-and-ready watering hole right on the road leading past his ranch. Turner introduced himself and then, good ole boy that he can be, bought the house a round. He never seemed to connect with the cowboy regulars, however, and hasn't been seen in Stacey's since. A Toronto Blue Jays banner appears over Stacey's bar around World Series time, just in case the Braves' owner ever thinks he's made it with the locals. Not likely, since Ted and Jane have joined a celebrity contingent in the Bozeman area that includes Big Sky novelist Tom McGuane, Glenn Close, Meryl Streep, Tom Brokaw, Keifer Sutherland, Jeff Bridges, Dennis Quaid, Meg Ryan, Michael Keaton, and Brooke Shields. Conscious of how wary most Montanans are of outsiders, both Turner and Fonda have learned to tread cautiously without diminishing their impressive list of active local interests. Fonda is the only out-of-stater on the board of the Montana Nature Conservancy, and Turner has been increasingly active in funding a unique array of environmental, archaeological, and historical projects.

"I think studies show that the best hope for the state economy," Fonda told the *Bozeman Chronicle*, "is preserving the environment. My brother, Peter, lives right over these mountains," she explained, pointing toward the shimmering eleven-thousand-foot-high Spanish Peaks. "I've flown it in a light plane and cried at the clear-cutting. The devastation is heartrending, and it isn't necessary. There are ways to have sustainable logging, and I want to see us work on that so there may be not as many jobs, but they'll be secure."

Turner committed recently to acquiring a $20 million track of timberlands now owned by Plum Creek Timber Company, which he intends to donate to the Nature Conservancy. The project will incorporate 175,000 acres in a new reserve environmentally compatible with both logging and modest housing development.

In early 1992 the Turner Family Foundation donated $60,000 to the Montana Historical Society to further archaeological and Native American research on the Flying D. The society put together a team of geologists, archaeologists, soil experts, and Native American advisers after Turner and several Montana archaeologists found evidence of more than one hundred different sites, including ancient Salish-Kootenai, Blackfeet, Crow, and Chippewa Cree campsites, mining sites, and workshops dating as far back as five thousand years or more.

David Schwab, one of the society's leading archaeologists, believes the Flying D is so rich in prehistoric finds because of the abundance of the substance called chert found in the rich bottomland between the Madison and Gallatin rivers. Chert was once used by Montana's earliest inhabitants to make stone tools and weapons. "This land has unleashed a spiritual power," Schwab says, "for some of the Indians involved with our project. Looking out over the buffalo grazing on the rehabilitated natural grasslands of the Flying D, they feel they are looking at the land as it was before the white man arrived."

Turner is responsible to the Nature Conservancy for maintaining strict environmental standards on all of his ranch properties. Even his archaeological projects must comply with easement restrictions. He and Fonda have spent considerable time with local tribal leaders in an effort to secure Native American involvement in these undertakings. Fonda has even organized programs that bring Native Americans to the Flying D to teach them buffalo management, with the expectation that tribes can then begin building herds of their own on their reservations and participate in the same economic boom Turner anticipates for his commercial buffalo operation. Working with the Montana Historical Society, Turner has brought tribal elders out to the Flying D and sought their counsel in an extraordinary exchange of historical information. Salish elders have shared ancient tales and tribal myths of hunting, fishing, and mining in the Gallatin Valley with Turner and the scientists and educated them about ancient tribal plant uses, which in turn has aided in the restoration of the land to its original state. "This project provides some of the local tribes," Schwab explains, "a unique opportunity to reconnect with lost, aboriginal times." Moved by this knowledge of their ancestral heritage, many tribal leaders have developed an abiding respect for Turner and his land ethic.

"We call him Wovoka," says Curly Bear Wagner of the Blackfeet Cultural Planning Office. Wagner believes Turner is fulfilling the prophecy of the original Wovoka, a Paiute medicine man who introduced the Ghost Dance to his people. "Wovoka's teaching spread to other tribes near the end of the nineteenth century," Wagner says. "They believed they would be invincible to white men, and white men would be blown back to where they came from, and the buffalo would return and Indians would flourish again. It all died at Wounded Knee. But Ted Turner is the new Wovoka. He's bringing back the buffalo."

There has been no formal naming ceremony, no passing of the pipe or recitation of gnostic prayer—indeed, only a Paiute can pass down a Paiute name, particularly so revered a name as Wovoka. But Curly Bear Wagner says Turner is actually fulfilling the prophecy, and because of this, Wagner means for the name to suggest "a way of explaining that Turner can see into the future. He's seeing that this is going to be happening." The reintroduction of buffalo, says Wagner, will have very positive economic as well as cultural benefits for Montana's Native Americans, who will raise bison for the market that Turner will create. Wagner is also involved in the historical research project on the Flying D and says he was impressed, even moved, by the way "Turner's done away with most of the fencing and encouraged a natural habitat of grasses—letting grasses grow as they should."

Girard Yellow Wolf Baker, an assistant ranger at Custer National Forest, built an authentic Mandan tribal sweat lodge for Jane Fonda on the Flying D. Baker's gift, the only known structure of its kind anywhere off a reservation, is a reflection of the high regard many Native Americans now have for Fonda, whose early involvement in Native American rights issues in the 1970s was not always so welcome. Her efforts in working with members of Montana tribes like the Salish and the Mandan have impressed people like Salish-Kootenai cultural director Betty White.

"Fonda is interested in the tribe's new cultural center," she says. "It's exciting from our perspective. We put a great emphasis on preserving our environment because it sustains us in other ways. Fonda's interested in sustainable use of resources, and that's very close to our hearts." Jane Fonda is so sensitive to these new relationships that she has persuaded Turner to adopt the "palmahawk wave" as a replacement for his Atlanta Braves' controversial "tomahawk chop." The palmahawk is a smooth, palm-down gesture outward from the chest, the universal Native American sign of peace.

About a hundred miles due north of Bozeman, almost midway between Cascade and Great Falls, lies one of the most important historic sites in the state, the ten-thousand-year-old Ulm *pishkun*. "For nearly half a century," says Stan Meyer of the Cascade County Historical Society's *pishkun* committee, "old-timers around here have wanted to protect and secure the entire site." *Pishkun* is the Blackfeet word for "buffalo trap"—literally "deep blood kettle"—and the *pishkun* at Ulm, largest in the world, was used well before the horse was introduced to North America in the seventeenth century. Native Americans hunted buffalo by stampeding them over the mile-long cliff. About 170 acres of the buffalo jump have long been protected as part of the Ulm Pishkun State Park, but another 1,080 acres, including much of the bottomland below the cliffs, remained in private hands until 1992, when Ted Turner acquired the land. Buffalo bone deposits extend for over a mile along the base of the cliffs, where ancient Native American workshops and trading centers were established to clean and tan the buffalo skins and butcher the meat. Private commercial contractors mined the bones after World War II and ground them into fertilizer and livestock meal. Old-timers recall seeing as many as three dozen railcar hoppers full of buffalo bones being shipped out daily in the late 1940s on a special rail spur built next to the *pishkun*. Despite such exploitation, archaeologists believe both the size and age of the Ulm *pishkun* can provide invaluable information about some of the earliest peoples to inhabit the high plains region. A team from Montana State University, together with the Department of Fish, Wildlife, and Parks, has already set up archaeological digs on the property, which Turner was persuaded to acquire sight unseen.

When Turner announced he would build a new log ranch house on the Flying D, Bozeman was certain the couple, whose romance most locals followed diligently in the supermarket tabloids, was now determined to tie the knot in their adopted home state. Their new house, modest to a fault like most of Turner's residences, is a two-story, four-bedroom affair, built into a hill facing the perpetually snow-capped Spanish Peaks. Living quarters are on the ground floor, next to a garage large enough to house the two Jeeps Ted and Jane use whenever they are in residence. The second floor includes a large dining space and kitchen and a workout room and gym, where Fonda spends several hours a day whenever she is at the ranch. She has succeeded on occasion in getting Turner into the gym, but he much prefers riding, mountain biking, or windsurfing on the 14.6-acre trout lake he had constructed in front of the house and stocked with four thousand rainbow trout.

The entire southern exposure of the house, which Jane helped design, is a virtual wall of glass, facing the spectacular Spanish Peaks. A wooden deck runs around the outside upper level. Turner often sits here with his spyglass, spotting elk or brown bear in the foothills leading up into the Lee Metcalf Wilderness. He sited his lake so that a reflection of the peaks is visible from inside the house and even had ten feet taken off the top of a small mountain to ensure that his view was totally unobstructed.

Although he has often been perceived as a reckless gambler, dazzled by the glint of fool's gold until it turns out he has somehow discovered a motherlode, Turner is, in fact, a uniquely successful workaday lobbyist who is much more effective proselytizing than managing. Consequently he has always delegated more day-to-day responsibility than virtually any other chief executive anywhere. He has proved that he can hold his own against superior odds and presumably more sophisticated opponents, whether they be the major television networks, the professional sports organizations, or the Congress of the United States. He learned how to make his own rules when none yet existed, and he wanted to send his Superstation out across the country. He learned how to break the rules when he had to and has almost single-handedly coopted the FCC's potentially damaging "must carry" rule for his own use and benefit. Now, on behalf of the National Buffalo Association, he is back on the barricades, touting the advantages of bison over beef. Turner began lobbying almost as soon as he bought the Flying D, but he has now taken his case to the public and added talks on the health benefits of eating buffalo meat to his regular "stump speech" agenda.

When Ted Turner passed the half century mark in 1988, Turner Broadcasting was nearly twenty years old, and cable television was forty. All three institutions had become mainstream. In early 1990 Turner became the first Western broadcaster to be carried on Soviet television. By sending CNN out all over the USSR via Soviet satellite, Turner was able to splice together the final link in the global network he had envisioned for more than a decade. "I think news is becoming our most important asset," he said then. "Almost by default. That's the big thing. If you were managing one thing in the world, wouldn't the global flow of television news be about as big a thing as you can possibly—I mean, the first global broadcast network?" In 1990 he could say, "We're already there, but it needs a little more refinement and a little bit more coverage and a little bit wider spread, but it's happening. It's already happening."

Ten years earlier, in a speech before a group of American newspaper editors, Turner had rashly predicted that newspapers would be dead within the decade. "I had to eat a lot of crow for that statement," he told the same editors in 1990. "Newspapers will still be here in the year 2000," Turner admitted, "but you'll be delivered electronically. Printed newspapers will eventually become too expensive." He then took newspapers to task for their international coverage. "Ask Americans if they are well informed," he challenged the editors. "They would say yes. But you will all be the first to admit the average American's knowledge of the world is not very high." There was only the slightest hint in his address that a healthy dose of all-news television might alleviate the situation.

Almost masochistically, the newspaper industry continues to invite Turner into its midst to predict the imminent demise of print. Hollywood, however, found in Ted Turner an entirely different kind of prophet. Not some faceless mogul or one of the new-breed bottom-liners who migrated from Wall Street to Sunset and Vine, Turner was that rarest of commodities in the entertainment industry of the 1990s, a genuine showman. He was also damned good for business. Turner was willing to fund everything from pro-choice documentaries to large-scale vanity productions that even the largest stars could never get off the ground anywhere else in the industry. Moreover, he had paid his dues and firmly established his liberal credentials, all of which made him eminently acceptable to the new Hollywood establishment. He was no Rupert Murdoch, trying to tell the professionals how to make a movie. Turner liked the glamour and the glitz of big-time, big-name productions, and increasingly, he was not only willing, but able to pay for it. Scott Sassa, the new head of Turner Pictures and now the clear number three within Turner Broadcasting, summed up Turner's reaction to Hollywood: "He likes being out there." Turner was just a piece of the furniture in Atlanta, a curious, unpredictable *chien bizarre*. In Hollywood, Sassa confirmed, "He's a celebrity."

"He has been very good for television," says Grant Tinker, former head of NBC. "In the beginning he was a bit of a swashbuckler, and perhaps he wasn't taken as seriously by the media as he should have been. I don't know him well, but he seems to have calmed down since he first came on the scene."

Once Turner and Fonda began showing up together around Los Angeles, the town was abuzz with the wonder of this obvious match. It was such a natural, anyone who knew them had to agree, that it could have, should have, happened years ago. Fonda could still provide Turner with the entrée into Hollywood's aristocracy, though he was rapidly redefining what an entertainment aristocrat ought to be. And Turner gave Fonda the self-respect and the support she had never before received from a man. When she turned to him during CNN's tenth anniversary celebration and brought his chin up close to hers so she could be certain to kiss him on camera, it was all over but the shouting.

Tom Hayden was absorbing a punishing personal defeat at the polls when Ted Turner strolled into Tiffany's in Beverly Hills on election day 1990. Turner picked out a simple little opal set off by two diamonds, which he planned to place on Jane's finger on December 21, her fifty-third birthday. Columnist Liz Smith had the story of their engagement, however, five minutes after he had walked out into Rodeo Drive, forcing Turner to pop the question over a month early. "I've been married twice," Fonda said, "but I've never had an engagement ring before." Undeterred by the fact that opals, Jane's favorite gem, are often considered the very essence of bad luck, Fonda decided to unveil their engagement and her new ring at a Variety Club dinner honoring Ted once again as Man of the Year. Expecting a stir as they entered the ballroom of Atlanta's elegant Hotel Nikko, the couple failed to turn a single head. The large celebrity crowd was preoccupied watching actor Donald O'Connor perform a bit of foolish standup comedy at his table. Without hesitation, Turner pulled his fiancée back out into the lobby and waited until they could get the crowd's full attention before remaking their grand entrance.

The smart money back in Bozeman was now certain the ceremony would take place before Christmas, since that was when their new house on the Flying D would be finished. "We've heard the rumors, too," ranch secretary Debbie Greenwood told the *Bozeman Daily Chronicle.* "But if the press wants to fly over the ranch here, all they'll see are buffalo." Fonda, in fact, had decided to wait until her eighteen-year-old son, Troy Garity (né Hayden) finished high school in Santa Monica before even considering when or where the wedding would be.

"Dad has met his match," says Robert Edward "Teddy" Turner IV. "She's tough, she's independent, she doesn't need him for anything." If Teddy had any disagreement with Fonda, it's her predilection for not wanting to be known as an American. "She wants to be known as a *human*," he observes. "I'm an American. And I'm proud of it. When they play the national anthem, Jane's family won't stand up. My father stands up. *He's* an American."

Teddy was the first of the Turner offspring to be married. After graduation from The Citadel, he had gone to work as a cameraman/editor in CNN's Moscow bureau. A near fatal automobile accident there knocked out his lower teeth and broke all the bones in his face, leaving him with a faint scar on his upper lip, a slightly crooked smile, and a new sense of purpose in his life. Not to mention a wife. He had proposed to his college sweetheart from the hospital gurney as he was being wheeled into the operating room. She had flown to Moscow to bring him home.

"I gave him a chance to renege," Genie Turner acknowledges, "because he had drugs in him." But the couple were married in early 1988. After a rocky first couple of years together, including a year-long separation during which Teddy began to believe he might be reliving *his* father's life, they are now back together again, stronger than ever. "You grow up in a dysfunctional family, that's what you know," Teddy explains. "Genie came from a very normal family, and I needed that."

Six months after Ted and Jane announced their engagement, Laura Lee, Ted's eldest daughter, went to the altar. She married Rutherford Seydel II on May 4, 1991, in what turned out to be Atlanta's "wedding of the year." Two years older than Teddy, Laura Lee met her future husband when she accompanied her father to yet another awards dinner. Scott Seydel, a local insurance executive and private investor, was also being honored at the event. Seydel's young son, Rutherford, asked about Ted Turner's date. "That's not his date," Seydel replied. "That's his daughter." Less than eight months later, Laura and Rutherford announced their engagement.

Weddings were proving to be something close to defining moments for the Turner clan. Ted's two previous nuptial celebrations had been restrained, formal affairs, reflecting the stolid certainty of life in the early 1960s, when the world seemed at peace with itself and there was little inkling that polite society, like the country itself, might soon begin to come unstuck at the seams.

The invitations to Laura's wedding reception at Atlanta's exclusive, old-money Piedmont Driving Club read "Robert Edward Turner III invites . . ." Of course, Mr. Turner was not a member of the Piedmont Driving Club and had to call upon the father of the groom, who was. Laura's guests were somewhat surprised to see signs at the entrance of the club announcing the "Seydel Wedding," though it was obvious that the man playing host was also picking up all the bills.

Judy Nye Hallisy had not seen Laura for nearly a dozen years and surprised her daughter by showing up along with her own father, Harry G. Nye, Jr., and his second wife. So did Laura's eighty-year-old grandmother, Florence Rooney Turner, who brought Robert Carter, her second husband of three months. It was Jane Fonda, however, who nearly stole the show at Laura's wedding. Poured into a slinky black microdress, she held hands with Ted during the ceremony, joked with the bride and bridesmaids, charmed the guests with her genuine good humor, and mugged incessantly for the photographers. While her performance won rave reviews from the Turner family, it threatened to turn the whole affair into an attraction reminiscent of the mass nuptials Ted once staged at Fulton County Stadium on Wedlock & Headlock Day, one of the Atlanta Braves' less memorable promotions.

"I haven't been to many weddings," says Fonda's daughter, Vanessa Vadim, who seemed to be experiencing culture shock at the extraordinary excess of Laura's. "I went to my mother's. But they were in jeans and in the living room." Vanessa, however, would be part of two more important weddings within the next twelve months, her mother's and Jennie Turner's, which followed four months later.

Like Laura, Teddy had not seen his real mother for over a dozen years until she showed up at his sister's wedding with his young half brother, Peter. "It was weird," Teddy says, "because he's my half brother on the other side, but he looks just like me." Ted Turner's own half brother, Marshall Hartmann, had not been invited.

Seeing so many of his family together at Laura's wedding, however, had a profound effect on Ted, who resolved to improve the relationships he was now willing to admit may have been neglected for many years. "We just didn't know him when we were growing up," Teddy recalls. "He was never home for Christmas—the Sydney-Hobart race always started on December 26—and we never went on family vacations until I was in college. He was scared to death by the movie *Citizen Kane*. He thought he *was* Kane, a guy who has everything and ends up with nothing. A while back he realized the world was in trouble, but that he was also in trouble. His environmental awareness is easily mirrored by his desire to have more of a family. We've gotten closer in the last year or so," Teddy adds, "and that's largely due to Jane. She said, 'There are five brats living in my house, and I want to get to know them.' We were all very wary at first, but she's terrific. Very sensitive, very real."

Turner is still not particularly close to any of his offspring, but he has indeed made a conscientious effort to bring them all together. Shortly after Laura's wedding, he established the Turner Family Foundation, a philanthropic trust whose board consists of Turner and Fonda and each of Turner's five children. The board meets at least twice a year to review various philanthropic investments and consider new requests for funding; the foundation gave away approximately $1 million in 1991 and over $10 million in 1992. Turner plans to expand the trust substantially over the years.

Ted has also made his children and Fonda's feel welcome at the Flying D in Montana, where the couple now spend much of their free time. "The Flying D is really becoming the new family home," says Teddy. "We get together for holidays—but it's a big crowd. At Thanksgiving last year it was over twenty, all family. Jane and my father have really made a push to get the family, not back together, but more together. At Christmas, Thanksgiving, spring breaks. And, of course, the Braves have been doing pretty well lately, so we all get to see each other at the games."

In addition to spending more time with his children, Turner has also vested each of them with a $2 million trust fund. With his endowment in hand, Teddy decided to leave Turner Broadcasting nearly three years ago but couldn't bring himself to tell his father he wanted to strike out on his own. Instead he approached Dee Woods, who has long served as confidante and surrogate parent to the Turner children.

"I told him, 'This is your life,' " Woods recalled. " 'This is your chance to do your thing.' "

A year later Teddy sank nearly a third of his trust into the purchase of *Challenge America I* and launched a bid to become the first American ever to win the Whitbread 'Round the World Race, a grueling nine-month, 32,000-mile circumnavigation of the globe that winds through every ocean and touches every continent. It is arguably the longest, most fearful, and most dangerous sporting event in the world. It could also be seen as a way for thirty-year-old Teddy to beat his father at Turner's own game. Although Teddy says the Whitbread makes the week-long America's Cup look like child's play, he denies any hint of familial competition and hopes to convert his experience in the race into an ongoing sports marketing enterprise. He just loves sailing, he says, a love he learned not from his father, but from Jimmy Brown, as his father had before him.

Teddy Turner was five years old—and frightened out of his wits —the first time he crewed on an ocean racer. His father dumped him onto *American Eagle* in Ft. Lauderdale and picked him up over one thousand miles later in Long Island Sound. "How many fathers let their kids go at five years old and live with strangers for almost a month on a sailboat?" he asks. "One thing I thought as a kid was, This is terrible. Why can't we be like other families?

"I probably picked up a lot of offshore techniques from my dad," Teddy admits, "but it was Jimmy Brown who taught me how to sail. He raised my dad, and he raised all of the kids in my family. Jimmy has been around this family since he was eighteen. I was eleven when Jimmy first took me sailing in Newport Harbor during the 1974 America's Cup. I got a boat of my own and spent a lot of time sailing around Atlanta and in Newport again in 1977 and 1980, just wherever I could.

"I went to The Citadel because my father made me," Teddy says. Disappointed that the McCallie School no longer offered a military curriculum, Turner made certain that each of his three sons completed a compulsory tour of duty at the legendary military college in Charleston, South Carolina. Like his father, Teddy was captain of his college sailing team. Like Ted, he even married a member of a rival team; Genie had been a top sailor at the College of Charleston.

Teddy and his younger brothers spent their summers braving one-hundred-degree heat, stagnant water, poisonous snakes, mosquitoes, and alligators as they pulled pigweed out of the rice canals at Hope Plantation. It was all part of basic training in the Turner family boot camp, where hardship was expected and complaints forbidden. "He made them work," says Carolyn Godley, who manages Hope Plantation with her husband, Johnny. The

Godleys also take care of the brown bears Yogi and BooBoo, as well as assorted cougars, swans, and guinea fowl Turner has penned up on the property. "He even made those boys pick their own birds," says Mrs. Godley. "I can remember them just fussing as they pulled the feathers off the ducks they shot. He laid down the law: "If you kill it, you eat it."

Now that his boys are grown, Turner brings in professionals to pull the weeds on his properties in Montana. Working through the state's nonprofit Noxious Weed Fund, he has already contributed some $20,000 toward the removal of spotted knapweed from nearly a hundred acres of the Bar None. Knapweed invades the streams and displaces native plant life. Turner's funding provides for biocontrolled stream rehabilitation, as well as the introduction of certain insects intended to keep the knapweed under control. The real problem on the Flying D, however, is not knapweed, but a parasite called leafy spurge. Turner purchased two hundred head of sheep, which eat the spurge, then he left the coyotes who roam free over his ranch land to keep the sheep in check. "I'll keep the sheep," he said, "only as long as I can get 'em cheap. Until they've gotten rid of the leafy spurge or until the coyotes get them." His stream reclamation project on the Flying D is one of the largest in the state, and he has worked closely with Montana's Soil Conservation Service to preserve the streams that affect tributaries throughout the entire Gallatin-Madison Valley, now some of the very finest fly-fishing streams in the world. One SCS field officer remembers being on the Flying D one day in 1991 pulling up spurge by the side of Spanish Creek when a couple pulled up in a boat and started helping him—and ended up spending the rest of the long, hot summer day at the job without ever identifying themselves as the owner of the property and his fiancée.

Always in a hurry, a boy on a tear for over fifty years, Turner has roared through his life without a backward glance. He found the time to scrape down the bottoms of his racing yachts with Jimmy Brown and pull weeds out of a blue-ribbon trout stream, but always seemed to come up short on the domestic front. Ted Turner always had the best of intentions and knew his heart was in the right place, but there was never enough time. Now approaching his fifty-fifth birthday, he is no longer in such a hurry, no longer running away from his "greatest fear"—the fear of his own demise. He seems at last able to make the effort his father never could.

Until a very few years ago the people closest to Ted Turner would still often hear him talk of suicide whenever he became depressed. Other times he would talk convincingly of his conviction that he would almost certainly be killed before he turned fifty. Still, he has never bothered with any kind of personal security and still doesn't, despite the tight protection that now surrounds CNN's headquarters. "Years ago, I came up with what I was going to say to an assassin if he came to shoot me," Turner recounts. "You want to know what it is? 'Thanks for not coming sooner.' Pretty good, huh? He might laugh so much he'd decide not to shoot me."

Ted Turner no longer fears the assassin's bullet. He has reinvented himself by redirecting a lifelong preoccupation with self-destruction into a public career of saving the planet. A conservationist since his boyhood days in Savannah, Turner never ceases to lament the disappearance of the whales and sea turtles he used to see off the Savannah coast or the ducks that no longer crowd his beloved eastern flyway. He shoots less now, however, and allows only limited hunting on his Montana ranches. "I'm not anti-hunting," Turner told *Montana* magazine. "I killed a couple of blue grouse for dinner the other day. I've killed two elk since I bought the Flying D. But I didn't hunt at all last year. I got a license this year, but I don't even know if I'll bother using it. I've gotten so I like watching them more than shooting them."

In the early 1980s Turner began to comprehend just how serious environmental devastation had become. He credits his old friend Jacques Yves Cousteau for the inspiration to act on his instincts. Turner founded the Better World Society in 1985 to educate others about the problem but used the opportunity to inform himself and widen his already considerable circle of international contacts. Where once he talked of war as an efficient means of weeding out the weaker members of society, today he girds himself against the fate of his former hero, Alexander the Great, who drank himself to death at thirty-five when he could find no more worlds to conquer. Turner's personal pantheon today includes new heroes like Martin Luther King and Mahatma Gandhi. Since 1981 he has been a lifetime trustee of the King Institute for Non-Violence. Hank Aaron and Rubye Lucas were the first blacks ever to sit on the board of directors of a billion-dollar corporation and have been Turner's close friends as well as

TBS business associates for more than twenty years. He launched the first Goodwill Games in Moscow in 1986 and promptly lost millions in a genuine effort to promote world peace by bringing the United States and the Soviet Union together on the playing field. That the Games led to the agreement putting CNN on a Soviet satellite or that he now owns an invaluable off-year Olympics is not incidental—Turner firmly believes that he can do well by doing good. He is not above recognizing the value of his contributions and has recently been heard telling intimates, with an absolutely straight face, that he hopes someday to have achieved enough to deserve a Nobel Peace Prize.

"If we can't make the right choice after we have all the information," Turner will say, "then we don't deserve to live." For more than a decade he has devoted a good deal of his time and considerable energy to spreading that message. Sometimes, however, his promotional zeal gets ahead of him, as it did in 1990 when he established the Turner Tomorrow Awards. Intended to inspire writers around the world to submit their own "positive solutions to global problems," the effort degenerated into an unsavory spat over who should get the $500,000 cash prize Turner put up. Because he seldom offers any specific solutions or becomes an advocate on individual issues, Turner is sometimes written off as just another "checkbook messiah," infatuated with the sound of his own voice and overcome by his self-importance. However, his extraordinary high profile, substantial wealth, multiple interests, and lifetime of contacts, as well as his typically apolitical posture and, most of all, his control of a global television network, have provided him with entrée anywhere in the world. It was not accidental that CNN was able to remain in Baghdad after the start of the Gulf War, just as it was not accidental that Turner's news network is now used by presidents and prime ministers for direct, over-the-air diplomacy. Boris Yeltsin climbed up on a tank to halt the attempted 1991 Soviet coup and save his nation because he knew his image would be flashed around the world by CNN, signaling to hundreds of thousands of Muscovites that he was still in control and making hundreds of millions around the world part of the revolution that ended seventy-five years of Communist rule. Britain's John Major and U.S. president George Bush were both watching the action unfold, powerless to act until they were informed by CNN's unblinking, live coverage.

Turner sees himself not as a messiah, but as a communicator

and catalyst. He has never really outgrown the hero complex he developed as a boy, but today he usually tempers those dreams with the impressive reality of his accomplishments. "The culmination of his life," says Gerry Hogan, once an heir apparent at Turner Broadcasting and still on good terms with his former boss, "would be if our country gets into such a crisis that there is an outcry that Ted take over and save us all. He still carries that dream around every day."

"My dad used to say 'A few fleas are good for a dog,'" Turner told television interviewer David Frost. "I've made a number of transitions in my life," he added, "one of them from being relatively insecure to relatively secure—everything is relative.

"I was raised to be a political conservative, but I've become more of a progressive over the last fifteen years, as I've been exposed to more things. I've gone from rampant nationalist to rampant internationalist. I've gone from someone in the billboard business to someone in the television business, from someone who was racing sailboats to primarily—my number one hobby now is fly-fishing. It's almost a Zen experience. It's totally, totally different. From male chauvinist to being totally in favor of the equal sharing of power and responsibility—men and women. I'm going to be a totally different kind of husband this time. And I was different in my second marriage than my first. This will be my last one. Hopefully. At least I feel I'm sure of that. Of course, everybody is always that way.

"I caused a lot of pain to my second wife," Turner admits, "and if I could set anything right, I would have liked that marriage not to have occurred or to have made her happier. That's probably been my greatest regret. I also wish we'd gotten into the World Series a long time ago."

"Ted has grown into his fifties very gracefully," observes Bob Wussler. "And the stronger CNN and TBS have got, the more believable Ted has become. When I first met him, one of his long-time friends told me that Ted was a man who would see a lot of changes during any five-year period. Having been with him for ten years, I can agree that he does experience these changes. It's just that now practically any change he makes could have a profound effect on the world."

Turner, the man who was usually ten years ahead of his time, was exactly ten years late in bringing Atlanta the World Series he promised when he bought the Braves back in 1976. But, like so many of his other ventures, when it happened it was almost larger than life. In 1991 Turner's Atlanta Braves were defeated by the Minnesota Twins in one of the most closely contested World Series in baseball history. Three of the seven games went into extra innings, four were decided on the last pitch, and five were won in a team's last at-bat. The seventh and deciding game was tied in the tenth inning, with the Twins finally winning 1–0 to take the series. Baseball commissioner Fay Vincent called it "probably the greatest World Series ever." The real highlight, however, was the cutaway shot on network television that showed Ted Turner sound asleep on Jane Fonda's shoulder as one of his Atlanta Braves rounded the bases after hitting the only grand slam home run of the Series.

First I shape up the establishment,
Then I become a part of it.

ROBERT EDWARD TURNER III

Chapter Eighteen

The eighteen children in Ms. Sherry Flamand's second-grade class at Margaret Leary Elementary School were beside themselves as they lofted their helium-filled balloons into the brisk high-country winds near Butte, Montana. The balloons carried self-addressed postcards asking finders to fill in their names and locations and mail them back to the school. Seven-year-old Molly Marshall's balloon carried ninety miles in the air, high over the Continental Divide, over the Madison range and Big Sky, and over the Spanish Peaks before finally splashing down in the Gallatin River. Molly Marshall's postcard was the only one returned, and it bore the signatures of Ted Turner and Jane Fonda.

With Jimmy Brown in command of the details, Ted and Jane's wedding had gone off without a hitch. Turner settled a $10 million dowry of TBS stock on Jane Fonda as part of the couple's prenuptial agreement and thought he had kept things quiet enough at Avalon Plantation for CNN to score yet another scoop. Fonda came up with something completely different as a wedding present. Aware of Ted's new sense of family history—he had made an abortive attempt to bring his grandfather's old Mississippi cotton farm back into the family—Fonda arranged for a Salt Lake City genealogical research firm to put together a hasty history of the Turner clan. Ted was so pleased with the handsome parchment-bound genealogy that he ordered copies made for each of his children.

Shortly after Turner's mother passed away in early 1992, Ted took his new bride down to Savannah to see the old brick house on Abercorn Street where he had spent so much of his youth. He also took advantage of the occasion to address the annual meeting of the National Buffalo Association being held there, since he was now the country's largest commercial buffalo breeder and could account for nearly 10 percent of all the privately owned bison in the world.

The newlyweds spent as much time as they could in Montana, but the year ahead had already begun to close in on them. Fonda brought Evita, her $250,000 Arabian, and two other favorite horses to the Flying D from her ranch in Santa Barbara, which was now on the market. She was hard at work on several new film projects, including *Jury Duty*, a sequel to *9 to 5*, her smash hit with Lily Tomlin and Dolly Parton. She was about to launch her thirteenth workout video, this one for children. She was also producing *Lakota Woman*, a feature-length movie for television to be shot in Montana, which would be part of Turner Broadcasting's new $50 million multimedia Native American project. Turner had already completed five movies in Montana, making him one of the largest part-time employers in the state.

When they are at the ranch, the couple rise every day before seven. Both maintain frenetic schedules that leave the locals' heads spinning. Their days in Bozeman are spent in endless rounds of meetings, with Native American groups, environmental and historical organizations, local and state politicians, as well as the growing circle of displaced celebrities who have gravitated to the area. In winter, they manage to carve out time for a little skiing, although they prefer the groomed slopes of Big Sky to the more challenging Bridger's Bowl, the locals' favorite. Turner and Fonda are both now addicted to fly-fishing and have became fixtures at the Trout Unlimited meetings in Bozeman's Holiday Inn.

In early 1992 Turner's youngest child, Sarah Jean (Jennie) Turner, married J. Peek Garlington III in what *Town & Country* magazine called an "intimate wedding service in front of nearly 100 friends and family" at Atlanta's towering Cathedral of St. Philip. Twelve months later, in the early spring of 1993, Laura Lee and her husband were presented with a baby boy, Rutherford Seydel II, making Ted Turner a grandfather at fifty-four. Once his youngest son, Beauregard, had graduated from the Citadel that June, Turner and Fonda led a large CNN crew to the Earth Summit in Rio de Janeiro. This conference drew nearly nine thousand news reporters, the largest contingent of media personnel ever assembled, and included a Global Forum—a "people's assembly of thousands of special-interest environmental groups from 180 countries"—which Turner chaired.

Wearing a traditional Brazilian white cotton waistshirt and fondling silver worry beads, Turner held forth at the forum in his usual amiable, unconstructed style, keeping the crowd in check with his obvious sincerity and effusive charm, if not his detailed knowledge of the earth's environmental problems. He kept an uncharacteristically low profile, however, at this historic event, which attracted heads of state from 118 countries. Choosing not to participate in some of the more public gatherings on the agenda. "Ted Turner is not a joiner," explains Maurice Strong, former chairman of Turner's Better World Society and director general of this United Nations Earth Summit, when asked why Ted Turner seemed to do a disappearing act in Rio immediately after he and Jane had hosted a Global Forum reception on the rooftop of their hotel. "He was ten years ahead of everybody else on the environment," Strong explains. "Now he's leaving it up to others to follow through."

Privately Turner continued to seek out new recruits for the environmental wars and traveled to Carrerras, Mexico, to meet with Sir James Goldsmith, the British industrialist and conglomerator who had sold off most of his politically incorrect holdings to concentrate on "green" investments.

Turner also reiterated his serious intention of making a business out of buffalo. "I don't subscribe to the 'buffalo commons' ideas," Turner said, referring to the suggestion that much of the Great Plains be given back to the bison, "but I do think there's going to be a bigger and bigger market for buffalo meat." Shortly thereafter he closed on the purchase of another major property— the five-hundred-square-mile Ladder Ranch near Truth or Consequences, New Mexico. This latest acquisition made him one of the largest individual landowners in the West.

When Turner and Fonda had lunch in the Cuchillo Cafe just outside Ladder Ranch's north entrance, their individual eating habits became hot topics with the locals—Turner had a rare steak, seventy-year-old Rosa Orr reported, but Fonda stayed with her usual salad. "A few years ago they would have had a fight on their hands if they ever tried to bring buffalo onto that ranch," Orr comments. "But I'm just a crotchety old lady. Those two are really moving with the times."

His famous chiseled jaw still juts forward in petulant challenge, but Turner's hair and mustache are now snow white. Under Fonda's disciplined influence he is as firm and fit as most men ten years his junior. But the years of working hard and playing harder have taken their toll. "I've been through a lot of campaigns," Turner says. "I'm only fifty-four, but I've already got the mileage of a one-hundred-fifty-year-old man. I'm like a New York City taxicab that has three drivers driving twenty-four hours a day, seven days a week."

Ted Turner can count himself among the world's two hundred or so billionaires. He has his trophy wife and she happens to come complete with her own trophies. He also has roomfuls of his own. He has become almost as openly affectionate with his children as he is with Fonda. He is even developing close ties with her two children, Vanessa Vadim, and Troy Hayden. "You never thought of having fun with Dad before," says Teddy. "But now you can." When Turner is with his children at the Flying D or on one of his plantations, he can even be talked out of his usual compulsive routine, which regularly includes riding, hiking, biking, and windsurfing, sometimes all within the same day. Having survived reading his own business obituary at least twice in the past ten years, Turner is contemplating the day he can throw off the yoke his cable partners have placed him in and regain total control of Turner Broadcasting.

"My father told me," Turner has repeated year after year to his children, "he wanted to be a millionaire, have a yacht, and a plantation. By the time he was fifty, he had achieved all three. And he was having a difficult time." Turner has carefully arranged his own life to avoid any possibility that he might ever have to rest on his own laurels—that is a principal motivation behind his zealous proselytization for world peace and preservation. "It's almost like a religious fervor. I'm not going to rest until all the world's problems have been solved," he attests, suggesting that a lifetime crusade is one certain way of avoiding the suicide that ended his father's life. "I'm in great shape. I mean, the problems will survive me—no question about it."

What may finally do Ted Turner in, however, is boredom. "The worst sin, the ultimate sin for me," he says, "is to be bored."

Testing the limits of his board's veto power in 1991, Turner offered financier Carl Lindner $320 million for the financially troubled Hanna-Barbera animation studio. His board approved the acquisition only after Turner got former Drexel banker Leon Black to put up half of the purchase price. Hanna-Barbera brought into the TBS library more than three thousand half-hour cartoons, nearly 40 percent of all the animated film ever produced in the United States, including such television 'toon classics as "The Flintstones," "Yogi Bear," and "The Jetsons," as well as H-B's substantial animation production studios in the Philippines.

The Hanna-Barbera acquisition reconfirmed Turner's insistence on owning the product. "We control more of our own software," he says today with smug satisfaction, "than any other programming entity in the world." Hanna-Barbera had been shopped to every studio and broadcaster in the country but at $320 million was considered seriously overpriced. Once again, it was Turner's ability to build appreciation into an asset that proved how wrong the market could be. No sooner had the Hanna-Barbera deal closed than Turner announced TBS would turn his new cartoon library into a twenty-four-hour Cartoon Network. With channel capacity limited and new rate restrictions built into the new 1992 cable reregulation act, Turner's cable partners were chary of new network launches. In the end, however, they went along, chiefly because they still need Turner at least as much as he once needed them.

Within six months Turner's new Cartoon Network, which provided his usual dual revenue steams of advertising and subscriber fees, was delivering Nielsen numbers twice as high as the company's prelaunch projections. The new venture, in fact, finished in a dead heat with Turner's own Superstation as the most watched channel from midnight to six A.M. By simply substituting sound tracks, Turner expects to find a ready audience for his newest network around the world. "Cartoons," he says, "travel even better than American movies."

With the Cartoon Network an almost instant success, Turner began hinting broadly that there might be more such launches in the future. Only about one thousand of the more than four thousand films in his library have ever been shown on either WTBS or TNT and could support several "minipay" channels—low-priced pay per view movie networks that could further segment the market and help squeeze out additional profits from the TBS library.

"The one thing we do here," says Terry McGuirk, who has gravitated upward to the clear number two slot at Turner Broadcasting, "is start new networks, build new networks, and market them." Turner Broadcasting now has five—more than anyone else in the world. Soon there will be at least two—another news channel, CNN International, and a second movie channel. Time-Warner and TCI can talk all they want about the new "500-channel information highway" that is just around the corner. Turner is coining money today and is perfectly positioned for the future, whatever it might hold, simply because he already owns more "information"—movies, news, and sports—than anyone else in the world.

"We're really in the business of remarketing products," explains Scott Sassa as Turner Broadcasting begins expanding rapidly into new media projects beyond broadcasting. "We buy as much software as we can and then find as many ways as we can to get it out there."

Recycling the enormous volume of news and information generated by CNN each day, Turner has already surpassed Reuters as the largest news gathering agency in the world. CNN distributes live news packages to more than six hundred television stations worldwide. CNN's audio track provides core programming for CNN Radio, which is distributed to several hundred independent and government-owned broadcasters around the world. Turner has extended his reach into the U.S. educational market with a satellite-delivered news package, replete with printed classroom materials, which goes into nearly twenty thousand secondary and high schools across the country. CNN produces a highly regarded opinion poll in conjunction with *Time* magazine and also co-produces entertainment industry news programming with *Variety*. Turner recently launched the Airport Channel, a custom-packaged television news service that offers travelers updated headlines, news and weather. Turner is currently testing even more new distribution outlets, including an in-flight news channel and McTV for McDonald's. CNN coverage of world crises like the Gulf War and the collapse of Soviet communism also gets repackaged into books published by Turner Publishing. Turner Home Entertainment takes CNN news footage, TNT movies, and cartoon channel animation and repackages the lot for sale in videocassette format. Turner uses each of his networks assiduously to cross-promote his other products and services.

"We're a lot like the modern chicken farmer," Turner explains.

"They grind up the feet to make fertilizer. They grind up the intestines to make dog food. The feathers go into pillows. Even the chicken manure is made into fertilizer. They use every bit of the chicken. Well, that's what we try to do with the television product, use everything to its fullest extent." He has even capitalized on his controversial colorized film classics—airing old movies like *Casablanca* or *King Kong* on both WTBS and TNT in color *and* black and white, then selling videocassettes of both versions.

Turner Pictures is now one of the most prolific film studios in the country, last year producing twenty-four feature films for television. Turner's new animated feature, *Tom & Jerry—The Movie,* is the first Turner film made for theatrical distribution and will be followed in late 1993 by *Gettysburg,* in which Turner himself manages to realize a lifelong fantasy with a bit part as a dying Confederate officer. Clearly there will be more, whether Turner finally succeeds in buying a studio or merely grows Turner Pictures into a major studio of his own.

The growth of Turner's established cable channels, however, should slow considerably as the U.S. cable market approaches saturation. His three largest networks—CNN, WTBS, and TNT—already reach more than 95 percent of all cable households in the United States. With the domestic market now expected to expand by only 2–3 percent a year through the 1990s, Turner must depend on squeezing even more profit from his existing product and launching more new channels to sustain the kind of growth TBS has enjoyed during the past five years.

The real growth opportunity for Turner Broadcasting lies outside the United States. "The line extension of all our brands," says Scott Sassa, "that's a no-brainer. It's basically getting on satellite and getting out there and distributing the service. It's really just blocking and tackling, the basics of distribution." Only thirty-three years old, Sassa is part of the company's new senior management team that includes Terry McGuirk and CNN president Tom Johnson. Sassa led the charge into Latin America and created the company's model for multilingual expansion. Dubbing programming into Spanish and Portuguese, TNT Latin America turned a profit in 1992 after less than twelve months on the air. In early 1993 Turner stole a march on the rest of the world by launching the first commercial television station in Russia. Time-Warner, Disney, Spelling Entertainment, British Broadcasting, and several other Western media companies were outbid by Turner and his local partner, Eduard Sagalaev, former director general of the state-owned Ostankino Television Co. Programmed in Russian with TBS and TNT movies, cartoons, and CNN, Turner's Russian venture brings him full circle, since he plans to use satellite distribution to beam this new station throughout the confederation, creating Russia's own Superstation and the country's first privately owned, advertiser–sponsored television network.

Turner has been slow to expand into similar relationships with local broadcasters in other countries. "There was a logic in Atlanta," says former Turner International executive Charles Bonan, "that said we'll do it all ourselves. We had all kinds of offers from potential partners, but Ted wasn't interested. Now, of course, he's learned it's the only way to go." Turner has already moved to link up with local strategic partners and accelerate his expansion into continental Europe, and has developed local language partners in Germany, Sweden, and Denmark. Turner is convinced the appetite for his staple of news, American film classics, sports, and cartoons will be even greater overseas than it has proven to be in the United States and he is now determined to take his networks into local language wherever possible.

CNN supplies twice daily Spanish-language newscasts to Telemundo in the United States and is exploring a twenty-four-hour Spanish news network with several other partners. In 1992 TBS invested over $20 million in a new joint venture news channel in Germany. (That investment was a compromise for Turner, however, forced on him by Time-Warner. He had originally planned his own, wholly owned CNN-D German-language news channel, but was caught up short by his partner's veto power.)

With a sharp eye on growing competition, Turner plans to more than double CNN International's budget. He is building a new $5 million production facility in Atlanta to send different versions of CNN International to different time zones around the world. By 1994 nearly three-quarters of CNN International's content will be original material. Turner is also speeding up efforts to improve CNN's international reporting and programming. He has opened new CNN bureaus in Amman, Rio de Janeiro, New Delhi, Mexico City, and Johannesburg, bringing the total to twenty foreign bureaus, plus eight more within the United States. No other broadcast news organization even comes close to CNN's global news-gathering ability.

Since wider penetration of international markets will depend not only on broader coverage of world events, but also on local-language broadcasts, CNN has begun experimenting with subtitles as well as local-language voice-overs. "Competition has been good for CNN," says Tom Johnson. "It has given us a sense of added urgency."

CNN's potential is vast, but the network is building on an already strong base. In 1992 CNN earned more than either CBS, NBC, or ABC, let alone their respective news divisions; and the Cable News Network, including CNN International and Headline News, is expected to earn an astounding $250 million by 1994. Turner has kept CNN operating costs below $150 million, still considerably less than each of the three major broadcasting networks spends each year on news. All three major broadcast networks have approached Turner regarding some form of sharing costs or exchanging raw news footage, and these talks are ongoing. Salaries at Turner remain substantially lower than those at the broadcast networks, although the disparities have been shrinking. CNN now starts correspondents at $60,000–$70,000, while the broadcast networks typically pay new reporters approximately $100,000.

Turner has aggressively blocked out more and more satellite transponders to provide segmented delivery of CNN and his other networks around the world. CNN is now up on eight different birds, giving the network the largest, as well as the most flexible, footprint of any broadcast service in the world. By splitting up his signal in so many different ways, Turner can offer advertisers regional market coverage, often in local language. Unfortunately, customizing the news for each region or setting aside time for local newscasts, says CNN International's Peter Vesey, "is not an easy or an inexpensive thing to do." Nevertheless, Turner is the only broadcaster in the world providing continent-by-continent advertising breakouts. The ultimate goal, of course, is to provide local-language, country-by-country segmentation.

As recently as 1990, Turner Broadcasting's liabilities exceeded the company's assets by nearly half a billion dollars. In 1992 TBS booked its first net profit in seven years, declared its first dividend since 1975, and had more than $600 million in unused credit lines and more than $300 million in free cash flow from operations. The company still carries some $1.8 billion in long-term debt but has been servicing this liability with relative ease. Despite the still widespread belief that Turner's overweening ambition and impetuous purchase of MGM cost him control of his company, he still retains a 62 percent majority of TBS voting stock. Both TCI and Time-Warner are carrying significantly greater relative debt loads, and Time-Warner, despite its recently professed interest in Turner's entertainment channels (and shocking disinterest in CNN), has publicly declared its intention to "monetize" its approximately 19-percent equity interest in TBS should the opportunity present itself (Tele-Communications and Turner's other cable partners notwithstanding).

"Turner Broadcasting has really been transformed from an entrepreneurially led, very heavily leveraged, modestly profitable programmer," says media analyst Dennis Leibowitz of Donaldson, Lufkin & Jenrette, "to a world-class media company with tremendous financial strength."

A visionary, Harold Ross once said, is the fool who just walked into the room. It was not so long ago that Robert Edward Turner III was derided, as much for his crude, clownish ways as for his oversimplified view of the industry in which he chose to operate. "Ted Turner's vision, and the guts to stick to the vision," says Terry McGuirk, "still drives this company." Turner may be starting to look his age, McGuirk suggests, but none of Turner's close associates believes he is even remotely ready to retire.

Former CNN anchorman Dan Schorr agrees, but he believes Turner is "looking around for a way to account for his sins. He just happens to have a powerful new technology to work with. I think Ted's motivation is to pay back past slights, pay back all the critics. He still wants to vindicate himself."

"In 1980," recalls Irwin Mazo, Turner's first real business adviser, "Ted told me with utter conviction that he had four great ambitions. He said he was going to make that dinky little television station WTCG the fourth national network. He said he was going into the movie business—because they were producing trash on movies and TV. He also said he was going to be this country's wealthiest man. And finally he told me he was going to be president of the United States.

"I asked him how in hell he thought he could be president. 'You have no political base.' 'I've got the boob tube,' he told me. 'If this country falls flat on its face, I can go on the boob tube. That's power.'"

"President?" says former Turner Broadcasting executive Jim Roddey. "All this is a progression—Ted just keeps moving to larger arenas. In the old days he wasn't satisfied unless everyone in a room listened to him. Then it became everyone in town, then the state, then the country. Now it's the world."

"I would only run for president if it was the only way I could get this country to turn around," Turner says, parrying the question of his interest and availability. "My main concern is to be a benefit to the world, to build up a global communications system that helps humanity come together, to control population, to stop the arms race, to preserve our environment. I'm a deeper thinker. I've traveled all over. I have more access to information than anyone on the planet. When you realize your family, your friends, your society, and your planet is in a dire state of emergency, that has to change anyone with a responsible world outlook. I've thought about being president from time to time," Turner explains, "and people have asked me about it from time to time, but I like my present job a lot more. I said back in the early 1980s that I wanted to be Jiminy Cricket for America. You know, the country's conscience."

Dissatisfied with both parties' candidates in the early days of the 1992 presidential campaign, several prominent southern political power brokers, including John Jay Hooker and Hamilton Jordan, put together a short list of potential third-party candidates they could support in lieu of Bush or Clinton. After a good deal of scrutiny the list was winnowed down to just two names. Hooker placed a call to Larry King to line up air time, then he telephoned the first name on his list. A few days later H. Ross Perot appeared live on CNN's "Larry King Show" and announced he could be persuaded to run for president providing there was a sufficient indication of interest from all fifty states. The other name on Hooker's list was Larry King's boss.

A few months later Turner himself admitted he had briefly considered the White House "or at least vice president." Speaking before a TV Critics Association meeting in Los Angeles in early 1992, he said he had rejected the idea because, among other reasons, "my wife was already married to one politician, and she told me she wasn't going to be married to another one." He also said that he doubted he had the "proper temperament" for the job. John Jay Hooker is convinced that Turner, unlike Perot, would never have quit under fire in the middle of the race. "I think the country might even be able to live with the lithium," Hooker adds, noting that "1996 is not that far away."

"I'm still building my company," Turner says convincingly. "Governments move too slowly for me, and besides, I haven't done everything I want to with this business." Turner's partners are becoming preoccupied with new technologies, with an electronic information highway and the increasingly apparent conflict of interest that separates programmers from the distribution channels they control. "We're always looking at new possibilities," Turner told *The Wall Street Journal* in early 1993. "We do business with everybody in the entertainment business, and from time to time we talk with just about everybody."

Ever since losing out in his 1985 bid for CBS, Turner has shown a recurring interest in owning a major broadcast network. He came close in 1988 to seducing General Electric's NBC into acquiring a 25-percent interest in Turner Broadcasting but those discussions broke down over price. In 1989, he changed direction and began looking for a movie studio. Now, with GE once again acting like it wants to unload NBC, Turner has reopened the dialogue. His cable partners, particularly Tele-Communications, which holds 22.5 percent of TBS, have consistently opposed any move that would dilute their own interest in TBS or combine the company with a cable industry competitor; but the possibilities for synergy are obvious and hold not a little promise for Turner himself. Time-Warner, Turner's other large partner (with 18.9 percent) may be less intransigent and, because of its own relatively high leverage, less willing to block any intelligent combination.

New legislation restricting cable operators' interference in programming may also provide Turner with a way to overcome the insidious veto he has lived with for the past six years. When Capital Cities/ABC announced recently it would welcome a merger or other combination with another major source of programming, Turner's name kept popping up, and he did, in fact, closet himself with Dan Burke and the Cap Cities directorate. If only because of Cap Cities' strong cash position, the prospects for a transaction with TBS remains a promising possibility. But Paramount Communications and CBS have also revealed continuing high-level discussions with Turner, and his interest in the synergistic benefits offered by the rapidly eroding NBC is an open secret.

The combination of Turner Broadcasting System with any one of the major broadcast networks, most industry observers agree, would create very substantial cost savings and be a source of incremental new profits for Turner as well as the network. CNN could easily replace or complement a network's entire news operation, creating instant savings of $100–$200 million, which would fall straight into the profit column. The network, in turn, could provide Turner with the critical mass to support high-profile motion picture acquisitions and big-ticket sports events like the 1996 Summer Olympics. Since TBS has much of the physical production plant already in place in Atlanta, the network that winds up with Olympic television rights almost axiomatically has to make Turner his partner or spend several hundred million dollars replicating the production facilities Turner already possesses. Federal regulatory limitations and Turner's complex ownership structure may make any such combination difficult, but in the volatile, fluid worlds of information and entertainment, no strategic pairing can any longer be discounted. To that end, *The Wall Street Journal* was moved to speculate recently that even AT&T might be a realistic strategic partner for Ted Turner, assuming Ma Bell first doesn't merge with John Malone's Tele-Communications.

During his two-year whirlwind courtship of Jane Fonda, Turner frequently took the opportunity to introduce her around the TBS offices. "When we would get done going through the first several floors," he relates, "and were getting ready to get on the elevator, I'd tell her, 'You know, if I hadn't started the place, I couldn't have afforded to buy it. And if I hadn't started it, I would certainly not be qualified to work here in any capacity.'" Turner enjoys telling that story, and every time he does, he usually ends up asking his listener, "Now, tell me the truth. Wouldn't you really rather be Ted Turner? You're right," he'll say. "It's a hell of a lot of fun, but I'll tell you something, kiddo. It ain't as easy as it looks."

Acknowledgments

Despite the compelling nature of its subject, this book could never have been written without the enthusiastic support, generous assistance, and extraordinary efforts of a small army of friends and colleagues, not the least of whom include my understanding associates at Ladenburg, Thalmann; Betty Prashker of Crown Publishers; Jim Stein of the William Morris Agency; Ron Martin of the *Atlanta Constitution;* Bob Hope; Daniel Schecter; Royal Dubois (Duby) Joslin IV; Joseph Jackson of the New York Yacht Club; Lucy Rooney; Lori Henry; William Steverson of the McCallie School; Legarè VanNess; Judy Warner; Max Berley; Nicholas Paumgarten; B. J. Beach; Patricia Bolling; David O'Dett; Les Brown; Peter Ross Range; Van Bucher; Kimberley Reilly; Faith Evans; and Cary Ryan, whose keen eye and sharp pencil has ensured that honesty and accuracy were not lost in the morass of words that informs this portrait of a truly amazing individual.

Bibliography

Akiskal, Hagip S. "The Bi-Polar Spectrum: New Concepts in Classification and Diagnosis." In *Psychiatric Update: The APA Annual Review*. Washington, DC: The American Psychiatric Press, 1983.

Anderson, Christopher. *Citizen Jane: The Turbulent Life of Jane Fonda*. New York: Henry Holt and Company, 1990.

Auletta, Ken. *Three Blind Mice*. New York: Random House, 1991.

Bertrand, John, and Patrick Robinson. *Born to Win*. New York: William Morrow, 1985.

Botkin, B.A. *A Treasury of Southern Folklore*. New York: Crown Publishers, 1962.

Brooks, Cleanth. *The Language of the American South*. Athens, GA: University of Georgia Press, 1985.

Editors of Buzzworm. *1993 Earth Journal*. Boulder, CO: Buzzworm Books, 1992.

Carpenter, Donna Sammons, and John Feloni. *The Fall of the House of Hutton*. New York: Henry Holt & Co., 1989.

Clurman, Richard M. *To the End of Time*. New York: Simon & Schuster, 1992.

Clymer, Adam, ed. *The New York Times Year in Review 1986*. New York: New York Times Books, 1987.

Columbia Journalism Review. CNN Goes for the Gold. New York: September 1990.

Dear, Ian. *Ocean Racing, an Illustrated History*. New York: Hearst Main Books, 1985.

Dizard, Wilson P. *Old Media/New Media: Mass Communications in the Information Age*. New York: Longman, 1993.

Duke, Patty, and Gloria Hochman. *A Brilliant Madness*. New York: Bantam Books, 1992.

Eisler, Riane. *The Chalice & the Blade*. New York: Harper & Row, 1987.

Fields, Robert Ashley. *Take Me Out to the Crowd*. Huntsville, AL.: The Strode Publishers, 1977.

Fonda, Jane. *Jane Fonda's Workout Book*. New York: Simon & Schuster, 1981.

Gans, Herbert J. *Deciding What's News?* New York: Pantheon Books, 1979.

Greist, John H., MD, and James W. Jefferson, MD. *Depression and Its Treatment*. Washington, DC: American Psychiatric Press, 1992.

Harris, Joel Chandler: *The Complete Tails of Uncle Remus*. Boston: Houghton, Mifflin, 1955.

Hayden, Thomas. *Reunion: A Memoir*. New York: Random House, 1988.

Hope, Bob. *We Could Have Finished Last Without You*. Atlanta: Longstreet Press, 1991.

Jobson, Gary, with Ted Turner. *The Racing Edge*. New York: Simon & Schuster, 1979.

Josephson, Jessica J. *European Media Hard Data*. London: International Media Publishing, 1991.

Klein, Donald F., and Paul H. Wender. *Understanding Depression*. New York: Oxford University Press, 1993.

Kornbluth, Jesse. *Highly Confident*. New York: William Morrow, 1992.

Leapman, Michael. *Arrogant Aussie: The Rupert Murdoch Story*. Secaucus, NJ: Lyle, Stuart, 1985.

Loory, Stuart. *Seven Days That Shook the World*. New York: Turner Publishing, 1991.

Lundy, Jim. *Lead, Follow, or Get Out of the Way*. New York: Avant Books, 1986.

MacArthur, John R. *Second Front: Censorship and Propaganda in the Gulf War*. New York: Hill & Wang, 1992.

McLuhan, Marshall. *Understanding Media: The Extensions of Man*. New York: New American Library, 1964.

Mayer, Martin. *Making News*. New York: Doubleday, 1987.

Meyer, Michael. *The Alexander Complex*. New York: Times Books, 1989.

National Cable Television Association, Research & Policy Analysis Department. *Cable Television Developments*. Washington, DC, 1992.

Papolos, Demitri, and Janice Papolos. *Overcoming Depression.* New York: Harper Perennial, 1992.

Paul Kagan Associates. *The Cable TV Financial Databook.* Palo Alto, CA: 1992.

Postman, Neil, and Steve Powers. *How to Watch TV News.* New York: Penguin Books, 1992.

Richey, Michael W. *The Sailing Encyclopedia.* New York: Lippencott & Crowell, 1980.

Riggs, Doug. *Keelhauled.* Newport, RI: Seven Seas Press, 1986.

Rusher, William A. *The Coming Battle for the Media.* New York: William Morrow, 1988.

Shawcross, William. *Murdoch.* New York: Simon & Schuster, 1993.

Smith, Major General Perry M. *How CNN Fought the War.* New York: Birch Lane Press, 1991.

Stefoff, Rebecca. *Ted Turner: Television's Triumphant Tiger.* Ada, OK: Garrett Educational, 1992.

Stewart, James B. *Den of Thieves.* New York: Simon & Schuster, 1992.

Taylor, Philip M. *War & the Media.* Manchester, England: Manchester University Press, 1992.

Vaughan, Roger. *The Grand Gesture.* Boston: Little, Brown, 1975.

———. *Ted Turner: The Man Behind the Mouth.* Boston: Sail Books, 1978.

Wiener, Robert. *Live from Baghdad.* New York: Doubleday, 1992.

Wilson, Charles, ed. *Encyclopedia of Southern Culture.* New York: Doubleday, 1953.

Whittemore, Hank. *CNN: The Inside Story.* Boston: Little, Brown & Co., 1990.

Williams, Christian. *Lead, Follow, or Get Out of the Way.* New York: Times Books, 1981.

Zilbergold, Bernie. *Male Sexuality.* Boston: Little, Brown & Co., 1978.

Source Notes

Chapter One

1   "You'll know it when it happens . . .": Ted Turner, *Bozeman Chronicle* (Bozeman, Mont.), Dec. 22, 1991, p. 1.

3   "My father worked a lot. . . .": Ted Turner, *Atlanta Constitution.* Aug. 21, 1979, p. 21.

3   "It's an Uncle Remus–type relationship. . . .": *ibid.*

4   "It was a wonderful . . .": Peter Fonda, *People* magazine. Jan. 6, 1992, p. 32.

5   ". . . the Man of the Year . . .": Dolly Parton, *People* magazine, Jan. 27, 1992, p. 40.

5   "I got my thrift . . .": Ted Turner, *Atlanta Constitution*, July 17, 1970, p. 44.

6   "Simon Theophilus Turner . . .": Turner Family genealogy, commissioned by the L. W. Anderson Genealogical Library, Gulfport, Miss., and Frances G. Martin Certified Genealogical Record Searcher, Grenada, Miss., 1992.

6   ". . . one male and two female Negro slaves . . .": Mississippi State Census, 1850.

8   ". . . without the degree . . .": University of Mississippi Records Office, 1992.

8   "He looked enough like Ted Turner . . .": Lucy Rooney, personal interview, June 19, 1992.

12   "It was still pretty rough . . .": Ted Turner, *Atlanta Constitution*, May 12, 1973, p. 23.

14   "I'd have more trouble . . .": Irwin Mazo, personal interview, June 10, 1992.

15   "Ed could turn on an old friend . . .": Dr. Irving Victor, personal interview, July 31, 1992.

15   "Ed Turner was a wild man . . .": Marshall Hartmann, personal interview, Oct. 12, 1992.

15   "I think both of them . . .": *ibid.*

16   "I saw him get very strict . . .": Dr. Irving Victor, personal interview, July 31, 1992.

16   "Teddy was a little on the mischievous side . . .": Florence Rooney Turner, *Atlanta Constitution*, August 12, 1976, p. 21.

16 "Our black houseman . . .": *ibid.*

17 "We have a long tradition of tolerating . . .": Mills B. Lane, Jr., *Savannah News* (Savannah, Ga.), June 12, 1971, p. 14.

17 "I don't think Ted was any great student . . .": Florence Turner, *Atlanta Constitution*, June 21, 1976, p. 38.

17 "There was nothing I could do . . .": *ibid.*

18 "I love McCallie . . .": Ted Turner, in a speech at JFK School of Government, Harvard University, Nov. 13, 1992.

18 "Ted hated McCallie . . .": Florence Turner, *Atlanta Constitution*, June 21, 1976, p. 38.

18 "At first I was just a terrible cadet . . .": Ted Turner, *Atlanta Constitution*, June 12, 1977, p. 23.

18 "Ted was very much of a loner . . .": William Cook, personal interview, June 5, 1992.

19 "Ted was a determined . . .": Professor Houston Patterson, personal interview, July 7, 1992.

19 "I wouldn't call him a loner . . .": James S. McCallie, personal interview, June 22, 1992.

19 "He created quite a problem . . .": Elliott Schmidt, personal interview, June 16, 1992.

20 "I used to give him a lot of rope . . .": *ibid.*

20 "He was never quite in danger . . .": Spencer J. McCallie III, personal interview, July 14, 1992.

20 "I got the feeling . . .": Elliott Schmidt, personal interview, June 16, 1992.

21 "It is a terrible, terrible affliction . . .": Dr. Robert Lahita, personal interview, July 7, 1992.

21 "She came out of that coma . . .": Ted Turner, *Sports Illustrated*, "Going Strawwng," by Curry Kirkpatrick, Aug. 21, 1978.

21 "Of course, that seemed harsh . . .": Elliott Schmidt, personal interview, June 16, 1992.

22 "I used to fuss a lot . . .": Florence Turner, *Atlanta Constitution*, June 21, 1976, p. 38.

22 "I didn't have a lot of natural athletic ability . . .": Ted Turner, *Atlanta Constitution*, June 13, 1977, p. 28.

22 "When he sailed . . .": Florence Turner, *Atlanta Constitution*, June 21, 1976, p. 38.

23 "First thing you noticed . . .": Legarè VanNess, personal interview, Sept. 23, 1992.

23 "I was interested in one thing . . .": Ted Turner, *Atlanta Constitution*, June 13, 1977, p. 28.

23 "His father felt boys . . .": Professor Houston Patterson, personal interview, July 4, 1992.

23 "I can still remember . . .": Spencer McCallie, personal interview, July 14, 1992.

23 "I just wanted to be the best . . .": Ted Turner, *Atlanta Constitution*, June 13, 1977, p. 28.

24 "I had the greatest difficulty . . .": Professor Houston Patterson, personal interview, July 14, 1992.

24 "Ted was distraught . . .": Elliott Schmidt, personal interview, Oct. 14, 1992.

24 "He was always fighting . . .": Marshall Hartmann, personal interview, Nov. 12, 1992.

25 "He was always up to something . . .": *ibid.*

25 ". . . with a bottle of bourbon . . .": Alan Laymon, personal interview, June 2, 1992.

25 "I think we were both on social probation . . .": *ibid.*

25 "Basically, we all liked to get drunk . . .": Peter A. Dames, Sr., *Atlanta Constitution*, January 11, 1978, p. 1-A.

26 "I didn't really like it . . .": Ted Turner, *Channels* magazine, Jan. 1988, p. 27.

26 ". . . plagued the campus . . .": *Brown Daily Herald*, Oct. 15, 1956, p. 4.

26 "There was limited tolerance . . .": Alan Laymon, personal interview, June 4, 1992.

26 "Ted carried a pistol . . .": *ibid.*

27 "He was certainly not vicious . . .": William Kennedy, personal interview, July 7, 1992.

27 "Hey, I didn't mean anything . . .": Ted Turner, *Sports Illustrated*, August 21, 1978.

27 "We stashed it in the car . . .": Alan Laymon, personal interview, June 4, 1992.

27 "We were all called on the carpet . . .": William Kennedy, personal interview, July 7, 1992.

28 ". . . too loud, too red in the neck . . .": Roger Vaughan, *Ted Turner: The Man Behind the Mouth*. Norton, 1978, p. 162.

28 "You're crazy to get serious about . . .": Judy Nye Turner Hallisy, personal interview, May 26, 1992.

28 "There were probably a dozen . . .": William Kennedy, personal interview, July 7, 1992.

29 "He was a handful . . .": Professor John Rowe Workman, *Brown Daily Herald*, Oct. 14, 1981, p. 12.

29 Letter from Ed Turner. *Brown Daily Herald*, April 15, 1957, p. 8.

32 "Ed was beside himself . . .": Florence Turner, *Atlanta Constitution*, June 15, 1977, p. 43.

32 "He came into a classics final . . .": Alan Laymon, personal interview, June 4, 1992.

33 "I don't know if Ted burned it down . . .": *ibid.*

34 "But then I'd be retired . . .": Ted Turner, in *Saturday Evening Post*, "Ted Turner: Capt. Outrageous," by Joseph B. Cummins, Jr., Oct. 1980, p. 69.

34 "I wasn't sure how good I'd be at knuckling under . . .": *New York Post*, "Turner to Launch News Channel," by Staff Reporters, May 18, 1980, p. 67.

34 "Ted traveled with me for about . . .": Hudson Edwards, personal interview, Sept. 23, 1992.

35 "Ted didn't want to go down to Macon . . .": Judy Hallisy, personal interview, Aug. 25, 1992.

35 "At the beginning I thought . . .": Legarè VanNess, *ibid.*

36 "I bring home the money . . .": Judy Hallisy, personal interview, Aug. 25, 1992.

36 "The provider must have his way . . .": *ibid.*

36 "After a while, I felt my entire ego . . .": *ibid.*

36 "I threw cold water on Ted . . .": *ibid.*

37 "The Lord works in mysterious ways . . .": Dr. Irving Victor, personal interview, July 31, 1992.

37 "All right, then . . .": Irwin Mazo, personal interview, July 31, 1992.

38 "He wouldn't even let them . . .": Alan Laymon, personal interview, June 5, 1992.

39 "When Ed Turner took over our firm . . .": In Christian Williams, *Lead, Follow, or Get Out of the Way*, p. 38.

40 "Ed liked to keep Ted on a short string . . .": Hudson Edwards, personal interview, Sept. 23, 1992.

40 "Ed had pulled off a terrific deal . . .": Irwin Mazo, personal interview, Oct. 10, 1992.

40   "He had just sold most . . .": *ibid.*
40   "He was terribly upset . . .": Robert Naegele, *New York Times*, June 5, 1978, p. C-3.
41   "He said he'd made a big mistake . . .": Irwin Mazo, personal interview, Oct. 10, 1992.
41   "Look, Ed, I don't know very much . . .": Dr. Irving Victor, personal interview, July 31, 1992.
42   "You're pretty concerned about me . . .": *ibid.*
42   "Too wet behind the ears . . .": *ibid.*
43   "We argued bitterly . . .": Ted Turner, in Christian Williams, *Lead, Follow, or Get Out of the Way.* Times Books, 1981, p. 40.
43   "Ed thought Ted was just too young to run the business . . .": Robert Naegele, *New York Times*, June 5, 1978, p. C-3.
43   "My father always said never to set goals . . .": *The Economist*, "Ted Turner's Marvelous News Machine," June 21, 1980, p. 30.

Chapter Two

44   "He seemed his old self again . . .": Irving Victor, personal interview, August 12, 1992.
45   "I'll meet you there . . .": Irving Victor, personal interview, July 31, 1992.
46   "Ed Turner was a very rich man . . .": *ibid.*
47   "Ted called his father cowardly . . .": Robert Naegele, *New York Times*, June 5, 1978, p. C-3.
47   "Ted's first reaction . . .": Judy Hallisy, personal interview, May 28, 1992.
48   "Ed thought Ted was too young . . .": Robert Naegele, *New York Times*, June 5, 1978, p. C-3.
48   "Ted had always been on a crusade . . .": Judy Hallisy, personal interview, May 28, 1992.
48   "That fellow over there . . .": Irving Victor, personal interview, August 21, 1992.
48   "When they read out the will . . .": Irwin Mazo, personal interview, July 31, 1992.
49   "That's right, but your father said specifically . . .": Irving Victor, personal interview, July 31, 1992.
49   "Ted merely said he wasn't in a position . . .": *ibid.*
50   "I was sad, pissed, and determined . . .": Ted Turner, *Advertising Age*, "Ted Turner Mines the Skies," Nov. 1982, p. B-1.
51   "When Ted took over the business . . .": Irwin Mazo, personal interview, May 21, 1992.
51   "But all that is getting ahead of the story . . .": *ibid.*
52   "Ted rushed right into our lenders . . .": *ibid.*
52   "Ted competed down in Savannah . . .": Saul Krawcheck, personal interview, Nov. 13, 1992.
55   "Another sailor from Savannah . . .": *ibid.*
55   "You can't leave now! . . .": *ibid.*
55   "You're not leaving the business to me . . .": In Roger Vaughan, *Ted Turner: The Man Behind the Mouth.* Sail Books, 1978, p. 176.
56   "We could have a lot of fun . . .": Andy Green, personal interview, Aug. 19, 1992.
56   "It was a good thing Ted was already rich . . .": *ibid.*
57   "As it turned out . . .": *ibid.*
58   "Life is a game . . .": *Sports Illustrated*, "Going Strawwng," by Curry Kirkpatrick, Aug. 21, 1978, p. 75.
58   "Ted's strong point . . .": Dennis Conner, *No Excuse to Lose*, Simon & Schuster, New York, 1984.

59 "My father had worked like hell . . .": Ted Turner, *Atlanta Constitution*, June 12, 1979, p. 47

59 "He is an aggressive, natural businessman . . .": Irwin Mazo, personal interview, Sept. 1, 1992.

59 "But he has always been the best salesman in the company . . .": In Roger Vaughan, *The Grand Gesture*. Little, Brown, 1975, p. 102.

60 "A lot of times back then . . .": In Christian Williams, *Lead, Follow, or Get Out of the Way*. Times Books, 1981, p. 56.

60 "The worst four days of my life . . .": Irwin Mazo, personal interview, July 31, 1992.

61 "I never crewed for anyone . . .": *ibid.*

62 "Winning the SORC . . .": *New York Times*, March 30, 1966, p. 46.

62 "The elements of success . . .": *ibid.*

62 "The way to win the SORC . . .": *One Design and Offshore Yachtsman* magazine, "The 1966 Southern Ocean Racing Circuit," April 1966, p. 45.

63 "We were either going to win . . .": Ted Turner, *Miami Herald*, March 2, 1967, p. 42.

63 "Ted's not like the rest of us . . .": Legarè VanNess, personal interview, Sept. 23, 1992.

64 "I watched Ted put his father's business in order . . .": Irwin Mazo, personal interview, July 31, 1992.

64 "Ted Turner is without doubt . . .": James Roddey, personal interview, Oct. 12, 1992.

65 "I know it doesn't sound very brilliant . . .": *ibid.*

66 "We nearly wound up on the rocks off Cape Hatteras . . .": Tracey Nelson, *Sail* magazine, December 1969, p. 55.

66 "A young upstart . . .": *One Design and Offshore Yachtsman* magazine, May 1968, p. 26.

66 "Mr. Ted! Mr. Ted! . . .": Jimmy Brown, *Sail* magazine, December 1969, p. 55.

66 "Harold sailed with Ted several times . . .": Legarè VanNess, personal interview, Sept. 23, 1992.

68 "When I first walked into Turner's office . . .": Ken Danforth, personal interview, July 24, 1992 and July 31, 1992.

68 "Well, you passed . . .": *ibid.*

Chapter Three

71 "I never watched any television . . .": Ted Turner, *Atlanta Constitution*, Sept. 25, 1976, p. B-12.

72 "Tony Lott and those boys . . .": Irwin Mazo, personal interview, July 31, 1992.

72 "If this deal doesn't work out . . .": *ibid.*

73 "We were certain Ted . . .": *ibid.*

73 "It's even more messed up than the one in Atlanta . . .": *ibid.*, p. 67.

74 "Ted would launch a new project . . .": James Roddey, personal interview, Oct. 12, 1992.

75 "Ted thought he could promote . . .": William S. Sanders, *Broadcasting* magazine, Aug. 17, 1977, p. 66.

75 "I could see the whole show . . .": *ibid.*

76 ". . . victory over superior forces . . .": Ted Turner, *Atlanta Constitution*, May 24, 1979, p. 32.

77 "The three other commercial stations . . .": Ted Turner, *Broadcasting* magazine, Aug. 17, 1977, p. 66.

77 "Ted didn't mind overpaying . . .": Tom Ashley, personal interview, June 5, 1992.

78 "We felt we could shake them up . . .": Ted Turner, *Broadcasting* magazine, Aug. 17, 1977, p. 66.

79 "Ted programmed the whole station . . .": Gerald Hogan, *ibid.*, p. 67.

79 "Our audience may not be big . . .": Ted Turner, *ibid.*

80 ". . . the new television deal . . .": Bob Hope, personal interview, July 15, 1992.

81 "It was kind of a joke . . .": In Christian Williams, *Lead, Follow, or Get Out of the Way*, p. 87.

82 "I think Roger Vaughan tried . . .": Judy Hallisy, personal interview, May 26, 1992.

82 "And I would have had her, too . . .": In Roger Vaughan, *Ted Turner: The Man Behind the Mouth.* p. 168.

82 "Working with Ted was no bowl of cherries . . .": Tom Ashley, personal interview, June 5, 1992.

83 "It was amazing . . .": Irwin Mazo, personal interview, June 10, 1992.

84 "At one point . . .": Tom Ashley, personal interview, June 11, 1992.

Chapter Four

88 "Ah! The good old time . . .": In Roger Vaughan, *The Grand Gesture*. Little, Brown, 1975, p. 117.

89 "He had won big . . .": In Christian Williams, *Lead, Follow, or Get Out of the Way*. Times Books, 1981, p. 89.

89 "Damn the cable! . . .": Ted Turner, *Sailing World* magazine, "The Seabreeze Unspoiled," July 1975, p. 57.

89 "Ted is always winning . . .": Carl Helfrich, Jr., *Miami Herald*, March 23, 1973, p. 54.

90 "Yeah, a couple of guys . . .": Ted Turner, *Sailing World* magazine, "The Seabreeze Unspoiled," July 1975, p. 57.

90 ". . . a hell of a sailor . . .": George Hinman, "The Grandest Prize," CBS-TV, 1974.

91 "Not by a damn sight . . .": Robert Derecktor, in Roger Vaughan, *The Grand Gesture*, p. 129.

91 "We kept asking him the same question . . .": James Lipscomb, "The Grandest Prize," CBS-TV, 1974.

91 ". . . figured a breakthrough design . . .": Britton Chance, Jr., *Providence Journal*, June 23, 1974.

92 "Listen, Turner, just because . . .": In Roger Vaughan, *The Grand Gesture*, p. 133.

93 "Brit, do you know why there are no fish . . .": Ted Turner, *Sailing World* magazine, "The Natural," May 1975, p. 48. (Line first attributed to Legarè VanNess, June 1974.)

93 "Ted did a great job . . .": In Roger Vaughan, *The Grand Gesture*, p. 292.

94 "He certainly doesn't get it from me . . .": In Roger Vaughan, *The Grand Gesture*, p. 287.

94 "Ted Turner was the real hero . . .": In Roger Vaughan, *The Grand Gesture*, p. 275.

95 "Then count me out, again . . .": Robert McCullough, personal interview, July 1975.

96 "I'm backing Ted Hood . . .": Robert McCullough, personal interview, Jan. 1975.

96 ". . . unreality and lack of planning . . .": In Roger Vaughan, *The Grand Gesture*, p. 294.

96 "I don't know if *Mariner* was good . . .": *ibid.*

98 "Ted ran WTCG like a radio station . . .": James Roddey, personal interview, Oct. 14, 1992.

98 "He came into my office one day . . .": Donald Andersson, *Channels* magazine, "Turner Carries the Day," May 1988, p. 44.

98 "Would it help if I bought the Braves? . . .": *ibid.*

98 "One night after about three beers . . .": Ted Turner, *Atlanta Constitution*, Jan. 24, 1978, p. 48.

98 "I can remember the exact moment . . .": Bob Hope, personal interview, Oct. 10, 1992.

99 "Dial-a-Prayer was busy . . .": Lewis Grizzard, *Atlanta Constitution*, "Braves' Bob Hope Isn't Joking," June 14, 1975, p. 31.

99 "Mr. Donahue simply gave me a copy . . .": Bob Hope, *We Could've Finished Last Without You.* Longstreet Press, 1991, p. 79.

100 "Got it! . . .": *ibid.*

100 "And no one . . .": Robbin Ahrold, *Broadcasting* magazine, June 27, 1977, p. 21.

103 "What Ted was doing . . .": Jeffrey Reisse, personal interview, July 30, 1992.

104 "I am crazy . . .": Terence McGuirk, *The Economist*, "More Gall than Cash," April 24, 1979, p. 54.

105 "Of course I did . . .": *ibid.*

107 "I was late . . .": Ted Turner, "60 Minutes," CBS-TV, 1977.

107 "He's one of the most refreshing . . .": Harry Reasoner, "60 Minutes," CBS-TV, 1977.

108 "It wasn't just the networks . . .": Robert Wussler, personal interview, Dec. 13, 1992.

108 "Ted plunged us into the Superstation . . .": Donald Andersson, *Channels* magazine, "Turner Carries the Day," May 1988, p. 45.

Chapter Five

109 "I don't want to see any more 'Loserville' headlines . . .": Ted Turner, *Atlanta Constitution*, Jan. 14, 1976, p. 34.

109 "I'm a dedicated and hardworking person . . .": *ibid.*

110 "There's never been an owner like him. . . .": Phil Niekro, *Atlanta Constitution*, April 21, 1976, p. C-4.

110 "I don't care if he was born here . . .": Robert Howsam, *Atlanta Constitution*, May 3, 1976, p. 24.

110 "I bought the Braves . . .": Ted Turner, *Atlanta Constitution*, "Ordinary Rookie," April 5, 1976, p. D-4.

111 "Where's my ten thousand dollars? . . .": Ted Turner, *Atlanta Constitution*, Furman Bisher's Column, Oct. 7, 1976, p. C-1.

111 "It may cost you more . . .": Robert Lurie, *Atlanta Constitution*, Furman Bisher's Column, Oct. 7, 1976, p. C-1.

111 "Everybody is going to be there . . .": Ted Turner, *Atlanta Constitution*, Furman Bisher's Column, Oct. 7, 1976, p. C-1.

112 "There's no law against showing . . .": *ibid.*

112 "I'll tell you what he's going to do . . .": Bob Hope, *We Could've Finished Last Without You.* Longstreet Press, 1991.

113 "I don't know what to do with this . . .": Reporter, KNX-FM, *Atlanta Constitution*, Dec. 10, 1976, p. 21.

113 "Ted's lost it . . .": Bob Hope, *We Could've Finished Last Without You*, pp. 150–151.

113 "You're absolutely out of your mind, Ted . . .": Bob Hope, personal interview (Oct. 10, 1992) and *We Could've Finished Last Without You*, pp. 150–151.

114 "I don't think the penalty . . .": Ted Turner, *Atlanta Constitution*, Jan. 3, 1977, p. 14 (includes comments by Robert Green and Jesse Hill).

Chapter Six

116 "We were good sailors on a dog . . .": Marty O'Meara, *Newsweek*, "Captain Courageous," Sept. 12, 1977, p. 77.

116 "They thought it was my swan song . . .": Ted Turner, *Sports Illustrated*, "Terrible Ted Takes Command," July 4, 1977, p. 45.

117 "Everything I do is a war . . .": Ted Turner, *Soundings*, July 7, 1977, pp. 5, 6, and 7.

119 "If I have to watch them lose . . .": Ted Turner, *Atlanta Constitution*, July 6, 1977, p. D-2.

120 "Tacks are like snowflakes . . .": *ibid.*

121 "We chuckled over that . . .": Commodore Robert McCullough, *Sports Illustrated*, July 21, 1977, p. 67.

121 "If he's ever selected . . .": Donald McNamara, *Providence* (R.I.) *Journal*, Aug. 20, 1977, p. 14.

121 ". . . no-good liar . . .": *ibid.*

121 "I've been a good customer . . .": In Roger Vaughan, *Ted Turner: The Man Behind the Mouth*. Sail Books, 1978, p. 84.

122 "I came down from my room. . . .": In Vaughan, *Ted Turner: The Man Behind the Mouth*, p. 85.

122 "If you want to 'Beat the Mouth . . .' ": In Vaughan, p. 102.

122 "It was obvious. . . .": Offending Member (of NYYC), in Vaughan, p. 102.

123 "Don't let Turner tell you . . .": Lee Loomis, *Providence Journal*, July 5, 1977, p. 38.

123 "At this point, I can't feel strongly. . . .": Lowell North, *Newport News*, Aug. 17, 1977, p. 14.

123 "Gentlemen, congratulations . . .": Comm. George Hinman, *Newport News*, Aug. 31, 1977, p. 8.

124 "We had a lot to show. . . .": Ted Turner, *Newsweek*, "Captain Courageous," Sept. 12, 1977, p. 77.

124 "If being against stuffiness and pompousness . . .": Ted Turner, *Time*, "Defending the America's Cup," Sept. 19, 1977, p. 84.

124 "There will never be a time . . .": Ted Turner, *Newport News*, Sept. 7, 1977, p. 9.

125 "I'm not sure I should comment on that. . . .": Comm. Robert Mosbacher, *Newport News*, Sept. 3, 1977, p. 14.

125 "No one else has ever . . .": In Bob Bavier, *America's Cup Fever*. Yachting Books/Ziff-Davis, 1981, p. 48.

125 "One Sunday in July . . .": Roger Vaughan, *Sail* magazine, Sept. 1978, p. 104.

126 "Ted's personality swings were extreme . . .": John Rousmaniere, *No Excuse to Lose*. W. W. Norton, 1984, p. 51.

126 "It was real communication. . . .": Gary Jobson, *Sail* magazine, September 1978, p. 102.

127 "Turner talked incessantly. . . .": Roger Vaughan, *Sail* magazine, September 1978, p. 104.

127 "There have even been a few bad moments . . .": Ted Turner, *Newsweek*, "The Mouth Roars," Sept. 5, 1977, p. 88.

128 "Brown Lost. . . .": Ted Turner, *Atlanta Constitution*, Sept. 18, 1977, p. C-4

128 "It was that outrageously uninhibited . . .": Doug Riggs, *Keelhauled*. Seven Seas Press, 1986, p. 201.

129 "Turner's been sailing almost . . .": Gary Jobson, *Time* magazine, "The Mouth Takes the Helm," Sept. 19, 1977, p. 85.

129 "But we've still got to fight the pressure . . .": Ted Turner, *Sports Illustrated*, "Cup Frenzy," Sept. 19, 1977, p. 78.
129 "Ted loves to be ahead. . . .": *Sports Illustrated*, "A Cup of Tea," by Coles Phinizy, Sept. 19, 1977, p. 28.
130 "Fame is like love . . .": Ted Turner, *People* magazine, Sept. 12, 1977, p. 30.
130 "If you have ever heard eleven grown men cry . . .": Ted Turner, *Newport News*, Sept. 10, 1977, p. 14.
130 "Ted, all these girls . . .": Jane Turner, *Atlanta Constitution*, Sept. 13, 1977, p. C-23.
130 "I can't help it. . . .": Ted Turner, *Atlanta Constitution*, Sept. 13, 1977, p. C-23.
130 "I'm not sure I ought to wait here. . . .": In *Atlanta Constitution*, Sept. 13, 1977, p. C-23.
131 "Ted Turner won't take a car . . .": *ibid.*
131 "Yeah. . . . It's crazy, isn't it?": Ted Turner, *Atlanta Constitution*, Sept. 13, 1977, p. C-23.
131 "We're used to our boat, our sails . . .": *Providence Journal*, Sept. 15, 1977, p. 32.
132 "Now you've got your crowds . . .": Gary Jobson, *Sail* magazine, Sept. 1978, p. 104.
132 "Show me your tits. . . .": In Roger Vaughan, *Ted Turner: The Man Behind the Mouth.* p. 203.
133 "It's your boat, Ted. . . .": Bill Ficker, *Providence Journal*, Sept. 18, 1977, p. 33.
133 "I—I never loved sailing. . . .": In Roger Vaughan, *Ted Turner: The Man Behind the Mouth*, p. 207. Also, *Providence Journal*, Sept. 18, 1977, p. 33. Also, "60 Minutes," CBS-TV, October. 1977.
134 "We, too . . . would also like to thank . . .": In Roger Vaughan, *Ted Turner: The Man Behind the Mouth.* p. 207.
134 ". . . The New York Yacht Club should . . .": Patrick Robinson, *Born to Win*, Hearst Marine Books, 1985, p. 59.
135 ". . . when I come back, I won't change anything. . . .": *Providence Journal*, "Turner Is What He Is," by Mark Patinkin, Sept. 19, 1977, p. AA-8.
135 ". . . with a huge assist from his tactician . . .": Alan Bond, *Sports Illustrated*, Sept. 19, 1977, p. 24.

Chapter Seven

136 "After all . . . winning the America's Cup . . .": Ted Turner, *Atlanta Constitution*, Sept. 24, 1977, p. C-1.
137 "Suggestive letters . . . They tell him they like . . .": Dee Woods, *Atlanta Constitution*, Nov. 28, 1977, p. B-15.
138 "Ted has five kids. . . .": Sexiest Man in Atlanta Poll, *Atlanta Constitution*, Dec. 1, 1977.
138 "Let's not leave viewers with a false impression. . . .": In Roger Vaughan, *Ted Turner: The Man Behind the Mouth.* p. 213.
138 "I have heard that you are a little . . .": In Roger Vaughan, *Ted Turner: The Man Behind the Mouth*, p. 213.
138 "Everybody wants to be a star. . . .": Ted Turner, *Sports Illustrated*, Oct. 12, 1977, p. 45.
138 "I'm not a fire-eating, maniacal madman. . . .": *ibid.*
139 "You were terrific. . . .": Ted Turner, *Broadcasting* magazine, Jan. 12, 1978, p. 23.
139 "You ain't such a bad boy yourself, Snyder. . . .": *ibid.*
139 "One of my responsibilities . . .": Sid Pike, *Atlanta Constitution*, Oct. 14, 1977, p. D-13.

139 "I don't think winning is everything. . . .": In *Sail* magazine, "The Defense: On the Razor's Edge," by John McNamara, August 1980, p. 81.

140 "I am appearing here as a broadcaster. . . .": Ted Turner in the Congressional Record, Feb. 21, 1979, pp. 1, 123.

141 "I used to worry about him. . . .": Jane Smith Turner, *Atlanta Constitution*, March 21, 1977, p. B-34.

142 "I was reared by a mother who was a mother. . . .": Jane Turner, *ibid.*

142 "Jane Smith knew all the right people. . . .": Geraldine Moore, personal interview, August 12, 1992.

142 "I used to, when we were first married. . . .": Jane Turner, *Atlanta Constitution*, March 21, 1977, p. B-34.

143 "I'm used to hiding out. . . .": Jane Turner, *Atlanta Constitution*, June 2, 1980, p. B-12.

143 "After a few years . . .": Geraldine Moore, personal interview, August 12, 1992.

144 "Sometimes it was boring that Ted wasn't here. . . .": Jane Turner, *Atlanta Constitution*, March 21, 1977, p. B-34.

144 "Ted Turner is the anachronism. . . .": Roger Vaughan, *Ted Turner: The Man Behind the Mouth*, p. 189.

144 "I've seen them, the groupies. . . .": Jane Turner, *Atlanta Constitution*, June 2, 1980, p. B-12, Also Roger Vaughan, *Ted Turner: The Man Behind the Mouth*, pp. 187–188.

145 "Blackaller, come on. Give me a break. . . .": In Christian Williams, *Lead, Follow, or Get Out of the Way*. Times Books, 1981, p. 162.

145 "Nothing personal, Ted . . .": In Christian Williams, *Lead, Follow*, p. 163.

146 "You're right, Blackaller. Beating everybody. . . .": In Christian Williams, *Lead, Follow*, p. 163.

147 "Finistere, Sole, Fastnet. Severe winds . . .": *Time* magazine, Aug. 17, 1979, p. 36.

147 "We're going to have a lot of breeze! . . .": In *Motorboat & Sailing*, "Fastnet," by Ted Turner, September 1979, p. 25.

147 "I felt a little bit like Noah. . . .": *Motorboat & Sailing*, September 1979, p. 26.

147 "Our steering wheel, complete with a man attached . . .": Arthur Moss, *Time* magazine, "Death In The South Irish Sea," August 27, 1979, p. 36.

147 "Waves were like cliffs. . . .": In *Motorboat & Sailing*, September 1979, p. 25.

148 "The idea of jumping . . .": Frank Worley, *Time* magazine, August 27, 1979, p. 36.

149 "Do you realize they all think we're dead? . . .": Christian Williams, *Lead, Follow*, p. 232.

149 ". . . the worst I have ever been through . . .": Edward Heath, *Time*, August 27, 1979, p. 36.

149 "It was rough! Rough! . . .": Ted Turner, *New York Times*, August 24, 1979, p. D-5.

149 "It was a storm precisely like this. . . .": Ted Turner, BBC-TV, August 22, 1979. Also, *Daily Telegraph*, August 23, 1979, p. 48.

Chapter Eight

152 "Since CBS News cannot be self-supporting . . .": Frank Stanton, *Broadcasting* magazine, Nov. 12, 1975, p. 28.

153 "I came up with the concept for a news channel . . .": Ted Turner, *Time* magazine, "Shaking up the Networks," August 9, 1972, p. 52.

153 "Successful entrepreneurs . . . find innovative ways . . .": Peter Drucker, *Business Monthly* magazine, Sept. 1989, p. 43.

156 "News? I can't do news. . . .": Ted Turner, quoted by Reese Schonfeld, personal interview, June 23, 1992.

156 "He was having a good laugh . . .": Reese Schonfeld, personal interview, June 23, 1992.

157 "I hate the news. News is evil. . . .": Ted Turner, quoted by Bob Hope, personal interview, July 15, 1992.

158 "Then we can show the most gory murder . . .": *ibid.*

149 "Hey, Reese! . . . You want to do this thing?": Ted Turner, quoted by Reese Schonfeld, personal interview, June 22, 1992.

159 "Ted planned to give me the whole treatment. . . .": Reese Schonfeld, personal interview, June 25, 1992.

159 ". . . the biggest single mistake of my career . . .": Nick Nicholas, *New York* magazine, July 23, 1985, p. 67. Also, *Broadcasting* magazine, May 22, 1987, p. 32.

160 "Anybody who thinks I'm not serious . . .": Ted Turner, *Atlanta Constitution*, July 15, 1979, p. B-14.

160 "If it wasn't for Channel 17 . . .": *ibid.*

161 "We've got to have more breaking news . . .": Reese Schonfeld, personal interview, June 25, 1992.

161 "Just keep me in the picture . . .": Ted Turner, quoted by Reese Schonfeld, personal interview, June 25, 1992.

161 "Y'all come meet Reese . . .": In Hank Whittemore, *CNN: The Inside Story*, p. 43.

161 "You've got to line up some names. . . .": Ted Turner, quoted by Reese Schonfeld, personal interview, June 25, 1992.

162 "We need names. . . .": Reese Schonfeld, personal interview, July 17, 1992.

162 "Who's Dan Rather?": Ted Turner, quoted by Reese Schonfeld, personal interview, July 17, 1992.

163 "I only knew what I'd read in *Time* magazine. . . .": Daniel Schorr, personal interview, Sept. 22, 1992.

163 "I started in asking a lot of questions. . . .": *ibid.*

164 "Look, I have a press conference. . . .": Ted Turner, quoted by Daniel Schorr, personal interview, Sept. 22, 1992.

164 "Then Turner started shouting . . .": Daniel Schorr, personal interview, Sept. 22, 1992.

164 "Write that down and I'll sign it. . . .": Ted Turner, quoted by Daniel Schorr, personal interview, Sept. 22, 1992.

164 "I wrote my own protection into the agreement. . . .": Daniel Schorr, personal interview, Sept. 22, 1992.

166 "It wasn't just the money. . . .": Reese Schonfeld, personal interview, June 25, 1992.

166 "Reese walked around forever with his idea for an all-news channel. . . .": Dave Walker, personal interview, Sept. 1, 1992.

166 "Once he actually announced CNN . . .": Les Brown, personal interview, May 27, 1992.

167 "Who the hell set this up, Reese? . . .": Ted Turner, quoted by Reese Schonfeld and Les Brown, together with various *New York Times* editors, personal interview, May 27, 1992.

167 "Yes . . . But if we don't, we'll never know. . . .": Reese Schonfeld. Also, Les Brown, personal interview, May 27, 1992.

167 "Awwriiight!": Ted Turner, quoted by Reese Schonfeld, personal interview, June 22, 1992.

169 ". . . social and athletic institution . . .": *Atlanta Constitution*, May 28, 1980, p. B-3.

170 ". . . as good as anything at Black Rock . . .": Reese Schonfeld, personal interview, June 22, 1992.

171   "There is risk . . . in everything you do. . . .": Ted Turner, *Newsweek*, "Turner Tackles TV News," June 16, 1980, p. 59.

171   "We are searching the heavens . . .": In Hank Whittemore, *CNN: The Inside Story*. Little, Brown, 1990, p. 79.

172   "Turner called us all into his office. . . .": Ted Kavanau, personal interview, Sept. 16, 1992.

172   "This order puts us back on the satellite. . . .": Ted Turner, *Atlanta Constitution*, March 6, 1980, p. B-11.

173   ". . . in no event shall Turner's right to retain use . . .": court order of Judge Ernest Tidwell, U.S. Federal District Court, Atlanta, Ga., March 5, 1980, in *Atlanta Constitution*, March 5, 1980, p. D-11.

173   "There was no precedent for this kind of building. . . .": Carl Heifrich, Jr., *Atlanta Constitution*, Feb. 4, 1980, p. C-3.

174   "CNN was basically a three-year project. . . .": Mike Briles, *Atlanta Constitution*, May 17, 1980, p. 22.

174   "We think it will fly. . . .": Irving Kahn, *Atlanta Constitution*, March 7, 1980, p. C-3.

174   "There's little question there will be an audience. . . .": Paul Kagan, *Multi-Channel News*, March 1980, p. 15.

175   "You hear a lot about him. . . .": William Pitney, *Wall Street Journal*, May 23, 1980, p.1.

175   "The largest opening paid circulation of any service . . .": Ted Turner, *Broadcasting* magazine, March 12, 1980, p. 34.

175   "Turner is trying too hard. . . .": Chris Burns, *Cablevision* magazine, March 1980, p. 24.

175   "By the end of our first month . . .": Ted Turner, *Cablevision* magazine, March 1980, p. 25. Also, *Multi-Channel News*, March 1980, p. 18.

176   "We aren't just starting up a new network. . . .": Ted Kavanau, *Wall Street Journal*, May 23, 1980, p.1.

176   "We threw those kids into hotels and motels. . . .": Ted Kavanau, personal interview, Sept. 16, 1992.

176   "That early crop of veejays . . .": Fran Heaney, personal interview, August 20, 1992.

177   "CNN was probably the best job I've ever had. . . .": Chris Pula, personal interview, Sept. 19, 1992.

177   "No matter how difficult it seems . . .": Ted Kavanau, personal interview, Sept. 16, 1992.

178   "We're not going to be the Cronkite news. . . .": Ted Kavanau, *Broadcasting* magazine, March 24, 1980, p. 24.

178   "When I was a kid . . .": In *Wall Street Journal*, "Screen Test," by John Huey, May 23, 1980, p. 1.

179   "Ted considers himself a devoted husband . . .": Jane Turner, *Time* magazine, "Shaking up the Networks," August 9, 1982, p. 56.

180   "Let's rock and roll, everybody!" *Atlanta Constitution*, "CNN Launch" by Richard Zoglin, June 2, 1980, p. D-1.

180   ". . . those wonderful black ladies . . .": Reese Schonfeld, personal interview, June 22, 1992.

180   ". . . a telepublishing event marking . . .": *Atlanta Constitution*, "CNN Launch," by Richard Zoglin, June 2, 1980, p. D-1.

181   ". . . Just one year, twenty-two days . . .": Reese Schonfeld, *Atlanta Constitution*, "CNN Launch," by Richard Zoglin, June 2, 1980, p. D-1.

181 *"Awww*riiight! ... At least I think we're on the air...." : Ted Turner, *Atlanta Constitution*, "CNN Launch," by Richard Zoglin, June 2, 1980, p. D-1.
181 "We need an opening statement ...": In Hank Whittemore, *CNN: The Inside Story*, p. 144.
181 "No, they should define the mission ...": *ibid.*
181 "Let 'em just open with the news ...": *ibid.*
181 "Good evening. I'm David Walker...." : *ibid.*
181 "And I'm Lois Hart...." : *ibid.*
182 "God sent us that story...." : Reese Schonfeld, personal interview, June 22, 1992.
183 "Ted, how did you like the way ...": In Hank Whittemore, *CNN: The Inside Story*, p. 149.
183 "That'll show them we don't bow down to advertisers...." : *ibid.*
184 "I am scared...." : Ted Turner, *Panorama* magazine, June 1980, p. 32.
185 "I'm going to travel around to every foreign ...": *Atlanta Constitution*, "CNN Launch," by Richard Zoglin, June 2, 1980, p. D-1.
185 "Nobody believed him, did they? ...": Reese Schonfeld, personal interview, June 22, 1992. Also *Atlanta Constitution*, June 19, 1980, p. C-12.

Chapter Nine

186 "This is the first time I've sailed the boat...." : Ted Turner, *Atlanta Constitution*, Oct. 27, 1979, p. 1-A.
187 "... ninety percent of where I want to be ...": Ted Turner, *Atlanta Constitution*, May 31, 1980, p. C-1.
187 "No matter who wins this summer ...": Ted Turner, *Sail* magazine, March 1980, p. 28.
188 "We own Newport...." : Ted Turner, *Newport News*, June 10, 1980, p. 1.
189 "Why don't you come down to Atlanta and work for me?": Ted Turner, quoted by Barbara Pyle, *Atlanta Business Chronicle*, April 1992, p. 31.
189 "Maybe I will ...": Barbara Pyle, *Atlanta Business Chronicle*, April 1992, p. 31.
189 "I have a feeling Dennis can get people...." : Norris Hoyt, *Yachting* magazine, June 1980, p. 38.
190 "It was very light air, and you ...": *Australia* crewman, *Yachting* magazine, July 1980, p. 42.
190 "I think Ted sails best if he feels his back is up...." : Dennis Conner, *Atlanta Constitution*, "Conner: He's Prepared," by Beau Cutts, August 23, 1980, p. 1-C.
190 "When we talked about coming back two and a half ...": Gary Jobson, *Yachting* magazine, June 1980, p. 54.
190 "Ted is someone who has lots on his mind...." : Gary Jobson, *Atlanta Constitution*, May 30, 1980, p. 1-C.
190 "Ted's charisma ... often leads people to underestimate ...": Dennis Conner, *Atlanta Constitution*, Aug. 23, 1980, p 1-C.
191 "Ted was totally outclassed by *Freedom*...." : Russell Long, *Newsweek*, "No Excuse to Lose," Aug. 25, 1980, p. 54.
191 "Whenever they come, we'll be glad ...": Ted Turner, *Providence Journal*, Aug. 23, 1980, p. 13.
191 "We do appreciate ...": *Atlanta Constitution*, "For Cup Crew, Defeat Hurts," by Mark Patinkin, Aug. 28, 1980, p. D-1.
191 "It hurts worse than he'll tell you...." : Marty O'Meara, *Atlanta Constitution*, Aug. 28, 1980, p. D-1.
191 "Well ... I think that's it...." : Gary Jobson, *Atlanta Constitution*, Aug. 28, 1980, p. D-1.

191 "I think so. . . .": Ted Turner, *Atlanta Constitution*, Aug. 28, 1980, p. D-1.
192 "Reese Schonfeld was the guy who really made CNN . . .": Lois Hart, personal interview, August 12, 1992.
193 ". . . they rewrote the rules . . .": Lois Hart, personal interview, August 12, 1992.
193 "You'd be sitting there in the middle . . .": Fran Heaney, personal interview, August 20, 1992.
193 "He would generally come down and get . . .": Dave Walker, personal interview, Sept. 1, 1992.
193 "I don't know whether he was dating her. . . .": Fran Heaney, personal interview, August 20, 1992.
194 "He overspent on videotape machines. . . .": Ted Kavanau, personal interview, Sept. 16, 1992.
195 "What we are seeing . . .": Dave Walker, personal interview, Sept. 1, 1992.
195 "Pick up the phone. . . .": quoted by Lois Hart, personal interview, Aug. 11, 1992.
195 "So I picked up the phone . . .": Lois Hart, personal interview, Aug. 11, 1992.
195 "If you like doing newsies' news . . .": Ed Turner, *Multi-Channel News*, August 1980, p. 24.
195 "This is not going to be a diversion . . .": *Atlanta Constitution*, "Superstation Launches News," by Richard Zoglin, July 21, 1980, p. B-1.
196 "But why let people think they can . . .": Reese Schonfeld, personal interview, June 22, 1992.
197 "But since we are likely to have competition . . .": Ted Turner, quoted by Reese Schonfeld, personal interview, June 22, 1992.
197 "I don't think Turner is in the sort of trouble . . .": Walter Pirey, *Atlanta Constitution*, Jan. 3, 1981, p. D-2.
197 "There are just two subjects you absolutely cannot even mention. . . .": Reese Schonfeld, personal interview, June 22, 1992.
198 "Without telling either his bankers or his lawyers. . . .": Dan Schecter, personal interview, July 28, 1992.
199 ". . . equal to or better than network news coverage . . .": A. C. Nielsen survey, commissioned by CNN, Jan. 1, 1982.
199 "We don't think there should be pools . . .": *Atlanta Constitution*, "Turner's Folly," by Richard Zoglin, May 14, 1981, p. C-3.
199 "We don't want them in the pool . . .": *Atlanta Constitution*, "CNN Struggles to Be Taken Seriously," by Richard Zoglin, Nov. 18, 1980, p. C-2.
199 ". . . the networks and the White House conspired . . .": *Atlanta Constitution*, "Turner Sues Three Networks," by Susan Wells, May 11, 1981, p. A-1.
200 "From the beginning of Washington journalism . . .": Fred Friendly, *Broadcasting* magazine, "Hearing on CNN Suit," July 14, 1981, p. 23.
200 ". . . to determine whether it has a detrimental effect . . .": Ted Turner, *Atlanta Constitution*, May 11, 1981, p. A-16.
200 "All three networks are operating in lock-step . . .": Ted Turner, *Atlanta Constitution*, May 12, 1981, p. A-9.
201 "We're at war with everybody. . . .": *Atlanta Journal*, "Turner Sues Networks," by Ann Woolner, May 11, 1981, p. 1.
201 "I'll give you a dish. . . .": Ted Turner, quoted by Daniel Schorr, personal interview, Sept. 22, 1992.
201 "Don't worry . . .": Sidney Topol, quoted by Daniel Schorr, personal interview, Sept. 22, 1992.
202 "It was . . . Atlanta's preference for features . . .": *Atlanta Constitution*, "CNN's Washington Bureau Struggles," by Richard Zoglin, Nov. 4, 1980, p. B-1.
202 ". . . a matter of volume . . .": *ibid.*

202 "I'm through with sailing. . . .": *Washington Post*, "Turner Through with Sailing," by Angus Phillips, May 12, 1981, p. 3-D.

202 "Look, what do you think about scrapping . . .": Jim Mattingly, *Washington Post*, May 12, 1981, p. 3-D.

203 "We probably sailed in three hundred races. . . .": Gary Jobson, *Washington Post*, May 12, 1981, p. 3-D.

203 "It is possible the company will break even . . .": *Atlanta Journal*, "TBS Meeting Reflects Turner Style," by Tom Walker, June 24, 1981, p. B-1.

204 "CNN made us all wonder whether we should . . .": Bill Leonard, personal interview, Aug. 19, 1992.

204 "Well, what do you guys have in mind . . .": Ted Turner, quoted by Bill Leonard, personal interview, Aug. 19, 1992.

204 "We'd be very interested in selling you CNN . . .": Ted Turner, quoted by Bill Leonard, personal interview, Aug. 19, 1992.

205 "We were pretty arrogant in those days . . .": Bill Leonard, personal interview, Aug. 19, 1992.

205 "I'm sorry we can't do business. . . .": Ted Turner, quoted by Bill Leonard, personal interview, Aug. 19, 1992.

205 "He was a very fresh guy . . .": Bill Leonard, personal interview, Aug. 19, 1992.

206 "They're in for the fight of their lives . . .": *Atlanta Constitution*, "Cable TV Battle Taking Focus," by Richard Zoglin, August 24, 1981, p. C-7.

Chapter Ten

207 "Ted's happy—we're at war again . . .": In Hank Whittemore, *CNN: The Inside Story*, Little, Brown, 1990, p. 203.

207 "It's a preemptive first strike! . . .": *ibid.*, p. 202. Also, *Broadcasting* magazine, Aug. 19, 1981, p. 34.

208 "CNN does a nice, straightforward basic . . .": Richard Wald, *Time* magazine, "Shaking Up the Networks," Aug. 9, 1982, p. 53.

208 "I know we can never win a war of attrition . . .": *Time* magazine, Aug. 9, 1982, p. 54.

209 "And grabbing every single . . .": Ted Kavanau, personal interview, Sept. 16, 1992.

210 "Raw footage only . . . and no ABC correspondents . . .": Roone Arledge, *Broadcasting* magazine, Aug. 16, 1981, p. 13.

211 "Anybody who goes with them . . .": In Hank Whittemore, *CNN: The Inside Story*, p. 210.

211 "Kavanau was a fabulous character . . .": Fran Heaney, personal interview, Aug. 20, 1992.

212 "Working with Reese was no bed of roses . . .": Ted Kavanau, personal interview, Sept. 16, 1992.

214 "Turner was prepared to fire me on the spot . . .": Reese Schonfeld, personal interview, June 22, 1992.

214 "Reese was pretty aggressive . . .": Fran Heaney, personal interview, Aug. 22, 1992.

214 "Watching all of this with a certain bemusement . . .": Les Brown, *New York Times*, Nov. 14, 1981, p. 47.

215 "Turner will enjoy a short-term advantage. . . .": Compton Advertising survey, Nov. 1981.

215 "Most men might then sell out and go away . . .": *Forbes* magazine, "Cable News Wars," Nov. 24, 1981, p. 53.

215   "Mad Dog Kavanau had created a news network . . .": Fran Heaney, personal interview, Aug. 22, 1992.

215   "Hello again, and Happy New Year . . .": Chuck Roberts, signing on Headline News Network, 12:01 A.M., Jan. 1, 1982.

215   "I will not let you fail . . ." Ted Kavanau, personal interview, Sept. 16, 1992.

216   "So much for Ted Turner's complaints . . .": Richard Zoglin, *Atlanta Constitution*, Jan. 6, 1982, p. B-1.

216   ". . . denies the public . . .": U.S. District Court decree by Judge Orinda Evans, Atlanta, Ga., March 12, 1982.

216   ". . . no inequality of personnel, equipment . . .": Settlement agreement between CNN, ABC, CBS, and NBC, *Atlanta Constitution*, March 26, 1982, p. B-5.

216   ". . . with Daniel Schorr and Charles Bierbauer . . .": Martin Mayer, *Making News*, Doubleday, New York, 1987, p. 301.

217   ". . . one of the nation's most celebrated entrepreneurs . . .": Judge John M. Canella, *Atlanta Constitution*, March 26, 1982, p. C-5.

217   ". . . most of it is nothing more than ingratiating . . .": Richard Zoglin, reviewing *Lead, Follow, or Get Out of the Way*, by Christian Williams, for the *Atlanta Constitution*, Dec. 2, 1981.

217   "Turner's life has many aspects . . .": Jack Romanos, *Publishers Weekly*, May 30, 1986, p. 20.

218   "When I make a decision . . .": Ted Turner, told to BBC-TV, "The Man from Atlanta," May 1982.

218   "We symbolize the end of network news . . .": Ted Turner, *Atlanta Constitution*, March 10, 1982, p. D-5.

218   "The response was fantastic . . .": Henry Gillespie, *Atlanta Constitution*, March 10, 1982, p. D-5.

218   "We're very interested for all seven . . .": Jeff Davidson, *Atlanta Constitution*, March 10, 1992, p. D-5.

220   "Is that what we've become?": William S. Paley, quoted by Ernest Leiser, personal interview, Oct. 12, 1992. Also, *New York Times Magazine*, "The Little Network That Could," by Ernest Leiser, June 12, 1988, p. 30.

220   "He had fought their battles and built their programming . . .": Arthur Sando, *Broadcasting* magazine, July 24, 1982, p. 12.

221   ". . . every possible news story . . .": *Washington Post*, "CNN Front and Center," by Trish Trescott, July 2, 1982, p. D-3.

221   "With one hand . . . ABC embraces cable . . .": Ted Turner, *Broadcasting* magazine, Aug. 22, 1982, p. 23.

221   "Network television's staple of sleazy sex and violence . . .": Ted Turner, *Atlanta Journal*, March 2, 1982, p. 32.

222   "Network television is responsible . . .": Ted Turner, in a speech to Milwaukee Advertising Club, May 15, 1982, *Advertising Age*, May 21, 1982, p. 47.

222   "American television network executives . . .": Ted Turner, in a speech to Veterans of Foreign Wars convention, Philadelphia, June 19, 1982, *Atlanta Constitution*, June 24, 1982, p. C-3.

222   "A large part of our populace is sick . . .": Ted Turner, testimony to U.S. Congressional Subcommittee on Violence in Television, Washington, D.C., June 2, 1982, *Atlanta Constitution*, June 9, 1982, p. D-9.

223   "It was a little hard to take this guy seriously . . .": Les Brown, personal interview, May 27, 1992.

223   "He made a lot of noise . . .": Richard Zoglin, personal interview, July 15, 1992.

224   "Fidel says he's been watching . . ." Ted Turner, *Atlanta Constitution*, Feb. 7, 1982, p. C-7.

225 "Space is universal . . .": In *Broadcasting* magazine, March 14, 1982, p. 23.

225 "Nobody ever calls . . .": Ted Turner, told to BBC-TV, "The Man from Atlanta," May 1982.

225 "I told the president . . .": Ted Turner, *Atlanta Constitution*, April 24, 1982, p. D-3. Also in Whittemore's *CNN: The Inside Story*, p. 233.

225 "I realized I was just ambling . . .": Ted Turner, quoted by Richard Zoglin, personal interview, July 15, 1992.

226 "I interviewed Turner right after his first trip to Cuba . . .": Richard Zoglin, personal interview, July 15, 1992.

226 ". . . sustain heavy financial losses at first . . .": ABC spokesperson, *Wall Street Journal*, June 30, 1982, p. B-21.

226 "I'm supporting old Ted . . .": Marc Nathanson, *Time* magazine, "The Big TV News Gamble," Aug. 9, 1982, p. 54.

227 "It's a great deal for Turner no matter how you cut it . . .": Bonnie Cook, *Broadcasting* magazine, Oct. 12, 1983, p. 37.

227 "CNN's reporters are not million-dollar names . . .": Prof. Andrew Stern, *Columbia Journalism Review*, Oct. 1983, p. 24.

227 "The one thing everybody feared . . .": Richard Zoglin, personal interview, July 15, 1992.

228 "I was in the midst of closing . . .": Alfred Geller, personal interview, July 15, 1992.

229 "Ted felt he should have been talked . . .": In Hank Whittemore, *CNN: The Inside Story*, p. 238.

229 ". . . Turner's name on the door and . . .": Reese Schonfeld, personal interview, June 22, 1992.

229 "A lot of us felt it was all over . . .": Mary Alice Williams, personal interview, June 2, 1992.

229 "He made it the most exciting time . . .": Daniel Schorr, personal interview, Sept. 22, 1992.

229 "Burt Reinhardt was a much more cautious, stodgy person. . . .": *ibid.*

230 ". . . bankrupting the company . . .": Ted Turner *Atlanta Constitution*, Jan. 6, 1983, p. D-7.

230 "He wanted me to put together . . .": Reese Schonfeld, personal interview, June 22, 1992.

230 "I am very, very concerned . . .": In Hank Whittemore, *CNN: The Inside Story*, p. 244.

231 "They were furious . . .": Daniel Schorr, personal interview, Sept. 22, 1992.

233 ". . . disparaged Turner as a lunatic . . .": In Ken Auletta, *Three Blind Mice*, Random House, 1991, p. 56.

233 "If you guys ever want to get . . .": Reese Schonfeld, personal interview, Nov. 2, 1992.

234 ". . . the classic error of fighting a new technology . . .": John Malone, *Multi-Channel News*, March 1984, p. 34.

234 "You're not doing this just to get even? . . .": Bill Daniels, quoted by Reese Schonfeld, personal interview, Nov. 2, 1992.

234 "Turner had been on the phone . . .": Reese Schonfeld, personal interview, July 21, 1992.

234 "Why do you guys want to compete with me . . .": Ted Turner to NBC, quoted by Reese Schonfeld, personal interview, July 21, 1992.

235 "The threat was enough . . .": Reese Schonfeld, personal interview, July 21, 1992.

236 "If any of those corporate chiefs . . .": Tom Ashley, personal interview, August 3, 1992.

237 "Do you think I'm crazy . . .": *Atlanta Constitution*, "Jane Turner's Life in the Fast Lane," by Beverly Hills, June 23, 1982, p. C-3.

237 "They weren't exactly vacations . . .": Mary Ann Loughlin, personal interview, July 12, 1992.

237 "It's the only thing that lasts . . .": *Time* magazine, "Vicarious Is Not the Word," by Jon Skow, Aug. 9, 1982, p. 57.

238 "If you close your eyes . . .": *Business Month*, "Once More with Cheek," by Gwenda Blair, July/August 1988, p. 33.

238 "The idea that Ted would take away . . .": Daniel Schorr, personal interview, Sept. 22, 1992.

238 "I mean . . . this one had to be a pro . . .": Lois Hart, personal interview, Aug. 11, 1992.

239 "I don't wish I had more time to reflect . . .": *Sports Illustrated*, "What Makes Ted Run?" by Gary Smith, June 23, 1986, p. 74.

239 "When I was younger . . .": Ted Turner, *The New Yorker*, "Signoff," Sept. 12, 1988, p. 25.

240 "He turned it down, of course . . .": Alan Laymon, personal interview, May 25, 1992.

240 ". . . a 'bachelor of philosophy' degree . . .": Pres. Vartan Gregorian, personal interview, June 22, 1992.

240 "Ted had always been a 'closet environmentalist' . . .": Barbara Pyle, *Atlanta Business Chronicle*, "Barbara Pyle: TBS' Environmental Conscience," June 12, 1989.

240 "I started studying the world . . .": Ted Turner, told to BBC-TV, "The Man from Atlanta," May 1982.

240 "Nobody believes him, do they?" Larry Wright, *Atlanta Constitution Sunday Magazine*, May 24, 1980, p. 21.

Chapter Eleven

242 "You're missing the third button . . .": *Business Month*, "Once More With Cheek," by Gwenda Blair, July/August 1988, p. 30.

243 ". . . end run around the whole compromising process . . .": John B. Summers, *New York Times*, "Turner's Capitol Lobbying Draws Ire," Dec. 19, 1982, p. 24-A.

244 "How do you figure a guy . . .": Peter Ross Range, *Playboy* magazine, interview by Range, August 1978, p. 67.

244 "Wow! *Playboy!* That's big time . . .": Ted Turner, *Playboy* magazine, November 1982, p. 60.

244 ". . . a fanatically positive thinker . . .": Peter Ross Range, introducing second *Playboy* interview with Ted Turner, *Playboy* magazine, November 1982. p. 59. Also, personal interviews with Range, May 28, 1992, and Nov. 23, 1992.

245 "I didn't get to meet Paley . . .": Ted Turner, *Playboy*, November 1982, p. 68, pp. 154–156.

247 ". . . distortions of a vindictive reporter. . . .": *Atlanta Constitution*, "Ted Strikes Again," by Andrew Mollison, July 1, 1983, p. A-12.

247 "Poor George . . . would have to take his hot dog . . .": Gov. Joe Frank Harris, *Atlanta Constitution*, April 3, 1983, p. C-1.

248 ". . . Incredible numbers of women Turner ran through . . .": Bob Hope, personal interview, July 15, 1992.

248 "You had to feel for that lady . . .": *ibid.*

249 ". . . terrorizing the other America's Cup syndicates . . .": In *Atlanta* magazine, "The Woman Who Tamed Ted Turner," by Vincent Coppolla, November 1989, p. 114.

249 "JJ was the best-looking thing on the dock . . .": *ibid.*

249 "My relationship with Tom was over . . .": *ibid.*

250 "I've seen them . . . the groupies . . .": Jane Turner, *Newsweek*, "Ted Turner Tackles TV News," June 16, 1980, p. 64.
250 "She was, ah, packaged right . . .": In *Atlanta* magazine, November 1989, p. 114.
250 "I remember being in the ladies' room at Techwood . . .": Fran Heaney, personal interview, Aug. 20, 1992.
251 "It was Ted's fear that I might get soft . . .": In Christian Williams, *Lead, Follow, or Get Out of the Way*, Times Books, 1981, p. 155.
251 "We met everybody from Dr. Seuss to the chairman . . .": In *Atlanta* magazine, November 1989, p. 114.
252 "JJ had real potential . . .": *ibid.*
253 "It was okay for him to go home to his wife . . .": *ibid.*
253 "What I do is help men . . .": Dr. Frank Pittman, *Time* magazine, "CNN's Ted Turner," Jan. 6, 1992, p. 37.
254 "He lay down on the bed . . .": Ted Turner to David Frost, "Talking with David Frost," PBS Television program aired Jan. 2, 1991.
254 "Ed once told me . . . that he wanted Ted . . .": Judy Hallisy, personal interview, May 26, 1992.
254 "He was tremendously difficult . . .": Dr. Irving Victor, personal interview, May 27, 1992.
255 "When he did spend time with the family . . .": Teddy Turner IV, *Time* magazine, Jan. 6, 1992, p. 37.
255 "The patient's goal . . .": Dr. Frank Pittman, *Time* magazine, Jan. 6, 1992, p. 37.
255 "Mood disorders . . . are the 'common cold' of major . . .": Dr. Demitri Papolos, *Overcoming Depression*, Harper Perennial/HarperCollins, 1992, p. 3.
257 ". . . greatest fear—the fear of death . . .": Ted Turner, *Time* magazine, Jan. 6, 1992.
257 "He saw himself . . . as part of a tragedy . . .": James Roddey, *Time* magazine, Jan. 6, 1992, p 35.
257 "Before, it was sometimes pretty scary . . .": JJ Ebaugh, *Time* magazine, Jan. 6, 1992, p. 36.
257 "Many patients incorrectly look on lithium as a 'mind control' drug . . .": Dr. Donald F. Klein, personal interview, May 20, 1992.
258 "Lithium interacts to correct a pathological . . .": Dr. Hagip Akiskal, *Overcoming Depression*, p. 127.
258 "He has seen more manic depressives . . .": Dr. Demitri Papolos, *Overcoming Depression*, p. 125.
258 "The aspect of manic-depressive behavior . . .": Dr. Donald F. Klein, *Understanding Depression*, Oxford University Press, New York, 1993, p. 94. Also, personal interview with Dr. Klein, May 20, 1992.
259 "He felt his father had died tragically . . .": Dee Woods, *Time* magazine, Jan. 6, 1992, p. 36.
259 "I had counted on him . . .": Ted Turner, *Time* magazine, Jan. 6, 1992, p. 36.

Chapter Twelve

260 "It's a pretty crazy company . . .": *Atlanta Constitution*, "Turner Coolly Accepts Challenges," by Emily Rubin, July 18, 1982, p. C-1.
261 ". . . conceptual investment . . .": *ibid.*
261 "In recent months . . .": Ted Turner, in his 1983 report to (TBS) shareholders. Also, *Atlanta Constitution*, May 24, 1983, p. D-5.
261 "The sale of ESPN . . . was completed . . .": *Atlanta Constitution*, "Turner Happy to Lose out on ESPN," by Beau Cutts, May 1, 1984, p. D-1.

262 "I suppose, in a strictly emotional sense . . .": *Atlanta Constitution*, "Turner's Put ESPN in a Bind," by Thomas Stinson, June 9, 1984, p. D-1.

262 "We're going after everything—basketball . . .": *ibid.*, June 9, 1984, p. D-1.

263 "I'm quite aware that it will be controversial . . .": *Atlanta Constitution*, "Will WTBS Air Soviet Games?" by John Carman, July 6, 1984, p. D-3.

263 "Let's say Turner's image in the cable industry . . .": Robert Hosfeldt, *Multi-Channel News*, June 1984, p. 23.

263 "There is no doubt we admire Ted Turner . . .": Ed Allen, *Broadcasting* magazine, June 23, 1984, p. 25.

264 ". . . sleazy . . .": Ted Turner, referring to Warner Communications, *Cablevision* magazine, June 1984, p. 15.

264 "If you add up all the advertising dollars . . .": Greg Blaine, *Broadcasting* magazine, June 21, 1983, p. 33.

264 ". . . to see if I could acquire MGM . . .": Ted Turner, *Channels* magazine, Nov. 1987, p. 24.

265 "Those networks . . . need to be gotten into the hands . . .": *Washington Post*, "Turner Renews Attacks," by the Associated Press, June 28, 1984, p. C-1.

266 ". . . Inconsequential . . .": Tench C. Coxe, referring to Turner's talks with both Sen. Jesse Helms and Fairness in Media, *Wall Street Journal*, Jan. 21, 1984, p. B-5.

266 *'The Wall Street Journal* published a denial by Turner . . .": *Wall Street Journal*, Jan. 21, 1984, p. B-5.

269 ". . . attacking a major part of the media may be ill advised. . . .": Fred Joseph, *BusinessWeek*, March 14, 1985, p. 34.

270 "This new proposal . . .": Howard F. Roycroft, *BusinessWeek* magazine, "Even the Networks May Be Fair Game," March 18, 1985, p. 29.

272 "While Hutton wouldn't be considered . . .": *Wall Street Journal*, commenting on a possible takeover of CBS, March 21, 1985, p. B-3.

272 ". . . extremist . . . without proper conscience . . . utterly no financial . . .": Thomas Wyman, *Broadcasting* magazine, March 25, 1985, p. 7.

272 "We are in a position . . . to react promptly . . .": Thomas Wyman, *Advertising Age*, March 25, 1985, p. 35.

273 "Mr. Turner simply does not have sufficient moral character . . .": Thomas Wyman, *Broadcasting* magazine, March 25, 1985, p. 7.

273 "Labels like 'Turbulent Ted' and 'Captain Outrageous' just don't apply . . .": Richard MacDonald, *New York Times*, "Formidable Turner Stalks a Network," April 5, 1985, p. B-1.

274 "Buying CBS stock is like buying a dollar for fifty cents. . . .": Ivan Boesky, *BusinessWeek* magazine, "Inside Wall Street," April 15, 1985, p. 144.

274 ". . . to the best of our knowledge, there is no financial . . .": Thomas Wyman, *Broadcasting* magazine, March 19, 1985, p. 67.

274 "I'm not allowed to comment on this proposal . . .": Ted Turner, *Wall Street Journal*, "Turner's Bid for CBS," April 19, 1985, p. 3.

274 "We tried to design a security package . . .": *Barron's*, "No Money Down," by Lauren Rublin, April 22, 1985, p. 15.

275 "This offer frankly borders on the ludicrous. . . .": *Barron's*, April 22, 1985, p. 16.

275 "Given this scenario . . . could Turner's deal . . .": *ibid.*

275 "It's great press, and it's something that sells . . .": Fred Silverman, in *Variety*, April 15, 1985, p. 13.

275 "There are two points to remember . . .": Daniel Schorr, in *Variety*, April 15, 1985, p. 13.

275 ". . . grossly inadequate and financially imprudent . . .": Joseph Fogg, *Broadcasting* magazine, May 6, 1985, p. 40.

276 "... moral fitness to run a network ...": Thomas Wyman, *U.S. News & World Report*, "CBS' Cool Commander in Chief," May 6, 1985, p. 15.

276 "... misstated earnings for 1983 and 1984...." CBS spokesperson, *Variety*, April 24, 1985, p. 163.

276 "... no plans to take the company private....": CBS filing with the Securities and Exchange Commission, April 23, 1985.

276 "The minute Turner takes over CBS ...": CBS spokesperson, *Variety*, April 24, 1985, p. 182.

276 "We intend to challenge his fitness, not just to operate ...": CBS legal team member, *BusinessWeek*, "How CBS Plans to Keep Raiders at Bay," April 15, 1985, p. 144.

277 "... serious conflict of interest ...": Thomas Wyman, *Variety*, April 24, 1985, p. 163.

277 "In light of the long list of pejorative statements ...": *ibid.*

277 "Terrible Ted's Network Obsession," *Wall Street Journal*, April 19, 1985, p. 1.

278 "What Tom's doing now? Fighting ...": William Spoor, *U.S. News & World Report*, May 6, 1985, p. 15.

279 "Anyone who tries an unfriendly takeover ...": Salim B. Lewis, *Fortune*, "The CBS Takeover Defense: It's Top Rated," May 13, 1985, p. 36.

279 "CBS is more than a business ...": William S. Paley, *Broadcasting* magazine, May 6, 1985, p. 40.

280 "Bill Bevins and I practically lived together for four or five months....": George Vandeman, personal interview, July 22, 1992.

280 "Now that Turner's proved the numbers work ...": Michael Arends, *Broadcasting* magazine, June 24, 1985, p. 30.

280 "Once we began to show investors ...": George Vandeman, personal interview, July 22, 1992.

281 "CBS will never be the same again ...": Charles Ferris, *Forbes*, "The Network Game," July 15, 1985, p. 128.

281 "We had already been offered ...": Dan Good, personal interview, Dec. 30, 1992.

282 "Sure, you need a 67 percent shareholder approval ...": *Forbes*, July 15, 1985, p. 129.

282 "We spent a lot of time with Turner down there....": Dan Good, personal interview, Dec. 30, 1992.

283 "... creative protection ...": Thomas Wyman, *Forbes*, July 15, 1985, p. 129.

283 "We can't even offer Prudential two hundred cents on the dollar ...": Hutton adviser, *Broadcasting* magazine, July 15, 1985, p. 32.

284 "... vigorous legal challenge ...": *Broadcasting* magazine, July 15, 1985, p. 31.

284 "You have to look at it as part of the whole....": Dan Good, personal interview, Dec. 30, 1992.

284 "... a partial recapitalization, a partial cutback ...": Ted Turner, *Broadcasting* magazine, July 15, 1985, p. 32.

285 "We had meetings everywhere....": George Vandeman, personal interview, July 22, 1992.

285 "I remember our first meeting....": Tom Belford, personal interview, August 4, 1992.

286 "It was a mystery....": Reed Irvine, *The Progressive*, "What Price Glory?" June 1985, p. 12.

286 "No mystery at all ...": Robert Wussler, *Channels* magazine, "The Turner Empire," November 1987, p. 24.

286 "What's wrong? ...": *Chicago Tribune*, "TV Set for Goodwill Games," June 1, 1986, p. C-1.

286 "Wussler, that's what's wrong. . . .": *ibid.*

287 "I thought I'd get blown out of the water. . . .": *ibid.*

287 "Let's do it! . . .": *ibid.*

287 ". . . the worst president in American history . . .": United Press International, "Turner's Olympics," June 2, 1985, p. 1.

287 ". . . the chairman of Turner Broadcasting . . .": CNN newscast, July 29, 1985, 7 P.M.

287 "We could see a shift in the wind . . .": George Vandeman, personal interview, July 22, 1992.

288 "Hutton was just days away from announcing a new, cash-heavy . . .": Dan Good, personal interview, Dec. 30, 1992.

288 "Without MGM, there was a question mark with advertisers. . . .": *New York Times*, "Ted Turner's Screen Test," March 30, 1986, p. F-8.

289 "The game I'm in is building assets. . . .": *Atlanta Journal*, "TV News Building Downtown," June 17, 1985, p. C-7.

290 "We're getting more than a third of the greatest . . .": Ted Turner, *New York Times*, March 30, 1986, p. F-8.

290 "If you'll throw in those other old movies . . .": *ibid.*

290 "Looking back . . . we knew $29 was high . . .": Bill Bevins, *New York Times*, March 30, 1986, p. F-8.

290 "The probability . . . that we would have been able to save . . .": *ibid.*

290 "We went right around the clock . . .": George Vandeman, personal interview, July 22, 1992.

291 "Normally you have from the time you sign . . .": *ibid.*

291 "I don't want to sit here forever wondering . . .": Kirk Kerkorian, *New York Times*, p. F-8.

291 "In twenty-twenty hindsight, the fact that the studio . . .": Bill Bevins, *New York Times*, March 30, 1986, p. F-8.

292 "Mr. Kerkorian is no dummy. . . . He knew what he wanted to sell. . . .": Ted Turner, *New York Times*, March 30, 1986, p. F-8.

295 "Dogs, hell . . . You couldn't *feed* these films to 295s. . . .": Bill Bevins, *New York Times*, March 30, 1986, p. F-8.

296 "When you suffer the kinds of losses we suffered . . .": *ibid.*

300 "They asked Ted to be the featured speaker . . .": George Vandeman, personal interview, July 22, 1992.

301 "He was very charismatic. . . . And on top of everything else . . .": Alan Ladd, personal interview, August 4, 1992.

Chapter Thirteen

304 "I'm putting on a full-court press now. . . .": Ted Turner, *Variety*, August 7, 1985, p. 3.

304 "Let's party! . . .": In Hank Whittemore, *CNN: The Inside Story*, Little, Brown, 1990, p. 272.

305 "There is no way to be fully and immediately . . .": *Los Angeles Times*, "The Man Hollywood Loves to Hate," April 30, 1989, p. 9.

305 "Oh, my God! No! . . .": In Hank Whittemore, *CNN: The Inside Story*, p. 272.

306 "Suddenly every news editor in the world was . . .": Mary Ann Loughlin, personal interview, July 12, 1992.

306 ". . . at the incredible creation of Ted Turner . . .": Dick Williams, *Atlanta Constitution*, July 15, 1986, p. D-3.

306 ". . . would change the face of TV journalism. . . .": In Hank Whittemore, *CNN: The Inside Story*, p. 273.

306 "MGM is absolute history with him now. . . .": Taylor Glover, *Atlanta Constitution*, Sept. 13, 1986, p. D-7.

307 "Ted Turner still runs the show. . . .": United Press International wire story, "Turner Executive Committee," by Joe Parham, Oct. 6, 1989.

308 ". . . dangerously mounting hysteria . . .": Roger Vaughan, *The Grand Gesture*. Little, Brown, 1975, p. 84.

308 "I told my dad that Turner was coming to Stanford. . . .": Lisa Blackaller, personal interview, June 2, 1992.

309 "Ted had told Janie over and over . . .": Sandy Ebaugh, *Atlanta* magazine, November 1989, p. 115.

309 "I mean, when you leave your wife . . .": Ted Turner, *Broadcasting* magazine, Aug. 17, 1987, p. 46.

310 "Our earliest societies were based . . .": Riane Eisler, *Atlanta* magazine, November 1988, p. 116.

311 "He had no partners his whole life. . . .": JJ Ebaugh, *Atlanta* magazine, November 1988, p. 116.

311 "There's no question I've changed . . .": Ted Turner, *Broadcasting* magazine, Aug. 17, 1987, p. 46.

311 "He came to town fully clothed . . .": *Newsweek*, "Turner's Windless Sails," Feb. 9, 1987, p. 46.

312 "His reputation in Hollywood . . .": *Newsweek* editorial comment, Feb. 9, 1987, p. 46.

312 "Even if Turner had access to the entire colorization . . .": *Newsweek*, Feb. 9, 1987, p. 47.

312 ". . . destruction of America's cinema masterpieces . . .": *Los Angeles Times*, "The Man Hollywood Loves to Hate," April 30, 1989, p. 11.

313 "In the first six months after we colorize . . .": *Newsweek*, Feb. 9, 1987, p. 47.

313 "Turner saw stars in his eyes and felt MGM . . .": *Newsweek*, Feb. 9, 1987, p. 47.

314 "I've been authorized by Gene Jankowski to discuss . . .": Van Gordon Sauter, personal interview, Aug. 26, 1992.

315 ". . . drinks too much, spends money like a madman . . .": In Richard Clurman, *To the End of Time*. Simon & Schuster, 1992, p. 79.

315 ". . . amused by Turner, but just didn't like . . .": *ibid*.

315 "It may have been the biggest business mistake . . .": In Richard Clurman, *To the End of Time*, p. 79.

316 "With this investment . . . Turner Broadcasting . . .": Ted Turner, *Broadcasting* magazine, July 3, 1987, p. 35.

317 "I like to think that we're Brer Rabbit . . .": Ted Turner, *Broadcasting* magazine, Aug. 17, 1987, p. 46.

317 "That's step one in Turner's recovery plan. . . .": Don West, personal interview, June 23, 1992.

317 "People assumed it was a 'bailout,' . . .": Ted Turner, *Broadcasting* magazine, Aug. 17, 1987, p. 46.

318 "We felt that a financially healthy TBS . . .": Tim Neher, *Financial World*, Sept. 14, 1987, p. 14.

318 "If we hadn't rescued Ted Turner . . .": John Malone, *Newsweek*, Feb. 9, 1987, p. 46.

318 "All of a sudden . . . he had twenty-seven new partners . . .": JJ Ebaugh, *Atlanta* magazine, November 1988, p. 118.

318 "My power is somewhat diminished . . .": Ted Turner, *Broadcasting* magazine, Aug. 17, 1987, p. 46.

319 "Ted has been on the edge financially . . .": Nick Nicholas, *Multi-Channel News*, September 1988, p. 23.

319 ". . . take millions of this company's dollars . . .": Michael Fuchs, *Newsweek*, Feb. 9, 1987, p. 46. Also, *Broadcasting* magazine, Oct. 14, 1988, p. 43.

319 "These are smart guys. . . .": Don West, personal interview, June 23, 1992.

319 "The cable industry . . . is faced with what might be called . . .": Bill Daniels, personal interview, Sept. 22, 1992.

320 ". . . he might be dismissed today as a buffoon. . . .": Ken Auletta, *Three Blind Mice*. Random House, 1991, p. 585.

321 ". . . deals of the decade . . .": *Institutional Investor* magazine, March 1991, p. 32.

321 "They must feel like bozos. . . .": Ted Turner, *Financial World*, April 18, 1989, p. 65.

321 "If we hadn't been undercapitalized . . .": *ibid.*

Chapter Fourteen

322 ". . . world's longest free-standing escalator . . .": CNN tour presentation, July 12, 1992.

324 "[Ted] stayed nineteen until about two or three . . .": Bill Daniels, *Washington Post*, "CNN's Turner," July 18, 1988, p. B-4.

324 "When I was a young man . . . I was a good man . . .": Ted Turner, "Talking with David Frost," Television interview aired on PBS, Jan. 2, 1991. Also, *Washington Post*, July 18, 1988, p. B-4.

324 "It was a friendship . . . that just crept up on me. . . .": JJ Ebaugh, *Atlanta* magazine, November 1988, p. 115.

324 "He put up the most aggressive . . .": *ibid.*

325 "It took her a while . . . even after Ted said . . .": Sandy Ebaugh, *Atlanta* magazine, November 1988, p. 115.

325 "I started to listen . . .": Ted Turner, *Time* magazine, "Man of the Year," Jan. 6, 1992, p. 38.

325 "I learned to give and take . . . better than . . .": *Atlanta* magazine, November 1988, p. 118.

325 "I knew I would never have an equal share . . .": *Atlanta* magazine, November 1988, pp. 88, 115, 116, 117.

326 ". . . kind and respectful . . . There's a certain amount . . .": *Atlanta* magazine, November 1988, p. 118.

326 "We don't do limos . . .": *Atlanta* magazine, November 1988, p. 120.

326 ". . . seemed profoundly changed. . . . He's the only one . . .": Riane Eisler, personal interview, Nov. 14, 1992.

327 "When you have critical issues like nuclear arms . . .": *The New Yorker*, Sept. 12, 1988, p. 26.

327 "Jean-Michel Cousteau screened a film there. . . .": Thomas Belford, personal interview, August 4, 1992.

328 ". . . ultimate movie—a 'peace epic' . . .": Lori Henry, personal interview, June 22, 1992. Also, Fran Heaney, personal interview, Aug. 20, 1992.

329 "You cannot expect producers to produce programming . . .": *Atlanta Constitution*, Sept. 15, 1982, p. D-5.

329 "If I make a program for a million dollars . . .": *ibid.*

329 "We haven't really gotten into that. . . .": *ibid.*

329 "We'll have to crawl before we walk. . . .": *Business Month*, July–August 1988, p. 36.

330 "It's just like Procter and Gamble or General Foods . . .": *ibid.*

330 "You've still go that twenty-seven-million household disparity. . . .": *ibid.*

330   "That kind of success . . . is unprecedented. . . .": *Corporate Finance*, "Ted Turner Roars Back into the Black," December 1989, p. 56.

331   "Turner is now viewed . . .": *Corporate Finance*, December 1989, p. 57.

331   "Turner Broadcasting has a great one-two combination. . . .": *ibid.*

331   "If this guy ever goes to jail . . .": Jesse Kornbluth, personal interview, June 22, 1992.

332   "Ted is impulsive. . . .": Michael Fuchs, *Financial World*, April 18, 1989, p. 63.

332   "I knew a lot of my partners pretty well before . . .": Ted Turner, *Broadcasting* magazine, Aug. 17, 1987, p. 66.

332   "In 1980 . . . the politicians acted like they were . . .": Bernard Shaw, *Washington Post*, July 18, 1988, p. B-1.

332   "We are the host hotel. . . .": Ted Turner, *Washington Post*, July 18, 1988, p. B-1.

333   ". . . practical as well as theoretical caring . . .": Riane Eisler, *Atlanta* magazine, November 1988, p. 115.

334   "I had a lot to do with Nicaragua. . . .": Ted Turner, *Business Month*, "Once More with Cheek," July–August 1988, p. 32.

334   "Hey, guys. The rest of us are really concerned about you all. . . .": Ted Turner, *Insight* magazine, June 19, 1989, p. 48.

334   ". . . politics reacts to what people want. . . .": *Seattle Times*, "The Greening of Ted Turner," July 1, 1990, p. 8.

335   "There's no way the U.S. government could have initiated . . .": *Seattle Times*, July 1, 1990, p. 9.

335   "Over one hundred countries participate in the news network in some form. . . .": *Insight* magazine, June 19, 1989, p. 49.

335   ". . . Soviet apologist . . .": *National Review*, September 1988, p. 31,

335   ". . . tool of right-wing fascists . . .": *The Nation*, March 15, 1989, p. 23.

335   "I'm fifty . . . It's amazing how it sneaks up on you. . . .": *Washington Post*, "Ted Turner, On Top of the World," by Tom Shales, p. C-1.

337   ". . . very nice, very pleasant relationship. . . .": Yue-Sai Kan, personal interview, June 28, 1992.

337   "I'll be in Los Angeles all next week. . . .": Lori Henry, personal interview, June 22, 1992.

338   "I'm sure Mr. Turner is a very nice man. . . .": Lori Henry, personal interview, June 22, 1992.

338   "He lives for romance. . . . But it's always 'C'est moi . . .' ": JJ Ebaugh, *Atlanta Constitution*, May 2, 1990, p. B-5.

Chapter Fifteen

339   ". . . the most important instrument of communication in the world . . .": In Hank Whittemore, *CNN: The Inside Story*, Little, Brown, 1990, p. 289.

340   "Overnight the capital of this great country . . .": In Hank Whittemore, *CNN: The Inside Story*, p. 290.

340   ". . . does signal some sort of government movement. . . .": In Hank Whittemore, *CNN: The Inside Story*, p. 295.

341   "As an observer of the Ministry of Telecommunications . . .": In Hank Whittemore, *CNN: The Inside Story*, p. 296.

341   "Karl Marx, Meet Marshall McLuhan. . . .": Jonathan Alter, writing in *Newsweek*, May 21, 1990, p. 45.

341   "An historic piece of television. . . .": *Orange County* (California) *Register*, May 22, 1990, p. 47.

341   "CNN performed a great national and even international service. . . .": Fred Friendly, *Columbia Journalism Review*, September/October 1990, p. 25.

341 "A big, continuing story is the best thing. . . .": Ted Turner, *BusinessWeek*, July 17, 1989, p. 106.

341 "The three major broadcast networks' monopoly . . .": William Small, *Washington Journalism Review*, July 1990, p. 15.

341 "CNN has opened up a whole new communications . . .": Marlin Fitzwater, *New York Times*, Aug. 12, 1989, p. C-23.

343 "Five years from now . . . I don't anticipate CNN . . .": Ted Turner, *BusinessWeek*, July 17, 1989, p. 104.

344 "Ted Turner *is* the CNN strategic planning department. . . .": Lou Dobbs, *Columbia Journalism Review*, September/October 1990, p. 24.

344 "The perception abroad . . . had always been that CNN . . .": Peter Vesey, *The Economist*, May 9, 1992, p. 90.

345 "I've said this a million times. . . .": *Los Angeles* magazine, "Terrible Ted Tries Again," by Ivor Davis, April 1990, p. 79.

345 "The last time you saw me . . .": Ted Turner, *Los Angeles* magazine, April 1990, p. 80.

345 "Ted's Better World Society . . .": Linda Berman, *Los Angeles* magazine, April 1990, p. 80.

346 ". . . had been captivated by Jane right from their first meeting. . . .": Bob Wussler, personal interview, Dec. 15, 1992.

347 "Ted Turner came up with the idea for 'Network Earth'. . .": Teya Ryan, *MSO* magazine, October 1990, pp. 26–27.

347 "Man needs to make peace both with himself . . .": Ted Turner, acceptance speech at Radio & Television News Directors Association dinner honoring Turner as recipient of Paul White Award, Sept. 20, 1989. Also, *American Film*, "Ted Turner: Into the 1990's," by Greg Dawson, January/February 1989, p. 52.

348 ". . . bundle of contradictions, who does not fit . . .": Daniel Schorr, personal interview, Sept. 22, 1982.

348 "It was a terrible realization for me to come to. . . .": Ted Turner, Associated Press wire story, Feb. 15, 1988, p. 2.

348 ". . . a poor man's Armand Hammer . . .": *The National Review*, March 1989, p. 17.

348 "Turner's no Jesse Helms . . .": James Cain, *Atlanta Constitution*, "The Education of Mr. Turner," May 15, 1990 (AP wire release).

349 "The first thing I want to tell you guys . . .": Vicki Martell, personal interview, Sept. 23, 1992.

350 "When you travel with Ted . . .": Vicki Martell, personal interview, Sept. 23, 1992.

350 "On the surface, there's still the same bluster, the same . . .": *Forbes* magazine cover story on Turner, Jan. 4, 1993, editor's letter, p. 7.

350 "I am desperately trying to hook the world together . . .": Ted Turner, *Electronic Media* magazine, "TBS Readies for the Next Big Leap," May 6, 1991, p. 21.

352 "I was a political woman before I met Tom. . . .": Jane Fonda, *Esquire*, "Jane and Ted's Excellent Adventure," February 1991, p. 72.

352 "The idea of Ted ever waiting for anyone . . .": Bob Wussler, personal interview, Dec. 30, 1992.

352 "Turner knows how to treat a lady. . . .": Longtime friend of Fonda, told to *Los Angeles Times*, Jan. 23, 1991, p. C-13.

352 "I think what intrigues everyone about them . . .": Julie Alexander King, *People* magazine, Nov. 21, 1990, p. 25.

353 ". . . thought Roosevelt and Truman were communists . . .": Ted Turner, *Washington Post*, July 18, 1988, p. B-4.

353 "As a young girl . . . most of my dreams . . .": In Christopher Anderson, *Citizen Jane*. Henry Holt & Co., 1990, p. 37.
354 "Lee Strasberg stopped me . . . and said he saw . . .": In Anderson, *Citizen Jane*, p. 61.
354 "Jack Warner, the head of the studio, sent a message . . .": In Anderson, *Citizen Jane*, p. 69.
355 "I always think about it. . . . But I never would do it. . . .": In Anderson, *Citizen Jane*, p. 80.
355 "I couldn't believe it. . . . All my life I'd been brought up . . .": In Anderson, *Citizen Jane*, p. 121.
356 "Daughter? . . . I don't have a daughter. . . .": In Anderson, *Citizen Jane*, p. 123.
356 "I guess because of my father. . . .": Jane Fonda, *New York Times*, Jan. 22, 1967.
356 "No one ever walks out on a Fonda. . . .": In Christopher Anderson, *Citizen Jane*, p. 139.
356 "She will leave you. . . .": In Christopher Anderson, *Citizen Jane*, p. 139.
356 "Jane eagerly complied, seeming . . .": In Anderson, *Citizen Jane*, p. 157.
357 "I began to love people. . . .": In Anderson, *Citizen Jane*, p. 166.
357 "Mr. Ted likes to win. . . . No way he likes being a loser. . . .": In Christian Williams, *Lead, Follow, or Get Out of the Way*, Times Books, 1981, p. 48.
357 "That first night out . . .": In Williams, *Lead, Follow*, p. 46.
357 "There was ice forming everywhere. . . .": In Williams, *Lead, Follow*, p. 47.
358 "After it looked like we would have a lot of wind . . .": In Williams, *Lead, Follow*, p. 47.
358 "When Vanessa was born . . . it was as if the sun . . .": In Anderson, *Citizen Jane*, p. 168.
358 "I wasted the first thirty-two years . . .": In Anderson, *Citizen Jane*, p. 178.
359 "I always had a deep-rooted psychological need . . .": In Anderson, *Citizen Jane*, p. 177.
359 "You don't mind if I turn on? . . .": Rex Reed, *New York Times*, Jan. 25, 1970, p. 36.
359 "We were the sloth generation . . .": *ibid.*
359 "We are very friendly . . . with all my husband's wives and mistresses . . .": Rex Reed, *ibid.*
360 "I took off on that trip a liberal . . .": Jane Fonda, *Chicago Sun-Times*, May 9, 1971, p. 45.
360 ". . . my erstwhile, my alleged daughter . . .": In Christopher Anderson, *Citizen Jane*, p. 224.
360 "I feel as if I were baby-sitting for Lenin. . . .": Roger Vadim, *Detroit Free Press*, Dec. 6, 1970, p. 14.
360 "And, yes, I'm afraid it will be a bloody one. . . .": In Christopher Anderson, *Citizen Jane*, p. 236.
360 ". . . the hardest thing for me is to take the subway. . . .": Jane Fonda, *Detroit Free Press*, Dec. 6, 1970, p. 14.
360 "She walks around with a solemn Red Guard face . . .": *Life* magazine, John Frook, March 21, 1971, p. 75.
361 "To understand Tom and Jane . . . all you have to know . . .": In Christopher Anderson, *Citizen Jane*, p. 251.
361 ". . . the Mork and Mindy of the New Left. . . .": *Hollywood Reporter*, July 15, 1972.
362 ". . . Will you, Jane, marry Tom, and will you try . . .": Hayden-Fonda wedding vows, *Los Angeles Times*, Jan. 20, 1973, p. 29.
362 "The choice . . . was between being a good mother and wife . . .": In Christopher Anderson, *Citizen Jane*, p. 261.

362   "Overnight . . . money became the driving impulse. . . .": In Anderson, *Citizen Jane*, p. 296.

362   ". . . enough like other women to be able . . .": In Anderson, *Citizen Jane*, p. 303.

362   "Tom . . . is going to be president. . . .": Jane Fonda, *Washington Star*, Feb. 1, 1974.

362   "It was very, very touching. . . . Fonda was so overwhelmed. . . .": Tom Hayden, *People* magazine, Aug. 30, 1982, p. 45.

363   "Don't forget . . . I am the number one major late starter. . . .": In Christopher Anderson, *Citizen Jane*, p. 323.

Chapter Sixteen

364   "She's decathecting from Hollywood . . .": Longtime Fonda associate, *People* magazine, Oct. 2, 1990, p. 66.

364   "TV TYCOON MENDS FONDA'S BROKEN HEART: *London Daily Mail*, Nov. 4, 1990.

365   "I sent them a note. . . .": Ed ("No Relation") Turner, *Atlanta Constitution*, Nov. 10, 1990, p. C-7.

365   "I knew she was a protester in Vietnam. . . .": Ted Turner, *Atlanta Constitution*, "A Sort of Colorized Rhett Butler," Dec. 10, 1989, p. 1.

365   "The relationship is a natural. . . .": Jane Fonda, *People* magazine, Nov. 12, 1991, p. 75.

365   "It's hard to have your life dissected. . . .": Ted Turner, *People* magazine, *ibid.*, p. 75.

366   "He's serious about this—very serious. They have a lot in common. . . .": JJ Ebaugh, *Atlanta Constitution*, Jan. 14, 1992, p. C-5.

366   "Fortunately I have a fair amount of business in L.A. . . .": *Esquire*, "Ted and Jane's Excellent Adventure," by Jerry Adler, February 1991, p. 72.

366   "I think they're appropriate for each other. . . .": *Esquire*, February 1991, p. 70.

3660   "Where are we? . . .": Ted Turner, *Los Angeles Times*, June 3, 1992, p. 47.

366   "Instead of hanging out with Jane at the Academy Awards . . .": Furman Bisher, writing in the *Atlanta Constitution*, May 12, 1990, p. C-3.

367   ". . . mellowed so damned much since he met Fonda. . . .": *Atlanta Constitution*, Phil Kloer, July 13, 1991, p. G-1.

367   "I'll be here as long as I live. . . .": *Atlanta Constitution*, "Capt. Courageous Takes a Lower Profile," by Melissa Turner, Nov. 14, 1991, p. A-1.

367   "Do whatever you want. . . .": *Esquire*, February 1991, p. 72.

368   "She's not used to being treated like a lady. . . .": *ibid.*

368   "Listen up! . . .": *Esquire*, February 1991, p. 69.

368   "Isn't it funny . . . that the woman they used to call 'Hanoi Jane' . . .": *Esquire*, February 1991, p. 70.

370   "I'm not going to go out and hire Michael Gartner. . . .": *Channels* magazine, "The Soul of a News Machine," by J. Max Robins, March 1990, p. 29.

370   "If we could somehow pull it off . . .": Robert Wiener, *Live from Baghdad*. Doubleday, 1992, p. 17.

371   "It's as though we were in training all this time for just this story . . .": Ed Turner, *New York Times*, Feb. 11, 1991, p. D-8.

371   "You have a meeting like that . . . and relationships are cemented. . . .": Eason Jordan, *New York Times*, *ibid.*, p. D-8.

372   "Everything's fine at home, except the kids have the sniffles. . . .": Robert Wiener, *Live from Baghdad*, p. 1.

372   "Listen, guys, absolutely nothing's changed. . . .": Wiener, *Live from Baghdad*, p. 2.

373 "... good friend Bernard Shaw would get out quickly. ...": John MacArthur, *Second Front: Censorship and Propaganda in the Gulf War*. Hill & Wang, 1992, p. 185.
373 "Robert, I am not, repeat, not going to order ...": Robert Wiener, *Live from Baghdad*, p. 11.
373 "I assume this call is monitored. ...": Wiener, *Live from Baghdad*, p. 12.
373 "I know what you're driving at, Tom. ...": Wiener, *Live from Baghdad*, p. 12.
374 "... absolutely nothing is happening. ...": Peter Jennings, "ABC Evening News," *Washington Post*, Jan. 17, 1991, p. C-1.
374 "We've got to run. ...": Bernard Shaw, broadcast on "CBS Evening News," *Washington Post*, Jan. 17, 1991, p. C-1.
374 "The best reporting that I've seen so far on what is transpiring ...": Secretary of Defense Richard Cheney, *Washington Post*, Jan. 17, 1991, p. C-1.
374 "... used to be called the 'little network that could. ...' ": Peter Jennings, on "ABC Evening News," *Washington Post*, Jan. 17, 1991, p. C-1.
374 "Within minutes of that first bomb burst ...": *Entertainment Weekly*, Feb. 1, 1991, p. 23.
375 "They cut to Bernie Shaw because it was clear ...": *ibid*.
375 "The reason I stayed in Baghdad. ...": Peter Arnett, *New York Times*, "Network's Anger with CNN Deepens," Feb. 12, 1991, p. C-18. Also, *Washington Post*, March 11, 1991, p. D-1.
376 "It's different ... but it's a service. ...": Stephen Hess, *Washington Post*, "Iraqis Allow Arnett to Stay," Jan. 21, 1991, p. C-8.
377 "CNN has been ground zero for critics. ...": Tom Johnson, *Broadcasting* magazine, March 4, 1991, p. 29.
377 "What CBS did during the Gulf War. ...": General Michael Dugan, USAF, ret., *New York* magazine, "Who Won the Media War?" March 18, 1991, p. 27.
377 "There is no 'enemy ...' ": Bernard Shaw, *Washington Journalism Review*, March 1991, p. 28.
378 "Everybody dies sooner or later. ...": John MacArthur, *Second Front*, p. 225.
378 "I saw him only once—in the cafeteria. ...": Major General Perry Smith, USAF, ret., *How CNN Fought the War*. Birch Lane Press, 1991, p. 179.
379 "CNN will continue to be what has been described ...": Tom Johnson, *Atlanta Constitution*, April 11, 1991, p. D-1.
379 "Once the bombing started. ...": Len King, *Washington Journalism Review*, March 1991, p. 30.
380 "Welcome to 'Larry King Live ...' ": Announcer, on CNN's "Larry King Live" television show, broadcast Oct. 8, 1990.
380 "Jane ... before we talk about the video ...": "Larry King Live," Oct. 8, 1990.
380 "As far as I can see, it's going great. ...": "Larry King Live," Oct. 8, 1990.
380 "What, Ted, could you tell us about Jane? ...": "Larry King Live," Oct. 8, 1990.
380 "I would say that she's a sweet, kind, down-to-earth person. ...": "Larry King Live," Oct. 8, 1990.
380 "And Jane ... what surprised you the most about Ted? ...": "Larry King Live," Oct. 8, 1990.
380 "How funny he is. ...": "Larry King Live," Oct. 8, 1990.

Chapter Seventeen
381 "You are all my neighbors now, whether you like it or not. ...": *Bozeman Daily Chronicle* (Bozeman, Mont.), "Neighborly Gesture," editorial, July 7, 1989.
381 "Turner is a conscientious neighbor. ...": Bill Don Brainard, *Bozeman Daily Chronicle*, Jan. 5, 1989, p. 1.

382 "I find it to be my second most favorite thing to do. ...": Ted Turner, *Bozeman Daily Chronicle*, April 7, 1991, p. 1.

383 "That's what everyone wants. ...": *Montana* magazine, "View from the Flying D," by Dan Burkhart, June 1992, p. 63.

384 "I just never liked cattle ... even though my dad had them. ...": *ibid.*

384 "Unlike cattle, bison don't just eat the best grass ...": *Montana* magazine, June 1992, p. 66.

384 "For Turner to tell us how to ranch ...": Malcolm Story, *People* magazine, Oct. 14, 1991, p. 121.

385 "That is potentially quite a problem. ...": Rep. Vernon Westlake, *Bozeman Daily Chronicle*, March 13, 1992, p. 8.

385 "If they get out ... naturally I'll be responsible. ...": Ted Turner, *Bozeman Daily Chronicle*, Sept. 22, 1991, p. 7.

385 "It takes less hired help, but Turner will have to pay ...": Dennis Rowe, *Bozeman Daily Chronicle*, Aug. 6, 1991, p. 3.

385 "The only reason those elk are there at all ...": Ted Turner, *Bozeman Daily Chronicle*, *ibid.*, Aug. 6, 1991, p. 7.

386 "If the Fish and Game Commission wanted to put grizzly ...": Ted Turner, *Montana* magazine, June 1992, p. 64.

386 "... an extreme conservationist. ... You can't rely ...": Linda Haseltine, *Bozeman Daily Chronicle*, July 20, 1989, p. 8.

387 "The Flying D is a handsome, high-quality place. ...": Bob Kiesling, *Bozeman Daily Chronicle*, July 20, 1989, p. 8.

387 "I'm spending more time in Montana ...": Ted Turner, *Montana* magazine, June 1992, p. 65.

387 "I've invested plenty of bucks ...": Ted Turner, *Bozeman Daily Chronicle*, July 20, 1989, p. 7.

387 "... one of the most complete geological ...": Jack Horner, personal interview, Jan. 12, 1992.

388 "Turner is very interested in our efforts ...": *ibid.*

388 "... who want to come in and tell us how ...": Rep. Ronald Marlenee, *Bozeman Daily Chronicle*, Feb. 14, 1989, p. 5.

389 "Ted Turner owns more of Montana than all of the Japanese ...": Montana state government official, quoted in *Outside* magazine, Oct. 1991, p. 27.

389 "I think studies show that the best hope for the state economy ...": Jane Fonda, *Bozeman Daily Chronicle*, Sept. 22, 1991, p. 7.

390 "This land has unleashed a spiritual power ...": David Schwab, *Bozeman Daily Chronicle*, Nov. 17, 1991, p. 3.

390 "We call him Wovoka. ...": Curly Bear Wagner, personal interview, Jan. 12, 1992. Also, *Montana* magazine, "View from the Flying D," June 1992, p. 65.

391 "Fonda is interested in the tribe's new cultural center. ...": Betty White, *Montana* magazine, June 1992, p. 67.

392 "For nearly half a century ...": Stan Meyer, *Bozeman Daily Chronicle*, March 8, 1992, p. 7.

393 "I think news is becoming our most important asset. ...": Ted Turner, *Broadcasting* magazine, Aug. 17, 1987, p. 60.

394 "I had to eat a lot of crow for that statement. ...": *Editor and Publisher* magazine, Nov. 17, 1990, p. 14.

394 "He likes being out there. ... He's a celebrity. ...": Scott Sassa, *Los Angeles* magazine, March 1990, p. 82.

394 "He has been very good for television. ...": Grant Tinker, *Los Angeles* magazine, March 1990, p. 82.

395 "I've been married twice. . . .": Jane Fonda, *The Washington Post*, August 13, 1991, p. B-2.

395 "We've heard the rumors, too. . . .": Debbie Greenwood, *Bozeman Daily Chronicle*, Oct. 15, 1991, p. 13.

396 "Dad has met his match. . . .":Teddy Turner IV, *Atlanta Constitution*, Jan. 19, 1992, p. M-1.

396 "I gave him a chance to renege. . . .": Genie Turner, *Atlanta Constitution, ibid.*, p. M-1.

396 "That's not his date. . . . That's his daughter. . . .": Rutherford Seydel, *Atlanta* magazine, April 1991, p. 21.

397 "I haven't been to many weddings. . . .": Vanessa Vadim, *People* magazine, Jan. 6, 1992, p. 32.

397 "It was weird . . . because he's my half brother. . . .": Teddy Turner IV, personal interview, Oct. 17, 1992.

398 ". . . She said, 'There are five brats . . .' ": Teddy Turner IV, *Atlanta Constitution*, Jan. 19, 1992, p. M-3.

398 "I told him, 'This is your life. . . .' ": Dee Woods, *Atlanta Constitution*, Jan. 19, 1992, p. M-3.

399 "How many fathers let their kids go at five years old . . .": Teddy Turner IV, *Atlanta Constitution*, Jan. 19, 1992, p. M-3.

399 "He made them work . . .": Carolyn Godley, *Atlanta Constitution*, Jan. 19, 1992, p. M-3.

400 "I'll keep the sheep. . . .": Ted Turner, *Bozeman Daily Chronicle*, Sept. 22, 1991, p. 7. Also, *Montana* magazine, June 1992, p. 66.

401 "I've killed two elk since I bought the Flying D. . . .": Ted Turner, *Montana* magazine, June 1992, p. 64.

402 "If we can't make the right choice after we have all the information . . .": Ted Turner, speech at Duke University, November 1991.

403 "The culmination of his life . . .": Gerald Hogan, *Television Business International*, Oct. 1991, p. 25. Also, *Time* magazine, Jan. 6, 1992, p. 39.

403 "My dad used to say 'A few fleas are good for a dog. . . .' ": "Talking with David Frost" television show, broadcast on PBS Jan. 2, 1992.

404 ". . . probably the greatest World Series ever. . . .": Fay Vincent, *Sporting News*, Nov. 10, 1991.

Chapter Eighteen

407 "Ted Turner is not a joiner. . . .": Maurice Strong, personal interviews, Oct. 2, 1992, and Oct. 12, 1992.

407 "I don't subscribe to the 'buffalo commons' idea. . . .": Ted Turner, *Bozeman Daily Chronicle*, "Baron of Bison," Sept. 22, 1991, p. 1

408 "A few years ago they would have had a fight on their hands. . . .": Rosella Orr, *Bozeman Daily Chronicle*, "Neighbors Buzz about Ted and Jane Ranch Buy in New Mexico," Aug. 4, 1992, p. 3.

408 "I've been through a lot of campaigns. . . .": Ted Turner, *Forbes* magazine, "What New Worlds to Conquer?" Jan. 4, 1993, p. 23.

408 "You never thought of having fun with Dad before. . . .": Teddy Turner IV, *Time* magazine, Jan. 6, 1992, p. 38.

408 "My father told me . . . he wanted to be a millionaire. . . .": Ted Turner, *Time* magazine, Jan. 6, 1992, p. 38.

408 "The worst sin, the ultimate sin for me . . .": Ted Turner, *Forbes* magazine, Jan. 4, 1993, p. 87.

409 "We control more of our own software ...": Ted Turner, *Forbes*, Jan. 4, 1993, p. 85.

409 "Cartoons ... travel even better than American movies. ...": Ted Turner, *Forbes*, Jan. 4, 1993, p. 87.

410 "... is start new networks, build new networks, and market them. ...": Terry McGuirk, *Forbes*, Jan. 4, 1993, p. 86.

410 "We buy as much software as we can. ...": Scott Sassa, *Forbes*, Jan. 4, 1993, p. 85.

410 "We're a lot like the modern chicken farmer. ...": Ted Turner, *Forbes*, Jan. 4, 1993, p. 85.

411 "The line extension of all our brands ...": Scott Sassa, *Forbes*, Jan. 4, 1993, p. 87.

412 "There was a logic in Atlanta ... that said we'll do it all by ourselves. ...": Charles Bonan, personal interview, June 13, 1992.

413 "Competition has been good for CNN. ...": Tom Johnson, *Broadcasting* magazine, March 4, 1991, p. 25.

413 "... is not an easy or inexpensive thing. ...": Peter Vesey, *Television Business International*, Feb. 1992, p. 28.

414 "Turner Broadcasting has really been transformed ...": Dennis Leibowitz, *Forbes* magazine, Jan. 4, 1993, p. 84.

414 "Ted Turner's vision, and the guts to stick to the vision ...": Terry McGuirk, *Forbes*, Jan. 4, 1993, p. 87.

414 "... is looking around for a way to account for his sins. ...": Daniel Schorr, personal interview, Sept. 22, 1992.

414 "In 1980 ... Ted told me with utter conviction ...": Irwin Mazo, personal interview, June 10, 1992. Also, July 31, 1992 and Sept. 1, 1992.

414 "All this is a progression ...": James Roddey, personal interview, Sept. 16, 1992. Also, *Pinnacle* magazine, "Ted Turner Takes on the World," by John Molavalli, September/October 1990, p. 25.

415 "I would only run for president ...": Ted Turner, *Broadcasting* magazine, April 9, 1990, p. 76.

415 "... my wife was already married to one politician. ...": Ted Turner, *Atlanta Constitution*, Jan. 25, 1992, p. C-7.

415 "I think the country might even be able to live with the lithium ...": John Jay Hooker, personal interview, Dec. 9, 1992.

415 "I'm still building my company. ...": Ted Turner, *Forbes* magazine, Jan. 4, 1993, p. 84. Also, *Wall Street Journal*, Feb. 13, 1993.

417 "When we would get done going through the first several floors ...": Ted Turner, *Pinnacle* magazine, September/October 1990, p. 8.

417 "Now tell me the truth. Wouldn't you really rather be Ted Turner? ...": Christian Williams, *Lead, Follow, or Get Out of the Way*, p. 274.

Index